D0899215

LYNN QUITMAN TROYKA

With the assistance of Cy Strom

Simon & Schuster Handbook for Writers

THIRD CANADIAN EDITION

TORONTO

For David, who makes it all incredibly special

National Library of Canada Cataloguing in Publication Data

Troyka, Lynn Quitman, 1938–
Simon & Schuster handbook for writers

3rd Canadian ed.
Includes index.
ISBN 0-13-060465-8

1. English language—Rhetoric—Handbooks, manuals, etc. 2. English language—Grammar—Handbooks, manuals, etc. I. Strom, Cy, 1954–. II. Title.

PE 1408.T76 2001 808'.042 C2001-903248-X

ISBN 0-13-060465-8

Vice President, Editorial Director: Michael Young
Editor-in-Chief: David Stover
Marketing Manager: Sharon Loeb
Developmental Editor: Matthew Christian
Production Editor: Avivah Wargon
Copy Editor: Cy Strom
Proofreaders: Lisa Berland, Tara Tovell
Production Coordinator: Peggy Brown
Page Layout: B.J. Weckerle
Permissions Research: Susan Wallace-Cox
Creative Director: Mary Opper
Cover Design: Lisa LaPointe
Cover Image: Vincent Van Gogh (1853-1890), "The Sower," Rijksmuseum Kroller-Muller, Otterio, Netherlands/A.K.G., Superstock

5 06 05 04 03

Printed and bound in Canada.

Contents

11 Agreement 247

12 Using Adjectives and Adverbs 266

17 Coordination and Subordination *340*

18 Parallelism *353*

19 Variety and Emphasis *363*

24 Commas 419

25 Semicolons 449

26 Colons 455

27 Apostrophes 460

28 Quotation Marks 467

29 Other Punctuation Marks 477

30 Capitals, Italics, Abbreviations, and Numbers *489*

PART V: Writing Research *507*

31 Using Sources and Avoiding Plagiarism *508*

32 The Processes of Research Writing 528

33 Successful Online Research 567

34 MLA, APA, CM, CBE, and COS Documentation Styles 584

Preface

In writing the *Simon & Schuster Handbook for Writers*, I remain convinced that students are empowered by knowledge and deserve unwavering respect as emerging writers.

This is the third Canadian edition of the *Simon & Schuster Handbook for Writers*; its U.S. counterpart is now in its sixth edition. As in previous editions, I've designed this revision of the *Handbook* for three purposes: as a classroom text, a self-instruction manual, and a reference book. My greatest wish for students who use this book is that they succeed as writers and joyfully fulfil their potential in academic, personal, workplace, and public settings.

In writing the *Handbook*, I've sought to be inclusive of all people. Role stereotyping and sexist language are avoided; *man* is never used generically for the human race (rare exceptions may appear in quotations from published writers); male and female writers are represented equally in examples; and many ethnic groups are represented in the mix of student and professional writing examples.

To unify this new edition of the *Handbook*, my stance throughout is that writing emerges from context, not from isolated components. I've written the exercises in connected discourse, not in random sentences collected together. As students do the exercises, they experience what real writers face when they revise and edit. For exercise content, I've drawn from subjects across the curriculum, choosing those with intrinsic interest for all students. Similarly, I've formed clusters of examples with related content so that students can focus on the instruction instead of on a new topic with each new example.

The *Simon & Schuster Handbook for Writers*, Third Canadian Edition, has followed the inspiration of the U.S. Sixth Edition in adding extensive new material. The Third Canadian Edition is nevertheless based closely on the previous Canadian editions and retains their core features. To acquaint you with this new edition, the rest of this introduction is divided into sections:

- **"How to Locate" Guide** lists the navigation tools that help students easily locate what they want to find.
- **New Features** lists the abundant, exciting additions to the Third Canadian Edition.
- **Core Features** lists the many popular elements that I have retained from my previous editions.

But first, a personal note: When I was an undergraduate years ago, handbooks for student writers weren't widely available or used. Questions about writing nagged at me, but I couldn't find a book to answer them. On top of my being curious about the "why" of English and its conventions, my less-than-precise ear for language annoyed me. I worried that I guessed too often, and I felt frustrated by my ignorance. The semester before I graduated, I happily discovered a dusty, thin book on a little-used library shelf that answered some—though not all—of my questions. Back then, I could never have imagined that someday I myself might write a considerably expanded, modern version of a handbook for writers. Once I completed the *Simon & Schuster Handbook for Writers* (I started writing the U.S. First Edition in 1983, and it was published in 1987), I was amazed that I had had the nerve to begin. This proves to me—and I hope to students—that with persistence and patience, anyone can master English and writing.

In that spirit, I hope faculty and students alike will join in the conversation my pages seek to invite. Please e-mail me at <**LQTBook@aol.com**>. I look forward to your starting our conversation.

Lynn Quitman Troyka

"HOW TO LOCATE" GUIDE FOR THE THIRD CANADIAN EDITION

HOW TO LOCATE LISTS OF THE BOOK'S CONTENTS

The Overview of Contents inside the front cover is a condensed version of the entire contents. Students can open the book to see instantly what chapter and section they are looking for. A complete Table of Contents precedes this preface, and a detailed Index starts on page Index-1.

HOW TO LOCATE THE BOOK'S SEVEN MAJOR TOPICS

Each of the seven Parts of this handbook contains one major topic: Writing an Essay; Understanding Grammar and Writing Correct Sentences; Writing Effectively; Using Punctuation and Mechanics; Writing Research; Writing Across the Curriculum and in the Public World; and Writing When English Is a Second Language. The Overview of Contents refers students quickly to the seven Parts and the chapters contained in each.

HOW TO LOCATE A SPECIFIC CHAPTER

The chapters in this handbook are numbered in sequence from 1 to 47. Within each chapter, the comprehensive coverage is divided into short "chunks" of information. Each section, or chunk, is assigned a number-letter code: the chapter number followed by a lower-case letter, beginning with *a* and continuing in alphabetical order to the end of the chapter. (For example, in Chapter 1, the sections are 1a, 1b, 1c, up to 1f; and in Chapter 47, the sections are 47a to 47c.) Each number-letter code appears alongside the heading of its section. These number-letter codes are also used to cross-reference to sections of the book where students can find more information. Number-letter codes also sit at the top outside corner of each page as well as in all contents lists.

HOW TO LOCATE MATERIAL ON EACH PAGE

The main headings in each chapter appear in blue type, and each heading is identified by its number-letter code. Also, the last heading on the page is repeated in the running head at the top of every right-hand page. For more detail about navigating a page, see How to Use Your Handbook, inside the back cover.

HOW TO USE THE BOOK'S SPECIAL ELEMENTS

Because students today are strongly oriented toward the visual, I have created many visual displays for guidelines, checklists, sentence patterns, summaries, flowcharts, illustrations, and more. Each item is designed to help students learn new material and to refresh their memories afterward. In addition, the *Handbook* draws on research findings concerning cognition and learning by employing these aids:

- Numbered sequentially throughout the book, 179 tinted charts work as thumbnail sketches or summaries of key information. An alphabetical list of these charts follows the Index.
- An ✤ALERT✤ system signals students about related information. For example, a brief Punctuation Alert in an explanation of coordination points out a particular function of the comma. The ✚ symbol indicates a Computer Tip, and ◆ announces an ESL Note for students for whom English is a second (or third, etc.) language.

- A degree mark (°) follows all terms that are defined in the Terms Glossary, located immediately before the Index at the back of the *Handbook*. This identification feature allows students to concentrate on the matter at hand, with the assurance that a needed definition is easy to find.
- Each of the seven Parts concludes with a list of Weblinks that contain guidelines and information relevant to the topics covered in that Part. Students who explore these links will find that many of them present a wide variety of related topics, as well.

NEW FEATURES OF THE THIRD CANADIAN EDITION

NEW 

COMPREHENSIVE, INTERACTIVE WEB SITE, FREE, to accompany the *Simon & Schuster Handbook for Writers*, Third Canadian Edition. Designed specifically to help anyone using either the *Simon & Schuster Handbook for Writers*, Third Canadian Edition, or the *Simon & Schuster Quick Access for Writers*, Canadian Edition, it includes numerous components:

- Hundreds of application exercises for self-grading, including editing, fill-in-the-blank, essay, multiple choice, and matching.
- "Blue Pencil" exercises, providing grammar and punctuation practice in the context of complete paragraphs.
- Several comprehensive diagnostic tests for students to assess their strengths and weaknesses in all areas of grammar and punctuation.
- Helpful Weblinks (URLs) for every Part or major topic to offer supplemental resources and activities.
- An online reference library that provides information on how to search, evaluate, and document online sources.
- A **new,** innovative section dedicated to helping students write different types of papers. It provides students with tips, book references, sample student papers, and more. To assist students even if they aren't navigating the site via a particular chapter, it's organized two different ways: (1) "What type of paper are you writing?" and (2) "Where are you in the writing process?"

NEW Expanded coverage of Research Writing, with six chapters instead of five.

- A **new** separate chapter, "Successful Online Research," with information about searching the Web and the Internet, narrowing a search, avoiding plagiarism, and evaluating online sources (Chapter 33).
- A **new** section on Columbia online style (COS) documentation, in the chapter that also presents the documentation styles used by the MLA and APA, as well as the Chicago Manual (CM) and Council of Biology Editors (CBE) styles (Chapter 34).
- **Revised** Chapter 32, "The Processes of Research Writing," now featuring new sections on formulating a research question and on the role of new technologies in research, and updates on Canadian government Web sites.

NEW Public writing, incorporated into Chapter 40, "Business Writing," via guidelines on composing e-mail messages and memos in and outside of the formal business environment, in addition to letters, job application letters, and résumés.

NEW A section on tools for writers (Chapter 1) talks about computers, a personal bookshelf of reference volumes, and other resources for writers.

NEW Over 20% of the exercise content is new for this edition, with selected exercises featuring options for both individual and collaborative work.

NEW Additional Computer Tips, ESL Notes, and Alerts throughout the text help students incorporate technology, assist students for whom English is a second language, and highlight interactions between two or more grammatical and rhetorical issues.

CORE FEATURES OF THE THIRD CANADIAN EDITION

- Starts with six chapters about writing essays, explaining that the writing process is rarely linear, varying always with the writer, the topic, and the writing situation.
- Illustrates a variety of writing processes with *nine* complete student essays: one with an informative purpose (Chapter 3); two with a persuasive purpose (Chapter 6); one as a critical response to a reading (Chapter 5); two MLA-style research papers, one on a general topic (Chapter 35) and one on a literary topic (Chapter 38); one APA-style research paper; and three literature-based papers, including the literary research paper mentioned above.
- Offers detailed explanations of critical thinking and reading, as they relate to writing. Extensively class-tested, Chapter 5 explains the crucial differences between summary and synthesis, with a

discussion paced to assist students in grasping each cognitive process and to help them understand the higher level thinking demanded by synthesis.

- Devotes a full chapter to argument, with each of two students taking a different position on the same topic. The Toulmin model and the classical model receive equal coverage.
- Covers all topics of grammar, style, language, punctuation, and mechanics.
- Demonstrates that research writing combines three processes: conducting research, understanding the results of that research, and writing a paper based on that research.
- Contains *two* complete MLA-style research papers. In Chapter 35, a paper about multiple intelligences is accompanied by a narrative of the student's research writing process, with annotations and commentary alongside each page of the paper. In Chapter 38, a literary research paper discusses the narrative poem *Towards the Last Spike* by Canadian poet E. J. Pratt.
- Contains a 1500-word sample student essay discussing an acclaimed Canadian literary work: the play *Goodnight Desdemona (Good Morning Juliet)* by Ann-Marie MacDonald (Chapter 38).
- Includes a complete APA-style research paper about biological clocks, accompanied by a brief narrative of the student's writing process.
- Supplies a huge number of MLA and APA documentation examples, with much more for users of Internet and other electronic sources and with directories for examples of in-text citations, similar to those already used for MLA Works Cited and APA References.
- Presents five chapters for students to use when they are writing across the curriculum, including an expanded chapter on business writing.
- Addresses the concerns of multilingual students, with many ESL Notes throughout the book and a longer discussion in six chapters.
- Placed on the second page preceding the inside back cover, Response Symbols include commonly used proofreading marks in addition to the traditional correction symbols.

SUPPLEMENTS FOR THE THIRD CANADIAN EDITION

Pearson Education Canada now offers an *even wider choice* of student supplements and instructor supplements to help faculty augment and customize their courses.

FOR STUDENTS

- COMPREHENSIVE, INTERACTIVE WEBSITE to accompany the *Simon & Schuster Handbook for Writers*, Third Canadian Edition, <**www.pearsoned.ca/troyka**>

- *Simon & Schuster Workbook for Writers*, Third Canadian Edition. ISBN 0-13-067587-3
- The New York Times *Themes of the Times* distributed exclusively by Prentice Hall. ISBN 0-13-690181-6
- *Rough Drafts: An Activity Book to Accompany the Simon & Schuster Handbook for Writers*, Sixth U.S. Edition. ISBN 0-13-041610-X
- *A Writer's Guide to Research and Documentation*. ISBN 0-13-032641-0
- *A Writer's Guide to Writing in the Disciplines and Oral Presentations*. ISBN 0-13-018931-6
- *A Writer's Guide to Document and Web Design*. ISBN 0-13-018929-4
- *A Writer's Guide to Writing about Literature*. ISBN 0-13-018932-4
- *English on the Internet 2001: Evaluating Online Resources*. ISBN 0-13-019484-0.

FOR INSTRUCTORS

- *Instructor's Manual* for the *Simon & Schuster Handbook for Writers*, Third Canadian Edition. ISBN 0-13-067586-5
- *WebCT*, *BlackBoard*, and *Course Compass* adapted for the *Simon & Schuster Handbook for Writers*, Third Canadian Edition. They feature extensive content in each of these course platforms, saving instructors time in preparing online courses.
- *Daedalus Online* is a Web site that provides an online environment for collaboration, with prompts for a variety of writing assignments and other user-friendly material. For more information, visit <**http://www.prenhall.com/daedalus**>.
- Prentice Hall Resources for Teaching Writing (available in print and online):
    - *Teaching Writing Across the Curriculum* by Art Young, Clemson University. ISBN 0-13-081650-7.
    - *Computers and Writing* by Dawn Rodrigues, University of Texas at Brownsville. ISBN 0-13-084034-3.
    - *Portfolios* by Pat Belanoff, State University of New York, Stony Brook. ISBN 0-13-572322-1.
    - *Journals* by Christopher C. Burnham, New Mexico State University. ISBN 0-13-572348-5
    - *Collaborative Learning* by Harvey Kail, University of Maine, and John Trimbur, Worcester Polytechnic Institute. ISBN 0-13-028487-4.
    - *English as a Second Language* by Ruth Spack, Tufts University. ISBN 0-13-028559-5.
    - *Distance Education* by W. Dees Stallings, University of Maryland, University College. ISBN 0-13-088656-4.

Acknowledgments

For me, the best part of writing acknowledgments is my chance to thank publicly all students who generously gave me permission to show their writing as exemplary models in the *Simon & Schuster Handbook for Writers*, Third Canadian Edition. Each is now officially a "published writer." My congratulations!

I also thank the hundreds of students who have met with me in groups or who have written me to share their experiences with, and suggestions for, my handbooks. I take their words very seriously, and whatever flaws remain on these pages are my responsibility alone.

Central to my composing process for this new edition of the *Simon & Schuster Handbook for Writers* were four exceptional colleagues. Esther DiMarzio, Kishwaukee College, wrote most of the new exercises for the U.S. Sixth Edition and shared her wise, creative insights into the teaching and learning of writing. Harriet Prentiss, Development Editor, was the penultimate structural editor and chief consultant as I updated this edition. Cynthia Nordberg contributed hugely to the *Annotated Instructor's Edition* of the *Handbook*, as I explain in that volume's Preface. For this Third Canadian Edition of the *Simon & Schuster Handbook for Writers*, Cy Strom of Colborne Communications Centre in Toronto once again applied his keen intelligence and talented pen, adapting exercises and other materials to the Canadian context.

Additionally, I was privileged to draw on the expertise of top-notch people to participate in the enterprise. I am very grateful to Beverly Buster, University of South Florida, for updating the *Simon & Schuster Workbook for Writers*, Sixth Edition; Lyneé Lewis Gaillet, Georgia State University, for journal updates; Linda Julian, Furman University, for updating *Strategies and Resources for Teaching Writing* to accompany the *Handbook;* Erin Karper, Purdue University, for an early draft of my new chapter on document design in the U.S. Sixth Edition; William J. McCleary, retired, State University of New York at

Brockport, for collaborative exercises; Sean Nighbert, St. Philip's College, for the first draft of my chapter on online research and for preparing Web site material for <www.prenhall.com/troyka>; Meredith Weisberg, Purdue University, for journal updates; and Christine Manion, Marquette University, for the first draft of my new chapter on oral presentations in the U.S. Sixth Edition.

My special thanks go to the faculty reviewers for the U.S. Sixth Edition: Stephanie Chamberlain, Southeast Missouri State University; Patrick T. Dolan, Arapahoe Community College; Sarah H. Harrison, Tyler Junior College; Anna R. Holston, Central Texas Community College; Richard F. Johnson, William Rainey Harper College; Mary Lynch Kennedy, State University of New York at Cortland; Charles Poston, Fairmont State College; Lauren Sewell Coulter, University of Tennessee at Chattanooga; Beverly J. Slaughter, Brevard Community College; Dr. Jan E. VanStavern, Dominican College of San Rafael; Stephen Wilhoit, University of Dayton; Heywood L. Williams-Crisson, Longview Community College. I'm grateful, too, to the following students at Kishwaukee College who wrote very helpful reviews: Cheryl Casey, Naomi Campbell Faivre, Amy Houtz, Angela Johanasson, Carolina Avendano Landaverde, Lauma Ribinska, Tara Senkowski, Harvest Sutherland, Daniel Underwood, Kim Coleman, and Kimberly Wilkerson. My thanks go also to the reviewers of the Third Canadian Edition: Gail Hartfield, Northern Alberta Institute of Technology; Susan Lieberman, Grant MacEwan Community College; and Robert Myles, McGill University.

I also renew my gratitude for their contributions to my previous handbook editions: Don Jay Coppersmith, Internet Consultant; Jo Ellen Coppersmith, Utah Valley State College; Esther DiMarzio, Kishwaukee College; Ann B. Dobie, University of Southwestern Louisiana; Michael J. Freeman, Director of the Utah Valley State College Library; Scott Leonard, Youngstown State University; Dorothy V. Lindman, Brookhaven College; Alice Maclin, DeKalb College; Barbara Matthies, Iowa State University; Patricia Morgan, Louisiana State University; Kirk Rasmussen, Utah Valley State College; Mary Ruetten and Barbara Gaffney, University of New Orleans; Matilda Delgado Saenz; Paulette Smith, Reference Librarian, Valencia Community College; Judith Stanford, Rivier College; Cy Strom, Colborne Communications Centre; and Lisa Lavery Wallace, Attorney at Law.

Behind the pages of this edition reside many voices of wise colleagues. I am particularly grateful to members of the Regional Advisory Boards for Prentice Hall and Lynn Troyka, who set aside precious days in their busy lives to discuss key issues with me. In the Southeast, they were Peggy Jolly, University of Alabama at Birmingham; Stephen Prewitt, David Lipscomb University; Mary Anne Reiss, Elizabethtown Community College; Michael Thro, Tidewater Community College at Virginia Beach;

and the late, treasured Sally Young, University of Tennessee at Chattanooga. In the Southwest, they were Jon Bentley, Albuquerque Technical-Vocational Institute; Kathryn Fitzgerald, University of Utah; Maggy Smith, University of Texas at El Paso; Martha Smith, Brookhaven College; and Donnie Yeilding, Central Texas College. In Florida they were Kathleen Bell, University of Central Florida; David Fear, Valencia Community College; D. J. Henry, Daytona Beach Community College; Marilyn Middendorf, Embry-Riddle Aeronautical University; Phillip Sipiora, University of South Florida; and Valerie Zimbaro, Valencia Community College.

My thanks also to reviewers of my earlier editions: Nancy Westrich Baker, Southeast Missouri State University; Bradley Bleck, University of Nevada; J. Norman Bosley, Ocean Community College; Phyllis Brown, Santa Clara University; Judith A. Burnham, Tulsa Community College; Robert S. Caim, West Virginia University at Parkersburg; Ann L. Camy, Red Rocks Community College; Joe R. Christopher, Tarleton State University; Marilyn M. Cleland, Purdue University, Calumet; Thomas Copeland, Youngstown State University; Rita Eastburg, College of Lake County; Joanne Ferreira, State University of New York at New Paltz and Fordham University; Carol L. Gabel, William Paterson University; Anne Gervasi, DeVry Institute of Technology; Joe Glaser, Western Kentucky University; Michael Goodman, Fairleigh Dickinson University; Mary Multer Greene, Tidewater Community College at Virginia Beach; Julie Hagemann, Purdue University, Calumet; John L. Hare, Montgomery College; Lory Hawkes, DeVry Institute of Technology, Irving; Lorraine Higgins, University of Pittsburgh; Janet H. Hobbs, Wake Technical Community College; Frank Hubbard, Marquette University; Rebecca Innocent, Southern Methodist University; Ursula Irwin, Mount Hood Community College; Denise Jackson, Southeast Missouri State University; Margo K. Jang, Northern Kentucky University; Margaret Faye Jones, Nashville State Technical Institute; Myra Jones, Manatee Community College; Judith C. Kohl, Dutchess Community College; James C. McDonald, University of Southwestern Louisiana; Darlene Malaska, Youngstown Christian University; Christine Manion, Marquette University; Martha Marinara, University of Central Florida; Michael J. Martin, Illinois State University; Susan J. Miller, Santa Fe Community College; Rosemary G. Moffett, Elizabethtown Community College; Bethany Paige Nowviskie, University of Virginia; Jon F. Patton, University of Toledo; Pamela T. Pittman, University of Central Oklahoma; Nancy B. Porter, West Virginia Wesleyan College; Kirk Rasmussen, Utah Valley State College; Edward J. Reilly, St. Joseph's College; Peter Burton Ross, University of the District of Columbia; Eileen Schwartz, Purdue University, Calumet; Lisa Sebti, Central Texas College; Eileen B. Seifert, DePaul University; John S. Shea, Loyola University at Chicago; Tony

Silva, Purdue University; Bill M. Stiffler, Harford Community College; Jack Summers, Central Piedmont Community College; Vivian A. Thomlinson, Cameron University; Matt Turner, Iowa State University; William P. Weiershauser, Iowa Wesleyan College; Joe Wenig, Purdue University; Carolyn West, Daytona Beach Community College; and Roseanna B. Whitlow, Southeast Missouri State University. Skilled reviewers of previous Canadian editions include Elaine Bander, Dawson College; Ronald W. Cooley, University of Saskatchewan; Cherry Dalley, Cabot College; Jeffery Donaldson, McMaster University; W. H. (Bill) Fricker, Northern Alberta Institute of Technology; Enid Gossin, Seneca College; Gabriele Helms, University of British Columbia; Gladys Hindmarch, Capilano College; Ingrid Hutchinson, Fanshawe College; Carol McCandless, Capilano College; and M. Dale Wilkie, University of Alberta.

My special gratitude goes to a group of eminent colleagues who contributed to the *Annotated Instructor's Edition (AIE)* of the U.S. Sixth Edition of the *Simon & Schuster Handbook for Writers.* For their scholarly bibliographic essays that set the context for my handbook, I thank Barbara Gleason, City College of the City University of New York; Catherine L. Hobbs, University of Oklahoma; Irwin Weiser, Purdue University; Margot I. Soven, La Salle University; and Joy Reid, University of Wyoming. D. J. Henry, Daytona Beach Community College, wrote the description in the margins of Chapter 35 of her practical application of portfolio assessment theory to the first-year composition classroom.

Pearson Education Canada provided me with a highly talented and enthusiastic group of collaborators. David Stover, Editor-in-Chief and Acquisitions Editor, supplied the vision and skill to put the plan for the *Simon & Schuster Handbook for Writers,* Third Canadian Edition, into effect. Matthew Christian, Developmental Editor, guided the project with uncommon intelligence and managerial acumen. Avivah Wargon, Supervising and Production Editor, and Peggy Brown, Production Coordinator, are the dedicated and sympathetic team who coordinated the book's production. Lisa Berland, who served as Developmental Editor for the Second Canadian Edition, this time contributed her sharp eye and analytic talents to the task of reading the book's proofs. Tara Tovell, who read second proofs, and Stephanie Fysh, indexer, also made significant contributions.

At U.S. Prentice Hall, I worked with a heroic, exceedingly intelligent team. Leah Jewell, English Editor in Chief, a visionary gifted with exceptional common sense, was the leader. Shelly Kupperman, Production Editor and Senior Project Manager, shared her amazing ability to care passionately, stay calm and productive in the midst of maelstroms, and polish all details to a lustrous shine. Vivian Garcia, Assistant Editor, was ideal as editorial coordinator because she is astute, dynamic, informed, and a delight to work with; while Stephanie Carpenter, Assistant Development Editor, jumped on the moving train of my handbook with grace and gusto, quickly becoming indispensable. Brandy Dawson, Senior Marketing Manager, participated beyond what her title suggests, for she is a keen-minded, enthusiastic bard who brings to the table news of the road along with fresh ideas. Others whose support sustained me are Phil Miller, President of Humanities and Social Sciences; Barbara Kittle, Director of Production and Marketing; Mary Rottino, Managing Editor; Leslie Osher, Creative Design Director; Beth Gillett Mejia, Director of Marketing; Ximena P. Tamvakopoulos, Senior Art Director; Mary Ann Gloriande, Assistant Manufacturing Manager; Nick Sklitsis, Manufacturing Manager; Bud Therien, AVP/Publisher; and Editorial Assistant Jennifer M. Collins and Marketing Assistant Christine Moodie. I would also like to thank both Judy Kiveat and Diane Nesin for their sharp eyes and dedication to excellence in copyediting and proofreading the U.S. Sixth Edition.

Family and friends strengthen all facets of my life by allowing me to share their lives and affections. Ida Morea, my Administrative Assistant and friend, is a joy who graces each day with her wonderful warmth, loyalty, excellence, and readiness to dive into whatever is at hand. My sister and friend, Edith Klausner, graces me with her bountiful spirit and outstanding values as a progressive educator. Others I treasure in my family include my sister-in-law and brother-in-law Rita and Hy Cohen; my niece Randi Klausner Friedman and Kenny, Casey, Max, and Alexandra; my nephew Michael Klausner and Barbara, Jill, Gregory, and Claire; my nephew Steven Klausner and Ariele, Daniel, and Jessica; my cousins Alan Furman and Lynne, Adam, and Joshua; Elaine and Lee Dushoff; Martha and Chuck Schliefer; Zina Rosenthal; the late, sorely missed Gideon Zwas; Tzila Zwas and Gila, and Eyal; and my late parents, Belle and Sidney Quitman. My "adopted" family, most especially extraordinary Kristen and Dan, Lindsey, and Ryan Black, are a cherished, vital part of my life. My dear friends stand by me in ways large and small. They are Susan Bartlestone; Elliot Goldhush; Myra Kogen; JoAnn and Tom Lavery; Betty Renshaw; Magdalena Rogalskaja; Avery Ryan and Jimmy, Gavin, and Ian; Shirley and Don Stearns; Marilyn and Ernest Sternglass; Elsie Tischler; Lisa and Nathaniel Wallace; and Muriel Wolfe. Most of all, I thank my husband and dearest friend, David Troyka, for his vibrant love, unwavering moral support, and energizing spirit of adventure.

About the Author

Lynn Quitman Troyka, Ph.D., taught for many years at the City University of New York (CUNY), including Queensborough Community College; the Center for Advanced Studies in Education at the Graduate School; the graduate program in Language and Literacy at City College; and as Senior Research Associate in the Instructional Resource Center.

Dr. Troyka has published in journals such as *College Composition and Communication, College English, Journal of Basic Writing*, and *Writing Program Administration*, and in books from Southern Illinois University Press, Random House, the National Council of Teachers of English (NCTE), and Heinemann/Boynton/Cook. She is an author in composition/rhetoric for the *Encyclopedia of English Studies and Language Arts*, Scholastic, 1993; and in basic writing for the *Encyclopedia of Rhetoric*, 1994. She served as editor of the *Journal of Basic Writing* from 1985 to 1988. She has also conducted seminars and workshops at hundreds of colleges and universities and at national and international meetings.

Dr. Troyka is the author of numerous textbooks, including the *Simon & Schuster Quick Access Reference for Writers*, Canadian Edition, Prentice Hall, 2000; the *Simon & Schuster Handbook for Writers*, Third Canadian Edition, Prentice Hall, 2002; *Structured Reading*, Fifth Edition (with Joseph W. Thweatt), Prentice Hall, 1999; *Steps in Composition*, Seventh Edition (with Jerrold Nudelman), Prentice Hall, 1999; and seven others.

Dr. Troyka is a past national chair of the Two-Year College English Association (TYCA) of NCTE, the Conference on College Composition and Communication (CCCC), the College Section of NCTE, and the Writing Division of the Modern Language Association (MLA). She is the recipient of the 2001 Exemplar Award of CCCC, the highest award given for scholarship, teaching, and service. She was named 1993 Rhetorician of the Year, and she received the Nell Ann Pickett Award for Service in 1995 from TYCA.

She chaired the Task Force on the Future of CCCC and the CCCC Project Mentor Committee, and she currently serves on the NCTE Leadership Committee for Preparing Future Faculty (PFF), a project of the Council of Graduate Schools and the American Association of Colleges and Universities.

"All this information," says Dr. Troyka, "tells what I've done, not who I am. I am a teacher. Teaching is my life's work, and I love it."

CREDITS

Arthur Andrew, excerpt from *The Rise and Fall of a Middle Power.* © 1993 Arthur Andrew. By permission of James Lorimer & Company Limited.

W. H. Auden, "Prologue: The Birth of Architecture" from *Collected Poems,* edited by Edward Mendelson. © 1965 by W. H. Auden. Reprinted with the permission of Random House, Inc. and Faber & Faber.

Jane E. Brody, excerpt from "A Hoarder's Life: Filling the Cache—and Finding It!" from *The New York Times* (November 19, 1991). © 1991 by The New York Times Company. Reprinted with the permission of *The New York Times.*

Harry Bruce, excerpt from "The Softball Was Always Hard," © Harry Bruce. Reprinted by arrangement with Bella Pomer Agency.

Sharon Butala, excerpt from "Rural Saskatchewan: Creating the Garden" from *Voices: Essays on Canadian Families,* edited by Marian Lynn (Nelson Canada). © 1995 Sharon Butala. With permission of the author.

Gerald Secor Couzens, excerpt from "If Lightning Strikes" from *Newsday* (August 13, 1988). © 1988 by Newsday. Reprinted with permission.

Northrop Frye, excerpt from Commission to the Graduating Class of 1988 in *Vic Report* 1991, edited by Alexandra Johnston. Published by permission of the Board of Regents, Victoria University, Toronto.

Robert Fulford, excerpt from "The Grand Illusion," *Saturday Night,* June 1984. Copyright © 1984 *Saturday Night.* Reprinted by permission.

Douglas Goold and Andrew Willis, excerpt from *The Bre-X Fraud,* used by permission, McClelland & Stewart Ltd., *The Canadian Publishers.*

Wayne Grady, excerpts from *Chasing the Chinook.* © 1998 by Wayne Grady. Reprinted by permission of Penguin Books Canada Limited.

Richard Gwyn, excerpt from *The 49th Paradox,* used by permission, McClelland and Stewart Ltd., *The Canadian Publishers.*

Robert Harris, excerpt from *What to Listen for in Mozart.* © Simon & Schuster.

Sydney J. Harris, "Sports Only Exercise Our Eyes" from *The Best of Sydney J. Harris.* © 1975 by Sydney J. Harris. Reprinted with the permission of Houghton Mifflin Company. All rights reserved.

Michael Ignatieff, excerpt from *Blood and Belonging*. Copyright © 1993 by Michael Ignatieff. Reprinted by permission of Penguin Books Canada Limited.

Mark Kingwell, excerpt from *Marginalia: A Cultural Reader* (Toronto: Penguin Canada, 1999). Copyright © 1999 Mark Kingwell. With permission of the author.

Michele Landsberg, excerpt from *Michele Landsberg's Guide to Children's Books*. Copyright © 1985 by Michele Landsberg. Reprinted by permission of Penguin Books Canada Limited.

Robert J. Lipsyte, excerpts from "The Emasculation of Sports" from *The New York Times Magazine* (May 2, 1995). © 1995 by The New York Times Company. Reprinted with the permission of *The New York Times*.

Randolph H. Manning, excerpt from "Fighting Racism with Inclusion" from *Newsday* (October 7, 1990). © 1990 by Newsday. Reprinted with permission.

Kenneth McRoberts, excerpt from *Misconceiving Canada: The Struggle for National Unity* reprinted with permission of Oxford University Press.

Ovide Mercredi, excerpt from "Self-Government as a Way to Heal," from *In the Rapids* by Ovide Mercredi and Mary Ellen Turpel. Copyright © 1993 by Ovide Mercredi and Mary Ellen Turpel. Reprinted by permission of Penguin Books Canada Limited.

Farley Mowat, excerpt from "The Nature of the North," from *Canada North*. Permission granted by Farley Mowat Limited.

Alice Munro, excerpt from "Royal Beatings," from *Who Do You Think You Are?* Copyright © 1977 by Alice Munro. Reprinted by permission of William Morris Agency, Inc. on behalf of the Author.

Jo Goodwin Parker, excerpts from "What Is Poverty?" from George Henderson, *America's Other Children*. © 1971 by the University of Oklahoma Press. Reprinted with the permission of the publishers.

Geoff Pevere and Grieg Dymond, excerpt from *Mondo Canuck* (Toronto: Prentice Hall Canada, 1996). By permission of Prentice Hall Canada.

Lisa Pratt, excerpt from "A Slice of History" from *Newsday Magazine* (April 29, 1990). © 1990 by Newsday. Reprinted with permission.

Roger Rosenblatt, excerpt from "What Brand of Laughter Do You Use?" from *The New York Times* (November 17, 1991). © 1991 by The New York Times Company. Reprinted with the permission of *The New York Times*.

Witold Rybczynski, excerpt from *Home*. Copyright © Witold Rybczynski.

Screen shots of UnCover database © 1998 The UnCover Company.

Screen shots of University of Toronto online catalogue courtesy of University of Toronto Library.

Screen shot from Balloon Pages on the World Wide Web: The World Wide Web Balloon Pages is the gateway to nearly all balloon Web sites in cyberspace. It's compiled by Joop de Wilde, a Dutch balloon pilot, jdewilde@euronet.nl

Screen shot of Yahoo! reproduced with permission of Yahoo! Inc. Copyright © 2000 by Yahoo! Inc. YAHOO! and the YAHOO! Logo are trademarks of Yahoo! Inc.

John Warde, excerpt from "Safe Lifting Techniques" from *The New York Times* (March 11, 1990). © 1990 by The New York Times Company. Reprinted with the permission of *The New York Times*.

Ronald Wright, excerpt from *Stolen Continents*. © 1992. Reprinted by permission of Penguin Books Canada Limited.

Jean Vanier, excerpt from *Becoming Human*. Copyright © 1998 by Jean Vanier. Reprinted by permission of Stoddart Publishing Co. Limited.

Margaret Visser, excerpt from *The Rituals of Dinner*, published in Canada by HarperCollinsPublishers Ltd. © 1991 by Margaret Visser. All rights reserved.

PART

I

Writing an Essay

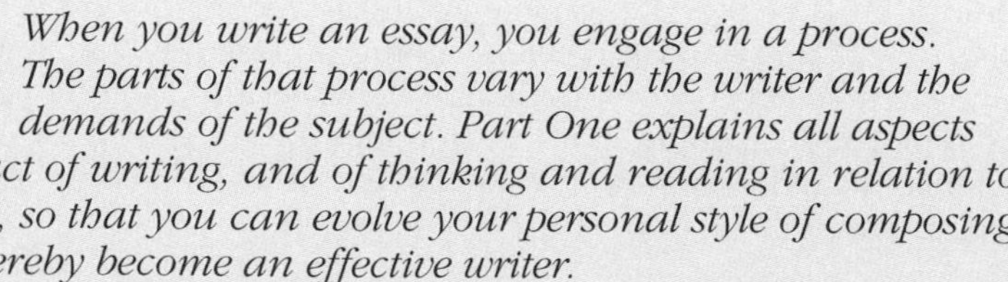

When you write an essay, you engage in a process. The parts of that process vary with the writer and the demands of the subject. Part One explains all aspects of the act of writing, and of thinking and reading in relation to writing, so that you can evolve your personal style of composing and thereby become an effective writer.

1 Thinking About Purposes and Audiences

Why write? In this age of cell phones, e-mail, and the Internet, why do you need the ability to write well? The answer has overlapping parts, starting with the inner life of a writer and moving outward.

Writing is a way of thinking and learning. Writing gives you unique opportunities to explore ideas and understand information. By writing, you come to know subjects well and make them your own. Even thirty years later, many people can recall details about the topics and content of essays they wrote in college or university, but far fewer people can recall specifics of a classroom lecture or a textbook chapter. Writing helps you learn and gain authority over knowledge. As you share what you learn, you also teach. When you write for a reader, you play the role of a teacher, someone who knows the material sufficiently well to organize and present it clearly.

Writing is a way of discovering. The act of writing allows you to make unexpected connections among ideas and language. As you write, thoughts emerge and interconnect in ways unavailable until the physical act of writing begins. An authority on writing, James Britton, describes discovery in writing as "shaping at the point of utterance." Similarly, well-known writer E. M. Forster talked about discovery during writing by asking, "How can I know what I mean until I've seen what I said?" You can expect many surprises of insight that come only when you write and rewrite, each time trying to get closer to what you want to say.

Writing creates reading. Writing is a powerful means of communication. It creates a permanent, visible record of your ideas for others to read and ponder. Reading informs and shapes human thought. In an open society, everyone is free to write and thereby to create reading for other people. For that freedom to be exercised, however, the ability to write cannot be concentrated in a few people. All of us need access to the power of the written word.

Writing ability is needed by educated people. In college and university, you must write many different types of assignments. In the workplace, most jobs, even in today's technological society, require writing skill for preparing documents ranging from letters to formal reports. Throughout your life, your writing reveals your ability to think clearly and to use language effectively.

1a Understanding the elements of writing

Writing can be explained by its elements: *Writing is a way of communicating a message to a reader for a purpose.* Each word in this definition carries important meaning. **Communicating** in writing means sending a message that has a destination. The **message** of writing is its content, which originates in your motivation as a writer to engage in one or more of these activities: *observing, remembering, reporting, explaining, exploring, interpreting, speculating, evaluating,* and *reflecting.* The **reader,** usually called the audience, is explained in section 1c. **Purposes** for writing are discussed in section 1b.

1b Understanding purposes for writing

Writing is often defined by its **purpose.** Writing purposes have to do with goals, sometimes referred to as *aims of writing* or *writing intentions.* Thinking about purposes for writing means thinking about the motivating forces that move people to write. As a student, you might assume that your only purpose for writing is to fulfil a class assignment. More is involved, however. Your academic writing will almost certainly address at least one of the major purposes discussed in this section.

The overarching categories for the major purposes for writing are shown in Chart 1. The purposes of writing *to express yourself* and *to create a literary work* contribute importantly to human thought and culture (see 1b-1). This handbook concentrates on the two purposes most prominent and practical in your academic life: *to inform a reader* (1b-2) and *to persuade a reader* (1b-3).

As a writer in college or university, you are challenged to shape the content of your material and the style of your writing to suit your writing purpose.

You have many choices of writing strategies for presenting your message with clarity and impact. These strategies include narrating, describing, illustrating, defining, analyzing and classifying, comparing

PURPOSES FOR WRITING* 1

- to express yourself
- to inform a reader
- to persuade a reader
- to create a literary work

and contrasting, drawing an analogy, considering cause and effect, and others; see Chapter 4, especially section 4f.

1 Writing to express yourself

Expressive writing is usually the private recording of your thoughts and feelings. (When expressive writing is intended for public exposure, it becomes more like *literary writing*.) Consider this personal journal entry written by one of the students whose essay appears in Chapter 6; even though it is his private writing, it is published here with his permission.

> When we lived in Manitoba, the fall and winter holidays were my touchstones—the calendar moved along in comforting sequence. I wrapped the snow and foods and celebrations around me like a soft blanket. I burrowed in. Now that we live in Victoria, I don't need that blanket. But I surely do miss it.
>
> —DANIEL CASEY, student

2 Writing to inform a reader

Informative writing seeks to give information and, frequently, to explain it. This writing is known also as **expository writing** because it expounds on, or sets forth, ideas and facts. *Informative writing focuses mainly on the subject being discussed.*

Informative writing includes reports of observations, ideas, scientific data, facts, statistics. It can be found in textbooks, encyclopedias, technical and business reports, nonfiction, newspapers, and magazines.

When you write to inform, you are expected to offer information with a minimum of bias. You aim to educate, not to persuade. Like all effective teachers, you need to present the information completely,

*Adapted from James L. Kinneavy, *A Theory of Discourse*. New York: Norton, 1980.

clearly, and accurately. The material should be verifiable by additional reading, talking with others, or personal experience. For example, consider this passage that aims to inform the reader.

> In 1914 in what is now Addo Park in South Africa, a hunter by the name of Pretorius was asked to exterminate a herd of 140 elephants. He killed all but 20, and those survivors became so cunning at evading him that he was forced to abandon the hunt. The area became a preserve in 1930, and the elephants have been protected ever since. Nevertheless, elephants now four generations removed from those Pretorius hunted remain shy and strangely nocturnal. Young elephants evidently learn from the adults' trumpeting alarm calls to avoid humans.
>
> —CAROL GRANT GOULD, "Out of the Mouths of Beasts"

As informative writing, this passage works because it *focuses* clearly on its topic (elephant behaviour), presents *verifiable facts*, and is written in a *reasonable tone.*

CHECKLIST FOR INFORMATIVE WRITING 2

- Is its information clear?
- Is its information complete and accurate?
- Does it present facts, ideas, and observations that can be verified?
- Is the writer's tone reasonable and free of distortions?

3 Writing to persuade a reader

Persuasive writing seeks to convince the reader about a matter of opinion. This writing is sometimes called **argumentative** because it argues a position. (Because the techniques of written argument can be especially demanding on a writer, this handbook devotes all of Chapter 6 to them.)

Persuasive writing focuses mainly on the reader, whom the writer wants to influence. When you write to persuade, you deal with debatable topics. Persuasive writing seeks to change the reader's mind or at least to bring the reader's point of view closer to the writer's. Even the writer who feels sure that the reader's position on the subject will never change is expected to argue as convincingly as possible.

To be persuasive, you cannot merely state an opinion. Your reader expects you to offer convincing support for your point of view. Such support often relies upon information that explains and defends a point of view. Persuasive writing, therefore, often calls for informative writing (see 1b-2) to provide the evidence that lends strength to an argument. Examples of persuasive writing include editorials, letters to the editor, reviews, sermons, business or research proposals, opinion essays in magazines, and books that argue a point of view. Consider this passage written to persuade.

> The search for some biological basis for math ability or disability is fraught with logical and experimental difficulties. Since not all math under-achievers are women, and not all women are mathematics-avoidant, poor performance in math is unlikely to be due to some genetic or hormonal difference between the sexes. Moreover, no amount of research so far has unearthed a "mathematical competency" in some tangible, measurable substance in the body. Since "masculinity" cannot be injected into women to test whether or not it improves their mathematics, the theories that attribute such ability to genes or hormones must depend for their proof on circumstantial evidence. So long as about seven percent of the Ph.D.'s in mathematics are earned by women, we have to conclude either that these women have genes, hormones, and brain organization different from those of the rest of us, or that certain positive experiences in their lives have largely undone the negative fact that they are female, or both.
>
> —SHEILA TOBIAS, *Overcoming Math Anxiety*

As persuasive writing, this passage works because it presents *information* on math ability without distortion; expresses a *point of view* that relies on sound reasoning; offers *evidence;* and tries to *influence the reader to agree* with the point of view.

CHECKLIST FOR PERSUASIVE WRITING 3

- Does it present a point of view about which opinions vary?
- Does it support its point of view with specifics?
- Is its point of view based on sound reasoning and logic?
- Are the points of its argument clear?
- Does it evoke the intended reaction from the reader?

EXERCISE 1-1

For each paragraph, decide if the dominant purpose is *informative* or *persuasive*. Then, answer the questions in Chart 2 or Chart 3 in relation to the paragraph, and explain your answers.

A. Diabetes mellitus could be treated—at least to the extent of reducing the elevated blood sugar and correcting the acidosis that otherwise led to diabetic coma and death—by the insulin preparation isolated by Banting and Best. Pellagra, a common cause of death among the impoverished rural populations in the South, had become curable with Goldberger's discovery of the vitamin B complex and the subsequent identification of nicotinic acid. Diphtheria could be prevented by immunization against the toxin of diphtheria bacilli and, when it occurred, treated more or less effectively with diphtheria antitoxin.

—LEWIS THOMAS, "1933 Medicine"

B. Noisy invasion of public spaces by yahoos is hardly a new problem, but unless my experience has been atypical, it seems to be nearing epidemic proportions. And the brutes are branching out. No longer content merely to destroy the sweet holy silence of the movie theatres, like nasty malignant cells, they're now everywhere—and they're out for blood. I see them on subway platforms, where their infernal amplified radios bring demented stares to other passengers' faces but never seem to arouse the offenders from their somnambulant stupor. I've pulled up beside roving packs of them at red lights, where they stare like zombies, blithely unaware that the decibel level of their tape decks is precipitating anxiety attacks in passers-by for miles. I've come face to face with them as close to home as a campsite in Algonquin Park and as far away as a surf-washed beach in Bali; recently I've even encountered them at live theatre. All of which convinces me there's something awry in the land.

—WENDY DENNIS, "A Tongue-Lashing for Deaf Ears"

C. Much of how the people live in rural Saskatchewan today continues to stem from the value system and the exigencies of pioneer life. The first settlers here almost immediately had to become self-sufficient, since the governmental system of land division ensured large distances between families at a time when transportation was always slow and uncertain, and in a climate where the weather was frequently too severe to allow travel. (That this system also ensured loneliness for the women who were always less mobile than the men is an underlying, but not fully articulated, theme in western Canadian life.) In most respects farm life at least has changed a great deal since those early days, and these changes have left the society in a general way still operating within a value system that does not always make sense in the new conditions.

—SHARON BUTALA, "Rural Saskatchewan: Creating the Garden"

EXERCISE 1-2

Consulting section 1b, assume that you have to write on each of these topics twice, once to inform and once to persuade your reader. Be prepared to discuss how your two treatments of each topic would differ.

1. diets
2. Canadian television
3. tattoos
4. tourists
5. cell phones

1c Understanding audiences for writing

Good writing is often judged by its ability to reach its intended **audience.** To be effective, informative and persuasive writing (see 1b) need to be geared to the fact that someone is "out there" to receive the communication. If you write without considering your reader, you risk communicating only with yourself.

As a writer for one or more readers, you need to consider who your audience is, especially concerning background. For example, in writing meant to persuade people to vote for a particular candidate, if you imply disrespect for people who stay home and raise children, you risk losing votes of many homemakers and their spouses. Or, if you wanted to persuade members of Parliament that homemakers should be eligible for a day-care subsidy, you would need to address some of the MPs' practical concerns, such as the impact of your proposal on the federal budget.

Also, as you write, you need to think about what you can assume an audience already knows. For example, a sales report filled with technical language assumes that its readers know the specialized vocabulary. The general reading public would have trouble understanding such a report. But if the material were rewritten without technical terms, general readers could understand it.

If you know or can reasonably assume even a few of the characteristics listed in Chart 4, your chances of reaching your audience improve. The more explicit your information about your audience, the better able you are to reach it. Often, of course, you can only guess at the details. Chart 4 can help you get started.

CHECKLIST OF BASIC AUDIENCE CHARACTERISTICS 4

WHAT SETTING ARE THEY READING IN?

- academic setting?
- workplace setting?
- public setting?

WHO ARE THEY?

- age, gender
- ethnic backgrounds, political philosophies, religious beliefs
- roles (student, parent, voter, wage earner, property owner, other)
- interests, hobbies

WHAT DO THEY KNOW?

- level of education
- amount of general or specialized knowledge about the topic
- probable preconceptions brought to the material

◆ ESL NOTE: If you come from outside North America, you may be surprised by the directness with which people speak and write in Canada. If so, I hope you'll read my open letter to multilingual students and what it says about honouring their cultures; it starts Part Seven of this handbook. Your own tradition may expect elaborate and/or ceremonial written language; tactful, indirect discussions, with the central point of an academic essay reserved for the middle; and, possibly, digressions from the main point. In contrast, Canadian writers and readers expect language and style to be direct and straightforward, with little embellishment. Canadian college and university instructors expect essays to contain a thesis statement (usually at the end of the introductory paragraph); to demonstrate a tightly organized presentation of information from one paragraph to the next; to back up generalizations with strong supporting details; and to contain a logical concluding paragraph. Also, you are expected to use "standard English grammar" that follows the rules used by educated speakers. Accurate choice of words and correct spelling are also expected. ◆

1 Understanding the general reading public

The **general reading public** is composed of educated, experienced readers, people who frequently read newspapers, magazines, and books. These readers often have some general information about the subject you are dealing with, but they enjoy learning something new or seeing something from a different perspective. The general reading public expects material to be clear and to be free of advanced technical information.

2 Understanding specialists as readers

Specialists are members of the general reading public who have expert knowledge on specific subjects. In writing for specialists, you are expected to know the specialty and also to realize that your readers have advanced expertise.

Specialized readers often share not only knowledge but also assumptions, interests, and beliefs. For example, they may be members of a club that concentrates on a hobby, such as amateur astronomy or orchid raising. They may have similar backgrounds, such as having immigrated from another country or having worked at a similar job. They may have similar views on matters related to religion and politics. When you write for readers who share specialized knowledge, you have to balance the necessity to be thorough with the demand not to go into too much detail about technical terms and special references.

3 Understanding your peers as readers

In some writing classes, instructors divide students into **peer response groups**. Such groups usually mean that your fellow students give you feedback on your writing drafts. This arrangement can prove very useful to you, because responses from peer groups allow you to benefit from others' ways of reading your writing—with the added advantage of seeing or hearing other students' writing for the same assignment. (If your instructor does not use peer response groups, check whether you are permitted to ask other students to help you. There can be a fine line between giving opinions and doing others' work for them.)

By responding in a peer group, you participate in a respected tradition of colleagues helping colleagues. Professional writers often seek to improve their rough drafts by asking other writers for comments. When you respond as a fellow student writer, you are not expected to be an expert. Rather, you can offer valuable responses as a practised reader and as a fellow writer who understands what other writers in your group are going through.

Specific setups for peer response groups can vary greatly among instructors, so be clear about exactly what is expected of you as both peer responder and writer in each situation. If your instructors distribute guidelines or directions for working in a peer response group, follow them carefully. One arrangement might call for students to pass around and read each others' drafts silently and then to jot helpful reactions or questions in the margins or on instructor-designed response forms. Another arrangement might have students reading their drafts aloud after which each person in the peer response group would respond either orally or on an instructor-designed form. Yet another arrangement might require response to only one feature of a draft.

If you have no experience in working as a member of a peer response group, or in the particular system for peer response required by your instructor, you can confidently assume you are not alone in feeling a bit lost. Consult the guidelines in Chart 5, watch what experienced people do (though some people can seem experienced when they are not), ask questions of your instructor (which demonstrates a positive, cooperative attitude), or dive in knowing you will learn as you go along.

GUIDELINES FOR PARTICIPATING IN PEER RESPONSE GROUPS 5

One basic principle guides your work in a peer response group: Approach it with an upbeat, constructive attitude, whether you are responding to someone else's writing or you are being responded to by others.

AS A RESPONDER

- Think of yourself in the role of a coach, not a judge.
- Consider your peers' writing as "works in progress."
- After hearing or reading a peer's writing, briefly summarize it as a check to determine that what you understand is what the writer intended.
- Start with what you think is well done. No one likes to hear only negative comments.
- Be honest in your suggestions for improvements. →

GUIDELINES FOR PARTICIPATING IN PEER RESPONSE GROUPS *(continued)* 5

- Ground your responses in an understanding of the writing process, remembering that you are dealing with drafts, not finished products. All writing can be revised (see 3c). Then the editing (3d) of surface features, such as spelling, can follow.
- Give concrete and specific responses. General comments such as "this is good" or "that is weak" say little. What specifically is good or bad? Ideas? Patterns of organization? Sentence styles? Word choice?
- Follow your instructor's system for getting your comments into writing so that your fellow writer can recall what you said. If one member of your group is supposed to take notes, speak clearly so the notes will be accurate.

AS A WRITER

- Adopt an attitude that encourages your peers to respond freely. Try to avoid defending your writing too aggressively.
- Remain open-minded when you hear responses. Your peers' comments can help you reread your writing in a fresh way that results in your writing a better revised draft.
- Ask for clarification if a comment is not clear to you. Ask for specifics, not generalities.
- As much as you encourage your peers to be honest, remember that the writing is yours. You are its "owner." You decide what comments to use or not use.

Now to the sometimes sticky issue of how to take criticism of your writing: Here is my personal advice for being able (or at least appearing able) to take constructive criticism gracefully. First, know that if criticism tends to jar your nerves, even when intended as constructive, you are not alone in your reaction. You have much company among professional writers if your initial reaction to criticism is defensive. Of course, if a response is purposely destructive or cruel, you and all others in your peer response group have every right to say so and ask that it be withdrawn or rephrased. Second, if a response is not clear to you, ask for clarification. You cannot learn what you do not understand. Third, realize that most students dislike having to criticize their peers. They fear they will lose friendships. They worry about being impolite, inaccurate, and plain wrong. If you want to set an atmosphere that encourages your peers to respond freely to you and therefore to be as helpful as possible, show that you can listen without being angry or feeling intruded upon. Finally, remember that whatever you have written is yours alone. You retain "ownership" of your writing always. Your revisions reflect your sense of what is needed to help it move closer to reaching your intended audience.

Understanding your instructor as a reader

Eventually, of course, your audience for a class assignment is your **instructor.** Your instructor is a member of the general reading public and also someone who recognizes that you are an apprentice. Your instructor knows that few students are experienced writers or complete experts on their subjects. Still, your instructor always expects your writing to reflect that you took time to learn the material thoroughly and to write about it well. In part, therefore, an instructor is a *judge,* someone to whom you must demonstrate that you are doing your best. Instructors are very experienced readers who can quickly recognize a minimal effort or a negative attitude (as when a paper carries a tone that suggests "Tell me what you want and I'll give it to you").

Think of your instructor as a representative reader typical of the audience you want to reach. *Inexperienced writers sometimes wrongly assume that instructors will fill in mentally what is missing on the page.* Instructors expect what they read to include everything that the writer wants to say or imply. Do not leave out material. Even if you write immediately after your instructor has heard you give an oral report on the same subject, write as if no one is aware of what you know.

Your instructor is also an *academic,* a member of a group whose professional life centres on intellectual endeavours. You must, therefore, write within the constraints of academic writing. For example, if you are told to write on a topic of your choice, you definitely do not have total freedom to choose. Your topic must have some intrinsic intellectual interest. For example, an essay should not merely give directions on how to cut a wedding cake or use an eraser.

1d Understanding the effect of tone

The **tone** of your writing is established by *what you say* and *how you say it.* Tone underlies much of written communication. This section gives a brief overview of tone, with references to longer discussions that you can consult elsewhere in this handbook.

The tone in your writing needs to be shaped to your purpose for writing (see 1b) and awareness of your audience (see 1c). Your tone reveals your attitude both toward the material about which you are writing and toward anyone you expect to read your writing. For example, if your tone implies that you feel superior to your readers, your material will be condescending and distasteful. Similarly, if your tone hints that you are uninformed or unsure, your readers will quickly lose confidence in what you are saying.

In your academic writing, you want to achieve a reasonable tone, both in the content of your material and in your choice of words. For example, readers may think a writer unreasonable who distorts information or tries to manipulate emotions unfairly by using slanted language (see 21a-4). Choose evenhanded or neutral words ("the politician being investigated for taking bribes") rather than biased ones ("the corrupt, deceitful politician"). Also, readers can infer from sexist language (see 21b) that a writer is insensitive to gender issues in word choice. Choose gender-neutral terms and language that represents both men and women fairly ("police officer," "the doctors and their spouses") rather than sexist language ("policeman," "the doctors and their wives"). Similarly, pretentious language (see 21e-1) reflects negatively on a writer because it can obscure the message. Choose straightforward words ("the concert") rather than overblown words ("the orchestral event").

As important, when you move from writing privately for yourself to writing for an audience, the level of formality (see 21a-1) in your writing should reflect your goal. Although readers enjoy lively language, they can be jarred by an overly informal tone being injected into a serious discussion. Readers of academic writing expect to be

GUIDELINES FOR HANDLING TONE IN YOUR WRITING 6

- Choose language appropriate to your subject and your readers.
- Choose words that work with your message, not against it.
- Use a highly informal tone only when you want to sound as if you are speaking conversationally.
- Avoid an overly formal, pretentious tone.
- Avoid sarcasm and other forms of nastiness.
- Use a formal tone or medium level of formality in your academic writing and when you write for supervisors, professionals, and other people you know from a distance.
- Whatever tone you choose, be consistent in each piece of writing.

treated respectfully. A medium level of formality is most effective. For example, in a newspaper report about the results of an election, you would not refer to the loser or winner as *guy* or *gal,* no matter how relaxed the candidate appeared. To control the tone in your writing, follow the guidelines in Chart 6.

EXERCISE 1-3

Using the topics listed here, work individually or with your peer response group to determine specific ways the tone of an essay would differ for these three audiences: an academic instructor, a close friend, and a supervisor at a job. Be ready to discuss in detail how the three essays on each topic would differ. For help, consult 1d.

1. a fair way to evaluate each person's work
2. benefits of having water sprinklers in each room
3. an explanation of why you were absent yesterday

1e Using outside sources for writing

An **outside source** is someone else's ideas, not yours. Outside sources include all that is located in libraries, credible material on the Internet (beware of using anything but what you can absolutely verify is credible; see Chart 142 in Chapter 32), and the spoken words of experts on your topic. When you can support with outside sources the validity of your information or of your point of view on a debatable topic, you bring more authority to what you are writing. But be very, very careful: Instructors have differing policies on whether or not students can draw on outside sources to support what they are writing. Some instructors forbid students to consult and use outside sources, except when a research paper (see Part Five) is assigned. Other instructors encourage students to do "source-based writing" for most assignments. Yet other instructors never want you to use outside sources for your writing. Whenever you are in doubt about an instructor's policy, ask for clarification and make sure you understand the answers you get.

One huge issue in students' using outside sources in their writing concerns the offence of **plagiarism**. Plagiarism occurs when a writer takes ideas or words from an outside source without specifically giving credit to that source. Giving credit means using the practice of documentation (see especially Chapter 34) in line with the accepted documentation style of each academic discipline. Plagiarism is such a major offence that it can lead to a student's instantly failing a course or being asked to leave a program of study.

Until recently, some students may have felt that they could "get away" with plagiarizing because no instructor could have read all the possible sources on a topic. Now, however, authors and instructors are fighting back. Today, Internet sites are being developed to scan documents and search the Internet to identify plagiarism. Such online tools look through search engine files, digitized library collections, and sites that sell research papers. The search quickly identifies not only exactly what has been plagiarized but also the source from which the material was taken.

Still, do not let this warning about plagiarism stop you from consulting outside sources. You can do so freely (within the limits of your instructor's policy, as discussed above) as long as you accurately and completely document where you found the ideas or words you are using. Refer to Chart 7 for major guidelines for using outside sources.

Many students wonder whether referring in their writing to outside sources carries the message that students cannot think or come up with ideas and words on their own. The opposite is true when outside sources are used well. Using outside sources well tests your ability to find relevant sources; to assess critically if the sources are creditable and therefore worthy of being used to support what you are writing; and to use skill in blending others' words reasonably and smoothly into the language you are using in your own writing. (Remember: *Always* use documentation.)

GUIDELINES FOR USING SOURCES IN WRITING 7

- Evaluate sources critically; not all are accurate, true, or honest. See section 5h-2, Chart 36.
- Represent the material in each source accurately. For guidance in quoting, paraphrasing, or summarizing source material, see Chapter 31.
- Synthesize source material, do not merely summarize (report) it. Make connections between the ideas and details in the source and your own ideas as stimulated by the source, or by a variety of sources. For guidance in how to synthesize, as part of critical thinking, see sections 5b and 5f.
- Credit each source by naming it clearly and completely. Ask your instructor what documentation method to use. Five widely used systems are described in Chapter 33.
- Never plagiarize. For help in avoiding plagiarism, see Chapter 31.

No matter what or how many outside sources you use, always know that *you* are your first source for writing. To plan and develop a point, you need first of all to draw on your own prior knowledge of the subject. You have been adding to your fund of knowledge throughout your life: reading, studying, listening to lectures and speeches, watching television, and exploring the Internet. Drawing on your prior knowledge is something you have been doing ever since you started putting pencil (or, way back, crayon) to paper. Also, you are the source of your thoughts, reactions, and opinions. They form the basis for all your writing, even when you use outside sources to bolster and lend authority to what you are writing.

1f Knowing the tools that can help you as a writer

Before you begin tackling your writing assignments, you can benefit greatly from knowing what tools are widely available to help you.

1 A computer for word processing

A computer's word-processing software can prove a big help at various stages of the writing process (Chapter 2). Although you can certainly write by hand or at a typewriter, methods that writers have been using for many years, you might find that writing on a computer is easier. If you don't own a computer, try to use one in your school's computer lab. Many instructors require final drafts to be typed on a computer, though some make allowances for students who find it impossible.

2 Your personal bookshelf

Your personal bookshelf needs to contain three essential volumes: a dictionary, a thesaurus, and a handbook for writers. A dictionary is indispensable. If possible, buy one. Most college and university bookstores offer a good variety of hardcover abridged or "college" dictionaries (20a-4). Before choosing one, browse through it for definitions you want to learn or to understand more clearly. A lightweight paperback abridged dictionary that you can carry with you can also be handy. Unabridged dictionaries (20a-3) list every word in English. The reference section of every library has one (usually on display) that everyone can consult.

Another valuable resource for writers is a thesaurus, which lists synonyms. The easiest to use are arranged alphabetically (20a-5).

A handbook for writers is also vital for you to have on your personal bookshelf. A handbook such as this one gives you detailed information about rules of grammar and punctuation, and other writing conventions. It also offers extensive advice about how to write successfully, whether for college or university, business, or the public. It shows you how to write and document research papers, step by step. Some handbooks, including this one, include guidance on how to write for a variety of courses other than English.

✚ COMPUTER TIP: At present, only one highly respected college dictionary—the *Merriam-Webster Collegiate Dictionary*—can be accessed online for free. The URL is <www.m-w.com/netdict.htm>. The same site gives you access to an online thesaurus. The *Oxford English Dictionary (OED)*, the most comprehensive unabridged English-language dictionary, is available online through paid subscription; students can have free access to it through academic libraries. To find out what is available when you need it, use the keyword "dictionaries" to activate a search engine—one or more Internet software programs that search and find material on any keyword you specify. ✚

3 Your college or university library

A college or university library, sometimes called a learning resources centre, is fully stocked with all manner of reference books, circulating books, resources for online access, and more. Spend some time getting to know what's available in your library. Then you can dive right in when the time comes.

Concentrate most on your library's reference section. It contains dozens, if not hundreds, of volumes. Essential resources include at least one set of encyclopedias; one or more almanacs; one or more up-to-date atlases; books of quotations (don't limit yourself to the classic *Bartlett's Familiar Quotations*); indexes to popular and scholarly periodicals; and the *Library of Congress Subject Headings (LCSH)*, volumes that list all categories of knowledge with subcategories for each. These resources can be centrally important as you write research papers and search out information for other purposes. Today, many—but not all—reference books are available in print and online.

4 Computer tools for writers

Word-processing programs, such as Microsoft Word and WordPerfect, include aids for writers. These programs are built into your software. They offer some advantages, but they also have severe limitations. Become familiar with both. In no case are such tools substitutes for your own careful editing and proofreading. Software, after all, cannot "think" and make reasonable distinctions.

- **Spell-check programs** show you words that do not appear in the dictionary in the software. These programs are a big help for spotting misspelled or mistyped words, but they will not call your attention to your having typed *west* when you intended to type *rest*.
- **Thesaurus programs**, like their print versions, give you synonyms for words. They cannot tell you which words fit well into your particular sentences, however. Whenever a synonym is unfamiliar or hazy, look it up in your dictionary. You do not want to use words that strike you as attractive options, but turn out to distort your meaning.
- **Grammar or style-check programs** check your writing against the software's strict interpretations of rules of grammar, word use, punctuation, and other conventions. You then see an alert saying that your writing differs from the program's standards. Can you always rely on those standards? No. While most alerts are useful for getting you to rethink the way you have said something, the final decision about how to deliver your message is yours. You might want to use a semicolon even when the program suggests a period; to retain a word even when the program says you need to be concise; and to accept a long sentence when it follows or is followed by a few very short sentences. Consult this handbook if you are unsure.

2 Planning and Shaping

2a Understanding the writing process

Many people assume that a real writer can pick up a pen or sit at a computer and magically write a finished product, word by perfect word. Experienced writers know better. They know that **writing is a process,** a series of activities that start the moment they begin thinking about a subject and end when they complete a final draft. Experienced writers know, also, that good writing is rewriting. Their drafts are filled with additions, deletions, rearrangements, and rewordings.

For example, below you can see how the paragraph you just read was reworked into final form. Notice that two sentences were dropped, two sentences were combined, one sentence was added, and various words were dropped, changed, or added. Such activities are typical of writing.

~~Chapter One discusses what writing is.~~ ~~This chapter explains how writing happens.~~ Many people assume that a real writer can ~~put pen to paper~~ (pick up a pen) or sit at ~~the keyboard of~~ a computer and (magically) write (a) finished product(, word by perfect word.) Experienced writers ~~all~~ know better. They know that writing is a process, ~~Writing is~~ a series of activities that start the moment (they begin) thinking about a subject ~~begins~~ and end when the(y) (complete the a) final draft. ~~is complete.~~ Experienced writers know, also, that good writing is rewriting. Their drafts are filled with additions, deletions, rearrangements, and rewordings.

Draft and Revision of Opening Paragraph in Chapter 2

AN OVERVIEW OF THE WRITING PROCESS 8

Planning calls for you to discover and compile ideas for your writing.

Shaping calls for you to organize your material.

Drafting calls for you to write your ideas in sentences and paragraphs.

Revising calls for you to evaluate your draft and rewrite it by adding, deleting, rewording, and rearranging.

Editing calls for you to check the technical correctness of your grammar, spelling, punctuation, and mechanics.

Proofreading calls for you to read your final copy to eliminate typing or handwriting errors.

Writing is an ongoing process of considering alternatives and making choices. The better you understand the writing process, the better you will write and the more you can enjoy writing. For the sake of explanation, the parts of the writing process are discussed separately in this chapter. In real life, the steps overlap, looping back and forth as each piece of writing evolves. Chart 8 summarizes the steps.

If you are a writer who likes to visualize a process, see the diagram below. A straight line would not be adequate because it would exclude the recursive nature of writing. The arrows on the diagram imply movement. Planning is not over when drafting begins, drafting is not necessarily over merely because the major activity shifts to revision, and editing sometimes inspires writers to see the need for additional revising—and perhaps some new planning.

As you work with the writing process, allow yourself to move freely through each stage to see what is involved. Then as you gain

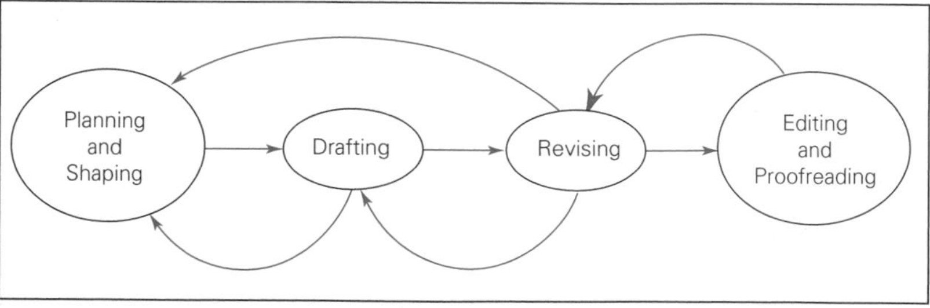

Visualizing the Writing Process

experience, begin to observe what works best for you. Once you have a general sense of the pattern of *your* writing process, you can adapt the process to suit each new situation that you encounter as a writer.

Most writers struggle some of the time with ideas that are difficult to express, sentences that will not take shape, and words that are not precise. Do not be impatient with yourself, and do not get discouraged. Writing takes time. The more you write, the easier it will be, but remember that experienced writers know that writing never happens magically.

An aside about the words used to discuss writing: Instructors refer to written products in different ways. Often the words are used interchangeably, but sometimes they have specific meanings for specific instructors. Listen closely and ask if you are unsure of what you hear. For example, the words *essay, theme,* and *composition* usually—but not always—refer to writing that runs from about 500 to 1000 words. This handbook uses *essay*. The word *paper* can mean anything from a few paragraphs to a long and detailed report or a complex research project. This handbook uses *paper* to refer to longer writing projects, such as research papers, that draw on many outside sources.

2b Adjusting for each writing situation

Writing begins with thinking about each **writing situation.** Your thinking involves answering the questions in Chart 9. Then you adjust your writing process (see 2a) to accommodate each particular writing situation.

The **topic** underlies all aspects of the writing situation. As you think through a topic, keep in mind the constraints of academic writing (see 2c). Whatever the topic, stick to it, and resist any temptation to bend it in another direction.

GUIDELINES FOR ANALYZING EACH WRITING SITUATION 9

- **Topic:** What will you be writing about?
- **Purpose:** What will be your purpose for writing?
- **Audience:** Who will be your audience?
- **Special requirements:** How much time were you given, and what length should the paper be?

The **purpose** of your college or university writing is usually *to inform* or *to persuade* (see 1b). Effective writing reflects a clear sense of purpose. Some writing assignments include or clearly imply a statement of purpose. For example, your purpose is informative if you are writing about the dangers of smoking. Conversely, your purpose is persuasive if you are writing an argument against smoking. Other assignments do not stipulate the writing purpose, which means you must choose either an informative or persuasive purpose based on the topic, what you want to say about it (often referred to as the *focus*), and how you develop what you want to say.

Your **audience** for college or university writing (see 1c) consists of all who will read it. To reach your audience effectively, you need to analyze who it might be. To do this, see the longer discussion in Chapter 1.

Special requirements influence every writing situation. These include the time allotted for the assignment, the expected length of the writing, and other practical constraints. If an assignment is due in one week, you have to expect that your instructor wants writing that shows more than one day's work. If the paper is due overnight, it has to be written more hastily, though never carelessly. If research is required, you have to build time for it into your schedule.

Your assignment is a major resource for you as you write. Refer to it often. Ideally, your instructor writes the assignment on the board or distributes it on paper. Some instructors, however, only announce an assignment, in which case you are expected to write it down. Try to record every word spoken, always ask questions if you need clarifications, and write down the answers you get or any given in response to other students' questions.

To give you examples of the writing process in progress, this chapter shows you the work of two actual students—Carol Moreno and Daniel Casey—as they plan and shape their essays. Then in Chapter 3, Carol Moreno's essay is discussed as it evolves through three drafts (shown in section 3f). Daniel Casey's essay is developed in Chapter 6, and its final draft appears in section 6i. On page 24 is the written statement of the assignment that each student received.

Moreno read her assignment with an eye toward analyzing the elements of her writing situation. The *topic* was a challenge she faced and tried to meet, a subject that Moreno realized she would have to narrow considerably (for her process of narrowing the topic, see 2c-3). For a writing *purpose,* Moreno tentatively chose an informative purpose, knowing that as she got further into her planning, she might change her mind. She saw that her instructor was to be her *audience* and that the *special requirements* of length and time were given in the assignment.

Carol Moreno was given this assignment: Write an essay of 700 to 800 words in which you discuss a challenge you faced and tried to meet. Your writing purpose can be informative or persuasive. Expect to write three drafts. Your first draft (in rough form, showing your comments to yourself and changes you made) and your second (cleanly typed) draft are due in one week. I will read your second draft as an "essay in progress" and will make comments to help you toward a third, final draft. That third, final draft (cleanly typed, double-spaced) is due one week after I hand back your second draft with my comments.

Daniel Casey was given this assignment: Write an essay of 500 to 700 words that argues about whether holidays have become too commercialized in North America. Your final draft is due in one week. Bring your earlier drafts to class for possible discussion.

Casey read his assignment to analyze his writing situation. He saw immediately that most elements were stated. The *topic* was commercialization of holidays in North America, and the *purpose* persuasive because students were expected to adopt and argue a position about the topic. The *audience* was the instructor, though Casey realized that the class might hear or see earlier drafts once the final draft was finished. The *special requirements* of length and time were given in the assignment.

EXERCISE 2-1

Consulting section 2b, for each assignment listed below, answer these questions: (a) What is its topic? (b) Is its purpose to inform or to persuade? (c) Who are your readers likely to be? (d) What special requirements of length and time are stated or implied?

1. *English:* Write a 500- to 700-word essay arguing for or against requiring two semesters of world literatures in translation for an English degree. This assignment is due in one week.
2. *Journalism:* Write a 300-word editorial for the student newspaper (to be published next week) praising or criticizing your school's policy on selling parking stickers to students and faculty. Draw on your personal experience, if any.
3. *Art:* You have twenty minutes in class to compare and contrast Greek and Roman styles of architecture.
4. *Chemistry:* Write a one-paragraph description of the process of hydration.

5. *Economics:* Write a 1000-word essay on the current and potential future effects of the Internet on economic trends. Draw on your reading. This assignment is due in two weeks.

2c Thinking through a topic for writing

Choosing a topic calls for making sound decisions. Experienced writers know that the quality of their writing depends on how they handle a topic. Always think through a topic before you rush in and get too deeply involved to pull out within the time allotted.

Of course, some assignments leave no room for making choices about the topic. You may be given very specific instructions such as "Explain how oxygen is absorbed from the lungs." Students need to do precisely what is asked, taking care not to wander off the topic. Only rarely, however, are writing-class assignments as specific as that one. Often, you will be expected to select your own topic (2c-1), broaden a narrow topic (2c-2), or narrow a broad topic (2c-3). The overriding principle always is **what separates most good writing from bad is the writer's ability to move back and forth between general statements and specific details.**

1 Selecting a topic on your own

Some instructors ask students to choose their own topic. In such situations, do not assume that all subjects are suitable for academic writing. Academic settings call for topics that can reflect your ability to think ideas through. For example, the old reliable essay about a summer vacation is probably not safe territory for a college or university essay if you have nothing extraordinary to report. Your essays need to dive into issues and concepts, and they should demonstrate that you can use specific, concrete details to support what you want to say.

When you choose a topic on your own, avoid topics so narrow that they give you little to say. For example, you would probably reach a dead end if you tried to write a 2500-word essay about what your sleeping cat looks like.

2 Broadening a narrow topic

You know that a topic is too narrow when you realize there is little to say after a few sentences, or when there is only one point to develop. When faced with a too-narrow topic, think about underlying concepts. For example, suppose you want to write about Wilfrid Laurier. If you chose "Wilfrid Laurier was the first French-speaking prime minister of Canada," you would be working with a single fact rather than a topic. To expand beyond such a narrow thought, you could think about the general area that your fact fits into—Canadian political history. Although that is too broad to be a useful topic, you are headed in the right direction. Next, you might think of a topic that relates to Laurier's political impact, such as "What effect did Wilfrid Laurier's francophone origins have on the success of the Liberal Party?" Depending on your writing situation (2b), you might need to narrow your idea further by focusing on Laurier's impact in a single area such as the question of national unity or the debate over religious education.

3 Narrowing an assigned topic

Narrowing a broad topic means thinking of subdivisions of the subject, of different areas within the subject. Most very broad subjects can be broken down in hundreds of ways, but you need not think of all of them. When one seems possible, think it through at the start so that you can decide whether you can develop it well in writing.

For example, if the subject is marriage, you might decide to talk about what makes marriages successful. But you cannot depend merely on generalizations such as "In successful marriages husbands and wives learn to accept each other's faults." You need to explain why accepting faults is important, and you need to give concrete illustrations of what you are talking about.

As you narrow a broad subject to obtain a writing topic, keep in mind the writing situation (see 2b) of each assignment. Think about what topics are possible and which of these you can handle well.

SUBJECT	*Music*
WRITING SITUATION	first-year composition class informative purpose instructor as audience 500 words, one week
POSSIBLE TOPICS	the moods music creates classical music of the Renaissance country and western music as big business
SUBJECT	*Cities*
WRITING SITUATION	sociology course persuasive purpose students and then instructor as audience 500 to 700 words, one week

POSSIBLE TOPICS comforts of city living
discomforts of city living
influence of the writings of Jane Jacobs on city planning

Carol Moreno narrowed the topic of her assignment (see page 24) because "a challenge you faced and tried to meet" was too general. To stimulate her thinking, Moreno used some of the techniques for gathering ideas presented in the rest of this chapter. She used an entry from her journal (shown in 2e), freewriting (in 2f), and mapping (in 2i). As a result, Moreno decided to write about the challenge of increasing her strength and stamina.

Daniel Casey did not have to narrow his topic because it was stated in his assignment (see page 24): the commercialization of holidays in North America. He did, however, have to choose a position to argue on the topic. What helped him the most were brainstorming (see his work in 2g), asking the "journalist's questions" (see his work in 2h), and using a subject tree (see his work in 2l).

2d Gathering ideas for writing

Techniques for gathering ideas, sometimes called *prewriting strategies* or *invention techniques,* can help you discover how much you know about a topic before you decide to write about it. Chart 10 lists various ways to gather ideas for writing and refers you to the sections in this handbook where you can learn more about each technique.

Students sometimes worry that they have nothing to write about. Often, however, students know far more than they give themselves credit for. The challenge is to uncover what is there but seems not to

WAYS TO GATHER IDEAS FOR WRITING 10

- Keeping an idea book and a journal (see 2e)
- Freewriting (see 2f)
- Brainstorming and talking it over (see 2g)
- Asking the journalist's questions (see 2h)
- Mapping (see 2i)
- Using a good Internet search engine (see Chapter 33)
- Incubating (see 2j)

be. As you use these various techniques for gathering ideas, find out which work best for *you* and *your* style of thinking.

No one technique of generating ideas always works for all topics. Experiment. If one method does not provide enough useful material, try another. Also, even if one strategy produces some good material, try another to turn up additional possibilities.

✚ COMPUTER TIPS: When freewriting (2f) or brainstorming (2g), consider using invisible writing by dimming the screen so that you cannot see what you are writing. This helps you avoid the temptation to edit while you are getting your ideas down. After a while, brighten the screen to look at what you wrote.

As you use idea-gathering techniques, do not delete material. Save your "rejected" work in a separate folder. Today's junk can become tomorrow's treasure. ✚

2e Keeping an idea book and a journal

Your ease with writing will grow as you develop the habits of mind that typify writers. Professional writers are always on the lookout for ideas to write about and for details to develop their ideas. They listen, watch, talk with people, and generally keep their minds open. For this reason, many writers always carry an **idea book**—a pocketsize notebook—to jot down ideas that spring to mind. Good ideas can melt away like snowflakes. Use an idea book throughout your college or university years, and watch your powers of observation increase.

Many writers write in a **journal.** Keeping a journal gives you the chance to have a "conversation on paper" with yourself. Fifteen minutes a day can be enough—before going to bed, between classes, on a bus. *You* are your audience, so the content and tone can be as personal and informal as you wish.

Unlike a diary, a journal is not merely for listing what you did that day. A journal is for your thoughts. You can draw on your reading, your observations, your dreams. You can respond to quotations, react to movies or plays, or think through your opinions, beliefs, and tastes.

Keeping a journal can help you in three ways. First, writing every day gives you the habit of productivity. The more you write, the more you get used to the feeling of words pouring out of you onto paper, the easier it will become for you to write in all situations. Second, a journal instils the habit of close observation and discovery. Third, a journal serves as an excellent source of ideas for many assignments.

Here is an excerpt of a journal entry Carol Moreno had written before she got the assignment to write an essay about facing a challenge (see page 24). When reading through her journal for ideas for her essay, Moreno realized that she had faced the challenge of needing to develop more strength and stamina.

September 30 I got to add 5 more reps
today and it's only the sixth weight
lifting class. I wasn't really surprised—
I can tell I'm stronger. I wonder if I'm
strong enough yet to lift Gran into the
wheelchair alone. I was so scared last
summer when I almost dropped her.
Besides being terrified of hurting her, I
thought that somehow the admissions
committee would find out and tell me I was too
weak to be accepted into nursing school. What
if I hadn't noticed the weight-lifting course
for P.E. credit!?! Weight lifting is the best
exercise I've ever done and I'm not getting
beefy looking either.

Excerpt from Carol Moreno's Journal

2f Freewriting

Freewriting is writing nonstop. It means writing down whatever comes into your mind without stopping to worry about whether the ideas are good or the spelling is correct. When you freewrite, do nothing to interrupt the flow. Do not censor any thoughts or flashes of insight. Do not go back and review. Do not cross out. Some days your freewriting might seem mindless, but other days it can reveal interesting ideas to you.

Freewriting helps get you used to the "feel" of pen moving across paper or of fingers in constant motion at a computer. Freewriting works best if you set a goal: perhaps writing for fifteen minutes or filling one or two pages. Keep going until you reach that goal, even if you have to write one word over and over until a new word comes to mind.

If you write on a computer, you can avoid the temptation to stop and criticize your writing by doing "invisible writing." Dim the screen so you cannot see your writing. The computer will still be recording your ideas, but you will not be able to see them until you brighten the screen again. To create the same effect writing by hand, use a worn-out ballpoint pen and a piece of carbon paper between two sheets of paper.

Focused freewriting means starting with a set topic. You can focus your freewriting in any way you like—perhaps with a phrase from your journal or a quotation you like. Using the focus as a starting point, write until you meet the time or page limit you have set as a goal. Again, do not censor what you say. Keep moving forward.

Like journals, freewriting can be a source for ideas and details to write about. Carol Moreno wanted to explore the topic of her experience in learning to lift weights. She felt it had potential for her essay assignment (on page 24). Here is an excerpt from her focused freewriting on "pumping iron."

Pumping iron—what the steroid jocks call it and exactly what I DO NOT want to be—a muscle cube. Great that Prof. Moore told us women's muscles don't bulk up much unless a weight lifting program is really intense—they just get longer. No bulk for me PLEASE. Just want upper body strength—oh, and the aerobic stuff from swimming, which makes me feel great. Lift, sweat, swim, lift, sweat, swim, lift, sweat, swim.

Excerpt from Carol Moreno's Freewriting

2g Brainstorming

Brainstorming means listing all the ideas associated with a topic that come to mind. The ideas can be listed as words, phrases, or even random sentences. Let your mind range freely, generating quantities of ideas before eliminating some.

You can brainstorm in one concentrated session or over several days, depending on how much time is available for the assignment. In courses that permit collaborative work, brainstorming in groups can work especially well because one person's ideas bounce off the next person's, and collectively more ideas get listed.

Brainstorming is done in two steps: First, you make a list, and then you try to find patterns in the list and ways to group the ideas into categories. Set aside any items that do not fit into groups. If an area interests you but its list is thin, brainstorm on that area alone. If you run out of ideas, ask yourself questions to stimulate your thinking. You might try exploratory questions about the topic, such as: What is it? What is it the same as? How is it different? Why or how does it happen? How is it done? What caused it or results from it? What does it look, smell, sound, feel, or taste like?

Daniel Casey's essay, discussed in Chapter 6, develops an argument concerning the benefits of the commercialization of holidays. For Casey's final draft, see section 6i. Realizing that his position was open to debate, Casey used the technique of brainstorming to help himself think through his opinion. Below is an excerpt from the ideas as they came to Casey at random. The items followed by an asterisk (*) are those Casey chose for the fourth paragraph—about the spirit of the holidays—of his essay, shown in section 6i.

EXCERPT FROM DANIEL CASEY'S BRAINSTORMED LIST

people feel cheerful*
the economy is stimulated
people give to charities
strangers exchange friendly greetings*
everyone gives and gets gifts
children love visiting Santa (and the Easter Bunny)*
festive atmosphere in stores*
sending greeting cards helps friends stay in touch*
arouses positive sentimental feelings
stimulates good will

Talking it over is based on the notion that two heads are better than one. The expression "bouncing ideas off each other" captures this idea. When you discuss your topic with someone interested in listening and making suggestions, you often think of new ideas. You can discuss what you have discovered using the techniques in this handbook (2d), or additional specific details to support a general statement, or anything else you want to explore. Ways of approaching a point of discussion include debating, questioning, analyzing (5d, 5e), synthesizing (5f), and evaluating.

Look for someone you trust to tell you if your ideas are complete and reasonable. If your instructor sets up peer response groups in your class, you might ask the other members to talk your topic over with you. Otherwise, talk with a good friend or another adult.

EXERCISE 2-2

Here is a brainstormed list for an assignment in a law class on causes of youth crime. Consulting section 2g, look over the list, and then group ideas. Some ideas may not fit into any group. You are welcome to add ideas to the list.

availability of weapons
TV
broken families
effects of poverty
legal reform
the schools
popular music lyrics
peer pressure
drug use
urgency of solving the problem
racism
the court system
the Young Offenders Act
lawyers
psychological troubles
statistics

2h Asking the journalist's questions

Journalist's questions ask *Who? What? When? Why? Where? How?* Asking these questions forces you to approach a topic from several different perspectives.

Daniel Casey used the journalist's questions to explore and expand his thinking about specific benefits of the commercialization of holidays in North America. His answers to the questions helped him decide that he had enough details to write an effective essay (for his final draft, see section 6i).

WHO	Who specifically benefits from the commercial aspects of holidays?
WHAT	What specific benefits result from commercialization of holidays?
WHEN	When specifically do beneficial holidays fall?
WHY	Why specifically do some people object to the commercial aspects of holidays?
WHERE	Where specifically can evidence of benefits be seen or felt?
HOW	How do specific commercial aspects of holidays create benefits?

2i Mapping

Mapping, also called *clustering* or *webbing,* is much like brainstorming (see 2g), but it is more visual and less linear. Many writers find that mapping frees them to think more creatively by associating ideas more easily.

To map, start with your topic circled in the middle of a sheet of unlined paper. Next, draw a line radiating out from the centre and label it with the name of a major subdivision of your topic. Circle it and from that circle radiate out to more specific subdivisions. When you finish with one major subdivision of your subject, go back to the centre and start again with another major division. As you go along, add anything that occurs to you for any section of the map. Continue the

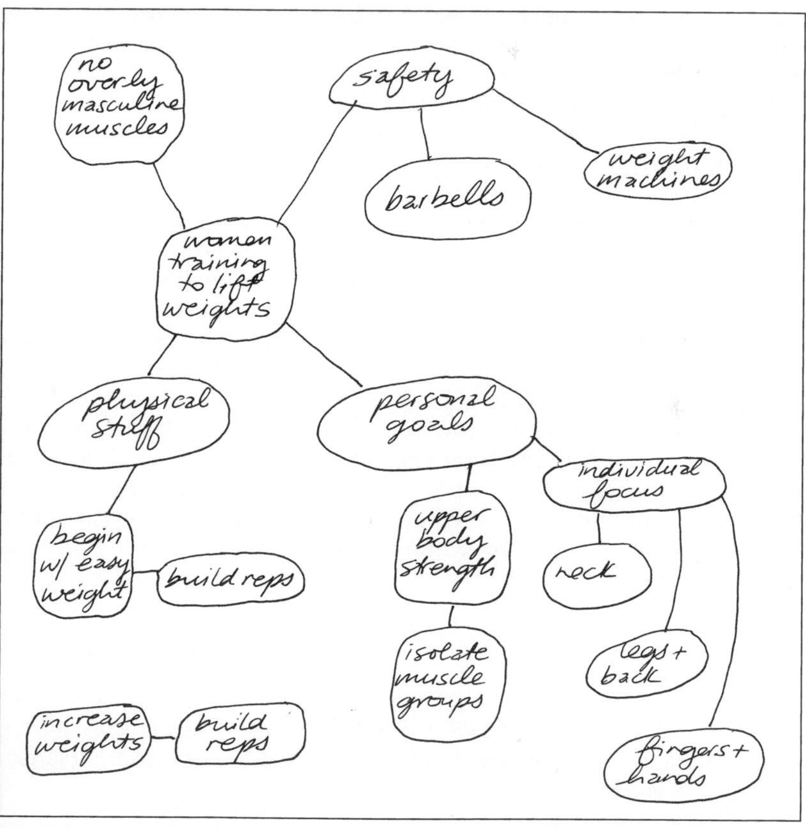

Carol Moreno's Mapping

process until you run out of ideas. The technique of mapping, by the way, also can be used the same way as using a subject tree (see 2l): to lay out the logical relationships of ideas to each other. But many writers seem to prefer to use mapping for discovering ideas already known but not remembered, as Carol Moreno did. You use the techniques as they suit you best.

Carol Moreno's mapping for ideas to use in her essay about women lifting weights is on page 33 (for the three drafts of her essay, see section 3f). After Moreno finished mapping, she was satisfied that she had enough information to use in her essay.

2j Using incubation

When you allow your ideas to **incubate,** you give them time to grow and develop. Incubation works especially well when you need to solve a problem in your writing (for example, if material is too thin and needs expansion, if material covers too much and needs pruning, or if connections among your ideas are not clear for your reader). Time is a key element for successful incubation. Arrange your time to make sure that you will not be interrupted. You need time to think, to allow your mind to wander, and then to come back and focus on the writing. Sometimes incubating an idea overnight permits sleep to help you discover or clarify an idea.

One helpful strategy is to turn attention to something entirely different from your writing problem. Concentrate *very hard* on that entirely different matter so that your conscious mind is totally distracted from the writing problem. After a while, relax and guide your mind back to the writing problem you want to solve.

Another strategy is to allow your mind to relax and wander, without concentrating on anything special. Open your mind to random thoughts, but do not dwell on any one thought very long. After a while, guide your mind back to the writing problem you are trying to solve. When you come back to the writing problem, you might see solutions that did not occur to you before.

EXERCISE 2-3

Consulting sections 2d through 2j, practise each method of gathering ideas at least once. Use your own topics or select from these: pizza, procrastinating, a dream vacation, meeting deadlines, playing a sport, telling jokes, libraries, chocolate, falling in love, world peace.

2k Shaping ideas

Shaping activities are related to the idea that writing is often called *composing*, the putting together of ideas to create a *composition*, one of the synonyms for *essay*. To shape the ideas that you have gathered, you need to group them (see 2l) and sequence them (see 2m).

As you shape ideas, keep in mind that the form of an essay is related to the classical notion of a story having a beginning, a middle, and an end. An academic essay always has an introduction, a body, and a conclusion. The length of each paragraph is in proportion to its function. Introductory and concluding paragraphs are generally shorter than body paragraphs, and no body paragraph should overpower the others by its length. (Writing paragraphs is discussed in Chapter 4.)

2l Grouping ideas by levels of generality

When you group ideas, you make connections and find patterns. As you create groups, use the concept of **levels of generality** to help you make decisions: One idea is more general than another if it falls into a larger, less specific category than the other. Remember that generality is a relative term. Each idea exists in the context of a whole relationship of ideas. An idea may be general in relationship to one set of ideas but specific in relation to another set.

For example, "bank account" is more general than "chequing account." In turn, "chequing account" is more general than "business chequing account" or "regular chequing account." And those terms are more general than "account 221222 at the EZ-Come-EZ-Go Bank."

To identify groups of ideas, review the material you accumulated while gathering ideas (see 2e through 2j). Look for general ideas. Then, group less general ideas under them. If your notes contain only general ideas, or only very specific details, return to techniques for gathering ideas to supply what you need. A standard tool for grouping ideas is to make a "subject tree" to see whether you have enough content to write about. A subject tree resembles a map (see 2i): It shows ideas and details in order from most general at the top to most specific at the bottom.

Daniel Casey used a **subject tree** while shaping his essay that takes the position that benefits result from the commercialization of holidays in North America (for his final draft, see section 6i). He used the subject tree to lay out the ideas in his third paragraph according to

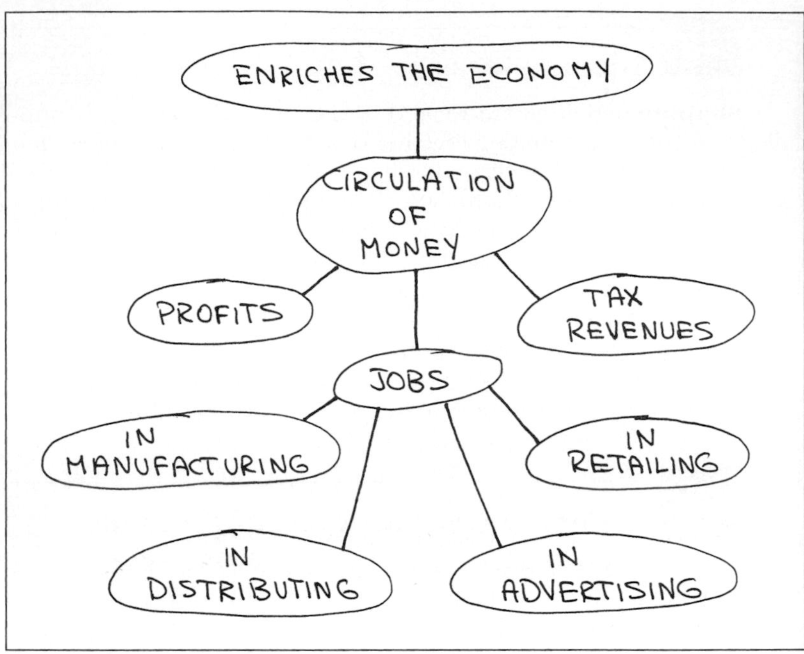

Daniel Casey's Subject Tree

their relative levels of generality. You can write out a subject tree for single paragraphs and for checking the interrelationships of the ideas in a whole essay. You use the techniques as they suit you best.

2m Sequencing ideas for writing

When you sequence ideas for writing, you decide what you want your readers to encounter first, second, and on until the last. When readers can follow your line of reasoning, they are more likely to understand the message that you want your material to deliver.

Within paragraphs, you can present ideas in any of the many ways explained in Chapter 4. Within an essay, the sequence in which you put those paragraphs reveals to your reader your evolving material. No one sequence or structure fits all academic essays, but certain elements are usually present. For the major elements in essays with persuasive purpose, see Chart 45 in section 6g. When you write essays with an informative purpose, be sure to include the elements in Chart 11. (Carol Moreno's essay in section 3f includes the elements in Chart 11.)

TYPICAL ELEMENTS IN AN ESSAY WITH AN INFORMATIVE PURPOSE 11

1. **Introductory paragraph:** leads into the topic of the essay, trying to capture the reader's interest. (For a discussion of introductory paragraphs, see 4g.)
2. **Thesis statement:** states the central message of the essay. In an academic essay, the thesis statement usually appears at the end of the introductory paragraph. (For a discussion of thesis statements, see 2n.)
3. **Background information:** provides a context for the points being made in the essay. Depending on its complexity, this information appears in its own paragraph or is integrated into the introductory paragraph. (For an example of integrating background information into the introductory paragraph, see Daniel Casey's essay in 6i. For an example of a separate paragraph for background information, see Carol Moreno's essay in 3f.)
4. **Points of discussion:** support the essay's thesis, each consisting of a general statement backed up by specific details. This material forms the core of the essay.
5. **Concluding paragraph:** ends the essay smoothly, flowing logically from the rest of the essay. (For a discussion of concluding paragraphs, see 4g.)

2n Shaping writing by drafting a thesis statement

A **thesis statement** is the central message of an essay. It is evidence that you have something definite to say about the topic. An effective thesis statement prepares your reader for the essence of what you discuss in an essay. As the writer, you want to compose a thesis statement with care so that it accurately reflects the content of your essay. If you find a mismatch between your thesis statement and the rest of your essay, revise to coordinate them better. The basic requirements for a thesis statement appear in Chart 12.

Some instructors ask for more than the basic requirements. For example, you might be required to put your thesis statement at the end of your introductory paragraph. (For an example, see the final draft of Carol Moreno's essay in 3f.) Also, many instructors require that the thesis statement be contained in one sentence. Other instructors permit

BASIC REQUIREMENTS FOR A THESIS STATEMENT 12

1. It states the essay's **subject**—the topic that you are discussing.
2. It reflects the essay's **purpose**—either to give your readers information or to persuade your readers to agree with you.
3. It includes a **focus**—your assertion that conveys your point of view.
4. It uses **specific language**—vague words are avoided.
5. It *may* briefly state the major subdivisions of the essay's topic.

two sentences if the material to be covered warrants such length. All requirements, basic and additional, are designed to help you think in structured patterns that communicate clearly with readers. Be sure not to confuse a title (see 3c-2) with a thesis statement.

◆ ESL NOTE: The use of a thesis statement to start an essay (or at least to come at the end of the introductory paragraph) is required in only some cultures, including Canada and the United States. Even if you are not used to writing a firm, outright thesis statement, you need to master the skill for your Canadian academic essays. ◆

Until you have written one or more drafts, all parts of a thesis statement might not accurately reflect what you say in the essay. To begin, make an **assertion**—a sentence stating your topic and the point you want to make about it. The exact wording of this assertion probably will not appear in your final draft, but it serves as a focus for your thinking as you progress through a **preliminary thesis statement** toward a fully developed one.

To write her essay about women lifting weights, Carol Moreno used this progression from basic assertion to final thesis statement.

NO I think women can "pump iron" like men. [This assertion is a start.]

NO If she is trained well, any woman can "pump iron" well, just like a man. [This preliminary thesis is more developed because it mentions training, but the word *well* is used twice and is vague, and the word *any* is inaccurate.]

NO In spite of most people thinking only men can "pump iron," women can also do it successfully with the right training. [This draft is better because it is becoming more specific, but "most people thinking only men" is not an aspect of the topic Moreno intends to explore. Also, the concept of building strength, a major aspect of Moreno's final draft, is missing.]

YES With the right training, women can also "pump iron" successfully to build strength. [This is the final version of Moreno's thesis statement. *Also* is a transitional word connecting the thesis statement to the sentence that comes before it in Moreno's introductory paragraph.]

The final version fulfils the requirements for a thesis statement described in Chart 12.

Here are more examples of thesis statements written for 500- to 700-word essays with an **informative purpose** (see section 1b-2). The ineffective versions resemble assertions or preliminary thesis statements. The effective versions are final thesis statements written by students after they had gathered and grouped ideas. The good versions fulfil the requirements in Chart 12.

TOPIC *classical music*

NO Classical music combines many different sounds.

YES Classical music can be played by groups of various sizes, ranging from chamber ensembles to full symphony orchestras.

TOPIC *women artists*

NO The paintings of women are getting more attention.

YES During the past ten years the works of artists Mary Cassatt and Rosa Bonheur have finally gained widespread critical acclaim.

For a persuasive purpose, Daniel Casey wrote this thesis statement for his essay about the commercialization of holidays (see section 6i):

> After all, commercial uses of holidays benefit the economy and lift people's spirits.

Casey's thesis statement reveals that the *topic* is commercialization of holidays, the *purpose* is to persuade, and the *focus* is the benefits of holidays' commercial uses.

Here are ineffective and effective thesis statements written for 500- to 700-word essays with a **persuasive purpose.** The ineffective versions resemble some types of preliminary thesis statements. The effective versions are final thesis statements written by students after they had gathered and grouped ideas. For example, the material here on city living is built on one of the "possible topics" evolved from narrowing the large subject of cities (see 2c-3). The good versions fulfil the requirements in Chart 12.

TOPIC	*discomforts of city living*
NO	The discomforts of living in a modern city are many.
YES	Rising crime rates, increasingly overcrowded conditions, and growing expenses make living comfortably in a modern city difficult.
TOPIC	*deceptive advertising*
NO	Deceptive advertising can cause many problems for consumers.
YES	Deceptive advertising can cost consumers not only money but also their health.

The *No* examples of thesis statements shown above suffer from being too broad. They are so general that they offer no focus, and readers cannot predict the essay's thrust.

Another type of ineffective thesis statement results from an overly narrow focus. In such cases, the thesis statement is closer in scope to a topic sentence that begins a paragraph.

NO	Car thefts on Silver Avenue between First and Second Streets are intolerable.
YES	Neighbours have overcome language obstacles and differences in customs to combat increasing car thefts on Silver Avenue.

EXERCISE 2-4

Each of the following sets of sentences offers several versions of a thesis statement. Within each set, the thesis statements progress from weak to strong. The fourth thesis statement in each set is the best. Based on the Basic Requirements listed in Chart 12, identify the characteristics of the fourth thesis statement in each set. Then explain why the other choices in each set are weak.

A. 1. Advertising is complex.
   2. Magazine advertisements appeal to readers.
   3. Magazine advertisements must be creative.
   4. To appeal to readers, magazine advertisements must skilfully use language, colour, and design.

B. 1. Many people swim regularly.
   2. Swimming is an aerobic exercise.
   3. Both young and old people swim to stay fit.
   4. Because it does not put excess stress on the body's joints, swimming is one of the rare aerobic exercises that can be done regularly into old age.

C. 1. *Hamlet* is a play about revenge.
   2. Hamlet must avenge his father's murder.
   3. Some characters in *Hamlet* want revenge.
   4. In *Hamlet*, Hamlet, Fortinbras, and Laertes all seek revenge.

D. 1. Maintaining friendships requires work.
   2. To have good friends, a person must learn how to be a good friend.
   3. To be a good friend, a person must value the meaning of friendship.
   4. Unless a person is sensitive to others and communicates with them honestly, that person will not be able to build strong friendships.

E. 1. Many people are uninterested in politics.
   2. Adults have become increasingly dissatisfied with the political process.
   3. Fewer adults than ever vote in local elections.
   4. Fewer postsecondary students expressed a strong preference or voted in the most recent municipal election than in either of the last two elections.

EXERCISE 2-5

Here are writing assignments, narrowed topics, and tentative thesis statements. Evaluate each thesis statement according to the Basic Requirements in Chart 12.

1. **Marketing assignment:** 700- to 800-word persuasive report on the school's cafeteria. *Audience:* the instructor and the cafeteria's manager. *Topic:* cafeteria conditions. *Thesis:* The cafeteria could attract more students if it improved the quality of its food, its appearance, and the friendliness of its staff.
2. **Art assignment:** 300- to 500-word analysis of an Inuit print. *Audience:* the instructor and other students in the class. *Topic:* Pitseolak Ashoona's *Perils of the Sea Travellers. Thesis: Perils of the Sea Travellers* is one of the most moving images of traditional Inuit life.
3. **Chemistry assignment:** 800- to 1000-word informative report about the ozone layer. *Audience:* the instructor and visiting students and instructors attending a seminar. *Topic:* recent research on the ozone layer. *Thesis:* Canada should increase efforts to slow the destruction of the ozone layer.
4. **Journalism assignment:** 200- to 300-word article about the school's drop-out problem. *Audience:* the instructor, the student body, and the administration. *Topic:* increasing drop-out rates. *Thesis:* The percentage of students who fail to complete their first year has doubled in the past ten years.
5. **Business writing assignment:** 400- to 500-word persuasive report about the career-counselling services available to you. *Audience:* students

in their final year, career counsellors, and the instructor. *Topic:* job placement for graduates. *Thesis:* Liberal arts graduates are hired mainly by business and industry.

2o Using collaborative writing

In some classes, instructors require students to collaborate in groups on a writing project. Why write collaboratively? Working in a group can stimulate people to think of ideas and to support each other during the writing process. Also, working collaboratively allows students to discuss their ideas and bounce them off each other, an activity that often inspires greater creativity and shared confidence.

The benefits of getting experience in writing collaboratively extend far beyond your college or university years. Many professions require people to serve on committees, to reach general agreement on how to proceed, and to contribute equally to a written report. For example, business marketing executives might be told to develop a new product, to conduct marketing research to predict the product's success, and then to write the results of their research in a final document that includes a plan for further action.

13

GUIDELINES FOR COLLABORATIVE WRITING

GETTING UNDERWAY

1. Get to know each other's names. If you exchange phone numbers, you can be in touch outside of class.
2. Participate in the group process. During discussions help to set a tone that encourages everyone to participate, including people who do not like to interrupt, who want time to think before they talk, or who are shy. If you are not used to contributing in a group setting, try to take a more active role.
3. Facilitate the collaboration. As a group, assign work to be done between meetings. Distribute the responsibilities as fairly as possible. Also, decide whether to choose one discussion leader or to rotate leadership.

GUIDELINES FOR COLLABORATIVE WRITING *(continued)* 13

PLANNING THE WRITING

4. After discussing the project, brainstorm (see 2g) or use other techniques to think of ideas (see 2d through 2j).
5. As a group, choose the ideas that seem best. Incubate (see 2j), if time permits, and discuss the choices again.
6. As a group, divide the project into parts and distribute assignments as fairly as possible.
7. As you work on your part of the project, take notes so that you can be ready to report to the group.
8. As a group, sketch an overview (if you choose to outline, see 2p) of the paper to get a preliminary idea of how best to use the material contributed by individuals.

DRAFTING THE WRITING

9. Draft°* a first paragraph or two. This material sets the direction for the rest of the paper. Each member of the group can draft a version, but agree on one draft for these paragraphs before getting too far into the rest of the draft. Your group might rewrite once the whole paper has been drafted, but a preliminary beginning helps to focus everyone.
10. Work on the rest of the paper. Decide whether each member of the group should write a complete draft or a different part of the whole. Use photocopies to share work.

REVISING THE WRITING

11. Read over the drafts. Check that everything useful has been incorporated into the draft.
12. Use the Revision Checklists in section 3c-3 to decide on revisions. Work as a group, or assign sections to subgroups. Use photocopies to share work.
13. Agree on a final version. Assign someone to prepare it in final form and make photocopies.

* Throughout this book, a degree mark (°) indicates that you can find the definition of the word in the Glossary of Terms in this handbook.

13

GUIDELINES FOR COLLABORATIVE WRITING *(continued)*

EDITING THE WRITING

14. As a group, review photocopies of the final version. Do not leave the last stages to a subgroup. Draw on everyone's knowledge of grammar, spelling, and punctuation. And use everyone's eyes to proofread.
15. Use the Editing Checklist in section 3d to make sure that the final version has no errors. If necessary, retype. No matter how well the group has worked collaboratively, or how well the group has written the paper, a sloppy final version reflects negatively on the entire group.

2p Knowing how to outline

Many writers find outlining a useful planning strategy. If you are working from an outline and make changes in organization as you write, be sure to revise your outline at the end if you are expected to submit it as part of an assignment. An outline helps pull together the results of gathering and ordering ideas and preparing a thesis statement. It also provides a visual guide and checklist. Some writers always use outlines; others prefer not to. Writers who do like outlines use them at various points in the writing process: for example, before drafting, to arrange material; during drafting, to keep track of evolving material; or while revising, to check the logic of an early draft's organization. Especially for academic writing, outlines can clearly reveal flaws: missing information, undesirable repetitions, digressions from the thesis. Some instructors require outlines because they want students to practise planning the arrangement and organization of a piece of writing.

An **informal outline** does not have to follow all the formal conventions of outlining. An informal outline is particularly useful for planning when the order within main ideas is still evolving or when topics imply their own arrangement, such as spatial arrangement for describing a room. An informal outline can also be considered a *working plan,* a layout of the major parts of the material intended for an essay. Here is part of an informal outline that served as a working plan for Carol Moreno when she was writing her essay on weight lifting for women. (For Moreno's techniques of gathering ideas for writing, see 2e, 2f, and 2i; for the three drafts of her essay, see 3f.) This excerpt includes the essay's thesis statement and fourth paragraph.

Thesis Statement: With the right training, women can also "pump iron" for increased strength and stamina.

using weights
- safety is vital
- free weights
  - don't bend at waist
  - do align neck and back
  - do look straight ahead
- weight machines—safety is easier

Sample Informal Outline

✚ COMPUTER TIP: You can informally outline an essay on a computer, especially after one draft. Read what you have written, and put a symbol near what seems most important. Then, look over the marked parts, and copy them to the bottom of your text so that you can see them grouped together. Shuffle them into several different sequences to discover which part should come first, second, and so on. ✚

A **formal outline** follows conventions concerning content and format. Use Chart 14 for a summary of the conventions of formal outlining. The conventions are designed to display material so that relationships among ideas are clear and so that the content is orderly. A formal outline can be a *topic outline* or a *sentence outline*. Each item in a topic outline is a word or phrase; each item in a sentence outline is a complete sentence. Formal outlines never mix the two.

Many writers who use formal outlines find that a sentence outline brings them closer to drafting than a topic outline does. For example,

CONVENTIONS OF FORMAL OUTLINES 14

FORMAL OUTLINE PATTERN

Thesis Statement:

I. First main idea
   A. First subdivision of the main idea
      1. First reason or example
      2. Second reason or example
         a. First supporting detail
         b. Second supporting detail
   B. Second subdivision of the main idea
II. Second main idea

a topic outline carries less information with the item "Gathering information" than does a sentence outline with the corresponding item "Gathering information is the first step to being well prepared."

Rules for formatting outlines

- **Introductory and concluding paragraphs.** The content of the introductory and concluding paragraphs is not part of a formal outline.
- **Numbers, letters, and indentations.** All parts of a formal outline are systematically indented. Capital roman numerals (I, II, III) signal major subdivisions of the topic. Indented capital letters (A, B) signal the next level of generality. Further indented arabic numbers (1, 2, 3) show the third level of generality. Indented lowercase letters (a, b) show the fourth level, if there is one. If an outline entry is longer than one line, the second line is indented as far as the first word of the preceding line.
- **More than one entry at each level.** At all points on an outline, there is no I without a II, no A without a B, and so on. Unless a category has at least two parts, it cannot be divided. If a category has only one subdivision, you need either to eliminate that subdivision or expand the material to at least two subdivisions.

NO

A. Free weights
    1. Safe lifting technique
B. Weight machines

YES

A. Free weights
B. Weight machines

YES

A. Free weights
    1. Unsafe lifting techniques
    2. Safe lifting techniques
B. Weight machines

- **Overlap.** Headings do not overlap. What is covered in subdivision 1 must be quite distinct from what is covered in subdivision 2. Said another way, all subdivisions are at the same level of generality; a main idea cannot be paired with a supporting detail.

NO

A. Free weights
    1. Weight machines

YES

A. Free weights
   1. Unsafe lifting techniques
   2. Safe lifting techniques
      a. Head alignment
      b. Neck and back alignment
B. Weight machines

- **Parallelism.** All entries within a level are parallel. For example, all might start with the *-ing* forms of verbs°. (For more about parallelism in outlines, see 18h.)

NO

A. Free weights
B. Using weight machines

YES

A. Free weights
B. Weight machines

YES

A. Using free weights
B. Using weight machines

- **Capitalization and punctuation.** Except for proper nouns°, only the first word of each entry is capitalized. In a sentence outline, end each sentence with a period. Do not punctuate the ends of entries in a topic outline.

Here is a topic outline of the final draft of Carol Moreno's essay on weight lifting for women (3f). A sentence outline follows so that you can compare the two types of outlines.

TOPIC OUTLINE

Thesis Statement: With the right training, women can also "pump iron" successfully for increased strength and stamina.

I. Avoiding massive muscle development
   A. Role of women's biology
      1. Not much muscle-bulking hormone
      2. Muscles get longer, not bulkier
   B. Role of combining exercise types
      1. Anaerobic (weight lifting)
      2. Aerobic (swimming)

II. Using weights safely
   A. Free weights
      1. Unsafe lifting technique
      2. Safe lifting technique
         a. Head alignment
         b. Neck and back alignment
   B. Weight machines (built-in safeguards)

III. Individualizing the program based on physical condition
   A. Role of resistance and reps
   B. Characteristics considered for personalizing the program
      1. Weight
      2. Age
      3. Physical condition
IV. Individualizing the program for other reasons
   A. Upper body strength
   B. Individual objectives
      1. Mine
      2. Car-crash victim's
      3. Physical therapist's

SENTENCE OUTLINE

Thesis Statement: With the right training, women can also "pump iron" successfully for increased strength and stamina.

I. The right training lets women who lift weights avoid developing massive muscles.
   A. Women's biology plays a role.
      1. Women don't produce much of a specific muscle-bulking hormone.
      2. Women's muscles tend to grow longer rather than bulkier.
   B. Combining exercise types plays a role.
      1. Anaerobic exercise, like weight lifting, builds muscle.
      2. Aerobic exercise, like swimming, builds endurance and stamina.
II. The right training shows women how to use weights safely to prevent injury.
   A. Free weights require special precautions.
      1. Bending at the waist and jerking a barbell up is unsafe.
      2. Squatting and using leg and back muscles to straighten up is safe.
         a. The head is held erect and faces forward.
         b. The neck and back are aligned and held straight.
   B. Weight machines make it easier to lift safely because they force proper body alignment.

III. The right training includes individualized programs based on a woman's physical condition.
   A. Progress comes from resistance and from repetitions tailored to individual capabilities.
   B. Programs consider a woman's physical characteristics.
      1. Her weight is considered.
      2. Her age is considered.
      3. Her physical conditioning is considered.

IV. The right training includes individualized programs based on a woman's personal goals.
   A. Certain muscle groups are targeted to increase women's upper body strength.
   B. Other muscle groups are targeted based on individual objectives.
      1. I wanted to strengthen muscles needed for lifting patients.
      2. An accident victim wanted to strengthen her neck muscles.
      3. A physical therapist wanted to strengthen her fingers and hands.

✚ COMPUTER TIP: Be careful with your computer's outlining function. In some word-processing programs, the function only places a bullet at the beginning of each paragraph. It pays no attention to levels of generality or whether the material relates to your topic. Other word-processing programs do a somewhat better job, but nothing substitutes for the human eye. ✚

EXERCISE 2-6

Here is a sentence outline. Consulting section 2p, revise it into a topic outline. Then decide which form you would prefer as a guide to writing, and explain your decision.

Thesis Statement: Common noise pollution, although it causes many problems in our society, can be reduced.

I. Noise pollution comes from many sources.
   A. Noise pollution occurs in many large cities.
      1. Traffic rumbles and screeches.
      2. Construction work blasts.
      3. Airplanes roar overhead.

   B. Noise pollution occurs in the workplace.
      1. Machines in factories boom.
      2. Machines used for outdoor construction thunder.
   C. Noise pollution occurs during leisure-time activities.
      1. Stereo headphones blare directly into eardrums.
      2. Film soundtracks bombard the ears.
      3. Music in discos assaults the ears.

II. Noise pollution causes many problems.
   A. Excessive noise damages hearing.
   B. Excessive noise alters moods.
   C. Constant exposure to noise limits learning ability.

III. Reduction in noise pollution is possible.
   A. Pressure from community groups can support efforts to control excessive noise.
   B. Traffic regulations can help alleviate congestion and noise.
   C. Pressure from workers can force management to reduce noise.
   D. People can wear earplugs to avoid excessive noise.
   E. Reasonable sound levels for headphones, soundtracks, and discos can be required.

3 Drafting and Revising

In the writing process, drafting and revising follow from planning and shaping, discussed in Chapter 2. **Drafting** means getting ideas onto paper in sentences and paragraphs. In everyday conversation, people usually use the word *writing* when they talk about the activities involved in drafting. In discussing the writing process, however, the word *drafting* is more descriptive. It conveys the idea that the final product of the writing process is the result of a number of versions, each successively closer to what the writer intends and to what will communicate clearly to readers. **Revising** means taking a draft from its preliminary to its final version by evaluating, adding, cutting, moving material, editing, and proofreading.

3a Getting started

If ever you have trouble getting started when the time arrives for drafting (or any other part of the writing process), you are not alone. When experienced writers get stalled, they recognize what is happening and deal with it. If you run into a writing block, it may be the result of one of these common myths about writing.

MYTH Writers are born, not made.

TRUTH Everyone can write. Writers do not expect to "get it right" the first time. Being a good writer means being a patient rewriter.

MYTH Writers have to be "in the mood" to write.

TRUTH If writers always waited for "the mood" to descend, few would write at all. After all, news reporters and other professional writers often have to meet deadlines.

MYTH Writers have to know how to spell every word and to recite the rules of grammar perfectly.

TRUTH Writers do not let spelling and grammar block them. They write and then check themselves. A good speller is someone who does not ignore the quiet inner voice that urges checking a dictionary. Similarly, writers use a handbook to check grammar rules.

MYTH Writers do not have to revise.

TRUTH Writers expect to revise. Once words are on paper, writers can see what readers see. This "re-vision" helps writers revise so that their writing delivers its intended message.

MYTH Writing can be done at the last minute.

TRUTH Drafting and revising take time. Ideas do not leap onto paper in final, polished form.

WAYS TO OVERCOME WRITER'S BLOCK 15

- **Avoid staring at a blank page.** Relax and move your hand across the page or keyboard. Write words, scribble, or draw while you think about your topic. The movement of filling the paper can help stimulate your mind to turn to actual drafting.
- **Visualize yourself writing.** Many professional writers say that they write more easily if they first picture themselves doing it. Before getting up in the morning, or when waiting for a bus, or walking to classes, summon a full visual image of yourself in the place where you usually write, with the materials you need, busy at work.
- **Picture an image or scene, or imagine a sound that relates to your topic.** Start writing by describing what you see or hear.
- **Write about your topic in a letter to a friend.** Relax and chat on paper to someone you like and feel comfortable with.
- **Try writing your material as if you were someone else.** Taking on a role may make you feel less inhibited about writing.
- **Start in the middle.** Begin with a body paragraph. Write from the centre of your essay out, instead of from beginning to end.
- **Use "focused freewriting"** (see 2f).
- **Change your method of writing.** If you usually use a computer, try writing by hand. When you write by hand, try to treat yourself to good-quality paper. The pleasure of writing on smooth, strong paper helps many experienced writers want to keep going.

Once you realize the truths behind myths about writing, you can try the time-proven ways that experienced writers use to get started when they are blocked. As you use these strategies, suspend judgment; do not criticize yourself when trying to get underway. The time for evaluation comes during revision, but revising too soon can stall some writers. While the writing that results from these ideas is most certainly not a final draft, having something on paper is a comfort—and can serve as a springboard to drafting.

As you write, seek out places and times of the day that encourage you to write. You might write best in a quiet corner of the library; at 4:30 a.m. at the kitchen table before anyone else is awake; or outside when people are walking by. Most experienced writers find that they concentrate best when they are alone, working without the risk of interruption. But occasionally background noise—in a crowded cafeteria, for example—might be comforting. Be sure, however, not to mislead yourself: You will not write well or efficiently while you are talking to other people, stopping now and then to jot down a sentence or two. Also, do not mistake delaying tactics for preparation: You do need a computer or pencil and paper to write, but you do not need fifteen perfectly sharpened pencils sitting in a neat row.

✚ COMPUTER TIP: Tailor your use of a computer to your personal needs. Some writers use a computer throughout the writing process. Other writers reserve the computer for revising and editing. ✚

3b Knowing how to draft

Once you have your ideas planned and shaped for an essay, you are ready to **compose** them on paper. When you compose, you put together sentences and paragraphs into a unified whole. A *first draft* is a preliminary draft. Its purpose is to get your ideas onto paper, not to refine grammar and style (they come later, during revision). First drafts are not meant to be perfect; they are meant to give you something to revise. According to your personal preferences and each writing situation, you can use any of these ways (or your own ways) of writing a first draft.

✚ COMPUTER TIP: Save or back up your work every one or two pages or every ten minutes. Also, consider printing out regularly so that you always have a hard copy. This gives you a record of your work, in case your disk develops problems. ✚

1. **Put aside all your notes from planning and shaping.** Write a **discovery draft**. As you write, be open to discovering ideas and

making connections that spring to mind during the physical act of writing. When you finish a discovery draft, you can decide to use it either as a first draft or as part of your notes when you write a structured first draft.

2. **Keep your notes from planning and shaping in front of you and use them as you write.** Write a structured first draft by arranging your notes in a preliminary sequence and working through them. Draft either the entire essay or blocks of one or two paragraphs at one time.
3. **Use a combination of approaches.** When you know the shape of your material, write according to that structure. When you feel "stuck" about what to say next, switch to writing as you would for a discovery draft.

The direction of drafting is forward: *keep pressing ahead*. If you are worried about the spelling of a word or a point in grammar, underline the material to check it later—and keep moving ahead. If you cannot think of an exact word, write an easy synonym and circle it to change later—and move on. If you are worried about your sentence style or the order in which you present the supporting details within a paragraph, write *Style?* or *Order?* in the margin and return to it later to revise—and press forward. If you begin to run dry, reread what you have written—but only to propel yourself to further writing, not to distract you into rewriting.

✚ COMPUTER TIP: Try to write a whole draft at one session, second-guessing and rewriting as little as possible. If you have questions, or think you may want to elaborate on something but cannot think how at the moment, insert a symbol that will alert you to "talk to yourself" later. When you finish the draft and begin revising, your symbols can help you focus on areas that need reworking. ✚

As you draft, use the essay's thesis statement (see 2n) as your springboard. A thesis statement has great organizing power, for it controls and limits what the essay will cover. Also, use your thesis statement as a connecting thread that unifies the essay. **Unity** is important for communicating clearly to an audience. An essay is unified when it meets two criteria: (1) the thesis statement clearly ties into all topic sentences: see 4b; and (2) the support for each topic sentence—the paragraph development—contains examples, reasons, facts, and details directly related to the topic and, in turn, to the thesis statement: see 4c.

Coherence is also important to communicate clearly to an audience. An essay is coherent when it supplies guideposts that communicate the relations among ideas. Coherence is achieved with transitional expressions, pronouns, repetition, and parallel structures. (see 4d).

When you write, plan your practical arrangements. For example, try to work in a place where you are comfortable and will not be disturbed. If someone comes along and interrupts, you might lose a train of thought or an idea that has flashed into your mind. Also, keep enough paper at hand so that you use only one side of each sheet of paper. Later you will need to spread your full draft in front of you so that you can physically see how the parts relate to one another. As you write, leave large margins and plenty of room between lines so that you have space to enter changes later on.

To give you examples of the writing process used by college and university students, this chapter discusses the drafting and revising of two students—Carol Moreno and Daniel Casey, each of whom wrote in response to the assignments shown on page 24. You can see three complete drafts of Moreno's essay in this chapter (section 3f). Also, you can see the final draft of Daniel Casey's essay in section 6i. For examples of Moreno's and Casey's uses of the techniques of planning and shaping before they began drafting, see sections 2b through 2p.

3c Knowing how to revise

To **revise** you must evaluate. You assess your first (or subsequent) draft and decide where improvements are needed. Then you make the improvements and evaluate each on its own as well as in the context of the surrounding material. The revision process continues until you are satisfied that the essay is the best that you can make it in the time available. Keep in mind that academic writing, especially through the vehicle of revision, is an engaging intellectual endeavour that encourages students to stretch to the maximum.

To revise successfully you need first to *expect to revise*. Some people think that anyone who revises is not a good writer. The opposite is true. Writing is largely revising. Experienced writers know that the final draft of any writing project shows on paper only a fraction of the decisions made from draft to successive draft. Revision means "to see again," to look with fresh eyes. Good writers can truly *see* their drafts and rework them so that they evolve and improve.

To revise successfully you need also to distance yourself from each draft. You need to read your writing with objective eyes. A natural reaction of many writers is to want to hold onto their every word, especially if they had trouble getting started with a draft. If you ever have such feelings, resist them and work on distancing yourself from the material. Before revising, give yourself some time for that rosy glow of authorial pride to dim a bit. The classical writer Horace recommended waiting nine years. Try to wait a few hours—or a day or two—before going back to look anew at your work.

If an objective perspective still eludes you, try reading your draft aloud; hearing the material can give you a fresh new sense of content and organization. Another useful method is to read the paragraphs in reverse order, starting with the conclusion; eventually, of course, you must read your essay from beginning to end, but to achieve distance you can temporarily depart from that sequence.

✚ COMPUTER TIPS: To move from your first draft to revision, use the Find or Search function to locate each place where you entered an "alert-to-yourself" (a symbol, a word, an underlining, etc.) as you were drafting (3b). Type into the search box whatever you used to alert yourself to the need to go back and revise. Then, click on Find Next and you will come to each place you used your alert. Take the time to rethink the matter and decide what to do.

As you are revising, if you suspect that you have overused a word or group of words, use the Find or Search function to discover if your suspicions are correct. If necessary, substitute other words. Beware, however, in using your computer's thesaurus: Many words in the thesaurus do not fit the specific context you have in mind. Always check the specific meaning of a synonym in your dictionary. ✚

1 Knowing the steps and activities of revision

Once you understand the attitudes that underlie the revision process, you are ready to move into actual revising.

To revise, you work to improve your draft at all levels: whole essay, paragraph, sentence, and word. A revised draft usually looks quite different from the preceding draft. To revise effectively you likely need to engage in all the activities in Chart 16 and Chart 17.

As you engage in each activity, keep in mind the whole picture. Changes affect more than the place revised. Check that your separate changes operate well in the context of the whole essay or a particular paragraph. As with drafting (see 3b), getting distance from your material allows you the chance to be more objective.

Revising is usually separate from editing (see 3d). Editing involves concentrating on important surface features such as correct spelling and punctuation. When revising, you pay attention to the meaning that you want your material to deliver effectively.

✚ COMPUTER TIP: Relieved of the sometimes tedious work of copying and recopying material, many writers feel more creative when they use a computer. Their ideas seem to flow more freely when each new thought

STEPS FOR REVISING 16

1. Shift mentally from suspending judgment (during idea gathering and drafting) to making judgments.
2. Read your draft critically to evaluate it. Be guided by the questions on the Revision Checklists in this chapter (see Charts 19 and 20) or by material supplied by your instructor.
3. Decide whether to write an entirely new draft or to revise the one you have. Do not be overly harsh. While some early drafts serve best as "discovery drafts" rather than first drafts, many early drafts provide sufficient raw material for the revision process to get underway.
4. Be systematic. Do not evaluate at random. You need to pay attention to many different elements of a draft, from overall organization to choice of words. Some writers prefer to consider all elements concurrently, but most writers work better when they concentrate on different elements sequentially during separate rounds of revision.

does not lead to a recopying job. Nevertheless, do not let yourself be seduced by the wonders of a computer. It is only a machine. A neatly printed page might "look" like a final draft, even when it is a very rough draft. Resist the urge to think that neatness means completion. ✚

2 Using the organizing power of your thesis statement and essay title during revision

As you revise, pay special attention to your essay's thesis statement and title. Both features can help you stay on the track. Also, they orient your reader to what to expect, which helps you communicate your message as clearly as possible.

If your **thesis statement** (see 2n, especially Chart 12) does not match what you say in your essay, you need to revise either the thesis statement or the essay—and sometimes both. A thesis statement must present the topic of the essay, the writer's particular focus on that topic, and the writer's purpose for writing the essay. The first draft of a thesis statement is often merely an estimate of what will be covered in the essay. Early in the revision process, check the accuracy of your estimate. Then use the thesis statement's controlling power to bring it and your essay in line with each other.

MAJOR ACTIVITIES DURING REVISION 17

- **Add.** Insert needed words, sentences, and paragraphs. If your additions require new content, return to idea-gathering techniques (see 2d through 2j).
- **Cut.** Get rid of whatever goes off the topic or repeats what has already been said.
- **Replace.** As needed, substitute new words, sentences, and paragraphs for what you have cut.
- **Move material around.** Change the sequence of paragraphs if the material is not presented in logical order (see 2m). Move sentences within paragraphs or to other paragraphs if any paragraph arrangement seems illogical (see 4d and 4e).

Each writer's experience with revising a thesis statement varies from essay to essay. Carol Moreno wrote a number of versions of her thesis statement before she started drafting. After writing her first draft, Moreno checked the thesis statement and satisfied herself that it communicated what she wanted to say. But she decided to change parts of her essay to conform more closely to her thesis statement. (For an example of a thesis statement being revised for a research paper from the first through the final draft, see 32r).

The **title** of an essay also plays an important organizing role during revision. An effective title sets you on your course and tells your reader what to expect. (Some writers like to start a first draft with a title at the top of the page to focus their thinking. As they revise drafts, they revise the title as needed.) An effective title might not come to mind until you have drafted, revised, and edited your essay, by which time your thinking about your topic has crystallized. Remember that a title is never the same as a thesis statement.

✤ PUNCTUATION ALERT: When you write the title of your paper at the top of the page or on a title page, do not use quotation marks to enclose it and do not underline it. ✤

Titles can be *direct* or *indirect*. A *direct title* tells exactly what the essay will be about. A direct title contains key words under which the essay would be catalogued in a library or other database system. The title of Carol Moreno's essay shown in 3f is direct: "Women Can Pump Iron, Too." Similarly, the title of Daniel Casey's essay in section 6i is direct: "Commercialism at Holiday Time Benefits Everyone." Each title is specific and prepares the reader for the topic of the essay.

A *direct title* should not be too broad. An overly broad title implies that the writer has not thought through the essay's content. An unsatisfactory title for Moreno's essay would be "Pumping Iron." Conversely, a direct title should not be too narrow. Equally unsatisfactory would be a title that is overly long—for example, by listing the topics of most of the essay's body paragraphs: "Women Pump Iron for Their Physical and Personal Objectives."

An *indirect title* is also acceptable in some situations, according to the writer's taste and instructor's requirements. An indirect title hints at the essay's topic. It presents a puzzle that can be solved by reading the essay. This approach can be intriguing for the reader, but the writer has to make sure that the title is not too obscure. For example, for Carol Moreno's essay a satisfactory indirect title would be "The Meaning of Muscles," but an unsatisfactory, overly indirect title would be "Equal Play."

Whether direct or indirect, a title stands alone. For example, Carol Moreno (whose essay's good title is "Women Can Pump Iron, Too") would have been wrong had she written as her essay's first sentence: "They certainly can" or "I am proof of that." Chart 18 gives guidelines for titles.

GUIDELINES FOR ESSAY TITLES 18

- Do not wait until the last minute to tack on a title. You might write a title before you start to draft or while you are revising, but always check as you review your essay, to make sure that the title clearly relates to the content of the evolving essay.
- For a direct title, use key words relating to your topic, but do not reveal your entire essay.
- For an indirect title, be sure that it hints accurately and that its meaning will be clear once a reader finishes your essay.
- Do not use quotation marks or underlining with the title (*unless* your title includes another title; see section 30f).
- Do not refer to your essay title with words like *it* or *this,* as if the title were part of the first sentence in the essay.

3 Using revision checklists

Revision checklists focus your attention as you evaluate your writing to revise it. Either use a checklist provided by your instructor, or compile your own based on the Revision Checklists in Chart 19

REVISION CHECKLIST: THE WHOLE ESSAY AND PARAGRAPHS

19

The answer to each question should be "yes." If it is not, you need to revise. The reference numbers in parentheses tell you what chapter or section of this handbook to consult.

1. Is your essay topic suitable and sufficiently narrow (2c-3)?
2. Does your thesis statement communicate your topic and focus (2n) and your purpose (1b)?
3. Does your essay reflect awareness of your audience (1c)?
4. Is your tone appropriate (1d)?
5. Is your essay logically organized (2m) and are your paragraphs logically arranged (4e)?
6. Have you cut material that goes off the topic?
7. Is your reasoning sound (5h–5j) and do you avoid logical fallacies (5k)?
8. Does your introductory paragraph prepare readers for what follows (4g)?
9. Does each body paragraph express its main idea in a topic sentence as needed (4b)? Are the main ideas clearly related to the thesis statement, and have you covered all that your thesis statement "promises" (2n)?
10. Are your body paragraphs sufficiently developed with concrete support for their main idea (4c)?
11. Have you used transitions effectively (4d-1, 4d-5)?
12. Do your paragraphs maintain coherence (4d)?
13. Does your conclusion provide a sense of completion (4g)?
14. Does your title reflect the content of the essay (3c-2)?

and Chart 20. The checklists here are comprehensive and detailed; feel free to adapt them to your writing assignments as well as to your personal weaknesses and strengths. Also, the checklists here move from the **larger elements** of the whole essay and paragraphs to the **smaller elements** of sentences and words. This progression for the sake of self-evaluation works well for many writers. (To see how Carol Moreno used these Revision Checklists, see section 3f.)

◆ ESL NOTE: If English is not your first language, you may want to consult Part Seven to check your use of verb–preposition combinations, articles, word order, verbals, and modal auxiliaries in addition to using the Revision Checklists. ◆

REVISION CHECKLIST: SENTENCES AND WORDS 20

The answer to each question should be "yes." If it is not, you need to revise. The reference numbers in parentheses tell you what chapter or section of this handbook to consult.

1. Have you eliminated sentence fragments (13)?
2. Have you eliminated comma splices and run-together sentences (14)?
3. Have you eliminated confusing shifts (15a)?
4. Have you eliminated misplaced and dangling modifiers (15b and 15c)?
5. Have you eliminated mixed and incomplete sentences (15d and 15e)?
6. Are your sentences concise (16)?
7. Do your sentences show clear relationships among ideas (17)?
8. Do you use parallelism to help your sentences deliver their meaning gracefully, and do you avoid faulty parallelism (18)?
9. Does your writing reflect variety and emphasis (19)?
10. Have you used exact words (20b)?
11. Is your usage correct (Usage Glossary)?
12. Do your words reflect an appropriate level of formality (21a-1)?
13. Do you avoid sexist language (21b), slang and colloquial language (21a-3), slanted language (21a-4), clichés (21d), and artificial language (21e)?

✚ COMPUTER TIPS: The Move or Cut and Paste functions of your computer make rearranging relatively painless. You may make endless versions of your draft until you are satisfied with the order. Try reordering your body paragraphs, splitting or joining some existing paragraphs, and moving your last paragraph to the first position. You may be surprised. Save the most promising versions, and perhaps ask your peers to react to them. Do not, however, be tempted to rearrange endlessly. Set limits or you will never finish. ✚

3d Knowing how to edit

When you **edit,** you are expected to check the technical correctness of your writing. You pay attention to surface features of your writing, such as grammar, spelling, and punctuation, and the correct use of capitals, numbers, italics, and abbreviations. Writers sometimes refer to editing as revising (see 3c). In this handbook, editing is discussed separately because editing focuses more on presentation than on meaning.

If you edit too soon in the writing process, you might distract yourself from checking to see if your material delivers its meaning effectively. You are ready to edit when you have a final draft that contains suitable content, organization, development, and sentence structure. Your job during editing is not to generate a new draft but to fine-tune the surface features of the draft you have. Once you have polished your work, you are ready to transcribe it into a final copy and proofread (see 3e) it.

Editing is crucial in writing. No matter how much attention you have paid to planning, shaping, drafting, and revising, you must edit carefully. Slapdash editing will distract your readers and, in writing for assignments, lower your grade.

Editing takes patience. Inexperienced writers sometimes rush editing, especially if they have revised well and feel that they have prepared a good essay. When you edit, resist any impulse to hurry. Matters of grammar and punctuation take concentration—and frequently they take time to check by looking up rules and conventions in this handbook. As you edit, be systematic. Use a checklist supplied by your instructor or one that you compile from the Editing Checklist in Chart 21.

EDITING CHECKLIST 21

The answer to each question should be "yes." If it is not, you need to edit. The reference numbers in parentheses tell you what chapter of this handbook to consult.

1. Is your grammar correct (7 to 15)?
2. Is your spelling correct, and are your hyphens correct (22)?
3. Have you correctly used commas (24)?
4. Have you correctly used all other punctuation (25 through 29)?
5. Have you correctly used capital letters, italics, abbreviations, and numbers (30)?

✚ COMPUTER TIPS: Many word-processing programs include tools for writers (a spell checker, style checker, thesaurus, etc.) to use as they edit. Each tool, however, has shortcomings serious enough to create new errors. Yet, if you use the tools intelligently with their shortcomings in mind, they can be very useful. (For a list, see 1f.)

- Whenever possible, edit on a hard copy. It is much easier to spot editing errors on a printed page than on a computer screen. After you finish editing, you can transfer your corrections to the computer file.
- Before you print out a draft of your writing during the editing (or revision) steps, double-space your document. The extra space gives you room to write in your changes clearly so that you can read them easily later.
- If you must edit on screen, highlight each group of two or three sentences and read each slowly. By working in small segments, you reduce the tendency to read too quickly and miss errors. ✚

3e Knowing how to proofread

When you **proofread,** you check a final version carefully before handing it in. To make sure that your work is an accurate and clean transcription of your final draft, proofread after you revise (see 3c) and edit (see 3d). If you try to proofread while you edit, one process might distract from the other.

Proofreading involves a careful, line-by-line reading of your writing. You may want to proofread with a ruler so that you can focus on one line at a time. Starting at the end also helps you avoid becoming distracted by the content of your paper. Another effective proofreading technique is to read your final draft aloud, to yourself or to a friend. This can help you hear and see errors that might have slipped past your notice.

In proofreading, look for letters or words inadvertently left out. If you handwrite your material, write legibly. If a page has numerous errors, redo the page. Do not expect your instructor to make allowances for crude writing or typing; if you cannot write legibly or type well, arrange to have your paper typed properly. No matter how hard you have worked on other parts of the writing process, if your final copy is inaccurate or messy, you will not reach your audience successfully.

✚ COMPUTER TIPS: You can use your computer as an aid in proofreading, but you should be aware of its shortcomings as well.

- Whenever possible, proofread on a hard copy. It is much easier to spot errors on a printed page than on a computer screen. After you finish proofreading, you can transfer your corrections to the computer file.
- Before you print out your writing for proofreading, double-space your document. The extra space gives you room to write in your changes clearly so that you can read them easily later.

- If you must proofread on screen, highlight each group of two or three sentences and read each slowly. By working in small segments, you reduce the tendency to read too quickly and miss errors. ✚

3f Case study: A student writing an essay

This section is a case study of a student, Carol Moreno, going through the process of writing an essay. As you examine her three drafts, refer back to her writing assignment on page 24. In addition, look at the discussion of how she shaped her ideas (see 2k) and wrote her thesis statement (see 2n). See 2p for sample outlines.

1 Writing and revising a first draft

Carol Moreno wrote about a challenge she faced and met. As a result of using planning techniques (see 2e, 2f, and 2i), she chose the topic of weight lifting for women who want to build up their strength. She decided that her writing purpose would be *to inform* (see 1b-2). She then wrote the first draft, expecting to revise it later.

As Moreno revised her first draft, she worked systematically through the larger elements of the whole essay and paragraphs, and then she turned to her sentences and words. As she did this, she referred to the Revision Checklists in Chart 19 and Chart 20. Here is Moreno's first draft, along with her notes to herself about revisions she wanted to make when she wrote her second draft.

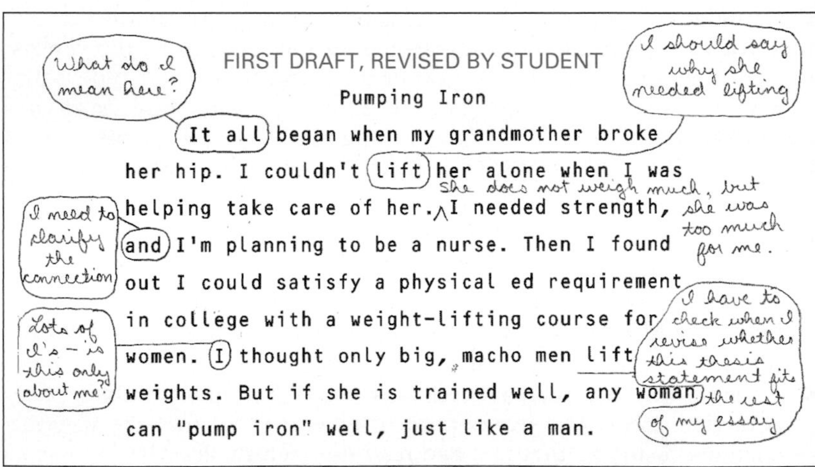

FIRST DRAFT, REVISED BY STUDENT

Pumping Iron

It all began when my grandmother broke her hip. I couldn't lift her alone when I was helping take care of her. ^ [She does not weigh much, but she was too much for me.] I needed strength, and I'm planning to be a nurse. Then I found out I could satisfy a physical ed requirement in college with a weight-lifting course for women. I thought only big, macho men lift weights. But if she is trained well, any woman can "pump iron" well, just like a man.

Move: This should be my third ¶. My second ¶ should give background

Hoping for strength and endurance

~~The first day of class we did not exercise. We talked about who we are and why we wanted to take the course. We heard about how to avoid~~ can lead to injury ~~by~~ unless lifters learning the safe use of free weights and weight machines. Free weights are barbells. ~~(barbells)~~ To be safe, no matter how little the weight, lifters must never raise a barbell by bending at the waist. Instead, they should squat, ~~grab~~ grasp the barbell, and then straighten up into a standing position. To avoid a ~~Twists~~ twist that can lead to serious injury ~~so~~ lifters must keep head erect, facing forward, back and neck aligned. Lifters use weight machines sitting down, which is a big advantage of the Nautilus and Universal. (I need to go into more detail here.)

(I have to bring in more than myself to say who we are) (move up to be ¶ 2 (background)) I was happy relieved that I won't develop overly masculine muscle mass. We learned that we can rely on women's biology. Our bodies produce only very small amounts of the hormones that enlarge muscles in men. ~~Normally,~~ With normal training women's muscles grow longer rather than bulkier. (I need to tie these together (check 4d)) Weight lifting is a form of anareobic (sp) exercise. It does not make people breathe harder or their hearts beat faster. Arobic (sp) exercise like running, walking, and swimming builds endurance, so I took up (Am I being too informal here?) swimming.

(dry topic sentence needs work) After safety comes our needs for physical strength. A well-planned, progressive weight-training program. ~~You~~ It begins with whatever weight ~~you~~ a person can lift comfortably and ~~then~~ gradually adds to the base weight so she gets stronger. What builds muscle strength is the number of "reps" ~~we do,~~ the lifter does, not necessarily an increase in the amount of resistance from adding ~~added~~ weight. In my class, we ranged from 18 to 43, scrawny to ~~fat~~ pudgy, and ~~lazy~~ couch potato to superstar, and we each developed a program that was OK (I'm not trying here) for us. Some women didn't listen to our instructor who (Start sentence here? Not sure.)

urged us not to ~~do~~ try more reps or weight than our programs called for even if ~~it~~ our first workouts seemed too easy. This turned out to be good advice because those of us who didn't listen woke up the next morning feeling as though our bodies had been twisted by evil forces.

~~After meeting~~ In addition to fitting to her physical capabilities, a weight lifter needs to design her personal goals. Most students in my group wanted to improve their upper body strength. Each student learned to use specific exercises to isolate certain muscle groups, for example we might work on our arms and abdomen (sp?) one day and our shoulders and chest the next day. ~~My goal is nursing, which I want to pursue. I want to help others, but I'm also very interested in the science I'll learn. I hear there is a lot of memorization, which I'm pretty good at. I also will have "clinical" assignments to give us hands-on experience in hospitals.~~ Because I had had such trouble lifting my grandmother, I added exercises to strengthen my legs and back. Another student added neck strengthening exercises. Someone else added finger and hand exercises.

I need specific examples of students

I'm off the topic

At the end of the course, we had to evaluate our progress. When I started, I could lift 10 pounds over my head for 3 reps. ~~, but~~ By the end I could lift 10 pounds over my head for 20 reps and 18 pounds for 3 reps. I am so proud of my accomplishments that still I work out three or four times a week. I am proof that any woman can become stronger and have more stamina.

I forgot to talk about my swimming

I need a stronger ending

2 Revising a second draft

After Carol Moreno had finished writing and entering notes to herself on her first draft (see 3f-1), she revised her work into a second draft and typed a clean copy to give to her instructor. As stated in the assignment (see page 24), Moreno's instructor considered the second draft an "essay in progress," so that all comments by the instructor were aimed at helping Moreno write an effective third, final draft.

Here is Moreno's second draft with two types of comments from the instructor: *questions* to stimulate Moreno to clarify and expand on ideas in the draft as well as section *codes*—the number-letter combinations—for Moreno to consult in this handbook.

SECOND DRAFT WITH INSTRUCTOR'S COMMENTS

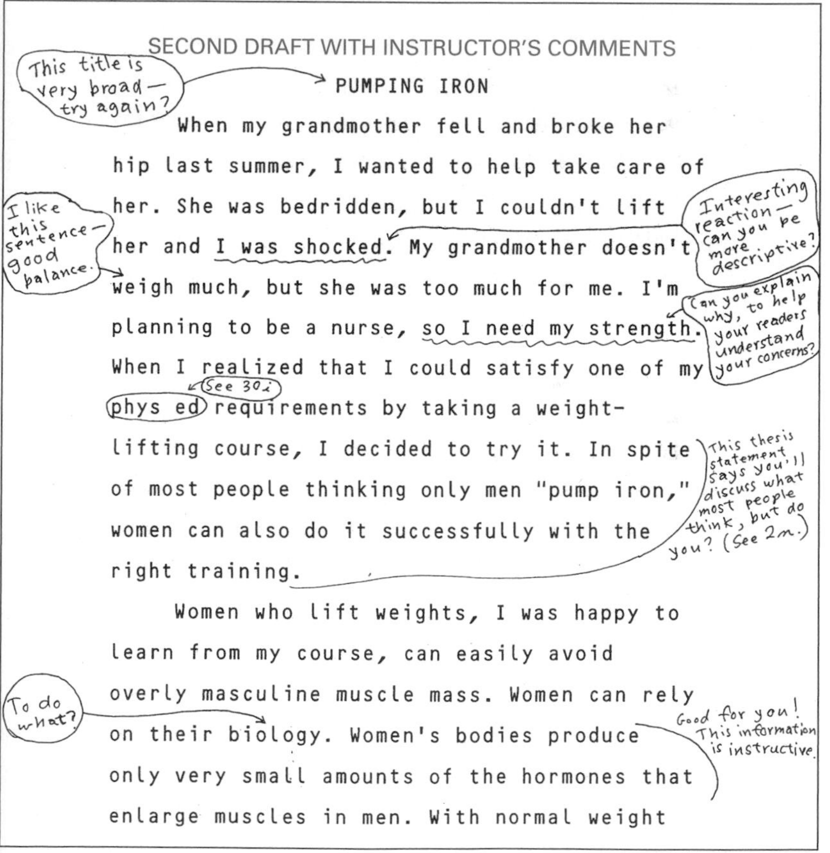

PUMPING IRON

When my grandmother fell and broke her hip last summer, I wanted to help take care of her. She was bedridden, but I couldn't lift her and I was shocked. My grandmother doesn't weigh much, but she was too much for me. I'm planning to be a nurse, so I need my strength. When I realized that I could satisfy one of my phys ed requirements by taking a weight-lifting course, I decided to try it. In spite of most people thinking only men "pump iron," women can also do it successfully with the right training.

Women who lift weights, I was happy to learn from my course, can easily avoid overly masculine muscle mass. Women can rely on their biology. Women's bodies produce only very small amounts of the hormones that enlarge muscles in men. With normal weight

This title is very broad—try again?
I like this sentence—good balance.
Interesting reaction—can you be more descriptive?
Can you explain why, to help your readers understand your concerns?
See 30i
This thesis statement says you'll discuss what most people think, but do you? (See 2m.)
To do what?
Good for you! This information is instructive.

→

training, women's muscles grow longer rather than bulkier. Also, women benefit most when they combine anaerobic exercise (weight lifting) with aerobic exercise. Anaerobic exercise strengthens and builds muscles, but it does not make people breathe harder or their hearts beat faster. Aerobic exercise like running, walking, and swimming builds endurance, not massive muscles. Thanks to my instructor, I balanced my weight-lifting workouts by swimming laps twice a week.

[With what result?] [Why use parentheses for key information?] [Only for a few seconds, or??] [Why? How?] [Is there a better word?]

Hoping for strength and endurance can lead to injury unless lifters learn the safe use of free weights and weight machines. Free weights are barbells. To be safe, no matter how little the weight, lifters must never raise a barbell by bending at the waist. Instead, they should squat, and then straighten up into a standing position. To avoid a twist can lead to a serious injury, lifters must do this: head erect and facing forward back and neck aligned. The big advantage of weight machines is that lifters must use them sitting down, so machines like the Nautilus and Universal pretty much force lifters to sit straight, which really does reduce the chance of injury.

[Can hope lead to injury?] [I can't "see" these.] [This image seems incomplete. Help?!] [See 15d-1.] [Read this aloud to hear that the action to do is missing.] [See 19b.]

Once a weight lifter understands how to lift safely, she needs to meet her personal needs. No one needs to be strong to get started. A well-planned, progressive weight-training program. It begins with whatever

[Do you want to use one word so much?] [See 13a]

weight a person can lift comfortably and gradually adds to the base weight as she gets stronger. What builds strength is the number of "reps" the lifter does, not necessarily an increase in the amount of resistance from adding weight. Our instructor helped the women in our class, who ranged from 18 to 43, scrawny to pudgy, couch potato to superstar, to develop a program that suited us. Our instructor urged us not to try more reps or weight than our programs called for, even if our first workouts seemed too easy. This turned out to be good advice because those of us who did not listen woke up the next morning feeling as though our bodies had been twisted by evil forces.

Meaning?

These adjectives are fun!

Fun again. Your voice (personality) comes through.

In addition to fitting a program to her physical capabilities, a weight lifter needs to design her personal goals. Most students in my group wanted to improve their upper body strength, so we focused on exercises to strengthen our arms, shoulders, abdomen, and chest. Each student learned to use specific exercises to isolate certain muscle groups, for example we might work on our arms and abdomen one day and our shoulders and chest the next day. Because I had such trouble lifting my grandmother, I added exercises to strengthen my legs and back. Another student added neck strengthening exercises. Someone else, planning to be a physical therapist, added finger and hand strengthening exercises.

Does one design a goal?

Good details.

Why important?

See 14a and 14e.

See 24b-3.

Excellent examples, Carol!

Why did she choose this?

How long was it?

At the end of the course, we had to evaluate our progress. When I started, I could lift 10 pounds over my head for 3 reps. By the end, I could lift 10 pounds over my head for 20 reps and 18 pounds for 3 reps. Also I could swim for 20 sustained minutes instead of the 10 at first. I am so proud of my accomplishments that I still work out three or four times a week. I am proof that any woman can benefit from "pumping iron." Not only will she become stronger and have more stamina, she will also feel very good.

See 24b-3

Can you communicate your enthusiasm to your reader more effectively?

Isn't this a bit flat?

Dear Carol,

You have truly earned the right to feel proud of yourself. You've also inspired me to consider weight training myself!

As you revise for your final drafts, I'd urge you to get more voice (your personality) into the essay. To do this, you don't have to become too informal; instead, find out how you felt about what you were doing and try to put that into words. Also, think about my questions and the codes that refer you to sections of the Troyka handbook. I will enjoy reading your final draft, I'm sure.

K.N.

3 Revising, editing, and proofreading a final draft

Moreno revised her essay in a third, final draft by working with the instructor's comments. Moreno started with the larger elements of the essay by thinking about the instructor's questions and suggestions. Next, Moreno used the codes—the number-letter combinations—that referred her to specific sections in this handbook concerning matters of word choice, style, grammar, and punctuation. She also referred to the Revision Checklists, Charts 19 and 20. Before typing a clean copy of her third, final draft, Moreno edited her writing by referring to the Editing Checklist in Chart 21. Here is the third, final draft of Moreno's essay. The labels in the margins are guideposts for you *only* in this handbook; do not use them on your final drafts.

THIRD, FINAL DRAFT BY STUDENT

title — Women Can Pump Iron, Too

introduction — When my grandmother fell and broke her hip last summer, I wanted to help take care of her. Because she was bedridden, she needed to be lifted at times, but I was shocked to discover that I could not lift her without my mother's or brother's help. My grandmother does not weigh much, but she was too much for me. My pride was hurt, and even more important, I began to worry about my plans to be a nurse specializing in care of elderly people. What if I were too weak to help my patients get around? When I realized that I could satisfy one of my Physical Education requirements by taking a weight-lifting course for women, I decided to try it. Many people picture only big, macho men wanting to lift weights, but times have changed. With the right training, women can also "pump iron" successfully to build strength.

thesis statement

→

background information

Women who lift weights, I was happy to learn from my course, can easily avoid developing overly masculine muscle mass. Women can rely on their biology to protect them. Women's bodies produce only very small amounts of the hormones that enlarge muscles in men. With normal weight training, women's muscles grow longer rather than bulkier. The result is smoother, firmer muscles, not massive bulges. Also, women benefit most when they combine weight lifting, which is a form of anaerobic exercise, with aerobic exercise. Anaerobic exercise strengthens and builds muscles, but it does not make people breathe harder or their hearts beat faster for sustained periods. In contrast, aerobic exercises like running, walking, and swimming build endurance, but not massive muscles, because they force a person to take in more oxygen, which increases lung capacity, improves circulatory health, and tones the entire body. Encouraged by my instructor, I balanced my weight-lifting workouts by swimming laps twice a week.

support: first aspect of training

Striving for strength can end in injury unless weight lifters learn the safe use of free weights and weight machines. Free weights are barbells, the metal bars that round metal weights can be attached to at each end. To be safe, no matter how little the weight, lifters must never raise a barbell by bending at the waist, grabbing the barbell, and then straightening up. Instead, they should squat, grasp the barbell, and then use their leg muscles to straighten into a standing position. To avoid a twist that can lead to serious injury, lifters must use this posture: head erect and facing forward, back and neck aligned. The big advantage of weight machines, which use weighted handles and bars hooked to wires and pulleys, is that lifters must use them sitting down. Therefore, machines like the Nautilus and Universal actually force lifters to keep their bodies properly aligned, which drastically reduces the chance of injury.

support: second aspect of training

Once a weight lifter understands how to lift safely, she needs a weight-lifting regimen personalized to her specific physical needs. Because benefits come from "resistance," which is the stress that lifting any amount of weight puts on a muscle, no one has to be strong to get started. A well-planned, progressive weight-training program begins with whatever weight a person can lift comfortably and gradually adds to the base weight as she gets stronger. What builds muscle strength is the number of repetitions, or "reps," the lifter does, not necessarily an increase in the amount of resistance from adding weight. Our instructor helped the women in the class, who ranged from 18 to 43, scrawny to pudgy, and couch potato to superstar, develop a program that was right for our individual weights, ages, and overall level

→

of conditioning. Everyone's program differed in how much weight to start out with and how many reps to do for each exercise. Our instructor urged us not to try more weight or reps than our programs called for, even if our first workouts seemed too easy. This turned out to be good advice because those of us who did not listen woke up the next day feeling as though our bodies had been twisted by evil forces.

support: third aspect of training

In addition to fitting a program to her physical capabilities, a weight lifter needs to design an individual routine to fit her personal goals. Most students in my group wanted to improve their upper body strength, so we focused on exercises to strengthen arms, shoulders, abdomens, and chests. Each student learned to use specific exercises to isolate certain muscle groups. Because muscles strengthen and grow when they are rested after a workout, our instructor taught us to work alternate muscle groups on different days. For example, a woman might work on her arms and abdomen one day and then her shoulders and chest the next day. Because I had had such trouble lifting my grandmother, I added exercises to strengthen my legs and back. Another student, who had hurt her neck in a car crash, added neck-strengthening exercises. Someone else, planning to be a physical therapist, added finger- and hand-strengthening exercises.

conclusion: outcome with call to action

At the end of our 10 weeks of weight training, we had to evaluate our progress. Was I impressed! I felt ready to lift the world. When I started, I could lift only 10 pounds over my head for 3 reps. By the end of the course, I could lift 10 pounds over my head for 20 reps, and I could lift 18 pounds for 3 reps. Also, I could swim laps for 20 sustained minutes instead of the 10 I had barely managed at first. I am so proud of my weight-training accomplishments that I still work out three or four times a week. I am proof that any woman can benefit from "pumping iron." Not only will she become stronger and have more stamina, she will also feel energetic and confident. After all, there is nothing to lose--except maybe some flab.

4 Writing Paragraphs

4a Understanding paragraphs

A **paragraph** is a group of sentences that work in concert to develop a unit of thought. Paragraphing permits you to subdivide material into manageable parts and, at the same time, to arrange those parts into a unified whole that effectively communicates its message.

Paragraphing is signalled by indentation. The first line is indented five spaces in a typewritten paper and one inch (about 2.5 cm) in a handwritten paper. (Business letters are sometimes typed in "block format," with paragraphs separated by a double space but no paragraph indentations. Generally block format is not appropriate for essays.)

The purpose of a paragraph helps to determine its structure. The most common purposes for academic writing are to inform and to persuade (see 1b). Some paragraphs introduce, conclude, or provide transitions. Most paragraphs, however, are **topical paragraphs,** also called *developmental paragraphs* or *body paragraphs.* They consist of a statement of a main idea, and specific, logical support for that main idea. Consider paragraph 1, a topical paragraph that seeks to inform. (To help discussion and reference in this chapter, a blue number appears at the left side of each sample paragraph.)

1 For most people, jellyfish are an ugly lump of stinging guck that washes up on the beach. But seeing them in action, you begin to understand why the world's 20 or so full-time jellyfish scientists view the creature as an elegantly beautiful specimen in which many mysteries of life might reside. "In a way, we're survivors of an earlier curiosity-driven group of naturalists—like those astronomers who used to count stars," says George Mackie, a University of Victoria–based zoologist who has been studying nerve function in the Portuguese man-of-war for 35 years and is invariably referred to as "the Grand Old Man of Jellies." "I'm doing this for the sheer love of

> it. Jellyfish are miracles of nature—so simple, yet they've survived
> 1 for so long. They are seen as limp and ineffectual creatures; I don't
> think that's fair."
>
> —RIC DOLPHIN, "Spineless Wonders"

Dolphin states his main idea in the second sentence. He then quotes an authority as support. This paragraph relates to the thesis° of the whole essay that although they seem simple, jellyfish are actually complex creatures that deserve close scientific attention.

Consider this topical paragraph that seeks to persuade. It, too, consists of a main idea and support.

> Many people have expressed uneasiness about the advertising
> enterprise in our time. To put the matter abruptly, the advertising
> industry is a crude attempt to extend the principles of automation to
> every aspect of society. Ideally, advertising aims at the goal of a
> 2 programmed harmony among all human impulses and aspirations
> and endeavors. Using handicraft methods, it stretches out toward
> the ultimate electronic goal of a collective consciousness. When all
> production and all consumption are brought into a pre-established
> harmony with all desire and all effort, then advertising will have
> liquidated itself by its own success.
>
> —MARSHALL MCLUHAN, *Understanding Media*

McLuhan states his main idea in the second sentence. The rest of the paragraph demonstrates his point and expands upon it.

Dolphin's and McLuhan's paragraphs demonstrate the three major characteristics of an effective paragraph. They are shown in Chart 22.

Understanding paragraph structure can help you at various points during your writing process. Before drafting (see 3b), you might decide to subdivide your material into paragraphs and to develop each in an effective way. If you prefer to plan less at first and instead write a "discovery" or a rough draft that gets all your ideas down on paper, you can later sort out your material and arrange it into manageable

MAJOR CHARACTERISTICS OF AN EFFECTIVE PARAGRAPH 22

- **Unity:** clear, logical relationship between the main idea of a paragraph and supporting evidence for that main idea (see 4b and 4c).
- **Coherence:** smooth progression from one sentence to the next within a paragraph (see 4d).
- **Development:** specific, concrete support for the main idea of the paragraph (see 4c).

paragraphs. When revising (see 3c), you might find that a particular paragraph is weak because it does not clearly state its main idea or it does not develop that idea well. Also, you might notice that although each paragraph is well structured on its own, the paragraphs do not work together very well. This chapter offers you paragraphing options to consider as you plan, draft, and revise your writing.

4b Writing unified paragraphs

A paragraph is **unified** when all its sentences clarify or help support the main idea. Unity is lost if a paragraph goes off the topic by including sentences unrelated to the main idea. Here is a paragraph about the novelist Jane Austen. It lacks unity because two sentences that were *deliberately added* to make this point regarding unity go off the topic.

NO

3 An Austen novel is a *tour de force,* at least by modern standards. Of course, Jane Austen did not feel the need to sprinkle her text with foreign phrases. Nothing extraordinary happens—no murders, escapades, or disasters. Instead of adventure or melodrama we read about the prosaic daily comedy of family life. There is little complexity to the plots (compared to Dickens, say), and the suspense, such as it is, arises chiefly out of questions of love and marriage. Jane Austen single-handedly invented, and brought to perfection, what could be called the domestic genre of novel-writing, the literary equivalent to the seventeenth-century Dutch school of interior painting. In contrast, Rembrandt, the pre-eminent Dutch painter of that era, avoided domesticity for its own sake.

In the preceding paragraph, the second and last sentences wander away from the topic of Austen's literary achievement. As a result, unity is lost. A reader quickly loses patience with material that rambles and therefore fails to communicate a clear message. Paragraph 4 is the original version as written by an award-winning author at McGill University. It is unified because all its sentences relate to the central subject.

YES

4 An Austen novel is a *tour de force,* at least by modern standards. Nothing extraordinary happens—no murders, escapades, or disasters. Instead of adventure or melodrama we read about the prosaic daily comedy of family life. There is little complexity to the plots (compared to Dickens, say), and the suspense, such as it is, arises chiefly out of questions of love and marriage. Jane Austen single-handedly invented, and brought to

perfection, what could be called the domestic genre of novel-writing, the literary equivalent to the seventeenth-century Dutch school of interior painting. Her books are, of course, much more than a faithful representation of
4 the period, just as Vermeer's paintings were more than illustrations of young Dutch women at home. Like Vermeer, de Witte, and the other Dutch domestic painters, Austen chose to stay strictly within the limits of the everyday, not because her talent was small, but because her imagination did not require a broader canvas.

—Witold Rybczynski, *Home*

The sentence that contains the main idea of a paragraph is called the **topic sentence.** It shapes and controls the content of the rest of the paragraph.

Some paragraphs use two sentences to present a main idea. In such cases, the topic sentence is followed by a **limiting** or **clarifying sentence,** which serves to narrow the paragraph's focus. In paragraph 4, the first sentence is its topic sentence, and the second sentence is its limiting sentence. The rest of the sentences support the main idea.

Professional essay writers do not always use topic sentences, because these writers have the skill to carry the reader along without explicit signposts. Student writers are often advised to use topic sentences so that their essays will be clearly organized and their paragraphs will not stray from the controlling power of each main idea.

Topic sentence at the beginning of a paragraph

Most informative and persuasive paragraphs place the topic sentence first so that a reader knows immediately what to expect.

The clock, Lewis Mumford has pointed out, is the key machine of the machine age, both for its influence on technics and for its influence on the habits of men. Technically, the clock was the first really automatic machine that attained any importance in the life of men. Previous to its invention, the common machines were of such nature that their operation depended on some external and unreliable force, such as human or animal muscles, water, or wind. It is true that
5 the Greeks had invented a number of primitive automatic machines, but these were used, like Hero's steam engine, either for obtaining "supernatural" effects in the temples or for amusing the tyrants of Levantine cities. But the clock was the first automatic machine that attained public importance and a social function. Clock-making began the industry from which men learnt the elements of machine-making and gained the technical skill that was to produce the complicated machinery of the Industrial Revolution.

—George Woodcock, "The Tyranny of the Clock"

Sometimes the main idea in the topic sentence starts a paragraph and is then restated at the end of the paragraph.

> *Every dream is a portrait of the dreamer.* You may think of your
> dream as a mirror that reflects your inner character—the aspects of your
> personality of which you are not fully aware. Once we understand
> 6 this, we can also see that every trait portrayed in our dreams has to
> exist in us, somewhere, regardless of whether we are aware of it or
> admit it. *Whatever characteristics the dream figures have, whatever
> behavior they engage in, is also true of the dreamer in some way.*
>
> —Robert A. Johnson, *Inner Work*

Topic sentence at the end of a paragraph

Some informative and persuasive paragraphs reveal the supporting details before the main idea. The topic sentence, therefore, comes at the end of a paragraph. This approach is particularly effective for building suspense and for dramatic effect. This arrangement forces readers to move through all the details before encountering the organizing effect of a main idea.

Paragraphs 7 and 8 end with a topic sentence. In paragraph 7, the main idea is fairly easy to predict as the specific suggestions accumulate. In paragraph 8, the main idea is less predictable, and it is thus more satisfying for some readers but more challenging for others.

> Burnout is a potential problem for any hard working and
> persevering student. A preliminary step for preventing student burnout
> is for students to work in moderation. Students can concentrate on
> school every day, provided that they do not overtax themselves.
> One method students can use is to avoid concentrating on a single
> 7 project for an extended period of time. For example, if students have
> to read two books for a midterm history test, they should do other
> assignments at intervals so that the two books will not get boring.
> Another means to moderate a workload is to regulate how many
> extracurricular projects to take on. *When a workload is manageable,
> a student's immunity to burnout is strengthened.*
>
> —Bradley Howard, student

> When I tell young softball players I played the game barehanded,
> they regard me warily. Am I one of these geezers who's
> forever jawing about the fact that, in his day, you had to walk through
> 8 six miles of snowdrifts just to get to school? Will I tediously lament the
> passing of the standing broad jump, and the glorious old days when
> the only football in the Maritimes was English rugger, and when
> hockey was an outdoor art rather than indoor mayhem, and at decent
> yacht clubs men were gentlemen and women were *personae non*

grata? No, but I will tell today's softball players that—with their fancy
8 uniforms, batters' helmets and, above all, gloves for every fielder—
the game they play is more tarted-up and sissy than the one I knew.

—HARRY BRUCE, "The Softball Was Always Hard"

Topic sentence implied

Some paragraphs make a unified statement without the use of a topic sentence. Writers must construct such paragraphs carefully so that a reader can easily discern the main idea.

> The Romans were entertained by puppets, as were the rulers
> of the Ottoman Empire with their favorite shadow puppet, Karaghoiz,
> teller of a thousand tales. In the Middle Ages, puppets were cast as
> devil and angel in religious mystery and morality plays until cast out
> 9 entirely by the church. For centuries, there has been a rich puppetry
> heritage in India that matches that country's multilayered culture.
> The grace of Bali is reflected in its stylized, ceremonial rod and
> shadow puppets. The Bunraku puppets of Japan, unequaled for
> technique anywhere in the world, require a puppet master and two
> assistants to create one dramatic character on stage.
>
> —DAN CODY, "Puppet Poetry"

Cody uses many examples to communicate the main idea that puppets have been popular in many cultures over time. A reader does not expect to puzzle over material, so implied topic sentences must be very clear, even though they are silent.

EXERCISE 4-1

Consulting sections 4a and 4b, identify all topic sentences, limiting sentences, and topic sentences repeated at the ends of paragraphs. If there is no topic sentence, compose an implied one.

A. A good college program should stress the development of high-level
reading, writing, and mathematical skills and should provide you with a
broad historical, social, and cultural perspective, no matter what subject
you choose as your major. The program should teach you not only the
10 most current knowledge in your field but also—just as important—
prepare you to keep learning throughout your life. After all, you will
probably change jobs, and possibly even careers, at least six times, and
you'll have other responsibilities, too—perhaps as a spouse and as a
parent and certainly as a member of a community whose bounds extend
beyond the workplace.

—FRANK T. RHODES, "Let the Student Decide"

B.

11 The once majestic oak tree crashes to the ground amid the destructive flames, as its panic-stricken inhabitants attempt to flee the fiery tomb. Undergrowth that formerly flourished smoulders in ashes. A family of deer darts furiously from one wall of flame to the other, without an emergency exit. On the outskirts of the inferno, fire fighters try desperately to stop the destruction. Somewhere at the source of this chaos lies a former campsite containing the cause of this destruction—an untended campfire. This scene is one of many which illustrate how human apathy and carelessness destroy nature.

—ANNE BRYSON, student

C.

12 Can you draw intricate distinctions on television? No. Can you say everything there is to be said, even everything you have to say, about a given topic? No. Can you back your way into the subject the way you might write the opening pages of a journal article? Also no. These are irritants to people trained in academic discourse, but they are not, in themselves, barriers to thought. On the contrary, I think it is the very sharpness of television discourse that dismays many intellectuals. It forces them to be direct. There is no time to gratify your ego by holding the floor, no opportunity to set the terms of the debate in your own favour, no licence for exclusive and proprietary language.

—MARK KINGWELL, "The Intellectual Possibilities of Television"

4c Supporting the main idea of a paragraph

As a writer, when you know how to achieve effective **paragraph development,** your material is far more likely to deliver its message to your reader. Most successful topical paragraphs that seek to inform or persuade (see 1b) contain a generalization, which is communicated in the topic sentence of the paragraph (see 4b). But more is needed. In writing most topical paragraphs, you must be sure to *develop the paragraph*. Development is provided by specific, concrete details that support the generalization. Without development, a topical paragraph contains only the broad claim of the generalization. It goes around in circles because it merely repeats the generalization over and over. It therefore does little to inform or persuade the reader.

Here is a paragraph that is unsuccessful because it contains one generalization restated four times in different words. Compare it with paragraph 1, an example of a successful paragraph, early in this chapter.

NO

13 For most people, jellyfish are an ugly lump of stinging guck that washes up on the beach. The average observer finds jellyfish disgusting. People have always been afraid of jellyfish because of their strange appearance and their sting. They seem like a lower form of life.

This *No* paragraph is stalled. It goes nowhere. Such material does not hold the reader's interest because it neither informs nor persuades.

When you write a topical paragraph, remember that **what separates most good writing from bad is the writer's ability to move back and forth between generalizations and specific details.** A successful topical paragraph includes a generalization and specific, concrete supporting details.

Details bring generalizations to life by providing concrete, specific illustrations. "RENNS" is a memory device you can use to check whether you have included sufficient detail in a topical paragraph. Chart 23 explains RENNS. A well-supported paragraph usually has only some kinds of RENNS; also, the supporting details do not need to occur in the order of the letters in RENNS. To see RENNS in action, read the many sample paragraphs in this chapter with an eye for the details. Consider paragraphs 14, 15, and 16 especially.

USING "RENNS" TO CHECK FOR SUPPORTING DETAILS 23

- **R**easons
- **E**xamples
- **N**ames
- **N**umbers
- **S**enses (sight, sound, smell, taste, touch)

Here is a paragraph that has three of the five types of RENNS. Locate as many RENNS as you can before you read the analysis that follows the paragraph.

14 A dramatic increase in the grizzly bear sightings in Alberta has touched off a heated dispute among wildlife experts that centres on a seemingly simple issue: Are there really more grizzlies or merely

14 more observers? More than 400 sightings were reported in Alberta in 1992, almost 10 times the number reported 10 years ago. The province's Department of Environmental Protection now estimates that 800 to 850 grizzly bears live in Alberta and that their number will reach 1000 by the turn of the century. Wildlife-conservation groups say the jump in sightings is mainly fuelled by greater activity by recreational users in the remote backcountry where grizzlies live. "My guess is, there are only 300 to 400 bears, and more likely, it's closer to the lower end," says Brian Horejsi, a conservation biologist with the group Speak Up For Wildlife.

—TERRY BULLICK, "When Is a Grizzly Not a Grizzly?"

Paragraph 14 succeeds because it does more than merely repeat its topic sentence, which is its first sentence. It develops the topic sentence to support the claim that grizzlies have not actually increased in number. It uses Numbers to document the apparent increase in sightings of grizzlies, but it uses Reasons to discount the claim that the rise in numbers means more actual bears. It has Names, such as Speak Up For Wildlife and the Department of Environmental Protection, which serve to support the claim.

Here is a paragraph that has four of the five types of RENNS. Locate as many RENNS as you can before you read the analysis of RENNS that follows the paragraph.

15 Tennyson called it a "flying flame." Benjamin Franklin termed it a "sudden and terrible mischief." In Roman mythology, the god Jupiter used spiky thunderbolts as letters to the editor when he chose to show displeasure with the poor mortals below. By whatever name, lightning is a spectacular natural event. Captured in photographs, its grandeur and beauty are safely petrified in static portraits of primal energy. In reality, at 24,000 to 28,000 degrees C, it is four times hotter than the surface of the sun. It can vaporize steel, plough up fields, shatter giant trees and scatter livid incendiary sparks over vast forests. Each day it kills 20 people.

—MICHAEL CLUGSTON, "Twice Struck"

Paragraph 15 succeeds because it illustrates its topic sentence, which is the fourth sentence. The paragraph develops its topic sentence with specific, concrete facts about the nature of lightning. It has Names, like Franklin and Tennyson, to testify to the power of the natural phenomenon. It has Numbers, such as those describing the temperature of lightning and the statistic that each day lightning kills twenty people. These Senses of sight and touch are appealed to in images of flame, "spiky thunderbolts," and intense heat. It also uses Examples, such as lightning's power to do powerful damage to steel, fields, and trees.

Some well-developed paragraphs have a single extended example to support the topic sentence.

> He was one of the greatest scientists the world has ever known,
> yet if I had to convey the essence of Albert Einstein in a single word,
> I would choose *simplicity*. Perhaps an anecdote will help. Once,
> caught in a downpour, he took off his hat and held it under his coat.
> 16 Asked why, he explained, with admirable logic, that the rain would
> damage the hat, but his hair would be none the worse for its wetting.
> This knack of going instinctively to the heart of the matter was the
> secret of his major scientific discoveries—this and his extraordinary
> feeling for beauty.
>
> —BANESH HOFFMAN, "My Friend, Albert Einstein"

EXERCISE 4-2

Reread the paragraphs in Exercise 4-1 and identify the RENNS (consult 4c) in each paragraph.

4d Writing coherent paragraphs

A paragraph is **coherent** when its sentences are related to each other, not only in content but also in grammatical structures and choice of words. To achieve coherence in your writing, write each sentence of a paragraph so that it flows sensibly from the one before. A coherent paragraph gives a reader a sense of continuity. Note in paragraphs 17 through 20 that each sentence continues from the previous sentence, by use of the techniques of coherence listed in Chart 24. As you draft and revise, monitor continuity in your paragraphs.

TECHNIQUES OF COHERENCE 24

- Use **transitional expressions** effectively (4d-1)
- Use **pronouns** effectively (4d-2)
- Use **deliberate repetition** effectively (4d-3)
- Use **parallel structures** effectively (4d-4)

1 Using transitional expressions

Transitional expressions are words and phrases that signal connections among ideas. By signalling how ideas relate to each other, you achieve coherence in your writing. Commonly used transitional expressions are listed in Chart 25. When you use them, be sure to vary your choices within each list to achieve variety in your writing.

✤ COMMA ALERT: Transitional expressions are usually set off with commas; see 24b-3. Here are some illustrations:

> **CONTINUITY BY ADDITION**
>
> Woodpeckers use their beaks to find food and to chisel out nests. **In addition,** they claim their territory and signal their desire to mate by drumming their beaks on trees.
>
> **CONTINUITY BY CONTRAST**
>
> Most birds communicate by singing. Woodpeckers, **however,** communicate by the duration and rhythm of the drumming of their beaks.
>
> **CONTINUITY BY RESULT**
>
> Woodpeckers communicate by drumming their beaks on dry branches or tree trunks. **As a result,** they can communicate across greater distances than songbirds can. ✤

Consider how the transitional expressions (shown in boldface) help to make this paragraph coherent.

> Certain aspects of Canadian cultural activity bear the stamp of this nation's rough, windswept, wilderness origins: ice hockey, wildlife prints, Farley Mowat, cottage-going, curling, toques. **To this list** we propose adding cuisine. **How else to account for** the enduring Canadian fondness for heavy, bland and non-nutritious fare than by noting that decades after there was any compelling reason to do so, Canadians still seem to eat purely for ballast: to bulk up to keep from being blown away. **Indeed,** it must be considered a providential
> 17 accident of history that no less a pioneer of high-calorie, comfort-and-convenience cuisine than James Lewis Kraft, founding father of processed cheese and namesake of the unstoppable Kraft Dinner, was born in 1875 in Stevensville, Ontario. **Moreover,** a Canuck invented that handy, fattening favourite—the chocolate bar. **Yes,** in 1910, Arthur Ganong, a St. Stephen, New Brunswick, mogul with a sweet tooth, decided he'd had enough of messing up his pockets with sticky, individual chocolates. **Within months,** the world's first bars of chocolate (conveniently wrapped in tin foil) were rolling off Ganong's factory's line.
>
> —GEOFF PEVERE AND GREIG DYMOND, *Mondo Canuck*

COMMON TRANSITIONAL EXPRESSIONS AND THE RELATIONSHIPS THEY SIGNAL 25

RELATIONSHIP	EXPRESSIONS
ADDITION	also, in addition, too, moreover, and, besides, furthermore, equally important, then, finally
EXAMPLE	for example, for instance, thus, as an illustration, namely, specifically
CONTRAST	but, yet, however, on the other hand, nevertheless, nonetheless, conversely, in contrast, still, at the same time
COMPARISON	similarly, likewise, in the same way
CONCESSION	of course, to be sure, certainly, granted
RESULT	therefore, thus, as a result, so, accordingly
SUMMARY	hence, in short, in brief, in summary, in conclusion, finally
TIME SEQUENCE	first, second, third, next, then, finally, afterwards, before, soon, later, meanwhile, subsequently, immediately, eventually, currently
PLACE	in the front, in the foreground, in the back, in the background, at the side, adjacent, nearby, in the distance, here, there

2 Using pronouns

When you use pronouns that clearly refer to nouns or other pronouns (see Chapter 10), you help your reader follow the bridges you build from one sentence to the next. Consider how the pronouns, shown in boldface, help make the following paragraph coherent.

> The funniest people I know are often unaware of just how
> ticked off **they** are about things until **they** start to kid around about
> them. Nature did not build **these** people to sputter or preach; instead,
> in response to the world's irritations, **they** create little plays in their
> 18 minds—parodies, cartoons, fantasies. When **they** see how funny
> **their** creations are, **they** also understand how really sore **they** were
> at **their** sources. **Their** anger is a revelation, one that works backward
> in the minds of an audience: the audience starts out laughing and
> winds up fuming.
>
> —Roger Rosenblatt, "What Brand of Laughter Do You Use?"

3 Using deliberate, selective repetition

You can achieve coherence by repeating key terms in a paragraph. A key term is usually one related to the main idea in the topic sentence or to a major detail in one of the supporting sentences. Repeating a key term now and then helps your reader follow your material. This technique must be used sparingly, however, because you risk being monotonous. The shorter a paragraph, the less likely that repeated words will be effective.

Consider how the careful reuse of key terms (shown in boldface) helps make this paragraph coherent.

19 Anthropologist Elena Padilla, author of *Up from Puerto Rico,* describing Puerto Rican **life** in a poor and squalid district of New York, tells **how** much people know about each other—**who** is to be trusted and **who** not, **who** is defiant of the law and **who** upholds it, **who** is competent and well informed and **who** is inept and ignorant—and **how** these things are known from the **public life** of the sidewalk and its associated enterprises. These are matters of **public** character. But she also tells **how** select are those permitted to drop into the kitchen for a cup of coffee, **how** strong are the ties, and **how** limited the number of a person's genuine confidants, those **who** share in a person's **private life** and **private affairs.** She tells **how** it is not considered **dignified** for everyone to know one's **affairs.** Nor is it considered **dignified** to snoop on others beyond the face presented in **public.** It does violence to a person's **privacy** and rights. In this, the people she describes are essentially the same as the people of the mixed, Americanized city street on which I **live,** and essentially the same as the people **who live** in high-income apartments or fine town houses, too.

—Jane Jacobs, *The Economy of Cities*

4 Using parallel structures

Parallel structures can help you achieve coherence in a paragraph. **Parallelism** is created when grammatically equivalent forms are used several times. The repeated tempos and sounds of parallel structures reinforce connections among ideas and create a dramatic effect. Be aware, however, that a thin line exists between effective parallelism (see Chapter 18) and lack of conciseness (see Chapter 16).

In paragraph 20, the authors use many parallel structures (shown in boldface) including a parallel series of words: *the sacred, the secular, the scientific*. They also use parallel phrases°: *sometimes smiled at, sometimes frowned upon*. They end the paragraph with a group of six parallel clauses°, starting with *banish danger with a gesture.*

> Superstitions are **sometimes smiled at** and **sometimes**
> **frowned upon** as observances characteristic of the old-fashioned, the
> unenlightened, children, peasants, servants, immigrants, foreigners
> or backwoods people. Nevertheless, they give all of us ways of
> moving back and forth among the different worlds in which we
> 20 live—**the sacred, the secular,** and **the scientific.** They allow us
> to keep a private world also, where, smiling a little, we can **banish**
> **danger with a gesture** and **summon luck with a rhyme, make**
> **the sun shine in spite of storm clouds, force the stranger to**
> **do our bidding, keep an enemy at bay,** and **straighten the paths**
> **of those we love.**
>
> —MARGARET MEAD AND RHODA METRAUX, "New Superstitions for Old"

5 Using coherence techniques to create connections among paragraphs

The same techniques for achieving coherence in a paragraph apply to communicating relationships among paragraphs in an essay. Transitional expressions, pronouns, deliberate repetition, and parallel structures can all link ideas from paragraph to paragraph throughout an essay.

Passage 21 shows two paragraphs and the start of a third paragraph from a book examining Canada's identity as a nation. Repeated words connecting these paragraphs include *nation, nationalism, history, historical,* and *Canadian(s).* The "From that year on" sentence tightly links the first and second paragraphs: A reader does not know what year is meant or what important events made it a turning point without reading the first paragraph. The opening sentence of the third paragraph creates another strong link by repeating the term *nationalism,* the word that concludes the second paragraph. This concept, introduced in the first two paragraphs, is qualified and nuanced in the final paragraph.

> As a nation, Canada was born again in 1957. The year lies
> across our history like a fault-line: Diefenbaker won his first election;
> Pearson won his Nobel Peace Prize; Walter Gordon brought down his
> 21 report on foreign ownership; and the Canada Council was established.
> These events, along with Quebec's Quiet Revolution, which began
> three years later, created the Canada of today, a society that seems to
> contain only a few trace elements of what Earle Birney called in the
> 1940s "a highschool land/deadset in adolescence."

From that year on, Canadian-American relations were redefined by a force for which there was no historical antecedent. This was the force, at first tentative and apologetic, then increasingly vocal, then rancorous, then celebratory, of Canadian nationalism.

21 This nationalism was always firmly rooted in pragmatism. Whenever times got tough or the price of flag-waving seemed likely to be too high, Canadians lowered their banners. This was predictable. Far more interesting was the way the minimum acceptable low-water mark of nationalist expression demanded by Canadians of their governments kept getting raised.

—RICHARD GWYN, *The 49th Paradox*

EXERCISE 4-3

Consulting section 4d, identify the techniques of coherence—words of transition, pronouns, deliberate repetition, and parallel structures—in each paragraph.

A. Kathy sat with her legs dangling over the edge of the side of the hood. The band of her earphones held back strands of straight copper hair which had come loose from two thick braids that hung down her back. She swayed with the music that only she could hear, making circles in
22 the warm air, her shoulders raised. Her arms reached out to her side; her opened hands reached for the air; her closed hands brought the air back to her. Her arms reached over her head; her opened hands reached for a cloud; her closed hands brought the cloud back to her. Her head moved from side to side; her eyes opened and closed to the tempo of the tunes. Kathy was motion.

—CLAIRE BURKE, student

B. Newton's law may have wider application than just the physical world. In the social world, racism, once set into motion, will remain in motion unless acted upon by an outside force. The collective "we" must be the outside force. We must fight racism through education. We must
23 make sure every school has the resources to do its job. We must present to our children a culturally diverse curriculum that reflects our pluralistic society. This can help students understand that prejudice is learned through contact with prejudiced people, rather than with the people toward whom the prejudice is directed.

—RANDOLPH H. MANNING, "Fighting Racism with Inclusion"

C. The Classical period—Mozart's era—coincided with the political
24 upheavals of the French Revolution, and the two were closely linked.

As polished and restrained as Classical music might seem today, it is
24 important to remember that it was revolutionary in its own time. It created
a revolution for simplicity, for direct communication, for common humanity
against aristocratic exclusiveness in music.

—Robert Harris, *What to Listen for in Mozart*

EXERCISE 4-4

Consulting sections 4c and 4d, develop three of the following topic sentences into paragraphs that are unified with RENNS and techniques of coherence. After you have finished, list the RENNS and the techniques of coherence you have built into each paragraph.

1. Too many people use the word *globalization* without really knowing what it means.
2. What constitutes garbage in Canada says a great deal about Canadian culture.
3. Society does not train parents adequately for their role.
4. Learning to cook involves more than just learning to follow recipes.
5. The friends we make at college (or university) will remain important in our later lives and careers.

4e Arranging a paragraph

Arranging a paragraph means putting its sentences into an order logical for communicating the message of the paragraph clearly and effectively. This section shows you the most common choices for arrangements of topical paragraphs. Choices include sequencing according to time and to location; moving from general to specific, from specific to general, and from least to most important; and progressing from problem to solution.

As you write, you might prefer to postpone your final decisions about the arrangement of your paragraphs until after you have written a first draft. As you revise, you can experiment to see how your sentences can be arranged for greatest impact.

According to time

A paragraph arranged according to time is put into a *chronological sequence*. It tells what happened or what is happening during a period of time.

25 Other visitors include schools of dolphin swimming with synchronized precision and the occasional humpback whale. Before 1950, these 14-meter marine mammals were a common sight in the waters of the Great Barrier Reef as they passed on their annual migration between Antarctic waters and the tropics, where their calves were born. Then in the 1950s whaling stations were set up on the New South Wales and Queensland coasts, and together with the long-established Antarctic hunts by the Soviet Union and America, whales were slaughtered in their thousands. By the time the whaling stations on the eastern Australian coast closed in the early 1960s, it was estimated that only two hundred remained in these waters. Today, their numbers are slowly increasing, but sightings are still rare.

—ALLAN MOULT, "Volcanic Peaks, Tropical Rainforest, and Mangrove Swamps"

According to location

A paragraph arranged according to location is put into a *spatial sequence*. It describes the position of objects relative to one another, often from a central point of reference. The topic sentence usually establishes a location that serves as the orientation for all other places mentioned. The other sentences in the paragraph often use transitional expressions (see Chart 25) that indicate *place*.

26 The old store, lighted only by three fifty-watt bulbs, smelled of coal oil and baking bread. In the middle of the rectangular room, where the oak floor sagged a little, stood an iron stove. To the right was a wooden table with an unfinished game of checkers and a stool made from an apple-tree stump. On shelves around the walls sat earthen jugs with corncob stoppers, a few canned goods, and some of the two thousand old clocks and clockworks Thurmond Watts owned. Only one was ticking; the others he just looked at.

—WILLIAM LEAST HEAT MOON, *Blue Highways*

From general to specific

An arrangement of sentences from the general to the specific is the most common organization for a paragraph. Seen in many of the examples earlier in this chapter, a general-to-specific arrangement begins with a topic sentence (and perhaps is followed by a limiting or clarifying sentence) and ends with specific details.

27 The problem with vitamin D in Canada is one of geography and climate. Because the sun is low on the horizon during winter, it passes through more of the Earth's atmosphere; the atmosphere acts as a filter and shuts out most of the low-wavelength UV rays that we need to make vitamin D. That, plus shorter day length and our

27 tendency to cover our bodies with clothing, means that from October to April we don't get nearly enough sunlight to produce natural vitamin D. If we don't take large doses of artificial vitamin D, in the form of fish oils (halibut and cod livers are best, but there are no more cod, and any fatty fish will do) and egg yolk, then we get poor bone development and repair. Dark or tanned skin is also a poorer producer of vitamin D than fair or untanned skin.

—WAYNE GRADY, *Chasing the Chinook*

From specific to general

A less common arrangement moves from the specific to the general. Like paragraphs 7 and 8 earlier in this chapter, a paragraph with such an arrangement ends with a topic sentence and begins with the details that support the topic sentence.

28 Replacing the spark plugs probably ranks number one on the troubleshooting list of most home auto mechanics. Too often this effort produces little or no improvement, as the problem lies elsewhere. Within the ignition system the plug wires, distributor unit, coil, and ignition control unit play just as vital a role as the spark plugs. However, performance problems are by no means limited to the ignition system. The fuel system and emissions control system also help determine engine performance, and each of these systems contains several components which equal the spark plug in importance. The do-it-yourself mechanic who wants to provide basic care for a car should be able to do more than change the spark plugs.

—DANNY WITT, student

From least to most important

A sentence arrangement that moves from the least to the most important is known as *climactic order* because it saves the climax for the end. This arrangement can be effective in holding the reader's interest because the best part comes at the end. In informative and persuasive writing, this type of arrangement usually calls for the topic sentence at the beginning of the paragraph, although sometimes the topic sentence works well at the end. Here is a climactic paragraph that begins with a topic sentence. ("The Department" in the paragraph is Canada's Department of External Affairs.)

29 The significance of General de Gaulle's famous *"Vive le Québec libre"* spoken from a balcony in Montreal in 1967 was debated in the Department as it was throughout the country. Mr. Pearson declared the general's utterance to be unacceptable, and de Gaulle promptly left the country without completing his visit. Although there were some dissenting voices, particularly to the effect that the government had overreacted, there was general agreement that the General's

statement was not a slip of the tongue. After General de Gaulle's visitation, the government could no longer assume that the influence
29 of France would always be benign so far as Canada was concerned. Now one thing had become clear: Canada's relations with France had become a matter of prime concern not just within the Department, but at all its diplomatic posts.

—ARTHUR ANDREW, *The Rise and Fall of a Middle Power* (James Lorimer & Company Ltd.)

From problem to solution

An effective arrangement can be to present a problem and move quickly to a suggested solution. The topic sentence presents the problem and the next sentence—the limiting or clarifying sentence—presents the main idea of the solution. The rest of the sentences give the specifics of the solution.

When I first met them, Sara and Michael were a two-career couple with a home of their own, and a large boat bought with a large loan. What interested them in a concept called voluntary simplicity was the birth of their daughter and a powerful desire to raise her themselves. Neither one of them, it turned out, was willing to restrict what they considered their "real life" into the brief time before work and the tired hours afterward. "A lot of people think
30 that as they have children and things get more expensive, the only answer is to work harder in order to earn more money. It's not the only answer," insists Michael. The couple's decision was to trade two full-time careers for two half-time careers, and to curtail consumption. They decided to spend their money only on things that contributed to their major goal, the construction of a world where family and friendship, work and play, were all of a piece, a world, moreover, which did not make wasteful use of the earth's resources.

—LINDA WELTNER, "Stripping Down to Bare Happiness"

EXERCISE 4-5

For each paragraph, arrange the sentences into a logical sequence. Begin by locating the topic sentence and placing it at the beginning of the paragraph. As you work, consult sections 4b and 4c.

PARAGRAPH A

1. Remember, many people who worry about offending others wind up living according to other people's priorities.
2. Learn to decline, tactfully but firmly, every request that does not contribute to your goals.
3. Of all the time-saving techniques ever developed, perhaps the most effective is the frequent use of the word *no.*

4. If you point out that your motivation is not to get out of work but to save your time to do a better job on the really important things, you'll have a good chance of avoiding unproductive tasks.

—Edwin Bliss, "Getting Things Done: The ABC's of Time Management"

Paragraph B

1. Supporters of malls point out their convenience for shoppers, with their many large stores and ample parking.
2. However, critics say that malls encourage people to drive rather than walk.
3. These arguments suggest that defenders of malls hold a "suburban" ideal of the city, in contrast to the "urban" ideal of their opponents.
4. In addition, large malls break up the traditional city streetscape formed by a variety of small shops and businesses.
5. Shopping malls have been both praised and criticized.
6. They argue that a city with few pedestrians is an impersonal city.

—Tanya Choi, student

Paragraph C

1. Significantly, scientists have found that radiated light activates a different part of the brain than reflected light.
2. Many people believe that reading a page on a computer screen is no different than reading a printed page.
3. The result is that reading with radiated light causes both the reader's eye and the reader's mind to wander.
4. This belief is inaccurate, however, because a computer screen *radiates* light, while a paper page *reflects* light at the reader's eye.

—Lise Bernard, student

EXERCISE 4-6

Consulting sections 4b and 4e, identify the arrangement or arrangements that organize the sentences in each paragraph. Choose from time, location, general to specific, specific to general, least to most important, and problem to solution.

A. A combination of cries from exotic animals and laughter and gasps from children fills the air along with the aroma of popcorn and peanuts. A hungry lion bellows for dinner, his roar breaking through the confusing
31 chatter of other animals. Birds of all kinds chirp endlessly at curious children. Monkeys swing from limb to limb performing gymnastics for gawking onlookers. A comedy routine by orangutans employing old shoes and garments incites squeals of amusement. Reptiles sleep peacefully behind

glass windows, yet they send shivers down the spines of those who
31 remember the quick death many of these reptiles can induce. The sights
and sounds and smells of the zoo inform and entertain children of all ages.

—Deborah Harris, student

B. No one even agrees anymore on what "old" is. Not long ago, 30
was middle-aged and 60 was old. Now, more and more people are living
32 into their 70s, 80s and beyond—and many of them are living well, without any incapacitating mental or physical decline. Today, old age is defined
not simply by chronological years, but by degree of health and well being.

—Carol Tavris, "Old Age Is Not What It Used to Be"

C. There is something slightly inhuman and robotic about the reporters
who deliver the news to us on television. As a class they do not represent
humanity. TV newspeople are never ugly. They are never old and seldom
middle-aged. They are rarely overweight or bald and they do not wear
striking or ungainly clothing. They are never unhappy or ill at ease. They
are, without exception, middle class: no national TV reporter speaks with
33 a regional or working-class accent, or for that matter, a Rosedale honk
or a Westmount whine. Whatever eccentricities they may have are sup-
pressed. They are chosen not to reflect the audience but to reflect the way
producers believe—perhaps with good reason—that we want to see our
society represented. They appear to be picked as carefully as actors in a
play—except that directors of plays often look for striking or anomalous
characteristics and TV news producers never do.

—Robert Fulford, "The Grand Illusion"

EXERCISE 4-7

Often more than one arrangement can be effective for discussing a subject. Think through the topics listed here and consider what arrangement (one or more) might be effective for discussing the subject. Consulting section 4e, choose from general to specific, specific to general, least to most important, problem to solution, location, and time. Be ready to explain your choices. As long as you can give a convincing rationale, you will be correct.

1. how to impress a total stranger
2. buying a computer
3. preparing for a job interview
4. the problems with junk food
5. the appeal of horror movies

4f Using rhetorical strategies in paragraphs

Rhetorical strategies, or rhetorical patterns, are techniques for presenting ideas clearly and effectively. You choose a specific rhetorical strategy according to what you want to accomplish.

COMMON RHETORICAL STRATEGIES—OR PATTERNS—FOR PARAGRAPHS 26

- narration
- description
- process
- example
- definition
- analysis and classification
- comparison and contrast
- analogy
- cause-and-effect analysis

For the purpose of illustration, the rhetorical strategies in this section are discussed separately. In essay writing, however, they often overlap. For example, narrative writing often contains descriptions; explanations of processes often include comparisons and contrasts; and so on.

1 Using narration

Narrative writing tells about what is happening or what has happened. In informative and persuasive writing, narration is usually written in chronological sequence. Narrative paragraphs that illustrate other aspects of informative and persuasive writing include paragraphs 16, 29, and 49.

Here is another example of a narrative paragraph. Its main idea appears in the fourth sentence, describing the sudden rise in the target price of a gold mine's stocks.

34 There were ten major gold company analysts waching Bre-X stock in October 1995, when the price blew through $30 on October 20, a level that meant investors valued the company at more than $700 million. Normally, analysts move up their target price for a $30 stock by a few dollars at a time. Not with Bre-X. Targets rose in leaps and bounds. By October 23, 1995, Bre-X was changing hands

34 at $43 and Lévesque's Fowler, still enthralled by his "visual inspection," set out a one-year target of $62, which would rank Bre-X as one of the five largest gold companies in Canada. In Indonesia, the geologists stayed true to form. Rather than verifying the existing deposit, Felderhof and de Guzman continued to do step-out drilling. Three new holes were drilled that extended the size of the deposit to a strip 2.75 kilometres long. All three found gold. The stock soared on the news..

—DOUGLAS GOOLD AND ANDREW WILLIS, *The Bre-X Fraud*

2 Using description

Descriptive writing appeals to a reader's senses—sight, sound, smell, taste, and touch. Descriptive writing permits you to share your sensual impressions of a person, a place, or an object. Descriptive paragraphs that illustrate other aspects of informative and persuasive writing include paragraphs 17, 18, and 25. Here is another example of a descriptive paragraph.

35 Somewhere to the far north of Newfoundland, the St. Lawrence Seaway, Place Ville Marie, the Macdonald-Cartier Freeway, the bald-headed prairie and Stanley Park lies an unreal world, conceived in the mind's eye, born out of fantasy and cauled in myth. It is a weird and terrible land where nothing is as it may seem. Home of the iceworm and the igloo, of mad trappers and mushing Mounties, of pingos and polar bears, of the legions of the damned that were conjured into being by Robert Service, its voice is the baleful whisper of the aurora borealis, the eerie howl of Jack London's malemutes and the whining dirge of C.B.C.'s wind machines. It is a "white hell", "the ultimate desolation", a "howling wasteland", "the Land that God forgot" and "the Land God Gave to Cain." It is a region almost wholly of our contriving, and we have made of it so inimical a world that the truly alien moon, even as seen on television screens, seems to have more reality.

—FARLEY MOWAT, "The Nature of the North"

3 Using process

Process is a term used for writing that describes a sequence of actions by which something is done or made. Usually a process description is developed in chronological order. For an example, see paragraph 36. To be effective, process writing must include all steps. The amount of detail depends on whether you want to instruct the reader about how to do something or you want to offer a general overview of the process. Here is a process description written to give the reader a general picture. A process description that gives directions appears in paragraph 37.

36 Making chocolate is not as simple as grinding a bag of beans. The machinery in a chocolate factory towers over you, rumbling and whirring. A huge cleaner first blows the beans away from their accompanying debris—sticks and stones, coins and even bullets can fall among cocoa beans being bagged. Then they go into another machine for roasting. Next comes separation in a winnower, shells sliding out one side, beans falling from the other. Grinding follows, resulting in chocolate liquor. Fermentation, roasting and "conching" all influence the flavor of chocolate. Chocolate is "conched"—rolled over and over against itself like pebbles in the sea—in enormous circular machines named conches for the shells they once resembled. Climbing a flight of steps to peer into this huge, slow-moving glacier, I was expecting something like molten mud but found myself forced to conclude it resembled nothing so much as chocolate.

—Ruth Mehrtens Galvin, "Sybaritic to Some, Sinful to Others"

Here is a process description that gives the reader specific, step-by-step instructions.

37 Carrying loads of equal weight like paint cans and toolboxes is easier if you carry one in each hand. Keep your shoulders back and down so that the weight is balanced on each side of your body, not suspended in front. With this method, you will be able to lift heavier loads and also to walk and stand erect. Your back will not be strained by being pulled to one side.

—John Warde, "Safe Lifting Techniques"

4 Using examples

A paragraph developed by example uses illustrations to provide evidence in support of the main idea. Examples are highly effective for developing topical paragraphs. They supply a reader with concrete, specific information. Many of the sample paragraphs in this chapter are developed with examples, among them paragraphs 1, 6, 7, 16, and 27. Here is another paragraph with examples used to develop the topic sentence.

38 One major value of rain forests is biomedical. The plants and animals of rain forests are the source of many compounds used in today's medicines. A drug that helps treat Parkinson's disease is manufactured from a plant that grows only in South American rain forests. Some plants and insects found in rain forests contain rare chemicals that relieve certain mental disorders. Discoveries, however, have only begun. Scientists say that rain forests contain over a thousand plants that have great anticancer potential. To destroy life forms in these forests is to deprive the human race of further medical advances.

—GARY LEE HOUSEMAN, student

5 Using definition

A paragraph of definition develops a topic by explaining the meaning of a word or a concept. A paragraph of definition is an *extended definition*—it is more extensive than a dictionary denotation (although the paragraph may include a dictionary definition). An effective paragraph of definition does not use abstractions to explain abstractions. Here is a paragraph that offers an extended definition of tolerance.

39 The Latin root of the word "tolerance" refers to things that can be borne, endured, are supportable. The intrinsic meaning of "tolerance" is the capacity to sustain and endure, as of hardship. From this comes the inferential meaning of patience with the opinions and practices of those who differ. It is interesting that the word is used in connection with the coining of money and with machinery, to indicate the margin within which coins may deviate from the fixed standard, or dimensions or parts of machine from the norm.

—DOROTHY THOMPSON, "Concerning Tolerance"

6 Using analysis and classification

Analysis (sometimes called *division*) divides things up. Classification groups things together. A paragraph developed by analysis divides one subject into its component parts. Paragraphs of analysis written in this pattern usually start by identifying the one subject and continue by explaining that subject's distinct parts. For example, here is a paragraph that identifies a new type of zoo design and then analyzes changes in our world that have brought about that design.

40 The current revolution in zoo design—the landscape revolution—is driven by three kinds of change that have occurred during this century. First are great leaps in animal ecology, veterinary

medicine, landscape design, and exhibit technology, making possible
unprecedented realism in zoo exhibits. Second, and perhaps most
40 important, is the progressive disappearance of wilderness—the very
subject of zoos—from the earth. Third is knowledge derived from
market research and from environmental psychology, making possible
a sophisticated focus on the zoo-goer.

—MELISSA GREENE, "No Rms, Jungle Vu"

A paragraph developed by classification groups information according to some scheme. The separate groups must be *from the same class*—they must have some underlying characteristics in common. For example, different galaxies can be classified into three general groups based on their shape. Here is a paragraph that discusses the three types of galaxies.

There are three basic types of galaxies: spiral galaxies, like the
Milky Way; spherical swarms of stars called elliptical galaxies; and
loose collections of stars with no distinct structural form, called
irregular galaxies. The Large and Small Magellanic Clouds, the Milky
Way satellite galaxies, are irregulars. Two nearby ellipticals are
companions of the Andromeda Galaxy and are easily seen in
photographs. The smallest elliptical galaxies, called dwarf spheroidal
41 systems, have only a few thousand stars. But giant ellipticals are the
titans of the cosmos, with populations of up to 50 trillion stars. Spiral
galaxies have a comparatively small size range. The upper limit is
marked by NGC 6872 and UGC 2885, both roughly 10 times the
number of the Milky Way, while NGC 3928 is only about one-quarter
of our galaxy's diameter. Although spiral galaxies are outnumbered
by ellipticals, they *appear* to be most common because a typical
spiral is larger and brighter than an average elliptical. Irregular galaxies
are less numerous than spirals or ellipticals, and most are quite small.

—TERENCE DICKINSON, "Galactic Encounters"

7 Using comparison and contrast

Comparison deals with similarities, while contrast deals with differences. Paragraphs using comparison and contrast can be structured in two ways. A *point-by-point structure* allows you to move back and forth between the two items being compared. A *block structure* allows you to discuss one item completely before discussing the other.

Here is a paragraph structured point-by-point for comparison and contrast.

In the business environment, tone is especially important.
42 Business writing is not literary writing. Literary artists use unique
styles to "express" themselves to a general audience. Business people

42 write to particular persons in particular situations, not so much to express themselves as to accomplish particular purposes, "to get a job done." If a reader does not like a novelist's tone, nothing much can happen to the writer short of failing to sell some books. In the business situation, however, an offensive style may not only prevent a sale but may also turn away a customer, work against a promotion, or even cost you a job.

—JOHN S. FIELDEN, "What Do You Mean, You Don't Like My Style!"

PATTERNS FOR COMPARISON AND CONTRAST 27

POINT-BY-POINT STRUCTURE

Student body: college *A*, college *B*
Curriculum: college *A*, college *B*
Location: college *A*, college *B*

BLOCK STRUCTURE

College A: student body, curriculum, location
College B: student body, curriculum, location

Here is a block-form comparison of games and business.

43 Games are of limited duration, take place on or in fixed and finite sites and are governed by openly promulgated rules that are enforced on the spot by neutral professionals. Moreover, they are performed by relatively evenly matched teams that are counseled and led through every move by seasoned hands. Scores are kept, and at the end of the game, a winner is declared. Business is usually a little different. In fact, if there is anyone out there who can say that the business is of limited duration, takes place on a fixed site, is governed by openly promulgated rules that are enforced on the spot by neutral professionals, competes only on relatively even terms, and performs in a way that can be measured in runs or points, then that person is either extraordinarily lucky or seriously deluded.

—WARREN BENNIS, "Time to Hang Up the Old Sports Clichés"

8 Using analogy

Analogy is a type of comparison. It compares objects or ideas from different classes—things not normally associated. For example, a fatal disease has certain points in common with war. Analogy is particularly effective when you want to explain the unfamiliar in terms of the familiar. Often a paragraph developed with analogy starts with a simile or metaphor (see 21c) to introduce the comparison. Here is a paragraph developed by analogy that starts with a simile and then explains the effect of casual speech by comparing it to casual dress.

> 44 Casual dress, like casual speech, tends to be loose, relaxed and colorful. It often contains what might be called "slang words": blue jeans, sneakers, baseball caps, aprons, flowered cotton housedresses, and the like. These garments could not be worn on a formal occasion without causing disapproval, but in ordinary circumstances they pass without remark. "Vulgar words" in dress, on the other hand, give emphasis and get immediate attention in almost any circumstances, just as they do in speech. Only the skillful can employ them without some loss of face, and even then they must be used in the right way. A torn, unbuttoned shirt, or wildly uncombed hair can signify strong emotions: passion, grief, rage, despair. They are most effective if people already think of you as being neatly dressed, just as the curses of well-spoken persons count for more than those of the customarily foul-mouthed.
>
> —ALISON LURIE, *The Language of Clothes*

9 Using cause-and-effect analysis

Cause-and-effect analysis involves examining outcomes and reasons for those outcomes. Causes lead to an event or an effect, and effects result from causes. (Section 5i describes making reasonable connections between causes and effects.) Here is a paragraph developed through a discussion of how television (the cause) becomes indispensable (the effect) to parents of young children.

> 45 Because television is so wonderfully available as child amuser and child defuser, capable of rendering a volatile three-year-old harmless at the flick of a switch, parents grow to depend upon it in the course of their daily lives. And as they continue to utilize television day after day, its importance in their children's lives increases. From a simple source of entertainment provided by parents when they need a break from child care, television gradually changes into a powerful and disruptive presence in family life. But despite their increasing resentment of television's intrusions into their family life, and despite their considerable guilt at not being able to control their children's viewing, parents do not take steps to extricate themselves from television's domination. They can no longer cope without it.
>
> —MARIE WINN, *The Plug-In Drug*

EXERCISE 4-8

Consulting section 4f, identify the pattern or patterns each paragraph illustrates. Choose from narration, description, process, example, definition, analysis, classification, comparison and contrast, analogy, and cause and effect.

A. The contrast between English Canadian and Quebecois attitudes to
the United States is striking. In English Canada there has been an
anguished debate for generations as to whether Canadian culture can
preserve its distinctiveness amid the nightly electronic deluge of up to
46 sixty cable TV stations in most Canadian homes. At Videotron, Quebec's
largest cable TV company, they beam all the American soaps into Quebec
homes, but they know that the most popular shows—the ones that get
up to 80 percent of the Quebec population staying home at night—are the
ones written and acted in Quebec. As long as they can see what they
want in their own language, Quebecois believe their culture will be secure.

—MICHAEL IGNATIEFF, *Blood and Belonging*

B. Buctouche is a small town at the mouth of the Buctouche River in
New Brunswick. It is also the summer home of Antonine Maillet. I had
just translated Maillet's short novel *Christophe Cartier de la noisette, dit
Nounours,* and was about to embark on her monumental allegory *Le
huitième jour,* and I wanted to get the lay of the Acadian landscape. I
had a literary sense of the Buctouche area, but I wanted to see it and hear
it for myself. I stopped outside a low brick building, one of those five-and-
47 dime stores that sell cheap clothes and expensive souvenirs, including
small Acadian flags—the French *tricolore* with a yellow *Stella maris* in one
corner. When I went up to the cash, I asked, in my best French, which
house belonged to Antonine and received a long, friendly reply. To my
complete astonishment I could not understand a word of it. I had entered
a private realm, a kind of hidden valley that had its own customs, its
own flag and its own language. Some call this place the Republic of
Madawaska, but for more than 350 years it has been known as the land
of Acadia.

—WAYNE GRADY, *Chasing the Chinook*

C. In the case of wool, very hot water can actually cause some structural changes within the fiber, but the resulting shrinkage is minor. The
fundamental cause of shrinkage in wool is felting, in which the fibers
48 scrunch together in a tighter bunch, and the yarn, fabric, and garment follow suit. Wool fibers are curly and rough-surfaced, and when squished
together under the lubricating influence of water, the fibers wind around
each other, like two springs interlocking. Because of their rough surfaces, they stick together and cannot be pulled apart.

—JAMES GORMAN, "Gadgets"

D. After our lunch, we drove to the Liverpool public library, where I
was scheduled to read. By then, we were forty-five minutes late, and on
arrival we saw five middle-aged white women heading away toward an
old car across the street. When they recognized me, the women came
over and apologized: They were really sorry, they said, but they had to
leave or they'd get in trouble on the job. I looked at them. Every one of
49 them was wearing an inexpensive, faded house-dress and, over that, a
cheap and shapeless cardigan sweater. I felt honored by their open-
mindedness in having wanted to come and listen to my poetry. I thought
and I said that it was I who should apologize: I was late. It was I who felt,
moreover, unprepared: What in my work, to date, deserves the open-
minded attention of blue-collar white women terrified by the prospect of
overstaying a union-guaranteed hour for lunch?

—JUNE JORDAN, "Waiting for a Taxi"

E. Lacking access to a year-round supermarket, the many species—
from ants to wolves—that in the course of evolution have learned the
advantages of hoarding must devote a lot of energy and ingenuity to
protecting their stashes from marauders. Creatures like beavers and
honeybees, for example, hoard food to get them through cold winters.
50 Others, like desert rodents that face food scarcities throughout the year,
must take advantage of the short-lived harvests that follow occasional
rains. For animals like burying beetles that dine on mice hundreds of
times their size, a habit of biting off more than they can chew at the
moment forces them to store their leftovers. Still others, like the male
MacGregor's bowerbird, stockpile goodies during mating season so they
can concentrate on wooing females and defending their arena de l'amour.

—JANE BRODY, "A Hoarder's Life: Filling the Cache—And Finding It"

4g Writing introductory, transitional, and concluding paragraphs

Introductory, transitional, and concluding paragraphs are generally shorter than the topical paragraphs with which they appear.

Introductory paragraphs

In informative and persuasive writing, an introductory paragraph sets the stage and prepares a reader for what lies ahead. An introduction provides a bridge from the reader's mind to yours. In so doing, it needs to arouse the reader's interest in your subject. An introduction must clearly relate to the rest of your essay. If it points in one direction and your essay goes off in another, your reader will be confused, even annoyed, and will likely stop reading.

For academic writing, many instructors require that an introductory paragraph include a statement of the thesis of the essay, so that the central idea of the essay is clearly available early on. Many instructors want students to demonstrate from the start that all parts of any essay are related. Professional writers do not necessarily include a thesis statement° in their introductory paragraphs; with experience comes skill at maintaining a line of thought without overtly stating a central idea. Student writers, however, often need to practise explicitly and demonstrate openly external clues to essay organization. As you write successive drafts of an essay, expect to revise your introduction, in whole or part, so that it works well in concert with your other paragraphs.

When instructors require a thesis statement, they often want it to be in the last sentence or two of the introductory paragraph. Here is an example of an introductory paragraph with a thesis statement (shown in italics).

> Most sprinters live in a narrow corridor of space and time. Life
> rushes at them quickly, and success and failure are measured by
> 51 frustrating, tiny increments. Florence Griffith Joyner paints her running
> world in bold, colorful strokes. *For her, there's a lot of romance to
> running fast.*
>
> —CRAIG A. MASBACK, "Siren of Speed"

You can see additional examples of introductory paragraphs with a thesis statement in the last sentence in the student essays in sections 3f and 6i.

An introductory paragraph often includes one or more **introductory devices** that serve to stimulate a reader's interest in the subject of the essay. Usually the introductory device precedes the thesis statement. As you write your introductory paragraphs, keep in mind the guidelines in Chart 28.

Here is an introduction that uses two anecdotes before its thesis statement (shown in italics).

> On seeing another child fall and hurt himself, Hope, just nine
> months old, stared, tears welling up in her eyes, and crawled to her
> mother to be comforted—as though she had been hurt, not her
> friend. When 15-month-old Michael saw his friend Paul crying,
> Michael fetched his own teddy bear and offered it to Paul; when
> 52 that didn't stop Paul's tears, Michael brought Paul's security blanket
> from another room. *Such small acts of sympathy and caring, observed
> in scientific studies, are leading researchers to trace the roots of
> empathy—the ability to share another's emotions—to infancy,
> contradicting a longstanding assumption that infants and toddlers
> were incapable of these feelings.*
>
> —DANIEL GOLEMAN, "Researchers Trace Empathy's Roots to Infancy"

INTRODUCTORY PARAGRAPHS 28

STRATEGIES TO USE

- Providing relevant background information
- Relating a brief, interesting story or anecdote
- Giving a pertinent statistic or statistics
- Asking a provocative question or questions
- Using an appropriate quotation
- Making an analogy
- Defining a key term

STRATEGIES TO AVOID

- Obvious statements that refer to what the essay is about or will accomplish, such as "I am going to discuss the causes of falling oil prices"
- Apologies, such as "I am not sure this is right, but this is my opinion"
- Overworked expressions such as "Haste really does make waste, as I recently discovered" or "Love is grand"

The key to the effectiveness of an introductory device is how well it relates to the essay's thesis and to the material in the topical paragraphs. An introductory device must be well integrated into the paragraph, not mechanically slotted in for its own sake. Note how smoothly the message of the quotation in the following introduction becomes a dramatic contrast that leads into the thesis statement (shown in italics).

> "Alone one is never lonely," says May Sarton in her essay "The Rewards of Living a Solitary Life." Most people, however, do not share Sarton's opinion: They are terrified of living alone. They are
> 53 used to living with others—children with parents, roommates with roommates, friends with friends, husbands with wives. When the statistics catch up with them, therefore, they are rarely prepared. *Chances are high that most adult men and women will need to know how to live alone, briefly or longer, at some time in their lives.*
>
> —TARA FOSTER, student

In the following paragraph, the author uses a question and some dramatic description to arouse interest and to set the stage for his thesis statement (shown in italics).

> 54 What should you do? You are out riding your bike, playing golf, or in the middle of a long run when you look up and suddenly see a jagged streak of light shoot across the sky, followed by a deafening clap of thunder. *Unfortunately, most outdoor exercisers do not know whether to stay put or make a dash for shelter when a thunderstorm approaches, and sometimes the consequences are tragic.*
>
> —GERALD SECOR COUZENS, "If Lightning Strikes"

Transitional paragraphs

A transitional paragraph usually consists of one or two sentences that help you move from a few pages on one subtopic to the next large group of paragraphs on a second subtopic. Transitional paragraphs are uncommon in short essays. In longer papers written for college or university, transitional paragraphs sometimes recapitulate the thesis° in the context of what was just discussed and what will follow.

Here is a two-sentence transitional paragraph written as a bridge between a lengthy discussion of people's gestures and the coming long discussion of people's eating habits.

> 55 Like gestures, eating habits are personality indicators, and even food preferences and attitudes toward food reveal the inner self. Food plays an important role in the lives of most people beyond its obvious one as a necessity.
>
> —JEAN ROSENBAUM, M.D., *Is Your Volkswagen a Sex Symbol?*

Concluding paragraphs

A concluding paragraph serves to bring your discussion to an end that logically follows from your thesis° and its discussion. A conclusion that is merely tacked onto an essay does not give the reader a sense of completion. An ending that flows gracefully and sensibly from what has come before it reinforces the writer's ideas and enhances an essay. A concluding paragraph often includes one or more **concluding devices.** As you write your concluding paragraphs, keep in mind the guidelines listed in Chart 29.

Here is a concluding paragraph that summarizes an essay that discusses pizza, including the many versions of pizzalike foods enjoyed by various cultures throughout time.

> 56 For a food that is traced to Neolithic beginnings, like Mexico's tortillas, Armenia's lahmejoun, Scottish oatcakes, and even matzohs, pizza has remained fresh and vibrant. Whether it is galettes, the latest thin-crusted invasion from France with bacon and onion toppings, or a plain slice of a cheese pie, the varieties of pizza are clearly limited only by one's imagination.
>
> —LISA PRATT, "A Slice of History"

CONCLUDING PARAGRAPHS 29

STRATEGIES TO USE

- Using any device appropriate for introductory paragraphs (see Chart 28)—but avoid using the same one in both the introduction and conclusion
- Summarizing the main points of the essay—but avoid a summary if the essay is less than three pages long
- Asking for awareness, action, or a similar resolution from readers
- Looking ahead to the future

STRATEGIES TO AVOID

- Introducing new ideas or facts that belong in the body of the essay
- Rewording your introduction
- Announcing what you have done, as in "In this paper, I have explained the drop in oil prices"
- Making absolute claims, as in "I have proved that oil prices do not affect gasoline prices"
- Apologizing, as in "Even though I am not an expert, I feel my position is correct" or "I may not have convinced you, but there is good evidence for my position"

This paragraph concludes an essay that argues for the recognition of First Nations governments in Canada. It reinforces the essay's message with a call for justice and cooperation.

> What we are looking for is not just power to deal with the social problems we face but reconciliation with Canada. We are trying to find a way of creating harmony in the country. The way you achieve that is to produce justice; our people have to feel justice,
> 57 not just think about it. We have to experience it before we can believe it. There is absolutely no way that First Nations governments can meet the needs of the First Nations peoples without the help of the provinces or the federal government. What we are asking is to become partners working towards the same future.
>
> —OVIDE MERCREDI, "Self-Government as a Way to Heal"

EXERCISE 4-9

Consulting section 4g, write an introduction and conclusion for each essay informally outlined below. To gain additional experience, write an alternative introductory and concluding paragraph for one of the essays.

A. Reading for fun

Thesis: People read many kinds of books for pleasure.

Topical paragraph 1: murder mysteries and thrillers
Topical paragraph 2: romances and westerns
Topical paragraph 3: science fiction

B. Computer games

Thesis: Interactive video games require players to exercise their skills of dexterity, intelligence, and imagination.

Topical paragraph 1: manual dexterity
Topical paragraph 2: intelligence
Topical paragraph 3: imagination

C. Surfing the Web

Thesis: The contents of the World Wide Web reveal people's obsessions at the start of the twenty-first century.

Topical paragraph 1: sites with offensive content
Topical paragraph 2: chat rooms and hobbies
Topical paragraph 3: financial investments and auctions

EXERCISE 4-10

Reread the paragraphs in Exercise 4-8 and do the following:

1. Consulting section 4b, identify all topic sentences, limiting sentences, and implied topic sentences.
2. Consulting section 4c, identify all RENNS.
3. Consulting section 4d, identify all techniques of coherence.
4. Consulting section 4e, identify paragraph arrangements.

5 Critical Thinking, Reading, and Writing

This chapter shows you how to participate actively in the ongoing exchanges of ideas and opinions that you encounter in college, university, and beyond. To participate, you need to understand **critical thinking** as a concept (see 5a) and as an activity (see 5b); **critical reading** as a concept (see 5c) and as an activity (see 5d through 5f); **writing critically** (see 5g); and **reasoning critically** (see 5h through 5k).

5a Understanding critical thinking

Thinking is not something you choose to do, any more than a fish "chooses" to live in water. To be human *is* to think. But while thinking may come naturally, awareness of *how* you think does not. Thinking about thinking is the key to **critical thinking.** When you think critically, you take control of your conscious thought processes. Without such control, you risk being controlled by the ideas of others. Indeed, critical thinking is at the heart of a liberal (from the Latin word for *free*) education.

The word **critical** here has a neutral meaning. It does not mean taking a negative view or finding fault, as when someone criticizes another person for doing something wrong. The essence of critical thinking is thinking beyond the obvious—beyond the flash of visual images on a television screen, the alluring promises of glossy advertisements, the evasive statements by some people in the news, the half-truths of some propaganda, the manipulations of slanted language and faulty reasoning.

Critical thinking is an attitude as much as an activity. If you face life with curiosity and a desire to dig beneath the surface, you are a critical thinker. If you do not believe everything you read or hear, you are a critical thinker. If you find pleasure in contemplating the puzzle of conflicting ideologies, theories, personalities, and facts, you are a critical thinker.

5b Engaging in critical thinking

Critical thinking is a process that evolves from becoming fully aware of something to reflecting on it to reacting to it. You use this sequence often in your life, even if you have never called the process "critical thinking." You engage in it when you meet someone new and decide whether you like the person; when you read a book and form an opinion of it; when you learn a new job and then evaluate the job itself as well as your ability to do the work.

Applied in academic settings, the general process of critical thinking is described in Chart 30. That process holds not only for thinking critically but also for reading critically (see 5c and 5e) and writing critically (see 5g).

As with the writing process (see 2a), the steps of the critical thinking process are not rigidly in place. Each element is described separately in this handbook to help you understand its operation, but in reality the elements are intertwined. Expect, therefore, to sometimes combine steps, reverse their order, and return to parts of the process needed anew.

STEPS IN THE CRITICAL THINKING PROCESS 30

1. **Summarize:** Extract and restate the material's main message or central point at the literal level (see 5d-1). (For a discussion of the differences between summary and synthesis, see 5f; for guidelines on writing a summary, see 31e.)
2. **Analyze:** Consider the whole and then break it into component parts so that you can examine them separately. By seeing them as distinct units, you can come to understand how they interrelate. Read "between the lines" to make inferences (see 5d-2) about the unstated assumptions. Also, evaluate tone, slant, and clarity of distinctions between fact and opinion (see 5d-3); quality of evidence (see 5h); and rigour of reasoning (see 5i and 5j) and logic (see 5k).
3. **Synthesize:** Pull together what you have summarized and analyzed to connect it to what you already know (your prior knowledge) or what you are currently learning. Create a new whole that reflects your ability to see and explain relationships among ideas (see also 5f).
4. **Evaluate:** Judge the quality of the material. Resist the common urge to evaluate before you summarize, analyze, and synthesize.

✤ ALERT: Summary (step 1 in Chart 30) and synthesis (step 3) are two different processes. Be careful not to think that your summary is a synthesis. For fuller discussion of the differences, see 5f. ✤

5c Understanding the reading process

If you understand **the reading process,** you can effectively come to "know," to compose meaning. Reading is not a passive activity. It involves more than looking for words. Reading is an active process—a dynamic, meaning-making encounter involving the interaction of the page, eye, and brain. When you read, your mind actively makes connections between what you know already and what is new to you. By this process you comprehend and absorb new material.

Reading calls for **making predictions.** As you read, your mind is always involved in guessing what is coming next. Once it discovers what comes next, it either confirms or revises its prediction and moves on. For example, if you encountered a chapter title "The Heartbeat," your predictions could range from romance to how the heart pumps blood. As you read on, you would confirm or revise your prediction according to what you found—you would be in the realm of romance if you encountered a paragraph about lovers and roses, and you would be in the realm of biology if you encountered material that included diagrams of the physiology of the heart.

Predicting during reading happens at split-second speed without the reader's being aware of it. Without predictions, the mind would have to consider infinite possibilities for assimilating every new piece of information; with predictions, the mind can narrow its expectations to reasonable proportions.

Deciding on your **purpose for reading** before you begin to read can help your prediction process. Purposes for reading vary. Most reading in college and university is for the purpose of learning new information, appreciating literary works, or reviewing notes on classes or readings. These types of reading involve much *rereading;* one encounter with the material rarely suffices.

Your purpose in reading determines the speed at which you can expect to read. When you are hunting for a particular fact, you can skim the material until you come to what you want. When you read about a subject that you know well, your mind is familiar with the material, so you can move somewhat rapidly, slowing down when you come to new material. When you are unfamiliar with the subject, your mind needs time to absorb the new material, so you have to proceed slowly.

5d Engaging in the reading process

During the reading process, full meaning emerges on the three levels described in Chart 31. Be careful as a reader not to stop at the literal level. Only when you go to the next two levels is complete understanding possible.

STEPS IN THE READING PROCESS 31

1. **Read for literal meaning:** Read "on" the lines to see what is stated (see 5d-1).
2. **Read to make inferences:** Read "between" the lines to see what is not stated but implied (see 5d-2).
3. **Read to evaluate:** Read "beyond" the lines to assess the soundness of the writer's reasoning, the accuracy of the writer's choice of words, and the fairness of the writer's treatment of the reader (see 5d-3).

1 Reading for literal meaning

Reading for literal meaning, sometimes called *reading "on" the line*, calls for you to understand what is said. It does not include impressions or opinions about the material. The literal level concerns (1) the key facts, the line of reasoning in an argument, or the central details of plot and character; and (2) the minor details that lend texture to the picture.

Whenever you encounter a complex writing style, take time to "unpack" the sentences. Try to break them down into shorter units or reword them into a simpler style. Do not assume that all writing is clear merely because it is in print. Authors write with a rich variety of styles, and not all are equally accessible on a first reading.

When you find a concept that you need to think through, take the time to come to know the new idea. Although no student has unlimited time for reading and thinking, rushing through material to "cover" it rather than understand it costs more time in the long run.

Chart 32 offers suggestions that can help you comprehend most efficiently what you are reading.

WAYS TO HELP YOUR READING COMPREHENSION 32

- **Make associations:** When reading about an unfamiliar subject, link the new material with what you already know. If necessary, build your store of prior knowledge by first reading easier material on the subject.
- **Make it easy to focus:** If your mind wanders, be fiercely determined to concentrate. Do whatever it takes: Arrange for silence or music, for being alone or in a crowded library's reading room, for reading at your best time of day (some people concentrate better in the morning, others in the evening).
- **Allot the time you need:** Unless you have allotted sufficient time to work with new material, you cannot comprehend it. Discipline yourself to balance classes, working, socializing, and participating in family activities with the unavoidable, time-consuming, yet totally engaging demands of reading, learning, and studying. Nothing prevents your success as much as lack of time.
- **Master the vocabulary:** If you are unfamiliar with key terms in your reading, you cannot fully understand the concepts. Try to figure out meanings using context clues (see 20c-2). Many textbooks list important terms and their definitions (often in a "glossary") at the end of each chapter or at the back of the book. Always have a good dictionary at hand (see 20a).

2 Reading to make inferences

Reading to make inferences, sometimes called *reading "between" the lines,* means understanding what is implied but not stated. Often you have to infer information, or background, or the author's purpose. Consider this passage:

> How to tell the difference between modern art and junk puzzles many people although few are willing to admit it. The owner of an art gallery in Chicago had a prospective buyer for two sculptures made of discarded metal and put them outside his warehouse to clean them up. Unfortunately, some junk dealers, who apparently didn't recognize abstract expressionism when they saw it, hauled the two 300-pound pieces away.
>
> —ORA GYGI, "Things Are Seldom What They Seem"

The literal meaning is that many people cannot tell the difference between art and junk. A summary of the passage is that two abstract metal sculptures were carted away as junk when an art dealer left them outside a warehouse to clean them.

Now read the material inferentially. You can begin with the unexplained statement "few are willing to admit" they do not know the difference between art and junk. Reading between the lines, you realize that people feel embarrassed *not* to know; they feel uneducated, or without good taste, or perhaps left out.

With this inference in mind, you can move to the last two sentences, in which the author offers not only the literal irony (see 21c) of the art's being carted away as junk, but also the implied irony that the people who carted it away are not among those who might feel embarrassed. This implied irony suggests that the people either do not care if they know the difference between art and junk (after all, they assumed it was junk and went on their way) or they "apparently" (a good word for inference making) want to give the impression that they do not know the difference. Thus, it is the art dealer who ends up being embarrassed, for it is he who created the problem by leaving the sculptures unattended outdoors.

The process of inferring adds texture and invaluable background to facilitate your interpretation of a passage. As you read to make inferences, consult Chart 33.

CHECKLIST FOR MAKING INFERENCES DURING READING 33

1. What is being said beyond the literal level?
2. What is implied rather than stated?
3. What words need to be read for their implied meanings (connotations) as well as for their stated meanings (denotations)? (For more about word meanings, see 20b-1.)
4. What information does the author expect me to have before I start to read the material?
5. What information does the author expect me to have about his or her background, philosophy, and the like?
6. What does the author seem to assume are my biases?
7. What do I need to be aware of concerning author bias?

3 Reading to evaluate

Evaluative reading, sometimes called *reading "beyond" the lines,* calls for many skills, including recognizing the impact of the author's tone, detecting prejudice, and differentiating fact from opinion.

Recognizing whether an author's tone is appropriate

Tone is communicated by all aspects of a piece of writing, from the writer's choice of words to the content of the message (see 1d). An author's tone should be appropriate to the author's purpose° and audience°. For example, most academic writing should not use language that is either informal or overly stiff and formal (see 21a-1).

Most authors use a serious tone, but sometimes they use humour to get their point across; if you read such material exclusively for its literal meaning, you will miss the point. In this passage, Stephen Leacock describes his reaction to a review of his writing. Although Leacock pretends to take the criticism seriously, his tone and language betray his amusement at attempts to reduce humorous writing to rhetorical formulas.

> An English reviewer writing in a literary journal, the very name of which is enough to put contradiction to sleep, has said of my writing, "What is there, after all, in Professor Leacock's humour but a rather ingenious mixture of hyperbole and myosis?"
>
> The man was right. How he stumbled upon this trade secret, I do not know. But I am willing to admit, since the truth is out, that it has long been my custom in preparing an article of a humorous nature to go down to the cellar and mix up half a gallon of myosis with a pint of hyperbole. If I want to give the article a decidedly literary character, I find it well to put in about half a pint of paresis. The whole thing is amazingly simple.
>
> —STEPHEN LEACOCK, *Further Foolishness*

Most readers are wary of a highly emotional tone whose purpose is not to give information but to incite the reader.

NO Urban renewal must be stopped! Urban redevelopment is ruining this country. Money-hungry capitalists are robbing treasures from law-abiding citizens! Corrupt politicians are murderers, caring nothing about people being thrown out of their homes into the streets.

Writers of such material do not respect their readers, for such writers assume that readers do not recognize screaming in print when they see it. Discerning readers instantly know the tone here is emotional and unreasonable. The exaggerations (robbing treasures, politicians as murderers) hint at the truth of some cases, but they are generalizations too extreme to be taken seriously.

On the other hand, if a writer's tone sounds reasonable and moderate, readers are more likely to pay attention.

YES Urban renewal is revitalizing our cities, but it has caused some serious problems. While investors are trying to replace slums with decent housing, they must also remember that they are displacing people who do not want to leave their familiar neighbourhoods. Surely a cooperative effort between government and the private sector can lead to creative solutions.

Detecting prejudice or bias

In writing, **prejudice** or **bias** is revealed in negative opinions based on beliefs rather than on facts or evidence. Negative opinions might be expressed in positive language, but the underlying assumptions are negative.

Prejudicial statements are like these: *Poor people like living in crowded conditions because they are used to the surroundings; Women are not aggressive enough to succeed in business.* Often writers imply their prejudices rather than state them outright. Detecting underlying negative opinions that distort information is important for critical reading, because discerning readers must call into question any argument that rests upon a weak foundation. (See also Hasty Generalization in 5k.)

Differentiating fact from opinion

Facts are statements that can be verified. A person may use experiment, research, and/or observation to verify facts. *Opinions* are statements of personal beliefs. Because they contain ideas that cannot be verified, opinions are open to debate.

An author sometimes intentionally blurs the difference between fact and opinion, and a discerning reader must be able to tell the difference. Sometimes that difference is quite obvious. Consider these statements:

A. A woman can never make a good mathematician.

B. Although fear of math is not purely a female phenomenon, girls tend to drop out of math sooner than boys, and adult women experience an aversion to math and math-related activity that is akin to anxiety.

Because of the word *never*, statement *A* is clearly an opinion. Statement *B* seems to be factual. Knowing who made these statements can sometimes help a reader distinguish between fact and opinion.

Statement *A* was made several years ago by a male mathematician living in Russia, as reported by David K. Shipler, a well-respected veteran reporter on Russian affairs for the *New York Times*. Statement *B* appears in a book called *Overcoming Math Anxiety* by Sheila Tobias, a university professor who has undertaken research studies to find out why many people dislike math. Tobias' research may confirm statement *B* as fact.

To differentiate between fact and opinion, reflect on the material and *think beyond the obvious*. For example, is "Strenuous exercise is good for your health" a fact? Although the statement has the ring of truth, it is not a fact. People with severe arthritis or heart trouble could be harmed by some forms of exercise. Also, what does "strenuous" mean—a dozen pushups, jogging, aerobics, or playing tennis?

EXERCISE 5-1

Consulting section 5d, decide if each statement is a fact or an opinion. When the author and source are provided, explain how that information influences your judgment.

1. Jogging promotes good mental health.
2. Cotton clothing is more comfortable than polyester clothing.
3. "Every journey into the past is complicated by delusions, false memories, false namings of real events." (Adrienne Rich, poet, *Of Woman Born*)
4. Edmund Hillary performed two major feats: He not only led the first successful climb to the top of Mount Everest but he also led the first group to cross the Antarctic continent from sea to sea.
5. "History is the branch of knowledge that deals systematically with the past." (*Webster's New World Dictionary,* Third College Edition)
6. "Any peace is honourable." (Morley Safer, *Toronto Star*)
7. The earth's temperature is gradually rising.
8. Slaves in ancient Egypt were often killed when they finished building a pyramid so that they could not reveal the entrances to thieves who would loot the tombs.
9. "Our cities tend to be functional but nondescript, anchored against the wind, with nothing to please the eye. Quebec City is an exception." (Mordecai Richler, *Oh Canada! Oh Quebec!*)
10. "Since the mid-1960s, hepatitis—meaning, simply, the inflammation of the liver—has become a major health problem. As many as 500 million people carry hepatitis B or C, the most serious forms. Up to 500,000 of them live in Canada." (Anita Elash, *Maclean's*)

EXERCISE 5-2

Consulting section 5d, after you read this passage, (1) list all literal information, (2) list all implied information, and (3) list the opinions stated.

EXAMPLE The study found many complaints against the lawyers were not investigated, seemingly out of a "desire to avoid difficult cases."

—NORMAN F. DACEY

Literal information: Few complaints against lawyers are investigated.
Implied information: The words "difficult cases" imply a coverup: lawyers, or others in power, hesitate to criticize lawyers for fear of being sued, or for fear of a public outcry if the truth about abuses and errors were revealed.
Opinions: None—all is factual because it refers to, and contains a quote from, a study.

A. I remember a weekend in Ottawa in the 1970s, when I helped to organize a meeting with men in prison; a group of ex-inmates and offenders, prison guards, policemen, prison chaplains, prison directors, and psychologists. We shared together, ate together, slept in dormitories. Nobody carried any label or sign showing to which group they belonged. We were together as persons, not as representatives of a group. It was, if you like, an image for me of how we actually behave towards each other when we have no "markers" to tell us what we are supposed to feel towards someone. It was also a small indication of what society might look like, and how it might function, if we could overcome our prejudices.

—JEAN VANIER, *Becoming Human*

B. The kind of constitution and government Gandhi envisaged for an independent India was spelled out at the forty-fifth convention of the All-India Congress, which began at Karachi on March 27, 1931. It was a party political convention the like of which I had not seen before—nor seen since—with its ringing revolutionary proclamations acclaimed by some 350 leaders, men and women, just out of jail, squatting in the heat under a tent in a semicircle at Gandhi's feet, all of them, like Gandhi, spinning away like children playing with toys as they talked. They made up the so-called Subjects Committee, selected from the five thousand delegates to do the real work of the convention, though in reality, it was Gandhi alone who dominated the proceedings, writing most of the resolutions and moving their adoption with his customary eloquence and surprising firmness.

—WILLIAM L. SHIRER, *Gandhi: A Memoir*

5e Engaging in critical reading

The concept of **critical reading** parallels that of critical thinking (see 5a and 5b). To read critically is to think about what you are reading while you are reading it. Do not let words merely drift by as your eyes scan the pages. To prevent that, use approaches such as reading systematically (see 5e-1) and reading actively and closely (see 5e-2).

1 Reading systematically

To **read systematically** is to use a structured plan for delving into the material. Your goal is to come to know and truly understand the material and—equally important—to be able to discuss it and even write about it. Guidelines for reading systematically start below and continue on the next page.

1. **Preview:** Before you start reading, look ahead. Glance over the pages you intend to read so that your mind can start making predictions (see 5c). As you look over the pages, ask yourself questions that the material stimulates. Do not expect to answer all the questions at this point; their purpose is to focus your thoughts.
   - To preview a textbook, first survey the whole book by reading chapter titles for an overview (book titles can be misleading). Next, survey the chapter you are assigned by reading all headings large and small; boldface words (in darker print); and all visuals and their captions, including photographs, drawings, tables, figures, and charts. If a glossary is at the end of the chapter, scan it for words you do and do not know.
   - To preview material that has few or no headings, read and ask questions of the book and (if any) chapter titles; of the author's name and any introductory notes about the author, such as those that precede the essays in many books of collected essays; and of pivotal paragraphs, such as the first few paragraphs and (unless you are reading for suspense) the last pages or paragraphs. If a preface or introduction begins a book, skim it.
2. **Read:** Read the material actively and closely as explained in 5e-2. Seek the full meaning at all levels explained in 5d. Most of all, expect to reread. College- and university-level material

can rarely be fully understood and absorbed in one reading. Budget your time so that you can make many passes through the material.

3. **Review:** Go back to the spots you looked at when you previewed the material. Look, too, at other pivotal places that you discovered. Ask yourself the same sort of questions, this time answering them as fully as possible. If you cannot, reread for the answers. For best success, review in chunks—small sections that you can capture comfortably. Do not try to cover too much at once.
   - To stimulate your concentration during reading, keep in mind that you intend to review. This awareness will help you to stay alert. Also, the next day, and again about a week later, repeat your review—always adding new material that you have learned since the previous review. As much as time permits, re-review at intervals during a course. The more reinforcement, the better.
   - Collaborative learning can help you reinforce what you learn from reading. Ask a friend or classmate who knows the material to discuss it with you, even test you. Conversely, offer to teach the material to someone; you will quickly discover whether or not you have mastered it well enough to communicate it.

2 Reading actively and closely

The secret to **reading actively and closely** is to annotate as you read. *Annotating* means writing notes to yourself in a book's margins, underlining or highlighting key passages, and using asterisks and other codes to alert you to special material. A well-annotated book is usually a well-read book.

Most readers annotate only after they have previewed the material and read it once, as explained in 5e-1. You might find, however, that you like to have a pencil in your hand from the moment you start to read. Experiment to find what works best for you.

Active reading calls for making annotations that relate to the content and meaning of the material. Restate major points "in a nutshell" in the margin. When you review, they will stand out. If you underline or highlight, be sure to jot in the margin key words or phrases that will jog your memory when you need to recall what is important. Extract meaning on the literal, inferential, and evaluative levels (see 5d). The excerpt on page 123 shows active-reading annotations in blue ink.

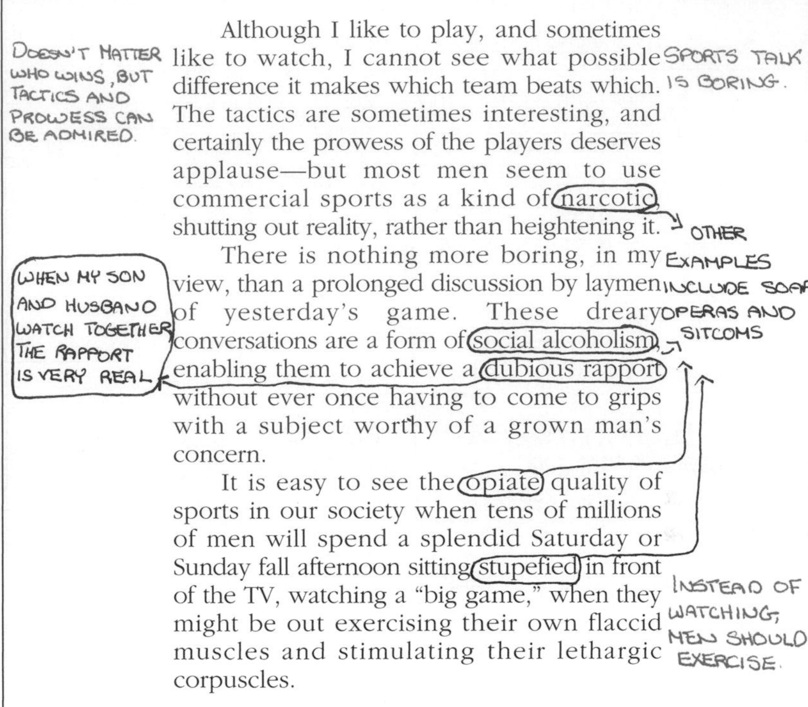

Although I like to play, and sometimes like to watch, I cannot see what possible difference it makes which team beats which. The tactics are sometimes interesting, and certainly the prowess of the players deserves applause—but most men seem to use commercial sports as a kind of narcotic, shutting out reality, rather than heightening it.

There is nothing more boring, in my view, than a prolonged discussion by laymen of yesterday's game. These dreary conversations are a form of social alcoholism, enabling them to achieve a dubious rapport without ever once having to come to grips with a subject worthy of a grown man's concern.

It is easy to see the opiate quality of sports in our society when tens of millions of men will spend a splendid Saturday or Sunday fall afternoon sitting stupefied in front of the TV, watching a "big game," when they might be out exercising their own flaccid muscles and stimulating their lethargic corpuscles.

DOESN'T MATTER WHO WINS, BUT TACTICS AND PROWESS CAN BE ADMIRED.
SPORTS TALK IS BORING.
OTHER EXAMPLES INCLUDE SOAP OPERAS AND SITCOMS
WHEN MY SON AND HUSBAND WATCH TOGETHER THE RAPPORT IS VERY REAL
INSTEAD OF WATCHING, MEN SHOULD EXERCISE.

Annotations of excerpt from essay shown in Exercise 5-3 [blue for content (active reading) and black for synthesis (close reading)].

Close reading calls for making annotations that record the connections you make between the material and your prior knowledge and experience. Close reading can also elicit questions and opinions about the material. This is your chance to think on paper. It opens a conversation between you and the author. If this is a relatively new practice for you, do not lose your nerve or get discouraged. Let your mind range across ideas that you associate with what you are reading. Consider yourself a partner in the making of meaning, a full participant in the exchange of ideas, opinions, and experiences that typify a higher education. The excerpt above shows close-reading annotations in black ink.

If you feel unable to write in a book—even though the practice of annotating texts dates back to the Middle Ages—try keeping a "double-entry notebook." On one side of each sheet of paper write "close-reading" notes on the content; on the other side, enter "active-reading" notes detailing the connections you make. Be sure to include

S. HARRIS ESSAY. "SPORTS ONLY"

CONTENT	CONNECTIONS I MAKE
¶1 H. LIKES SPORTS AND EXERCISE. HE EVEN BUILT A TENNIS COURT FOR HIS SUMMER HOME.	H. ISN'T "EVERYMAN." IT TAKES BIG BUCKS TO BUILD ONE'S OWN TENNIS COURT.
¶2 H. THINKS THE AVERAGE NORTH AMERICAN MALE IS OBSESSED WITH SPORTS.	THAT "AVERAGE" (IF THERE IS SUCH A THING) MALE SOUNDS A LOT LIKE MY HUSBAND.
¶3 ATHLETICS/SPORTS ARE ONE STRAND, NOT THE WEB, OF SOCIETY.	IT'S WORTH THINKING WHY SPORTS HAVE SUCH A MAJOR HOLD ON MEN. AND WHY NOT WOMEN, ON "AVERAGE"? (THIS MIGHT BE A TOPIC FOR A PAPER SOMEDAY.)

Double-entry notebook excerpt, based on first three paragraphs of the essay in Exercise 5-3 [left side for content (active reading) and right side for synthesis (close reading)].

information that identifies the passages referred to so that you can easily relocate them. Below is a short example from a double-entry notebook (the symbol ¶ stands for "paragraph").

EXERCISE 5-3

Below and on the next two pages is the complete, brief essay from which the excerpt in the example above was taken. The essay was first published as an informal opinion in a newspaper column. Annotate the entire essay, with notes about content in one colour (such as blue) and your notes synthesizing the material in another (such as red).

Sports Only Exercise Our Eyes

Sydney J. Harris

Before I proceed a line further, let me make it clear that I enjoy physical exercise and sports as much as any man. I like to bat a baseball, dribble a basketball, kick a soccer ball and, most of all, swat a tennis ball. A man who scorned physical activity would hardly build a tennis court on his summer-house grounds, or use it every day.

Having made this obeisance, let me now confess that I am puzzled and upset—and have been for many years—by the almost obsessive interest in sports taken by the average North American male.

Athletics is one strand in life, and even the ancient Greek philosophers recognized its importance. But it is by no means the whole web, as it seems to be in our society. If North American men are not talking business, they are talking sports, or they are not talking at all.

This strikes me as an enormously adolescent, not to say retarded, attitude on the part of presumed adults. Especially when most of the passion and enthusiasm center around professional teams which bear no indigenous relation to the city they play for, and consist of mercenaries who will wear any town's insignia if the price is right.

Although I like to play, and sometimes like to watch, I cannot see what possible difference it makes which team beats which. The tactics are sometimes interesting, and certainly the prowess of the players deserves applause—but most men seem to use commercial sports as a kind of narcotic, shutting out reality, rather than heightening it.

There is nothing more boring, in my view, than a prolonged discussion by laymen of yesterday's game. These dreary conversations are a form of social alcoholism, enabling them to achieve a dubious rapport without ever once having to come to grips with a subject worthy of a grown man's concern.

It is easy to see the opiate quality of sports in our society when tens of millions of men will spend a splendid Saturday or Sunday fall afternoon sitting stupefied in front of the TV, watching a "big game," when they might be out exercising their own flaccid muscles and stimulating their lethargic corpuscles.

Ironically, our obsession with professional athletes not only makes us mentally limited and conversationally dull, it also keeps us physically inert—thus violating the very reason men began engaging in athletic competitions. It is tempting to call this malaise of "spectatoritis" childish—except that children have more sense, and would rather run out and play themselves.

5f Distinguishing between summary and synthesis

A crucial distinction in critical thinking, critical reading, and critical writing resides in the **differences between summary and synthesis.**

Summary comes before synthesis (see Chart 30 in 5b) in the critical thinking process. To summarize is to extract the main message or central point of a passage. A summary does not include supporting evidence or details. It is the gist, the hub, the seed of what the author is saying; it is not your reaction to it.

You summarize informally in a conversation and more formally in a speech. When you write a summary, use the guidelines in Chart 135 in section 31e. They apply generally to the kind of summarizing you do in content annotations (see 5e-2), in writing an essay that draws on only one source (see 5g), and in a research paper based on multiple sources (see Chapters 31, 34, and 35).

Synthesis comes after analysis, summary, and interpretation (see Chart 30 in 5b). To synthesize is to weave together ideas from more than one source; to connect ideas from one or more sources to what you already know from your having read, listened, and experienced life; to create a new whole that is your own as a result of your thinking about diverse yet related ideas. Unsynthesized ideas and information are like separate spools of thread, neatly lined up, possibly coordinated, but not integrated. Synthesized ideas and information become threads woven into a tapestry that creates a new whole. Synthesis is the evidence of your ability to tie ideas together in the tapestry of what you learn and know and experience.

When you synthesize unconsciously, your mind connects ideas by thought processes mirrored in the rhetorical strategies discussed in section 4f. To synthesize, consciously apply these strategies. For example, compare ideas in sources; contrast ideas in sources; create definitions that combine and extend definitions in individual sources; apply examples or descriptions from one source to illustrate ideas in another; find causes and/or effects described in one source that explain another.

✤ ALERT: "Synthesis by summary"—a mere listing of who said what about a topic—is not true synthesis. It does not create new connections among ideas. ✤

Here is an example of synthesis connecting the essay in Exercise 5-3 to the excerpt below by Robert Lipsyte. (Lipsyte, a sports columnist for the *New York Times*, published his long essay in the spring of 1995 at the end of a nine-month-long major-league baseball strike. He asserts that sports have become too commercialized and no longer inspire loyalty, teach good sportsmanship, or provide young people with admirable role models.)

> Baseball has done us a favor. It's about time we understood that staged competitive sports events—and baseball can stand for all the games—are no longer the testing ground of our country's manhood and the theater of its once seemingly limitless energy and power.
>
> As a mirror of our culture, sports now show us spoiled fools as role models, cities and colleges held hostage and games that exist only to hawk products.
>
> The pathetic posturing of in-your-face macho has replaced a once self-confident masculinity.
>
> —ROBERT LIPSYTE, "The Emasculation of Sports"

SYNTHESIS BY COMPARISON AND CONTRAST
Both Harris and Lipsyte criticize professional sports, but their reasons differ. In part, Harris thinks that people who passively watch sports on TV and rarely exercise are destroying their physical health. Lipsyte sees something less obvious, but potentially more sinister: the destruction of traditional values in sports. No longer are athletes heroes who inspire; they are puppets of sports as "big business."

SYNTHESIS BY DEFINITION
The omission of women from each writer's discussion seems a very loud silence. Considered together, these essays define sports as a male preoccupation and undertaking. Harris condemns only men for their inability to think and talk beyond sports and business, an insulting and exaggerated description made even less valid by the absence of women. Lipsyte, even in the 1995 atmosphere of women excelling in many team and individual sports, claims that we have lost a "once self-confident masculinity." An extended definition would include women, even though they might prefer to avoid the negative portraits of Harris and Lipsyte.

A synthesis belongs to the person who made the connections; someone else might make entirely different connections. Still, any synthesis needs to be sensibly reasoned and informed by an individual intelligence.

Try these techniques for stimulating your mind to recall prior knowledge and work toward creating a synthesis. (The critical response essay by a student, Anna Lozanov, in 5g, is an excellent example of making connections between reading and one's personal experience.)

- Use the technique of mapping (see 2i) to lay out and discover relationships between elements in the material and between the material and other ideas that come to mind.
- Use your powers of play. Mentally toss ideas around, even if you make connections that seem outrageous. Try opposites (for example, read about athletes and think about the most unathletic person you know). Try turning an idea upside down (for example, read about the value of being a good sport and list the benefits of being a bad sport). Try visualizing what you are reading about, and then tinker with the mental picture (for example, picture two people playing tennis and substitute dogs playing frisbee or seals playing ping pong). The possibilities are endless—make word associations, think up song lyrics, draft a TV advertisement. The goal is always to jump-start your thinking so that you see ideas in new ways.
- Discuss your reading with someone else. Summarize its content and elicit the other person's opinion or ideas. Deliberately debate that opinion or challenge those ideas. Discussions and debates can get your mind moving.

EXERCISE 5-4

Here is an excerpt from an essay by Robert Lipsyte. (Another excerpt from this essay is shown on page 127.) The words in brackets are added in this handbook to supply background information some readers might need.

> We have come to see that [basketball star Michael] Jordan, [football star] Troy Aikman, and [baseball star] Ken Griffey have nothing to offer us beyond the gorgeous, breathtaking mechanics of what they do. And it's not enough, now that there is no longer a dependable emotional return beyond the sensation of the moment itself. The changes in sports—the moving of franchises, free agency—have made it impossible to count on a player, a team, an entire league still being around for next year's comeback. The connection between player and fan has been irrevocably destabilized, for love and loyalty demand a future. Along the way, those many virtues of self-discipline, responsibility, altruism and dedication seem to have been deleted from the athletic contract with America.
>
> —Robert Lipsyte, "The Emasculation of Sports"

Consulting sections 5e-2 and 5f, do this:

1. Summarize the excerpt here.
2. Annotate it for its content and for the connections you make to its content.

3. Draft a synthesis connecting this essay and the essay by Sydney J. Harris reprinted in Exercise 5-3.

5g Writing a critical response

A **critical response** essay has two missions: first, to summarize a source's central point or main idea; second, to respond to the source's main idea with your reactions based on your synthesis (see 5b and 5f).

A well-written critical response accomplishes these two missions with grace and style. That is, it does not say "My summary is ..." and "Now, here's what I think...." Your goal is to write a well-integrated essay. Its length and whether you respond to a single passage or to an entire work vary with the assignment. Chart 34 gives general guidelines for writing a critical response.

GUIDELINES FOR WRITING A CRITICAL RESPONSE 34

- Write a summary of the main idea or central point of what you are responding to (whether you are responding to part or all of a source).
- Write a smooth transition between that summary and your response. Although a statement bridging the two parts of a critical response paper need not observe all the formal requirements of a thesis statement (see 2n), it should at least subtly signal the beginning of your response.
- Respond to the source, basing your reaction on the influences of your own experience, your prior knowledge, and your opinions.
- Fulfil all documentation requirements. See Chapter 34 for coverage of four widely used documentation systems (MLA, APA, CM, and CBE), and ask your instructor which to use.

Here is a critical response essay written by Anna Lozanov, a university student. The assignment was to read and respond to the brief essay "Sports Only Exercise Our Eyes" by Sydney J. Harris shown in Exercise 5-3. Lozanov's bridge statement comes at the beginning of the third paragraph: "Just this weekend, however, I had an occasion to reconsider the value of sports." The Work Cited at the end of the essay uses MLA documentation style (see 34c) to identify the source. The numbers in parentheses in the essay indicate the pages in the cited work where the quoted words can be found.

Critical Response by Anna Lozanov

to "Sports Only Exercise Our Eyes" by Sydney J. Harris

Except for a brief period in high school when I was wild about a certain basketball player, I never gave sports much thought. I went to games because my friends went, not because I cared about football or baseball or track. I certainly never expected to defend sports, and when I first read Sydney Harris's essay "Sports Only Exercise Our Eyes," I thoroughly agreed with him. Like Harris, I believed that men who live and breathe sports are "mentally limited and conversationally dull" (111).

For the entire thirteen years of my marriage I have complained about the amount of time my husband, John, spends watching televised sports. Of course, I've tried to get him to take an interest in something else. There was the time as a newlywed when I flamboyantly interrupted the sixth game of the World Series--wearing only a transparent nightie. Then, in 1978, I had the further audacity to go into labour with our first child--right in the middle of the Grey Cup. Even the child tried to help me cure my husband of what Harris calls an "obsession" (111). Some months after the fateful game, the kid thoroughly soaked his father, who was concentrating so intently on the Tigers' struggle for the American League pennant that he didn't even notice! Only a commercial brought the dazed sports fan back into the living room from Tiger Stadium.

Just this weekend, however, I had an occasion to reconsider the value of sports. Having just read the Harris essay, I found myself paying closer attention to my husband and sons' Saturday afternoon television routine. I was surprised to discover that they didn't just "vegetate" in front of the TV; during the course of the afternoon, they actually discussed ethics, priorities, commitments, and the consequences of abusing one's body. When one of the commentators raised issues like point shaving and using steroids, John and the kids talked about cheating and using drugs. When another commentator brought up the issue of skipping one's final year to go straight to the pros, John explained the importance of a university education and discussed the short career of most professional football players.

Then, I started to think about all the times I've gone to the basement and found my husband and sons performing exercise routines as they watched a game on TV. Even our seven year old, who loathes exercise, pedals vigorously on the exercise bike while the others do sit-ups and curls. Believe it or not, there are times when they're all exercising more than just their eyes.

I still agree with Harris that many people spend too much time watching televised sports, but after this weekend, I certainly can't say that all of that time is wasted--at least not at my house. Anything that can turn my couch potatoes into thinking, talking, active human beings can't be all bad. Next weekend, instead of putting on a nightie, I think I'll join my family on the couch.

Work Cited

Harris, Sydney J. "Sports Only Exercise Our Eyes." The Best of Sydney J. Harris. Boston: Houghton, 1975. 111-12.

5h Assessing evidence critically

The cornerstone of all reasoning is evidence. Readers expect writers to provide solid evidence for any assertion made or conclusion reached. Writers who successfully communicate their messages use evidence well to support their assertions or conclusions. Evidence consists of facts, statistical information, examples, and opinions of experts.

1 Evaluating evidence

Chart 35 lists guidelines for evaluating evidence that you read and for deciding what evidence to include in your writing. A discussion of each guideline in the chart follows:

- **Is the evidence sufficient?** A general rule for both readers and writers is the more evidence, the better. As a reader, you can usually have more confidence in the results of a survey that draws on a hundred respondents than in a survey involving only ten. As a writer, you may convince your reader that violence is a serious problem in high schools on the basis of two specific examples, but you will be more convincing if you can give five examples—or, better still, statistics for a school district, a city, or a nation.
- **Is the evidence representative?** As a reader, assess objectivity and fairness; do not assume them because words are in print. Do not trust a claim or conclusion about a group based on only a few members rather than on a truly representative or typical sample. A pollster surveying national political views would not get representative evidence by asking questions of the first 1500 people to walk by a street corner in Calgary because that group would not truly represent the varied regional, racial, political, and ethnic makeup of the electorate. As a writer, make sure the evidence you offer represents your claim fairly; do not base your point on exceptions.
- **Is the evidence relevant?** Determining relevance can demand subtle thinking. Suppose you read evidence that one hundred students who had watched television for more than two hours a day throughout high school earned significantly lower scores on a college entrance exam than one hundred

GUIDELINES FOR EVALUATING EVIDENCE 35

- Is the evidence sufficient?
- Is the evidence representative?
- Is the evidence relevant?
- Is the evidence accurate, whether from primary or secondary sources?
- Are the claims qualified fairly based on the evidence?

students who had not. Would you conclude that students who watch less television perform better on college entrance exams? Perhaps, closer examination of the evidence might reveal other differences between the two groups—differences in geographical region, family background, socioeconomic group, quality of schools attended. Therefore, the evidence would not be relevant to that conclusion about TV watching and college entrance exams.

- **Is the evidence accurate?** Without accuracy, evidence is useless. Evidence must come from reliable sources, whether they are *primary sources* or *secondary sources* (see 5h-2). Equally important, reliable evidence must be presented carefully so that it does not misrepresent or distort information.
- **Is the evidence qualified?** Evidence rarely justifies claims that use words such as *all, certainly, always,* or *never.* Conclusions are more reasonable when qualified with words such as *some, many, a few, probably, possibly, perhaps, may, usually,* and *often.* Remember that today's "facts" may be revised as time passes, information changes, and knowledge grows.

2 Understanding differences between primary and secondary sources as evidence

Primary sources present first-hand evidence based on your own or someone else's original work or direct observation. First-hand evidence has the greatest impact on a reader. Consider this eyewitness account:

> Poverty is dirt.... Let me explain about housekeeping with no money. For breakfast I give my children grits with no oleo or cornbread without eggs and oleo. This does not use up many dishes. What dishes there are, I wash in cold water and with no soap. Even the cheapest soap has to be saved for the baby's diapers. Look at my hands, so cracked and red. Once I saved for two months to buy a jar of Vaseline for my hands and the baby's diaper rash. When I had saved enough, I went to buy it and the price had gone up two cents. The baby and I suffered on. I have to decide every day if I can bear to put my cracked sore hands into the cold water and strong soap. But you ask, why not hot water? Fuel costs money. If you have a wood fire it costs money. If you burn electricity, it costs money. Hot water is a luxury. I do not have luxuries....
>
> —JO GOODWIN PARKER, in *America's Other Children*

As a reader and as a writer, remember that not all eyewitness accounts are equally reliable. What is it about Parker's account that makes you trust what she says? She is specific. She is also authoritative. It is doubtful that anyone would have invented the story about being two cents short of the price of a jar of Vaseline. As a writer of personal observations, you need to be as specific as possible—to prove that you truly saw what you say you saw. Use language that appeals to all five senses: Describe sights, sounds, and experiences that could have been seen, heard, or experienced only by someone who was there. Show your readers *your* cracked, red hands.

As evidence, primary sources that meet the guidelines in Chart 35 provide invaluable reports of observations. Few will ever see the surface of the moon or the top of Mt. Everest. People rely, therefore, upon the first-hand reports of the astronauts and mountain climbers who have been there. Indeed, much of history depends heavily on letters, diaries, and journals—the reports of eyewitnesses who saw events unfold.

Surveys, polls, and experiments are some of the means by which people extend their powers of observation beyond what can be "seen" in the everyday sense of the word. Jo Parker could look at her hands. Who can see, however, the attitude of the public toward marriage, toward a political candidate, toward inflation? For evidence on such matters, polls or surveys are necessary. They constitute primary evidence and must be carefully controlled—through weighing, measuring, or quantifying information that would otherwise not be available.

Secondary sources report, describe, comment on, or analyze the experiences or the work of others. As evidence, a secondary source is at least once removed from the primary source. It reports *about* the original work, the direct observation, or the first-hand experience. Still, such evidence can have great value and enormous impact. Consider this second-hand, reported observation.

> The immediate causes of death from nuclear attack are the blast wave, which can flatten heavily reinforced buildings many kilometers away, the firestorm, the gamma rays and the neutrons, which effectively fry the insides of passersby. A school girl who survived the American nuclear attack on Hiroshima, the event that ended the Second World War, wrote this first-hand account:
>
> > Through a darkness like the bottom of hell, I could hear the voices of the other students calling for their mothers. And at the base of the bridge, inside a big cistern that had been dug out there, was a mother weeping, holding above her head a naked baby that was burned bright red all over its body.... But every single person who passed was wounded, all of them, and there was no one, there was no one to turn to for help. And the singed hair on the heads of the people was frizzled and whitish and covered with dust. They did not appear to be human, not creatures of this world.
>
> —CARL SAGAN, *Cosmos*

As with Parker's eyewitness account, the strength or value of a second-hand account hinges on the reliability of the reporter. That reliability is a function of how specific, accurate, and authoritative the observations are. Here the standard maxim "consider the source" becomes crucial. An expert's reputation must stem from some special experience (as the parents of many children could be "experts" on child rearing) or training (as an accountant could be an expert on taxes). Because the author of the example paragraph, Carl Sagan, is a respected scientist, scholar, and writer, his report of the schoolgirl's eyewitness account is likely to be reliable, authoritative, worthwhile secondary evidence.

Sagan is a secondary source because although readers can feel quite confident that Sagan is fully and fairly representing what the schoolgirl said, *no one* can be sure of that without seeing her original account. If you were to use Sagan's version of her account as evidence, it would be third-hand evidence: one person (you) further removed from another (Sagan) and yet further from the original source (the schoolgirl). In college or university, you must often depend on secondary sources (for example, most textbooks), but sometimes you are expected to use primary sources (for example, a published diary, scientists' journal articles reporting their research, works of literature). Chart 36 gives guidelines for evaluating a secondary source.

GUIDELINES FOR EVALUATING A SECONDARY SOURCE 36

- **Is the source authoritative?** Was it written by an expert or a person whom you can expect to write credibly on the subject?
- **Is the source reliable?** Does the material appear in a reputable publication—in a book published by an established publisher or a respected journal or magazine?
- **Is the source well known?** Do you find the source cited elsewhere as you read about the subject? (If so, the authority of the source is probably widely accepted.)
- **Is the information well supported?** Is the source *based on* primary evidence? If secondary evidence, is it authoritative and reliable?
- **Is the tone balanced?** Is the language relatively objective (therefore more likely reliable) or slanted (probably not reliable)?
- **Is the source current?** Is the material current (therefore more likely reliable), or has later authoritative and reliable research made it outdated? ("Old" is not necessarily unreliable. In many fields, classic works of research remain authoritative for decades or even centuries.)

✣ ALERT: You can use the guidelines in Chart 36 to evaluate electronic sources as well as conventional print sources. Be skeptical about any Internet source that cannot be verified according to these guidelines. ✣

EXERCISE 5-5

Consulting section 5h, decide the following: (a) Would each passage constitute primary or secondary evidence? (b) Is the evidence acceptable? Why or why not?

1. I went one morning to a place along the banks of the Madeira River where the railroad ran, alongside rapids impassable to river traffic, and I searched for any marks it may have left on the land. But there was nothing except a clearing where swarms of insects hovered over the dead black hen and other items spread out on a red cloth as an offering to the gods of macumba, or black magic. This strain of African origins in Brazil's ethnic character is strong in the Northwest Region.

   —William S. Ellis, "Brazil's Imperiled Rain Forest"

2. Most climatologists believe that the world will eventually slip back into an ice age in 10,000 to 20,000 years. The Earth has been unusually cold for the last two to three million years, and we are just lucky to be living during one of the warm spells. But the concern of most weather watchers looking at the next century is with fire rather than ice. By burning fossil fuels and chopping down forests, humans have measurably increased the amount of carbon dioxide in the atmosphere. From somewhere around 300 parts per million at the turn of the century, this level has risen to 340 parts per million today. If the use of fossil fuels continues to increase, carbon dioxide could reach 600 parts per million during the next century.

   —Steve Olson, "Computing Climate"

EXERCISE 5-6

Individually or with a peer response group choose one thesis statement below and then list the kinds of primary and secondary sources you might consult to support the thesis (guess intelligently, but you need not be certain the sources exist). Then decide which sources would be considered *primary* and which *secondary*.

Thesis statement 1: The history of this college (or university) is very straightforward.

Thesis statement 2: The history of this college (or university) is complicated.

5i Assessing cause and effect critically

Cause and effect is a mode of thinking that seeks to establish some relationship, or link, between two or more specific pieces of evidence. Regardless of whether you begin with a cause or an effect, you are working with this basic pattern:

BASIC PATTERN FOR CAUSE AND EFFECT

Cause A ⟶ produces ⟶ effect B

You may seek to understand the effects of a known cause (for example, studying two more hours each night):

More studying ⟶ produces ⟶ ?

Or you may attempt to determine the cause or causes of a known effect (for example, recurrent headaches):

? ⟶ produces ⟶ recurrent headaches

If you want to use reasoning based on a relationship of cause and effect, evaluate the connections carefully. As you evaluate cause-and-effect relationships, keep in mind the guidelines in Chart 37. A discussion of each guideline in the chart follows:

- **Is there a clear relationship between events?** When you read or write about causes and effects, carefully think through the reasoning. Related causes and effects happen in sequence: A cause exists or occurs before an effect. *First* the wind blows; *then* a door slams; *then* a pane of glass in the door breaks. But just because the order of events implies a cause-and-effect relationship, that relationship does not necessarily exist. Perhaps someone slammed the door shut. Perhaps someone threw a baseball through the glass pane. A cause-and-effect relationship must be linked by more than chronological sequence. The fact that *B* happens after *A* does not prove that *A* causes *B*.

GUIDELINES FOR ASSESSING CAUSE AND EFFECT 37

- Is there a clear relationship between events?
- Is there a pattern of repetition?
- Are there multiple causes and/or effects?

- **Is there a pattern of repetition?** To establish that *A* causes *B*, there must be proof that every time *A* is present, *B* occurs—or that *B* never occurs unless *A* is present. The need for a pattern of repetition explains why Health Canada sponsors or performs many tests before declaring a new food or medicine safe for human consumption.
- **Are there multiple causes and/or effects?** Avoid oversimplification. The basic pattern of cause and effect—single cause, single effect (*A* causes *B*)—rarely represents the full picture.

It is oversimplifying to assume that a falling crime rate is strictly due to high employment rates. Similarly, one cause can produce **multiple effects:**

Cause A ——→ produces ——→ { effect 1, effect 2, effect 3 }

Oversimplification of effects usually involves focusing on one effect and ignoring others. For example, advertisements about a liquid diet drink focus on its most appealing effect: rapid weight loss. But they ignore other less desirable effects such as loss of nutrients and vulnerability to rapidly regaining the weight.

5j Assessing reasoning processes critically

To think critically you need to be able to understand reasoning processes so that you can recognize and evaluate them in your reading and use them correctly in your writing. **Induction** and **deduction** are reasoning processes. They are natural thought patterns that people use every day to think through ideas and to make decisions. The differences between the two processes are summarized in Chart 38.

1 Recognizing and using inductive reasoning

Induction is the process of arriving at general principles from particular facts or instances, as summarized in Chart 39. Suppose that

COMPARISON OF INDUCTIVE AND DEDUCTIVE REASONING 38

	INDUCTIVE REASONING	DEDUCTIVE REASONING
ARGUMENT BEGINS	with specific evidence	with a general claim
ARGUMENT CONCLUDES	with a general claim	with a specific statement
CONCLUSION IS	reliable or unreliable	true or false
PURPOSE IS	to discover something new	to apply what is known

SUMMARY OF INDUCTIVE REASONING 39

Inductive reasoning moves from the specific to the general. It begins with the evidence of specific facts, observations, or experiences and moves to a general conclusion.

- Inductive conclusions are considered *reliable* or *unreliable,* not true or false. An inductive conclusion indicates probability, the degree to which the conclusion is likely to be true—not certainty.
- An inductive conclusion is held to be reliable or unreliable in relation to the quantity and quality of the evidence (see 5e) supporting it.
- Induction leads to new "truths." Induction can support statements about the unknown on the basis of what is known.

you go to the local Motor Vehicle Licence Agency to renew your driver's licence, and you have to stand in line for two hours until you get the document. Then a few months later, when you return to the Agency for new licence plates, a clerk gives you the wrong advice, and you have to stand in two different lines for three hours. Another time you go there in response to a letter asking for information, and you discover that you should have brought your car registration form, although the letter failed to mention that fact. You conclude that the Agency is inefficient and seems not to care about the convenience of its patrons. You have arrived at this conclusion by means of induction.

2 Recognizing and using deductive reasoning

Deduction is the process of reasoning from general claims to a specific instance. If several unproductive visits to the Motor Vehicle Licence Agency have convinced you that the Agency cares little about the convenience of its patrons (as the experiences described in 5j-1 suggest), you will not be happy the next time you must return. Your reasoning might go something like this:

> The Agency wastes people's time.
> I have to go to the Agency tomorrow.
> Therefore, tomorrow my time will be wasted.

You reached the conclusion—"therefore, tomorrow my time will be wasted"—by means of deduction.

Deductive arguments have three parts: two **premises** and a **conclusion.** This three-part structure is known as a **syllogism.** The first premise of a deductive argument may be a fact or an assumption. The second premise may also be a fact or an assumption.

Whether or not an argument is **valid** has to do with the argument's form or structure. Here the word *valid* is not the general term people use in conversation to mean "acceptable" or "well grounded." In the context of reading and writing logical arguments, the word *valid* has a very specific meaning. A deductive argument is *valid* when the conclusion logically follows from the premises. The following argument is valid.

VALID

PREMISE 1	When it snows, the streets get wet. [fact]
PREMISE 2	It is snowing. [fact]
CONCLUSION	Therefore, the streets are wet.

The following argument is invalid.

INVALID

PREMISE 1	When it snows, the streets get wet. [fact]
PREMISE 2	The streets are wet. [fact]
CONCLUSION	Therefore, it is snowing.

The invalid argument has acceptable premises because the premises are facts. The argument's conclusion, however, is wrong. It ignores other reasons for why the streets may be wet. The street could be wet from rain, from street-cleaning trucks that spray water, or from people using hoses to cool off the pavement or to wash their cars.

Because the conclusion does not follow logically from the premises, the argument is invalid.

The following argument is also invalid. The conclusion does not flow from the premises (the car may not start for many reasons other than a dead battery).

INVALID

PREMISE 1	When the battery is dead, a car will not start. [fact]
PREMISE 2	My car will not start. [fact]
CONCLUSION	My battery is dead.

When a premise is an assumption, the premise must be able to be defended with evidence. The following argument is valid. Its conclusion flows logically from the premises. An argument's validity, however, is independent of its truth. Is premise 1 true? Different economists will offer different opinions. *Only if both premises are true is an argument true.* This argument may be true or false depending on whether the first premise is true or false. The writer must support the claim that is the first premise.

VALID (AND POSSIBLY TRUE)

PREMISE 1	When the unemployment rate rises, an economic recession occurs. [assumption: the writer must present evidence in support of this statement]
PREMISE 2	The unemployment rate has risen. [fact]
CONCLUSION	An economic recession will occur.

The following argument is valid. Its conclusion follows from its premises. Is the argument, however, true? Because the argument contains an assumption in its first premise, the argument can be true only if the premise is proved true. Such proof is not possible. Therefore, although the argument is valid, it is not true.

VALID (BUT NOT TRUE)

PREMISE 1	If you buy a Supermacho 357 sports car, you will achieve instant popularity. [assumption]
PREMISE 2	Kim just bought a Supermacho 357 sports car. [fact]
CONCLUSION	Kim will achieve instant popularity.

In any deductive argument, beware of premises that are implied but not stated—called **unstated assumptions.** Remember that an argument can be logically valid even though it is based on wrong assumptions. The response to such an argument is to attack the assumptions, not the conclusion. Often the assumptions are wrong. For example, suppose a corporation argued that it should not be required to install pollution control devices because the cost would cut into its profits. This argument rests on the unstated assumption that no corporation should do something that would lower its profits. That assumption is wrong, and so is the argument. But it can be shown to be wrong only when the assumptions are challenged.

Similarly, if someone says that certain information has to be correct because it was printed in a newspaper, the person's deductive reasoning is flawed. Here the unstated assumption is that everything in a newspaper is correct—which is not true. Whenever there is an unstated assumption, supply it and then check to make sure it is true. Deductive reasoning is summarized in Chart 40.

SUMMARY OF DEDUCTIVE REASONING 40

Deductive reasoning moves from the general to the specific. The three-part structure that makes up a deductive argument includes two premises and a conclusion drawn from them.

- A deductive argument is valid if the conclusion logically follows from the premises.
- A deductive conclusion may be judged true or false. If both premises are true, the conclusion is true. If the argument contains an assumption, the writer must prove the truth of the assumption to establish the truth of the argument.
- Deductive reasoning applies what the writer already knows. Though it does not yield anything new, it builds stronger arguments than does inductive reasoning because it offers the certainty of a conclusion's being true or false.

EXERCISE 5-7

Consulting section 5j-2, ignore for the moment whether the premises seem to you to be true, but determine if each conclusion is valid. Explain your answer.

1. Engineering students are pragmatic.
   Mary-Ellen is an engineering student.
   Mary-Ellen must be pragmatic.
2. When a storm is threatening, small-craft warnings are issued.
   A storm is threatening.
   Small-craft warnings will be issued.
3. The Governor General's Awards are given to outstanding literary works.
   Margaret Atwood's *The Robber Bride* did not win the Governor General's Award for Fiction.
   The Robber Bride is not an outstanding literary work.

4. All provinces send representatives to federal–provincial conferences.
   The Northwest Territories sends representatives to federal–provincial conferences.
   The Northwest Territories is a province.
5. All risks are frightening.
   Changing to a new job is a risk.
   The change to a new job is frightening.
6. Before a file can be copied onto a floppy disk, the disk must be formatted.
   This floppy disk contains a file.
   This floppy disk has been formatted.
7. You should not believe all that you read on the Internet.
   This article was downloaded from the Internet.
   You should not believe this article.
8. Prairie politicians tend to be famed for their charismatic speaking style.
   John Diefenbaker, Tommy Douglas, and Joe Clark are Prairie politicians.
   Therefore, John Diefenbaker, Tommy Douglas, and Joe Clark are all famed for their charismatic speaking style.
9. All members of Parliament are entitled to subsidized haircuts.
   Elaine Laurendeau is a member of Parliament.
   Elaine Laurendeau is entitled to subsidized haircuts.
10. All great chefs are men.
    Madame Benoît was a great chef.
    Madame Benoît was a man.

5k Recognizing and avoiding logical fallacies

Logical fallacies are flaws in reasoning that lead to illogical statements. They tend to occur most often when ideas are being argued, although they can be found in all types of writing. Most logical fallacies masquerade as reasonable statements, but they are in fact attempts to manipulate readers by reaching their emotions instead of their intellects, their hearts rather than their heads. Most logical fallacies are known by labels; each indicates a way that thinking has gone wrong during the reasoning process.

Hasty generalization

A **hasty generalization** occurs when someone generalizes from inadequate evidence. If the statement "My hometown is the best place in the province to live" is supported with only two examples of why it is pleasant, the generalization is hasty. **Stereotyping** is a type of hasty generalization that occurs when someone makes prejudiced, sweeping claims about all of the members of a particular religious, ethnic, racial, or political group: "Everyone from country *X* is dishonest." **Sexism** occurs when someone discriminates against people on the basis of sex. (See 11q and 21b for advice on how to avoid sexist language, a form of sexism, in your writing.) One often-heard combination of stereotyping and sexism occurs when a car driven by a woman has hit a car driven by a man, and the man says, "That's just like a woman."

False analogy

A **false analogy** is a comparison in which the differences outweigh the similarities, or the similarities are irrelevant to the claim the analogy is intended to support. "Old Joe Smith would never make a good prime minister because an old dog cannot learn new tricks." Homespun analogies like this often seem to have an air of wisdom about them, but just as often they fall apart when examined closely.

Begging the question

An argument that **begs the question** states a claim, but the support is based on the claim, so the reasoning is circular. Sometimes, the support simply restates the claim: "Wrestling is a dangerous sport because it is unsafe." "Unsafe" conveys the same idea as "dangerous"; it does not provide evidence to support the claim that wrestling is dangerous. Another question-begging argument offers a second statement as support, but the support for the second statement is the argument in the first statement: "Wrestling is a dangerous sport because wrestlers get injured. Anyone as big and strong as a wrestler would not get injured if the sport were safe." Begging the question also occurs in statements such as "Wrestlers love danger." There is an unstated assumption that wrestling is dangerous as well as an assumption that no proof is called for because the audience shares the opinion that wrestling is dangerous.

Irrelevant argument

An **irrelevant argument** is called ***non sequitur*** in Latin, which translates as "it does not follow." This flaw occurs when a conclusion does not follow from the premises: "Marie Trudel is a forceful speaker, so she will make a good mayor." It does not follow that someone's ability to be a forceful speaker means that person would be a good mayor.

False cause

The fallacy of **false cause** is called ***post hoc, ergo propter hoc*** in Latin—which means "after this, therefore because of this." This fallacy results when someone assumes that because two events are related in time, the first one *causes* the second one. This cause-and-effect fallacy is very common. "A new weather satellite was launched last week, and it has been raining ever since" implies—illogically—that the rain (the second event) is a result of the satellite launch (the first event).

Self-contradiction

Self-contradiction occurs when two premises are used that cannot simultaneously be true: "Only when nuclear weapons have finally destroyed us will we be convinced of the need to control them." This statement is self-contradictory in that no one would be around to be convinced if everyone had been destroyed.

Red herring

A **red herring,** sometimes referred to as **ignoring the question,** sidetracks an issue by bringing up a totally unrelated issue: "Why worry about pandas becoming extinct when we should be concerned about the plight of the homeless?" Someone who introduces an irrelevant issue hopes to distract the audience as a red herring might distract bloodhounds from a scent.

Argument to the person

An **argument to the person,** also known as ***ad hominem,*** attacks a person's appearance, personal habits, or character instead of dealing with the merits of the individual's arguments, ideas, or opinions. "We could take her position in favour of jailing child abusers seriously if she were not so nasty to the children who live next door to her" is one type of *ad hominem* attack. The suggestions, not the person who makes them, must be dealt with. The person who argues is *not* the argument.

Guilt by association

Guilt by association is a kind of *ad hominem* attack implying that an individual's arguments, ideas, or opinions lack merit because of that person's activities, interests, or associates. The claim that because Jack belongs to the International Hill Climbers Association, which declared bankruptcy last month, he is unfit to be mayor uses guilt by association.

Jumping on the bandwagon

Jumping on the bandwagon, also known as **going along with the crowd** or **argument *ad populum,*** implies that something is right because everyone is doing it, that truth is determined by majority vote: "Smoking is not bad for people because millions of people smoke."

False or irrelevant authority

Using **false or irrelevant authority,** sometimes called **argument *ad verecundiam,*** means citing the opinion of an "expert" who has no claim to expertise about the subject at hand. This fallacy attempts to transfer prestige from one area to another. Many television commercials rely on this tactic—a famous tennis player praising a brand of motor oil or a popular movie star lauding a brand of cheese.

Card-stacking

Card-stacking, also known as **special pleading,** ignores evidence on the other side of a question. From all the available facts, the person arguing selects only those that will build the best (or worst) possible case. Many television commercials use this strategy. When three slim, happy consumers rave about a new diet plan, they do not mention that (a) the plan does not work for everyone and that (b) other plans work better for some people.

The either-or fallacy

The either-or fallacy, also known as **false dilemma,** offers only two alternatives when more exist. Such fallacies often touch on emotional issues and can therefore seem accurate at first. When people reflect, however, they quickly come to realize that more alternatives are available. Here is a typical example of an either-or fallacy: "Either go to university or forget about getting a job." This statement implies that a university education is a prerequisite for all jobs, which is not true.

Taking something out of context

Taking something out of context separates an idea or fact from the material surrounding it, thus distorting it for special purposes. Suppose a critic writes about a movie saying, "The plot was predictable and boring but the music was sparkling." Then an advertisement for the movie says, "Critic calls this movie 'sparkling.'" The critic's words have been taken out of context—and distorted.

Appeal to ignorance

Appeal to ignorance assumes that an argument is valid simply because it has not been shown to be false. Conversely, something is not false simply because it has not been shown to be true. Appeals to ignorance can be very persuasive because they prey on people's superstitions or lack of knowledge. Here is a typical example of such flawed reasoning: "Since no one has proven that depression does not cause cancer, we can assume that it does." The absence of opposing evidence proves nothing.

Ambiguity and equivocation

Ambiguity and **equivocation** describe expressions that are not clear because they have more than one meaning. An ambiguous expression may be taken either way by the reader. A statement such as "They were entertaining guests" is ambiguous. Were the guests amusing to be with or were people giving hospitality to guests? An equivocal expression, by contrast, is one used in two or more ways within a single argument. If someone argued that the prime minister *played a role* in constitutional negotiations and then, two sentences later, said that the prime minister was *playing a role* when he called himself a supporter of the "distinct society" clause to satisfy Quebec, the person would be equivocating.

SUMMARY OF LOGICAL FALLACIES 41

- hasty generalization
- false analogy
- begging the question
- irrelevant argument
- false cause
- self-contradiction
- red herring
- argument to the person
- guilt by association
- jumping on the bandwagon
- false or irrelevant authority
- card-stacking
- the either-or fallacy
- taking something out of context
- appeal to ignorance
- ambiguity and equivocation

EXERCISE 5-8

Consulting section 5k, identify and explain the fallacy in each item. If the item does not contain a logical flaw, circle its number.

EXAMPLE Seat belts are the only hope for reducing the death rate from automobile accidents. [This is an *either-or fallacy* because it assumes that nothing but seat belts can reduce the number of fatalities from car accidents.]

1. Joanna Hayes should write a book about international espionage. She has starred in three films that show the inner workings of foreign spy rings.
2. It is ridiculous to have spent thousands of dollars to rescue those two whales from being trapped in the Arctic ice. Why, look at all of the people trapped in jobs that they don't like.
3. Every time my roommate flosses her teeth, her boyfriend comes by. Clearly, he likes her to keep her teeth clean.
4. Our history is not violent because we live in a peaceful country.
5. The local political coalition to protect the environment would get my support and that of many other people if its leaders did not drive cars that get poor gasoline mileage.
6. UFOs must exist because no reputable studies have proven conclusively that they do not.
7. Getting a postsecondary diploma leads to good health. Statistics show that university graduates live longer than high-school graduates.
8. Learning to manage a corporation is exactly like learning to ride a bicycle: Once you learn the skills, you never forget how, and you never fall.
9. The Great Depression of the 1930s exceeded the worst economic crisis possible.
10. Reading good literature is the one way to appreciate culture.

6 Writing Argument

When writing **argument** for your college or university courses, you seek to convince a reader to agree with you concerning a topic open to debate. The terms *persuasive writing* and *argumentative writing* often are used interchangeably. When a distinction is made between them, persuasive writing is the broader term. It includes advertisements, letters to editors, emotional pleas in speeches or writing, and formal written arguments. The focus of this chapter is formal written argument as usually assigned in college and university courses.

A written argument states and supports one position about the debatable topic. Support for that position depends on evidence, reasons, and examples chosen for their direct relation to the point being argued. One section of the written argument might present and attempt to refute other positions on the topic, but the central thrust of the essay is to argue for one point of view.

Taking and defending a position in a written argument is an engaging intellectual process, especially when it involves a topic of substance about which universal agreement is unlikely. The ability to think critically by analyzing, synthesizing, and evaluating (see Chart 30 in section 5b) is challenged by the activity of examining all sides of a topic, choosing one side to defend, and marshalling convincing support for that one side.

If you are among the people who find any type of arguing distasteful, you are not alone. But rest assured that written argument differs drastically from everyday, informal arguing. Informal arguing sometimes originates in anger and might involve bursts of temper or unpleasant emotional confrontations. Written argument, in contrast, can always be a constructive activity. When you write an argument, you can disagree without being disagreeable. An effective written argument sets forth its position calmly, respectfully, and logically. Any passion that underlies a writer's position is evident not from angry words but from the force of a balanced, well-developed, clearly written discussion.

SECTIONS OF THIS HANDBOOK TO USE WHEN WRITING AN ARGUMENT 42

- Checklist for persuasive writing (1b-3)
- Audiences for writing (1c)
- Establishing a suitable tone (1d)
- Choosing a topic (2c)
- The writing process: planning and shaping (Chapter 2)
- The writing process: drafting and revising (Chapter 3)
- Writing paragraphs (Chapter 4)
- Reading and thinking critically (Chapter 5)
- Using evidence to think critically (5h)
- Analyzing cause and effect (5i)
- Using inductive and deductive reasoning (5j)
- Avoiding logical fallacies (5k)

The ability to argue reasonably and effectively is an important skill that people need not only in their studies but throughout their lives—in family relationships, with friends, and in the business world. People engage in debates (perhaps more often in speaking than in writing) that call for an exchange of solidly supported views. Once you become adept at the techniques of written argument, you can use them equally effectively for oral argument.

Much of the material in the earlier chapters of this handbook can help you compose a written argument. A list of useful sections is given in Chart 42. This chapter concentrates on the special demands of writing argument. The writing of two student essays is discussed in this chapter, and the final draft of each essay appears in section 6i.

6a Choosing a topic for a written argument

When you choose a topic for written argument, be sure that it is open to debate. Be careful not to confuse matters of information with matters of debate. Facts are matters of information, not debate. An essay becomes an argument when it takes a position concerning the fact or other piece of information.

FACT Students at this college **are required** to take physical education.

POSITION OPEN TO DEBATE	Students at this college **should not be required** to take physical education.
OPPOSITE POSITION OPEN TO DEBATE	Students at this college **should be required** to take physical education.

A written argument could take one of these opposing positions and defend it. The essay could not argue for two or more sides, though it might mention other points of view and attempt to refute them.

When you are assigned a written argument, be sure to read and think through the assignment carefully. Instructors construct assignments for written argument in a number of ways. You might be given both the topic and the position to take on that topic. In such cases, you are expected to fulfil the assignment whether or not you agree personally with the given point of view. You are judged on your ability to marshal a defence of the assigned position and to reason logically about it. Another type of assignment is unstructured, requiring you to choose the debatable topic and the position to defend. In such cases, the topic that you choose should be **suitable for postsecondary writing** (see 2c-1), not trivial (for example, not the best way to chew gum). The topic should be **narrowed sufficiently** (see 2c-3) to fit the writing situation. You are judged on your ability to think of a debatable topic of substance, to narrow the topic so that your essay can include general statements and specific details, to choose a defensible position about that topic, and to present and support your position convincingly. If you cannot decide what position you agree with personally because all sides of a debatable topic have merit, do not get blocked. You need not make a lifetime commitment to your position. Rather, concentrate on the merits of one position, and present that position as effectively as possible.

The two sample essays at the end of this chapter were written in response to the assignment shown in the box below. This assignment states the topic but asks students to take a position about it.

> *Lindsey Black and Daniel Casey were given this assignment:* Write an essay of 500 to 700 words that argues about whether holidays have become too commercialized in North America. Your final draft is due in one week. Bring your earlier drafts to class for possible sharing and discussion.

Black and Casey analyzed the four aspects of the **writing situation** (see 2b) reflected in the assignment. The essay *topic* is stated (whether holidays have become too commercialized in North America). The essay's *purpose* is persuasive, but students are free to choose the position to argue for (the student can choose to argue that the holidays have become too commercialized *or* that they have not become too commercialized). The *audience* for the essay is not specified and is therefore assumed to be the instructor and, perhaps, other members of the class. The *special requirements* include the essay's length (between 500 and 700 words) and the time for getting the essay into final draft (one week).

6b Developing an assertion and a thesis statement for a written argument

An **assertion** is a statement that gives a position about a debatable topic and that can be supported by evidence, reasons, and examples (including facts, statistics, names, experiences, and experts). The thinking process that moves you from a topic to a defensible position calls, first, for you to make an assertion about the topic. The exact wording of the assertion often does not find its way into the essay, but the assertion serves as a focus for your thinking and your writing.

TOPIC	*The commercialization of holidays*
ASSERTION	Holidays have become too commercialized.
ASSERTION	Holidays have not become too commercialized.

Before you decide on an assertion—the position that you want to argue—you need to explore the topic. Do not rush into deciding on your assertion. Try to wait until you have as full a picture as possible. Consider all sides. Remember that **what mainly separates most good writing from bad is the writer's ability to move back and forth between general statements and specific details.** Try to avoid a position that limits you to *only* general statements or to *only* specific details. In deciding on your assertion, use the memory device of RENNS (see 4c) to see whether you can marshal sufficient details to support your generalizations.

Even if you know immediately what assertion you want to argue for, do not stop there. The more you think through all sides of the topic, the broader will be the perspective that you bring to your writing. Also, as you think through your position and consider alternative points of view, be open to changing your mind and taking an opposite position. Before too long, however, do settle on a position; switching positions at the last minute lessens your chances of writing an effective essay.

To stimulate your thinking about the topic and your assertion about it, use the techniques for gathering ideas explained and illustrated in sections 2e through 2j. Jot down your thoughts as they develop. Do not lose the unique opportunity that the act of writing gives you to discover new ideas and fresh insights. Writers of effective arguments often list for themselves the various points that come to mind, using two columns to represent visually two contrasting points of view. (Head the columns with labels that emphasize contrast: for example, *agree* and *disagree* or *for* and *against.*) The lists can then supply ideas during drafting and revising.

Whenever possible—if your instructor approves—use outside resources for developing an assertion. These include talking with other people and conducting research in the library or on the Internet. As you talk with people, interview them rather than argue with them. Your goal is to come to know opposing points of view, so resist any temptation to "win" a verbal argument.

Next, using your assertion as a base, you compose a thesis statement (see 2n) to use in the essay. It states the position that you present and support in the essay. To write this essay about holiday commercialism shown in 6i, Daniel Casey used this progression from basic assertion to final thesis statement.

> I think holiday commercialism is a good thing. [This assertion is a start.]
>
> All commercial uses of holidays are very good for our economy and people's spirits. [This preliminary thesis is more developed because it gives a reason—economic and emotional benefits—but the word *all* is misleading and the vocabulary level of *very good* needs work.]
>
> In spite of what some people think, commercial uses of holidays benefit the economy and people's spirits. [This draft is better, but "what some people think" was not an aspect of the topic Casey intended to explore. Also, *benefit spirits* needs revision.]
>
> Such commercial uses of holidays benefit the economy and lift people's spirits. [This is the final version of Casey's thesis statement; *Such* is a transitional word connecting the thesis statement to sentences in the introductory paragraph that describe several holiday activities.]

The final version meets the requirements listed in Chart 12 in section 2n.

EXERCISE 6-1

Develop an assertion and a thesis statement for a written argument on each of the following topics. You may choose any defensible position.

EXAMPLE **Topic:** *Book censorship in high school*
Assertion: *Books should not be censored in high school.*
Thesis statement: *When books are taken off high school library shelves and are dropped from high school curricula, students are denied exposure to an open exchange of ideas.*

1. television
2. prisons
3. drugs and athletics
4. diets for weight loss
5. grades

6c Considering the audience for written argument

The purpose of written argument is to convince a reader—the audience—of a matter of opinion. Key factors in considering audience are discussed in 1c. When you write argument, consider one additional factor about audience: the degree of agreement expected from the reader.

When a topic is emotionally charged, chances are high that any position being argued will elicit either strong agreement or strong disagreement. For example, topics such as abortion, capital punishment, and gun control arouse very strong emotions in many people. Such topics are emotionally loaded because they touch on matters of personal beliefs, including religion and individual rights. A topic such as the commercialization of holidays (see the two essays in section 6i) is somewhat less emotionally loaded. Even less emotionally loaded, yet still open to debate, are topics such as whether everyone needs a postsecondary education or whether Computer X is better than Computer Y.

The degree to which a reader might be friendly or hostile can influence what strategies you use to try to convince that reader. For example, when you anticipate that many readers will not agree with you, consider using techniques of **Rogerian argument.** Rogerian argument has been adapted from the principles of communication developed by psychologist Carl Rogers. Communication, according to Rogers, is eased when people find common ground in their points of view. The common ground in a debate over capital punishment might be that both sides find crime to be a growing problem today. Once both sides agree about the problem, they might have more tolerance for the divergence of opinion concerning whether capital punishment is a deterrent to crime.

6d Using the classical pattern for written argument

No one structure fits all written argument. For college and university courses, most written arguments include certain elements. Lindsey Black's essay in section 6i uses a structure based on the **classical pattern of argument** developed by the ancient Greeks and Romans and still highly respected today. Daniel Casey's essay in section 6i uses a modified form of that structure. Chart 43 will help you recognize the elements in a written argument.

ELEMENTS IN THE CLASSICAL PATTERN FOR WRITTEN ARGUMENT 43

1. **Introductory paragraph:** sets the context for the position that is argued in the essay. (For a discussion of introductory paragraphs, see 4g.)
2. **Thesis statement:** states the position being argued. In a short essay, the thesis statement often appears at the end of the introductory paragraph. (For a discussion of thesis statements, see 2n.)
3. **Background information:** gives the reader basic information needed for understanding the position being argued. This information can be part of the introductory paragraph (as in Daniel Casey's essay in section 6i) or can appear in its own paragraph (as in Lindsey Black's essay in section 6i).
4. **Reasons or evidence:** supports the position being argued. This material is the core of the essay. If the support consists of evidence, consult the discussion in 5h. Also, be sure that your reasoning is logical (see 5k). Each type of evidence or reason usually consists of a general statement backed up with specific details or examples. Depending on the length of the essay, one or two paragraphs are devoted to each reason or type of evidence.

   The best sequence for presenting the complete set of reasons and types of evidence depends on the impact you want to achieve. Moving from evidence most familiar to the reader to evidence least familiar helps the reader move from the known to the unknown. This order might catch the reader's interest early on. Moving from evidence least important to evidence most important might build the reader's suspense. (For more about various types of paragraph arrangement, see 4e.) ➜

ELEMENTS IN THE CLASSICAL PATTERN FOR WRITTEN ARGUMENT (*continued*) 43

5. **Anticipation of likely objections and responses to them:** mentions positions opposed to the one being argued and rebuts them briefly. In classical argument, this "refutation" appears in its own paragraph, immediately before the concluding paragraph (as in Lindsey Black's essay). An alternative placement is immediately after the introductory paragraph, as a bridge to the rest of the essay; in such arrangements the essay's thesis statement falls either at the end of the introductory paragraph or at the end of the "refutation" paragraph (as in Daniel Casey's essay in section 6i). In still another arrangement, each paragraph that presents a type of evidence or reason (item 4 in this list) also mentions and responds to the opposing position.
6. **Concluding paragraph:** brings the essay to an end that flows logically and gracefully from the rest of the essay. It does not cut off the reader abruptly. (For a discussion of concluding paragraphs, see 4g.)

6e Using the Toulmin model for argument

The Toulmin model for argument has recently gained popularity among teachers and students because it clarifies the major elements in an effective argument. The terms used in the Toulmin model may seem unfamiliar, even intimidating, at first. But worry not. The concepts that the terms describe are ones you have encountered before. What is new is placing those concepts into the vocabulary and structure of the Toulmin model.

The essential elements of the Toulmin model are presented in Chart 44.

The elements in Chart 44 can be identified in Daniel Casey's written argument shown in 6i:

- Casey's claim: Commercial uses of holidays benefit the economy and lift people's spirits.
- Casey's support: (1) Economic prosperity creates circulation of money, which in turn creates jobs. (2) Holidays are festive times that cheer people up with decorations, costumes, gift-giving, and a friendly atmosphere. (3) Successful businesses improve everyone's quality of life by sponsoring charitable causes, parades, fireworks displays, and cultural events.

ELEMENTS IN THE TOULMIN MODEL OF ARGUMENT 44

TOULMIN'S TERM	MORE FAMILIAR TERMS
the claim	the main point or central message, usually disclosed in the thesis statement
the support	data or other evidence, from broad reasons to specific details
the warrant	underlying assumptions, usually not stated but clearly implied; readers infer assumptions

- Casey's warrants: (1) Benefiting the economy is an important objective from which everyone gains. (2) Even the spiritual aspects of the holidays are not paramount.

The concept of a warrant may seem difficult to understand. It can help to think of warrants as related to the concept of reading to make inferences, a key part of reading critically (see 5d). Like inferences, which you make by reading "between the lines," warrants are an author's assumptions that you must infer from the stated argument.

To help you figure out the warrant that underlies an argument you are writing or reading, try placing it into one of Toulmin's three broad categories for warrants: (1) A warrant based on **authority** rests on respect for the credibility and trustworthiness of the person; (2) a warrant based on **substance** rests on the reliability of factual evidence; (3) a warrant based on **motivation** rests on the values and beliefs of the audience and the writer. Daniel Casey's warrant listed above is a motivational warrant because it is not based on authority or factual evidence—it is based on the writer's valuing of economic prosperity over spiritual considerations.

The concepts in the Toulmin model can help you read arguments with a critical eye. The concepts are equally useful for you as a writer. As you draft and revise your written argument, evaluate what you are saying by checking whether you can analyze it for the elements in the Toulmin model. If you can't your argument needs work.

6f Defining terms in written argument

When you **define terms,** you explain what you mean by key terms that you use. **Key terms** are words that are central to the message that you want to communicate. The meaning of some key terms is readily evident. Key terms open to interpretation, however, should be made specific enough to be clear.

NO Commercialism at holiday time is **bad.**

YES Commercialism at holiday time is **ruining the spirit of the holidays.**

YES Commercialism at holiday time **tempts too many people to spend more money than they can afford.**

Some key terms might vary with the context of a discussion and should be explained in an essay. Abstract words such as *love, freedom,* and *democracy* have to be explained because they have different meanings in different contexts. Daniel Casey opens his essay (see 6i) with the words *signs of commercialism*. Although each word by itself is familiar, the term is not. Casey therefore gives examples to illustrate the concept. In so doing, he creates an effective introduction by bringing the reader to a quick understanding of his topic. Casey uses *economy,* a word with many meanings, in the topic sentence of the third paragraph of his essay. He defines *economy* as the *ongoing circulation of money* and explains how that circulation operates. In this way, Casey makes clear that he is not referring to any of the other meanings of *economy.*

Many students ask whether they should use dictionary definitions in an essay. Looking words up in a dictionary to understand precise meanings is a very important activity for writers. Quoting a dictionary definition, however, is not always wise. Dictionary definitions tend to be overused in student writing, and they are often seen as the "easy way out." Using an **extended definition** is usually a more effective approach, which is what Casey did for *economy* in the third paragraph of his essay. If you do use a dictionary definition in your writing, be sure to work it into your material gracefully. In general, do not rely on it for your opening sentence. Also, be aware that references to a dictionary must be complete. Each dictionary has its own name, such as the *Gage Canadian Dictionary* or the *Canadian Oxford Dictionary.*

6g Reasoning effectively in written argument

When you reason effectively, you increase your chances of persuading your reader to agree with you. In many instances, of course, you cannot expect actually to change your reader's mind. The basis for a debatable position is often personal opinion or belief, neither of which can be expected to change as the result of one written argument. Nevertheless, you still have an important goal: to convince your reader that your point of view has merit. People often "agree to disagree," in the best spirit of intellectual exchange. Round-table discussions among various experts heard on the CBC or PBS are conducted in such a spirit.

The opposite positions taken by Lindsey Black and Daniel Casey (see 6i) concerning commercialism at holiday time stem from their personal beliefs and perceptions of the world. Black feels that commercialism is ruining the holidays. Casey recognizes the existence of commercialism, but he sees it as beneficial. The chance of either person convincing the other is slight. What can happen, however, is that each person can respect the quality of the other's argument.

An argument of good quality relies on three types of appeals to reason: the logical, the emotional, and the ethical. Chart 45 gives a summary of how to use the three appeals.

The most widely used appeal in written argument is the **logical appeal,** called *logos* by the ancient Greeks. Logical reasoning is sound reasoning. This type of reasoning is important in all thinking and writing. Chapter 5 of this handbook, therefore, is a close companion to this chapter. Logical reasoning calls for using evidence well, as explained in 5h. Logical reasoning also means analyzing cause and effect correctly, as explained in 5i. A sound argument uses patterns of inductive reasoning and deductive reasoning, as explained in 5j. A sound argument also clearly distinguishes between fact and opinion, as explained in 5d-3. Finally, sound reasoning means avoiding logical fallacies, as explained in 5k.

Written argument for college and university courses relies heavily on logic. Both Lindsey Black and Daniel Casey (see 6i) used logical reasoning throughout their essays. While the reader might not agree with the reasons or types of evidence presented, the reader can respect the logic of their arguments.

GUIDELINES FOR REASONING EFFECTIVELY IN WRITTEN ARGUMENT 45

- **Be logical:** Use sound reasoning.
- **Enlist the emotions of the reader:** Enlist the values and beliefs of the reader, usually by arousing "the better self" of the reader.
- **Establish credibility:** Show that you as the writer can be relied upon as a knowledgeable person with good sense.

The **emotional appeal,** called *pathos* by the ancient Greeks, can be effective when used in conjunction with logical appeals. The word *emotional* has a specific meaning in this context. It means arousing and enlisting the emotions of the reader. Often it arouses the "better self" of the reader by eliciting sympathy, civic pride, and other feelings based on values and beliefs. Effective emotional appeals use description and examples to stir emotions, but they leave the actual stirring to the reader. Restraint is more effective than excessive sentimentality.

Both Casey and Black (see 6i) use emotional appeals in their essays, but always in conjunction with a logical presentation of material. Casey appeals to the emotions when in his fifth paragraph he mentions stores giving toys to children in hospitals. But he does not overdo it. He does not say that anyone who disagrees with him hates children and feels no pity for their suffering from dreadful illnesses that ravage their tiny bodies. If he had indulged in such excesses, the reader would resent being manipulated and therefore would probably reject his argument. Black appeals to the emotions when she writes in her second paragraph about the origins of the holiday spirit. With restraint, she mentions the meaning of each holiday. She does not attempt to tell the reader how to feel; she simply points out facts that support the logic of her argument and that might also stir the reader's pride in country and heritage.

The **ethical appeal,** called *ethos* by the ancient Greeks, means establishing the ethics and credibility of the writer. Credibility is gained if the writer uses correct facts, undistorted evidence, and accurate interpretations of events. Readers do not trust a writer who states opinions as fact or who makes a claim that cannot possibly be supported. The statement "A child who does not get gifts for Christmas suffers a trauma from which recovery is impossible" is an opinion as well as an exaggeration. It has no place in written argument.

Ethical appeals cannot take the place of logical appeals, but the two types of appeals work well together. One effective way to make an ethical appeal is to draw on personal experience. (Some college and university instructors do not want students to write in the first person, so ask your instructor before you use it.) If you use personal experience, always be sure that it relates directly to a generalization that you are supporting. Also, be aware that a personal experience can say as much about the writer as about the experience. For example, if Casey had been a volunteer at a hospital when gifts from a local business were distributed, the story of the experience not only would have supported his claim in his fifth paragraph, but also would have illustrated his good character.

6h Establishing a reasonable tone in written argument

To be reasonable, you have to be fair. By anticipating opposing positions and responding to them (see 6c), you have a particularly good chance to show that you are fair. When you alert your reader to other ways of thinking about the issue, you demonstrate that you have not ignored other positions. Doing this implies respect for the other side, which in turn makes the tone (see 1d) of the essay more reasonable.

To achieve a reasonable tone, choose your words carefully. Avoid words that exaggerate. Use figurative language, such as similes and metaphors (see 21c), to enhance your point rather than distort it. No matter how strongly you disagree with opposing arguments, never insult the other side. Name-calling is impolite, shows poor self-control, and demonstrates poor judgment. The more emotionally loaded a topic (for example, abortion, capital punishment, and gun control), the more might be the temptation to use angry words. Words such as *stupid* or *pigheaded,* however, say more about the writer than about the issue.

Artificial language (see 21e) also ruins a reasonable tone. In contrast, appropriate figurative language (see 21c), such as well-chosen similes and metaphors, enhances your point.

6i Writing and revising a written argument

Lindsey Black chose the position that holidays have become too commercialized. Daniel Casey, on the other hand, chose the position that the commercialization of holidays has advantages. The final draft of each essay appears at the end of this chapter. The labels identify the structural elements of written argument discussed in 6d.

In an early draft, Black wrote an introduction that included the background information on the holidays, now in her second paragraph. When she revised, she moved the information to a separate paragraph because she saw that the introductory paragraph was too long and the thesis statement was being overshadowed. Also, she felt that a separate paragraph giving background information had the additional advantage of giving her the space to use an emotional appeal (see 6g). An early draft of Black's third paragraph consisted only of the topic sentence and the last three sentences of the final draft. When she revised, Black saw that she needed more examples to support the generalization in her topic sentence. She added the material about greeting cards and about time and stress.

REVISION CHECKLIST FOR WRITTEN ARGUMENT 46

1. Does the thesis statement concern a debatable topic (see 6b)?
2. Is the material structured well for a written argument (see 6d)?
3. Do the reasons or evidence support the thesis statement? Are the generalizations supported by specific details (see 6d)?
4. Are opposing positions mentioned and responded to (see 6d)?
5. Are terms defined (see 6f)?
6. Are the appeals to reason used correctly and well (see 6g)?
7. Is the tone reasonable (see 6h)?

Casey wrote a discovery draft (see 3b) to explore further the ideas that he evolved while planning his essay: for his brainstorming, see section 2g; for his use of the journalist's questions, see section 2h; for the sequencing of his ideas, see section 2m. As he wrote his draft, he discovered, for example, that he needed to define the term *signs of commercialism* by giving specific examples. He also found that he had two reasons he could develop in support of his thesis: an enriched economy and an enhanced spirit. He wanted a third reason, so he interviewed some friends who worked in a shopping mall, and they mentioned what some of the stores do for the community at holiday time. The second paragraph of Casey's essay was the next-to-last paragraph in an early draft. He moved it when he revised because he decided that it built an effective bridge to his thesis statement.

As both Black and Casey revised, they consulted the Revision Checklists in 3c to remind them of general principles of writing, and they looked over the checklist in Chart 46.

EXERCISE 6-2

Choose a topic below, and write an essay that argues for a debatable position about the topic. Apply all the principles you have learned in this chapter.

1. genetically modified foods
2. nuclear power
3. French immersion programs
4. celebrity endorsements
5. day-care centres
6. surrogate mothers
7. the monarchy
8. school prayer
9. optimism
10. western alienation

Lindsey Black

Professor Gregory

English 101

April 10, 20XX

Commercialism Is Ruining the Holidays

introduction: identification of the situation

Holidays should be special occasions that have religious, historical, and cultural significance. Increasingly, however, holidays in North America are turning into little more than business opportunities. From coast to coast, the jingles and beeps of cash registers drown out the traditional sounds of holiday observance. The spirit of the holidays is being destroyed by commercialism.

thesis statement

background: origins and significance

The origins of the holiday spirit are varied in Canada and the United States. Thanksgiving reminds us to be grateful for our blessings, and holidays like Canada Day or the Fourth of July stimulate pride in the founding of the country. Labour Day is a tribute to workers. Remembrance Day in Canada and Memorial Day in the United States honour soldiers who died in defence of their country. Christmas and Easter have great religious significance to Christians. Holidays used to be occasions for people to come together and celebrate their heritages. Today, however, the overriding message of the holidays is "spend money."

→

evidence: one type

The most visible evidence that commercialism now dominates holidays is the unfortunate emphasis on spending money in preparation for religious holidays. For example, buying and mailing Christmas cards has become standard practice for individuals, families, and industry. How many people can ignore the social and the business pressures to mail cards? The commitment of money and time for this activity is not small. The gift situation is equally stressful. Although exchanging gifts on Christmas or Hanukkah was always part of the celebration, the thought behind the present used to be the point. Today, however, advertising--particularly on television--sets a high standard of expectations. Can home-baked cookies compare to a microwave oven? Can hand-drawn, handwritten cards be as impressive as elaborate greeting cards that play music?

evidence: another type

Other evidence that commercialism is ruining holidays is the emphasis on shopping for bargains rather than on activities related to cultural history. Huge sales held before holidays, and often on the holiday itself, are advertised heavily in newspapers, on television, and on radio. The emphasis on shopping before Christmas and then on Boxing Day sales tends to overshadow the true spirit of the season. The image of the family gathering on Thanksgiving Day is being replaced with the image of the family shopping the day after Thanksgiving. Some special days, in fact, seem to have been created with the sole purpose of making money--for instance, Valentine's Day, Mother's and

Father's Day, and the more recent Grandparents' Day. While these are not technically holidays, such occasions illustrate how business seizes on an opportunity to make a profit.

major likely objections and responses to them

In spite of all this, not all people are troubled by the spirit of commercialism on holidays. Many people enjoy the festivity of exchanging cards and gifts. Some people feel that the chance to buy at sales helps them stay within their budgets and therefore enjoy life more. What these people do not realize is that the festive spirit of giving can quickly turn sour when large amounts of money are suddenly not available for necessities. Also, these people do not realize that holiday sales tend to lure shoppers into spending more money than they had planned, often for things that they did not think they needed until they saw them "on sale."

conclusion: call for awareness

Holiday celebrations in North America today have more to do with the wallet than the spirit. Some people refuse to participate in the frenzy of a commercial interpretation of holidays, of course. But for too many people, holidays are becoming stressful rather than joyful, and upsetting rather than uplifting.

Daniel Casey

Professor Gregory

English 101

April 10, 20XX

Commercialism at Holiday Time Benefits Everyone

introduction: gives background

Signs of commercialism at holiday time are easy to see in North America. Christmas decorations begin their call to consumers in October. Labour Day reminds shoppers to prepare for the seasonal change in clothing fashions. Halloween and Easter mean children can expect treats from the Great Pumpkin or the Easter Bunny.

presentation and refutation of opposite view

Some people disapprove of these commercial uses of holidays in North America. These people feel that the meaning of a holiday gets lost when television is blaring news of the latest holiday sale or expensive gift item. Many people also feel that the proliferation of gifts and greeting cards creates stressful pressure on budgets and ruins any pleasure derived from giving and receiving. No one, however, has to forget the meaning of a holiday simply because commerce is involved. In fact, commercialism can increase people's enjoyment of the holidays. After all, commercial uses of holidays benefit the economy and lift people's spirits.

thesis statement

reason: one effect

Commerce at holiday time in North America enriches the economy. Prosperity is based on the ongoing circulation of money, which holidays encourage. When people spend money on gifts and holiday products, jobs are created. The jobs are in many sectors of the economy: manufacturing, distribution, advertising, and retailing. Jobs help people support their families. Profits help business and industry grow. Salaries and profits bring about tax revenues that support schools, police, hospitals, and other government services.

reason: second effect

In addition to economic benefits, commercial activity enhances the spirit of holidays. Most people feel more cheerful at holiday time. Everyone takes part in one big party. Advertising related to holidays, along with stores filled with holiday products, creates an atmosphere of festivity across the nation. Being able to say "Happy Thanksgiving" or "Merry Christmas" to strangers while shopping breaks down barriers and helps everyone feel part of one big family. The festivity on the streets, in malls, and in stores is infectious. Giving and getting gifts and greeting cards helps people stay in touch with each other and express their feelings. Children look forward all year to wearing a store-bought costume for Halloween, sitting on Santa's lap in a department store, and talking to the Easter Bunny at the local shopping mall.

reason: third effect

The holiday activities that help businesses prosper also inspire many businesses to improve everyone's quality of life. Many companies, for example, organize collections of clothing and preparation of hot meals for needy people at holiday time. Toy stores often give away toys for

→

Christmas and Hanukkah to children in hospitals and in caretaking homes. Santa Claus parades in virtually every city annually delight people of all ages. In small towns and large cities, many businesses sponsor fireworks, mounted and displayed safely by professionals, to celebrate Canada Day. Good will and good business go together to everyone's benefit at holiday time.

conclusion: summary of main points

While commercialism can detract from the true meaning of a holiday, it does not have to. People can discipline themselves to balance the spiritual with the commercial. People should recognize that the advantages of a stimulated economy and a collective festive spirit are worth the effort of such self-discipline.

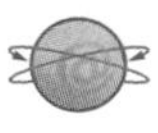

web.uvic.ca/wguide/Pages/EssaysToc.html
The Essay

owl.english.purdue.edu/handouts/general/index.html
Planning and Writing an Essay

www.wuacc.edu/services/zzcwwctr/paragraphs.txt
Building Paragraphs: The Paragraph as a Miniature Essay

www.utoronto.ca/writing/notes.html
Taking Notes from Research Reading

webware.princeton.edu/Writing/wc4d.htm
Developing an Argument

www.utoronto.ca/writing/computer.html
Using the Computer to Improve Your Writing

leo.stcloudstate.edu/
LEO: Literary Education Online

PART

II Understanding Grammar and Writing Correct Sentences

When you understand grammar and write correct sentences, you increase your chances of communicating your meaning clearly. Part Two focuses on these elements of communication. The descriptions of grammar in Chapters 7 through 12 give you one tool for discussing language. The explanations of correct sentences in Chapters 13 through 15 give you the foundation on which you can build a personal writing style that is effective and graceful.

7 Parts of Speech and Sentence Structures

PARTS OF SPEECH

Knowing **parts of speech** gives you a basic vocabulary for identifying words and understanding how language works. Sections 7a through 7i explain the **noun, pronoun, verb, adjective, adverb, preposition, conjunction,** and **interjection.** As you use this material, be aware that no part of speech exists in a vacuum. To identify a word's part of speech correctly, see how the word functions in the sentence you are analyzing. Often, the same word functions differently in different sentences.

We ate **fish.** [*Fish* is a noun. It names a thing.]

We **fish** on weekends. [*Fish* is a verb. It names an action.]

7a Recognizing nouns

A **noun** names a person, place, thing, or idea: student, school, textbook, education. For a list of types of nouns, see Chart 47. Nouns function as subjects°,* objects°, and complements°.

✤ ALERT: Words that appear with nouns often tell how much or many, whose, which one, and similar information. These words include **articles** (*a, an, the*) and other **determiners** or **limiting adjectives.** For more about these words, see 7e and Chapter 43ESL. ✤

*Throughout this book, a degree mark (°) indicates that you can find the definition of the word in the Terms Glossary in this handbook.

NOUNS		47
PROPER	names specific people, places, or things (first letter is always capitalized)	**Jim Carrey, Paris, Buick**
COMMON	names general groups, places, people, or things	**singer, automobile**
CONCRETE	names things experienced through the senses: sight, hearing, taste, smell, and touch	**landscape, pizza, thunder**
ABSTRACT	names things not knowable through the senses	**freedom, shyness**
COLLECTIVE	names groups	**family, team**
NONCOUNT OR MASS	names uncountable things	**water, time**
COUNT	names countable items	**lake, minute**

◆ ESL NOTE: Sometimes a **suffix** (a word ending) can help you identify the part of speech. Usually, words with these suffixes are nouns: *-ness, -ence, -ance, -ty,* and *-ment.* For more on suffixes, see 20c-1 and 22d. ◆

7b Recognizing pronouns

A **pronoun** takes the place of a noun°. The word (or words) a pronoun replaces is called its **antecedent.** Pronouns have three different forms, known as **cases:** subjective case, objective case, and possessive case. For more details about pronoun case, see Chapter 9. For types of pronouns, see Chart 48.

David is an accountant. [noun]

He is an accountant. [pronoun]

The finance committee needs to consult **him.** [The pronoun *him* refers to its antecedent, *David.*]

PRONOUNS 48

PERSONAL *I, you, they, her, its, ours,* and others	refers to people or things	**I** saw **her** take your book to **them.**
RELATIVE *who, which, that*	introduces certain noun clauses° and adjective clauses°	The book **that** I lost was valuable.
INTERROGATIVE *who, whose, what, which,* and others	introduces a question	**Who** called?
DEMONSTRATIVE *this, these, that, those*	points out the antecedent°	Whose books are **these**?
REFLEXIVE; INTENSIVE *myself, themselves,* and other *-self* or *-selves* words	reflects back to the antecedent; intensifies the antecedent	They claim to support **themselves.** I **myself** doubt it.
RECIPROCAL *each other, one another*	refers to individual parts of a plural antecedent	We respect **each other.**
INDEFINITE *all, anyone, each,* and others	refers to nonspecific persons or things	**Everyone** is welcome here.

EXERCISE 7-1

Consulting sections 7a and 7b, underline and label all nouns (N) and pronouns (P). Circle all articles.

N N N N
EXAMPLE Treadmills can be (a) way to fitness and rehabilitation.

1. Not only humans use them.
2. Scientists conduct experiments by placing lobsters on treadmills.
3. Scientists can study a lobster when it is fitted with a small mask.
4. The lobster may reach speeds up to a kilometre an hour.
5. Through the mask, researchers can monitor the heartbeat of the crustacean that they are studying.

7c Recognizing verbs

Main verbs express action, occurrence, or state of being.

I **dance.** [action]

The audience **became** silent. [occurrence]

Your dancing **was** excellent. [state of being]

✤ ALERT: If you are not sure whether a word is a verb, try putting the word into a different tense°. If the sentence still makes sense, the word is a verb. (For an explanation of verb tense, see 8g.)

NO He is a **changed** man. He is a **will change** man. [The sentence does not make sense when the verb *will change* is substituted, so *changed* is not functioning as a verb.]

YES The store **changed** owners. The store **will change** owners. [Because the sentence still makes sense when the verb *will change* is substituted, *changed* is functioning as a verb.] ✤

For a detailed discussion of all verb types and the information that they convey, see Chapter 8.

EXERCISE 7-2

Consulting section 7c, underline all verbs.

EXAMPLE A distinctive group of self-published magazines <u>is called</u> simply "zines."

1. Many young writers found regular mass-market magazines boring and irrelevant.
2. Some of them created their own small magazines, or "zines," for readers with the same interests and tastes.
3. Most zines contain cartoons, short stories, and personal essays.
4. Typically, zines are given odd names like *Ottawa's Plague* and *I Hate My Generation.*
5. Their creators shock their small group of readers with satire, bizarre fantasies, and wild rumours about popular rock bands.

7d Recognizing verbals

Verbals are verb parts functioning as nouns°, adjectives°, or adverbs°. For types of verbals, see Chart 49.

VERBALS AND THEIR FUNCTIONS		49
INFINITIVE *to* + simple form° of verb	1. noun°	**To eat** now is inconvenient.
	2. adjective° or adverb°	Still, we have far **to go.**
PAST PARTICIPLE *-ed* form of regular verb° or equivalent in irregular verb°	adjective°	**Boiled, filtered** water is usually safe to drink.
PRESENT PARTICIPLE *-ing* form of verb	1. noun° (called a gerund°)	**Running** is a popular sport.
	2. adjective°	**Running** water may not be safe.

◆ ESL NOTE: For information about using gerunds and infinitives, see Chapter 46ESL. ◆

7e Recognizing adjectives

Adjectives modify—that is, they describe or limit—nouns°, pronouns°, and word groups that function as nouns. For a detailed discussion of adjectives, see Chapter 12.

I saw a **green** tree. [*Green* modifies the noun *tree.*]

It was **leafy.** [*Leafy* modifies the pronoun *it.*]

The flowering trees were **beautiful.** [*Beautiful* modifies the noun phrase *the flowering trees.*]

Descriptive adjectives, like *leafy* and *green,* can show levels of intensity: *green, greener, greenest; leafy, more leafy, most leafy.* **Proper adjectives** are formed from proper nouns°: *American, Victorian.*

◆ ESL NOTE: Usually, words with these suffixes are adjectives: *-ful, -ish, -less,* and *-like*. For more about suffixes, see 20c-1 and 22d. ◆

Determiners are sometimes called **limiting adjectives.** They "limit" nouns by conveying information such as whether a noun is general (***a*** *tree*) or specific (***the*** *tree*). They also tell which one (***this*** *tree*), how many (***twelve*** *trees*), whose (***our*** *tree*), and similar information.

The determiners, *a, an,* and *the* are also called **articles.** *The* is a **definite article.** Before a noun, *the* conveys that the noun refers to a specific item (***the*** *plan*). *A* and *an* are **indefinite articles.** They convey that a noun refers to an item in a nonspecific or general way (***a*** *plan*).

✤ ALERT: Remember to use *a* when the word following it starts with a consonant sound: ***a c****arrot,* ***a b****roken egg,* ***a h****ip;* use *an* when the word following it starts with a vowel sound: ***an e****gg,* ***an o****ld carrot,* ***an h****onour.* For more on articles, see Chapter 43ESL. ✤

Chart 50 lists determiners. Some words in the chart also function as pronouns. To identify a word's part of speech, see how it functions in a sentence.

> **That** car belongs to Harold. [*that* = demonstrative adjective]
>
> **That** is Harold's car. [*that* = demonstrative pronoun]

DETERMINERS (LIMITING ADJECTIVES) 50

ARTICLES *a, an, the*	**A** reporter working on **an** assignment is using **the** telephone.
DEMONSTRATIVE *this, these, that, those*	**Those** students rent **that** house.
INDEFINITE *any, each, few, other, some,* and others	**Few** films today have complex plots.
INTERROGATIVE *what, which, whose*	**What** answer did you give?
NUMERICAL *one, first, two, second,* and others	The **fifth** question was tricky.
POSSESSIVE *my, your, their,* and others	**My** violin is older than **your** cello.
RELATIVE *what, which, whose, whatever,* and others	We don't know **which** road to take.

7f Recognizing adverbs

An **adverb** modifies—that is, describes or limits—verbs°, adjectives°, other adverbs, and entire sentences. For a detailed discussion of adverbs, see Chapter 12.

Chefs plan meals **carefully.** [*Carefully* modifies the verb *plan.*]

Vegetables provide **very** important vitamins. [*Very* modifies the adjective *important.*]

Those potato chips are **too** heavily salted. [*Too* modifies the adverb *heavily.*]

Fortunately, people are learning that salt can be harmful. [*Fortunately* modifies the entire sentence.]

Descriptive adverbs can show levels of intensity, usually by adding *more* (or *less*) and *most* (or *least*): *more happily, least clearly.*

Conjunctive adverbs modify by creating logical connections in meaning, as shown in Chart 51. Conjunctive adverbs can appear in the first position of a sentence, in the middle of a sentence, or in the last position of a sentence.

Therefore, we consider Isaac Newton an important scientist.

We consider Isaac Newton, **therefore,** an important scientist.

We consider Isaac Newton an important scientist, **therefore.**

Relative adverbs are words such as *where* and *when* used to introduce adjective clauses°; see 7o-2.

CONJUNCTIVE ADVERBS AND THE RELATIONSHIPS THEY EXPRESS 51

RELATIONSHIP	WORDS
ADDITION	*also, furthermore, moreover, besides*
CONTRAST	*however, still, nevertheless, conversely, nonetheless, instead, otherwise*
COMPARISON	*similarly, likewise*
RESULT OR SUMMARY	*therefore, thus, consequently, accordingly, hence, then*
TIME	*next, then, meanwhile, finally, subsequently*
EMPHASIS	*indeed, certainly*

EXERCISE 7-3

Consulting 7d, 7e, and 7f, underline and label all adjectives (ADJ) and adverbs (ADV).

EXAMPLE Scientific (ADJ) evidence shows that massage (ADJ) therapy can dramatically (ADV) improve human (ADJ) health.

1. Premature babies who are massaged gently gain 47 percent more weight than babies who do not receive touch treatment.
2. Frequently, massaged premature babies go home from the hospital sooner, saving medical expense and parental concern.
3. Also, daily massage helps many people with stomach problems digest their food easily because important hormones are released during the rubdown.
4. People with HIV infection find their weakened immune system significantly improved by targeted massage.
5. In addition, massage treatments have helped people with asthma breathe more easily.

7g Recognizing prepositions

Prepositions include common words such as *in, under, by, after, to, on, over,* and *since.* Prepositions function with other words in **prepositional phrases.** Prepositional phrases often set out relationships in time or space: *in April, under the orange umbrella.*

In the fall, we will hear a concert **by our favourite tenor.**

After the concert, he will fly **to Paris.**

Some words that function as prepositions also function as other parts of speech. To check whether a word is a preposition, see how it functions in its sentence.

The mountain climbers have not radioed in **since** yesterday. [preposition]

Since they have left the base camp, the mountain climbers can communicate with us only by radio. [subordinating conjunction: see 7h]

At first I was not worried, but I have **since** changed my mind. [adverb: see 7f]

◆ ESL NOTE: For a list of prepositions and the idioms they involve, see Chapter 45ESL. ◆

7h Recognizing conjunctions

A **conjunction** connects words, phrases°, or clauses°. **Coordinating conjunctions** join two or more grammatically equivalent structures.

We hike **and** camp every summer. [*And* joins two words.]

I love the outdoors, **but** my family does not. [*But* joins two sentences.]

COORDINATING CONJUNCTIONS AND THE RELATIONSHIPS THEY EXPRESS 52

RELATIONSHIP	WORDS
ADDITION	*and*
CONTRAST	*but, yet*
RESULT OR EFFECT	*so*
RESULT OR CAUSE	*for*
CHOICE	*or*
NEGATIVE CHOICE	*nor*

Correlative conjunctions function in pairs to join equivalent grammatical structures. They include *both...and, either...or, neither...nor, not only...but (also), whether...or,* and *not...so much as.*

Both English **and** French are spoken in many homes in Canada.

Not only students **but also** business people should study a second language.

Subordinating conjunctions introduce dependent clauses°, which are structures that are grammatically less important than those in an independent clause° within the same sentence. Subordinating conjunctions are listed in Chart 53.

Many people were happy **after** they heard the news.

Because it snowed, school was cancelled.

SUBORDINATING CONJUNCTIONS AND THE RELATIONSHIPS THEY EXPRESS 53

RELATIONSHIP	WORDS
TIME	*after, before, once, since, until, when, whenever, while*
REASON OR CAUSE	*as, because, since*
RESULT OR EFFECT	*in order that, so, so that, that*
CONDITION	*if, even if, provided that, unless*
CONTRAST	*although, even though, though, whereas*
LOCATION	*where, wherever*
CHOICE	*rather than, than, whether*

7i Recognizing interjections

An **interjection** is a word or expression that conveys surprise or another strong emotion. Alone, an interjection is usually punctuated with an exclamation point(*!*). As part of a sentence, an interjection is set off with a comma (or commas). In academic writing, use interjections sparingly, if at all.

Hooray! I got the promotion.

Oh, they are late.

EXERCISE 7-4

Consulting sections 7a through 7i, identify the part of speech of each numbered and underlined word. Choose from noun, pronoun, verb, adjective, adverb, preposition, coordinating conjunction, correlative conjunction, and subordinating conjunction.

Although[1] few[2] people realize that the coffee bean is drunk by[3] more people than any other beverage[4], it[5] is actually the second best-selling[6] item of international[7] commerce. Petroleum is the first[8] item. People[9] in the United States consume about 1.5 million tonnes of[10] coffee beans per year, more coffee than the entire world drank[11] only fifty years ago. Nevertheless[12], the

13 14 15
Swedish are the world's heaviest coffee consumers. In an average year,
16 17 18
each Swede consumes nearly 15 kilograms of coffee, and this consumption
19 20 21
is slowly rising. Therefore, if both Americans and Swedes continue to consume
22 23 24 25
coffee at this rate, coffee may eventually equal or surpass petroleum as the largest item of international commerce.

SENTENCE STRUCTURES

When you know how sentences are formed, you have one tool for understanding the art of writing.

7j Defining the sentence

The sentence has several definitions, each of which views it from a different perspective. On its most mechanical level, a sentence starts with a capital letter and finishes with a period, question mark, or exclamation point. A sentence can be defined according to its purpose. **Declarative sentences** make a statement: *Sky diving is dangerous.* **Interrogative sentences** ask a question: *Is sky diving dangerous?* **Imperative sentences** give a command: *Be careful when you sky dive.* **Exclamatory sentences** begin with *What* or *How* and express strong feeling: *How I love sky diving!* Grammatically, a sentence contains an **independent clause** (a group of words that can stand alone as an independent unit): *Sky diving is dangerous.* Sometimes a sentence is described as a "complete thought," but the concept of "complete" is too subjective to be reliable.

An infinite variety of sentences can be composed, but all sentences share a common foundation. Sections 7k through 7p present the basic structures of sentences.

7k Recognizing subjects and predicates

A sentence consists of two basic parts: a **subject** and a **predicate.**

The **simple subject** is the word or group of words that acts, is described, or is acted upon.

The **telephone** rang. [Simple subject, *telephone,* acts.]

The **telephone** is red. [Simple subject, *telephone,* is described.]

The **telephone** was being connected. [Simple subject, *telephone,* is acted upon.]

The **complete subject** is the simple subject and its modifiers (all the words that describe or limit it): ***The red telephone*** *rang.*

A **compound subject** consists of two or more nouns° or pronouns° and their modifiers: ***The telephone and the doorbell*** *rang.*

The **predicate** is the part of the sentence that contains the verb. The predicate tells what the subject is doing or experiencing or what is being done to the subject.

The telephone **rang.** [*Rang* tells us what the subject, *telephone,* did.]

The telephone **is** red. [*Is* tells what the subject, *telephone,* experiences.]

The telephone **was being connected.** [*Was being connected* tells what was being done to the subject, *telephone.*]

A **simple predicate** contains only the verb: *The lawyer* ***listened.*** A **complete predicate** contains the verb and its modifiers°: *The lawyer* ***listened carefully.*** A **compound predicate** contains two or more verbs: *The lawyer* ***listened and waited.***

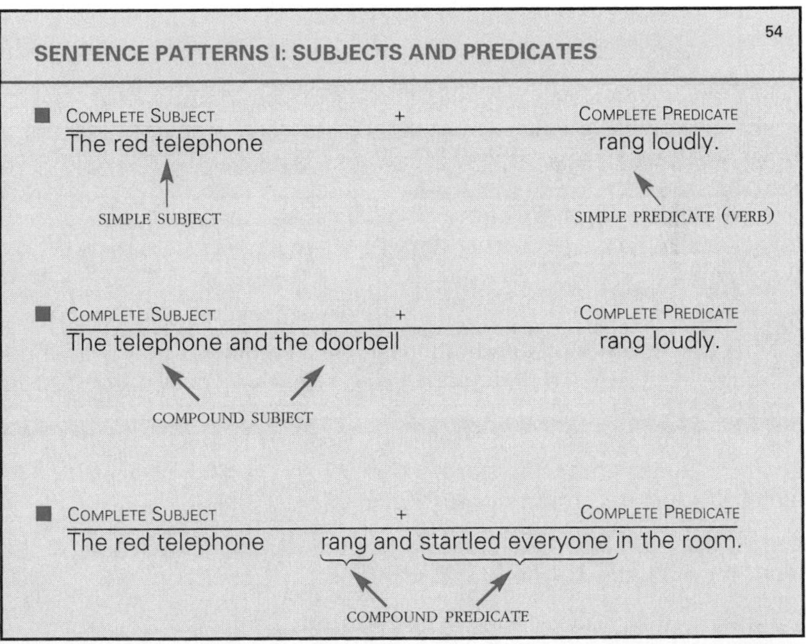

54
SENTENCE PATTERNS I: SUBJECTS AND PREDICATES
COMPLETE SUBJECT + COMPLETE PREDICATE
The red telephone
rang loudly.
SIMPLE SUBJECT
SIMPLE PREDICATE (VERB)
COMPLETE SUBJECT + COMPLETE PREDICATE
The telephone and the doorbell
rang loudly.
COMPOUND SUBJECT
COMPLETE SUBJECT + COMPLETE PREDICATE
The red telephone
rang and startled everyone in the room.
COMPOUND PREDICATE

✤ ALERT: In sentences that make a statement, the subject usually comes before the predicate. (One exception is inverted sentences°; see 19f). In sentences that ask a question, part of the predicate usually comes before the subject. For more about word order, see Chapter 44ESL. ✤

◆ ESL NOTE: Avoid repeating a subject with a personal pronoun in the same clause.

NO My grandfather, **he** lived to be eighty-seven.

YES My grandfather lived to be eighty-seven.

NO Winter storms that bring ice, sleet, and snow **they** can cause traffic problems.

YES Winter storms that bring ice, sleet, and snow can cause traffic problems. ◆

EXERCISE 7-5

Consulting section 7k, separate the complete subject from the complete predicate with a slash.

EXAMPLE One of the most devastating natural disasters of recorded history / began on April 5, 1815.

1. Mount Tambora, located in present-day Indonesia, erupted.
2. The eruption exploded the top 1200 metres of the mountain.
3. The blast was heard over 1400 kilometres away.
4. A thick cloud of volcanic ash circled the globe and reached North America the following summer.
5. The sun could not penetrate the cloud throughout the entire summer.

71 Recognizing direct and indirect objects

Direct objects and **indirect objects** occur in the predicate° of a sentence.

A **direct object** receives the action—it completes the meaning—of a transitive verb°. To find a direct object, make up a *whom?* or *what?* question about the verb.

An **indirect object** answers a *to whom? for whom? to what?* or *for what?* question about the verb. Chart 55 shows the relationships of direct and indirect objects in sentences.

◆ ESL NOTES: (1) In sentences with indirect objects that follow the word *to* or *for*, always put the direct object before the indirect object.

NO Will you please give **to John** this letter?

YES Will you please give this letter **to John**?

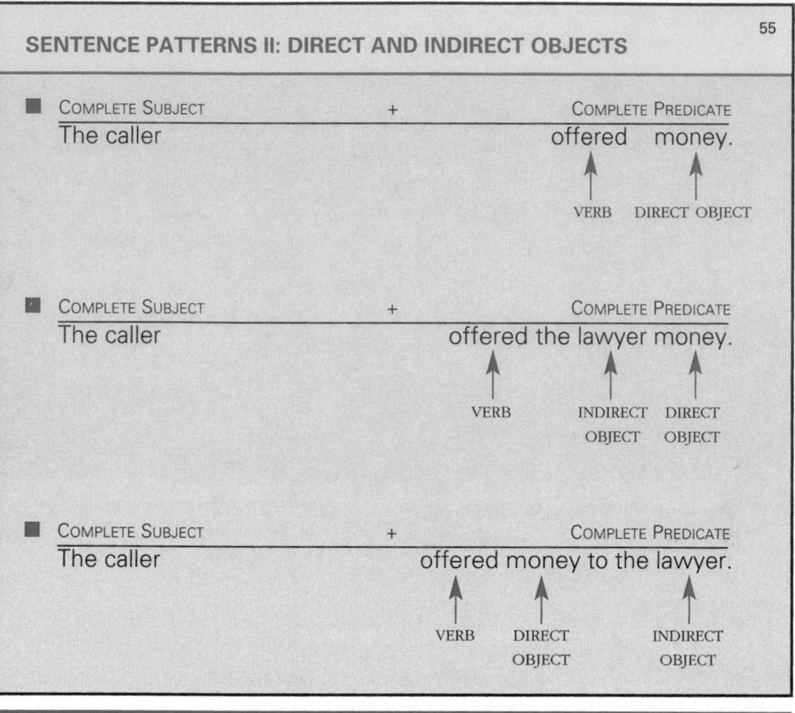

(2) When a pronoun is used as an indirect object, some verbs require *to* or *for* before the pronoun, and others do not.

NO Please explain me the rule. [*Explain* requires *to* before an indirect object.]

YES Please explain the rule to me.

NO Please give to me the letter.

YES Please give me the letter. [*Give* does not require *to* before an indirect object.]

Even when a verb does not require *to* before an indirect object, you may use *to* if you prefer. If you do, be sure to put the direct object before the indirect object.

YES Please give the letter to me. ◆

EXERCISE 7-6

Consulting section 7l, draw a single line under all direct objects and a double line under all indirect objects.

EXAMPLE Television-watching guarantees injury to people by the thousands every year, a British survey claims.

1. Gory scenes on television give some people such a severe fright that they faint.
2. Others are injured when they try ironing or perhaps painting while they give the television screen their full attention.
3. Last month, the survey reports, one person threw a glass at the screen and sprained his wrist.
4. Another person gave her knee a bad twist while dancing along with a music video.
5. Also, an enthusiastic sports fan jumped for joy and banged his head on a chandelier.

7m Recognizing complements, modifiers, and appositives

Recognizing complements

A **complement** occurs in the predicate° of a sentence. It renames or describes a subject° or an object°.

A **subject complement** is a noun°, pronoun°, or adjective° that follows a linking verb° (for an explanation of linking verbs, see 8a, especially Chart 60). Some systems of grammar use the term **predicate nominative** for a noun used as a subject complement and the term **predicate adjective** for an adjective used as a subject complement.

An **object complement** is a noun° or an adjective° that follows a direct object° (see section 7l) and either describes or renames it. Chart 56 shows the relationships of subject complements and object complements in sentences.

EXERCISE 7-7

Consulting section 7m-1, underline all complements and identify each as a subject complement (SUB) or an object complement (OB).

EXAMPLE Architect Frank Gehry's buildings have been called bizarre.

1. Frank Gehry's colleagues consider him brilliant for his work in designing remarkable structures.
2. In 1989, he was awarded the Pritzker Architecture Prize, which is said to be equivalent to winning a Nobel.

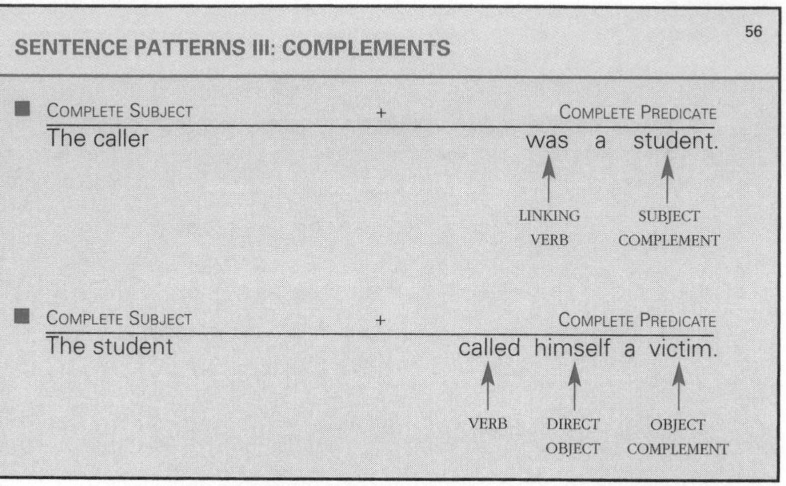

56
SENTENCE PATTERNS III: COMPLEMENTS
COMPLETE SUBJECT + COMPLETE PREDICATE
The caller
was a student.
LINKING VERB
SUBJECT COMPLEMENT
COMPLETE SUBJECT + COMPLETE PREDICATE
The student
called himself a victim.
VERB
DIRECT OBJECT
OBJECT COMPLEMENT

3. From a distance, his Guggenheim Museum in Bilbao, Spain, seems poised over the city like a huge, splashing silver whale.
4. Gehry was born Canadian, but he made his career in California.
5. For years he wondered why no Canadian individuals or institutions ever found him appropriate to design their projects.

2 Recognizing modifiers

A **modifier** is a word or group of words that functions as an adjective° or adverb°. Modifiers can appear in the subject° or the predicate° of a sentence.

The **large red** telephone rang. [Adjectives *large* and *red* modify the noun *telephone*.]

The lawyer answered **quickly.** [The adverb *quickly* modifies the verb *answered*.]

The person **on the telephone** was **extremely** upset. [The prepositional phrase° *on the telephone* modifies the noun *person*; the adverb *extremely* modifies the adjective *upset*.]

Therefore, the lawyer spoke **gently.** [The adverb° *therefore* modifies the independent clause° *the lawyer spoke gently*; the adverb *gently* modifies the verb *spoke*.]

Because the lawyer's voice was calm, the caller felt reassured. [The adverb clause° *because the lawyer's voice was calm* modifies the independent clause *the caller felt reassured*.]

3 Recognizing appositives

An **appositive** is a word or group of words that renames the noun° or pronoun° preceding it.

> The student's story, **a tale of broken promises,** was complicated. [*A tale of broken promises* is an appositive that renames the noun *story*.]
>
> The lawyer consulted an expert, **her law professor.** [*Her law professor* is an appositive that renames the noun *expert*.]
>
> The student, **Jamil Amin,** asked to speak to his lawyer. [*Jamil Amin* is an appositive that renames the noun *student*.]

✤ PUNCTUATION ALERT: When an appositive is not essential for identifying the noun or pronoun it renames (that is, when an appositive is nonrestrictive), use a comma or commas to set it off from whatever it renames and any words following it (see 24e). ✤

7n Recognizing phrases

A **phrase** is a group of related words that does not contain both a subject° and a predicate°. A phrase cannot stand alone as an independent unit. Phrases function as parts of speech. A **noun phrase** functions as a noun° in a sentence.

> The **modern population census** dates back to the **seventeenth century.**

A **verb phrase** functions as a verb° in a sentence.

> Two military censuses **are mentioned** in the Bible.
>
> The Romans **had been conducting** censuses every five years to establish tax liabilities.

A **prepositional phrase** always starts with a preposition° and functions as a modifier°.

> **After the collapse of Rome,** censuses were discontinued **until modern times.** [*After the collapse*, *of Rome*, and *until modern times* are all prepositional phrases.]
>
> William the Conqueror conducted a census **of landowners in newly conquered England in 1086.** [three prepositional phrases in a row beginning with *of, in, in*]

An **absolute phrase** usually contains a noun or pronoun and a participle°. It modifies the entire sentence to which it is attached.

Censuses being the fashion, Quebec and Nova Scotia took sixteen counts between 1665 and 1754.

Eighteenth-century Sweden and Denmark had complete records of their populations, **each adult and child having been accounted for.**

A **verbal phrase** is a word group that contains a verbal. Verbals are infinitives°, present participles°, and past participles°. **Infinitive phrases** function as nouns° or modifiers°. (An infinitive is the simple form° of a verb, usually preceded by the word *to;* see 8b.) **Participial phrases** function as adjectives°. Participial phrases can be formed from a verb's present participle (its *-ing* form) and from its past participle (the *-ed* form of a regular verb or the irregular form; see 8d).

In 1624, Virginia began **to count its citizens** in a census. [infinitive phrase = direct object]

Going from door to door, census takers interview millions of people. [participial phrase = adjective modifying *census takers*]

Amazed by some people's answers, the census takers always listen carefully. [participial phrase = adjective modifying *census takers*]

Gerund phrases function as nouns°. Telling the difference between a gerund phrase and a participial phrase using a present participle can be tricky because both use the *-ing* verb form. The key is to determine how the verbal phrase is functioning: a gerund phrase functions only as a noun°, and a participial phrase functions only as a modifier°.

Including each person in the census was important. [gerund phrase = noun used as the subject]

Including each person in the census, Abby spent many hours on the crowded city block. [participial phrase = modifier used as adjective describing *Abby*]

EXERCISE 7-8

Consulting section 7n, combine each set of sentences into a single sentence, converting one sentence in each set into a phrase. Choose from among noun phrases, verb phrases, prepositional phrases, participial phrases, and gerund phrases. You can omit, add, or change words. Most sets can be combined in several equally correct ways, but be sure to check that your combined sentence makes sense.

EXAMPLE North American pioneer literature is filled with many supposedly authentic accounts of wolves attacking humans. It does not, however, provide definite evidence that a wolf has ever killed a human in North America.

North American pioneer literature, filled with many supposedly authentic accounts of wolves attacking humans, does not, however, provide definite evidence that a wolf has ever killed a human in North America. [verbal (participial) phrase]

1. Wolves possess speed, stamina, and strength. They have rich vocal communication and body language and a highly developed sense of smell.
2. In Canada, wolves number about 60 000. They inhabit 90 percent of the country.
3. Many wolves live in Algonquin Park. This wilderness area is in the Canadian Shield. It was established as a protected area in 1893.
4. Some people have an image of Canada as a wilderness country. Less than 6 percent of Canada's land is actually legally protected as wilderness.
5. People often believe that travelling alone in wolf country is hazardous. They have read too much Jack London.
6. Wolves are wandering, secretive hunters. Their biology and behaviour are thus difficult to study.
7. Wolves do much of their hunting in winter. They prey on moose and deer. They prey on these animals so that they can survive in this time of stress.
8. Wolves exhibit many cooperative characteristics. They mate for life and raise their young together.
9. Wolves can be playful with their pups. They rank second only to humans in their social bonding and care-giving skills.
10. Hunting or trapping of wolves goes on in fully 65 percent of Canadian wilderness areas. This fact is rarely acknowledged.

7o Recognizing clauses

A **clause** is a group of words that contains a subject° and a predicate°. Clauses are divided into two categories: **independent clauses** (also known as **main clauses**) and **dependent clauses** (also known as **subordinate clauses**).

1 Recognizing independent clauses

An **independent clause** contains a subject° and a predicate°. It can stand alone as a sentence because it is an independent grammatical unit (see 7j). Chart 57 shows the basic pattern.

SENTENCE PATTERNS IV: INDEPENDENT CLAUSES		57
	THE SENTENCE **INDEPENDENT CLAUSE**	
■ COMPLETE SUBJECT	+	COMPLETE PREDICATE
The telephone		rang.

2 Recognizing dependent clauses

A **dependent clause** contains a subject° and a predicate° but cannot stand alone as a sentence. A dependent clause must be joined to an independent clause (see 7o-1).

Some dependent clauses start with subordinating conjunctions such as *although, because, when, until.* A subordinating conjunction expresses a relationship between the meaning in the dependent clause and the meaning in the independent clause (see Chart 53). Clauses that start with subordinating conjunctions function as adverbs° and so are called **adverb clauses** (or sometimes **subordinate clauses**).

Adverb clauses usually answer some question about the independent clause: *how? why? when? under what circumstances?* Adverb clauses modify verbs°, adjectives°, other adverbs, and entire independent clauses.

✤ PUNCTUATION ALERT: When an adverb clause comes before its independent clause, the clauses are usually separated by a comma (see 24b-1). ✤

> **If the vote passes,** the city will install sewers. [The adverb clause modifies the verb *install;* the clause explains "under what conditions."]
>
> They are drawing up plans **as quickly as they can.** [The adverb clause modifies the verb *drawing up;* it explains "how."]
>
> The homeowners feel happier **because they know the flooding will soon be better controlled.** [The adverb clause modifies the entire independent clause; it explains "why."]

Adjective clauses (also called *relative clauses*) start with relative pronouns°, the most common of which are *who, which,* and *that,* or relative adverbs° such as *when* or *where.* An adjective clause modifies the noun° or pronoun° that it follows.

The car **that Jack bought** is practical. [The adjective clause describes the noun *car; that* refers to *car.*]

The day **when I can buy my own car** is getting closer. [The adjective clause modifies the noun *day; when* refers to *day.*]

Chart 58 shows common sentence patterns for adverb and adjective clauses.

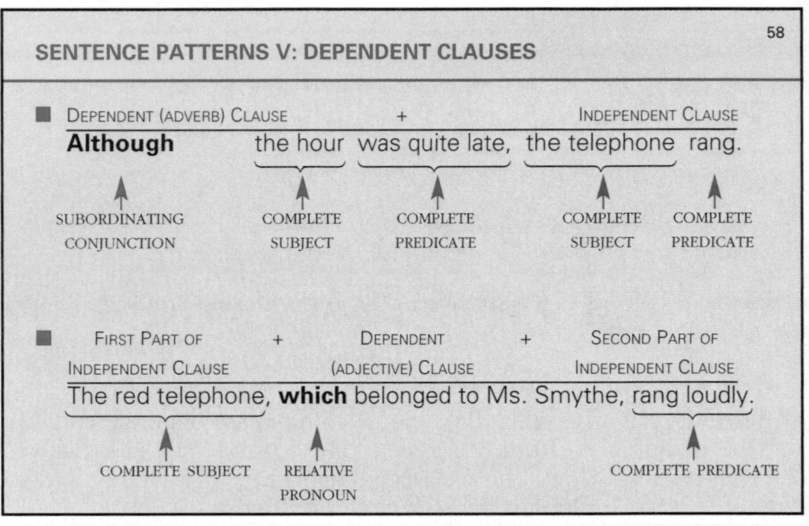

When you write adjective clauses, use *who, whom, whoever, whomever,* and *whose* when the antecedent° is a person or an animal with a name.

The di Pietros, **who collect cars,** are wealthy.

Their dog Bowser, **who is quite large,** is spoiled.

When you write adjective clauses, use *which* or *that* if the antecedent° is a thing or an animal. Either *which* or *that* begins restrictive° adjective clauses, and *which* begins nonrestrictive° ones.

✤ PUNCTUATION ALERT: When an adjective clause is nonrestrictive, use commas to separate it from the independent clause°. (A restrictive clause is essential to limit meaning; a nonrestrictive clause is nonessential; see 24e.)

The car **that I want to buy** has a cassette player.

The car **which I want to buy** has a cassette player. [The adjective clause is restrictive, and so either *that* or *which* may be used.]

My current car, **which I bought used,** needs major repairs. [The adjective clause is nonrestrictive, so it begins with *which* and is set off with commas.] ✤

Sometimes, *that* can be omitted from a sentence. For purposes of grammatical analysis, however, the omitted *that* is considered to be implied and therefore present.

The car [that] I buy will have to get good mileage.

✤ ALERT: Omitting the word *that* can make a sentence harder to understand. Be sure to use *that* when it makes your writing clearer.

NO I know Dale Smythe, who won a car in a raffle, is selling it.

YES I know **that** Dale Smythe, who won a car in a raffle, is selling it. ✤

EXERCISE 7-9

Consulting section 7o-2, underline the dependent clauses. Write ADJ at the end of adjective clauses and ADV at the end of adverb clauses.

EXAMPLE When cooks on São Miguel island in the Azores decide to prepare their favourite stew (ADV), they dig a hole on the shores of Lake Furnas.

1. Although São Miguel's Furnas volcano erupted thousands of years ago, the collapsed mountain top formed a lake bed that is still hot.
2. The ground around Lake Furnas acts as a natural oven because its temperature is more than 93°C.
3. To prepare the famous stew, which is called *cozido*, cooks assemble chicken, beef, sausage, and vegetables in a pan.
4. After the pan is tied in a cloth bag, it is buried in the hole.
5. The *cozido* simmers for about six hours, a cooking time that brings it to tasty perfection.

Noun clauses function as nouns. Noun clauses often begin with many of the same words as adjective clauses: *that, who, which,* and their derivatives, as well as *when, where, whether, why,* or *how*. Noun clauses, however, do not modify; they replace nouns.

Promises are not always dependable. [noun]

What politicians promise is not always dependable. [noun clause]

The electorate often cannot figure out the **truth.** [noun]

The electorate often cannot know **that the truth is being manipulated.** [noun clause]

Because they start with similar words, noun clauses and adjective clauses are sometimes confused with each other. A noun clause *is* a subject°, object°, or complement°. An adjective clause *modifies* a subject, object, or complement. The word starting an adjective clause has an antecedent° in the sentence. The word starting a noun clause does not.

> Politicians understand **whom they must please.** [Noun clause is an object; *whom* does not need an antecedent here.]
>
> Politicians **who make promises** sometimes fail to keep them. [Adjective clause modifies *politicians,* which is the antecedent of *who.*]

◆ ESL NOTE: Noun clauses in indirect questions are phrased as statements, not questions: *Kara asked why we needed the purple dye.* Avoid such sentences as *Kara asked why did* [or *do*] *we need the purple dye?* Tense, pronoun, and other changes may be necessary when a direct question is rephrased as an indirect question; see 15a-4. ◆

Elliptical clauses are grammatically incomplete for the deliberate purpose of concise prose (see Chapter 16). The term *elliptical* comes from the word *ellipsis,* meaning "omission." An elliptical clause delivers its meaning only if the context makes clear what the missing elements are. Common are *that* or *which* in adjective clauses, *that* in some noun clauses, subject and verb in adverb clauses, and the second half of comparisons.

> Engineering is one of the majors **[that] she considered.** [relative pronoun omitted from adjective clause]
>
> She decided **[that] she would prefer to major in management**. [relative pronoun omitted from noun clause]
>
> **After [he takes] a refresher course**, he will be eligible for a raise. [subject and verb omitted from adverb clause]
>
> Broiled fish tastes better **than boiled fish [tastes]**. [second half of the comparison omitted]

Sometimes an omission, although grammatically acceptable, interferes with the ability of a sentence to deliver its meaning, so omit nothing that helps to establish clarity.

EXERCISE 7-10

Consulting section 7o, use some of the subordinating conjunctions and relative pronouns from this list to combine each of the following pairs of sentences. Some pairs may be combined in a variety of ways. Create at least one elliptical construction. Subordinators may be used more than once, but try to use as many different ones as possible.

EXAMPLE Famine occurs. Insects or rodents destroy crops or stored food.

When insects or rodents destroy crops or stored food, famine occurs.

which	because	of which	since	if
while	as	how	that	although

1. Destruction of crops has been a problem for ages. The human race has an equally long history of trying to eliminate pests.
2. The earliest pesticides were not very effective. The earliest pesticides included sulphur, lead, mercury, and arsenic.
3. We now realize something. These original pesticides are poisonous.
4. They accumulate in the soil. They can limit or stop plant growth.
5. Some pests develop immunity to the chemicals. The pests are never completely destroyed.
6. The surviving pests reproduce quickly, passing on resistant genes. A new generation of resistant pests takes the place of those killed.
7. New pesticides are manufactured organic chemicals. The most famous is DDT, dichlorodiphenyltrichloroethane.
8. No one thought about something. DDT would contaminate and threaten the entire planet.
9. Some birds have trouble forming eggs. DDT accumulates in them.
10. In 1971 a special committee began reviewing pollutants. DDT was one.

7p Recognizing sentence types

Sentences can be **simple, compound, complex,** and **compound-complex.**

A **simple sentence** is composed of a single independent clause° with no dependent clauses°.

Charlie Chaplin was born in London on April 16, 1889.

A mime, he became famous for his character the Little Tramp.

A **compound sentence** is composed of two or more independent clauses. These clauses may be connected by a coordinating conjunction (*and, but, for, or, nor, yet,* or *so*) or by a semicolon alone or with a conjunctive adverb.

✤ PUNCTUATION ALERT: Use a comma before a coordinating conjunction connecting two independent clauses; see 24a.

His father died early, **and** his mother spent time in mental hospitals. ✤

Many people enjoy Chaplin films; others do not.

Many people enjoy Chaplin films; **however,** others do not.

A **complex sentence** is composed of one independent clause and one or more dependent clauses.

✤ PUNCTUATION ALERT: When a dependent clause comes before its independent clause, the clauses are usually separated by a comma (see 24b-1).

When times were bad, Chaplin lived in the streets. [dependent clause starting *When;* independent clause starting *Chaplin*]

When Chaplin was performing with a troupe that was touring the United States, he was hired by Mack Sennett, **who owned the Keystone Comedies.** [dependent clause starting *When;* dependent clause starting *that;* independent clause starting *he;* dependent clause starting *who*] ✤

A **compound-complex sentence** joins a compound sentence and a complex sentence. It contains two or more independent clauses and one or more dependent clauses.

Chaplin's comedies were immediately successful, **and** his salaries were huge **because of the enormous popularity of his tramp character, who was famous for his tiny mustache, baggy trousers, big shoes, and trick derby.** [independent clause starting *Chaplin's;* independent clause starting *his salaries;* dependent clause starting *because;* dependent clause starting *who*]

Once studios could no longer afford him, Chaplin co-founded United Artists, **and** then he was able to produce and distribute his own films. [dependent clause starting *Once;* independent clause starting *Chaplin;* independent clause starting *then he was able*]

EXERCISE 7-11

Consulting section 7p, identify each sentence as simple, compound, complex, or compound-complex.

EXAMPLE Medical doctors are constantly fighting a battle against harmful bacteria. (simple)

1. When bacteria develop resistance to an antibiotic drug, that drug can no longer fight those bacteria.
2. A simple experiment shows this resistance in action.
3. In the morning, a researcher puts a single bacterial cell into a glass dish that is known as a Petri dish.
4. Bacteria multiply rapidly, and this one cell will increase to 10 million bacterial cells by mid-afternoon.

5. In the Petri dish, these 10 million bacteria look like a heap of salt to the naked eye.
6. Then the researcher puts an antibiotic drug into the Petri dish, and the drug begins killing off the bacteria.
7. The heap of bacteria disappears quickly, but a few bacteria always survive contact with the antibiotic.
8. These surviving bacteria are immune to that antibiotic, and they are very dangerous because they pass on this immunity to all their descendants.
9. The bacteria once again multiply, and in a few hours, they build up another heap that looks just like the first one.
10. This time, however, the researcher finds that the antibiotic will not kill the growing pile of bacteria in the Petri dish.

8 Verbs

8a Understanding verbs

Verbs convey information about what is happening, what has happened, and what will happen. In English, a verb tells of an action, an occurrence, or a state of being.

Many people **overeat** on Thanksgiving. [action]

Mother's Day **fell** early this year. [occurrence]

New Year's Day **is** tomorrow. [state of being]

To understand more about the information verbs convey, see Chart 59. For types of verbs, see Chart 60.

INFORMATION VERBS CONVEY 59

PERSON	Who or what acts or experiences an action—**first person** (the one speaking), **second person** (the one being spoken to), or **third person** (the person or thing being spoken about).
NUMBER	How many subjects act or experience an action—**singular** (one) or **plural** (more than one).
TENSE	When an action occurs—in the **past, present,** or **future;** see 8g–8k.
MOOD	What attitude is expressed toward the action—**indicative, imperative,** or **subjunctive;** see 8l–8m.
VOICE	Whether the subject acts or is acted upon—**active voice** or **passive voice;** see 8n–8o.

TYPES OF VERBS	60
MAIN VERB	A verb expressing action, occurrence, or state of being. She **talked** to the group.
LINKING VERB	A main verb that conveys a state of being (*is*), relates to the senses (*taste*), or indicates a condition (*grow*) and that joins a subject to a word or words that rename or describe it. (More about linking verbs follows this chart.) She **was** happy about speaking.
AUXILIARY VERB	A verb that combines with a main verb to convey information about tense, mood, or voice. She **has** talked to them before. Modal auxiliary verbs° include *can, could, may, might, should, would, must,* and others that add shades of meaning such as ability or possibility to verbs (see 8e and Chapter 47ESL).
TRANSITIVE VERB	A verb that is followed by a direct object°—a noun° or pronoun° that completes the verb's message (see 8f). She **spoke** *French* to them.
INTRANSITIVE VERB	A verb that does not have a direct object completing its message (see 8f). She **talked** slowly.

Linking verbs are main verbs that indicate a state of being or a condition. They link a subject with a **subject complement**—a word (or words) that renames or describes the subject.

Some systems of grammar use the term **predicate nominative** for a subject complement that is a noun° or pronoun° renaming the subject and the term **predicate adjective** for a subject complement that is an adjective° describing the subject.

Some people consider a linking verb as an equal sign between a subject and its complement. Chart 61 presents an overview of linking verbs.

LINKING VERBS 61

- Linking verbs may be forms of the verb *to be* (*am, is, was, were*; see 8e for a complete list).

  Pierre Trudeau (SUBJECT) **was** (LINKING VERB) prime minister. (COMPLEMENT (PREDICATE NOMINATIVE: RENAMES SUBJECT))

- Linking verbs may deal with the senses (*look, smell, taste, sound,* and *feel*).

  Pierre Trudeau (SUBJECT) **sounded** (LINKING VERB) confident. (COMPLEMENT (PREDICATE ADJECTIVE: DESCRIBES SUBJECT))

- Certain other verbs that convey a sense of existing or becoming—*appear, seem, become, get, grow, turn, remain, stay,* and *prove,* for example—can be linking verbs.

  Pierre Trudeau (SUBJECT) **grew** (LINKING VERB) old. (COMPLEMENT (PREDICATE ADJECTIVE: DESCRIBES SUBJECT))

- To test whether a verb other than a form of *to be* is functioning as a linking verb, substitute *was* (for a singular subject) or *were* (for a plural subject) for the original verb. If the sentence makes sense, the original verb is functioning as a linking verb.

  NO Pierre Trudeau **grew** a beard → Pierre Trudeau **was** a beard. [*Grew* is not functioning as a linking verb.]

  YES Pierre Trudeau **grew** old → Pierre Trudeau **was** old. [*Grew* is functioning as a linking verb.]

VERB FORMS

8b Recognizing the forms of main verbs

A **main verb** names an action (*people **dance***), an occurrence (*Mother's Day **fell** early this year*), or a state of being (*New Year's Day **is** tomorrow*). Every main verb has five forms.

- The **simple form** conveys an action, occurrence, or state of being taking place in the present (*I **laugh***) or, with an auxiliary verb°, in the future (*I **will laugh***).

- The **past-tense form** is the basis for conveying an action, occurrence, or state completed in the past (*I **laughed***). Regular verbs° add *-ed* or *-d* to the simple form. Irregular verbs° vary; see Chart 62.
- The **past-participle form** in regular verbs uses the same form as the past tense. Irregular verbs vary; see Chart 62. To function as a verb, a past participle must combine with a subject° and one or more auxiliary verbs: ***I have laughed***. Otherwise, past participles function as adjectives°: ***crumbled*** *cookies*.
- The **present-participle form** adds *-ing* to the simple form (*laugh**ing***). To function as a verb, a present participle combines with a subject and one or more auxiliary verbs (*I **was laughing***). Otherwise, present participles function as adjectives (*my **laughing** friends*) or as nouns° (***laughing*** *is healthy*).
- The **infinitive** uses the simple form, usually but not always following *to* (*I started **to laugh***). The infinitive functions as a noun or an adjective, not a verb.

◆ ESL NOTE: When they function as parts of speech other than verbs, verb forms are called verbals° (see 7d). Present participles functioning as nouns are called gerunds°. For information about using gerunds and infinitives as objects after certain verbs, see Chapter 46ESL. ◆

8c Using the *-s* form of verbs

The *-s* form of a verb occurs in the third-person singular in the present tense°. The *-s* ending is added to a verb's simple form: *smell, smells*.

The bread **smells** delicious.

The verbs *be* and *have* are irregular verbs. For the third-person singular, present tense, *be* uses **is** and *have* uses **has.**

The cheesecake **is** popular.

The eclair **has** chocolate on top.

Even if you tend to drop the *-s* or *-es* ending when you speak, do not forget to use it when you write. Proofread carefully for the correct use of the *-s* form. (For an explanation of the *-s* form of verbs in subject–verb agreement, see 11b.)

EXERCISE 8-1

Consulting sections 8b and 8c, rewrite each sentence, changing the subject to the word given in parentheses. Change the form of the verb shown in italics to match this new subject. Keep all sentences in the present tense.

EXAMPLE The song of a bird *represents* different things to different listeners. (the songs of birds)

The songs of birds represent different things to different listeners.

1. The poet Keats *imagines* a songbird as a fellow poet creating beautiful art. (The poets Keats and Shelley)
2. To a biologist, however, singing birds *communicate* practical information. (a singing bird)
3. A male sparrow that *whistles* one melody to attract a mate *sings* a different tune to warn off other male sparrows. (Male sparrows)
4. Female redwing blackbirds usually *distinguish* a male redwing's song from a mockingbird's imitation, but a male redwing almost never *hears* the difference. (A female redwing blackbird) (male redwings)
5. Nevertheless, in experiments, female birds *are* sometimes fooled by a carved wooden male and a recorded mating song.

8d Using regular and irregular verbs

A **regular verb** forms its past tense and past participle by adding *-ed* or *-d* to the simple form. Most verbs in English are regular. Some English verbs are **irregular.** They form the past tense and past participle in various ways. For a list of the most common irregular verbs, see Chart 62.

✤ SPELLING ALERT: For information about when to change a *y* to an *i* when adding the *-ed* ending, see 22c. For information about when to double a final consonant before the *-ed* ending, see 22c. ✤

Speakers sometimes skip over the *-ed* sound, hitting the sound lightly or not at all. Even if you are not used to hearing or pronouncing this sound, do not forget to add it when you write. Proofread carefully for *-ed* endings.

NO The cake was **suppose** to be tasty.

YES The cake was **supposed** to be tasty.

About two hundred verbs in English are **irregular.** Unfortunately, a verb's simple form does not provide a clue about whether the verb is irregular or regular. Irregular verbs do not consistently add *-ed* or *-d* to form the past tense and past participle. Some irregular verbs change an internal vowel to make past tense and past participle: *sing, sang, sung*. Some change an internal vowel and add an ending other than *-ed* or *-d: grow, grew, grown*. Some use the simple form throughout: *cost, cost, cost*.

Although you can always look up the principal parts of any verb, memorizing any you do not know is much more efficient in the long run. The most frequently used irregular verbs are listed in Chart 62.

COMMON IRREGULAR VERBS 62

SIMPLE FORM	PAST TENSE	PAST PARTICIPLE
arise	arose	arisen
awake	awoke *or* awaked	awaked *or* awoken
be (is, am, are)	was, were	been
bear	bore	borne *or* born
beat	beat	beaten
become	became	become
begin	began	begun
bend	bent	bent
bet	bet	bet
bid (offer)	bid	bid
bid (command)	bade	bidden
bind	bound	bound
bite	bit	bitten *or* bit
blow	blew	blown
break	broke	broken
bring	brought	brought
build	built	built
burst	burst	burst
buy	bought	bought
cast	cast	cast
catch	caught	caught
choose	chose	chosen
cling	clung	clung
come	came	come

→

62

COMMON IRREGULAR VERBS *(continued)*

SIMPLE FORM	PAST TENSE	PAST PARTICIPLE
cost	cost	cost
creep	crept	crept
cut	cut	cut
deal	dealt	dealt
dig	dug	dug
dive	dived *or* dove	dived
do	did	done
draw	drew	drawn
drink	drank	drunk
drive	drove	driven
eat	ate	eaten
fall	fell	fallen
feed	fed	fed
feel	felt	felt
fight	fought	fought
find	found	found
flee	fled	fled
fling	flung	flung
fly	flew	flown
forbid	forbade *or* forbad	forbidden
forget	forgot	forgotten *or* forgot
forgive	forgave	forgiven
forsake	forsook	forsaken
freeze	froze	frozen
get	got	got *or* gotten
give	gave	given
go	went	gone
grow	grew	grown
hang (suspend)*	hung	hung
have	had	had

*When it means to execute by hanging, *hang* is a regular verb: "In wartime, armies routinely hanged deserters."

62

COMMON IRREGULAR VERBS *(continued)*

SIMPLE FORM	PAST TENSE	PAST PARTICIPLE
hear	heard	heard
hide	hid	hidden
hit	hit	hit
hurt	hurt	hurt
keep	kept	kept
know	knew	known
lay	laid	laid
lead	led	led
leave	left	left
lend	lent	lent
let	let	let
lie	lay	lain
light	lighted *or* lit	lighted *or* lit
lose	lost	lost
make	made	made
mean	meant	meant
pay	paid	paid
prove	proved	proved *or* proven
put	put	put
quit	quit	quit
read	read	read
rid	rid	rid
ride	rode	ridden
ring	rang	rung
rise	rose	risen
run	ran	run
say	said	said
see	saw	seen
seek	sought	sought
send	sent	sent
set	set	set
shake	shook	shaken
shine (glow)*	shone	shone
shoot	shot	shot

*When it means to polish, *shine* is a regular verb: "We shined our shoes."

→

COMMON IRREGULAR VERBS *(continued)* 62

SIMPLE FORM	PAST TENSE	PAST PARTICIPLE
show	showed	shown *or* showed
shrink	shrank	shrunk
sing	sang	sung
sink	sank *or* sunk	sunk
sit	sat	sat
slay	slew	slain
sleep	slept	slept
sling	slung	slung
speak	spoke	spoken
spend	spent	spent
spin	spun	spun
spring	sprang *or* sprung	sprung
stand	stood	stood
steal	stole	stolen
sting	stung	stung
stink	stank *or* stunk	stunk
stride	strode	stridden
strike	struck	struck
strive	strove	striven
swear	swore	sworn
sweep	swept	swept
swim	swam	swum
swing	swung	swung
take	took	taken
teach	taught	taught
tear	tore	torn
tell	told	told
think	thought	thought
throw	threw	thrown
understand	understood	understood
wake	woke *or* waked	waked *or* woken
wear	wore	worn
wring	wrung	wrung
write	wrote	written

EXERCISE 8-2

Consulting section 8d, in each blank write the correct past-tense form of the regular verb (simple form) in parentheses.

EXAMPLE Psychologists often (wonder) **wondered** about the saying that people's emotions are contagious.

(1) Researchers (report) _______ that people looking at pictures of smiling or angry faces unconsciously (imitate) _______ the same expressions. (2) The subjects who (display) _______ these facial expressions (experience) _______ the feelings that go with them. (3) People who (copy) _______ each other's gestures when talking also (transmit) _______ emotions to one another. (4) The researchers (describe) _______ the entire process in medical terms. According to the researchers, the people in the study ("catch") _______ an "emotional virus," which (seem) _______ to make it easier for them to get along.

EXERCISE 8-3

Consulting section 8d, in each blank write the correct past-tense form of the irregular verb (simple form) in parentheses. Use the list of irregular verbs in Chart 62.

EXAMPLE In the mid-1990s, the new information economy (lead) **led** big corporations to imitate smaller ones.

(1) Economic and social changes (teach) _______ older companies to copy new ones, as they (seek) _______ to swim with the dot-com sharks. (2) Those that (do) _______ not adapt soon (fall) _______ far behind. (3) Smart corporations (throw) _______ out their dress codes. (4) They (shrink) _______ their managerial staffs. (5) They (make) _______ themselves less hierarchical and more informal, as they (go) _______ after the most intelligent and creative graduates. (6) The visionaries who (understand) _______ these things (know) _______ from the start that the wired world (be) _______ the domain of teenagers and twenty-somethings. (7) Now, from Microsoft down to the smallest dot-com, the workers' skills counted, not the years they (spend) _______ in the organization. (8) In big high-tech firms, older managers (begin) _______ to learn from their younger subordinates. (9) The word (come) _______ down from the very top: Senior employees who once (wear) _______ business suits (put) _______ on blue jeans and (sling) _______ a knapsack over their shoulders. (10) Predictably, the managerial staff (take) _______ the directive to be informal more seriously than anyone else. (11) One visitor (say) _______ that she (know) _______ who the managers (be) _______ at IBM because they were the people wearing blue jeans!

8e Using auxiliary verbs

Auxiliary verbs, also called **helping verbs,** combine with main verbs° to make verb phrases°.

Auxiliary verbs deserve special attention because they occur very frequently in English. Also, the forms of the three most common auxiliaries—*be, do,* and *have*—vary more than usual; see Charts 63 and 64.

THE FORMS OF THE VERB *BE* 63

SIMPLE FORM	be	***-S* FORM**	is
PAST TENSE	was, were	**PRESENT PARTICIPLE**	being
PAST PARTICIPLE	been		

PERSON	PRESENT TENSE	PAST TENSE
I	am	was
you (singular)	are	were
he, she, it	is	was
we	are	were
you (plural)	are	were
they	are	were

✤ ALERT: The verb *be*, along with its various forms, can also function as a *linking verb* (see Chart 61). In joining a subject° to a subject complement°, it acts as a main verb° rather than an auxiliary verb. Academic writing requires standard forms and uses of the verb *be* as a main verb and as an auxiliary verb.

> The gym **is** [not *be*] a busy place. [*Gym* is the subject; *is* is the linking verb, which acts as a main verb; *busy place* is the subject complement.]
>
> The gym **is** [not *be*] filling with spectators. [*Gym* is the subject; *is* is the auxiliary verb and *filling* is the main verb; together *is filling* is a verb phrase.] ✤

64

THE FORMS OF THE VERBS *DO* AND *HAVE*

SIMPLE FORM	do	**SIMPLE FORM**	have
PAST TENSE	did	**PAST TENSE**	had
PAST PARTICIPLE	done	**PAST PARTICIPLE**	had
***-S* FORM**	does	***-S* FORM**	has
PRESENT PARTICIPLE	doing	**PRESENT PARTICIPLE**	having

◆ ESL NOTE: When an auxiliary verb is used with a main verb, the auxiliary may change form to agree with a third-person singular subject, but the main verb does not change.

> NO **Does** the library **closes** at 6:00?
>
> YES **Does** the library **close** at 6:00? ◆

The verbs *can, could, may, might, must, shall, should, will,* and *would* are **modal auxiliary verbs.** Modal auxiliaries work in concert with the simple form° of main verbs to communicate a meaning of ability, permission, obligation, advisability, necessity, or possibility.

> Exercise **can lengthen** lives. [possibility]
>
> The exercise **must occur** regularly. [necessity, obligation]
>
> People **should protect** their bodies. [advisability]
>
> **May** I **exercise?** [permission]
>
> She **can jog** for eight kilometres. [ability] ◆

◆ ESL NOTE: For more about modal auxiliary verbs and the meanings they communicate, see Chapter 47ESL. ◆

EXERCISE 8-4

Consulting section 8e, use auxiliary verbs from the list below to fill in the blanks. Use each auxiliary verb only once.

are ~~may~~ should can has do

EXAMPLE It **may** come as a surprise to discover that perfumes, hair sprays, and smelly soaps attract bears.

(1) Many people who camp in the wild know that the smell of food _______ often brought a hungry bear to a campsite. (2) Fewer people realize that curious bears _______ sometimes attracted to campsites that smell of perfume, hair spray, or soap. (3) Therefore, if you go camping in the woods or the mountains, you _______ avoid smelly cosmetics and put away all your food and garbage. (4) If you ever _______ meet a bear in the wild, stay calm and do not try to protect your food. (5) Talking to the animal in a quiet voice while backing off slowly is a better strategy than running away, because an excited bear _______ run as fast as a racehorse.

8f Using intransitive and transitive verbs

A verb is **intransitive** when an object° is not required to complete its meaning: *I **sing** loudly*. A verb is **transitive** when an object is necessary to complete its meaning: *I **need** a **guitar.*** Some verbs are transitive only (for example, *need, have, like, owe, remember*). Many verbs have both transitive and intransitive meanings. Other verbs are transitive only. Dictionaries usually label verbs as transitive (vt) or intransitive (vi). Chart 65 shows how transitive and intransitive verbs function.

The verbs *lie* and *lay* are particularly confusing. *Lie* is intransitive (it cannot be followed by an object). *Lay* is transitive (it must be followed by an object). Some of their forms, however, are similar. Get to know these forms so that you can use them with ease.

	LIE	LAY
SIMPLE FORM	lie	lay
PAST TENSE	lay	laid
PAST PARTICIPLE	lain	laid
***-S* FORM**	lies	lays
PRESENT PARTICIPLE	lying	laying

To *lie* means to recline, to place oneself down, or to remain; to *lay* means to place something down. Note from the examples that the word *lay* is both the past tense of *lie* and the present-tense simple form of *lay*.

65

COMPARISON OF INTRANSITIVE AND TRANSITIVE VERBS

INTRANSITIVE (OBJECT NOT NEEDED)

They **sat** together quietly. [*Together* and *quietly* are not direct objects°; they are modifiers°.]

The cat **sees** in the dark. [*In the dark* is not a direct object; it is a modifier.]

I can **hear** well. [*Well* is not a direct object; it is a modifier.]

TRANSITIVE (OBJECT NEEDED)

They **sent** a birthday card to me. [*a birthday card* = direct object]

The cat **sees** the dog. [*dog* = direct object]

I can **hear** you. [*you* = direct object]

INTRANSITIVE

PRESENT TENSE	The hikers **lie** down to rest.
PAST TENSE	The hikers **lay** down to rest.

TRANSITIVE

PRESENT TENSE	The hikers **lay** their backpacks on a rock. [*Backpacks* is an object.]
PAST TENSE	The hikers **laid** their backpacks on a rock. [*Backpacks* is an object.]

EXERCISE 8-5

Consulting section 8f, in each blank write the correct word from each pair in parentheses.

EXAMPLE Whenever I come home, I always check to see where my cat is (laying, lying) **lying**.

(1) Coming home from jogging one morning, I (laid, lay) ________ my keys on the counter and saw my cat, Andy, (laying, lying) ________ in a patch of sunlight on the living room floor. (2) When I (sat, set) ________ down beside him, he (raised, rose) ________ up on his toes, stretched, and then (laid, lay) ________ down a few feet away. (3) (Sitting, Setting) ________ there, I reached out to Andy, and my contrary cat jumped up onto the couch. As he landed, I heard a clicking noise. (4) I (raised, rose) ________ the bottom of the slipcover, and there (laid, lay) ________ my favourite earrings, the ones I thought I had lost last week. Deciding he had earned a special privilege, Andy curled up on a red silk pillow in the corner of the couch. (5) Since the earrings now (laid, lay) ________ safely in my pocket, I let him (lay, lie) ________ there undisturbed.

VERB TENSE

8g Understanding verb tense

Verbs use **tense** to express time. They do this by changing form. English has six verb tenses, divided into simple and perfect groups. The three **simple tenses** divide time into present, past, and future. The **present tense** describes what is happening, what is true at the moment, and what is consistently true: *Rick **wants** to speak Spanish fluently*. The **past tense** tells of an action completed or a condition ended: *Rick **wanted** to improve rapidly*. The **future tense** indicates action yet to be taken or a condition not yet experienced: *Rick **will want** to progress even further next year.*

The three **perfect tenses** also divide time into present, past, and future. They show more complex time relationships than do the simple tenses, as explained in 8i.

The three simple tenses and the three perfect tenses also have **progressive forms.** These forms show an ongoing or a continuing dimension to whatever the verb describes, as explained in 8j. Chart 66 summarizes verb tenses and progressive forms.

◆ ESL NOTE: Chart 66 shows that most verb tenses are formed by combining one or more auxiliary verbs° with the simple form°, the present participle°, or the past participle° of a main verb°. Auxiliary verbs are important in the formation of most tenses, so be sure not to omit them.

NO **I talking** to you.

YES **I am talking** to you. ◆

8h Using the simple present tense

The **simple present tense** uses the simple form of the verb (see 8b). It describes what happens regularly, what takes place in the present, and what is generally or consistently true. Also, it can express a future occurrence with verbs like *start, stop, begin, end, arrive*, and *depart.*

Calculus class **meets** every morning. [regularly occurring action]

Mastering calculus **takes** time. [general truth]

The course **ends** in eight weeks. [future event with end]

✤ VERB ALERT FOR WRITING ABOUT LITERATURE: Use the present tense to describe or discuss action in a work of literature, no matter how old the work; see 38b-2.

66

SUMMARY OF TENSES—INCLUDING PROGRESSIVE FORMS

	REGULAR VERB	IRREGULAR VERB	PROGRESSIVE FORM
		SIMPLE TENSES	
PRESENT	I talk	I eat	I am talking; I am eating
PAST	I talked	I ate	I was talking; I was eating
FUTURE	I will talk	I will eat	I will be talking; I will be eating
		PERFECT TENSES	
PRESENT PERFECT	I have talked	I have eaten	I have been talking; I have been eating
PAST PERFECT	I had talked	I had eaten	I had been talking; I had been eating
FUTURE PERFECT	I will have talked	I will have eaten	I will have been talking; I will have been eating

In Shakespeare's *Romeo and Juliet,* Juliet's father **wants** her to marry Paris, but Juliet **loves** Romeo. ✤

For action prior to or after the action you are describing or discussing, use the correct sequence of tenses as explained in 8k.

8i Forming and using the perfect tenses

The **perfect tenses** generally describe actions or occurrences completed, or to be completed, before a more recent point in time. They use the past participle (see 8b) together with auxiliary verbs° to form verb phrases°. For the present perfect, use *has* for third-person° singular subjects° and *have* for all other subjects, along with the past participle.

PRESENT PERFECT Our government **has offered** to help. [action completed but condition still in effect]

PRESENT PERFECT The drought **has created** terrible hardship. [condition completed and still prevailing]

PRESENT PERFECT We **have** always **believed** in freedom of speech. [condition true once and still true]

For the past perfect, use *had* with the past participle. For the future perfect, use *will have* with the past participle.

PAST PERFECT	As soon as the tornado **had passed,** the heavy rain started. [Both events occurred in the past; the earlier event, the tornado's passing, was completed before the later event, the rain's starting, took place, so the earlier event uses *had*.]
FUTURE PERFECT	Our chickens' egg production **will have reached** 500 per day by next year. [The event will be complete before a specified or predictable time.]

8j Forming and using progressive forms

Progressive forms show an ongoing action or condition. They also express habitual or recurring actions or conditions. They use the present participle° (the *-ing* form) of the verb together with the appropriate form of the verb *be* as an auxiliary verb°. (See Chart 66.)

For the present progressive, use the form of *be* that fits with the subject in person° and number°, plus the present participle: ***I am*** *thinking*, ***you are*** *thinking*, ***she is*** *thinking*. For the past progressive, use *was* or *were* to fit with the subject in person and number, plus the present participle: ***I was*** *thinking*, ***you were*** *thinking*, ***she was*** *thinking*. For the present perfect progressive, use *have been* or *has been* to fit with the subject. In all other progressive tenses, the auxiliary verbs do not change form to show person and number.

PRESENT PROGRESSIVE	The smog **is stinging** everyone's eyes. [event taking place now]
PAST PROGRESSIVE	Eye drops **were selling** well last week. [event ongoing in the past within stated limits]
FUTURE PROGRESSIVE	We **will be ordering** more eye drops than usual this month. [recurring event that will take place in the future]
PRESENT PERFECT PROGRESSIVE	Scientists **have been warning** us about air pollution for years. [recurring event that took place in the past and may still take place]
PAST PERFECT PROGRESSIVE	We **had been ordering** three cases of eye drops a month until the smog worsened. [recurring past event that has now ended]
FUTURE PERFECT PROGRESSIVE	In May, we **will have owned** this pharmacy for five years. [ongoing condition to be completed at a specific time in the future]

EXERCISE 8-6

Consulting sections 8g through 8j, select the verb in parentheses that best suits the meaning. If more than one answer is possible, be prepared to explain the differences in meaning between the choices.

EXAMPLE Before 1999, no head of state still holding office (has been charged, had been charged) with war crimes by an international court.

Before 1999, no head of state still holding office *had been charged* with war crimes by an international court.

1. In May 1999, Judge Louise Arbour (accused, was accusing) the then president of Yugoslavia of committing crimes against humanity.
2. The crimes with which he was charged (have occurred, occurred) during the conflicts following the breakup of Yugoslavia in the early 1990s.
3. Arbour (was acting, has been acting) in her role as chief prosecutor of the United Nations International Criminal Tribunal for the former Yugoslavia.
4. This court (is known, is being known) also as the Hague Tribunal, after the Dutch city where it (has been, is) based since its establishment.
5. Its mission (is, has been) to prosecute crimes committed by all sides in the former Yugoslavia.
6. The last time such a court (existed, was existing) was after World War II, when the Nuremberg and Tokyo war crimes tribunals (have judged, judged) the defeated side.
7. The Hague Tribunal (will succeed, will be succeeding) only by demonstrating that it always (is acting, acts) fairly toward all sides in every conflict.
8. Until her appointment to the Hague Tribunal in 1996, Arbour (was serving, has been serving) on the Ontario Court of Appeal. Before that, she (has been, had been) a leader of the Canadian Civil Liberties Association and a law professor at York University.
9. Arbour (is, was) a native of Quebec, however, and (is speaking, has spoken) English only since her early twenties.
10. In September 1999, Louise Arbour (has been appointed, was appointed) to the Supreme Court of Canada.

8k Using accurate tense sequence

Sequences of verb tenses help you deliver messages about actions, occurrences, or states that occur at different times. Using

accurate tense sequences—that is, showing time relationships correctly—is important for clear communication (see Chart 67).

✤ ALERT: When an independent-clause verb is in the future tense, do not use a future tense in the dependent clause.

NO The river **will flood** again next year unless we **will build** a better dam.

YES The river **will flood** again next year unless we **build** a better dam. [Dependent-clause verb *build* is in the present tense.]

YES The river **will flood** again next year unless we **have built** a better dam by then. [Dependent-clause verb *have built* is in the present perfect tense.] ✤

Tense sequences may include infinitives° or participles°. The **present infinitive** can name or describe an activity or occurrence coming either at the same time or after the time expressed in the main verb°.

I **hope to buy** a used car. [*To buy* comes at a future time. *Hope* is the main verb, and its action is now.]

I **hoped to buy** a used car. [*Hoped* is the main verb, and its action is over.]

I **had hoped to buy** a used car. [*Had hoped* is the main verb, and its action is over.]

SUMMARY OF SEQUENCE OF TENSES 67

WHEN THE INDEPENDENT-CLAUSE VERB IS IN THE SIMPLE PRESENT TENSE, FOR THE DEPENDENT-CLAUSE VERB:

- Use the present tense° to show same-time action.

  The director **says** that the movie **is** a tribute to Chaplin.

  I **avoid** shellfish because I **am** allergic to it.

- Use the past tense° to show earlier action.

  I **am** sure that I **deposited** the cheque.

- Use the present perfect tense° to show (1) a period of time extending from some point in the past to the present—often accompanied by *for* or *since*—or (2) an indefinite past time.

  They **say** that they **have lived** in Canada since 1979.

  I **believe** that **I have seen** that movie before.

SUMMARY OF SEQUENCE OF TENSES *(continued)* 67

- Use the future tense° for action to come.

  The book **is** open because I **will be reading** it later.

WHEN THE INDEPENDENT-CLAUSE VERB IS IN THE PAST TENSE, FOR THE DEPENDENT-CLAUSE VERB:

- Use the past perfect tense° to show earlier action.

  The sprinter **knew** that she **had broken** the record.

- Use the present tense to state a general truth.

  Christopher Columbus discovered that the world **is** round.

WHEN THE INDEPENDENT-CLAUSE VERB IS IN THE PRESENT PERFECT OR PAST PERFECT TENSE, FOR THE DEPENDENT-CLAUSE VERB:

- Use the past tense.

  The agar plate **has become** mouldy since I **poured** it last week.

  Sugar prices **had** already **declined** when artificial sweeteners first **appeared.**

WHEN THE INDEPENDENT-CLAUSE VERB IS IN THE FUTURE TENSE, FOR THE DEPENDENT-CLAUSE VERB:

- Use the present tense to show action happening at the same time.

  You **will be** rich if you **win** the prize.

- Use the past tense to show earlier action.

  You **will** surely **win** the prize if you **remembered** to mail the entry form.

- Use the present perfect tense to show future action earlier than the action of the independent-clause verb.

  The river **will flood** again next year unless we **have built** a better dam by then.

WHEN THE INDEPENDENT-CLAUSE VERB IS IN THE FUTURE PERFECT TENSE°, FOR THE DEPENDENT-CLAUSE VERB:

- Use either the present tense or the present perfect tense.

  Dr. Chang **will have delivered** 5000 babies by the time she **retires.**

  Dr. Chang **will have delivered** 5000 babies by the time she **has retired.**

The **present participle** (a verb's *-ing* form) can describe action happening at the same time.

> **Driving** his new car, the man **smiled.** [The driving and the smiling happened at the same time.]

To describe an action that occurs before the action in the main verb°, use the perfect infinitive° (*to have gone, to have smiled*); the past participle° (*gone, pleased*); or the present perfect participle° (*having gone, having smiled*).

> Candida **claimed to have written** fifty short stories in college. [First Candida wrote; then she claimed.]
>
> **Pleased** with the short story, Candida **mailed** it to several magazines. [First Candida was pleased; then she mailed.]
>
> **Having sold** one short story, Candida **invested** in a laptop. [First Candida sold a story; then she bought a laptop.]

EXERCISE 8-7

Consulting section 8k, select the verb form in parentheses that best suits the sequence of tenses. Be ready to explain your choices.

EXAMPLE When he (is, was) seven years old, Yo Yo Ma, possibly the world's greatest living cellist, (moves, moved) to the United States with his family.

When he *was* seven years old, Yo Yo Ma, possibly the world's greatest living cellist, *moved* to the United States with his family.

1. Yo Yo Ma, who (had been born, was born) in France to Chinese parents, (lived, lives) in Boston, Massachusetts, today and (toured, tours) as one of the world's greatest cellists.
2. Years from now, after Mr. Ma has given his last concert, music lovers still (treasure, will treasure) his many fine recordings.
3. Mr. Ma's older sister, Dr. Yeou-Cheng Ma, was nearly the person with the concert career. She had been training to become a concert violinist until her brother's musical genius (began, had begun) to be noticed.
4. Even though Dr. Ma eventually (becomes, became) a physician, she still (had been playing, plays) the violin.
5. The family interest in music (continues, was continuing), for Mr. Ma's children (take, had taken) piano lessons.
6. Although most people today (knew, know) Mr. Ma as a brilliant cellist, he (was making, has made) films as well.
7. One year, while he (had been travelling, was travelling) in the Kalahari Desert, he (films, filmed) dances of southern Africa's Bush people.

8. Mr. Ma first (becomes, became) interested in the Kalahari people when he (had studied, studied) anthropology twenty years ago at Harvard University.
9. When he shows visitors around Boston, Mr. Ma has been known to point out the Harvard University library where, he claims, he (fell asleep, was falling asleep) in the stacks when he (had been, was) a student.
10. Indicating another building, Mr. Ma admits that in one of its classrooms he almost (failed, had failed) German.

MOOD

8l Understanding mood

Mood refers to a verb's ability to convey "attitude" in a sentence. The most common mood in English is the **indicative mood.** It is used for statements about real things, or highly likely ones, and for questions about fact.

INDICATIVE The door to the tutoring centre opened.
She seemed to be looking for someone.
Do you want to see a tutor?

The **imperative mood** expresses commands and direct requests. When the subject is omitted in an imperative sentence—and it often is—the subject is implied to be either *you* or the indefinite pronoun *anybody, somebody,* or *everybody.*

✤ PUNCTUATION ALERT: A strong command is followed by an exclamation point; a mild command or a request is followed by a period (see 23a and 23e).

IMPERATIVE Please shut the door.
Watch out, that hinge is broken! ✤

The **subjunctive mood** can express speculations and other unreal conditions, conjectures, wishes, recommendations, indirect requests, and demands. Subjunctive verb forms are used much less often in English than they once were. Still, they are common for expressing unreal conditions or conjectures in *if* clauses° and in such phrases° as *far be it from me* and *come what may.*

SUBJUNCTIVE If **I were** you, I would ask for a tutor.

8m Using correct subjunctive forms

For the **present subjunctive,** use the simple form of the verb (see 8b) for all persons° and numbers°.

The prosecutor asks that **she testify** [not *testifies*] again.

It is important that **they be** [not *are*] allowed to testify.

For the **past subjunctive,** use the same form as the simple past tense: *I wish that **I had** a car.* The one exception is for the past subjunctive of *be:* use *were* for all persons and numbers.

I wish that **I were** [not *was*] leaving on vacation today.

They asked if **she were** [not *was*] leaving on vacation today.

1 Using the subjunctive in *if, as if, as though,* and *unless* clauses

In dependent clauses introduced by *if* and sometimes by *unless,* the subjunctive is often used to describe speculations or conditions contrary to fact.

If **it were** [not *was*] to rain, attendance at the race would be disappointing. [speculation]

In an *unless* clause, the subjunctive signals that what the clause says is highly unlikely.

Unless **rain were** [not *was*] to create floods, the race will be held this Sunday. [Floods are highly unlikely.]

The runner looked as if **he were** [not *was*] winded.

✤ ALERT: Not every clause introduced by *if, unless, as if,* or *as though* requires the subjunctive. Use the subjunctive only when the dependent clause describes a speculation or condition contrary to fact.

INDICATIVE	If **she is** going to leave late, **I will** drive her to the race. [Her leaving late is highly likely.]
SUBJUNCTIVE	If **she were** going to leave late, **I would** drive her to the race. [Her leaving late is speculative.] ✤

2 Using the subjunctive in *that* clauses for wishes, indirect requests, recommendations, and demands

When *that* clauses describe wishes, requests, demands, or recommendations, the subjunctive can convey the message.

I wish that this **race were** [not *was*] over. [wish about something happening now]

He wishes that **he had seen** [not *saw*] the race. [wish about something that is past]

The judges are demanding that the **doctor examine** [not *examines*] the runners. [demand for something that would happen in the future]

✤ ALERT: Modal auxiliary verbs like *would, could, might,* and *should* can convey speculations and conditions contrary to fact: *If the **runner were*** [not *was*] *faster, **we would** see a better race.* When the independent clause expresses a conditional statement with a modal auxiliary, be sure to use the appropriate subjunctive form, not another modal auxiliary, in the dependent clause.

NO	If **I would have** trained for the race, **I might have** won.
YES	If **I had** trained for the race, **I might have** won.✤

EXERCISE 8-8

Consulting sections 8l and 8m, fill in the blanks with the appropriate subjunctive form of the verb in parentheses.

EXAMPLE Imagining the possibility of brain transplants requires that we (to be) **be** open minded, as it (to be) **were**.

(1) If almost any organ other than the brain (to be) ________ the candidate for a swap, we would probably give our consent. (2) If the brain (to be) ________ to hold whatever impulses form our personalities, few people would want to risk a transplant. (3) Many popular movies have asked that we (to suspend) ________ disbelief and imagine the consequences should a personality actually (to be) ________ transferred to another body. (4) In real life, however, the complexities of a successful brain transplant require that not-yet-developed surgical techniques (to be) ________ used. (5) For example, it would be essential that during the actual transplant each one of the 500 trillion nerve connections within the brain (to continue) ________ to function as though the brain (to be) ________ lying undisturbed in a living human body.

VOICE

8n Understanding voice

Voice refers to verbs' ability to show whether a subject° acts or receives the action named by the verb. English has two voices: active and passive. In the **active voice,** the subject performs the action.

Most clams live in salt water. [The subject *clams* does the acting; clams *live.*]

They **burrow** into the sandy bottoms of shallow waters. [The subject *they* does the acting; they *burrow.*]

In the **passive voice,** the subject is acted upon, and the person or thing doing the acting often appears as the object° of the preposition° *by*. Verbs in the passive voice add forms of *be* and *have,* as well as *will,* as auxiliaries to the past participle° of the main verb°.

Clams **are considered** a delicacy by many people. [The subject *clams* is acted upon by *people,* the object of the preposition *by.*]

They **are** also **admired** by crabs and starfish. [The subject *they* is acted upon by *crabs and starfish,* the objects of the preposition *by.*]

When you write, your decisions about audience° and purpose° should influence the voice that you choose for a sentence. Misusing voice usually creates problems of writing style rather than problems of incorrect grammar. To make your writing clear, use voice consistently in sentences on the same topic. For ways to identify and correct confusing shifts in voice, see 15a-2.

8o Writing in the active voice, not the passive voice, except to convey special types of emphasis

Because the active voice emphasizes the doer of an action, active constructions are more direct and dramatic. Active constructions also use fewer words than passive constructions (see 16a-2). Most sentences in the passive voice can easily be converted to the active voice.

PASSIVE	African tribal masks are often imitated by Western sculptors.
ACTIVE	Western sculptors often imitate African tribal masks.

The passive voice, however, does have some uses. If you learn what they are, you can use the passive to advantage.

1 Using the passive voice when the doer of the action is unknown or unimportant

When no one knows who or what did something, the passive voice is useful.

The lock **was broken** sometime after four o'clock. [Who broke the lock is unknown.]

When the doer of an action is unimportant, writers often use the passive voice.

> In 1899, the year I was born, **a peace conference was held** at The Hague. [The doers of the action—holders of the conference—are unimportant to White's point.]
>
> —E. B. WHITE, "Unity"

2 Using the passive voice to focus attention on the action rather than on the doer of the action

The passive voice emphasizes the action, while the active voice focuses on the doer of the action. In a passage about important contributions to the history of science, you might want to emphasize a doer by using the active voice.

ACTIVE **Joseph Priestley discovered** oxygen in 1774.

But in a passage summarizing what is known about oxygen, you may want to make oxygen, rather than Priestley, the sentence subject. Doing so requires a passive-voice verb.

PASSIVE **Oxygen was discovered** in 1774 by Joseph Priestley.

PASSIVE The unsigned letter **was sent** before it **could be retrieved** from the mailroom. [Emphasis on events, not on the doers of the action.]

ACTIVE **The postal clerk sent** the unsigned letter before **I could retrieve** it from the mail room. [Emphasis is on the people rather than the actions.]

3 Using active or passive voice in the social and natural sciences

Many writers in scientific disciplines (see Chapter 39) overuse the passive voice. Yet style manuals for scientific disciplines agree with the advice given in this section: Prefer the active voice. "Verbs are vigorous, direct communicators," point out the editors of the *Publication Manual of the American Psychological Association* (the APA). "Use the active rather than the passive voice...."*

*American Psychological Association, *Publication Manual of the American Psychological Association,* 4th ed. (Washington: APA, 1994), 32.

EXERCISE 8-9

Consulting sections 8n and 8o, determine first whether each of these sentences is in the active or the passive voice. Second, rewrite the sentence in the other voice. Then decide which voice best suits the meaning, and be ready to explain your choice.

EXAMPLE In the West African country of Ghana, a few wood carvers are creating coffins that reflect their occupants' special interests. (*Active; change to passive.*)

In the West African country of Ghana, coffins that reflect their occupants' special interests *are being created* by a few wood carvers.

1. A coffin in the shape of a green onion was chosen by a farmer.
2. A hunter's family buried him in a wooden coffin shaped like a leopard.
3. A dead chief was carried through his fishing village by friends and relatives bearing his body in a large, pink, wooden replica of a fish.
4. Wood carver Paa Joe can turn out about ten coffins a year.
5. A few of these fantasy coffins have been displayed in museums, although most of them end up buried in the ground.

Focus on Revising

REVISING YOUR WRITING

If you have trouble with your verbs when you write, including unnecessary use of the passive voice, go back to your writing and locate the problems. Using this chapter as a resource, revise your writing to correct these kinds of problems: -*s* endings (see 8c); -*ed* endings (see 8d); auxiliary verbs (see 8e); transitive and intransitive verbs, including *lie* and *lay* (see 8f); tenses (see 8g–8j); tense sequences (see 8k); the subjunctive mood (see 8l–8m); active versus passive voice (see 8n–8o).

CASE STUDY: REVISING TO ELIMINATE VERB ERRORS

In these case studies, you can observe a student writer revising. Then, you have the chance to revise other student writing on your own.

Observation

A student wrote the following draft for a course called Popular Culture. The assignment called for choosing a popular cultural event in Canada and then writing about it. While this paragraph is well organized and offers good examples to support its topic, the draft's effectiveness is diminished by the presence of errors in verb forms and verb tense, and by the unnecessary use of the passive.

Read through the draft. The verb errors are highlighted and explained. Before you look at the student's revision, revise the material yourself. Then compare your revision with the student's.

The Calgary Stampede was an example of the persistence of a popular cultural event over a long period of time. The Stampede, actually a combination of exhibition and stampede, is held annually in much its present form since 1923, beginning with a parade and involving a rodeo and other events over the course of ten days.

simple past used; need present tense: 8h

present tense used; need present perfect progressive: 8j

→

The first exhibition, billed the "Greatest Outdoor Show on Earth," had taken place in 1886. It was accompany by the world-famous Stampede rodeo in 1912. The latter event was begun by Guy Weadick, an American trick roper who decided Calgary was a fit place for a big rodeo. Although initially a success, the event was not repeat until 1919 as a "Great Victory Stampede" marking the end of World War I. If Guy Weadick was to return, he would find that the Stampede still includes the traditional tests of cowboy versus animal. The chuckwagon races still are a popular spectator event.

With its many events, including bareback bronc riding, steer wrestling, and calf roping, the Stampede is one of the largest rodeos in the world with approximately $500 000 prize money. About 1 million visitors come to the Stampede every year, among them once the Queen and the Duke of Edinburgh, who attended many events and took part in square dancing. Just like Anne of Green Gables, the landscapes of Tom Thomson, or the RCMP Musical Ride, the Calgary Stampede had become a quintessential icon of Canadian identity.

past perfect used; need simple past: 8i

-ed missing: 8d

unneeded passive voice: 8n

-ed missing: 8d

subjunctive needed for *if* clause: 8m-1

past perfect used; need present perfect: 8i

Here is how the student revised the material to eliminate the verb errors. In revising from the unneeded passive voice to the active voice, the student had alternatives in word choice. Your revisions into the active voice might differ in wording from the student's.

The Calgary Stampede is an example of the persistence of a popular cultural event over a long period of time. The Stampede, actually a combination of exhibition and stampede, has been held annually in much its present form since 1923, beginning with a parade and involving a rodeo and other events over the course of ten days.

The first exhibition, billed the "Greatest Outdoor Show on Earth," took place in 1886. It was accompanied by the world-famous Stampede rodeo in 1912. Guy Weadick, an American trick roper, began the latter event when he decided Calgary was a fit place for a big rodeo. Although initially a success, the event was not repeated until 1919 as a "Great Victory Stampede" marking the end of World War I. If Guy Weadick were to return, he would find that the Stampede still includes the traditional tests of cowboy versus animal. The chuckwagon races still are a popular spectator event.

With its many events including bareback bronc riding, steer wrestling, and calf roping, the Stampede is one of the largest rodeos in the world with approximately $500 000 prize money. About 1 million visitors come to the Stampede every year, among them once the Queen and the Duke of Edinburgh, who attended many events and took part in square dancing. Just like Anne of Green Gables, the landscapes of Tom Thomson, or the RCMP Musical Ride, the Calgary Stampede has become a quintessential icon of Canadian identity.

Participation

A student wrote the following draft for a course called Introduction to Environmental Studies. The assignment was to write about an environmental problem created by developments in technology. The material is concise and logical, but the draft's effectiveness is diminished by errors in verb forms and verb tense and by the unnecessary use of the passive voice.

Read through the draft. Then revise it to eliminate the errors. Also, make any additional revisions you think would improve the content, organization, and style of the material.

Toronto's CN Tower had become the world's tallest free-standing bird killer. The tower, along with Toronto's many other skyscrapers, has prove a fascinating but fatal attraction for birds of all kinds. The birds dash to their deaths against the fully lit tower or flutter disoriented until falling exhausted to the earth.

➜

The CN Tower, when under construction, was worrying bird watchers because of its great size. The morning after the tower's completion, there were two hundred dead and injured birds laying around the tower's base. Officials at the tower agree to dim decorative lights and to shut off lights at eleven o'clock instead of two o'clock in the morning. Deaths have been reduced by this action, but the problem still is remaining.

More than forty buildings in Toronto are identified as notable bird killers. The Toronto-Dominion Centre, Commerce Court, and the Imperial Oil Building are well known for causing high mortality rates. Casualties were reduced, however, by dimming lights during spring and fall migrations.

Not only tall buildings kill birds. Many birds are falling prey to large picture windows on buildings in Toronto's Eglinton Park. Picture windows in office buildings like Hydro Place on University Avenue posed threats to birds that mistake reflections for reality. That building's mirrored surfaces threaten birds that migrated by day. Many robins and blue jays are also flying into the building's glass walls that reflect Queen's Park. Ironically, many birds fall as a result of human safety features; for instance, tall buildings frequently had lights to ward off low-flying airplanes.

As bird killers, man-made obstacles still rank small beside natural threats to migrators flying thousands of miles during the spring and fall. A sudden storm, for example, can wipe out thousands of birds. But, as more tall buildings rose in Toronto, the toll of birds is being looked at with grave concern. The hazard of tall buildings, combined with reduction in habitats and other human interference, may make the situation even worse.

9 Case of Nouns and Pronouns

9a Understanding case

Case refers to the different forms that nouns° and pronouns° take to deliver information. Case communicates how the noun or pronoun relates to other words in a sentence.

Nouns "show" case only in the possessive, by the use of the apostrophe: ***Nobu's*** *hat* (see Chapter 27). Pronouns have three cases: subjective case°, objective case, and possessive case°.

Personal pronouns, the most common type of pronouns, have **singular** and **plural** forms for all three cases. (See Chart 68.)

CASES OF PERSONAL PRONOUNS 68

	SUBJECTIVE		OBJECTIVE		POSSESSIVE	
PERSON	SING.	PLUR.	SING.	PLUR.	SING.	PLUR.
FIRST	I	we	me	us	my/mine	our/ours
SECOND	you	you	you	you	your/yours	your/yours
THIRD	he	they	him	them	his	their/theirs
	she		her		her/hers	
	it		it		its	

A pronoun in the **subjective case** functions as a subject°.

We were going to get married. [*We* is the subject.]

John and **I** wanted an inexpensive band to play at our wedding. [*I* is part of the compound subject *John and I*.]

He and **I** found an affordable one-person band. [*He* and *I* are compound subjects.]

A pronoun in the **objective case** functions as a direct object°, an indirect object°, or the object of a preposition°.

We saw **him** perform in a public park. [*Him* is the direct object.]

We showed **him** our budget. [*Him* is the indirect object.]

He wrote down what we wanted and shook hands with **us**. [*Us* is the object of the preposition *with*.]

A pronoun in the **possessive case,** or **possessive pronoun,** indicates possession or ownership. For a discussion of the possessive case before gerunds, see 9h.

The **musician's** contract was in the mail the next day. [*Musician's*, a noun in the possessive case, indicates ownership.]

The first signature on the contract was **mine**. [*Mine*, a pronoun in the possessive case, indicates ownership and refers to the noun *signature*.]

My fiancé signed **his** name next to **mine**. [*His* and *mine*, pronouns in the possessive case, indicate ownership and refer to the noun *name*.]

✤ PUNCTUATION ALERT: Do not use an apostrophe in a possessive pronoun (see 27b). ✤

The pronouns *who* and *whoever* also have forms for each case, as explained in 9e.

9b Using the same cases for pronouns in compound constructions as in simple constructions

A compound construction contains more than one subject° or object°.

He saw the eclipse of the sun. [single subject]

He and I saw the eclipse of the sun. [compound subject]

That eclipse astonished **us.** [single object]

That eclipse astonished **him and me.** [compound object]

A compound construction has no effect on the choice of pronoun case. A compound subject uses the subjective case, and a compound object uses the objective case. Sometimes, however, people make the mistake of switching cases for compounds. If you are unsure which case to use, try the "drop test." Temporarily drop all of the compound elements *except* the pronoun in question, as explained in Chart 69.

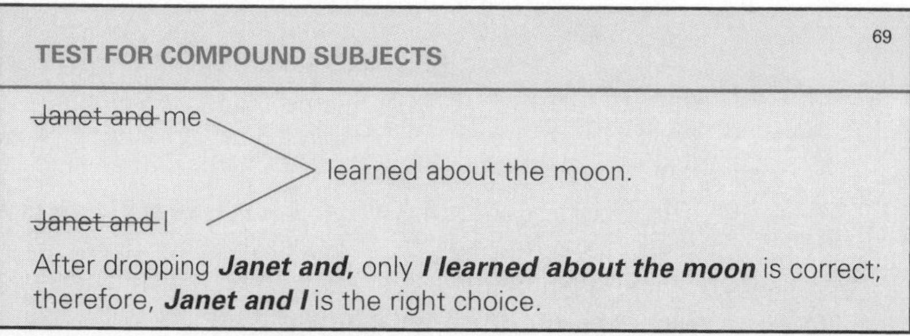

69
TEST FOR COMPOUND SUBJECTS
Janet and me
learned about the moon.
Janet and I
After dropping Janet and, only I learned about the moon is correct; therefore, Janet and I is the right choice.

This "drop test" also works when a compound subject contains only pronouns: ***She and I*** [not *Her and me, She and me*, or *Her and I*] *learned about the moon.*

The "drop test" in Chart 70 works for compound objects. Also, this test works when a compound object contains only pronouns: *The instructor told* ***her and me*** [not *she and I, her and I*, or *she and me*] *about the moon's phases.*

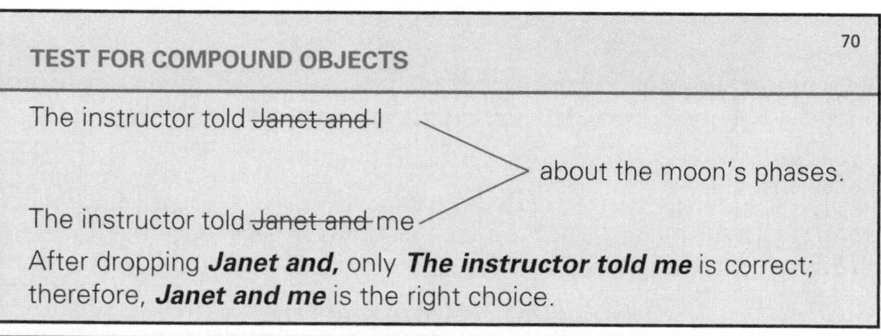

70
TEST FOR COMPOUND OBJECTS
The instructor told Janet and I
about the moon's phases.
The instructor told Janet and me
After dropping Janet and, only The instructor told me is correct; therefore, Janet and me is the right choice.

These principles apply to all sequences of pronouns (for example, the rules that govern *her and me* apply also to *me and her*). Also, when you write compound constructions that contain pronouns, do not mix pronouns in the subjective case with pronouns in the objective case: For example, do not use the combinations *him and I* (objective and subjective) or *she and me* (subjective and objective).

Even when pronouns in a prepositional phrase° are compound, they must be in the objective case.

NO The instructor gave an assignment **to Sam and I.** [*To* is a preposition; *I* is in the subjective case and cannot follow a preposition.]

YES The instructor gave an assignment **to Sam and me.** [*To* is a preposition; *me* is in the objective case, so it is correct.]

NO The instructor spoke **with he and I.** [*With* is a preposition; both *he* and *I* are in the subjective case and cannot follow a preposition.]

NO The instructor spoke **with him and I.** [*With* is a preposition; *him* is in the objective case, so it is correct. *I* is in the subjective case and cannot follow a preposition.]

YES The instructor spoke **with him and me.** [*With* is a preposition; *him* and *me* are both in the objective case, so this construction is correct.]

Between is a preposition that frequently leads people to pronoun error. A pronoun after *between,* like those after other prepositions, must always be in the objective case.

NO The instructor divided the work **between Sam and I.** [*Between* is a preposition; *I* is in the subjective case and cannot follow a preposition.]

YES The instructor divided the work **between Sam and me.** [*Between* is a preposition; *me* is in the objective case, so it is correct.]

When you are in doubt about pronoun case in prepositional phrases, use the "drop test" for compound objects in Chart 70.

EXERCISE 9-1

Consulting section 9b, select the correct pronoun from each pair in parentheses and write it in the blank.

EXAMPLE "Just between you and (I, me) **me**," said my workout partner, "I could stand to lose a few pounds."

I suggested that [1](us, we) _______ both consider going on a low-fat diet. Consulting a doctor first seemed like the right plan for Al and [2](I, me) _______, and so I made appointments for [3](he and I, him and me) _______ with Mary Standish, my own physician. [4](We, Us) _______ both were seen the next evening. After examining us separately, Dr. Standish told Al and [5](I, me) _______ that between [6](he and I, him and me) _______ [7](we, us) _______ should lose twelve kilograms. Dr. Standish gave a list of desirable and undesirable foods to [8](we, us) _______ two. Naturally, the desirable list seemed undesirable and the undesirable delicious, agreed Al and [9](I, me) _______. Al had a different problem. Because the diet was now the same goal for both [10](he and I, him and me) _______, he dreaded the competition between [11](we, us) _______ two. "Don't worry," I told Al. "It's not a matter of you versus [12](me, I) _______, because the big loser is the real winner!"

9c Matching noun and pronoun cases in appositives

The case rules hold when pronouns are renamed by appositives° and when they are appositive themselves. The pronouns and nouns must be in the same case. To check, temporarily drop the noun to see whether subjective or objective pronouns read correctly.

We ~~tennis players~~ / Us ~~tennis players~~ → practise hard.

After dropping *tennis players*, only *we* is correct; therefore, *We tennis players practise hard* is the right choice.

This test also works when the pronouns function as the appositive, coming after the noun: *The winners, **she** and **I*** [not *her* and *me*], *advanced to the finals.* Because they rename *winners,* which is the subject, the pronouns must be in the subjective case.

This test also works when the nouns and pronouns are in the objective case: *The coach tells **us*** [not *we*] *tennis players to practise hard. The crowd cheered the winners, **her** and **me*** [not *she* and *I*].

9d Avoiding the objective case after linking verbs

A **linking verb** connects a subject° to a word that renames it (see 8a). Linking verbs indicate a state of being (*am, is, are, was, were,* etc.), relate to the senses (*look, smell, taste, sound, feel*), or indicate a condition (*appear, seem, become, grow, turn, remain,* and *prove*).

Because a pronoun coming after any linking verb renames the subject, the pronoun must be in the subjective case.

The contest winner was **I.** [*I* renames *the contest winner,* the subject, so the subjective case is correct.]

The ones who will benefit are **they** and **I.** [*They* and *I* rename *the ones who will benefit,* the subject, so the subjective case is correct.]

Who is there? It is **I.** [*I* renames *it,* the subject, so the subjective case is correct.]

Although in speech and informal writing, the objective case is sometimes substituted in the constructions shown in the last two examples above, always use the subjective case in academic writing.

EXERCISE 9-2

Consulting sections 9a through 9d, select the correct pronoun of each pair in parentheses and write it in the blank.

EXAMPLE Dad, because your wedding anniversary is next week, (we, us) **we** sisters decided to get you and Mother a gift you will never forget!

(1) Anne and (me, I) _______ have given this a great deal of thought, especially in light of the conversations you and Mom have had with us about your stress at work. (2) You and Mom have always insisted that (we, us) _______ children save money for special occasions, and Anne asked (me, I) _______ if she and I could use our savings for a weekend getaway for you as the perfect anniversary gift. (3) It is (she and I, she and me) _______ who most worry about how (you and her, you and she) _______ are doing, so Anne and (I, me) _______ think this trip will be beneficial for everyone. (4) In fact, Dad, just last week, Mom mentioned to Anne how much she would love it if you and (she, her) _______ could spend some more time together. (5) It will really make Anne and (me, I) _______ feel great to do something nice for you and Mom. (6) So, Dad, you and Mom start packing for a weekend at your favourite bed and breakfast, a weekend you and (her, she) _______ desperately need and deserve. (7) Anne and (I, me) _______ will be waiting when you and Mom come home rested and free of stress.

9e Using *who*, *whoever*, *whom*, and *whomever*

The pronouns *who* and *whoever* are in the subjective case. The pronouns *whom* and *whomever* are in the objective case. (See Chart 71.) They do not change form.

CASES OF RELATIVE AND INTERROGATIVE PRONOUNS 71

SUBJECTIVE	OBJECTIVE	POSSESSIVE
who	whom	whose
whoever	whomever	—

1 Using *who, whoever, whom,* and *whomever* in dependent clauses

Pronouns such as *who, whoever, whom,* and *whomever* start many **dependent clauses°**. To determine what pronoun case is correct in a dependent clause, you need to find out whether the pronoun is functioning as a subject° or an object° in its own clause. Informal spoken English tends to blur distinctions between *who* and *whom,* so you may not want to rely entirely on what sounds right.

To check your use of *who* and *whom,* adapt the "drop test" introduced in section 9b. As Chart 72 shows, temporarily drop everything in the sentence up to the pronoun in question, and then make substitutions. Remember that *he, she, they, who,* and *whoever* are subjects, and *him, her, them, whom,* and *whomever* (the *-m* forms and *her*) are objects.

TEST FOR *WHO/WHOM* IN SUBJECTIVE CASE 72

EXAMPLE I wondered **(who, whom)** would vote.

DROP I wondered

TEST Temporarily substitute *he* and *him* (or *she* and *her*): "**He** would vote" or "**Him** would vote."

ANSWER **He.** Therefore, because *he* is subjective, *who,* which is also the subjective, is correct: "I wondered **who** would vote."

The subjective case is used even if words such as *I think* or *he says* come between the subject and verb. Ignore these expressions in determining the correct pronoun: *She is the candidate who [I think] will get my vote.* The "drop test" in Chart 73 also works for *whoever:*

73

TEST FOR *WHO/WHOM* IN OBJECTIVE CASE

EXAMPLE Often, a second pair of enumerators comes by to register residents (**who, whom**) the first enumeration missed.

DROP Often, a second pair of enumerators comes by to register residents.

TEST Try *they* and *them* in the resulting sentence: "The first enumeration missed **they**" or "The first enumeration missed **them.**"

ANSWER **Them.** Therefore, because *them* is objective, *whom*, which is also objective, is correct: "Often, a second pair of enumerators comes by to register residents **whom** the first enumeration missed."

Voter enumeration attempts to locate **whoever** is eligible to vote. ["***He*** (not *him*) is eligible to vote" proves that the subjective case of ***whoever*** is needed.]

The "drop test" in Chart 73 also works for *whomever:*

All voters can vote for **whomever** they wish. ["All voters can vote for ***him*** (not *he*)" proves that the objective case of ***whomever*** is needed.]

2 Using *who* and *whom* in questions

At the beginning of questions, use *who* if the question is about the subject° and *whom* if the question is about the object°. To determine case, recast the question into a statement using *he* or *him* (or *she* or *her*).

Who watched the space shuttle lift off? ["***He*** (not *Him*) watched the space shuttle lift off" uses the subjective case, so *Who* is correct.]

Ann admires **whom**? ["Ann admires ***him*** (not *he*)" uses the objective case, so *whom* is correct.]

Whom does Ann admire? ["Ann admires ***him*** (not *he*)" uses the objective case, so *whom* is correct.]

EXERCISE 9-3

Consulting section 9e, select the correct pronoun of each pair in parentheses and write it in the blank.

EXAMPLE (Whoever, Whomever) **Whoever** has been dragged out of bed by the need for a peanut butter sandwich can join millions of other people with similar cravings.

(1) There is nothing strange about a person (who, whom) experiences late-night cravings for favourite snacks. (2) (Whoever, Whomever) _______ has worried about such habits can take comfort from a researcher at an Ontario university. (3) Among the 1000 undergraduates (who, whom) _______ he studied, a large majority admitted that they craved specific foods. (4) Women (who, whom) _______ these cravings strike tend to desire chocolate and sweets; men usually crave high-protein foods like meat. (5) Few people (who, whom) _______ are told about this difference are very surprised. (6) What may be surprising is that researchers have found few pregnant women (who, whom) _______ crave dill pickles. (7) Nevertheless, (whoever, whomever) _______ researchers ask about cravings, the pickle myth is bound to come up.

9f Using the appropriate pronoun after *than* or *as*

A sentence of comparison may often imply rather than state a word or words following *than* or *as*. For example, the word *are* does not have to be expressed at the end of this sentence: *My two-month-old Saint Bernard is larger* ***than*** *most full-grown dogs [are].*

When a pronoun follows *than* or *as,* the pronoun case carries essential information about what is being said. For example, these two sentences convey two very different messages, simply because of the choice between the words *me* and *I* after *than.*

1. My sister loved that dog more **than me.**
2. My sister loved that dog more **than I.**

Because *me* is an objective-case pronoun, sentence 1 means "My sister loved that dog more *than she loved me.*" Because *I* is a subjective-case pronoun, sentence 2 means "My sister loved that dog more *than I loved it.*" To make sure that any sentence of comparison delivers its message clearly, either mentally fill in the words to check that you have chosen the correct pronoun case, or write in all the words after *than* or *as.*

9g Using pronouns with infinitives

An **infinitive** is the simple form° of a verb, usually, but not always, following *to: to laugh*. Objective-case pronouns serve as both subjects° and objects° of infinitives.

> Our tennis coach expects **me to serve.** [The word *me* is the subject of the infinitive *to serve,* and so it is in the objective case.]
>
> Our tennis coach expects **him to beat me.** [The word *him* is the subject of the infinitive *to beat,* and *me* is the object of the infinitive; so both are in the objective case.]

9h Using pronouns with *-ing* words

A **gerund** is a verb's *-ing* form functioning as a noun°. (***Brisk walking*** *is excellent exercise.*) When a noun or pronoun precedes a gerund, the possessive case is called for. (***Kim's brisk walking*** *built up his stamina.* ***His brisk walking*** *built up his stamina.*) In contrast, a present participle—a form that also ends in *-ing*—functions as a modifier. It does not take the possessive case. (*Kim,* ***walking briskly,*** *caught up to me.*)

The possessive case, therefore, communicates important information. Consider these two sentences, which convey two different messages, entirely as a result of the possessive:

1. The detective noticed the **man staggering.**
2. The detective noticed the **man's staggering.**

Sentence 1 means that the detective noticed the man; sentence 2 means that the detective noticed the staggering. The same distinction applies to pronouns:

1. The detective noticed **him staggering**.
2. The detective noticed **his staggering**.

In conversation, such a distinction is often ignored, but readers of academic writing expect that information will be precise. Consider the difference in the following two examples:

(AS SUBJECT) GERUND	The **premier's calling for a tax increase** surprised her supporters.
(AS MODIFIER) PARTICIPLE	The premier, **calling for a tax increase,** surprised her supporters.

EXERCISE 9-4

Consulting sections 9f, 9g, and 9h, select the correct pronoun of each pair in parentheses and write it in the blank.

EXAMPLE The two inventors of the Quebec dish known as poutine say that no one is more surprised than (they, them) **they** at its huge popularity.

Poutine was invented in 1957 when a truck driver named Eddy Lainesse pulled into Fernand Lachance's roadside diner and asked Lachance to serve [1](he, him) _______ an order of french fries with melted cheese curds. The diner was located in Quebec's dairy country, which accounts for [2](its, it) _______ having fresh cheese curds for sale. Although Lachance found [3](them, their) _______ appearing on a plate with french fries a strange idea, Lainesse was able to persuade [4](him, he) _______ to give it a try. The new dish was a triumph. Popular demand at Lachance's diner for an even more filling snack soon had [5](his, him) _______ adding gravy, the way it is served today throughout Quebec. Poutine's success—it is now on the menu of a nationwide hamburger chain and has been seen as far away as Florida—can be traced to [6](it, its) _______ being a classic fast food: heavy, high in cholesterol, and gooey. As far as Lainesse and Lachance are concerned, no one could be happier than [7](them, they) _______ that Quebec is now known for this humble dish, even if Quebeckers who value their province's reputation for fine dining are annoyed at [8](it, its) _______ winning such fame. What explains [9](their, them) _______ calling their invention "poutine," a slang word meaning a "mess"? When Lainesse first asked for the dish, Lachance was not nearly as sure as [10](him, he) _______ that it would work, and predicted, "If you do that, you'll get a real *poutine*."

9i Using *-self* pronouns

Reflexive pronouns° reflect back on the subject° or object°: *The detective disguised* ***himself.*** *He relied on* ***himself*** *to solve the mystery.*

Do not use reflexive pronouns to substitute for personal pronouns° as subjects or objects: *The detective and* ***I*** [not *myself*] *had a long talk. He wanted my partner and* ***me*** [not *myself*] *to help him.*

Intensive pronouns provide emphasis by making another word more intense in meaning: *The detective felt that his career* ***itself*** *was at stake.*

✤ USAGE ALERT: Avoid nonstandard forms of reflexive and intensive pronouns. Use *himself,* never *hisself;* use *themselves,* never *their self, theirselves, themself,* or *themselfs.* ✤

10 Pronoun Reference

A pronoun° always refers to a noun° or another pronoun, which is called the pronoun's **antecedent.** The term **pronoun reference** refers to this pronoun–antecedent relationship. For writing to communicate a clear message, each pronoun must relate directly to an antecedent.

Consider these sentences and lines in poetry in which each pronoun has a clear referent.

> **Facts** do not cease to exist just because **they** are ignored.
>
> —Aldous Huxley

> Whatever **women** do **they** must do twice as well as men to be thought half so good . . . luckily, it's not difficult.
>
> —Charlotte Whitton

> **I** knew a woman, lovely in **her** bones,
> When small birds sighed, **she** would sigh back at **them;**
>
> —Theodore Roethke, "I Knew a Woman"

74

HOW TO CORRECT FAULTY PRONOUN REFERENCE

- Make a pronoun refer clearly to a single nearby antecedent (see 10a).
- Place pronouns close to their antecedents (see 10b).
- Make a pronoun refer to a definite antecedent (see 10c).
- Do not overuse *it* (see 10d), and reserve *you* only for direct address° (see 10e).
- Use *who, which,* and *that* correctly (see 10f).

10a Making a pronoun refer clearly to a single antecedent

Be sure that each pronoun that you use refers clearly to a single, nearby antecedent. If you find that you need the same pronoun to refer to more than one antecedent, revise the passage by replacing some pronouns with nouns° so that all the remaining pronouns clearly refer to a single antecedent.

NO In 1911, **Roald Amundsen** reached the South Pole just thirty-five days before **Robert F. Scott** arrived. **He** [who? Amundsen or Scott?] had told people that **he** was going to sail for the Arctic but then **he** turned south for the Antarctic. On the journey home, **he** [who? Amundsen or Scott?] and **his** party froze to death just a few kilometres from safety.

YES In 1911, **Roald Amundsen** reached the South Pole just thirty-five days before **Robert F. Scott** arrived. **Amundsen** had told people that **he** was going to sail for the Arctic but then **he** turned south for the Antarctic. On the journey home, **Scott** and **his** party froze to death just a few kilometres from safety.

When you use more than one pronoun in a sentence, be sure that each has a clear antecedent.

Robert F. Scott used **horses** for **his** trip to the Pole, but **they** perished quickly because **they** were not suited for travel over ice and snow.

Said and *told,* when used with pronouns that refer to more than one person, are particularly likely to create confusion for readers. Quotation marks and slight rewording can clarify meaning.

NO Her mother told her she was going to visit the Yukon.

YES Her mother told her, "You are going to visit the Yukon."

YES Her mother told her, "I am going to visit the Yukon."

10b Placing pronouns close to their antecedents for clarity

If too much material comes between a pronoun and its antecedent, even though they may be logically related, unclear pronoun reference results. Readers lose track of the meaning of a passage if they have to trace back too far to find the antecedent of a pronoun.

NO **Alfred Wegener,** a highly trained German meteorologist and professor of geophysics and meteorology at the University of Graz in Austria, was the first person to suggest that all the continents on earth were originally part of one large land mass. According to this theory, the supercontinent broke up long ago and the fragments drifted apart. **He** named this supercontinent Pangaea. [Although *he* can refer only to *Wegener,* too much material intervenes between the pronoun and its antecedent.]

YES **Alfred Wegener,** a highly trained German meteorologist and professor of geophysics and meteorology at the University of Graz in Austria, was the first person to suggest that all the continents on earth were originally part of one large land mass. According to this theory, the supercontinent broke up long ago and the fragments drifted apart. **Wegener** named this supercontinent Pangaea.

Be cautious about beginning a new paragraph with a pronoun referring to a name in a prior paragraph. Repeating the name instead of using a pronoun for it can help your reader follow more easily the message that you want your material to deliver.

◆ ESL NOTE: Many languages omit a pronoun as a subject° because the verb° delivers the needed information. English, however, requires the use of the pronoun as a subject.

NO Political science is an important academic subject; **is** studied all over the world.

YES Political science is an important academic subject; **it is** studied all over the world. ◆

EXERCISE 10-1

Consulting sections 10a and 10b, revise so that each pronoun refers clearly to its antecedent. Either replace pronouns with nouns or restructure the material to clarify pronoun reference.

EXAMPLE Pierre Trudeau became prime minister of Canada the year after Expo 67, the world's fair that presented it as youthful, exciting, and self-confident. These were the qualities that he embodied, too.

Here is one acceptable revision: *Pierre Trudeau became prime minister of Canada the year after Expo 67, the world's fair that presented Canada as youthful, exciting, and self-confident. These were the qualities that Trudeau embodied, too.*

Trudeau exploded onto the scene as a sportscar-driving intellectual who—Canadians instantly recognized—was not like other politicians. He fascinated them, so they tolerated things from him that they would never accept from them: his dismissive shrugs, his arrogance, his insults. They were merely politicians; Trudeau was a star. Moreover, he combined them with an engaging playfulness. Most of them were delighted when he did an exaggerated pirouette behind the Queen's back at a royal reception.

Once, Trudeau had said "Just watch me." Journalists knew that Canada's "philosopher-king" was both spectacle and symbol to Canadians. They saw in him an idealized mirror of themselves. Significantly, when he retired, the critic Larry Zolf called the aging leader "our permanent Expo"—as though he were pure image.

Trudeau emerged again in the 1990s to launch his thunderbolts at Canada's new leaders, calling them "weaklings." When his son Michel died in 1998, he appeared frail and aged at his funeral. Then, when he died in late September 2000, Canadians acted much as Americans and British had at the deaths of Kennedy family members and of Princess Diana. They felt Trudeau's death as personally as they had felt their deaths. Mourning became a public spectacle.

Now they must ask themselves if this reaction represents their coming of age or is rather a sign of political immaturity. Perhaps when they say that he somehow touched them personally they are substituting emotions and wishes for political realism. Or perhaps Canadians have finally accepted their own identity and given it a necessary symbolic expression.

10c Making a pronoun refer to a definite antecedent

1 Not using a pronoun to refer to a noun's possessive form

A noun's possessive form cannot be the antecedent° to a pronoun, unless the pronoun is also in the possessive case.

NO The **geologist's** discovery brought **him** fame. [The pronoun *him* is not possessive and therefore cannot refer to the possessive *geologist's.*]

YES The **geologist** became famous because of **his** discovery.

YES The **geologist's** discovery was **his** alone.

2 Not using a pronoun to refer to an adjective

An adjective° cannot be an antecedent. A pronoun, therefore, cannot refer to an adjective.

NO Avery likes to study **geological** records. **That** will be her major. [*That* cannot refer to the adjective *geological*.]

YES Avery likes to study **geological** records. **Geology** will be her major.

3 Making *it, that, this,* and *which* refer to only one antecedent

When you use *it, that, this,* and *which,* check to see that the referent of these pronouns can be determined easily by your readers.

NO Comets usually fly by the earth at 160 000 km/h, whereas asteroids sometimes collide with the earth. **This** interests scientists. [Does *this* refer to the speed of the comets, comets flying by the earth, or asteroids colliding with the earth?]

YES Comets usually fly by the earth at 160 000 km/h, whereas asteroids sometimes collide with the earth. **This difference** interests scientists. [Adding a noun after *this* or *that* is an effective way to make your meaning clear.]

NO I told my friends that I was going to major in geology, **which** annoyed my parents. [What does *which* refer to?]

YES My parents were annoyed because I discussed my major with my friends.

YES My parents were annoyed because I chose to major in geology.

4 Using *they* and *it* precisely

The expression *they say* cannot take the place of stating precisely who is doing the saying. Your reader is entitled to more than a *they* to provide authority for a statement.

NO	**They** say that earthquakes are becoming more frequent.
YES	**Seismologists** say that earthquakes are becoming more frequent.

In speech, a common statement is *It said on the radio.* Because such expressions are inexact and wordy, they should be avoided in academic writing: ***The newspaper reports*** [not *It said in the newspaper*] *that minor earthquakes occur almost daily in California.*

5 Not using a pronoun in the first sentence of a work to refer to the work's title

When referring to a title, repeat or reword whatever part of the title you want to use.

TITLE Geophysics as a Major

FIRST SENTENCE

NO	This subject unites the sciences of physics, biology, and ancient life.
YES	Geophysics unites the sciences of physics, biology, and ancient life.

10d Not overusing *it*

It has three different uses in English.

1. *It* is a personal pronoun: *Kumar wants to visit the Canadian observatory where a supernova was discovered in 1987, but* ***it*** *is located in Chile.*
2. *It* is an expletive, a word that postpones the subject: ***It*** *is interesting to observe the stars.*
3. *It* is part of idiomatic expressions of weather, time, or distance: ***It*** *is sunny.* ***It*** *is midnight.* ***It*** *is not far to the hotel.*

All of these uses are acceptable, but combining them in the same sentence can create confusion.

NO	Because our car was overheating, **it** came as no surprise that **it** broke down just as **it** began to rain. [*It* is overused here even though all three uses—2, 1, and 3 above, respectively—are acceptable.]

YES **It** came as no surprise that our overheating car broke down just as the rain began to fall.

See section 16a-1 for advice about revising wordy sentences that use expletive structures, and see section 11f for advice about using singular verbs with *it* expletives.

◆ ESL NOTE: Be careful not to omit *it* from an expletive (also called a *subject filler*).

NO **Is** a lovely day.

YES **It is** a lovely day. ◆

10e Using *you* only for direct address

In academic writing, *you* is not a suitable substitute for specific words that refer to people, situations, and occurrences. Exact language is always preferable. Also, *you* used for other than direct address tends to lead to wordiness. This handbook uses *you* to address you directly as the reader; it never uses *you* to refer to people in general.

NO Uprisings in prison often occur when **you allow** overcrowded conditions to continue. [Are you, the reader of this handbook, allowing the conditions to continue?]

YES Uprisings in prison often occur when **the authorities allow** overcrowded conditions to occur.

NO In many provinces, **you have your prisons** with few rehabilitation programs. [Do you, the reader, have few programs? Also, are the prisons yours?]

YES In many provinces, **prisons have** few rehabilitation programs.

NO When **you** are crowned Queen of England, **you** automatically become Head of the Commonwealth. [Are you, the reader, planning to be crowned Queen of England?]

YES **Queen Elizabeth, when she was crowned** Queen of England, automatically **became** Head of the Commonwealth.

EXERCISE 10-2

Consulting sections 10a to 10e, rewrite each sentence so that all pronoun references are clear. If you consider a passage correct as written, circle its number.

EXAMPLE In a research study, it says that romantic love is a chemical process.

A research study claims that romantic love is a chemical process. [Revision avoids imprecise use of *it says.*]

1. Scientific evidence supports lovers' claims that they feel swept away.
2. When you fall in love, you are flooded with substances that your body manufactures.
3. It is surprising that love owes its "natural high" to phenylethylamine (PEA), a chemical cousin of the amphetamines, as well as to emotion.
4. As the body builds up a tolerance for PEA, it is necessary to produce more and more of it to create the euphoria of romantic love.
5. Although chocolate is high in PEA, gobbling it will not revive your wilting love affair.
6. Infatuation based on PEA lasts no longer than four years. This is when most divorces take place.
7. Chemicals called endorphins are good news for romantics. They promote long-term intimate attachments.
8. Endorphins' special effects on lovers allow them to exert a soothing, not an exciting, influence.
9. Oxytocin is called the "cuddle chemical" because it seems that it encourages mothers to nuzzle their babies.
10. Romantic love also owes a debt to this, for it promotes similar feelings in adult lovers.

10f Using *who*, *which*, and *that* correctly

Who refers to people or to animals with names or special talents.

John Polanyi, who was awarded the Nobel Prize in chemistry, speaks passionately in support of nuclear disarmament.

Lassie, who was known for her intelligence and courage, was actually played by a series of male collie dogs.

Which and *that* refer to animals, things, and sometimes anonymous or collective groups of people. Some writers use *which* both for restrictive clauses (clauses that add essential information to a sentence) and for nonrestrictive clauses (clauses that could be omitted from a sentence without changing the essential meaning). Other writers reserve *which* for nonrestrictive clauses and *that* for restrictive clauses. You can follow either practice as long as you are consistent in each piece of writing. For help in distinguishing between restrictive and nonrestrictive clauses, see 24e.

The zoos **that most delight children** display newborn animals as well as animals that can be touched safely. [*That* introduces information essential for understanding which zoos are being referred to.]

Zoos, **which delight most children,** have been attracting fewer visitors each year. [*Which* introduces information that could be dropped from the sentence without changing the essential message.]

Who can be used for restrictive and nonrestrictive clauses alike.

✣ COMMA ALERT: Set off nonrestrictive clauses with commas. Do not set off restrictive clauses with commas (see 24e). ✣

EXERCISE 10-3

Consulting section 10f, fill in the blanks with *who, which,* or *that.*

EXAMPLE Psychologists have found that most people **who** believe that the moon influences behaviour actually believe that others, not they themselves, are affected by the moon.

1. Does the moon really affect human behaviour? Ancient people believed the power _______ came from the moon was divine.
2. The word *lunatic,* _______ is derived from the Latin *luna,* suggests that people _______ are exposed to the moon become mad.
3. The moon, _______ has been credited by some researchers with influencing the stock market, is also thought by some experts to affect agricultural yields.
4. Some nurses _______ work in hospital delivery rooms claim it is the moon _______ stimulates labour pains to begin.
5. The moon may also affect certain groups of people, _______ include sleepwalkers and those _______ suffer from migraine headaches.

11 Agreement

In everyday speech, *agreement* indicates that people hold the same ideas. Grammatical agreement also is based on sameness. Applying the rules governing grammatical agreement can be tricky, so almost everyone consults a handbook now and then to check one or another rule.

This chapter discusses agreement between subjects and verbs (see 11a through 11l) and between pronouns and antecedents (see 11m through 11r).

SUBJECT–VERB AGREEMENT

11a Understanding subject–verb agreement

Subject–verb agreement means that a subject° and its verb° match in number (singular or plural) and in person (first, second, or third person). The major concepts in grammatical agreement are explained in Chart 75.

The **firefly glows** with luminescent light. [*firefly* = singular subject in the third person; *glows* = singular verb in the third person]

Fireflies glow with luminescent light. [*fireflies* = plural subject in the third person; *glow* = plural verb in the third person]

11b Using the final *-s* or *-es* either for plural subjects or for singular verbs

Subject–verb agreement often involves one letter: *s*. The basic pattern for agreement is shown in Chart 76. Keep in mind that the *-s* added to subjects and the *-s* added to verbs serve very different functions.

75

MAJOR CONCEPTS IN GRAMMATICAL AGREEMENT

- **Number,** as a concept in grammar, refers to *singular* and *plural.*
- The **first person** is the speaker or writer. *I* (singular) and *we* (plural) are the only subjects that occur in the first person.

SINGULAR	**I** see a field of fireflies.
PLURAL	**We** see a field of fireflies.

- The **second person** is the person spoken or written to. *You* (for both singular and plural) is the only subject that occurs in the second person.

SINGULAR	**You** see a shower of sparks.
PLURAL	**You** see a shower of sparks.

- The **third person** is the person or thing being spoken or written of. Most rules for subject–verb agreement involve the third person.

SINGULAR	The **scientist sees** a cloud of cosmic dust.
PLURAL	The **scientists see** a cloud of cosmic dust.

76

PATTERN FOR BASIC SUBJECT–VERB AGREEMENT

The **student works** long hours.

SINGULAR SUBJECT — SINGULAR VERB

The **students work** long hours.

PLURAL SUBJECT — PLURAL VERB

Most **plural subjects** are formed by adding an *-s* or *-es: lip* becomes *lip**s***; *princess* becomes *princess**es.*** Exceptions include most pronouns (*they, it*) and a few nouns that for singular and plural either do not change (*deer, deer*) or change internally (*mouse, mice; child, children*).

Singular verbs in the present tense of the third person are formed by adding *-s* or *-es* to the simple form of the verb: *laugh, laugh**s***; *kiss, kiss**es**.* Even the exceptions—the verbs *be* (*is*) and *have* (*has*)—end in *s*.

The **student disagrees** that **students watch** too much television.

Most part-time **jobs involve** ten or twenty hours a week.

Studying requires all remaining time.

Here is a memory device to help you visualize how, in most cases, the *s* works in agreement. The *-s* (or *-es*) can take only one path at a time, going either to the top or to the bottom.

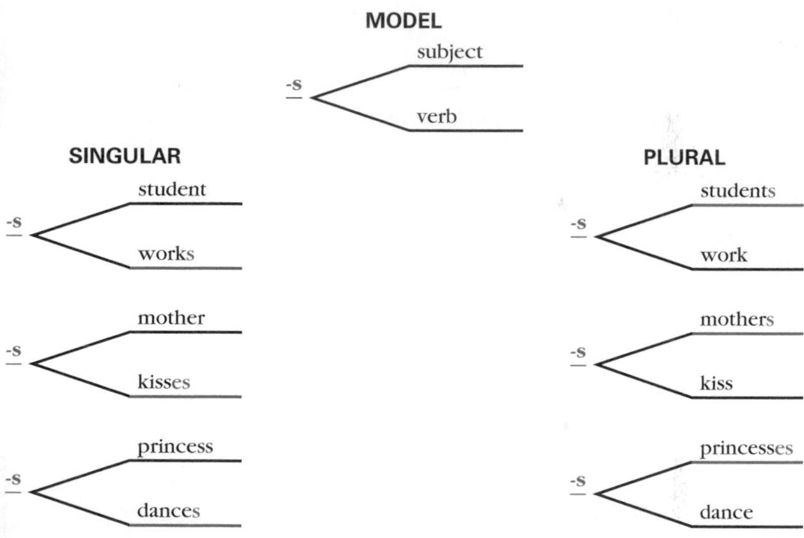

The principle of the memory device holds, even for the exceptions discussed earlier in this section: ***It*** (singular pronoun) ***is*** *late; the **mice*** (plural with internal change) ***are*** *sleeping*.

✤ ESL ALERT: Do not add *-s* to a main verb used with an auxiliary verb (a helping verb such as *be, do, can, might, must, would;* see 8e): *The coach **can walk*** [not *can walks*] *to campus.* ✤

EXERCISE 11-1

Consulting sections 11a and 11b, use the subject and verb in each set to write two complete sentences—one with the subject as a singular and one with the subject as a plural. Keep all verbs in the present tense.

1. dog bark	2. theory state	3. match might light	4. jet depart
5. man smile	6. it change	7. planet rotate	8. parade celebrate

11c For agreement, ignoring words between a subject and verb

Words that separate the subject° from the verb° do not affect what the verb should agree with. The pattern is shown in Chart 77. Such intervening material often appears as a prepositional phrase°. Eliminate all prepositional phrases from consideration when you look for the subject of a clause.

NO **Winners** of the regional contest **goes** to the national finals. [*Winners* is the subject. The verb must agree with it; *of the regional contest* is a prepositional phrase.]

YES **Winners** of the regional contest **go** to the national finals.

Be especially careful with a construction that starts *one of the*. This construction takes a singular verb, to agree with the word *one*. Do not be distracted by the plural noun that comes after *of the*.

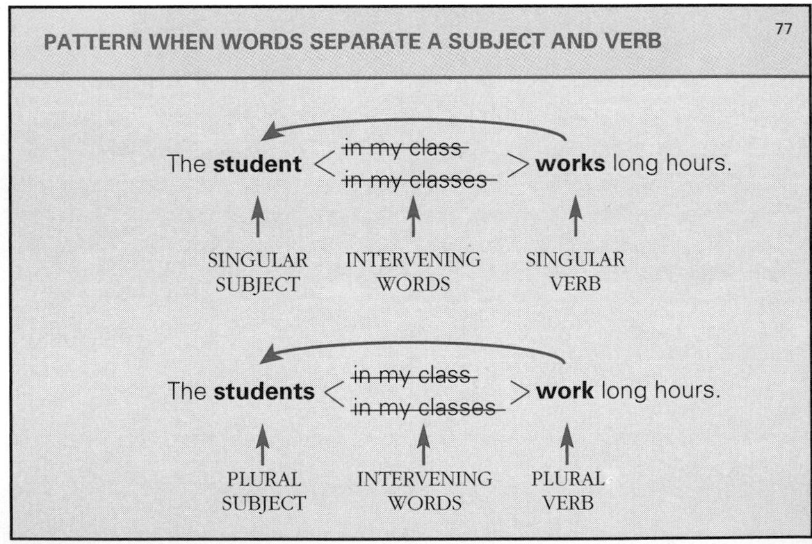

PATTERN WHEN WORDS SEPARATE A SUBJECT AND VERB
77
The student
in my class
in my classes
works long hours.
SINGULAR SUBJECT
INTERVENING WORDS
SINGULAR VERB
The students
in my class
in my classes
work long hours.
PLURAL SUBJECT
INTERVENING WORDS
PLURAL VERB

NO **One** of the problems **are** broken equipment.

YES **One** of the problems **is** broken equipment.

Similarly, to locate the subject of a sentence, eliminate any phrases that start with *including, together with, along with, accompanied by, in addition to, except,* and *as well as.* Be sure that the verb agrees with the subject, not with the intervening words.

NO **The moon,** *as well as* Venus, **are** visible in the night sky. [*The moon* is the subject. The verb must agree with it. Ignore *as well as Venus.*]

YES **The moon,** *as well as* Venus, **is** visible in the night sky.

11d Using verbs with subjects connected with *and*

When subjects are connected with *and,* they comprise a compound subject° (see 7k) and require a plural verb. Chart 78 shows this pattern.

The Cascade Diner *and* the Wayside Diner *have* [not *has*] fried halibut today.

An exception occurs when *and* joins parts that combine to form a single thing or person.

My ***best friend and neighbour*** **makes** [not *make*] excellent chili. [The best friend is the same person as the neighbour. If two different people were involved, *makes* would become *make.*]

Macaroni and cheese **contains** [not *contain*] pasta, protein, and many calories.

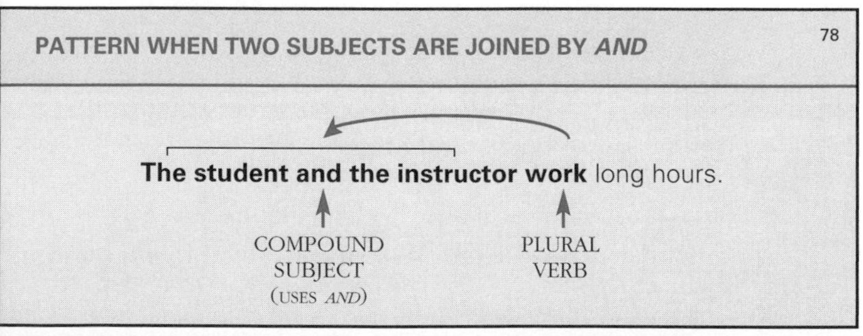

PATTERN WHEN TWO SUBJECTS ARE JOINED BY *AND*
78
The student and the instructor work long hours.
COMPOUND SUBJECT (USES *AND*)
PLURAL VERB

each, every

The words *each* and *every* remain singular even when they modify° a compound subject. Therefore, when *each* or *every* precedes a compound subject, the verb that follows it must be singular, not plural. (For information about verb agreement for *each* or *every* used alone, not as a modifier, see 11g.)

> ***Each* human hand and foot makes** [not *make*] a distinctive print.
>
> To identify lawbreakers, ***every* police chief, detective, and RCMP officer depends** [not *depend*] on such prints.

✤ USAGE ALERT: Use either *each* or *every*, not both together, to single out something: ***Each*** [not *each and every*] *robber has been caught.*✤

11e Making the verb agree with the nearest subject

When subjects are joined with *or, nor, either ... or, neither ... nor,* or *not only ... but (also),* make the verb agree with the subject closest to it. For subject–verb agreement, ignore everything before the final subject. Chart 79 shows this pattern with *or.*

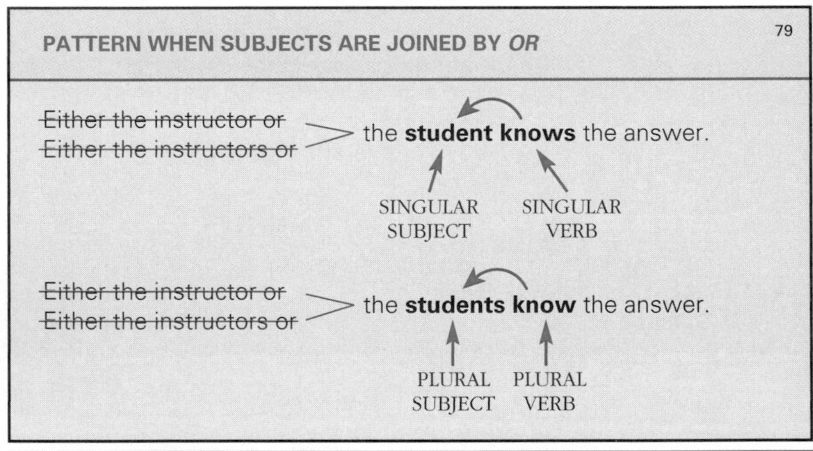

> ~~Not only the spider but also~~ **all other arachnids have** four pairs of legs.
>
> ~~Neither spiders nor~~ **flies tempt** my appetite.
>
> ~~Six clam fritters, four blue crabs, or~~ **one steamed lobster tempts** my appetite. [For less awkward wording, rearrange the items to place the plural subject next to the verb: *One steamed lobster, four blue crabs, or six clam fritters tempt my appetite.*]

11f Using verbs in inverted word order

In English, the subject of a sentence normally precedes its verb: *Astronomy is interesting*. Inverted word order means a change in the usual order. Most questions use inverted word order. Be sure to look *after* the verb, not before it, to check that the subject and verb agree.

Is astronomy interesting?

What **are** the **requirements** for the major?

Do Ravi and Mary study astronomy?

If you occasionally choose to write a sentence in inverted word order to convey emphasis (see 19f), be sure to locate the subject and then make the verb agree with it.

Into deep space **shoot** probing **satellites.** [The plural verb *shoot* agrees with the inverted plural subject *satellites*.]

On the television screen **appears** an **image** of Saturn. [The singular verb *appears* agrees with the inverted singular subject *image*.]

Expletive constructions use inverted word order. With the use of *there* or *it,* they postpone the subject. Check ahead in such sentences to identify the subject, and then make sure that the verb agrees with the subject. For advice on being concise by eliminating some expletives, see 16a-1.

There are nine **planets** in our solar system. [The verb *are* agrees with the subject *planets*.]

There is probably no **life** on eight of them. [The verb *is* agrees with the subject *life*.]

It plus a singular form of the verb *be* can be an expletive construction as well: ***It is*** *astronomers who want new telescopes.*

EXERCISE 11-2

Supply the correct present-tense form of the verb in parentheses. For help, consult 11b through 11f.

EXAMPLE Detectives and teachers (to know) **know** that experienced liars can fool almost anybody, but a new computer can discover who is telling the truth.

1. Police officers and teachers often (to wish) _______ they could "read" people's facial expressions.

2. Trained police officers or a smart teacher (to know) _______ that facial tics and nervous mannerisms (to show) _______ that someone is lying.
3. However, a truly gifted liar, along with well-coached eyewitnesses, (to reveal) _______ very little through expressions or behaviour.
4. There (to be) _______ forty-six muscle movements in the human face that create all facial expressions.
5. Neuroscientist Terrence Seinowski, accompanied by a team of researchers, (to be) _______ developing a computer program to recognize even slight facial movements made by the most expert liars.

11g Using verbs with indefinite pronouns

Many **indefinite pronouns** refer to unknown persons, things, quantities, or ideas—thus the label "indefinite." In context in a sentence, even indefinite pronouns that do not have a specific antecedent° can take on clear meaning. Most indefinite pronouns are singular and require a singular verb for agreement. Two indefinite pronouns, *both* and *many*, are always plural and require a plural verb. A few indefinite pronouns can be singular or plural. See Chart 80 for a list of indefinite pronouns and their numbers. (For advice on avoiding sexist language with indefinite pronouns, see 11q and 21b.)

SINGULAR INDEFINITE PRONOUNS

Everything about that intersection **is** dangerous.

But whenever **anyone says** anything, **nothing is** done.

Each of us **has** [not *have*] to shovel snow; **each is** [not *are*] expected to help.

Every snowstorm of the past two years **has** [not *have*] been severe; **every** one of them **has** [not *have*] caused massive traffic jams.

SINGULAR OR PLURAL INDEFINITE PRONOUNS

Some of our streams **are** polluted. [*Some* refers to the plural *streams,* so the plural verb *are* is correct.]

Some pollution **is** reversible, but **all** pollution **is** a threat to the balance of nature. [*Some* and *all* refer to the singular *pollution,* so the singular verb *is* is correct in both cases.]

All that environmentalists ask **is** to give nature a chance. [*All* has the meaning here of "the entire thing" or "the only thing," so the singular verb *is* is correct.]

Winter has driven the birds south; **all are** gone. [*All* refers to *birds,* so the plural verb *are* is correct.]

COMMON INDEFINITE PRONOUNS 80

ALWAYS PLURAL

both	many	

ALWAYS SINGULAR

another	every	no one
anybody	everybody	nothing
anyone	everyone	one
anything	everything	somebody
each	neither	someone
either	nobody	something

SINGULAR OR PLURAL DEPENDING ON CONTEXT

all	more	none
any	most	some

✤ USAGE ALERT: Do not mix singular and plural with *this, that, these* and *those*, as in *this kind, this type, these kinds,* and *these types. This* and *that* are singular, as are *kind* and *type; these* and *those* are plural, as are *kinds* and *types: **This*** [or ***That***] ***kind*** *of weather* ***makes*** *me shiver.* ***These*** [or ***Those***] ***kinds*** *of sweaters* ***keep*** *me warm.* ✤

11h Using verbs in context for collective nouns

A **collective noun** names a group of people or things: *family, group, audience, class, number, committee, team,* and the like. When the group acts as one unit, use a singular verb. When the members of the group act individually, thus creating more than one action, use a plural verb.

> **The senior class** nervously **awaits** final exams. [*Class* is acting as a single unit, so the verb is singular.]

The senior class were fitted for their graduation robes today. [Each member was fitted individually, so because there was more than one fitting the verb is plural.]

The couple in blue **is** engaged. [*Couple* refers to a single unit, so the verb is singular.]

The couple say their vows tomorrow. [Each of the two people will take a separate action, so because there is more than one action, the verb is plural.]

11i Making a linking verb agree with the subject—not the subject complement

Linking verbs indicate a state of being or a condition. They connect the subject to its **complement** (7m), which is a word that renames or describes the subject. You can think of a linking verb as an equal sign between a subject and its complement, called the **subject complement.**

The car **looks** new. [*The car = new; the car* is the subject, *looks* is the linking verb, and *new* is the subject complement.]

When you write a sentence that contains a subject complement, remember that the verb always agrees with the subject. For the purposes of agreement, ignore the subject complement.

NO **The worst part** of owning a car **are** the bills. [The subject is *the worst part,* with which the verb *are* does not agree; the subject complement is *the bills.*]

YES **The worst part** of owning a car **is** the bills. [The subject *the worst part* agrees with the verb *is;* the subject complement is *the bills.*]

11j Using verbs that agree with the antecedents of *who, which,* and *that*

The pronouns *who, which,* and *that* have the same form in singular and plural. Before deciding whether the verb° should be singular or plural, find the pronoun's antecedents°.

The scientist will share the income from her new patent with the graduate **students who work** with her. [*Who* refers to *students,* so the plural verb *work* is used.]

George Jones is **the student who works** in the science lab. [*Who* refers to *student,* so the singular verb *works* is used.]

Be especially careful when you use *one of the* or *the only one of the* in a sentence before *who, which,* or *that.* If the pronoun refers to *one,* use a singular verb. If the pronoun refers to what comes after *one of the,* use a plural verb.

Tracy is one of the students **who talk** in class. [*Who* refers to *students,* so *talk* is plural.]

Jim is the only one of the students **who talks** in class. [*Who* refers to *one,* so *talks* is singular.]

EXERCISE 11-3

Consulting sections 11g through 11j, supply the correct present-tense form of the verb in parentheses.

EXAMPLE Everybody on a class trip to the coastal waters of the Pacific Ocean (to enjoy) **enjoys** an opportunity to study dolphins in their natural habitat.

1. A class of students in Marine Biology (to take) _______ notes individually while watching dolphins feed off the British Columbia coast.
2. Everyone in the class (to listen) _______ as a team of dolphin experts (to explain) _______ some of the mammal's characteristics.
3. A group of dolphins, called a pod, usually (to consist) _______ of 10 000 to 30 000 members.
4. One unique characteristic of a dolphin's brain (to be) _______ the sleep patterns that (to keep) _______ one-half of the brain awake at all times.
5. All (to need) _______ to stay awake to breathe or else they would drown.

11k Using verbs with amounts, fields of study, and other special nouns

1 Using singular verbs with amounts

Subjects that refer to sums of money, distance, or measurement are considered singular and take singular verbs.

Two hours is not enough time to finish that project. [time]

Three hundred dollars is what we must pay. [sum of money]

Three-quarters of an inch is needed for a perfect fit. [measurement]

Five kilometres is a short sprint for some serious joggers. [distance]

2 Using singular verbs with fields of study

Fields of study are singular in meaning and so need singular verbs, despite their plural appearance: *economics, mathematics, physics, statistics.*

Statistics is required of science majors. [*Statistics* is a field of study, so the singular verb *is* is correct.]

Statistics show that a teacher shortage is coming. [*Statistics* refers to separate pieces of information, so the plural verb *show* is correct.]

3 Using singular or plural verbs with special nouns

Words such as *athletics, ethics, news,* and *measles* are singular, despite their plural appearance. Also, *the United States of America* is singular (see also 42c). However, *politics* and *sports* take either singular or plural verbs, depending on the meaning of the sentence.

The **news gets** better each day. [*News* is singular, so the singular verb *gets* is correct.]

Sports is a good way to build physical stamina. [*Sports* is one general activity, so the singular verb *is* is correct.]

Three **sports are offered** at the recreation centre. [*Sports* are separate activities, so the plural verb *are offered* is correct.]

Some words require a plural verb even though they refer to one thing: *jeans, pants, scissors, clippers, tweezers, eyeglasses, thanks,* and *riches*. If, however, the word *pair* is used in conjunction with *jeans, pants, scissors, clippers, tweezers,* or *eyeglasses,* a singular verb is required to agree with *pair.*

My slacks need pressing.

My pair of slacks needs pressing.

Series and *means* have the same form in singular and plural, so the meaning determines whether the verb is singular or plural.

Six new television series are beginning this week.

A series of disasters is plaguing our production.

11l Using singular verbs for titles of written works, companies, and words as terms

Even when plural° and compound nouns° occur in a title, the title itself indicates one work or entity. Therefore, titles of written works are singular and require singular verbs.

Fugitive Pieces by Anne Michaels **is** a prize-winning novel.

If a word that is plural is referred to as a term, it requires a singular verb.

***We* implies** that I am included.

I've come to think that ***scattered showers* is** a meteorologist's euphemism for *drenching thunderstorms.*

EXERCISE 11-4

Consulting sections 11k and 11l, supply the correct present-tense form of the verb in parentheses.

EXAMPLE Everyone (to use) **uses** phrases involving colour in daily conversations, such as the expressions "someone has the blues" or "they were caught red-handed."

1. Hardly anyone (to realize) _______ that in such phrases, *red-handed* or *the blues* has a significant and generally unknown meaning.
2. Explanations about the origins of phrases like *red-letter day* (to be) _______ often a surprise.
3. An assortment of language experts (to agree) _______ that because special dates, such as national holidays, were often printed in red on calendars, people started to use the expression *red letter* when talking about any special day.
4. There are many other curious uses of such colour words; one (to be) _______ "the greenroom," a waiting room for guests who are going to appear on a TV talk show.
5. People rarely meet an individual who (to know) _______ that the term *greenroom* originated in the nineteenth century, when theatres always used green paint for an actor's dressing room.

PRONOUN–ANTECEDENT AGREEMENT

11m Understanding pronoun–antecedent agreement

Pronoun–antecedent agreement means that pronouns (such as *it, they, their;* see 7b) must "match" in form with their **antecedents**—the nouns°, noun phrases°, or other pronouns to which they refer. To agree grammatically, pronouns must match in number (singular or plural) and in person (first, second, or third person); Chart 81 shows these relationships. For explanations of major concepts in grammatical agreement, consult Chart 75 in section 11b.

Agreement between pronouns and antecedents must be clear so that readers are not distracted by having to figure out the intended

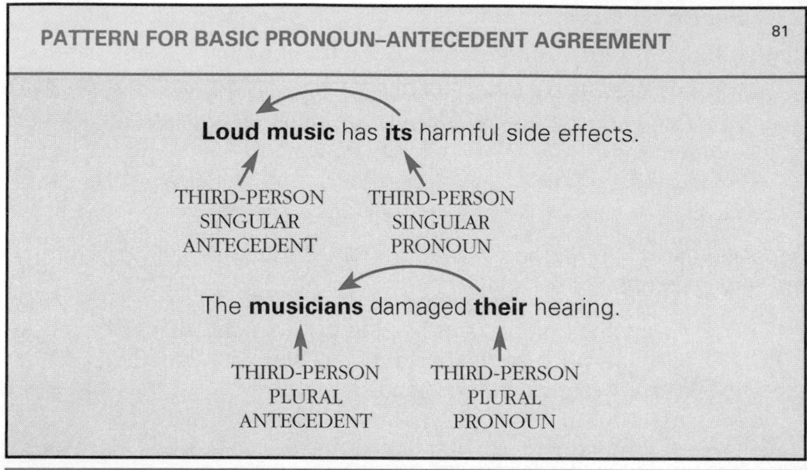

meaning of a sentence. (For related material on subjects and verbs, see section 11a. Also, for advice about staying consistent in person and number, see section 15a-1.)

PATTERN FOR BASIC PRONOUN–ANTECEDENT AGREEMENT
81
Loud music has its harmful side effects.
THIRD-PERSON SINGULAR ANTECEDENT
THIRD-PERSON SINGULAR PRONOUN
The musicians damaged their hearing.
THIRD-PERSON PLURAL ANTECEDENT
THIRD-PERSON PLURAL PRONOUN

> The **firefly** glows with luminescent light when **it** emerges from **its** nest at dusk. [The singular pronouns *it* and *its* match their singular antecedent *firefly.*]

> **Fireflies** glow with luminescent light when **they** emerge from **their** nests at dusk. [The plural pronouns *they* and *their* match their plural antecedent *fireflies.*]

11n Using pronouns with antecedents connected with *and*

When two or more antecedents are connected with *and,* they require a plural pronoun, even if the separate antecedents are singular. (For related material on subjects and verbs, see 11d.)

> **The Cascade Diner *and* the Wayside Diner** closed for New Year's Eve to give **their** [not *its*] employees the night off. [separate diners]

An exception occurs when *and* joins singular nouns that combine to form a single thing or person.

> My **best friend *and* neighbour** makes **his** [not *their*] excellent chili every Saturday. [The best friend is the same person as the neighbour. If two different people were involved, *his* would become *their*—and *makes* would become *make.*]

each, every

The words *each* and *every* are singular. When *each* or *every* precedes antecedents joined by *and,* the pronoun must be singular. (For related material on subjects and verbs, see 11d. Also, for advice about pronoun agreement for *each* or *every* used alone, see 11p.)

> ***Each* human hand and foot** leaves **its** [not *their*] distinctive footprint.

The same rule holds when the construction *one of the* follows *each* or *every*: ***Each one of the* robbers** left **his** [not *their*] fingerprints at the scene.

11o Making the pronoun agree with the nearest antecedent

Antecedents joined by *or, nor,* or correlative conjunctions (such as *either ... or, not only ... but [also];* for a list, see 7h) often mix singular and plural. For the purposes of agreement, ignore everything before the final antecedent. (For related material on subject–verb agreement, see 11e.) The pattern in Chart 82 illustrates this principle.

> Each night after the restaurant closes, either the resident mice or **the owner's cat** manages to get **itself** a good meal of leftovers.

> Each night after the restaurant closes, either the owner's cat or **the resident mice** manage to get **themselves** a good meal of leftovers.

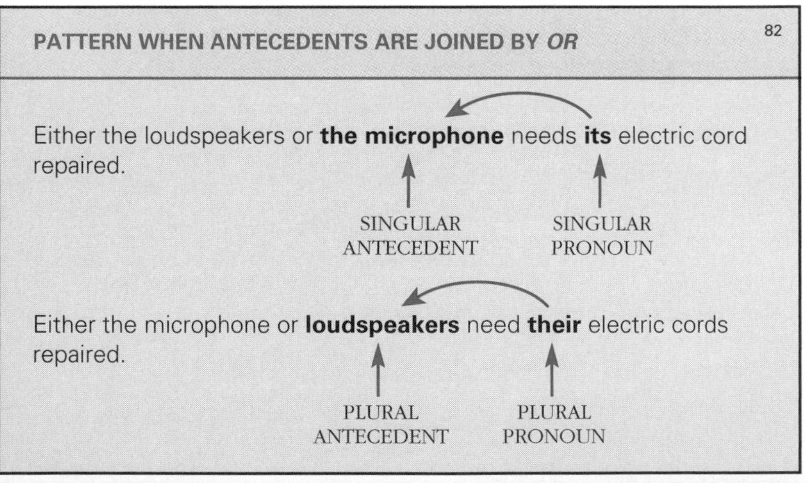

PATTERN WHEN ANTECEDENTS ARE JOINED BY OR
82
Either the loudspeakers or the microphone needs its electric cord repaired.
SINGULAR ANTECEDENT
SINGULAR PRONOUN
Either the microphone or loudspeakers need their electric cords repaired.
PLURAL ANTECEDENT
PLURAL PRONOUN

11p Using pronouns with indefinite-pronoun antecedents

Many indefinite pronouns refer to unknown persons, things, quantities, or ideas—thus the label "indefinite." In context within a sentence, even indefinite pronouns that do not have a specific antecedent take on clear meaning. Most indefinite pronouns are singular. Two indefinite pronouns, *both* and *many*, are plural and thus function as plurals when they are antecedents. A few indefinite pronouns can be singular or plural, depending on the meaning of the sentence. (For a list of indefinite pronouns grouped by number, see Chart 80 in section 11g. For advice on avoiding sexist language with indefinite pronouns, see 11q and 21b.)

SINGULAR INDEFINITE PRONOUNS

Everyone taking this course hopes to get **his or her** [not *their*] degree within a year.

Anybody wanting to wear a cap and gown at graduation must have **his or her** [not *their*] measurements taken.

Each student **is** [not *are*] hoping for a passing grade.

Each of the students handed in **his or her** [not *their*] final term paper.

Every student **needs** [not *need*] encouragement now and then.

Every student in my classes **is** [not *are*] studying hard.

SINGULAR OR PLURAL INDEFINITE PRONOUNS

When winter break arrives for students, **most** leave **their** dormitories for the comforts of home. [*Most* refers to *students*, so the plural pronoun *their* is correct.]

As for the luggage, **most** is already on **its** way to the airport. [*Most* refers to *luggage*, so the singular pronoun *its* is correct.]

None fear that **they** will fail. [The entire group does not expect to fail, so a plural noun is correct.]

None fears that **he or she** will fail. [No one individual expects to fail, so a singular pronoun is correct; note that *he or she* always functions as a singular pronoun (see Chart 83).]

11q Avoiding sexist pronoun use

In the past, grammatical convention specified using masculine pronouns to refer to indefinite pronouns: "*Everyone* open *his* book." Today, people are conscious that the pronouns *he, his, him,* and *himself* exclude women, who comprise over half the population. Chart 83 shows three ways to avoid using masculine pronouns when referring to males and females together. (For advice on how to avoid other types of sexist language, see 21b.)

Questions often arise concerning the use of *he or she* and *his or her.* In general, writers find these gender-free pronoun constructions awkward. To avoid them, many writers make the subject plural. Doing this becomes problematic when the subject is best stated as a singular indefinite pronoun° (see Chart 80). Informal writing is moving toward the use of the plural pronouns *they, them,* and *their* with the singular indefinite pronoun. In your academic writing, however, it is still best not to follow this informal practice.

83

WAYS TO AVOID USING ONLY THE MASCULINE PRONOUN TO REFER TO MALES AND FEMALES TOGETHER

Solution 1: Use a pair of pronouns—but try to avoid a pair more than once in a sentence or in many sentences in a row. When you use a *he or she* construction, remember that it acts as a singular pronoun.

> **Everyone** hopes that **he or she** wins the scholarship.
>
> With the explosion of medical information, a **doctor** usually has time to read in only **his or her** specialty.

Solution 2: Revise into the plural.

> **Many people** hope that **they** win the scholarship.
>
> With the explosion of medical information, few **doctors** have time to read outside **their** specialties.

Solution 3: Recast the sentence.

> Everyone hopes to win the scholarship.
>
> With the explosion of medical information, few specialists have time for general reading.

11r Using pronouns with collective-noun antecedents

A **collective noun** names a group of people or things, such as *family, group, audience, class, number, committee,* and *team.* When the group acts as one unit, use a singular pronoun to refer to it. When the members of the group act individually, thus performing more than one action, use a plural pronoun.

> **The audience** was cheering as **it** stood to applaud the performers. [The audience was acting as one unit, so the singular pronoun *it* is correct.]
>
> **The audience** put on **their** coats and walked out. [Here the members of the audience were acting as individuals, so all the actions are counted as many individual actions. Therefore the plural pronoun *their* is correct.]
>
> **The family is** spending **its** vacation in the Laurentians. [All the family members went to one place together.]
>
> **The family are** spending **their** vacations in the Laurentians, the Rockies, and the Swiss Alps. [Each family member went to a different place.]

EXERCISE 11-5

Consulting sections 11a through 11l, choose the correct form of the verb in parentheses.

EXAMPLE Of the 30 000 plant species on earth, the rose (to be) **<u>is</u>** the most universally known.

1. Each plant species (to invite) _______ discussion about origins and meanings; when talk turns to flowers, the rose is usually the first mentioned.
2. More fragrant and colourful (to be) _______ other types of flowers, yet roses (to remain) _______ the most popular worldwide.
3. Each of the types of roses (to symbolize) _______ beauty, love, romance, and secrecy.
4. There (to be) _______ over 200 pure species of roses and thousands of mixed species, thirty-five of which (to flourish) _______ in the soil of North America.
5. It is impossible to determine exactly where or when the first rose (to be) _______ domesticated, because roses have existed for so many centuries; however, one of the earliest references dates back to 3000 B.C.
6. One such myth from Greek mythology (to suggest) _______ that the rose first appeared with the birth of Aphrodite, the goddess of love and beauty.
7. Another myth, which focuses on the rose's thorns, (to say) _______ that an angry god shot arrows into the stem to curse the rose forever with arrow-shaped thorns.
8. While theories of this kind (to explain) _______ the significance and evolution of the rose, few people can explain the flower's enduring popularity.
9. Even today, a couple (to demonstrate) _______ love by exchanging red roses.
10. The rose, of all flowers, (to have) _______ the most devoted following.

EXERCISE 11-6

Consulting sections 11p through 11r, choose the proper pronoun to agree with its antecedent.

EXAMPLE Many people wonder what gives certain leaders (his or her, their) **their** spark and magnetic personal appeal.

1. The cluster of personal traits that produces star quality is called *charisma*, a state that bestows special power on (its, their) _______ bearers.
2. Charisma is the quality that allows an individual to empower (himself, herself, himself or herself, themselves) _______ and others.
3. Power and authority alone do not guarantee charisma; to produce it, (it, they) _______ must be combined with passion and strong purpose.
4. A charismatic leader has the ability to draw other people into (his, her, his or her, their) _______ dream or vision.
5. Charisma trainers advise would-be leaders to start by bringing order to (his, her, his or her, their) _______ activities; in stressful times, anyone who appears to have some part of (his, her, his or her, their) _______ life under control makes others relax and perform (his, her, his or her, their) _______ responsibilities better.

12 Using Adjectives and Adverbs

12a Distinguishing between adjectives and adverbs

Both **adjectives** and **adverbs** are modifiers—words or groups of words that describe other words.

ADJECTIVE The **brisk** *wind* blew. [Adjective *brisk* modifies noun *wind.*]

ADVERB The wind *blew* **briskly.** [Adverb *briskly* modifies verb *blew.*]

SUMMARY OF DIFFERENCES BETWEEN ADJECTIVES AND ADVERBS 84

WHAT ADJECTIVES MODIFY	EXAMPLE
nouns	The **busy** *lawyer* took a **quick** *look* at the members of the jury.
pronouns	*She* felt **triumphant,** for *they* were **attentive**.
WHAT ADVERBS MODIFY	**EXAMPLE**
verbs	The lawyer *spoke* **quickly** and **well.**
adverbs	The lawyer spoke **very** *quickly*.
adjectives	The lawyer was **extremely** *busy*.
independent clauses	**Therefore,** the *lawyer* rested.

The key to distinguishing between adjectives and adverbs is understanding that they modify different words or groups of words. As Chart 84 demonstrates, if you want to modify a noun° or pronoun°, use an adjective. If you want to modify a verb°, an adjective, or another adverb, use an adverb.

Inexperienced writers sometimes interchange adjectives and adverbs because of the *-ly* ending. Even though many adverbs do end in *-ly* (eat *swiftly,* eat *frequently,* eat *hungrily*), some do not (eat *fast,* eat *often,* eat *seldom*). To complicate matters further, some adjectives end in *-ly* (*lovely* flower, *friendly* dog). The *-ly* ending, therefore, is not a reliable way to identify adverbs.

EXERCISE 12-1

Consulting section 12a, first underline and label all adjectives (ADJ) and adverbs (ADV). Then go back and draw an arrow from each adjective and adverb to the word or words it modifies.

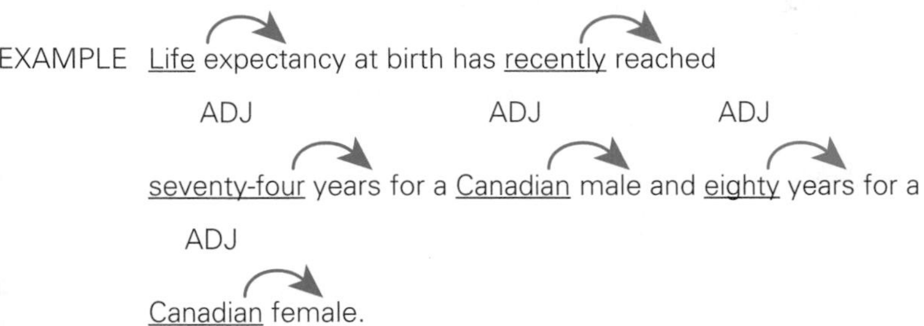

ADJ
ADV
EXAMPLE Life expectancy at birth has recently reached
ADJ
ADJ
ADJ
seventy-four years for a Canadian male and eighty years for a
ADJ
Canadian female.

1. Before the Industrial Revolution, mortality rates were high, extremely variable, and dependent upon crop conditions and rapidly spreading epidemics.
2. A 1990 survey indicates that more seniors are living independently; for this age group, life has improved dramatically because of pensions, increased mobility, and improved general health.
3. Alarmingly, the suicide rate among young Canadian men has risen greatly over the past twenty years and it is notably higher than the suicide rate for women.
4. Age-specific mortality rates for the native population are higher than those for the Canadian population in almost all age categories; consequently, life expectancy for natives is less than for the population as a whole.
5. Today, we are hardly able to appreciate that children four generations ago could reasonably expect to be orphaned before reaching maturity, or that parents often lost one or more of their children.

12b Using adverbs—not adjectives—to modify verbs, adjectives, and other adverbs

Do not use adjectives as adverbs. Always use adverbs to modify verbs, adjectives, and other adverbs.

NO The candidate inspired us **great.** [Adjective *great* cannot modify verb *inspired.*]

YES The candidate inspired us **greatly.** [Adverb *greatly* can modify verb *inspired.*]

NO The candidate felt **unusual** energetic. [Adjective *unusual* cannot modify adjective *energetic.*]

YES The candidate felt **unusually energetic.** [Adverb *unusually* can modify adjective *energetic.*]

NO The candidate spoke **exceptional forcefully.** [Adjective *exceptional* cannot modify adverb *forcefully.*]

YES The candidate spoke **exceptionally forcefully.** [Adverb *exceptionally* modifies adverb *forcefully.*]

12c Not using double negatives

A **double negative** is a statement with two negative modifiers, the second of which repeats the message of the first. (This form, nonstandard today, was standard in the days of Chaucer and Shakespeare.) Negative modifiers include *no, never, not, none, nothing, hardly, scarcely,* and *barely.*

NO The factory workers will **never** vote for **no** strike.

YES The factory workers will **never** vote for **a** strike.

The words *not, no,* and *nothing* are particularly common in double negatives.

NO The union members did **not** have **no** money in reserve.

YES The union members did **not** have **any** money in reserve.

YES The union members had **no** money in reserve.

Take special care to avoid double negatives with contractions of the word *not* (such as *isn't, don't, didn't,* or *haven't*). The negative message is conveyed by the contraction; do not add a second negative. (For advice about when contractions are appropriate, see 27c.)

NO	He did**n't** hear **nothing.**
YES	He did**n't** hear **anything.**
NO	They have**n't** had **no** meeting.
YES	They have**n't** had **any** meeting.

12d Using adjectives—not adverbs—as complements after linking verbs

Linking verbs connect a subject° to a complement (see 7m-1). Always use an adjective, not an adverb, as the complement.

The guests looked **happy.** [subject *guests* = adjective *happy*]

Problems can arise with verbs that function sometimes as linking verbs and sometimes as action verbs, depending on the structure of the sentence. Examples of such verbs are *look, feel, smell, taste, sound,* and *grow.*

Zora **looks happy.** [*looks* = linking verb; *happy* = adjective]

Zora **looks happily** at the sunset. [*looks* = action verb; *happily* = adverb]

Bad—Badly

The words *bad* (adjective) and *badly* (adverb) are particularly prone to misuse with linking verbs.

For Describing a Feeling

NO	The student felt **badly.**
YES	The student felt **bad.**

For Describing a Smell

NO	The food smelled **badly.**
YES	The food smelled **bad.**

Good—Well

Good is always an adjective. *Well* is an adjective referring to good health, but it is an adverb in all other contexts.

You look **well** = You look to be in good health. [*well* = adjective]

You write **well** = You write skilfully. [*well* = adverb]

Except when *well* is an adjective referring to health, use *good* only as an adjective and *well* only as an adverb.

NO She sings **good.** [*sings* = action verb; adverb, not adjective, required; *good* is an adjective]

YES She sings **well.** [*well* = adverb]

EXERCISE 12-2

Consulting sections 12a through 12d, choose the correct uses of negatives and of adjectives and adverbs.

EXAMPLE Online translation programs are one of the (undoubtedly, undoubted) **undoubted** triumphs of the information age.

(1) From what I have read, computer translation programs were (original, originally) _______ (secretly, secret) _______ developed during the Cold War to translate masses of sensitive documents (quick, quickly) _______ from Russian into English. (2) By the late 1980s, (commercially, commercial) _______ developers began to bring out their products, proving that automatic computer-based translation was (practically, practical) _______ and reliable. (3) I was intrigued to discover that today, (free, freely) _______ available online translation programs work with (nearly, near) _______ twenty languages. (4) Such programs (apparently, apparent) _______ can bring (linguistically, linguistic) _______ competence within reach of any Internet user. (5) This is some of the latest technology from the region where a (high, highly) _______ sophisticated analysis of human language meets advanced software development. (6) I decided that one way to verify just how (well, good) _______ this cutting-edge technology actually is would be to have an online program translate a sentence into French and then back into English. (7) I felt (eager, eagerly) _______ to test my theory, so I (expectantly, expectant) _______ typed the following into the on-screen translation box: "It was raining cats and dogs, so I spent the day cooped up at home." (8) No one (could, could not) _______ have been more shocked than I was to see this result: "It rained of the cats and from the dogs, thus I spent the day locked to the top of the house."

12e Using correct comparative and superlative forms of adjectives and adverbs

When comparisons are made, descriptive adjectives and adverbs often carry the message. Adjectives and adverbs, therefore, have forms that communicate relative degrees of intensity.

1 Using correct forms of comparison for regular adjectives and adverbs

Most adjectives and adverbs show degrees of intensity by adding *-er* and *-est* endings or by combining with the words *more, less, least* (see Chart 85). A few adjectives and adverbs are irregular, as explained in 12e-2.

FORMS OF COMPARISON FOR REGULAR ADJECTIVES AND ADVERBS 85

FORM	FUNCTION
■ Positive	Used when nothing is being compared
■ Comparative	Used when two things are being compared, with *-er* ending or *more/less*
■ Superlative	Used when three or more things are being compared, with *-est* ending or *most/least*

POSITIVE	COMPARATIVE	SUPERLATIVE
green	greener	greenest
happy	happier	happiest
selfish	less selfish	least selfish
beautiful	more beautiful	most beautiful

Her tree is **green.**

Her tree is **greener** than his tree.

Her tree is the **greenest** tree on the block.

The choice of whether to use *-er, -est* or *more, most, less, least* depends largely on the number of syllables in the adjective or adverb.

- With **one-syllable words,** the *-er* and *-est* endings are most common: *large, larger, largest* (adjective); *far, farther, farthest* (adverb).
- With **three-syllable words,** *more, most, less, least* are used.
- With **adverbs of two or more syllables,** *more, most, less, least* are used: *easily, more easily, most easily.*
- With **adjectives of two syllables,** practice varies: some take the *-er, -est* endings; others combine with *more* and *most.*

One general rule covers two-syllable adjectives ending in *-y:* use the *-er, -est* endings after changing the *-y* to *i: pretty, prettier, prettiest.*

For other two-syllable adjectives, form comparatives and superlatives intuitively, based on what you have heard or read for a particular adjective.

✤ ALERT: Be careful not to use a **double comparative** or **double superlative.** The words *more, most, less, least* cannot be used if the *-er* or *-est* ending has been used.

He was **younger** [not *more younger*] than his brother.
Her music was the **loudest** [not *more loudest*] on the stereo.
People danced **more easily** [not *more easier*] to her music. ✤

2 Using correct forms of comparison for irregular adjectives and adverbs

A few comparative and superlative forms are irregular. They are listed in Chart 86. Memorize them so that they always spring easily to mind.

The Perkinses saw a **good** movie.
The Perkinses saw a **better** movie than the Smiths did.
The Perkinses saw **the best** movie that they had ever seen.
The Changs had **little** trouble finding jobs.
The Changs had **less** trouble finding jobs than the Smiths did.
The Changs had **the least** trouble finding jobs of everyone.

IRREGULAR COMPARATIVES AND SUPERLATIVES 86

POSITIVE [1]	COMPARATIVE [2]	SUPERLATIVE [3+]
good (adjective)	better	best
well (adjective and adverb)	better	best
bad (adjective)	worse	worst
badly (adverb)	worse	worst
many	more	most
much	more	most
some	more	most
little	less	least

✤ USAGE ALERTS: Do not use *less* and *fewer* interchangeably. Use *less* with noncountable items or values that form one whole. Use *fewer* with numbers or anything that can be counted: *They consumed* ***fewer calories;*** *the sugar substitute had* ***less aftertaste.***

Do not use comparative and superlative adverbs with absolute adjectives° such as *unique* and *perfect.* Something either is or is not one of a kind or faultless. No degrees of intensity are involved: *This teapot is* ***unique*** [not *the most unique*]; *the glazing is* ***perfect*** [not *the most perfect*]. ✤

EXERCISE 12-3

Consulting section 12e, do two things: First, complete this chart. Next, write sentences that set a context for each word in the completed chart.

EXAMPLE *little:* Towering redwoods dwarfed the little Douglas fir.

POSITIVE [1]	COMPARATIVE [2]	SUPERLATIVE [3+]
little		
	greedier	
		most complete
gladly		
		fewest
	darker	
some		

12f Avoiding too many nouns as modifiers

Sometimes nouns—words that name a person, place, thing, or idea—function as modifiers° of other nouns: *truck driver, train track, security system.* These very familiar terms create no problems. However, when nouns pile up in a sequence of modifiers, the reader has difficulty figuring out which nouns are being modified and which nouns are doing the modifying. As you revise such sentences, you can use any of several routes to clarify your material.

Sentence Rewritten

NO I asked my advisor to write **two college recommendation** letters for me.

YES I asked my advisor to write **letters of recommendation** to **two colleges** for me.

One Noun Changed to Possessive Case and Another to Adjective Form

NO The **university psychology lab facilities** are available to students doing advanced **cognition research projects**.

YES The **university's** psychology lab facilities are available to students doing advanced **cognitive** research projects.

Noun Changed to Prepositional Phrase

NO Our **student advisor training program** has won awards for excellence.

YES Our training program **for student advisors** has won awards for excellence. [Notice that this change requires the plural *advisors*.]

EXERCISE 12-4

Consulting all sections of this chapter, select the better choice from each set of words in parentheses so that these sentences are suitable for academic writing.

EXAMPLE A modern sculpture by Haida artist Bill Reid, done in a style that seems (traditionally, traditional) **traditional,** depicts his people's legend of the creation of mankind.

1. According to the Haida people of the Queen Charlotte Islands, before the (most early, earliest) _______ humans appeared the world was the home of powerful beings.
2. One of these beings was the Raven, a playful bird who created the moon and the stars and did many other important deeds—but seldom out of the desire to do (good, well) _______ at his tasks.
3. (Fewer, Less) _______ of the Raven's creations were the product of his (well, good) _______ intentions than of his sense of mischief.
4. While flying over a (more remote, remote) _______ part of the islands, the Raven saw a clam shell lying on the beach and heard tiny creatures scrambling around inside it.
5. Although none of us (cannot, can) _______ hear it today, the Raven had a beautiful voice, which he could use for magical purposes, in addition to his hoarse cawing sound.
6. The (curious, curiously) _______ Raven used this beautiful voice to coax the creatures out of the shell, and so brought the first naked, helpless humans crawling (fearful, fearfully) _______ into the world.

13 Sentence Fragments

A sentence fragment occurs when a portion of a sentence is punctuated as a complete sentence. This chapter shows you how to distinguish between sentence fragments and complete sentences.

FRAGMENT	The telephone with redial capacity. [no verb°]
REVISED	The telephone has redial capacity.
FRAGMENT	Rang loudly for ten minutes. [no subject°]
REVISED	The telephone rang loudly for ten minutes.
FRAGMENT	At midnight. [no verb° or subject°]
REVISED	The telephone rang at midnight.
FRAGMENT	**Because** the telephone rang loudly. [dependent clause° starting with subordinating conjunction°]
REVISED	Because the telephone rang loudly, the family was awakened in the middle of the night.
FRAGMENT	**Which** really annoyed me. [dependent clause° with relative pronoun°]
REVISED	The telephone call was a wrong number, which really annoyed me.

Sentence fragments distort the message that you want your material to deliver.

NO The lawyer was angry. When she returned from court. She found the key witness waiting in her office. [Was the lawyer angry when she returned from court or when she found the witness in her office?]

YES The lawyer was angry when she returned from court. She found the key witness waiting in her office.

YES The lawyer was angry. When she returned from court, she found the key witness waiting in her office.

Many writers wait until the revising° and editing° stages of the writing process to check for sentence fragments. During drafting°, the goal is to get ideas down on paper or disk. As you draft, if you suspect a sentence fragment, underline or highlight the material. Then, you can easily find and check it later.

13a Testing for sentence completeness

If you write sentence fragments frequently, you need a system to check that your sentences are complete. Here is a test you can use.

TEST FOR SENTENCE COMPLETENESS 87

Question 1: **Is the word group a dependent clause°?** If yes, there is a fragment. To revise, see 13b.

NO Because the ship intended to cut a path through the ice. [a fragment]

Question 2: **Is there a verb°?** If no, there is a fragment. To revise, see 13c.

NO Thousands of whales in the Arctic Ocean because of an early winter. [a fragment]

Question 3: **Is there a subject°?** If no, there is a fragment. To revise, see 13c.

NO Raced to reach the whales. [a fragment]

QUESTION 1: Is the word group a dependent clause?

If the answer to Question 1 is "yes," you are looking at a sentence fragment. A **dependent clause** has a subject and a verb, but it begins with a subordinating word. It cannot stand alone as an independent unit; it must be joined to an independent clause to be part of a complete sentence.

One type of subordinating word is a **subordinating conjunction.** A subordinating conjunction comes at the beginning of a dependent clause. Here are frequently used subordinating conjunctions. (For a more complete list that also tells the relationship each word expresses, see Chart 53 in section 7h.)

after	because	since	when
although	before	unless	whenever
as	if	until	where

FRAGMENT **Because** she returned my books.

REVISED **Because** she returned my books, I can study.

FRAGMENT **When** I study.

REVISED I have to concentrate **when** I study.

✤ PUNCTUATION ALERT: When a dependent clause starting with a subordinating conjunction (an adverb clause) comes before an independent clause, a comma usually separates the clauses (see 24b-1).✤

Another type of subordinating word is a **relative pronoun.** The most common relative pronouns are *who, which,* and *that.*

FRAGMENT The test **that** we studied for.

REVISED The test **that** we studied for was cancelled.

FRAGMENT The professor **who** taught the course.

REVISED The professor **who** taught the course was ill.

Questions can begin with words such as *when, where, who,* and *which* without being sentence fragments: *When do you want to study? Where is the library? Who is your professor? Which class are you taking?*

QUESTION 2: Is there a verb?

If there is no verb, you are looking at a sentence fragment. Verbs convey information about what is happening, what has happened, or what will happen. In testing for sentence completeness, find a verb that can change tense° to communicate a change in time.

Yesterday, the telephone **rang.**

Now the telephone **rings.**

Verbals° do not function as verbs. Verbals are gerunds° (*-ing* forms as nouns°), present participles° (*-ing* forms as modifiers°), past participles° (*-ed* or irregular past forms as modifiers), and infinitives° (*to* forms). (See 7d and Chart 49.)

FRAGMENT Yesterday, the students registering for classes.

REVISED Yesterday, the students **were registering** for classes.

FRAGMENT	Now the students registering for classes.
REVISED	Now the students **are registering** for classes.
FRAGMENT	Informed about an excellent teacher.
REVISED	**They had been informed** about an excellent teacher.
FRAGMENT	Now the students to register for classes.
REVISED	Now the students **want** to register for classes.

QUESTION 3: Is there a subject?

If there is no subject, you are looking at a sentence fragment. To find a subject, ask the verb "who?" or "what?"

FRAGMENT	Studied hard for class. [Who studied? unknown]
REVISED	The students studied hard for class. [Who studied? students]
FRAGMENT	Contained some difficult questions. [What contained? unknown]
REVISED	The test contained some difficult questions. [What contained? the test]

Every sentence must have its own subject.

NO	The students formed a study group to prepare for the midterm exam. **And decided** to study together for the rest of the course.
YES	The students formed a study group to prepare for the midterm exam. **They decided** to study together for the rest of the course.

See the discussion of compound predicates in 13c.

Imperative statements—commands and some requests—are an exception. They are not sentence fragments. Imperative statements imply the word "you" as the subject.

Run! = (You) run!

Study hard. = (You) study hard.

Please return my books. = (You) please return my books.

Chart 88 summarizes information on correcting a sentence fragment once you have identified its grammatical structure.

HOW TO CORRECT SENTENCE FRAGMENTS 88

REVISION STRATEGY

- If the sentence fragment is a dependent clause°, join it to an adjacent independent clause° (see 13b).
- If the sentence fragment is a dependent clause, revise it into an independent clause (see 13b).
- If the sentence fragment is a phrase°, join it to an adjacent independent clause (see 13c).
- If the sentence fragment is a phrase, revise it into an independent clause (see 13c).

EXERCISE 13-1

Using the Test for Sentence Completeness in Chart 87 and section 13a, check each word group. If a word group is a sentence fragment, explain what makes it incomplete. If a word group is a complete sentence, circle its number.

EXAMPLE Because gold is shiny, flexible, and scarce. [dependent clause beginning with a subordinating word (*Because*) and lacking an independent clause to complete the thought; Question 1]

1. Making gold ideal for a variety of uses.
2. Since gold does not easily tarnish, corrode, or rust.
3. Provides brilliance to coins, jewellery, and artwork.
4. Because gold combines easily with the harder metals copper and silver.
5. Weighs twice as much as the equivalent volume of lead.
6. Ten grammes of gold can be rolled out to cover a surface nearly 10 metres square.
7. Or can be pulled into an 18-kilometre-long wire.
8. The melting point of gold is 1060°C.
9. Although tonnes of gold lie under the oceans.
10. The value of gold being less than the cost of mining gold from the ocean floor.

13b Revising dependent clauses punctuated as sentences

A **dependent clause** contains both a subject° and a verb° but also contains a subordinating word° (see the discussion of Question 1, following Chart 87). It cannot stand on its own as a sentence.

To correct a dependent clause punctuated as a sentence, you can either (1) join the dependent clause to an independent clause that comes directly before or after, or (2) drop the subordinating word. Whichever strategy you use, if necessary, add words to create an independent clause that makes sense.

FRAGMENT Icebreakers were required to serve as rescue ships. **Because the ice was thick.**

REVISED Icebreakers were required to serve as rescue ships because the ice was thick. [joined into one sentence]

FRAGMENT The noisy motors of the ships worried the crews. **Who feared the whales would panic.**

REVISED The noisy motors of the ships worried the crews. They feared the whales would panic. [relative pronoun dropped and *they* added to create an independent clause]

✤ USAGE ALERT: When trying to identify dependent clauses, be especially careful with words that indicate time—such as *after, before, since,* and *until.* In some sentences, they function as subordinating conjunctions, but in other sentences they function as adverbs° and prepositions°. Do not automatically assume when you see these words that you are looking at a dependent clause.

> **Before,** the whales had responded to classical music. This time it did not seem to work. [These are two complete sentences. In the first sentence, *before* is an adverb° modifying the independent clause° *the whales had responded to classical music.*]
>
> **Before** the whales responded to classical music, some crew members had tried new age music. [This is a complete sentence. *Before* is a subordinating conjunction° in the dependent clause° *before the whales responded to classical music.* If these words stood on their own, however, they would be a sentence fragment. They must be joined to an independent clause.] ✤

EXERCISE 13-2

Consulting sections 13a and 13b, find and correct any sentence fragments. If a sentence is correct, circle its number.

EXAMPLE Mordecai Richler was a novelist and essayist. Who was born in Montreal in 1931.

Mordecai Richler was a novelist and essayist who was born in Montreal in 1931.

1. Richler made his reputation with the satirical novel *The Apprenticeship of Duddy Kravitz*. Which is a hard-edged portrait of a young entrepreneur and hustler from Montreal's Jewish quarter.
2. Still, Richler must have had warm feelings for his old St. Urbain neighbourhood and the remarkable characters who inhabit it. Because mingled with the satire are sympathy and even nostalgia.
3. Unless people can be convinced otherwise. They will continue to believe that there is much of Richler himself in his funny, pathetic, yet engaging anti-heroes. Who try to make their way in an unsympathetic world.
4. Even though much of Richler's wit is aimed at people striving to escape their modest backgrounds. Satires like *Solomon Gursky Was Here* have not spared the Canadian elite, whom Richler shows with feet of clay and closets full of embarrassing secrets.
5. In a series of essays, Richler turned his pen against nationalist intellectuals in Quebec. If Richler insisted. That his essay *Oh Canada! Oh Quebec!* with its sad subtitle *Requiem for a Divided Country* was serious political analysis. Why did his publisher catalogue it as "humour"?

13c Revising phrases punctuated as sentences

A **phrase** is a group of words that lacks a subject°, a verb°, or both. A phrase cannot stand on its own as a sentence. To revise a phrase punctuated as a sentence, you may choose to (1) rewrite it to become an independent clause°, or (2) join it to an independent clause that comes directly before or after the phrase.

A phrase containing only a verbal (an infinitive°, a past participle°, or a present participle°) but no verb is a fragment, not a sentence.

FRAGMENT The mayor called a news conference last week. **To announce new programs for crime prevention and care for the homeless.** [*To announce* starts an infinitive phrase, not a sentence.]

REVISED The mayor called a news conference last week to announce new programs for crime prevention and care for the homeless. [joined into one sentence]

REVISED The mayor called a news conference last week. She wanted to announce new programs for crime prevention and care for the homeless. [rewritten]

FRAGMENT **Introduced by her assistant.** The mayor began with an opening statement. [*Introduced* starts a participial phrase, not a sentence.]

REVISED Introduced by her assistant, the mayor began with an opening statement. [joined into one sentence]

REVISED The mayor was introduced by her assistant. She began with an opening statement. [rewritten]

FRAGMENT **Hoping for strong public support.** She gave many examples of problems everywhere in the city. [*Hoping* starts a participial phrase, not a sentence.]

REVISED Hoping for strong public support, she gave many examples of problems everywhere in the city. [joined into one sentence]

REVISED She was hoping for strong public support. She gave many examples of problems everywhere in the city. [rewritten]

A **prepositional phrase** starts with a preposition°. It is not a sentence.

FRAGMENT Cigarette smoke made the conference room seem airless. **During the long news conference.** [*During* starts a prepositional phrase, not a sentence.]

REVISED Cigarette smoke made the conference room seem airless during the long news conference. [joined into one sentence]

REVISED Cigarette smoke made the conference room seem airless. It was hard to breathe during the long news conference. [rewritten]

An **appositive** is one or more words that rename a noun°. It is not a sentence.

FRAGMENT Most people respected the mayor. **A politician with fresh ideas and practical solutions.** [*A politician* starts an appositive, not a sentence.]

REVISED Most people respected the mayor, a politician with fresh ideas and practical solutions. [joined into one sentence]

REVISED Most people respected the mayor. She seemed to be a politician with fresh ideas and practical solutions. [rewritten]

A **compound predicate** contains two or more verbs°. To be part of a complete sentence, a predicate must have a subject. When the second half of a compound predicate is punctuated as a separate sentence, it is not a sentence.

FRAGMENT The reporters asked the mayor many questions about the details of her program. **And then discussed her answers among themselves.** [*And then discussed* is the start of a compound predicate, not a sentence.]

REVISED The reporters asked the mayor many questions about the details of her program and then discussed her answers among themselves. [joined into one sentence]

REVISED The reporters asked the mayor many questions about the details of her program. Then the reporters discussed her answers among themselves. [rewritten]

EXERCISE 13-3

Go back to Exercise 13-1 and revise any sentence fragments into complete sentences. In some cases you may be able to combine two fragments into one complete sentence.

EXERCISE 13-4

Consulting sections 13a, 13b, and 13c, revise this paragraph to eliminate any sentence fragments. In some cases, you can combine word groups to create complete sentences; in other cases, you must supply missing elements to revise word groups. Some sentences may not require revision. In your final version, check not only the individual sentences but also the clarity of the whole paragraph.

(1) An English inventor has developed a portable radio that needs no batteries. (2) And plays when it is wound up by hand. (3) This wind-up radio designed to be sold in Africa, where many villages have no electricity. (4) Also, batteries being expensive and hard to find in parts of Africa. (5) The radio playing for half an hour or more. (6) Before its owner has to spend a few seconds winding it up again. (7) For a portable radio, it is bulky, and its sound is not of top quality. (8) In countries with few newspapers or books, however, a radio seen as an important tool. (9) To provide information on health and other practical matters. (10) Besides, where most people are poor,

a radio is a much-desired luxury. (11) So it has become a status symbol. (12) In poor African villages, a radio ranking number three in prestige after a motorcycle and a bicycle. (13) These three status symbols able to make an unmarried man into an eligible bachelor. (14) According to some people, at least.

13d Revising sentence fragments in lists and examples

Sentence fragment problems sometimes come up when people write lists and examples. Unless a list or example is formatted as a column in point form, it must be part of a complete sentence.

You can connect a list fragment by attaching it to the preceding independent clause with a colon° or a dash°. You can correct an example fragment by attaching it to an independent clause (the punctuation you use—typically, a semicolon°, a dash, or a comma—will depend on the meaning) or by rewriting it as a complete sentence. (Chapters 24, 25, 26, and 29 discuss the uses of these punctuation marks.)

FRAGMENT You have a choice of desserts. **Carrot cake, butter tarts, apple pie, or peppermint ice cream.** [The list cannot stand on its own as a sentence.]

REVISED You have a choice of desserts: carrot cake, butter tarts, apple pie, or peppermint ice cream. [joined into one sentence with a colon]

REVISED You have a choice of desserts—carrot cake, butter tarts, apple pie, or peppermint ice cream. [joined into one sentence with a dash]

FRAGMENT There are several good places to go for brunch. **For example, the Bluenose Inn and Peggy's Retreat.** [Examples cannot stand on their own as a sentence.]

REVISED There are several good places to go for brunch—for example, the Bluenose Inn and Peggy's Retreat. [joined into one sentence with a dash]

REVISED There are several good places to go for brunch. For example, there are the Bluenose Inn and Peggy's Retreat. [rewritten with the addition of a main verb]

13e Recognizing intentional fragments

Professional writers sometimes intentionally use fragments for emphasis and effect.

> But in the main I feel like a brown bag of miscellany propped against a wall. Pour out the contents, and there is discovered a jumble of small things priceless and worthless. **A first-water diamond, an empty spool, bits of broken glass, lengths of string, a key to a door long since crumbled away, a rusty knife-blade, old shoes saved for a road that never was and never will be, a nail bent under the weight of things too heavy for any nail, a dried flower or two still a little fragrant.**
>
> —ZORA NEALE HURSTON, *How It Feels to Be Colored Me*

The ability to judge the difference between an acceptable and unacceptable sentence fragment comes from much exposure to reading the work of skilled writers. Many instructors, therefore, do not accept sentence fragments in student writing until a student can demonstrate the consistent ability to write well-constructed complete sentences.

EXERCISE 13-5

Consulting sections 13a through 13d, revise this paragraph to eliminate any sentence fragments. In some cases, you can combine word groups to create complete sentences; in other cases, you must supply missing elements to revise word groups. In your final version, check not only the individual sentences but also the clarity of the whole paragraph.

(1) Your car shuddering and jolting. (2) As a hubcap flies off one of the tires and clatters across the road. (3) Have just hit a pothole in the pavement. (4) Potholes, typically formed when water seeps into cracks in the road surface, freezes, and then melts. (5) Are usually found in northern regions. (6) However, can also be a problem in warmer climates. (7) Where heat and frequent rain may cause the pavement to collapse. (8) A research laboratory that has counted 16 million potholes. (9) Scarring the roads in the United States. (10) Each one a source of grief to countless drivers. (11) Canada's harsh climate, which guarantees that this country has its share, too. (12) Because potholes bring expense and even danger. (13) Governments are finding ingenious ways of dealing with them. (14) For example, a scheme in one province for volunteers to "adopt" a highway. (15) And pay for its upkeep. (16) No matter how many schemes their governments think up, however, all drivers want just one thing. (17) To see that fewer of their roads remain poorly maintained "orphans."

Focus on Revising

REVISING YOUR WRITING

If you write sentence fragments, go back to your writing and locate them. Then figure out why each is a sentence fragment by using the Test for Sentence Completeness in 13a. Next, revise each sentence fragment into a complete sentence, referring to 13a, 13b, and 13c.

CASE STUDIES: REVISING TO AVOID SENTENCE FRAGMENTS

In these case studies, you can observe a student writer revising. Then you have the chance to revise other student writing on your own.

Observation

A student wrote the following draft for a course called Introduction to the Novel. The assignment was to compose a brief essay about a novel that deals with a real event. This material is well organized as a narrative and tells an interesting story, but the draft's effectiveness is diminished by the presence of sentence fragments.

Read through the draft. The sentence fragments are highlighted. Before you look at the student's revision, revise the material yourself. Then compare your revision with the student's.

phrase—with *-ing* form of verb—punctuated as a sentence: 13c

Trying to reconstruct a memory that was erased from history by Salvadoran authorities. Claribel Alegría and her husband, Darwin "Bud" Flakoll, have recreated the tragic *la matanza* in their novel, *Ashes of Izalco*.

La matanza was the name given to a 1932 massacre of El Salvadoran adults and children. One which took the lives of 30 000 peasants and farm workers. Alegría vividly recalls

dependent clause punctuated as a sentence: 13b

the nightly shootings of innocent people. Who were killed because they were thought to be communists. Traumatized by the massacre. Alegría decided to write a novel with Flakoll about a love affair between two characters who had some connection to the massacre. The novel would allow readers to relive the event themselves. Something which had always been impossible for El Salvador's people. During and for many years after the massacre. The El Salvadoran government had censored any information about the event.

dependent clause punctuated as a sentence: 13b

phrase—with past participle of verb—punctuated as a sentence: 13c

dependent clause punctuated as a sentence: 13b

prepositional phrase punctuated as a sentence: 13c

When working on the novel, Alegría wrote only the voices of women. And only wrote in Spanish. Flakoll wrote the male voices in English. They each translated and revised each other's work. Creating a uniquely cross-cultural novel.

phrase—part of compound predicate—punctuated as a sentence: 13c

phrase—with *-ing* form of verb—punctuated as a sentence: 13c

The novel's success is largely due to its careful interpretation of events, an interpretation which was desirable to everyone who had once lived them. Because it allowed them to recapture a vital El Salvadoran memory. But even more important, *Ashes of Izalco* will also allow future generations to be informed of their country's past.

dependent clause punctuated as a sentence: 13b

Here is how the student revised the passage to eliminate the sentence fragments. In many places, the student could correct the error in more than one way. Your revision, therefore, might not be exactly like this one, but it should not contain any sentence fragments.

➜

Trying to reconstruct a memory that was erased from history by Salvadoran authorities, Claribel Alegría and her husband, Darwin "Bud" Flakoll, have recreated the tragic *la matanza* in their novel, *Ashes of Izalco*.

La matanza was the name given to a 1932 massacre of El Salvadoran adults and children, one which took the lives of 30 000 peasants and farm workers. Alegría vividly recalls the nightly shootings of innocent people, who were killed because they were thought to be communists. Traumatized by the massacre, Alegría decided to write a novel with Flakoll about a love affair between two characters who had some connection to the events. The novel would allow readers to relive the event themselves, something which had always been impossible for El Salvador's people, because during and for many years after the massacre, the El Salvadoran government had censored any information about the event.

When working on the novel, Alegría wrote only the voices of women and only wrote in Spanish. Flakoll wrote the male voices in English. Each translated and revised the other's work, creating a uniquely cross-cultural novel.

The novel's success is largely due to its careful interpretation of events, an interpretation which was desirable to everyone who had once lived them because it allowed them to recapture a vital El Salvadoran memory. But even more important, *Ashes of Izalco* will also allow future generations to be informed of their country's past.

Participation

A student wrote the following draft for a course called European History. The assignment was to discuss the political atmosphere of a European nation during the seventeenth century. This material is effectively organized for chronological presentation of information, and it uses specific details well. The draft's effectiveness, however, is diminished by the presence of sentence fragments.

Read through the draft. Then revise it to eliminate the sentence fragments. Also, make any additional revisions that you think would improve the content, organization, and style of the material.

In seventeenth-century England, from the death of Elizabeth I in 1603 to William of Orange's ascension to the throne in 1689. The monarchy of England was the cause of unrest and uncertainty.

Queen Elizabeth I died single and childless in 1603. Because she did not have a direct descendant. The throne passed to the Queen's cousin. Who was crowned James I. Discord over the relative power of Parliament and the crown emerged under James I. And erupted during the reign of James's son, Charles I. Incapable of resolving the conflicts, Charles I lost both the throne and his head to Oliver Cromwell's Puritan Revolution in 1649.

Holding fast to his anti-monarchy sentiments and refusing a crown. Oliver Cromwell did not establish a new line of English monarchs. Instead, he became Lord Protector of England. When Cromwell died, his son Richard lacked the charisma and political astuteness to hold on to power. As a result, the son of Charles I was recalled from France. Where he had fled to live in safety. He was crowned Charles II in 1660. And had very limited power, according to new laws passed by Parliament. Charles II sired no legitimate heirs, so the succession passed to his brother, James. An apparently able man with one serious political handicap in seventeenth-century England. He was Catholic, at a time when the English feared that the Pope was plotting to reclaim England and rule it from Rome. When the second wife of James baptized her newborn son Catholic. Unease over James's rule escalated rapidly. To ensure the safety of his wife and new son. James sent them to France and followed soon after. James's Protestant daughter Mary took the throne. With her husband William of Orange. A Dutchman who was a staunch supporter of Protestantism. Their union was so popular with the English that William continued to rule after Mary's death in 1694. Thus, the century that saw much upheaval and instability in England ended in relative calm.

14 Comma Splices and Run-Together Sentences

A **comma splice** (or **comma fault**) is an error that occurs when a comma by itself joins independent clauses°. A comma is correct between two independent clauses only when it is followed by a coordinating conjunction (*and, but, for, or, nor, yet,* and *so*). The word *splice* means "to fasten ends together." The end of one independent clause and the beginning of another should not be fastened together with a comma alone.

COMMA SPLICE	The iceberg broke off from the glacier, it drifted into the sea.

A **run-together sentence** is an error that occurs when two independent clauses° are not joined by a comma with a coordinating conjunction (*and, but, for, or, nor, yet,* and *so*) or by other punctuation. Two independent clauses cannot be united by running them together. A run-together sentence is also known as a *run-on sentence* or a *fused sentence.*

RUN-TOGETHER SENTENCE	The iceberg broke off from the glacier it drifted into the sea.

Comma splices and run-together sentences are two versions of the same problem: incorrect joining of two independent clauses. Both comma splices and run-together sentences distract readers from understanding the meaning you want your material to deliver.

If you tend to write comma splices and run-together sentences, it may be because you have trouble recognizing them. Interestingly, almost all such errors follow only a few patterns. Chart 89, which lists these patterns, shows you how to find and correct these errors.

HOW TO FIND AND CORRECT COMMA SPLICES AND RUN-TOGETHER SENTENCES

89

FINDING COMMA SPLICES AND RUN-TOGETHER SENTENCES

- Look for a pronoun° starting the second independent clause.

  NO The physicist Marie Curie discovered radium, **she** won two Nobel prizes.

- Look for a conjunctive adverb° (Chart 51 in 7f) or transitional expression° (Chart 25 in 4d-1) starting the second independent clause°.

  NO Marie Curie and her husband, Pierre, worked together at first, **however**, he died at age 47.

- Look for a second independent clause that explains/amplifies, contrasts with, or gives an example of, information in the first independent clause.

  NO Radium can cause cancer **radium is used to cure cancer.**

FIXING COMMA SPLICES AND RUN-TOGETHER SENTENCES

- Use a period (14b) or a semicolon (14e) between independent clauses.

  YES The physicist Marie Curie discovered radium. **She** won two Nobel Prizes.

- Use a comma + coordinating conjunction° between the clauses (14c).

  YES The physicist Marie Curie discovered radium, **and** she won two Nobel Prizes.

- Use a semicolon + conjunctive adverb or transitional expression between the clauses (14e).

  YES Marie Curie and her husband, Pierre, worked together at first; **however** he died at age 47.

- Revise one independent clause into a dependent clause° (14d).

  YES Radium, **which can cause cancer,** is also used to cure cancer.

14a Recognizing comma splices and run-together sentences

To recognize comma splices and run-together sentences, you need to be able to recognize an independent clause, a clause that contains a subject° and predicate° and that does not begin with a subordinating word°. An independent clause can stand alone as a sentence because it is an independent grammatical unit.

SUBJECT	PREDICATE
Alexander Graham Bell	was a Canadian inventor.

If you tend to write comma splices, here is a useful technique for proofreading your work. Cover all the words on one side of the comma and see if the words remaining constitute an independent clause. If they do, cover that clause and uncover all the words on the other side of the comma. If the second side of the comma is also an independent clause, you have written a comma splice. Also, to help yourself avoid writing comma splices, become familiar with correct uses for commas, explained in Chapter 24.

Writers often wait until the revising° and editing° stages of the writing process to check for comma splices and run-together sentences. While you are drafting°, if you suspect an error, quickly underline or highlight the material and keep drafting. Then, you can easily find and check it later.

Experienced writers sometimes use a comma to join very brief parallel independent clauses, especially if a negative sentence is followed by a positive sentence. *Mosquitoes do not bite, they stab.* Many instructors consider this form an error in student writing; you will never be wrong if you use a semicolon or period.

14b Using a period or semicolon to correct comma splices and run-together sentences

You can use a period or semicolon to correct comma splices and run-together sentences. For the sake of sentence variety and emphasis, however, do not always choose punctuation to correct this type of error. (Other methods are discussed in 14c and 14d.) Strings of too many short sentences rarely establish relationships and levels of importance among ideas.

COMMA SPLICE A shark is all cartilage, it does not have a bone in its body.

RUN-TOGETHER SENTENCE	A shark is all cartilage it does not have a bone in its body.
CORRECTED	A shark is all cartilage. It does not have a bone in its body. [A *period* separates the independent clauses.]
COMMA SPLICE	Sharks can smell blood from 400 metres away, they swim toward the source like a guided missile.
RUN-TOGETHER SENTENCE	Sharks can smell blood from 400 metres away they swim toward the source like a guided missile.
CORRECTED	Sharks can smell blood from 400 metres away; they swim toward the source like a guided missile. [A *semicolon* separates the independent clauses.]

✤ PUNCTUATION ALERTS: (1) Choose a semicolon only when the separate sentences are closely related in meaning. (See also 25a.) (2) Occasionally, when your meaning allows it, you can use a colon (Chapter 26) or a dash (Chapter 29) to join two independent clauses. ✤

14c Using coordinating conjunctions to correct comma splices and run-together sentences

You can connect independent clauses° with a coordinating conjunction (*and, but, or, nor, for, so,* and *yet*). If you are correcting a comma splice, keep the comma and insert a coordinating conjunction after it. If you are correcting a run-together sentence, insert a comma followed by a coordinating conjunction.

✤ PUNCTUATION ALERT: Use a comma before a coordinating conjunction that links independent clauses° (see 24a). ✤

✤ USAGE ALERT: When using a coordinating conjunction, be sure that it fits the meaning of the material. *And* signals addition, *but* and *yet* signal contrast, *for* and *so* signal cause, and *or* and *nor* signal alternatives.✤

COMMA SPLICE	Every living creature gives off a weak electrical charge in the water, special pores on a shark's skin can detect these signals.
RUN-TOGETHER SENTENCE	Every living creature gives off a weak electrical charge in the water special pores on a shark's skin can detect these signals.

CORRECTED	Every living creature gives off a weak electrical field in the water, and special pores on a shark's skin can detect these signals.
COMMA SPLICE	The great white shark supposedly eats humans, however most white sharks spit them out after the first bite.
RUN-TOGETHER SENTENCE	The great white shark supposedly eats humans however most white sharks spit them out after the first bite.
CORRECTED	The great white shark supposedly eats humans, but most white sharks spit them out after the first bite.

EXERCISE 14-1

Consulting sections 14a, 14b, and 14c, revise any comma splices or run-together sentences by using a period, a semicolon, or a coordinating conjunction and comma.

EXAMPLE Emily Carr was born in Victoria, British Columbia, in 1871, she died there in 1945.

Emily Carr was born in Victoria, British Columbia, in 1871; she died there in 1945.

1. Carr grew up in a disciplined, conventional household in a small and conservative city, however she went off to study art in San Francisco in 1891, after the death of her parents.
2. When she came home two years later, Carr set up a studio of her own, she roamed the beaches and forests of British Columbia sketching Indian totem poles and longhouses in their natural setting.
3. In 1910, Carr began her most important voyage she travelled to France where she developed the vivid postimpressionist style of painting for which she became known.
4. After Carr's return to Canada, her work showed new vigour clearly, her French experience had taught her how to interpret the powerful rhythms of Northwest Coast Indian art and the majesty of the region's mountains and forests.
5. Carr worked in obscurity until she was fifty-seven, she displayed her work that year in a national exhibition and, with the help of Lawren Harris and other members of the Group of Seven, she began to win wider recognition.

14d Revising an independent clause into a dependent clause to correct a comma splice or run-together sentence

You can revise a comma splice or run-together sentence by changing one of two independent clauses° into a dependent clause°. This method is suitable when one idea can logically be subordinated to the other.

One way to create a dependent clause is to insert a subordinating conjunction (such as *because* and *although*; for a complete list, see Chart 53 in section 7h). When using a subordinating conjunction, be sure that it fits the meaning of the material: for example, *as* and *because* signal reason, *although* signals contrast, *if* signals condition, and *when* signals time. This type of dependent clause is called an **adverb clause.**

COMMA SPLICE	Homer and Langley Collyer had packed their house from top to bottom with junk, police could not open the front door to investigate a missing-persons report on the brothers.
RUN-TOGETHER SENTENCE	Homer and Langley Collyer had packed their house from top to bottom with junk police could not open the front door to investigate a missing-persons report on the brothers.
CORRECTED	**Because Homer and Langley Collyer had packed their house from top to bottom with junk,** police could not open the front door to investigate a missing-persons report on the brothers.
COMMA SPLICE	Old newspapers, toys, car parts, and books filled every room to the ceiling, enough space remained for fourteen pianos.
RUN-TOGETHER SENTENCE	Old newspapers, toys, car parts, and books filled every room to the ceiling enough space remained for fourteen pianos.
CORRECTED	**Although old newspapers, toys, car parts, and books filled every room to the ceiling,** enough space remained for fourteen pianos.

✤ PUNCTUATION ALERTS: (1) If you put a period after a dependent clause that is not attached to an independent clause, you will create the error called a *sentence fragment;* see Chapter 13. (2) Generally, use a comma after an introductory dependent clause that starts with a subordinating conjunction; see 24b-1. ✤

Another way to create a dependent clause is to use a **relative pronoun** (*that, which, who*). This type of dependent clause is called an **adjective clause.**

COMMA SPLICE	The Collyers had been crushed under a pile of newspapers, the newspapers had toppled onto the brothers.
RUN-TOGETHER SENTENCE	The Collyers had been crushed under a pile of newspapers the newspapers had toppled onto the brothers.
CORRECTED	The Collyers had been crushed under a pile of newspapers **that had toppled onto the brothers.**

✤ PUNCTUATION ALERT: To determine whether you need commas to set off an adjective clause, check whether it is nonrestrictive (nonessential) or restrictive° (essential), as explained in 24e. ✤

EXERCISE 14-2

Consulting sections 14a through 14d, revise any comma splices or run-together sentences.

(1) Because millions of North Americans are now cruising the information superhighway, traffic pileups and confrontations are more likely. (2) The Internet connects thousands of online computer networks around the world it has created a new form of personal communication that requires new rules. (3) Just as on a real highway, not all users of the information highway observe "netiquette," the rules governing online courtesy. (4) Sometimes the faceless communication gives timid users confidence to speak their minds, however, at other times some users have less pleasant experiences. (5) A flame, for example, is an insulting message it is the online equivalent of a poison pen letter. (6) The quick response time of e-mail encourages hasty people to react hastily instant anger can be thoughtlessly expressed. (7) Flamers cannot always be identified, their real names are concealed by passwords. (8) Another prank is to impersonate another user by adopting his or her online name, as a result, there is no way to identify the person sending a fake message. (9) Internet lurkers are undesirable too they read other people's messages in the public spaces but are too fearful of being flamed to send their own messages.

14e Using a semicolon or a period before a conjunctive adverb or other transitional expression between independent clauses

Conjunctive adverbs and other transitional expressions link ideas between sentences. When these words fall between sentences, a period or semicolon must immediately precede them.

Conjunctive adverbs include such words as *however, therefore, also, next, then, thus, furthermore,* and *nevertheless* (for a complete list, see Chart 51 in section 7f). Remember that these words are *not* coordinating conjunctions, which work in concert with commas to join independent clauses (see 14c).

COMMA SPLICE	Buying or leasing a car is a matter of individual preference, **however,** it is wise to consider several points before making a decision.
RUN-TOGETHER SENTENCE	Buying or leasing a car is a matter of individual preference **however,** it is wise to consider several points before making a decision.
CORRECTED	Buying or leasing a car is a matter of individual preference; **however,** it is wise to consider several points before making a decision.

✤ PUNCTUATION ALERT: A conjunctive adverb at the beginning of a sentence is usually followed by a comma (see 24b-3). ✤

Transitional expressions include *for example, for instance, in addition, in fact, of course,* and *on the other hand* (see Chart 25 in section 4d-1 for a complete list).

COMMA SPLICE	Car leasing requires a smaller down payment**,** **for example,** in many cases you need only \$1000 or \$2000 and the first monthly payment.
RUN-TOGETHER SENTENCE	Car leasing requires a smaller down payment **for example,** in many cases you need only \$1000 or \$2000 and the first monthly payment.
CORRECTED	Car leasing requires a smaller down payment. **For example,** in many cases you need only \$1000 or \$2000 and the first monthly payment.

✤ PUNCTUATION ALERT: A transitional expression at the beginning of a sentence is usually followed by a comma (see 24b-3). ✤

A conjunctive adverb or other transitional expression can appear in more than one location within an independent clause°. In contrast, a coordinating conjunction (*and, but, or, nor, for, so,* and *yet*) can appear only between independent clauses that it joins.

> Car leasing grows more popular every year. **However,** leasers have nothing to show for their money when the lease ends. [conjunctive adverb at beginning of sentence]
>
> Car leasing grows more popular every year. Leasers, **however,** have nothing to show for their money when the lease ends. [conjunctive adverb in middle of sentence]
>
> Car leasing grows more popular every year. Leasers have nothing to show for their money, **however,** when the lease ends. [conjunctive adverb in middle of sentence]
>
> Car leasing grows more popular every year. Leasers have nothing to show for their money when the lease ends, **however.** [conjunctive adverb at end of sentence]
>
> Car leasing grows more popular every year, **but** leasers have nothing to show for their money when the lease ends. [coordinating conjunction *but* can appear only between two independent clauses]

EXERCISE 14-3

Consulting section 14e, revise any comma splices or run-together sentences caused by a conjunctive adverb or other transitional expression. If an item is correct, circle its number.

EXAMPLE The horror stories of the New England writer H. P. Lovecraft were little known during his lifetime however they gained a following of enthusiastic readers after his death in 1937.

The horror stories of the New England writer H. P. Lovecraft were little known during his lifetime. However, they gained a following of enthusiastic readers after his death in 1937.

1. Lovecraft wrote vividly of monsters from beyond space and time however, he insisted that he did not believe in the supernatural.
2. "The Shadow over Innsmouth" is Lovecraft's famous tale about the strange inhabitants of a New England port, specifically, they are part fish and part human.
3. Lovecraft wanted his invented historical backgrounds to sound factual so he often cited impressive-sounding reference works; of course, he simply made most of them up.
4. Many of Lovecraft's stories mention a volume of secret lore called the *Neocronomicon*, however, it was entirely a product of his imagination.
5. No such book exists nevertheless libraries still receive call slips for the *Neocronomicon* filled out by gullible Lovecraft readers.

EXERCISE 14-4

Consulting all sections in this chapter, revise all comma splices and run-together sentences, using as many different methods of correction as you can. If a sentence is correct, circle its number.

(1) Shortly after midnight on August 21, 1853, the bow of the H.M.S. *Breadalbane* was pierced by a huge shard of ice. (2) The wooden hull's copper sheathing was no protection against a summer storm in Canada's Arctic thus, within fifteen minutes the crew was standing on the pack ice, watching the last of their ship's three masts slip below the surface. (3) The *Breadalbane* was a sturdy Scottish-built merchant ship it had been pressed into service by the Royal Navy to help in the search for the missing Franklin Expedition. (4) Lord John Franklin's two ships and their crews had not returned from their attempt eight years earlier to navigate the Northwest Passage, they were never again seen alive by Europeans.

(5) The twenty-one sailors and officers of the *Breadalbane* were more fortunate they were plucked off the ice by their sister ship, the *Phoenix*. (6) They returned safely to England, however, their ship remained on the ocean floor, almost miraculously preserved by the freezing temperature. (7) Only in 1980 was the wreck located by Dr. Joseph MacInnis he had spent three years searching the southern coast of Beechey Island. (8) The following summer saw MacInnis return to continue studying the most northerly shipwreck ever discovered, it was also the best preserved wooden wreck. (9) MacInnis's team were forced to develop new diving and photographic techniques to use beneath the ice then in 1983 they employed an advanced arctic diving suit and miniature submersible vehicle to complete their exploration. (10) The underwater searchers found a ship that looks almost ready to set sail it still contains the crew's tools and personal effects, and above the deck hangs the signal lamp, forever dark.

Focus on Revising

REVISING YOUR WRITING

If you write comma splices or run-together sentences, go back to your writing and locate them. Then figure out why each is an error by using Chart 89 above section 14a on How to Find and Correct Comma Splices and Run-Together Sentences. Next, using the explanations in 14b through 14e, revise your writing to eliminate the errors.

CASE STUDIES: REVISING TO AVOID COMMA SPLICES AND RUN-TOGETHER SENTENCES

In these case studies, you can observe a student writer revising. Then you have the chance to revise other student writing on your own.

Observation

A student wrote the following draft for a course called Introduction to Business Studies. The assignment was to discuss a social problem that might arise in the workplace. This material is well organized and presents its information clearly and fully. However, the draft's effectiveness is diminished by comma splices and run-together sentences.

Read through the draft. The errors are highlighted and explained. Before you look at the student's revision, revise the material yourself. Then compare your revision with the student's.

In the past few years, women have made momentous strides in establishing themselves in the workplace. Yet, studies show that one understated factor may still be holding women back, they rarely seek relationships with women mentors. Instead, young women starting their careers choose men

comma splice with pronoun *they*: 14a

as role models. But there is a problem with choosing a male mentor it doesn't allow young women to get the gender-related advice they need in order to reach their highest potential.

run-together sentence with pronoun *it*:14a

Because of old-time attitudes and because others might think they are discussing discrimination, harassment, or other touchy subjects, women often feel uncomfortable talking with each other. However, there are other reasons why senior women feel uncomfortable mentoring their junior counterparts, they feel that failure in a younger protégée is a poor reflection on them. In addition, there is a mutual assumption between junior and senior women that they have nothing in common. Senior women often had to sacrifice their social and family life in order to get ahead thus most senior women are accustomed to working twelve-hour days. Junior women, on the other hand, have more opportunities to get ahead without sacrificing their families or personal lives, they are able to strike a balance between the office and home. Senior men have quite a different experience with their young protégés they see the young men as reminders of their earlier career days.

comma splice with pronoun *they:* 14a

run-together sentence with conjunctive adverb *thus:* 14a

comma splice with pronoun *they:* 14a

run-together sentence with explanation in second independent clause: 14a

Young women are constantly seeking to create a personal balance, they need mentors to whom they can relate →

comma splice with pronoun *they:* 14a

on a personal and professional level. One thing is evident, for a woman to succeed in the workplace, she will have to approach experienced women for advice, not their male counterparts.

comma splice with explanation in the second independent clause: 14a

Here is how the student revised the draft to correct comma splices and run-together sentences. In many places, the student could correct the errors in more than one way. Your revision, therefore, might not be exactly like this one, but it should deal with each error highlighted on the draft.

In the past few years, women have made momentous strides in establishing themselves in the workforce. Yet, studies show that one understated factor may still be holding women back: They rarely seek relationships with women mentors. Instead, young women starting their careers choose men as role models. But there is a problem with choosing a male mentor. It doesn't allow young women to get the gender-related advice they need in order to reach their highest potential.

Because of old-time attitudes and because others might think they are discussing discrimination, harassment, or other touchy subjects, women often feel uncomfortable talking with each other. However, there are other reasons why senior women feel uncomfortable mentoring their junior counterparts. They feel that failure in a younger protégée is a poor reflection on them. In addition, there is a mutual assumption between junior and senior women that they have nothing in common. Senior women often had to sacrifice their social and family life in order to get ahead. Thus, most senior women are accustomed to working twelve-hour days. Junior women, on the other hand, have more opportunities to get ahead without sacrificing their families or personal lives. They are able to strike a balance between the office and home. Senior men have quite a different experience with their young protégés. They see the young men as reminders of their earlier career days.

Young women, who are constantly seeking to create a personal balance, need mentors to whom they can relate on a personal and professional level. One thing is evident: For a woman to succeed in the workplace, she will have to approach experienced women for advice, not their male counterparts.

Participation

A student wrote the following draft for a course called Introduction to Magazine Writing. The assignment was to write a popular account of current research in one area of psychology. This material is well organized and uses specific examples well, but the draft's effectiveness is diminished by comma splices and run-together sentences.

Read through the draft. Then revise it to eliminate the comma splices and run-together sentences. Also, make any additional revisions that you think would improve the content, organization, and style of the material.

Psychologists' research has suggested that happiness is not dependent on money, a good job, or marriage instead happiness may be largely determined by an individual's genes, not outside factors.

Although life's ups and downs may affect a mood level, this emotional reaction to events is only temporary. Inevitably, the happy will be happy again, and the sad will be sad again. Researchers suggest that each individual has a set point for happiness it genetically determines the individual's mood level. It is said, in fact, that about half of an individual's sense of well-being is determined by his or her set point the remaining half comes from very recent pleasures or sorrows.

Studies show that money rarely has an impact on most people's happiness, however for the poor, the opposite is true. Lottery winners typically return to their pre-lottery mood level about a year after the win.

When testing the set-point concept on twins, researchers found that life circumstances hardly mattered at all, they accounted for a mere two percent of happiness variation. Although most researchers accept the validity of the set-point arguments, there is still the question of exactly how much an individual's happiness is determined by this factor.

It is suggested that those with more brain activity on the left pre-frontal area get more pleasure from ordinary life activities. In contrast, those with more activity on the right are more easily distressed or worried nevertheless people can increase their happiness level by incorporating personal pleasures—like reading a favourite book or visiting friends—into their daily routines. Researchers say that doing that will lift a person's mood much more significantly than winning the lottery ever could. Believe it or not.

15 Awkward Sentences

A sentence can seem structurally correct at first glance, as if no grammatical principles of English had been violated, but can still have internal flaws that keep it from delivering a sensible message. While you are drafting°, if you suspect that you have made one of these errors, quickly underline or highlight the material and move on. Then, you can easily find and check it later.

WAYS THAT SENTENCES SEND UNCLEAR MESSAGES 90

PROBLEM	SEE SECTION
■ Unnecessary shifts	
Person° and number°	15a-1
Subject° and voice°	15a-2
Tense° and mood°	15a-3
Direct discourse° and indirect discourse°	15a-4
■ Misplaced modifiers°	15b
■ Dangling modifiers°	15c
■ Mixed sentences	
Mixed constructions	15d-1
Faulty predication	15d-2
■ Incomplete sentences	15e

Many flaws that make sentences awkward can be hard to spot because of the way the human brain works. When writers know what they mean to say, they sometimes misread what is on the paper for what they intend. The mind unconsciously adjusts an error or fills in missing material. Readers, on the other hand, see only what is on the paper. For suggestions to help you see such flaws, see Chart 91.

NO Heated for 30 seconds, you get bubbles on the surface of the mixture. [This sentence says *you* are heated for 30 seconds.]

YES After the mixture is heated for 30 seconds, bubbles form on the surface.

NO The chemical reaction taking place rapidly creates a salt. [*Rapidly* could refer to the speed of the reaction or to the speed at which the salt is created; readers cannot know.]

YES The chemical reaction takes place rapidly and creates a salt.

YES The chemical reaction rapidly creates a salt.

PROOFREADING TO FIND SENTENCE FLAWS 91

- Finish your revision in enough time so you can put it aside and go back to it with fresh eyes that can spot flaws more easily.
- Work backwards, from your last sentence to your first, so that you can see each sentence as a separate unit free of a context that might lure you to overlook flaws.
- Ask an experienced reader to check your writing for sentence flaws. If you make an error discussed in this chapter, you likely make that error repeatedly. Once you become aware of it, you will have made a major step toward eliminating that type of error.
- Proofread an extra time exclusively for any error that you tend to make more than any other.

15a Avoiding unnecessary shifts

Shift is a term for an abrupt, unneeded change of person°, number°, subject°, voice°, tense°, mood°, or kind of discourse (direct° or indirect°). Unnecessary shifts blur meaning. Readers expect to stay on the track that you as the writer start them on. If you switch tracks, your readers become confused.

1 Staying consistent in person and number

Person in English consists of the *first person (I, we),* words that designate the speaker or writer; *second person (you),* the word that designates the one being spoken or written to; and *third person (he, she, it, they),* words that designate the person or thing spoken or written about. All common nouns° are third-person words. (For more about person, see Chart 75 in section 11b.)

NO **They** enjoy feeling productive, but when a job is unsatisfying, **you** usually become depressed. [*They* shifts to *you.*]

YES **They** enjoy feeling productive, but when a job is unsatisfying, **they** usually become depressed.

Number refers to *singular* (one) or *plural* (more than one). Do not start to write in one number and then shift for no reason to the other number. Such shifting gives your sentences an unstable quality.

NO Because most **people** are living longer, an **employee** in the twenty-first century will retire later. [The plural *people* shifts to the singular *employee.*]

YES Because most **people** are living longer, **employees** in the twenty-first century will retire later.

A common cause of inconsistency in person and number is shifts to *you* (second person) from *I* (first person) or from a noun (third person) such as *person, the public,* or *people.* In academic writing, reserve *you* for sentences that address the reader directly; use the third person for general statements.

NO **I** enjoy reading forecasts of the future, but **you** wonder which will turn out to be correct. [*I,* which is first person, shifts to *you,* which is second person.]

YES **I** enjoy reading forecasts of the future, but **I** wonder which will turn out to be correct.

NO By the year 2020, **North Americans** will pay twice today's price for a car, and **you** will get twice the gas efficiency. [*North Americans,* which is third person, shifts to *you,* which is second person.]

YES By the year 2020, **North Americans** will pay twice today's price for a car, and **they** will get twice the gas efficiency.

Another common shift in number is using *they* (the plural third-person pronoun) although its antecedent° is a singular third-person pronoun.

Only *he* or *she* (or *he or she*, which acts as a singular pronoun) or *it* can refer to a singular noun. Especially when you use words such as *employee* or *someone* in a general sense, without any specific "employee" or "someone" in mind, you might think that a "he" or "she" is not involved. Still, you have to choose a singular pronoun. Another choice is to change to the plural *employees*, in which case the plural pronoun *they* is correct. A third possibility is revising so that personal pronouns are unneeded.

NO When an **employee** is treated with respect, **they** usually feel highly motivated.

YES When an **employee** is treated with respect, **he or she** usually feels highly motivated.

YES When **employees** are treated with respect, **they** usually feel highly motivated.

YES **Employees** who are treated with respect usually feel highly motivated.

YES An **employee** who is treated with respect usually feels highly motivated.

Try to avoid sexist language when you use indefinite pronouns (such as *someone* or *everyone;* for a complete list, see Chart 80 in 11g); see 11q and especially 21b for advice about nonsexist language.

✤ VERB ALERT: After you have revised person or number, check the verbs in the sentence to see whether any verb needs a change in number as well (see 8c). In the examples just shown, all *Yes* choices contain verb changes. ✤

EXERCISE 15-1

Consulting section 15a-1, eliminate shifts in person and number. Be alert to shifts between, as well as within, sentences. Some sentences may not need revision.

(1) According to some experts, snobbery is measured by your mental attitude, not the extent of your worldly goods. (2) Because a snob is unsure of his or her social position, snobs are driven by what others think of them. (3) You tend to be too dependent on buying status symbols to define your place in the world, and snobs look down on others. (4) The origin of this word can be traced to the British Isles. (5) When commoners were first allowed to enter England's Cambridge University in the 1700s, each student was required to identify their social position. (6) The commoner had to use the Latin words *sine nobilitate*, meaning "without nobility." (7) Eventually, the students shortened this phrase to "s.nob," and the word came to signify persons aspiring to a higher social level.

2 Staying consistent in subject and voice

The **subject** of a sentence is the word or group of words that acts, is acted upon, or is described: ***People*** *laugh,* ***people*** *were entertained,* ***people*** *are nice.*

Some subject shifts are justified by the meaning of a passage: ***People*** *look forward to the future, but* ***the future*** *holds many secrets.*

Shift in subject is rarely justified when it is accompanied by a shift in **voice.** The voice of a sentence is either *active (People expect changes)* or *passive (Changes are expected).* (For information about active and passive voice, see 8n–8o.) Unnecessary shifts in subject and voice cause a sentence or longer stretch of writing to go out of focus.

NO Most **people expect** major improvements in the future, but some **hardships are also anticipated.** [The subject shifts from *people* to *hardships,* and the voice shifts from active to passive.]

YES Most **people expect** major improvements in the future, but **they also anticipate** some hardships.

YES Most people expect major improvements in the future but also anticipate some hardships.

3 Staying consistent in tense and mood

Tense refers to the ability of verbs to show time. Tense changes are required to describe time changes: *We will go to the movies after we finish dinner.* If a tense shift within or between sentences is illogical, clarity suffers. (For information about correct sequences of tenses, see section 8k.)

NO The campaign to clean up the movies **began** in the 1920s as civic and religious groups **try** to ban sex and violence from the screen. [The tense shifts from the past *began* to the present *try.*]

YES The campaign to clean up the movies **began** in the 1920s as civic and religious groups **tried** to ban sex and violence from the screen.

NO Producers and distributors **created** a film Production Code in the 1930s. At first, violating its guidelines **carried** no penalty. Eventually, however, films that **fail** to get the board's Seal of Approval **do not receive** wide distribution. [This shift occurs between sentences: The past tense *created* and *carried* shift to the present tense *fail* and *do not receive.*]

YES Producers and distributors **created** a film Production Code in the 1930s. At first, violating its guidelines **carried** no penalty. Eventually, however, films that **failed** to get the board's Seal of Approval **did not receive** wide distribution.

Mood refers to whether a sentence is a statement or question (*indicative mood*), a command or request (*imperative mood*), or a conditional or other-than-real statement (*subjunctive mood*); see section 8l. A shift between moods may blur the message of a passage.

NO The Production Code included two guidelines about violence. **Do not show** the details of brutal killings, and **movies should not be** explicit about how to commit crimes. [The verbs shift from the imperative mood *do not show* to the indicative mood *movies should not be.*]

YES The Production Code included two guidelines about violence: **Do not show** the details of brutal killings, and **do not show** explicitly how to commit crimes. [This revision uses the imperative mood for both guidelines.]

YES The Production Code included two guidelines about violence. **Movies were not to show** the details of brutal killings or explicit ways to commit crimes.

NO The Code writers worried that if a crime **were to be accurately depicted** in a movie, copycat crimes **will follow.** [The sentence shifts from the subjunctive mood *if a crime were to be depicted* to the indicative mood *copycat crimes will follow.*]

YES The Code writers worried that if a crime **were to be accurately depicted** in a movie, copycat crimes **would follow.**

4 Avoiding unmarked shifts between indirect and direct discourse

Indirect discourse reports speech or conversation and is not enclosed in quotation marks. **Direct discourse** repeats speech or conversation exactly and encloses the spoken words in quotation marks (see 24g). Sentences that merge indirect and direct discourse without quotation marks and without other necessary changes that mark words as either reported or quoted distort the intended message.

NO A critic said that board members were acting as censors and **what you are doing is dictatorial.** [The first clause is indirect discourse; the second clause shifts into unmarked direct discourse, garbling the message.]

YES A critic said that board members were acting as censors and **that what they were doing was dictatorial.** [This revision consistently uses indirect discourse.]

YES A critic said that board members were acting as censors and added, **"What you are doing is dictatorial."** [This revision uses indirect and direct discourse correctly, with quotation marks and other changes to distinguish reported words from spoken words.]

Changing a message from a direct-discourse version to an indirect-discourse version usually requires a change of verb tense° and other grammatical features. Simply removing the quotation marks is not enough.

NO He asked **did we enjoy** the movie? [This version has the verb form needed for direct discourse, but the pronoun *we* is wrong and quotation punctuation is missing.]

YES He asked **whether we enjoyed** the movie. [This version is entirely indirect discourse, and the verb has changed from *enjoy* to *enjoyed*.]

YES He asked, **"Did you enjoy** the movie?" [This version is direct discourse. It repeats the original speech exactly, with correct quotation punctuation.]

EXERCISE 15-2

Consulting section 15a, revise these sentences to eliminate all incorrect shifts. Some sentences can be revised several ways.

EXAMPLE During the Victorian era, all gentlemen worthy of the name are obliged to raise their hats to ladies.

During the Victorian era, all gentlemen worthy of the name *were* obliged to raise their hats to ladies.

1. The Victorian male's custom of tipping his hat had serious drawbacks, though; for instance, if you were carrying parcels you would have to set them down first.
2. In 1896, an inventor named James Boyle developed a self-tipping hat that solves the problem.
3. If a man nodded while wearing Boyle's invention, they activated a lifting mechanism concealed in the hat's crown.

4. Boyle claimed that since the novelty of the moving hat would attract attention, advertising also can be one of its uses.
5. He said that companies could place signs on the hats and you will be able to advertise any product innovatively and inexpensively.

EXERCISE 15-3

Consulting section 15a, revise this paragraph to eliminate incorrect shifts between, as well as within, sentences.

(1) When people think positively, your chances of success really do seem to go up. (2) A psychologist in Kansas confirms that optimists hold an advantage over a less hopeful person. (3) He finds that an optimist often does better than expected in school and could handle stress at work more easily than other people. (4) Other researchers praise the benefits of optimism in her study of patients who must cope with severe illnesses. (5) These psychologists designed a "hope scale" that ranks people according to their level of hopefulness and is used to place them among either the optimistic crowd or the less optimistic crowd. (6) The psychologists contend that optimists are not simply someone who thinks, "I'm a winner," and therefore says that things always turn out right for me in the end. (7) Rather, a true optimist combines confidence in his or her problem-solving abilities with the readiness to seek advice from friends. (8) True optimists had to be willing to motivate yourself so that important goals can be accomplished.

15b Avoiding misplaced modifiers

A **modifier** is a word or word group that describes another word or words. A **misplaced modifier** is positioned incorrectly in a sentence, therefore describing the wrong word, and thus distorting meaning. As you write and revise, always check to see that your modifiers are placed as close as possible to what they describe so that your reader will be able to follow your intended meaning.

1 Avoiding ambiguous placements

With **ambiguous placement,** a modifier is confusing to a reader because it can refer to two or more words in a sentence.

Limiting words (such as *only, not only, just, not just, almost, hardly, nearly, even, exactly, merely, scarcely, simply*) can change meaning according to where they are placed. When you use such words, position them precisely. Consider how different placements of *only* change the meaning of this sentence: *Professional coaches say that high salaries motivate players.*

> **Only** professional coaches say that high salaries motivate players. [No one else says this.]
>
> Professional coaches **only** say that high salaries motivate players. [The coaches probably do not mean what they say.]
>
> Professional coaches say **only** that high salaries motivate players. [The coaches say nothing else.]
>
> Professional coaches say that **only** high salaries motivate players. [Nothing except high salaries motivates players.]
>
> Professional coaches say that high salaries **only** motivate players. [High salaries do nothing other than motivate players.]
>
> Professional coaches say that high salaries motivate **only** players. [No others on the team, such as coaches and managers, are motivated by high salaries.]

Squinting modifiers are ambiguous because they can describe both what precedes and what follows them. For clarity, revise the sentence, making sure that the modifier is positioned where its meaning is precise.

NO The football player being recruited **fervently** believed each successive offer would be better. [What was **fervent,** the recruitment or the player's belief?]

YES The football player being recruited believed **fervently** that each successive offer would be better.

YES The football player being **fervently** recruited believed that each successive offer would be better.

2 Avoiding interrupting placements

Interrupting placements are awkward interruptions that seriously break the flow of a message and thereby distract your reader from understanding your material. A **split infinitive** is one type of awkward interruption. (An **infinitive** is a verb form that starts with *to: to convince, to create.*) When material comes between the *to* and its verb, it can interrupt meaning.

NO Orson Welles's radio drama "War of the Worlds" managed **to,** in October 1938, **convince** listeners that they were hearing an invasion by Martians.

YES In October 1938, Orson Welles's radio drama "War of the Worlds" managed **to convince** listeners that they were hearing an invasion by Martians.

Often the intervening word that splits an infinitive is an adverb ending in *-ly*. Many such adverbs sound awkward unless they are placed either before or after the infinitive.

NO People feared they would no longer be able **to happily live** in peace.

YES People feared they would no longer be able **to live happily** in peace.

Nevertheless, sometimes an adverb° fits best between *to* and the verb°. Many readers, therefore, are not distracted by split infinitives like this one:

Welles wanted **to realistically portray** a Martian invasion for the radio audience.

If you think your readers prefer that infinitives never be split, you can usually revise the sentence to avoid the split:

Welles wanted his "Martian invasion" **to sound** realistic for the radio audience.

Interruptions of subjects° and verbs, verb phrases°, and verbs and objects° can disturb the smooth flow of a sentence.

NO The **announcer,** because the script, which Welles himself wrote, called for perfect imitations of emergency announcements, **opened** with a warning that included a description of the "invasion." [subject–verb interrupted]

YES Because the script, which Welles himself wrote, called for perfect imitations of emergency announcements, **the announcer opened** with a warning that included a description of the "invasion."

NO Many churches **held** for their frightened communities **"end of the world" prayer services.** [verb–direct object interrupted]

YES Many churches **held "end of the world" prayer services** for their frightened communities.

EXERCISE 15-4

Consulting section 15b, revise these sentences to correct any ambiguous, wrong, or awkward placements. If a sentence is correct, circle its number.

EXAMPLE The invention of the first car took place in 1885, one of the greatest accomplishments in history.

The invention of the first car, *one of the greatest accomplishments in history,* took place in 1885.

1. The origins of the automobile can, if we look back in history, be found in 1769 in France.
2. The Frenchman Nicholas Cugnot, because of his determination to travel without the assistance of animals, built the first self-propelled vehicle.
3. Cugnot's invention only was powered by steam.
4. During a trial drive, the vehicle, which was run by a huge steam boiler that hung in front of its single front wheel and which was difficult to steer and hard to stop, knocked over a rock wall.
5. The invention of various types of gas-combustion engines, beginning in 1860, provided an alternative to clumsy steam power.
6. Two other inventors, Karl Benz and Gottlieb Daimler, were, in Germany, trying to invent a gas-driven vehicle.
7. Only they lived about 100 kilometres apart, but they did not know each other.
8. Benz is finally the man who produced the first car and was given credit for the invention of the automobile.
9. The first car rolled, after the finishing touches had been added, out of a workshop in a small German town.
10. It rattled and banged down the street to loudly and dramatically announce a revolution in transportation.

EXERCISE 15-5

Consulting section 15b, combine each list of word groups to create all the possible logical sentences (each list offers more than one possibility). Insert commas as needed. Use a slash to indicate where each word or group of words ends. Explain differences in meaning, if any, among the alternatives you create.

EXAMPLE runners
than couch potatoes do
have lower blood pressure
for the most part

A. For the most part, / runners / have lower blood pressure / than couch potatoes do. /

B. Runners / have lower blood pressure, / for the most part, / than couch potatoes do. /

C. Runners, / for the most part, / have lower blood pressure / than couch potatoes do. /

D. Runners / have lower blood pressure / than couch potatoes do, / for the most part. /

1. studied
   an entertainment lawyer
   corporate and copyright law
   the student
   to become
   intensively

2. introduced the
   happily
   muscular artist
   the matchmaker
   to the
   wrestler

3. climbed
   the limber teenager
   a tall palm tree
   to pick a ripe coconut
   quickly

4. and cause mini-avalanches
   ski patrollers
   set explosives
   often
   to prevent big avalanches

5. chicken soup
   according to folklore
   helps
   cure colds

15c Avoiding dangling modifiers

A **dangling modifier** describes or limits a word or words that are not stated in a sentence. Because a reader will "attach" the information in the dangling modifier to a noun° or pronoun° that *does* appear in the sentence, the writer's intended meaning is lost.

Dangling modifiers can be hard for a writer to spot. Aware of the intended meaning, the writer unconsciously supplies the missing material, but the reader usually sees only the error and realizes that the meaning is flawed. You can correct a dangling modifier by revising the sentence so that the intended subject° is stated.

NO **Reading Faulkner's short story "A Rose for Emily,"** the ending surprised us. [The *reading* cannot be done by an *ending*.]

YES **Having read Faulkner's short story "A Rose for Emily," we** were surprised by the ending.

YES We read Faulkner's short story "A Rose for Emily" and were surprised by the ending.

NO **When courting Emily, the townspeople** gossiped about her. [*The townspeople* were not courting Emily.]

YES **When Homer Barron was courting Emily, the townspeople** gossiped about her.

Dangling modifiers are sometimes caused by unnecessary use of the passive voice° (see 8n–8o).

NO **To earn money, china-painting lessons** were offered by Emily to wealthy young women. [*China-painting lessons* cannot earn money.]

YES **To earn money, Emily** offered china-painting lessons to wealthy young women.

EXERCISE 15-6

Consulting section 15c, identify and correct any dangling modifiers in these sentences. If a sentence is correct, circle its number.

EXAMPLE Starting out as a short-order cook, the work can be confusing at first to a trainee.

Starting out as a short-order cook, *a trainee can find the work confusing at first.*

1. Cooking in a busy coffee shop or diner, a quick pair of hands is a necessity for a short-order cook.
2. To do a good job, the ability to concentrate is also a must for a short-order cook.
3. Especially at lunchtime, customers expect their meals *yesterday morning.*
4. While preparing several orders at once, kitchen utensils and ingredients have to be located at a moment's notice.
5. Although often hard to keep straight, a long list of orders and recipes must be remembered by the cook.
6. When first learning the job, orders like "wreck two" and "cowboy" may be puzzling.
7. After catching on to the diner staff's slang, "wreck two" for an order of two scrambled eggs and "cowboy" for a Western omelet will make sense.
8. Crammed with food and utensils, an inexperienced cook may see a diner's small kitchen as a stressful place to work.
9. The pressures of the job can begin to become manageable, however, by learning how to plan ahead for the busy times.
10. Along with the diner's other workers, the opportunity also exists to enjoy the funny slang, joking conversations, and even the hectic pace.

15d Avoiding mixed sentences

A **mixed sentence** consists of parts that do not make sense together because the writer has lost track of the beginning of a sentence while writing the end. Careful proofreading, including reading aloud, can help a writer avoid this error.

1 Revising mixed constructions

A **mixed construction** starts out taking one grammatical form and then changes, derailing the meaning of the sentence.

NO Because television's first large-scale transmissions included news programs quickly became popular with the public. [The opening dependent clause° starts off on one track, but the independent clause° goes off in another direction. What does the writer want to emphasize—the first transmissions or the popularity of news programs?]

YES Television's first large-scale transmissions included news programs, which quickly became popular with the public. [The idea of the first transmissions is emphasized.]

YES Because television's first large-scale transmissions included news programs, television quickly became popular with the public. [The idea of the popularity of the news programs is now emphasized.]

NO By increasing the time allotment for network news to thirty minutes increased the prestige of network news programs. [A prepositional phrase°, such as *by increasing,* cannot be the subject of a sentence.]

YES Increasing the time allotment for network news to thirty minutes increased the prestige of network news programs. [Dropping the preposition *by* clears up the problem.]

YES By increasing the time allotment for network news to thirty minutes, the network executives increased the prestige of network news programs. [Inserting a logical subject, *the network executives,* clears up the problem; an independent clause° is now preceded by a modifying prepositional phrase°.]

The phrase *the fact that* is sometimes the cause of a mixed sentence.

NO The fact that quiz show scandals in the 1950s prompted the networks to produce even more news shows.

YES The fact is that quiz show scandals in the 1950s prompted the networks to produce even more news shows. [The added *is* clarifies the meaning.]

YES Quiz show scandals in the 1950s prompted the networks to produce even more news shows. [Dropping *the fact that* clarifies the meaning.]

2 Revising faulty predication

Faulty predication, sometimes called *illogical predication,* occurs when a subject° and its predicate° do not make sense together.

NO The **purpose** of television **was invented** to entertain people.

YES The **purpose** of television was to entertain people.

YES **Television was invented** to entertain people.

One key cause of illogical predication is a breakdown in the connection between a subject and its complement°. (A subject complement can be a noun°, a pronoun°, a noun clause° renaming a sentence subject, or an adjective° describing a sentence subject; see 7m-1.)

In the following *No* example, the subject complement *credible* could logically describe Lloyd Robertson, but *Lloyd Robertson* is not the subject. The subject is *characteristic,* so the meaning calls for a subject complement that renames some characteristic of Lloyd Robertson as a newscaster: thus, *credibility* instead of *credible.*

NO Lloyd Robertson's outstanding **characteristic is credible** as a newscaster.

YES Lloyd Robertson's outstanding **characteristic is credibility** as a newscaster. [The noun *credibility* renames *characteristic.*]

YES **Lloyd Robertson is credible** as a newscaster. [The adjective *credible* describes the subject *Lloyd Robertson.*]

Illogical predication is a problem in many constructions that include *is when* or *is where.* Avoid these phrases.

NO A disaster **is when** television news shows get some of their highest ratings.

YES Television news shows get some of their highest ratings during a disaster.

Also, avoid *reason ... is because* constructions. Use *reason ... is that* instead. Remember that *because* means "for the reason that," so *reason ... is because* literally means "reason ... is for the reason that," which is repetitious.

NO One **reason** television news captured widespread attention **is because** it covered the Vietnam War thoroughly.

YES One **reason** television news captured widespread attention **is that** it covered the Vietnam War thoroughly.

YES Television news captured widespread attention **because** it covered the Vietnam War thoroughly.

EXERCISE 15-7

Consulting section 15d, revise the mixed sentences below so that the beginning of each sentence fits logically with its end. If a sentence is correct, circle its number.

EXAMPLE In 1937, under the sponsorship of Lord Tweedsmuir, who was the Governor General at the time, sponsored the launching of the Governor General's Literary Awards.

In 1937, Lord Tweedsmuir, who was the Governor General at the time, sponsored the launching of the Governor General's Literary Awards.

1. The reason that Governor General Lord Tweedsmuir is better known in some quarters as John Buchan is because under that name he wrote *The Thirty-Nine Steps,* a spy novel that was filmed by Alfred Hitchcock.
2. The Governor General's Awards that he helped establish have become the greatest desirability of any literary awards in Canada, and as a result, the categories of works for which they are awarded have undergone frequent expansion and revision.
3. The fact that at first, only books in English were eligible for the awards, a situation that many believed to be a serious oversight.
4. The solution to this problem was remedied in 1959, when the Canada Council began to administer the awards and established an identical set of Governor General's Awards for works in French.
5. A controversial episode was when the refusal of an award in 1968, when Leonard Cohen declined the prize for his *Selected Poems, 1956–1968* and said, "Much in me strives for this honour, but the poems themselves forbid it absolutely."
6. About the same time, a less enigmatic explanation for refusing the award was given by several nationalistic Quebec writers announced they were rejecting it for political reasons.

7. However, in 1992 Cohen accepted the newly instituted Governor General's Performing Arts Award, so apparently his songs, unlike his poems, did permit that honour.
8. Although the judgment and taste of the awards' juries have sometimes been questioned, but we can note in their favour that recipients have included important writers such as Margaret Atwood, Northrop Frye, Alice Munro, Mavis Gallant, and Robertson Davies.
9. When we examine this list of writers stands up well against the winners of any literary award.
10. Every year, a gala ceremony is where the current Governor General presents the literary prizes first awarded by Lord Tweedsmuir, the writer of suspense stories who became the monarch's representative in Canada.

15e Avoiding incomplete sentences

An **incomplete sentence** is missing words, phrases°, or clauses° necessary for grammatical correctness or sensible meaning. Such omissions blur your meaning, and your reader has to work hard to understand your message.

Using elliptical constructions carefully

An **elliptical construction** deliberately leaves out, rather than repeats, one or more words that appear elsewhere in the sentence. *I have my book and Joan's,* for example, is an acceptable way to express *I have my book and Joan's book.* An elliptical construction is correct only if the sentence contains the *exact* word or words omitted from the elliptical construction. Thus, *I have my book and Joan's* cannot be used to express the thought that Joan, for example, has many *books.*

NO In the 1980s, software expertise and communications equipment **were becoming** two major Canadian exports, and comedy talent a third. [The words *were becoming* cannot take the place of *has become,* which the subject *comedy talent* requires.]

YES In the 1980s, software expertise and communications equipment **were becoming** two major Canadian exports, and comedy talent **was becoming** a third.

YES In the 1980s, software expertise and communications equipment **became** two major Canadian exports, and comedy talent a third. [The verb *became* is correct both with *software expertise and communications equipment* and with *comedy talent* and thus can be omitted after *comedy talent.*]

NO Talented expatriates have **appeared** and **written for** *Saturday Night Live, David Letterman*, and other shows that gave television comedy a new, ironic attitude. [This sentence implies *for* after *appeared*, but *appeared* requires *in*, not *for*.]

YES Talented expatriates have **appeared in** and **written for** *Saturday Night Live, David Letterman*, and other shows that gave television comedy a new, ironic attitude.

2 Making comparisons complete, unambiguous, and logical

In writing a comparison, be sure to include all words needed to make clear the relationship between the items or ideas being compared.

NO Individuals with high concern for achievement make **better** business executives. [*Better* implies a comparison, but none is stated.]

YES Individuals with high concern for achievement make **better** business executives **than** do people with little interest in personal accomplishments.

NO Most personnel officers value high achievers more than risk takers. [Unclear: more than risk takers value high achievers, or more than personnel officers value risk takers?]

YES Most personnel officers value high achievers more than they value risk takers.

YES Most personnel officers value high achievers more than risk takers do.

NO A risk taker's chance of success is very different. [Different from what?]

YES A risk taker's chance of success is very different **from a high achiever's.**

NO Achievers value success **as much,** if not more than, a high salary. [Comparisons using *as* ... *as* require the second *as*.]

YES Achievers value success **as much as,** if not more than, a high salary.

In speech, sentences such as *That was such a difficult exam, You're so smart,* or *I'm too upset* are common. These constructions use *so, too,* and *such* as intensifiers. In academic writing, be sure to supply the completing information or take out the intensifier.

NO Risk takers are often **such** innovative people.

YES Risk takers are often **such** innovative people that some businesses seek them out as employees.

YES Risk takers are often innovative people.

3 Proofreading for inadvertently omitted little words

Little words—articles°, pronouns°, conjunctions°, and prepositions°—needed to make sentences complete tend to drop out when a writer is rushing or is distracted. If you tend to omit small words, proofread your work an extra time exclusively to discover the missing words.

NO On May 2, 1808, citizens Madrid rioted against French soldiers.

YES On May 2, 1808, **the** citizens **of** Madrid rioted against French soldiers.

NO On following day, captured rioters were taken into country and shot.

YES On **the** following day, captured rioters were taken into **the** country and shot.

NO The Spanish painter Francisco Goya recorded both the riot the execution in a pair of pictures painted 1814.

YES The Spanish painter Francisco Goya recorded both the riot **and** the execution in a pair of pictures painted **in** 1814.

EXERCISE 15-8

Consulting section 15e, revise this paragraph to create correct elliptical constructions, to complete comparisons, and to insert any missing words.

(1) A giant tsunami is as destructive and even larger than a tidal wave. (2) The word *tsunami* is Japanese for "harbour wave," for this kind wave appears suddenly in harbour or bay. (3) It begins with rapid shift in ocean floor caused by an undersea earthquake or volcano. (4) The wave this produces in the open sea is less than one metre high, but it can grow to a height of thirty metres as it rushes and strikes against the shore. (5) For this reason, tsunamis are much more dangerous to seaside towns than ships on the open sea. (6) In 1960, a huge tsunami that struck coasts of Chile, Hawaii, and Japan killed total of 590 people.

Focus on Revising

REVISING YOUR WRITING

If you write sentences that send unclear messages, go back to your writing and locate the errors. Using this chapter as a resource, revise your writing to eliminate unnecessary shifts (15a), misplaced modifiers (15b), dangling modifiers (15c), mixed sentences (15d), and incomplete sentences (15e).

CASE STUDIES: REVISING TO CORRECT SENTENCES THAT SEND UNCLEAR MESSAGES

In these case studies, you can observe a student writer revising. Then you have the chance to revise other student writing on your own.

Observation

A student wrote the following draft for a course called Introduction to Child Development. The assignment was to compose a brief account of a developmental problem and the practical means that could be used to address it. This draft outlines the problem clearly and gives a concise, well-organized account of its treatment. The draft's effectiveness is diminished, however, by the presence of sentences that send unclear messages by unnecessary shifts, misplaced modifiers, dangling modifiers, mixed sentences, and incomplete sentences.

Read through the draft. The unclear messages are highlighted and explained. Before you look at the student's revision, revise the material yourself. Then compare what you and the student did.

ambiguous comparison: 15e-2

dangling modifier: 15c

unnecessary shift in person: 15a-1

Children with many friends, researchers suggest, have an easier time adjusting to life's challenges. By not interacting with friends, getting into trouble and dropping out of school become more likely for children. Friends cannot be seen as a luxury for children; you have to see them as a necessity for healthy child development. ➜

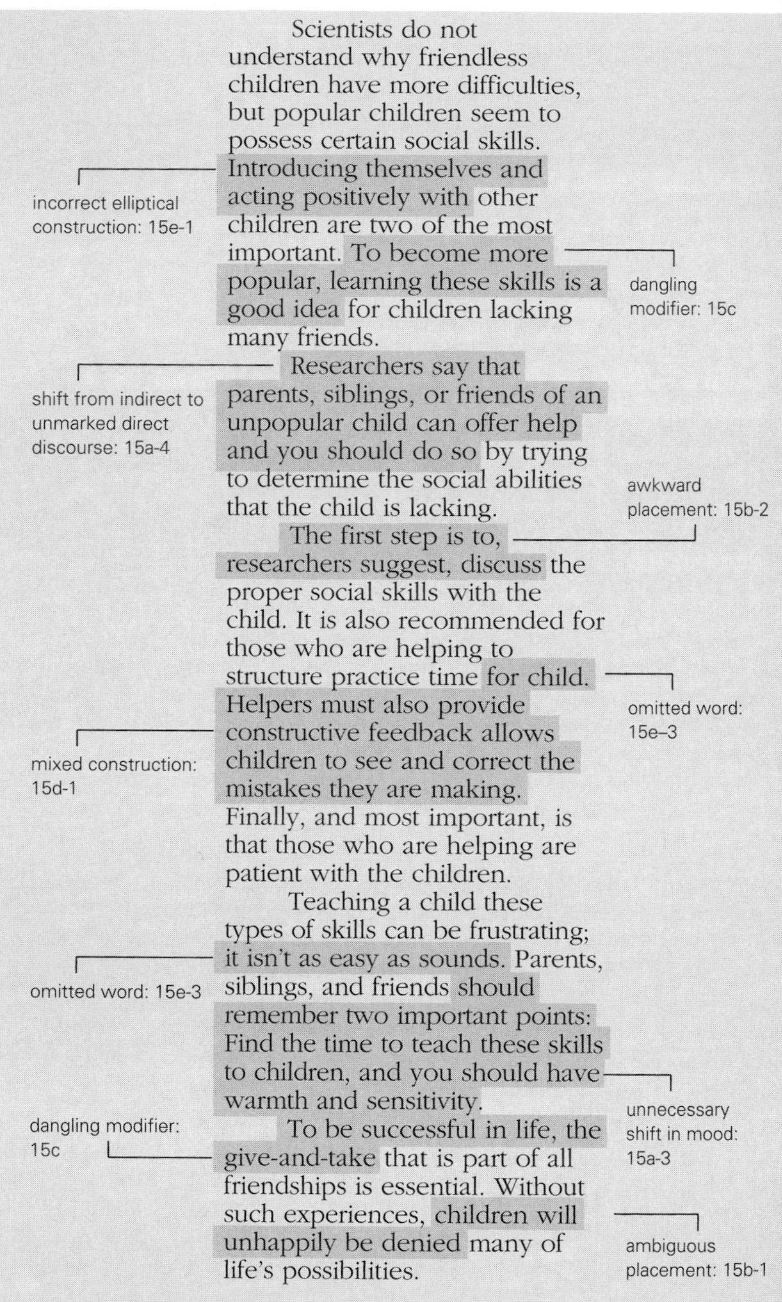
Scientists do not understand why friendless children have more difficulties, but popular children seem to possess certain social skills. Introducing themselves and acting positively with other children are two of the most important. To become more popular, learning these skills is a good idea for children lacking many friends.
incorrect elliptical construction: 15e-1
dangling modifier: 15c
Researchers say that parents, siblings, or friends of an unpopular child can offer help and you should do so by trying to determine the social abilities that the child is lacking.
shift from indirect to unmarked direct discourse: 15a-4
awkward placement: 15b-2
The first step is to, researchers suggest, discuss the proper social skills with the child. It is also recommended for those who are helping to structure practice time for child. Helpers must also provide constructive feedback allows children to see and correct the mistakes they are making. Finally, and most important, is that those who are helping are patient with the children.
omitted word: 15e–3
mixed construction: 15d-1
Teaching a child these types of skills can be frustrating; it isn't as easy as sounds. Parents, siblings, and friends should remember two important points: Find the time to teach these skills to children, and you should have warmth and sensitivity.
omitted word: 15e-3
unnecessary shift in mood: 15a-3
To be successful in life, the give-and-take that is part of all friendships is essential. Without such experiences, children will unhappily be denied many of life's possibilities.
dangling modifier: 15c
ambiguous placement: 15b-1

Here is how the student revised the draft to correct the errors. In a few places, the student could correct the errors in more than one way. Your revision, therefore, might not be exactly like this one, but it should deal with each error highlighted on the draft.

Children with many friends, researchers suggest, have an easier time adjusting to life's challenges than do children with few or no friends. By not interacting with friends, children are more likely to get into trouble and drop out of school. Friends cannot be seen as a luxury for children; they must be seen as a necessity for healthy child development.

Scientists do not understand why friendless children have more difficulties, but popular children seem to possess certain social skills. Introducing themselves to and acting positively with other children are two of the most important. To become more popular, children lacking friends should learn these skills.

Researchers say that parents, siblings, or friends of an unpopular child can offer help and that what they need to do is to determine the social abilities that the child is lacking.

The first step, researchers suggest, is to discuss the proper social skills with the child. It is also recommended for those who are helping to structure practice time for the child. Helpers must also provide constructive feedback, which allows children to see and correct the mistakes they are making. Finally, and most important, is that those who are helping are patient with the children.

Teaching a child these types of skills can be frustrating; it isn't as easy as it sounds. Parents, siblings, and friends must have time, warmth, and sensitivity.

To be successful in life, children need to experience the give-and-take that is part of all friendships. Unhappily, without such experiences, children will be denied many of life's possibilities.

Participation

A student wrote the following draft for a course called Introduction to International Relations. The assignment was to analyze one area of Canada's involvement in the international arena. This draft makes its point clearly and provides supporting evidence. The draft's effectiveness is diminished, however, by the presence of mixed sentences, incomplete sentences, and sentences that send unclear messages because of unnecessary shifts, misplaced modifiers, and dangling modifiers.

Read through the draft. Then revise it to eliminate the errors. Also, make any additional revisions that you think would improve the content, organization, and style of the material. ➜

If Canada's system free medical care symbolizes the Canadian identity at home, then Canada's role in peacekeeping represents its identity overseas, according to some people. Canada has put much effort and gained much prestige from its contributions. Yet despite Canada's long history of leadership in United Nations peacekeeping missions, by the year 2000, they ranked behind more than twenty countries in the number of personnel serving in international trouble spots. This put Canada behind countries such as Bangladesh and Nigeria, and also puts us behind several European states. Still, Canada has kept the high reputation it established early on.

Showing initiative and originality, the Nobel Peace Prize that Lester Pearson won was for putting together the United Nations force in the Sinai Desert in 1956. The role of this force was intended to observe the ceasefire between Egypt and Israel. In 1960, Canadians participated in a brief United Nations peacekeeping mission to the newly independent Congo. Four years later, merely, Canada sent a large force to patrol the ceasefire lines between the Greek and Turkish populations in Cyprus. However, later missions are not always as successful.

As an example was the United Nations effort in Bosnia and Croatia, where the fighting was still continuing and there was no peace to keep. Canadian soldiers later said that we felt sickened and ashamed at witnessing the violence going on around us. Tragically, they were powerless to stop it. This situation put these soldiers under severe psychological stress. Being exposed to toxic substances near the battlefield, the health of many peacekeepers was also affected, and of course there were injuries and deaths.

Despite such problems, and in spite its limited defence budget, Canada contributes in any way it can. Having pioneered many of the practices used in international peacekeeping, Canada now trains other nations' peacekeepers. It also lends UN missions technical personnel, including RCMP officers, who work in communications, supply, and other specialized fields. Canadians who support international peacekeeping hope that resting on its laurels, there is a danger that Canada will let its contribution slide.

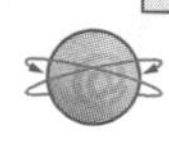

ccc.commnet.edu/grammar
Guide to Grammar & Writing
www.uottawa.ca/academic/arts/writcent/hypergrammar/
Hyper Grammar
www.urich.edu/~writing/wweb.fragment.html
Sentence Fragments and Complete Sentences
www.lynchburg.edu/public/writcntr/guide/grammar/fusedsen.htm
Fused Sentences and Comma Splices
www.wisc.edu/writing/Handbook/CommonErrors.html
Grammar and Style: An Editing Checklist (twelve common errors)

PART III Writing Effectively

Writing effectively means that you advance beyond correctness to writing characterized by style and grace. Part Three shows you how various techniques of writing style and awareness of the impact of word choice can enhance the delivery of your message. As you use Chapters 16 through 22, remember that writers seek to combine both form and content in their writing to create memorable prose.

16 Conciseness

Conciseness describes writing that is direct and to the point. Wordy writing is its opposite. Wordiness irritates readers, who must clear away excess words before sentences can deliver their messages. Concise writing can be achieved by eliminating wordy sentence structures (see 16a); dropping unneeded words (see 16b); and omitting redundancies (see 16c). Usually, the best time to do this is while you are revising°.

16a Eliminating wordy sentence structures

Wordy sentence structures make writing seem abstract and uninteresting. Whenever possible, revise to achieve conciseness.

1 Revising unnecessary expletive constructions

An **expletive construction** consists of *it* or *there* along with a form of the verb°* *be* placed before the subject° in a sentence. In some contexts, an expletive construction can create anticipation and provide emphasis, but usually expletive constructions are merely wordy. Removing the expletive and revising slightly eliminates wordy sentence structures.

NO	**It was** on Friday that we missed class.
YES	On Friday, we missed class.
YES	We missed class on Friday.
NO	**There was** a new teacher waiting for us.
YES	A new teacher was waiting for us.

*Throughout this book, a degree mark (°) indicates that you can find the definition of the word in the Glossary of Terms in this handbook.

◆ ESL NOTE: The *it* in an expletive construction is not a pronoun° referring to a specific antecedent°. The *it* is an "empty" word that fills the subject° position in a sentence but does not function as the actual subject. The actual subject appears after the expletive construction: ***It** was the **teacher** who answered the question.* (A more concise version is *The **teacher** answered the question.*)◆

◆ ESL NOTE: The *there* in an expletive construction does not designate a place. The *there* indicates merely that something exists. Expletive constructions with *there* shift the sequence of the subject and verb in a sentence, so that the actual subject appears after the expletive construction: ***There** are many **teachers** who can answer the question.* (A more concise version is *Many **teachers** can answer the question.*)◆

2 Revising unnecessary passive constructions

In the **active voice,** the subject of a sentence *does* the action named by the verb°.

ACTIVE — **Professor Higgins teaches** public speaking. [*Professor Higgins* is the subject, and he does the action: he *teaches.*]

In the **passive voice,** the subject of a sentence *receives* the action named by the verb.

PASSIVE — **Public speaking is taught** by Professor Higgins. [*Public speaking* is the subject, which receives the action *taught.*]

The active voice adds liveliness as well as conciseness. The simplest way to revise from passive to active is to make the doer of the action the subject of the sentence. (In the passive, the doer of an action is usually identified in a phrase starting with *by.*)

NO — Volunteer work **was done by the students** for extra credit in sociology. [The students are doers of the action, but they are not the subject of the sentence.]

YES — The **students did** volunteer work for extra credit in sociology.

NO — The church basement **was decorated by the choir** for the party. [The choir is the doer of the action, but it is not the subject of the sentence.]

YES — The **choir decorated** the church basement for the party.

Sometimes you can revise a sentence from passive voice to active voice by using a new verb. This method works especially well when you want to keep the same subject.

PASSIVE	**The Central Powers were defeated** in World War I.
ACTIVE	**The Central Powers lost** World War I.
PASSIVE	Many **soldiers were stricken** with influenza.
ACTIVE	Many **soldiers caught** influenza.

Writers sometimes, however, deliberately use the passive voice in sentence after sentence in the mistaken belief that it sounds "mature" or "academic."

NO	One very important quality developed by an individual during a first job is self-reliance. This strength was gained by me when I was allowed by my supervisor to set up and conduct my own survey project.
YES	During their first job, many individuals develop the very important quality of self-reliance. I gained this strength when my supervisor allowed me to set up and conduct my own survey project.
YES	During a first job, many people develop self-reliance, as I did when my supervisor let me set up and conduct my own survey project.

Be particularly alert for the passive voice that misleads readers because it hides information about who acts: *Cracks in the foundation of the structure had been found, but they were not considered serious.* The sentence leaves out important information telling who found cracks and who decided that they were not serious.

Writers may sometimes have no choice but to use the passive voice, as when the doer of an action is unknown or when naming the doer would disrupt the focus of a sentence (see 8n–8o).

3 Combining sentences and reducing clauses and phrases

As you revise, check your writing for conciseness. To counteract wordiness, you can often combine sentences and reduce clauses° and phrases°.

Combining sentences

Look carefully at sets of sentences in your writing. You may be able to fit the information in one sentence into another sentence.

TWO SENTENCES

The *Titanic* was discovered seventy-three years after being sunk by an iceberg. The wreck was located in the Atlantic by a team of French and American scientists.

COMBINED SENTENCE

Seventy-three years after being sunk by an iceberg, the *Titanic* was located in the Atlantic by a team of French and American scientists.

TWO SENTENCES

The stern of the ship was missing and there was some external damage to the hull. Otherwise, the *Titanic* seemed to be in excellent condition.

COMBINED SENTENCE

Aside from its missing stern and external damage to its hull, the *Titanic* seemed to be in excellent condition.

For more advice about combining sentences, see Chapter 17.

Shortening clauses

Keep your meaning clear when you shorten clauses. Making your writing concise should never get in the way of clarity.

You can sometimes shorten an adjective clause° simply by dropping the opening relative pronoun° and verb°.

The *Titanic,* **which was a huge ocean liner,** sank in 1912.

The *Titanic,* **a huge ocean liner,** sank in 1912.

Sometimes you can reduce a clause to a single word.

The scientists held a memorial service for the passengers and crew members **who had died.**

The scientists held a memorial service for the **dead** passengers and crew members.

You can create elliptical constructions° to reduce clauses. Be sure to omit only those words that are clearly implied (see 15e-1).

When they were confronted with disaster, some passengers behaved heroically, **while others behaved selfishly.**

Confronted with disaster, some passengers behaved heroically, **others selfishly.**

Shortening phrases

Sometimes you can shorten phrases° to shorter phrases or to single words.

More than fifteen hundred **travellers on that voyage** died in the shipwreck.

More than fifteen hundred **passengers** died in the shipwreck.

Objects found inside the ship **included unbroken** bottles of wine and expensive **undamaged** china.

Found undamaged inside the ship were bottles of wine and expensive china.

4 Using strong verbs and avoiding nouns formed from verbs

Strong verbs° directly convey an action. *Be* and *have* are not strong verbs because they tend to create wordiness. When you revise weak verbs to strong ones, often you can increase the impact of your writing as you reduce the number of words in your sentences.

WEAK VERB

The proposal before the city council **has to do with** locating the sewage treatment plant outside city limits.

STRONGER VERBS

The proposal before the city council **suggests** locating the sewage treatment plant outside city limits.

The proposal before the city council **argues against** locating the sewage treatment plant outside city limits.

WEAK VERBS

The board members **were of the opinion** that the revisions in the code **were not** changes they could accept.

STRONGER VERBS

The board members **said** that they **could not accept** the revisions in the code.

✤ ALERT: When you revise, look carefully at verbs with the pattern *be* + adjective° + *of* (*be aware of, be capable of, be fearful of*). Many of these phrases can be replaced with one-word verbs: ***I envy*** [not *am envious of*] *the council president's ability to speak in public*. Always avoid certain of these phrases: for example, always use ***appreciate*** [not *be appreciative of*], ***illustrate*** [not *be illustrative of*], and ***support*** [not *be supportive of*].

NO The council president **was supportive of** the council's attempts to lower property taxes.

YES The council president **supported** the council's attempts to lower property taxes. ✤

When you look for weak verbs to revise, look also for nominals (nouns derived from verbs, usually by added suffixes° such as *-ance, -ment,* or *-tion*). Turning a nominal back into a verb reduces words and increases impact.

NO We **oversaw the establishment of** a student advisory committee.

YES We **established** a student advisory committee.

NO The building **had the appearance of** having been renovated.

YES The building **appeared** to have been renovated.

5 Using pronouns for conciseness

Replacing nouns° with pronouns° can reduce wordiness. When changing nouns to pronouns, be sure that each pronoun's antecedent is unambiguous (see 10a–10c) and that each pronoun agrees with its antecedents (see 11m–11p).

NO Queen Elizabeth II served as a driver and mechanic in World War II. **Elizabeth** joined the Auxiliary Territorial Service in 1944, while **the future queen** was still a princess. Although **Princess Elizabeth** did not know how to drive, she quickly learned how to strip and repair many kinds of engines.

YES Queen Elizabeth II served as a driver and mechanic in World War II. **She** joined the Auxiliary Territorial Service in 1944, while **she** was still a princess. Although **she** did not know how to drive, she quickly learned how to strip and repair many kinds of engines.

EXERCISE 16-1

Consulting section 16a, combine each set of sentences to eliminate wordy constructions.

EXAMPLE A creative idea, says psychologist Robert Epstein, can be like a rabbit. The rabbit runs by fast. We glimpse only the rabbit's ears or tail.

A creative idea, says psychologist Robert Epstein, can be like a rabbit that runs by so fast we glimpse only its ears or tail.

1. There is evidence that suggests that there is only one difference between creative people and the rest of us. It is creative people who are always poised to capture the new ideas we might not catch right away.
2. Creative thinking has to do with seizing opportunities. Creative thinking has to do with staying alert. Creative thinking has to do with seeking challenges and pushing boundaries.
3. The goal is that the idea be caught first and that the idea be evaluated later. A fleeting thought is captured by the alert person by writing it down at once. The goal is not to worry whether the thought will have eventual value.
4. There is an important part of creativity, and that is daydreaming, which is an activity allowing thoughts to bubble up spontaneously. These creative thoughts surprise us with their freshness.
5. Creativity can be unlocked in us by our trying something different. It is possible to turn pictures sideways or upside down to see them in new ways. We can mould clay while we think about a writing problem that is difficult.
6. It is stressed by the psychologist Robert Epstein that there are many exciting advances in everything. The advances are in fields from astrophysics to car design to dance. The advances creatively combine ideas that are from widely different sources.
7. Epstein gave his students the assignment of a problem. The problem called for the retrieval of a ping-pong ball. It was located at the bottom of a vertical drainpipe that was sealed at the bottom.
8. Some of the tools that the students had been given by Epstein were too short to reach the ball. Other tools that the students had been given were too wide to fit into the pipe.
9. The students were stumped at first. The students tried unsuccessfully to capture the ball with the tools. Then the students stepped back from the immediate situation. The students saw the big picture and began thinking creatively.
10. Water was poured down the drainpipe by the students. The ball achieved flotation and rose to the top. The ball was retrieved by the students there.

16b Eliminating unneeded words

For conciseness, eliminate unneeded words that clutter sentences. Also, revise imprecise language. Never let six inexact words take the place of one precise word.

When a writer tries to write very formally or tries to reach an assigned word limit, **padding** usually results. Sentences loaded with **deadwood** contain empty words and phrases that increase the word count but lack meaning. If you find deadwood, clear it away.

PADDED ~~In fact,~~ the television station ~~which is situated in the local area~~ has won a great many awards ~~as a result of its having been involved in the~~ coverage of ~~all kinds of~~ controversial issues.

CONCISE The local television station has won many awards for its coverage of controversial issues.

PADDED The bookstore ~~entered the order for~~ the books ~~that the instructor has said will be utilized~~ in the course ~~sequence.~~

CONCISE The bookstore ordered the books for the course.

Chart 92 lists typical empty words that are among the worst offenders. The chart also offers revised versions. Apply the principles found here to similar items not listed.

GUIDE FOR ELIMINATING EMPTY WORDS AND PHRASES 92

EMPTY WORD OR PHRASE	WORDY EXAMPLE	REVISION
as a matter of fact	*As a matter of fact,* statistics show that many marriages end in divorce.	Statistics show that many marriages end in divorce.
due to the fact that	Mary Stuart did not say the monarch's oath when she became queen of Scotland *due to the fact that* she was just six days old.	Mary Stuart did not say the monarch's oath when she became queen of Scotland because she was just six days old.
in a very real sense	*In a very real sense,* the drainage problems caused the house to collapse.	The drainage problems caused the house to collapse.

➜

GUIDE FOR ELIMINATING EMPTY WORDS AND PHRASES (*continued*) 92

factor	The project's final cost was an essential *factor* to consider.	The project's final cost was essential to consider.
manner	The child touched the snake in a reluctant *manner.*	The child touched the snake reluctantly.
nature	His comment was of an offensive *nature.*	His comment was offensive.
type of	Gordon took a relaxing *type of* vacation.	Gordon took a relaxing vacation.
seems	It *seems* that the union called a strike over health benefits.	The union called a strike over health benefits.
tendency	The team had a *tendency* to lose home games.	The team often lost home games.
in the process of	We are *in the process of* reviewing the proposal.	We are reviewing the proposal.
exist	The crime rate that *exists* is unacceptable.	The crime rate is unacceptable.
in light of the fact that	*In light of the fact that* jobs are scarce, I am going back to school.	Because jobs are scarce, I am going back to school.
for the purpose of	Work crews were dispatched *for the purpose of* fixing the potholes.	Work crews were dispatched to fix the potholes.
in the case of	*In the case of* the proposed water tax, residents were very angry.	Residents were very angry about the proposed water tax.

GUIDE FOR ELIMINATING EMPTY WORDS AND PHRASES (*continued*) 92

in the event that	*In the event that* you are late, I will leave.	If you are late, I will leave.
the point I am trying to make	*The point I am trying to make* is that news reporters should not invade people's privacy.	News reporters should not invade people's privacy.

EXERCISE 16-2

Consulting section 16b, eliminate unnecessary words or phrases. Be especially alert for empty words that add nothing to meaning.

EXAMPLE Folk wisdom has a tendency to be untrue.

Folk wisdom is often untrue.

(1) As a matter of fact, it seems as though a great many folk beliefs that are popular are, in a very real sense, dead wrong. (2) For example, ophthalmologists make the statement that reading in the dark will not have the effect of ruining a person's eyes. (3) In the case of spicy foods, specialists have proven that foods of this sort are not necessarily bad for the stomach, even for people who have been treated as ulcer patients. (4) What about our mothers' warning that exists about catching colds when we are in the process of becoming chilled? (5) It is certainly quite true that more people have a tendency to get sick in winter than people do in summer. (6) It seems that lower temperatures are not a factor that deserves the blame, however. (7) In view of the fact that cold weather often has a tendency to drive people indoors and to bring people together inside, this factor has the appearance of increasing our odds of infecting one another. (8) Finally, there has been a long-standing tradition that states that the full moon has the effect on people of making them crazy. (9) Investigations that were made by researchers who were tireless and careful came to the ultimate conclusion that there is no such relationship in existence.

16c Revising redundancies

Planned repetition can create a powerful rhythmic effect (see 19g). The dull drone of unplanned repetition, however, can bore a reader and prevent the delivery of your message. Unplanned repetition is called **redundancy.**

Certain redundant word pairs are very common. Avoid expressions like *each and every, null and void, forever and ever,* and *final and conclusive.* Other common redundancies are *perfectly clear, few* (or *many*) *in number, consensus of opinion,* and *reason is because.*

NO Bringing the project to **final completion** three weeks early, the new manager earned our **respectful regard** when **the project was completed.**

YES **Completing** the project three weeks early, the new manager earned our **respect.**

YES The new manager earned our **respect** for **completing** the project three weeks early.

NO **Astonished,** the architect **circled around** the building in **amazement.**

YES **Astonished,** the architect **circled** the building.

YES The architect **walked around** the building **in amazement.**

Notice how redundancies deaden a sentence's impact.

NO The council members **proposed a discussion** of the amendment, but that **proposal for a discussion** was voted down after they had **discussed** it for a while.

YES The council members' proposal to discuss the amendment was eventually voted down.

NO The **consensus of opinion** among those of us who saw it is that the carton was **huge in size.**

YES Most of us who saw the carton agree that it was huge.

◆ ESL NOTE: In all languages, words often carry an unspoken message—an *implied meaning*—that is assumed by native speakers of the language. Implied meaning can cause redundancy in writing. For example, *I walked to the store* ***on foot*** is redundant; in English, *to walk* implies *on foot.* A good dictionary gives information about implied meaning of words (see the list of dictionaries in 20a). ◆

EXERCISE 16-3

Consulting section 16c, eliminate redundant words and phrases. Then revise the paragraph so that it is concise.

EXAMPLE Oral history is an important legacy that can be handed down to future generations who come later.

Oral history is an important legacy for future generations.

(1) Now is the time to interview and talk to each and every family elder about the events and happenings of their lives. (2) The reason for the urgency is because the aging process of growing older can interrupt our dialogue with elderly relatives faster and more rapidly than we could or should be able to imagine. (3) To give just one example, in the 1980s, Ellen Miller, a woman in her forties, started to begin audiotaping her mother's memories and reminiscences of Berlin during the era of the early 1900s. (4) Before Miller had the chance to videotape some sessions, however, Alzheimer's disease had robbed her mother of her speech and memory. (5) Upon her mother's death at the age of eighty-eight years, Miller sat down, listened again and heard once more the familiar gentle voice telling stories and tales of far-off days on another continent that vividly evoked those times. (6) Then and there Miller decided on the spot to make a film that would bring together these audiotapes combined with family photographs, her own narration, and her mother's favourite Beethoven piano sonata. (7) Ellen Miller advises those who want to capture and preserve their family history on tape to bring family heirlooms and photographs when the recording sessions are being held. (8) The interviewer should ask questions that are specific and particular and not vague, and the interviewer should keep his or her own comments to a minimum.

17 Coordination and Subordination

Coordination and **subordination** help your writing gracefully communicate relationships between ideas. While you are drafting°, concentrate on getting your ideas onto paper. When you are revising°, you can explore the full potential of coordination and subordination for enriching your writing style.

TWO IDEAS	The sky turned dark grey. The wind died suddenly.
COORDINATED VERSION	The sky turned dark grey, and the wind died suddenly.
SUBORDINATED VERSION	As the sky turned dark grey, the wind died suddenly. [The *wind* is the focus.]
SUBORDINATED VERSION	As the wind died suddenly, the sky turned dark grey. [The *sky* is the focus.]

COORDINATION

17a Understanding coordination

Coordination can produce harmony by bringing together related but separate elements to function smoothly in unison. Sections 17a through 17d explain coordination of independent clauses°. Coordinate sentences communicate balance in, or sequence of, the ideas that they contain. You can apply these same principles to the coordination of words, phrases°, and dependent clauses° (see also the explanation of parallelism, Chapter 18).

Patterns for coordinate sentences, also known as *compound sentences,* are shown in Chart 93. When you choose to coordinate sentences in your writing, keep these principles in mind:

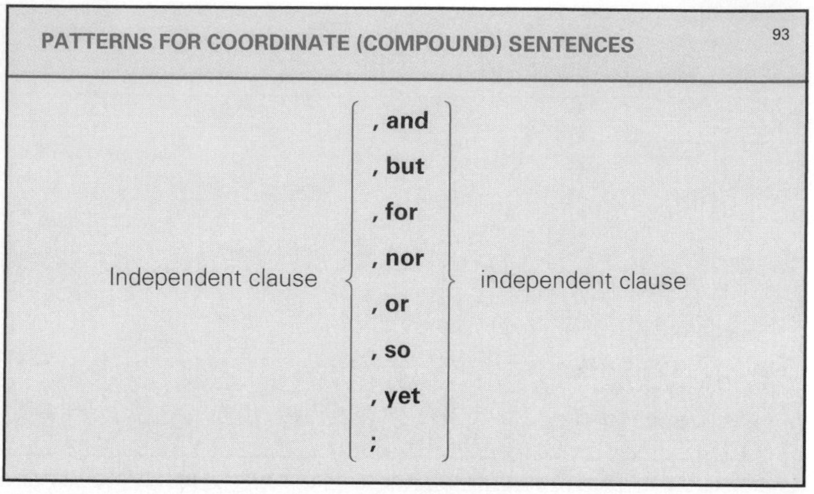

PATTERNS FOR COORDINATE (COMPOUND) SENTENCES 93

Independent clause { , and / , but / , for / , nor / , or / , so / , yet / ; } independent clause

- A coordinate sentence consists of two grammatically equivalent independent clauses.
- Coordinating independent clauses must be justified by the meaning that you want your sentence to communicate.
- The independent clauses must be joined either by a coordinating conjunction (see Chart 93) or by a semicolon (see 25a and 25b).
- The coordinating conjunction must accurately express the relationship (see Chart 94) between the ideas in the independent clauses.
- If you are tempted to coordinate more than two independent clauses, do so with much care (see 17d-1 and 19b-2).

✤ CONJUNCTION ALERT: Do not confuse coordinating conjunctions with conjunctive adverbs such as *also, however,* and *therefore* (for a complete list, see Chart 51 in section 7f). When conjunctive adverbs connect independent clauses, they function as explained in 7f and 14e.✤

✤ PUNCTUATION ALERT: You will never be wrong if you use a comma before a coordinating conjunction that joins two independent clauses (see 24a).

The sky turned dark grey, **and** the wind died suddenly.
The November morning had just begun, **but** it looked like dusk.✤

COORDINATING CONJUNCTIONS AND THE RELATIONSHIPS THEY EXPRESS 94

RELATIONSHIPS	WORDS
addition	*and*
contrast	*but, yet*
result or effect	*so*
reason or choice	*for*
choice	*or*
negative choice	*nor*

17b Using coordinate sentences to show relationships

Deliberately writing a string of short sentences can create impact. In most cases, however, a series of short sentences does not communicate well the relationships among ideas. Coordination can help you avoid writing a series of short sentences that have unclear relationships.

Unclear Relationships

We decided not to go to class. We planned to get the notes. Everyone else had the same plan. Most of us ended up failing the quiz.

Clear Relationships

We decided not to go to class, **but** we planned to get the notes. Everyone else had the same plan, **so** most of us ended up failing the quiz.

Overuse of coordination, however, can bore a reader with its unbroken rhythm (see 17d-2). For another technique to help you avoid an unwanted series of short sentences, see the discussion of subordination in 17e through 17h.

17c Using coordinate sentences for effect

Coordinate sentences can help you communicate an unfolding of events, a sequence, or a list.

> There is Ontario patriotism, Quebec patriotism, or Western patriotism, each based on the hope that it may swallow up the others, **but** there is no Canadian patriotism, **and** we can have no Canadian nation when we have no Canadian patriotism.
>
> —HENRI BOURASSA, *The Nationalist Movement in Quebec*

In this passage, coordination underlines the contrasts that are drawn.

> What sets a canoeing expedition apart is that it purifies you more rapidly and inescapably than any other. Travel a thousand miles by train **and** you are a brute; pedal five hundred on a bicycle **and** you remain basically a bourgeois; paddle a hundred in a canoe **and** you are already a child of nature.
>
> —PIERRE ELLIOTT TRUDEAU, "The Ascetic in a Canoe"

17d Avoiding the misuse of coordination

1 Avoiding illogical coordination

Coordination is illogical when ideas in the compounded independent clauses° are not related. Your reader expects one part of a coordinate construction to lead logically to the other.

NO Computers came into common use in the 1970s, and they sometimes make costly errors.

The statement in each independent clause is true, but the ideas are not related closely enough. The two ideas should not be coordinated. Here are ideas that do coordinate logically.

YES Computers came into common use in the 1970s, and they are now indispensable for conducting business.

YES Modern computer systems are often very complex, and they sometimes make costly errors.

2 Avoiding the overuse of coordination

Overused coordination creates writing that reads as if the writer simply wrote down whatever came into his or her head. Readers become impatient and quickly lose interest.

NO Dinosaurs could have disappeared for many reasons, and one theory holds that the climate suddenly became cold, and another theory suggests that a sudden shower of meteors and asteroids hit the earth, so the impact created a huge dust cloud that caused a false winter. The winter lasted for years, and the dinosaurs died.

YES Dinosaurs could have disappeared for many reasons. One theory holds that the climate suddenly became cold, and another suggests that a sudden shower of meteors and asteroids hit the earth. The impact created a huge dust cloud that caused a false winter. The winter lasted for years, killing the dinosaurs.

Writers may overuse coordination if they fail to feature some ideas more prominently than others. Such writing tends to drone on monotonously. (See 17e through 17h)

◆ ESL NOTE: If your instructor tells you that your sentences are too long and complex, practise limiting them. Follow the advice of many ESL teachers: Revise any sentence containing a combination of more than three independent and dependent clauses. ◆

EXERCISE 17-1

Consulting sections 17a through 17d, revise these sentences to eliminate illogical or overused coordination. If you think a sentence needs no revision, explain why.

EXAMPLE Fencing, now a competitive sport worldwide, was once a form of combat, and today's fencers disapprove of those who identify fencing with fighting.

Fencing, now a competitive sport worldwide, was once a form of combat, but today's fencers disapprove of those who identify fencing with fighting.

1. As depicted in movies, fencing sometimes appears to be reckless swordplay, and fencing requires precision, coordination, and strategy.

2. The first fencing competitions in the fourteenth century were small, and because fencing was very popular, it was one of the few sports included in the first modern Olympic Games in 1896, and fencing has been part of the Olympics ever since.
3. Fencing equipment includes a mask, a padded jacket, a glove, and one of three weapons—foil, épée, or sabre—and a fencer's technique and targets differ depending on the weapon used and the fencer's experience.
4. Generally, a fencer specializes in one of the three weapons, but some competitors are equally skilled with all three.
5. The object of fencing is to be the first to touch the opponent five times, and a "president," who is sometimes assisted by a number of judges, officiates at competitions.

EXERCISE 17-2

Consulting sections 17a through 17d, revise this paragraph. Choose which ideas seem to have equal weight and could therefore be contained in compound sentences. Your final version should have no more than two compound sentences—all other sentences should be left as they are.

Bicycle couriers represent the newest flourishing of urban subculture. They are a cosmopolitan phenomenon. They swarm the downtowns of big cities from Berlin to Vancouver. European bicycle couriers favour a streamlined, high-tech look, all vinyl and Spandex and severe haircuts. The North American branches of the tribe prefer a neo-primitive look. They are likely to sport nose rings, jangling handmade accessories, and flying dreadlocks. As often as not, couriers assemble the jewellery they wear from a bicycle repair kit. This subculture has transformed the bicycle helmet into a fashion statement. Once this practical piece of headgear was disparaged as "uncool."

SUBORDINATION

17e Understanding subordination

Subordination expresses the relative importance of ideas in a sentence by making a less important idea grammatically less prominent than a more important one. Sections 17e through 17h explain subordination of dependent° and independent clauses°: The more important idea appears in the independent clause—a group of words that can stand alone as a grammatical unit; the subordinated idea appears in the dependent clause—a group of words that cannot stand alone as a grammatical unit. What information you choose to subordinate depends on the meaning that you want a sentence to deliver.

Major patterns of subordination with dependent clauses are shown in Chart 95. Two types of dependent clauses are adverb clauses and adjective clauses (see Chart 95). An **adverb clause** is a dependent clause that starts with a subordinating conjunction°. Each subordinating conjunction has a specific meaning that expresses a relationship between the dependent clause and the independent clause, as shown in Chart 96.

An **adjective clause** is a dependent clause that can start with a relative pronoun (*who, which, that*), a relative adverb° (such as *where*), or a preposition° before a "relative" word (for example, ***to*** *whom*, ***above*** *which*).

PATTERNS OF SUBORDINATION WITH DEPENDENT CLAUSES 95

SENTENCES WITH ADVERB CLAUSES

- **Adverb clause,** independent clause.

  After the sky grew dark, the wind died suddenly.

- Independent clause, **adverb clause.**

  Birds stopped singing, **as they do during an eclipse.**

- Independent clause **adverb clause.**

  The shops closed **before the storm began.**

SENTENCES WITH ADJECTIVE CLAUSES

- Independent clause **restrictive (essential)*** **adjective clause.**

  The weather forecasts warned of a storm **that might bring a seventy-centimetre snowfall.**

- Independent clause, **nonrestrictive (nonessential)*** **adjective clause.**

  Spring is the season for tornadoes, **which rapidly whirl their destructive columns of air.**

- Beginning of independent clause **restrictive (essential)*** **adjective clause** end of independent clause.

  Anyone **who lives through a tornado** recalls the experience.

- Beginning of independent clause, **nonrestrictive (nonessential)*** **adjective clause,** end of independent clause.

  The sky, **which had been clear,** was turning grey.

*For an explanation of restrictive (essential) and nonrestrictive (nonessential) elements, see 24e.

SUBORDINATING CONJUNCTIONS AND THE RELATIONSHIPS THEY EXPRESS 96

RELATIONSHIPS	WORDS
time	*after, before, once, since, until, when, whenever, while*
reason or cause	*as, because, since*
purpose or result	*in order that, so, so that, that*
condition	*even if, if, provided that, unless*
contrast	*although, even though, though, whereas*
location	*where, wherever*
choice	*rather than, whether*

17f Choosing the subordinate conjunction appropriate to your meaning

Subordinating conjunctions express the relationship between major and minor ideas in sentences (see Chart 96). Consider the influence of the subordinating conjunction in each of the following sentences.

> **After you have handed it in,** you cannot make any changes in your report. [time]
>
> **Because you have handed it in,** you cannot make any changes in your report. [reason]
>
> **Unless you have handed it in,** you cannot make any changes in your report. [condition]
>
> **Although you have handed it in,** you can make changes in your report. [contrast]
>
> I want to read your report **so that I can evaluate it.** [purpose]
>
> **Since you handed in your report,** three more people have handed in theirs. [time]
>
> **Since I have seen the report,** I can comment on it. [cause]

17g Using subordination to show relationships

Subordination directs your reader's attention to the idea in the independent clause° while at the same time using the idea in the dependent clause° to provide context and support. Consider these examples (dependent clauses are in boldface).

> **As soon as I saw the elephant,** I knew with perfect certainty that I ought not to shoot it.
>
> —George Orwell, "Shooting an Elephant"

> **If they are very lucky,** the passengers may catch a glimpse of dolphins playfully breaking water near the ship.
>
> —Elizabeth Gray, student

Subordination usually communicates relationships among ideas more effectively than a group of separate sentences does. In the clear version that follows, the first four short sentences have been combined into two complex sentences°. The last sentence, which is left short, now makes a stronger impact.

Unclear Relationships

In 1910, my grandfather and his hired hand got caught in a dangerous snowstorm on the prairies. They were looking for cattle. They were lost and thought they were going to freeze to death. Suddenly they saw a light through the snow. Survival then seemed certain.

Clear Relationships

In 1910, my grandfather and his hired hand got caught in a dangerous snowstorm on the prairies **while they were looking for cattle.** They were lost and thought they were going to freeze to death **when suddenly they saw a light through the snow.** Survival then seemed certain.

EXERCISE 17-3

Consulting sections 17e through 17g, combine each pair of sentences, using an adjective clause to make one idea subordinate to the other. Then revise each sentence so that the adjective clause becomes the independent clause. Use the relative pronoun given in parentheses.

EXAMPLE Aristides was an ancient Greek politician famous for his honesty and judgment. He was known as Aristides the Just. (who)

a: Aristides, who was an ancient Greek politician famous for his honesty and judgment, was known as Aristides the Just.

b: Aristides, who was known as Aristides the Just, was an ancient Greek politician famous for his honesty and judgment.

1. A law in ancient Athens allowed voters to banish politicians from the city. It asked citizens to write the name of an unpopular politician on their ballots. (that)
2. A voter was filling out a ballot when Aristides the Just walked by. The voter needed help in spelling "Aristides." (who)
3. Aristides knew the voter did not recognize him. He asked why the voter wanted to banish that particular politician. (who)
4. The voter said he resented hearing someone called "the Just" all the time. He handed Aristides his ballot. (who)
5. Aristides' reaction lived up to his nickname "the Just." His reaction was to write his own name on the voter's ballot even though that person's vote helped banish Aristides. (which)

17h Avoiding the misuse of subordination

1 Avoiding illogical subordination

Subordination is illogical when the subordinating conjunction does not make clear the relationship between the independent and dependent clause (see Chart 96). The following sentence is illogical.

NO Because Beethoven was deaf when he wrote his final symphonies, they are musical masterpieces.

Revising from *because* to *although* creates logical subordination. *Although* implies that the symphonies are masterpieces in spite of Beethoven's deafness.

YES Although Beethoven was deaf when he wrote his final symphonies, they are musical masterpieces.

2 Avoiding the overuse of subordination

Overused subordination crowds too many images or ideas together, making readers lose track of your intended message. If you have used more than two subordinating conjunctions or relative pronouns° in a sentence, question whether your meaning is clear. In the following example, the base sentence *A new technique for eye surgery has been developed* is crowded with dependent clauses. The *Yes* version breaks up one long sentence into three sentences. Two dependent clauses remain, while the second sentence is a simple sentence°. Some words have been moved to new positions. With a variety of sentence structures (see 19a), the material is easier to read and the relationships among ideas are clearer.

NO A new technique for eye surgery, which is supposed to correct nearsightedness, which previously could be corrected only by glasses, has been developed, although many doctors do not approve of it because it can create unstable vision.

YES A new technique for eye surgery, which is supposed to correct nearsightedness, has been developed. Previously, nearsightedness could be corrected only by glasses. Because it can create unstable vision, many doctors do not approve of it, however.

EXERCISE 17-4

Consulting section 17h, correct illogical or excessive subordination in this paragraph. As you revise, use not only some short sentences but also some correctly constructed adverb clauses. Also, apply the principles of coordination discussed in 17a through 17d, if you wish.

Because too many young ape mothers in zoos were rejecting or abusing their infants, zoo keepers decided to stop their usual practice of separating mother and infant from the rest of the ape community which was done so that the infant would supposedly be safe from harm from other apes. In the new arrangement, group settings were established that included older, experienced loving ape mothers as well as other infants and young mothers so that the abusive mothers could learn from good role models how to love and care for their infants and so that each mother would have childrearing support from the equivalent of aunts and cousins. The experiment was successful, and some pediatricians, who are doctors who specialize in child care, tried a similar program for abusive human mothers, which worked well even though the human mothers took far longer than the ape mothers to learn and use good mothering techniques.

17i Balancing subordination and coordination

Coordination and subordination can sometimes be used in concert with each other.

> **When Laura Secord overheard the American plans for attack,** she realized she had to warn the British **and,** with only her lantern, she set out to walk the thirty kilometres from Queenston to Beaver Dams.

Varying sentence types can improve your ability to emphasize key points in your writing. Consider the following paragraph, which demonstrates a good balance in the use of coordination and subordination. It contains compound sentences (see 17a–17d), sentences that consist of dependent and independent clauses (see 17e–17h), and simple sentences°.

> **When I was growing up,** I lived on a farm just across the field from my grandmother. My parents were busy trying to raise six children and to establish their struggling dairy farm. It was nice to have Grandma so close. **While my parents were providing the necessities of life,** my patient grandmother gave her time to her shy, young granddaughter. I always enjoyed going with Grandma and collecting the eggs that her chickens had just laid. Usually she knew which chickens would peck, **and** she was careful to let me gather the eggs from the less hostile ones.
>
> —PATRICIA MAPES, student

Avoid using both a coordinating *and* a subordinating conjunction to express one relationship.

NO **Although** the story was well written, **but** it was too unbelievable.

YES Although the story was well written, it was too unbelievable.

YES The story was well written, but it was too unbelievable.

EXERCISE 17-5

Consulting all sections of this chapter, use subordination and coordination to combine these sets of short, choppy sentences. You may use more than one sentence in some of your answers.

EXAMPLE Thirst is the body's way of surviving. Every cell in the body needs water. People can die by losing as little as 15 to 20 percent of their body's water supply.

Thirst is the body's way of surviving, for every cell in the body needs water, and people can die by losing as little as 15 to 20 percent of their body's water supply.

1. Blood contains 83 percent water. Blood provides indispensable nutrients for the cells. Blood carries water to the cells. Blood carries waste away from the cells.
2. Insufficient water means that cells cannot be fuelled or cleaned. The body becomes sluggish.
3. An adult can survive eleven days without water. Bodily functions are seriously disrupted by a lack of water for more than one day. The body loses water. The blood thickens. The heart must pump harder. Thickened blood is harder to pump through the heart.
4. Some drinks replace the body's need for fluids. Alcohol or caffeine in drinks leads to dehydration.
5. People know that they should drink water often. They can become moderately dehydrated before they even begin to develop a thirst.

EXERCISE 17-6

Consulting all sections of this chapter, revise this passage by using coordination and subordination.

Harlequin Enterprises sells more than 700 million books a year. It markets them throughout the world. The company is a Canadian success story. It claims to have made "the language of love universal, crossing social, cultural and geographical borders with an ease unrivalled by any other publisher." Harlequin's success lies in its ability to market a formula. The heroines and heroes of all the books fulfil certain criteria of age, appearance, and profession. The romances follow a prescribed pattern. Fans of Harlequin's books do not care. They buy the new titles faithfully each month.

18 Parallelism

This chapter advises you how to avoid **faulty parallelism** (18b through 18e) and how to use the grace and power of **parallelism** to strengthen your writing (18f and 18g). It also explains parallelism in outlines and lists (18h).

Many writers attend to parallelism when they revise°. If while you are drafting° you think that your parallelism is faulty or that you can enhance your writing style by using parallelism, underline or highlight the material and keep your focus on getting ideas onto paper. When you revise, you can work on the places that you marked.

18a Understanding parallelism

Parallelism in writing, related to the concept of parallel lines in geometry, calls for the use of equivalent grammatical forms to express ideas of equal importance. An **equivalent grammatical form** is a word or group of words that matches—is parallel to—the structure of a corresponding word or group of words, as explained in Chart 97.

Also, when you are expressing ideas of equal weight in your writing, parallel sentence structures can echo that fact and offer you a writing style that uses balance and rhythm to help deliver your meaning.

> **They come like foxes** through the woods. **They attack like lions. They take flight like birds,** disappearing before they have really appeared.
>
> —JÉRÔME LALEMANT, in *The Jesuit Relations*

The Jesuit missionary and martyr conveys the sense of stealth, courage, and speed of the Iroquois by using similes from the natural world. He sets out his images in parallel structure.

PARALLEL STRUCTURES 97

PARALLEL WORDS

Recommended exercise includes **running, swimming,** and **cycling.** [The **-ing** words are parallel in structure and equal in importance.]

PARALLEL PHRASES

Exercise helps people **to maintain healthy bodies** and **to handle mental pressure.** [The *to* phrases are parallel in structure and equal in importance.]

PARALLEL CLAUSES

People exercise **because they want to look healthy, because they need to have stamina,** or **because they hope to live longer.** [The *because* clauses are parallel in structure and equal in importance.]

18b Using words in parallel form

To achieve a graceful form, make words parallel—put them in the same grammatical form. Also, using words in parallel form can enhance the impact of the meaning (see 18f and 18g).

NO	The strikers had tried **pleading, threats,** and **shouting.**
YES	The strikers had tried **pleading, threatening,** and **shouting.**
YES	The strikers had tried **pleas, threats,** and **shouts.**

18c Using phrases and clauses in parallel form

To make word groups parallel, put them in the same grammatical form. Using phrases and clauses in parallel form can enhance the impact of the meaning (see 18f and 18g).

NO The committee members **read the petition, discussed its major points,** and **the unanimous decision was to ignore it.**

YES The committee members **read the petition, discussed its major points,** and **unanimously decided to ignore it.** [revised to parallel phrases]

NO **The signers heard that their petition had not been granted, they became very upset,** and then **staged a protest demonstration.**

YES **The signers heard that their petition had not been granted, they became very upset,** and then **they staged a protest demonstration.** [revised to parallel clauses]

YES **The signers heard that their petition had not been granted, became very upset,** and then **staged a protest demonstration.** [revised to parallel phrases]

18d Using parallel structures with coordinating and correlative conjunctions and with *than* and *as*

1 Using parallel forms with coordinating conjunctions

The coordinating conjunctions are *and, but, or, nor, for, yet,* and *so* (for the relationship each expresses, see Chart 94 in section 17a). To avoid faulty parallelism, be sure that elements joined by coordinating conjunctions are parallel in grammatical form.

NO **Love and being married** go together.

YES **Love and marriage** go together.

YES **Being in love and being married** go together.

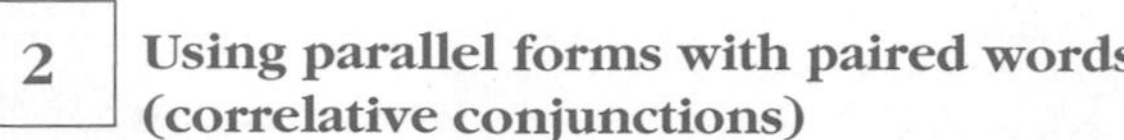

2 Using parallel forms with paired words (correlative conjunctions)

Correlative conjunctions are pairs of words such as *not only ... but (also), either ... or,* and *both ... and* (for more, see 7h). To make elements joined by correlative conjunctions parallel, put them in the same grammatical form. As you check your writing, pay particular attention to where you put the first half of the pair.

NO Differing expectations for marriage **not only** can lead to disappointment **but also** to anger.

YES Differing expectations for marriage **not only can lead to** disappointment **but also can cause** anger.

YES Differing expectations for marriage can lead **not only** to disappointment **but also** to anger.

—NORMAN DUBOIS, student

If the same verb applies to both parts, put the verb before the first part of the pair.

3 Using parallel forms with *than* and *as*

When you use *than* and *as* for comparisons, be sure that elements are parallel in grammatical form. Also, make sure that these comparisons are complete (see 15e-2).

NO **Having a solid marriage** can be more satisfying **than** the **acquisition of wealth.**

YES **Having a solid marriage** can be more satisfying **than acquiring wealth.**

YES **A solid marriage** can be more satisfying **than wealth.**

NO A solid marriage can be **as satisfying**, if not **more satisfying than,** the acquisition of wealth**.**

YES A solid marriage can be **as satisfying as,** if not **more satisfying than,** the acquisition of wealth.

—EUNICE FERNANDEZ, student

18e Repeating function words in parallel elements

In a series of two or more parallel elements, be consistent in the second and subsequent elements about repeating or omitting function words. These include articles (*the, a, an*); the *to* of the infinitive° (for example, *to* love); and prepositions (for example, *of, in, about*). If you think that repeating such words clarifies your meaning or might help your reader catch the parallelism that you intend, use them.

NO **To assign** unanswered letters their proper weight, **free us** from the expectations of others, **to give us** back to ourselves—here lies **the great, the singular** power of self-respect.

YES **To assign** unanswered letters their proper weight, **to free us** from the expectations of others, **to give us** back to ourselves—here lies **the great, the singular** power of self-respect.

—JOAN DIDION, "On Self-Respect"

When you use *who, which,* or *that* to start a series of clauses°, be sure to repeat or omit the words consistently in subsequent clauses.

> I have in my own life a precious friend, a woman of 65 **who has** lived very hard, **who is** wise, **who listens** well, **who has** been where I am and can help me understand it; **and who represents** not only an ultimate ideal mother to me but also the person I'd like to be when I grow up.
>
> —JUDITH VIORST, "Friends, Good Friends—and Such Good Friends"

> We looked into the bus, **which was** painted blue with orange daisies, **had** picnic benches instead of seats, and **showed** yellow curtains billowing out its windows.
>
> —KERRIE FALK, student

18f Using parallel and balanced structures for impact

Parallel structures emphasize the meaning that sentences deliver. **Deliberate, rhythmic repetition** of parallel, balanced word forms and word groups reinforces the impact of a message. (For information about misused repetition, see 16c.) Consider the impact of this passage:

> **It is a good country for** the honest, industrious artisan. **It is a fine country for the** poor labourer who, after a few years of hard toil, can sit down in his own log-house and look abroad on his own land and see his children well settled in life as independent freeholders. **It is a good country for** the rich speculator who can afford to lay out a large sum in purchasing land in eligible situations; for if he has any judgement he will make a hundred per cent as

interest for his money after waiting a few years. But **it is a hard country for** the poor gentleman whose habits have rendered him unfit for manual labour.

—CATHERINE PARR TRAILL, *The Backwoods of Canada*

If Traill had expressed the same idea with only minimal parallelism, her message would have been weaker. Her structures reinforce the power of her message, and give her final sentence more weight because it is a slight variation on the parallel form. An ordinary structure would not have been as effective: "It is a good country for the honest, industrious artisan. The poor labourer ... will also do well. If a rich speculator can afford to lay out a large sum, ... he will make a hundred per cent as interest for his money after waiting a few years. The poor gentleman whose habits have rendered him unfit for manual labour will probably not become rich here."

A **balanced sentence** has two parallel structures, usually potential sentences in their own right, with contrasting content. A balanced sentence is a coordinate sentence (see 17a), characterized by opposition in the meaning of the two structures, sometimes with one cast in the negative: *Mosquitoes do not bite; they stab.* Consider the impact of this sentence:

By night, the litter and desperation disappeared as the city's glittering lights came on; by day, the filth and despair reappeared as the sun rose.

—JENNIFER KIRK, student

Similarly, consider the impact of this famous sentence, which adds unusual word order (*ask not,* instead of *do not ask*) to its parallelism and balance.

Ask not what your country can do for you, ask what you can do for your country.

—JOHN F. KENNEDY

✤ COMMA ALERT: Authorities differ about using a comma or semicolon between the parts of a balanced sentence. In your academic writing, to avoid seeming to make the error of a comma splice (see Chapter 14), you are safer if you use a semicolon (or revise in other ways). ✤

18g Using parallel sentences for impact in longer passages

Parallel, balanced sentences in longer passages can create a dramatic unity through carefully controlled repetition of words and word forms. Consider this rich passage of repeated words, concepts, and rhythms.

You ask me what is **poverty? Listen** to me. Here I am, dirty, **smelly,** and with no "proper" underwear on and with the **stench** of my rotting teeth near you. I will tell you. **Listen** to me. **Listen** without pity. I cannot use your pity. **Listen** with understanding. Put yourself in my dirty, worn-out, ill-fitting shoes, and hear me.

Poverty is getting up every morning from a dirt- and illness-stained mattress. The sheets have long since been used for diapers. **Poverty** is living in a **smell** that never leaves. **This is a smell** of urine, sour milk, and spoiling food sometimes joined with the strong **smell** of long-cooked onions. Onions are cheap. If you have **smelled** this **smell,** you did not know how it came. **It is the smell** of the outdoor privy. **It is the smell** of young children who cannot walk the long dark way in the night. **It is the smell** of the mattresses where years of "accidents" have happened. **It is the smell** of the milk which has gone sour because the refrigerator long has not worked, and it costs money to get it fixed. **It is the smell** of rotting garbage. I could bury it, but where is the shovel? Shovels cost money.

—Jo Goodwin Parker, "What Is Poverty?"

EXERCISE 18-1

Reread the Jo Goodwin Parker passage above. Then, consulting sections 18a through 18f, discover all parallel elements in addition to those shown in boldface.

EXERCISE 18-2

Consulting sections 18a through 18f, revise these sentences to eliminate errors in parallel structure.

EXAMPLE Difficult bosses not only affect their employees' performance but their private lives are affected as well.

Difficult bosses affect *not only their employees' performances but their private lives as well.*

1. According to psychologist Harry Levinson, the five main types of bad boss are the workaholic, the kind of person you would describe as bullying, a person who communicates badly, the jellyfish type, and someone who insists on perfection.
2. As a way of getting ahead, to keep their self-respect, and for simple survival, wise employees handle problem bosses with a variety of strategies.
3. To cope with a bad-tempered employer, workers can both stand up for themselves and reasoning with a bullying boss.
4. Often bad bosses communicate poorly or fail to calculate the impact of their personality on others; being a careful listener and to be sensitive to others' responses are qualities that good bosses possess.

5. Employees who take the trouble to understand what makes their boss tick, engage in some self-analysis, and staying flexible are better prepared to cope with a difficult job environment than suffering in silence like some employees.

EXERCISE 18-3

Consulting sections 18a through 18f, combine the sentences in each numbered item, using techniques of parallelism.

EXAMPLE A few years ago Canadians witnessed a renaissance of skateboarding. Skateboarding inspired its own clothing styles. In fact, a skateboard culture also was developed.

A few years ago Canadians witnessed a renaissance of skateboarding, which not only inspired its own clothing styles but also developed its own culture.

1. Cities became filled with whirling skateboarders; they flew on their skateboards. These skateboarders hopped curbs and would leap boldly up and down stairs. They also careened unsteadily down railings.
2. Not long afterward began the reign of in-line skates. They were built for speed. Young adults adopted them to commute and also in order to show off their style.
3. Skateboarders, who had a preference for gymnastic feats, were unlike the people who used in-line skates. These people favoured a graceful, undulating style marked by sweeping strides.
4. Late in the 1990s, small-wheeled scooters became popular. Adults liked them. They also became popular with young children.
5. Any town that has a sidewalk has certainly seen children wobbling on these scooters. If a town is big enough to have a rush hour, people there probably have seen businesspeople on motorized versions, trying to beat the traffic.

EXERCISE 18-4

Find the parallel elements in the following passages. Next, using your own topics, imitate the parallelism of two of the passages.

1. The time will come when that national spirit which has been spoken of will be truly felt among us, when we shall realize that we are four million Britons who are not free, when we shall be ready to take up that freedom, and to ask what the late prime minister of England assured us we should not be denied—our share of national rights.

—EDWARD BLAKE, *A National Sentiment!*

2. It was the 18th of October, 1830, in the morning, when my feet first touched the Canadian shore. I threw myself on the ground, rolled in the sand, seized handfuls of it and kissed them, and danced around, till, in the eyes of several who were present, I passed for a madman.

—JOSIAH HENSON (an escaped slave and the model for Harriet Beecher Stowe's Uncle Tom), *An Autobiography*

3. It was Sunday morning at 11 o'clock and David Suzuki was on the radio, warning of the environmental catastrophe looming around his listeners. A generation ago most of us would have been in church at this time; and here we were in church again. Dr. Suzuki's programme, with its visions of Armageddon and its call to repentance and conversion, was surely a sermon.

—DAVID CAYLEY, "The Beer Can or the Highway?"

18h Using parallelism in outlines and lists

Items in formal outlines and lists must be parallel in grammar and structure. (For information about other issues of outline format and about how to develop an outline, see 2p.)

FORMAL OUTLINE NOT IN PARALLEL FORM

Reducing Traffic Fatalities

I. Stricter laws
   A. Top speed should be 80 km/h on highways.
   B. Higher fines
   C. Requiring jail sentences for repeat offenders
II. The use of safety devices should be mandated by law.

FORMAL OUTLINE IN PARALLEL FORM

Reducing Traffic Fatalities

I. **Passing** stricter speed laws
   A. **Making** 80 km/h the top speed on highways
   B. **Raising** fines for speeding
   C. **Requiring** jail sentences for repeat offenders
II. **Mandating** by law the use of safety devices

Although a nonparallel outline might serve as an informal, scratch outline for a writer's private purposes in the early stages of the writing process, only a parallel outline is acceptable as a final draft.

FORMAL LIST NOT IN PARALLEL FORM

Workaholics share these characteristics:

1. They are intense and driven.
2. Strong self-doubters
3. Labour is preferred to leisure by workaholics.

FORMAL LIST IN PARALLEL FORM

Workaholics share these characteristics:

1. **They are** intense and driven.
2. **They have** strong self-doubts.
3. **They prefer** labour to leisure.

EXERCISE 18-5

Consulting section 18h, revise this outline into parallel form.

Planning for Your First Paycheque

- I. How to live within your means
  - A. You should keep track of current expenses
  - B. Working out a sensible breakdown of your paycheque among savings and expenses
  - C. Credit cards and their uses
- II. Investing for your future
  - A. Awareness of your company pension plan
  - B. Learn about stocks, bonds, and other investments
  - C. A long-term investment portfolio: first steps

19 Variety and Emphasis

19a Understanding variety and emphasis

Achieving variety and emphasis can move your writing beyond correctness to style and grace. Your writing style has **variety** when your sentence lengths and patterns vary; see 19b and 19c. Your writing style is characterized by **emphasis** when your sentences are constructed to communicate the relative importance of their ideas.

Using techniques of variety and emphasis, you help readers distinguish between major and minor points; recognize tone (1d, 5d-3), which gives depth to your message; and enjoy a pleasing writing style. Usually the best time to apply the principles of variety and emphasis is while you are revising°.

19b Varying sentence length

A variety of sentence lengths communicates clear distinctions among ideas. Such a style can help your readers understand the focus of your material. Also, such a style avoids the unbroken rhythm of monotonous sentence length, which can lull your reader into inattention.

1 Revising strings of too many short sentences

Strings of too many short sentences rarely establish relationships and levels of importance among ideas. Readers cannot easily make distinctions between major and minor points. Such strings, unless deliberately planned in a longer piece of writing for occasional impact (see 19b-3), suggest that the writer has not thought through the material and decided what to emphasize. The style tends to read like that of young children.

NO Soto and his like invaded North America. They invaded from the south. Other invaders began to probe the continent's colder latitudes. In 1534, a middle-aged Breton named Jacques Cartier sailed up the St. Lawrence. He kidnapped two boys. They had gone out fishing from a distant Iroquoian town. The boys spent a winter in France. Then they led Cartier farther west. They came to where tides cease and the St. Lawrence narrows below a tall bluff. Here was their home, Stadacona, where Quebec City now stands.

YES While Soto and his like were invading North America from the south, others began to probe its colder latitudes. In 1534, a middle-aged Breton named Jacques Cartier sailed up the St. Lawrence and kidnapped two boys out fishing from a distant Iroquoian town. After a winter in France, the boys led Cartier farther west, to where tides cease and the St. Lawrence narrows below a tall bluff. Here was their home, Stadacona, where Quebec City now stands.

—Ronald Wright, *Stolen Continents*

In the revised version, the sentence structures permit key ideas to be featured.

2 Revising a string of too many compound sentences

A **compound sentence** consists of two or more independent clauses° connected with a coordinating conjunction° or a semicolon (see 17a). Too often, compound sentences are monotonous and do not communicate the relationships among ideas.

NO Science fiction writers are often thinkers, and they are often dreamers, so they let their imaginations wander. Jules Verne was such a writer, and he predicted space ships and atomic submarines, but most people did not believe airplanes were possible.

YES Science fiction writers are often thinkers and dreamers who let their imaginations wander. Jules Verne was one such writer. He predicted space ships and atomic submarines before most people believed airplanes were possible.

3 Revising for a suitable mix of sentence lengths

To emphasize one idea among many others, you can express it in a sentence noticeably different in length or structure from the sentences surrounding it. Consider this passage, which carries its emphasis in one short sentence among longer ones:

> Today is one of those excellent January partly cloudies in which light chooses an unexpected landscape to trick out in gilt, and then shadow sweeps it away. **You know you are alive.** You take huge steps, trying to feel the planet's roundness arc between your feet. Kazantzakis says that when he was young he had a canary and a globe. When he freed the canary, it would perch on the globe and sing. All his life, wandering the earth, he felt as though he had a canary on top of his mind, singing.
>
> —ANNIE DILLARD, *Pilgrim at Tinker Creek*

A long sentence among shorter ones is equally effective.

> Mistakes are not believed to be part of the normal behavior of a good machine. **If things go wrong, it must be a personal, human error, the result of fingering, tampering, a button getting stuck, someone hitting the wrong key.** The computer, at its normal best, is infallible. I wonder whether this can be true.
>
> —LEWIS THOMAS, "To Err Is Human"

EXERCISE 19-1

Consulting sections 19a and 19b, revise these sets of sentences to vary the sentence lengths effectively.

1. Biometeorology is a science. It examines weather's unseen power over living things. The science concentrates on the effects of weather patterns on human behaviour and health. Many researchers study these effects. They are attempting to find a connection between the two. One such researcher is William Ferdinand Peterson. He has spent the past twenty years collecting statistics and anecdotes. He wrote the book *The Patient and the Weather*. His research focuses on the invisible elements of air. These elements include passing fronts. These elements include falling barometric pressure. The elements include shifting wind directions.
2. Feared winds and all their variations—from katabatic to chinook to Santa Ana—are frequently considered the cause of every illness that can be imagined by many people in every country. In Russia, high winds and the frequency of strokes seem related, and in Italy southern winds and heart attacks seem connected, and in Japan, researchers have noticed an increase in asthma attacks whenever the wind changes direction.

19c Using an occasional question, mild command, or exclamation

To vary your sentence structure and to emphasize material, you can call on four basic sentence types. The most common English sentence is **declarative.** A declarative sentence makes a statement—it declares something. Declarative sentences offer an almost infinite variety of structures and patterns.

A sentence that asks a question is called **interrogative.** Occasional questions can help you involve your reader. A sentence that issues a mild or strong command is called **imperative.** Occasional mild commands are particularly helpful for gently urging your reader to think along with you. A sentence that makes an exclamation is called **exclamatory.**

✤ PUNCTUATION ALERT: A mild command ends with a period. A strong command or an exclamation ends with an exclamation mark (see 23e). ✤

Consider the following paragraph, which uses the three basic sentence types found most frequently in academic writing: declarative, interrogative, and imperative.

> Imagine what people ate during the winter as little as seventy-five years ago. They ate food that was local, long-lasting, and dull, like acorn squash, turnips, and cabbage. Walk into an American supermarket in February and the world lies before you: grapes, melons, artichokes, fennel, lettuce, peppers, pistachios, dates, even strawberries, to say nothing of ice cream. Have you ever considered what a triumph of civilization it is to be able to buy a pound of chicken livers? If you lived on a farm and had to kill a chicken when you wanted to eat one, you wouldn't ever accumulate a pound of chicken livers.
>
> —PHYLLIS ROSE, "Shopping and Other Spiritual Adventures in America Today"

EXERCISE 19-2

The paragraph below effectively varies sentence lengths and uses a question and a command. The result emphasizes the key points. Write an imitation of this paragraph, closely following all aspects except the topic. Choose your own topic.

EXAMPLE If your topic were gardens, your first sentence might be: *Why do most people plant tomatoes in their gardens when they know they will harvest many more tomatoes than the average family wants to eat in a whole year?*

Why do most North Americans spend $95 a year to operate their clothes dryers when Nature provides free energy for the same task? Consider the humble clothesline and clothespins. They cost about $30 for a lifetime and solar power is free, unlike an electric dryer, which can cost as much as $500. In an increasingly mechanized indoor life, people who hang their clothes on the line are obliged to notice the weather. Today is a perfect morning for drying, they think. Or: Will it rain this afternoon? Another line in the basement or spare room works well in rainy weather and in winter. Indoor drying has the further benefit of humidifying the house; ten kilos of wet wash contributes about four litres of water to the air.

19d Choosing the subject of a sentence according to your intended emphasis

The subject° of a sentence establishes the focus for that sentence. The subject you choose should correspond to the emphasis that you want to communicate to your reader.

Each of the following sentences, all of which are correct grammatically, contains the same information. Consider, however, how changes of the subject (and its verb°) influence meaning and impact.

> **Our study showed** that 25 percent of undergraduates' time is spent eating or sleeping. [Focus is on the study.]
>
> **Undergraduates eat or sleep** 25 percent of the time, according to our study. [Focus is on the undergraduates.]
>
> **Eating or sleeping occupies** 25 percent of undergraduates' time, according to our study. [Focus is on eating and sleeping.]
>
> **Twenty-five percent** of undergraduates' time **is spent** eating or sleeping, according to our study. [Focus is on the percentage of time.]

19e Adding modifiers to basic sentences for variety and emphasis

Adding modifiers° to basic sentences can provide you with a rich variety of sentence patterns.

1 Expanding basic sentences with modifiers

Sentences that consist only of a subject and verb usually seem very thin. You might use a very short sentence for its dramatic effect in

WAYS TO EXPAND A BASIC SENTENCE 98

BASIC SENTENCE	The river rose.
ADJECTIVE	The **swollen** river rose.
ADVERB	The river rose **dangerously.**
PREPOSITIONAL PHRASE	**In April,** the river rose **above its banks.**
PARTICIPIAL PHRASES	**Swollen by melting snow,** the river rose, **flooding the farmland.**
ABSOLUTE PHRASE	**Trees swirling away in the current,** the river rose.
ADVERB CLAUSE	**Because the snows had been heavy that winter,** the river rose.
ADJECTIVE CLAUSE	The river, **which runs through vital farmland,** rose.

emphasizing an idea (see 19b-3). When you want to avoid a very short sentence, however, you can expand the basic sentence as illustrated in Chart 98. Your decision to expand a basic sentence will depend on the focus of each sentence and how it works in concert with its surrounding sentences.

EXERCISE 19-3

Consulting section 19e-1, expand each sentence by adding (a) an adjective°, (b) an adverb°, (c) a prepositional phrase°, (d) a participial phrase°, (e) an absolute phrase°, (f) an adverb clause°, and (g) an adjective clause°.

1. We bought a house.
2. The roof leaked.
3. I remodelled the kitchen.
4. Neighbours brought food.
5. Everyone enjoyed the barbecue.

2 Positioning modifiers to create variety and emphasis

Research on learning suggests that readers are more likely to retain the words and ideas placed at the very beginning or the very end of a sentence. Although you do not have unlimited choices about where to place modifiers, you often have options. Try to place them according to the emphasis that you want to achieve. At the same time, be sure to place your modifiers precisely within sentences so that you avoid the error of misplaced modifiers (see 15b).

A sentence that starts with a subject° and verb° and then provides additional information with modifiers that appear after the subject and verb is called a **cumulative sentence.** The cumulative sentence is the most common sentence structure in English; it is called "cumulative" because information accumulates. Sometimes the cumulative sentence is referred to as a **loose sentence** because it lacks the tightly planned structure of other sentence varieties. Such sentences, easy to read because they reflect how humans receive and pass on information, often do not provide impact, however.

In contrast, a **periodic sentence,** also called a *climactic sentence,* is highly emphatic. It builds up to the period, reserving the main idea for the end of the sentence. It draws the reader in as it builds to its climax. Periodic sentences can be very effective, but if they are overused they lose their punch.

PERIODIC If we had not felt that, after coming to this conclusion, we were bound to set aside our private opinions on matters of detail, if we had not felt ourselves bound to look at what was practicable, not obstinately rejecting the opinions of others nor adhering to our own; if we had not met, I say, in a spirit of conciliation, and with an anxious, overruling desire to form one people under one government, **we never would have succeeded.**

—John A. Macdonald, 1868

CUMULATIVE **We never would have succeeded** if we had not felt that, after coming to this conclusion, we were bound to set aside our private opinions on matters of detail, if we had not felt ourselves bound to look at what was practicable, not obstinately rejecting the opinions of others nor adhering to our own; if we had not met, I say, in a spirit of conciliation, and with an anxious, overruling desire to form one people under one government.

Another way to vary sentence structures is to start sentences with introductory words, phrases°, or clauses°.

WORD	**Fortunately,** I taught myself to read before I had to face boring reading drills in school. —ANDREW FURMAN, student
PHRASE	**Along with cereal boxes and ketchup labels,** comic books were the primers that taught me how to read. —GLORIA STEINEM
CLAUSE	**Long before I wrote stories,** I listened for stories. —EUDORA WELTY, *One Writer's Beginnings*

Often, modifiers may appear in several different positions within a sentence. Positioning modifiers offers you a chance to enhance your writing style with variety and emphasis. Here are sentences with the same modifiers in various positions. If you use this technique, be very careful to avoid placing modifiers in positions that create ambiguous meaning (see 15b-1).

Angrily the physician slammed down the chart, **sternly** speaking to the patient.

The physician slammed down the chart **angrily,** speaking **sternly** to the patient.

The physician **angrily** slammed down the chart, speaking to the patient **sternly.**

✤ PUNCTUATION ALERT: For a discussion of commas with introductory material, see 24b. ✤

19f Inverting standard word order

Standard word order in the English sentence places the subject° before the verb°. Because this pattern is so common, it is set in people's minds, so any variation creates emphasis. Inverted word order places the verb before the subject. Used too often, inverted word order can be distracting; but used sparingly, it can be very effective.

STANDARD	**The mayor walked** in. **The premier walked** out.
INVERTED	In **walked the mayor.** Out **walked the premier.**
STANDARD	**Responsibilities begin** in dreams.
INVERTED	In dreams **begin responsibilities.**

—DELMORE SCHWARTZ

19g Repeating important words or ideas to achieve emphasis

You can repeat some words to help emphasize meaning, but choose the words carefully. Repeat only those words that contain a main idea or that use rhythm to focus attention on a main idea. Consider this passage, which uses deliberate repetition to deliver its meaning.

> The **knowledge** that you can have is inexhaustible, and what is inexhaustible is benevolent. The **knowledge** that you cannot have is of the riddles of birth and death, of our future destiny and the purposes of God. Here there is no **knowledge,** but illusions that restrict freedom and limit hope. Accept the mystery behind **knowledge.** It is not darkness but shadow.
>
> —NORTHROP FRYE, Convocation Address, 1988

Frye repeats the word *knowledge* in different contexts to distinguish between the kinds of knowledge available to humans and to show the importance of respecting the limits of our knowledge. His repetition of *inexhaustible,* his use of the parallel phrases *The knowledge that you can have ... The knowledge that you cannot have,* and his linking of important concepts with the conjunctions *and* and *but* set up a series of rhythms that give this passage an almost prophetic power, in keeping with its subject matter.

Use deliberate repetition sparingly, with central words, and only when your meaning justifies the technique. Consider this passage, which is the result of limited vocabulary and a dull, unvaried style. Although few synonyms exist for the words *an insurance agent, car,* and *model,* some do. Also, the sentence structure has no variety.

NO **An insurance agent** can be an excellent advisor when you want to buy a **car. An insurance agent** has records on most **cars. An insurance agent** knows which **models** tend to have most accidents. **An insurance agent** can tell you which **models** are the most expensive to repair if they are in a collision. **An insurance agent** can tell you which **models** are most likely to be stolen.

YES If you are thinking of buying a new car, an insurance agent can be an excellent advisor. An insurance broker has complete records on most automobiles. For example, he or she knows which models are accident prone. Did you know that some car designs suffer more damage than others in a collision? If you want to know which automobiles crumple more than others and which are least expensive to repair, ask an insurance agent. Similarly, some models are more likely to be stolen, so find out from the person who specializes in dealing with claims.

EXERCISE 19-4

Consulting all sections of this chapter, revise this paragraph to achieve emphasis through varied sentence length and deliberate repetition. You can reduce or increase the number of sentences, and you can drop words to reduce unneeded repetition. Each writer's revision will vary somewhat, but try to include at least one revision to a question or exclamation (19c) and one revision to an inverted word order (19f).

The chimney is one of civilization's great technological innovations. The chimney represents a major step up from a hole in the roof or a slit in the wall. The heating of houses was not an urgent problem in the warm climates of ancient Egypt and Mesopotamia. Scholars believed this until a palace was uncovered during a recent excavation of the great lost city of Mari on the upper Euphrates River in ancient Mesopotamia. The palace, which was 4000 years old, was peppered with chimneys. Two thousand years later the Romans came along. The Romans were engineering geniuses. The Romans developed elaborate chimneys as part of their hot-air heating systems. The Roman empire declined in the fourth century A.D., and after then no one from the former colonies knew how to make chimneys. For four centuries western Europe had no chimneys. So the simple question has always been how chimneys finally got to western Europe. Nobody is quite sure, but here is what a current theory holds. Around A.D. 800, chimneys were brought by Syrian and Egyptian traders. They were from the East.

20 Understanding the Meaning of Words

North American English, evolving over centuries into a rich language, reflects the contributions of many cultures. Distinctly North American words originated colloquially—in spoken language—and words from all the cultures settling on this continent became part of the language. Food names, for example, show how other languages and cultures loaned words to English. Africans brought the words *okra* and *gumbo;* Spanish and Latin American peoples contributed *tortilla* and *taco.* From German we got *hamburger* and *pretzel;* Italian supplied *spaghetti* and *antipasto;* and Yiddish is responsible for *gefilte fish* and *bagel.*

French language and culture have especially influenced the Canadian variety of North American English. This influence perhaps is felt less in the language of cuisine (itself a loan word from French) than in terms dealing with the environment, outdoor activities, and political or social institutions. Many English-speaking Canadians are familiar with French-Canadian dishes such as *poutine* and *tourtière,* and the expressions *café au lait* and *crêpes* have been adopted into English in Canada and elsewhere. Nevertheless, the most characteristic borrowings from French used in Canadian English are words such as *portage, voyageur, lacrosse, francophone, Métis,* and *concession* road. The languages of the Aboriginal peoples of Canada have also enriched the English spoken here with words such as *kayak, pemmican, chinook,* and *caribou.*

Etymology is the study of the origins and historical development of words, including changes in form and meaning. For example, *alphabet* originates from the names of the first two letters in Greek: *a = alpha, b = beta.* The meanings of some words change with time. For example, W. Nelson Francis points out in *The English Language,* the word *nice* "has been used at one time or another in its 700-year history to mean ... foolish, wanton, strange, lazy, coy, modest, fastidious, refined, precise, subtle, slender, critical, attentive, minutely accurate, dainty, appetizing, agreeable."

To use English well, you want to be aware of the kinds of information that dictionaries offer (20a), to know how to choose exact words (20b), and to use strategies that actively build your vocabulary (20c).

20a Using dictionaries

Good dictionaries show how language has been used and is currently being used. Each dictionary entry gives the meaning of the word and much additional important information. Many dictionaries also include essays on the history and use of language.

Understanding all parts of a dictionary entry

A dictionary entry usually includes items 1 through 11, and sometimes 12 and 13, discussed below. As you use the list, consult three or four entries in one of the dictionaries listed in section 20a-4.

1. **Spelling.** If more than one spelling is shown, the first is the most commonly used, and the others are acceptable.
2. **Word Division.** Dots (or bars, in some dictionaries) separate the syllables of a word. Writers can hyphenate at syllables as long as the rules in section 22d are not violated.
3. **Pronunciation.** If more than one pronunciation is given, the first is the most common, and the others are acceptable. Phonetic symbols are usually used to show pronunciation. A guide to the pronunciation of the symbols appears in the front of most dictionaries, and some dictionaries provide a brief guide to the most common symbols at the bottom of pages.
4. **Part of Speech Labels.** Abbreviations, explained in the front of many dictionaries, indicate parts of speech. Many words can function as more than one part of speech.
5. **Grammatical Forms.** This information tells of variations in grammar: for a verb°, its principal parts and form variations; for a noun°, its plural if formed other than by adding only *-s*; for an adjective° or adverb°, its comparative and superlative forms°.
6. **Etymology.** This information traces the way that the word has evolved through other languages over the years to become the word and meaning in current use.
7. **Definitions.** If a word has more than one meaning, the definitions are numbered in most dictionaries from the oldest to the newest meaning. A few dictionaries start with the most common use.

8. **Usage Labels.** If the use of a word is special, a usage label explains how the word should be used. Chart 99 explains the most common usage labels in dictionaries.
9. **Field Labels.** When a word applies to a specialized area of study, such as chemistry or law, an abbreviation alerts a reader to the specialized meaning. For example, along with its everyday meanings, the word *centre* has specialized meanings in these fields: sports, mechanics, the military, and politics.
10. **Related Words.** Words based on the defined word appear, with their part of speech, at the end of the definitions.
11. **Synonyms and Antonyms,** if any. Synonyms are words that are close in meaning. They are listed with their subtle differences explained. Also, for each word in the list of synonyms, a cross-reference appears at that word's entry so that the reader can tell where to find the complete list. Antonyms are words that are opposite in meaning to the word defined. Any antonyms are listed after any synonyms.

USAGE LABELS 99

LABEL	DEFINITION	EXAMPLE
COLLOQUIAL	Characteristic of conversation and informal writing	**pa** [father] **ma** [mother]
SLANG	Not considered part of standard language, but sometimes used in informal conversation	**whirlybird** [helicopter]
OBSOLETE	No longer used; occurred in earlier writing	**betimes** [promptly, quickly]
POETIC	Found in poetry or poetic prose	**o'er** [for *over*]
DIALECT	Used only in some geographical areas	**tickle** [Newfoundland: a narrow channel or entrance to a harbour]

12. **Idioms,** if any. When the defined word is an idiom, either in itself or when combined with other words, it has a meaning that differs from its usual meaning. For example, in *Webster's New World Dictionary,* the entry for *ceiling* lists and defines the idiom *hit the ceiling.* If an idiom is considered slang or colloquial, a usage label (see item 8 above and section 20a-2) alerts the reader.

13. **Examples.** Some definitions provide an example sentence that illustrates the defined word in use.

2 Understanding usage labels

Usage refers to the customary manner of using particular words or phrases. As a writer, you can refer to the **usage labels** in a dictionary to help you decide when a word is appropriate for use. For example, a word labelled *slang* usually is not suitable for academic writing, unless you are writing about the word itself. A word labelled *poetic* is likely to be found in poetry, not in prose.

The concept of usage also applies to the customary manner of using certain words (for example, *among* versus *between*). For a list and explanation of such words, see the Usage Glossary toward the back of this handbook.

3 Using unabridged dictionaries

Unabridged means "not shortened." Of the various kinds of dictionaries, unabridged dictionaries have the most in-depth, accurate, complete, and scholarly entries. They give many examples of current uses and changes in meanings of the word over time. They include infrequently used words that abridged dictionaries (see 20a-4) often omit.

The most comprehensive, authoritative unabridged dictionary of English is the *Oxford English Dictionary (OED).* Its second edition has twenty volumes defining more than 616 500 words and terms. The *OED* traces each word's history, using quotations to illustrate changes in meaning and spelling over the life of the word. The second edition consists of three parts: (1) the first edition of the *OED,* largely unchanged; (2) the contents of the four supplements that accompanied the first edition; and (3) approximately 5000 newer words or terms. The second edition of the *OED* is kept up-to-date in an online version, which is available through paid subscription; students can have free access to it through academic libraries. A third edition is also in progress. Its revisions are being incorporated into the online *OED*.

Its comprehensive historical information about English words and examples of their use make the *OED* a specialized dictionary (20a-5) as well as an unabridged dictionary. In addition to the usual dictionary features, the *OED* offers a complete history of the words it defines.

Many college and university students use the one-volume *Webster's Third New International Dictionary of the English Language*. This highly respected work has more than 470 000 entries and is especially strong in new scientific and technical terms. It uses quotations to show various meanings, and its definitions are given in order of their appearance in the language.

Using abridged dictionaries

Abridged means "shortened." Abridged dictionaries contain the most commonly used words. They are convenient in size and economical to buy, and they serve as practical reference books for writers and readers. Many good abridged dictionaries are referred to as "college" editions because they serve the needs of most college and university students.

Three such dictionaries developed specifically for Canadian users are the *Gage Canadian Dictionary* (revised and expanded, 2000), the *ITP Nelson Canadian Dictionary of the English Language* (1997), and the *Canadian Oxford Dictionary* (2002). These dictionaries all contain approximately 140 000 to 150 000 entries, with an emphasis on distinctive Canadian spellings, vocabulary, pronunciation, and usage, including variants and regionalisms. They also include names of people and places, abbreviations, and foreign phrases. Word definitions in these dictionaries point out idioms and nuances of meaning and may be supplemented with synonyms and antonyms. Definitions are accompanied by word etymologies. Each of these three dictionaries contains an essay on the origins and peculiarities of Canadian English and an appendix with a variety of useful information. The slimmer *Penguin Canadian Dictionary* (1990), with approximately 75 000 entries, is another useful source for distinctive Canadian vocabulary and pronunciation.

For many years, the standard student reference book and spelling arbiter for British style in Canada has been the *Concise Oxford Dictionary*. Another abridged dictionary commonly used here is *Webster's New World Dictionary of American English*, Revised College Edition.

◆ ESL NOTE: A useful dictionary for students who speak English as a second language is the *Dictionary of Contemporary English* published by Longman. For a list of specialized dictionaries, see 20a-5. ◆

5 Using specialized dictionaries of English

A specialized dictionary focuses on a single area, such as slang, word origins, synonyms, antonyms, usage, or almost any other aspect of language. Most college and university libraries include all or some of the volumes listed here:

SPECIALIZED DICTIONARIES

SYNONYMS	*Roget's 21st Century Thesaurus: In Dictionary Form*
SLANG AND COLLOQUIALISMS	*Dictionary of Slang and Unconventional English,* ed. Eric Partridge
	Dictionary of American Slang, ed. Harold Wentworth and Stuart Berg Flexner [out of print, but available in many libraries]
	The Thesaurus of Slang, by Esther Lewin and Albert E. Lewin
	NTC's Dictionary of American Slang and Colloquial Expressions, by Richard A. Spears
ETYMOLOGIES	*Dictionary of Word and Phrase Origins,* ed. William Morris and Mary Morris
	Origins: A Short Etymological Dictionary of Modern English, ed. Eric Partridge [out of print, but available in many libraries]
CANADIANISMS	*Dictionary of Canadianisms on Historical Principles,* ed. Walter Avis et al.
USAGE	*Oxford Guide to Canadian English Usage,* ed. Margery Fee and Janice McAlpine
REGIONALISMS	*Dictionary of American Regional English,* ed. Frederic Cassidy
IDIOMS	*A Dictionary of American Idioms,* by Adam Makkai
	Dictionary of English Idioms, published by Longman Inc.

6 Using CD-ROM and online dictionaries

Several major dictionaries are available on CD-ROM, including *The Merriam Webster Collegiate Dictionary, The Random House College Dictionary,* and the second edition of *The Oxford English Dictionary* (the *OED*). The *Gage Canadian Dictionary* is available on CD-ROM together with *The Canadian Encyclopedia*. Consult your university or college library for others, as well as for links to reliable online dictionaries.

20b Choosing exact words

The English language offers a wealth of words to choose among as a writer. **Diction,** the term for choice of words, affects the clarity and impact of the message that you want your sentences to deliver. As a writer, you want to use words that exactly fit the particular context of each piece of writing.

1 Understanding denotation and connotation

When you look up a word in the dictionary to find out what it means, you are looking for its **denotation.** For example, the denotation of the word *semester* is "a period of time of about eighteen weeks that makes up part of a school or college year."

Readers expect words to be used according to their established meanings for their established functions. Exactness is essential. When you use a thesaurus or dictionary of synonyms, be aware that subtle shades of meaning create distinctions among words that have the same general definition. These small differences in meaning allow you to be very precise in choosing just the right word, but they also oblige you to make sure that you know what precise meanings your words convey. For instance, describing a person famous for praiseworthy achievements in public life as *notorious* would be wrong. Although *notorious* means "well-known" and "publicly discussed"—which famous people are likely to be—*notorious* also carries the meaning "unfavourably known or talked about." Wilfrid Laurier is *famous,* not *notorious*. The Donnellys, on the other hand, are *notorious*.

Here is another example. *Obdurate* means "not easily moved to pity or sympathy," and its synonyms include "inflexible, obstinate, stubborn, hardened." The synonym *hardened* for *obdurate,* however, might prompt someone unfamiliar with *obdurate* to use the word incorrectly.

NO Footprints showed in the *obdurate* concrete.

Here are two correct uses of *obdurate:*

YES The supervisor remained *obdurate* in refusing to accept excuses.

YES My *obdurate* roommates will not let my pet boa constrictor live in the bathtub.

✤ COMPUTER ALERT: Be especially careful about using a software program's thesaurus. Recent versions of sophisticated programs have thesauruses that offer synonyms for many words and that make substitutions easy. However, unless you know the exact meaning of an offered synonym, as well as its part of speech, you may introduce a grammatical error or a "wrong word" error into your writing. For example, one word-processing program's thesaurus offers the choices *low, below, beneath,* and *subterranean* as synonyms for *deep* with the sense of low (down, inside). None of these words, however, could replace *deep* in many sentences, including this one: *Mine shaft #4 is too deep* [not too *low, below, beneath,* or *subterranean*] *to be filled with sand or rocks.* ✤

Connotation refers to ideas implied, but not directly indicated, by a word. Connotations convey associations as emotional overtones beyond the direct, explicit definition of a word. For example, the word *home* usually evokes more emotion than does its denotation "a dwelling place" or its synonym *house. Home* may have very pleasant connotations of warmth, security, the love of family. Or *home* may have unpleasant connotations of an institution for elderly or sick people. As a student writer, be aware of the potential of connotation to help your words deliver their meaning. Connotations are never completely fixed, for they can vary with different contexts for a word. Still, people can communicate effectively because most words have relatively stable connotations and denotations in most contexts.

Being sensitive to the differences between the denotation and connotation of a word is essential for critical thinking. Critical thinkers must first consider material at its literal level (see 5d-1). Doing so calls for dealing with the denotation of words. Next, critical thinkers must move to the inferential level (see 5d-2)—to what is implied although not explicitly stated. Connotations of words often carry the inferential message, as illustrated in Chart 100.

COMPARING DENOTATION AND CONNOTATION

100

Sample Word	**Denotation**	**Connotation**
ADDITIVE	an added substance	something unnatural, especially in food; perhaps harmful to health
CHEAP	inexpensive	of products, low quality; of people, stingy
NUCLEAR REACTOR MELTDOWN	melting of fuel rods in a nuclear reactor, releasing dangerous radiation	spectre of imminent death or eventual cancer; poisoning of food chain

EXERCISE 20-1

Consulting section 20b-1, separate the words in each set into one of three groups: *Neutral* if you think the word has no connotations; *Positive* if you think it has good connotations; *Negative* if you think it has bad connotations. If you think a word fits in more than one group, put it under each heading that applies, and be ready to explain your choices. If you are unsure of a word, consult your dictionary.

EXAMPLE sensitive, touchy, tender, thin-skinned, impressionable

Neutral: impressionable; Positive: sensitive; Negative: touchy, thin-skinned

1. carefree, exuberant, light-hearted, frivolous, rash, high-spirited, riotous, animated, reckless, joyful
2. thrifty, economical, frugal, stingy, tight-fisted, prudent, foresighted, penny-pinching, money-conscious
3. lawyer, attorney, shyster, learned counsel, ambulance chaser, advocate, legal practitioner, public defender, prosecutor
4. smell, odour, fragrance, stink, aroma, scent, stench, whiff, perfume, smoke, incense
5. flexible, yielding, wishy-washy, adaptable, tolerant, indulgent, undemanding, weak, submissive, imitative
6. alone, lonely, single, solitary, individual, deserted, independent, isolated, unique

2 Using specific and concrete language to bring life to general and abstract language

Specific words identify individual items in a group (*Oldsmobile, Honda, Ford*). **General** words relate to an overall group (*car*). **Concrete** words identify persons and things that can be perceived by the senses—seen, heard, tasted, felt, smelled (the *black padded vinyl dashboard* of my car). **Abstract** words denote qualities, concepts, relationships, acts, conditions, ideas (*transportation*).

As a writer, you want to choose words suitable for your writing purpose° and your audience°. Usually, specific and concrete words bring life to general and abstract words. Whenever you choose general and abstract words, be sure to supply enough specific, concrete details and examples to illustrate effectively your generalizations and abstractions. Consider how sentences with general words come to life when they are revised with words that refer to specifics.

GENERAL	My car has a great deal of power, and it is very quick.
SPECIFIC	My Trans Am with 220 horsepower can go from zero to eighty in six seconds.
GENERAL	The car gets good gas mileage.
SPECIFIC	The Dodge Lancer uses about 7 litres of gas per 100 kilometres on the highway and 8 litres per 100 kilometres in the city.
GENERAL	Her car is comfortable and easy to drive.
SPECIFIC	When she drives her new Buick Regal on a five-hour trip, she arrives refreshed and does not need a long nap to recover, as she did when she drove her ten-year-old Upusho.

Specific language is not always preferable to general language, nor is concrete language always preferable to abstract language. Effective writing usually combines them. Consider the following from an effective essay comparing cars:

General and Specific Combined

GENERAL / SPECIFIC / SPECIFIC / GENERAL
My car, a **220-horsepower Trans Am,** is **quick.** It accelerates

SPECIFIC / SPECIFIC
from **0 to 80** kilometres per hour in **6 seconds**—but it uses

SPECIFIC / SPECIFIC
13 litres of gas per 100 kilometres. The **Dodge Lancer,** on the

GENERAL / GENERAL
other hand, gets **very good** gas **mileage:** It uses about

SPECIFIC / GENERAL
7 litres per 100 kilometres in **highway driving** and

SPECIFIC / GENERAL / SPECIFIC
8 litres per 100 kilometres when **traffic** is **bumper-to-bumper**

GENERAL / SPECIFIC
or when **car trips** are **frequent and short.**

Do not overdo being specific and concrete. If you want to inform a nonspecialist reader about possible automobile fuels other than gasoline, *do* name the fuels and be very specific about their advantages and drawbacks. *Do not* go into a detailed, highly technical discussion of the chemical profiles of the fuels. Always base your choices on an awareness of your purpose for writing (see 1b) and your audience (see 1c).

EXERCISE 20-2

Consulting section 20b-2, revise the following paragraph by providing specific and concrete words and phrases to explain and enliven the ideas presented here in general and abstract language. As needed, you can revise these sentences to accommodate your changes in language.

The house for rent was exactly what I wanted. It had trees on the lawn and a driveway for my car. It had a porch, and flowers grew near the doorway. I was thrilled that the rent was even less money than I had hoped to spend. The real estate broker said I could move in that very day. I called a friend, who owned a truck, and asked him to help me move in. We got started that afternoon and almost finished unpacking all the boxes by that evening.

20c Increasing your vocabulary

The benefits of increasing your vocabulary are many. The more words you know, the more easily and the faster you can read. A large, rich vocabulary also helps you understand ideas and communicate them clearly and effectively in your writing. Use the techniques described in Chart 101.

TECHNIQUES FOR BUILDING YOUR VOCABULARY 101

TO FIND WORDS

- Use a highlighter pen to mark all unfamiliar words in textbooks and other reading material. Then define the words in the margin so you can study the meaning in context. Use context clues (see 20c-2) to figure out definitions, or look up the words in a dictionary. Write each word and its definitions on an index card or in a notebook.
- Listen carefully to learn how speakers use the language. Jot down new words to look up later. Write each word and its definitions on an index card or in a notebook.

TO STUDY WORDS

- Select some words that you intend to study each week. Put the date next to the word so that you can keep track of your goals. Whenever you look up a word in your dictionary, put a small checkmark next to it. When you accumulate three checkmarks next to a word, it is time to learn that word.
- Set aside time each day to study your selected words. Carry your cards or notebook to study in spare moments each day.
- Use mnemonics (see 22b) to help you memorize words. Set a goal of learning eight to ten new words a week. Use the words in your writing and, when possible, in conversation.
- Go back to words from previous weeks, whenever possible. List any words you have not learned well. Study them again, and *use* them.

1 Knowing prefixes and suffixes

Knowing common prefixes and suffixes is an excellent way to learn to decode unfamiliar words and increase your vocabulary.

Prefixes are syllables in front of a **root** word that modify its meaning. *Ante-* (before) placed before *room* gives *anteroom,* a waiting room leading to a larger room.

Suffixes are syllables added to the end of a root word that modify its meaning. For example, *excite* plus *-able* means "able to be excited," and *excite* plus *-ment* means "the state of being excited." The part of speech of a word is often signalled by the suffix.

2 Using context clues to figure out word meanings

Familiar words that surround an unknown word can give you hints about the meaning of the new word. Such **context clues** include four main types.

1. **Restatement context clue.** You can figure out an unknown word when a word you know repeats the meaning: *He jumped into the fray and enjoyed every minute of the fight. Fray* means "fight." Sometimes a restatement is set off by punctuation. For example, parentheses contain a definition in this sentence: *Fatty deposits on artery walls combine with calcium compounds to cause* arteriosclerosis *(hardening of the arteries).* Sometimes a technical term is set off by punctuation after the definition of a term is given. For example, dashes set off a term after it is defined in this sentence: *The upper left part of the heart—the left* atrium—*receives blood returning from circulation.*
2. **Contrast context clue.** You can figure out an unknown word when an opposite or contrast is presented: *We feared that the new prime minister would be a* menace *to society, but she turned out to be a great peacemaker. Menace* means "threat"; the contrast that explains *menace* is *but she turned out to be a great peacemaker.* As you read, watch for words that express contrast (such as *but, however, nevertheless;* for a complete list see Chart 25 in 4d-1).
3. **Example context clue.** You can figure out an unfamiliar word when an example or illustration relating to the word is given: *They were* conscientious *workers, making sure that everything was done correctly and precisely.* A dictionary

defines *conscientious* as "motivated by a desire to do what is right." The words "done correctly and precisely" are close to that meaning.

4. **General sense context clue.** You can use an entire passage to get a general sense of difficult words. For example, in *Nearly forty million North Americans are overweight; obesity has become an epidemic,* chances are good that *epidemic* refers to something happening to many people. Sometimes a "general sense context clue" will not make clear a word's exact denotation. For example, you might guess that *epidemic* indicates a widespread threat, but you might miss the connection of the word *epidemic* with the concept of disease. Interpreting the meaning of a word from the general sense carries the risk of allowing subtle variations that distinguish one word from another to slip by. You might want, therefore, to check the exact definition in a dictionary.

21 Understanding the Effect of Words

As words communicate meaning (see Chapter 20), they have an effect on the people reading or hearing them. As a writer, you want to choose words carefully. Sometimes the choices available to you are clearly either right or wrong, but often the choices are subtle. The guidelines discussed in this chapter can help you make good choices.

21a Using appropriate language

Using appropriate language means paying special attention to **tone** (see 1d) and **diction** (see 20b). As a writer, you want the words that you use to communicate your meaning as clearly and effectively as possible. Your choice of words and sentence styles (see Chapters 16–19) work together to create your individual writing style.

1 Using appropriate levels of formality

Informal and highly formal levels of writing differ clearly in tone. They use different vocabulary and sentence structures. Tone in writing indicates the attitude of the writer toward the subject and toward the audience. Tone may be highly formal, informal, or somewhere in between.

An **informal** tone occurs in e-mail or letters to friends. A **highly formal** tone, in contrast, occurs in sermons and proclamations. Academic writing uses a **medium** or **semiformal** tone: It is reasonable and even-handed, clear and efficient, and its vocabulary is appropriate for an academic audience.

INFORMAL — Ya know stars? They're a gas!

MEDIUM OR SEMIFORMAL — Gas clouds slowly changed into stars.

FORMAL The condensations of gas spun their slow gravitational pirouettes, slowly transmogrifying gas cloud into star.

—CARL SAGAN, "Starfolk: A Fable"

The informal example would be appropriate in a letter to a close friend or in a journal. The writer's attitude toward the subject is playful and humorous. The medium or semiformal example would be appropriate in most academic and professional situations. The writer's attitude toward the subject is serious and straightforward. The formal example is addressed to an audience with knowledge of scientific phenomena and an appreciation of figurative language (21c).

2 Using edited English for academic writing

The language standards that you are expected to use in academic writing are those of **edited English** as used in Canada: the accepted written language of most textbooks and many major newspapers, and of serious magazines. Such language conforms to widely established rules of grammar, sentence structure, punctuation, and spelling. Because advertising language and other language intended to reach and sway a large audience often ignore conventional usage, readers often encounter written English that varies from the standard. Such published departures from edited English are not acceptable in academic writing.

3 Avoiding slang and colloquial or regional language for most academic writing

Slang consists of coined words and new meanings attached to established terms. Slang words and phrases usually pass out of use quickly, although occasionally they become accepted into standard usage. **Colloquial** language is characteristic of casual conversation and informal writing: *The student flunked chemistry* instead of *the student failed chemistry.*

Canadian slang has been influenced by that of the United States and Britain, but uniquely Canadian expressions do exist: *sodbuster, high muckymuck,* and from the world of hockey, *cream, deke,* and *rink rat.* At no time does slang communicate accurate meanings in academic or business writing.

Regional language (also called *dialectal language*) is specific to some geographic areas. *Coal oil* in one part of the country, for example, is *kerosene* in another. The *Saskatoon berry* is also known as the *shadberry,* the *juneberry,* or the *serviceberry*. Dialects are different from slang because dialectic differences reflect geographical regions and socioeconomic status. Using a dialect when writing for the general reading public tends to shut some people out of the communication. Except when dialect is the topic of the writing, academic writing rarely accommodates dialect well.

Although slang, colloquial words, and regional language are neither substandard nor illiterate, they are usually not appropriate for academic writing. Replacing them in your academic writing allows you to communicate clearly with the large number of people who speak and write in medium or semiformal levels of language (see 21a-1).

4 Avoiding slanted language

To communicate clearly, choose words that convince your audience of your fairness as a writer. When you are writing about a subject on which you hold strong opinions, it is easy to slip into biased or emotionally loaded language. Such **slanted language** usually does not persuade a careful reader to agree with your point. Instead, it makes the reader wary or hostile. For example, suppose you are arguing against the practice of scientific experimentation on animals. If you use language such as "laboratory Frankensteins" who "routinely and viciously maim helpless kittens and puppies," you are using slanted language. You want to use words that make your side of an issue the more convincing one. Once you start using slanted, biased language, readers feel manipulated rather than reasoned with.

21b Avoiding sexist language

Sexist language assigns roles or characteristics to people on the basis of gender. Its opposite, **gender-neutral language**, represents both men and women fairly Most women *and* men today feel that sexist language unfairly discriminates against both sexes. Sexist language inaccurately assumes all nurses and homemakers are female (and therefore refers to them as "she") and all physicians and wage earners are male (and therefore refers to them as "he"). One widespread occurrence of sexist language is the use of the pronoun *he* to refer to someone of unidentified sex. Although tradition holds that *he* is correct in such situations, using only masculine pronouns to represent the human species excludes women and thereby distorts reality.

If you want to avoid sexist language in your writing, follow the guidelines in Chart 102. Also, avoid demeaning, outdated stereotypes, such as *women are bad drivers* or *men are bad cooks.* Do not describe a woman by her looks, clothes, or age (unless you do the same for men). Do not use the first name of one spouse when you use a title (such as *Mr.* or *Mrs.*) and the last name for the other spouse: *Phil Miller* [not Mr. Miller] *and his wife, Jeannette, always travel on separate planes* or *Jeannette and Phil Miller live in Manitoba.*

EXERCISE 21-1

Consulting section 21b, revise the following sentences by changing sexist language to gender-neutral language.

1. Many of man's most important inventions are found not in scientific laboratories but in the home.
2. Among these inventions are the many home appliances that were designed in the early 1900s to simplify women's housework.
3. Every housewife should be grateful to the inventors of labour-saving appliances such as vacuum cleaners, washing machines, and water heaters.

HOW TO AVOID SEXIST LANGUAGE 102

- Avoid using only the masculine pronoun to refer to males and females together. Use a pair of pronouns.

NO A doctor has little time to read outside **his** specialty.

YES A doctor has little time to read outside **his or her** specialty.

The "he or she" construction acts as a singular pronoun, and it therefore calls for a singular verb when it serves as the subject of a sentence. Try to avoid using the "he or she" construction, especially more than once in a sentence or in consecutive sentences. Revising into the plural may be a better solution.

NO A successful doctor knows that **he** has to work long hours.

YES Successful doctors know that **they** have to work long hours.

You may also recast a sentence to omit the gender-specific pronoun.

NO Everyone hopes that **he** will win the scholarship.

YES Everyone hopes to win the scholarship.

HOW TO AVOID SEXIST LANGUAGE *(continued)* 102

- Avoid the use of *man* when men and women are clearly intended in the meaning.

  NO **Man** is a social animal.
  YES **People** are social animals.
  NO Dogs are **man's** best friend.
  YES Dogs are **human's** best friends.
  Dogs are **people's** best friends.
  Dogs are **our** best friends.

- Avoid stereotyping jobs and roles by gender when men and women are included.

NO	YES
chairman	chair, chairperson
policeman	police officer
businessman	businessperson, business executive
statesman	diplomat, prime minister, statesperson

  NO teacher ... **she;** principal ... **he**
  YES teachers ... **they;** principals ... **they**

- Avoid expressions that exclude either sex.

NO	YES
mankind	humanity
the common man	the average person
man-sized sandwich	huge sandwich
old wives' tale	superstition

- Avoid using demeaning and patronizing labels.

NO	YES
lady lawyer	lawyer
male nurse	nurse
gal Friday	assistant
coed	student

  NO My **girl** will send it.
  YES My **secretary** will send it.
  Ida Morea will send it.

4. Before such appliances became available, a family was fortunate if the husband could afford to hire a cleaning lady or a maid to help with the housework.
5. Otherwise, each family member had tasks to do that could include washing his clothes by hand or carrying hot water for bathing up or down the stairs.
6. Once family members were freed from these difficult duties early in the twentieth century, women had more time to spend with their children.
7. Also, now everyone in the household had more time for his favourite pastimes and hobbies.
8. None of the inventors of modern home appliances could have guessed what far-reaching effects his inventions would have on our society.
9. Every worker, from labourer to businessman, could return each day to a home where there was not nearly as much heavy housework waiting to be done.
10. Even more important, with less housework to do, women could now leave the home to take jobs as office girls and sometimes even lady doctors and lawyers.

21c Using figurative language

Figures of speech use words for more than their literal meanings, yet they are not merely decorative. **Figurative language** enhances meaning. It makes comparisons and connections that draw on one idea or image to explain another, as shown in Chart 103.

As you use figurative language, avoid mixed metaphors, which blend images that do not work well together.

NO Recent years have given professional women a **foothold** on the **window of opportunity**.

YES Recent years have **opened** a **window of opportunity** for professional women.

There is rarely a place for irony in your academic writing, and you should always avoid its close relative, sarcasm. Readers will realize that you are being nasty.

NO He was a regular Albert Einstein with my questions. [This is sarcastic if you mean the opposite.]

YES He had trouble understanding many of my questions.

TYPES OF FIGURATIVE LANGUAGE 103

- **Analogy:** a comparison of similar traits between dissimilar things (The length of an analogy can range from one sentence to a paragraph to an entire essay; see 4f-8.)

  The tool that you saw yesterday in the robotics laboratory, worked with a ball and socket joint—in effect, a mechanical shoulder.

- **Irony:** the use of words to suggest the opposite of their usual sense

  Told that the car repair would cost $2000 and take at least two weeks, she said, "Oh, that would be wonderful!"

- **Metaphor:** a comparison between otherwise dissimilar things without using the word *like* or *as* (Be alert to avoid the error of a mixed metaphor, explained in 21c.)

  The rush-hour traffic bled out of all the city's major arteries.

- **Overstatement** (also called *hyperbole*): deliberate exaggeration for emphasis

  Andrew Marvell says praising his love's eyes and forehead could take 100 years.

- **Personification:** the assignment of a human trait to a nonhuman thing

  The book begged to be read.

- **Simile:** a direct comparison between otherwise dissimilar things, using the word *like* or *as*

  Langston Hughes says that a deferred dream dries up like a raisin in the sun.

- **Understatement:** deliberate restraint for emphasis

  It gets a little warm when the temperature reaches 35 degrees.

EXERCISE 21-2

Consulting section 21c, identify each figure of speech. Also, revise any mixed metaphors.

1. In these challenging times, the road ahead for our corporation is going to be a patchwork quilt of complexity.
2. Having spent the whole day on the beach, he came home as red as a lobster.

3. If I eat one more bite of that chocolate cake, I'll explode.
4. What I love best about you is that you use all the hot water every time you take a shower.
5. The daisies nodded their heads in the hot sun.
6. Stormy clouds covered the full moon like a veil.
7. Think of the environment as a human body, where small problems in one part do not much affect other parts, any more than a paper cut causes most of us more than an instant's pain and a heartfelt "Ouch!" Problems throughout a system like the air or the oceans, however—say, pollution building up beyond the system's ability to cleanse itself—can kill the entire organism just as surely as cholesterol building up in arteries can kill you or me.
8. That actor displayed the entire range of human emotions from A to B.
9. My heart stopped when I opened the gift my parents gave me.
10. Our supervisor said that reorganizing the department according to our recommendations would be trading a headache for an upset stomach.

21d Avoiding clichés

A **cliché** is a worn-out expression that has lost its capacity to communicate effectively. Many clichés are similes or metaphors, once clever, which have grown trite from overuse: *dead as a doornail, gentle as a lamb, straight as an arrow*. If you have heard words over and over again, so has your reader. If you cannot think of a way to rephrase a cliché, delete the phrase entirely.

On the other hand, English is full of frequently used word groups that are not clichés (for example, *up and down* and *in and out*). Common patterns are not clichés and need not be avoided.

EXERCISE 21-3

Consulting section 21d, revise these clichés. Use the idea in each cliché for a sentence of your own in plain English.

1. The bottom line is that Carl either raises his grade point average or finds himself in hot water.
2. Carl's grandfather says, "When the going gets tough, the tough get going."
3. Carl may not be the most brilliant engineering major who ever came down the pike, but he has plenty of get-up-and-go.
4. When they were handing out persistence, Carl was first in line.
5. The $64 000 question is: Will Carl make it safe and sound, or will the school drop him like a hot potato?

21e Avoiding artificial language

Sometimes student writers think that ornate words and complicated sentence structures make writing impressive. Experienced writers, however, work hard to communicate as clearly and directly as they can. Try to make your writing as accessible as possible to your readers. Extremely complex ideas or subject areas may require complex terms or phrases to explain them, but in general the simpler the language, the more likely your readers will understand it.

1 Avoiding pretentious language

Pretentious language is too showy, calling undue attention to itself with complex sentences and polysyllabic words. Academic writing does not call for big words used for their own sake. Overblown words are likely to obscure your message.

> As I alighted from my vehicle, my clothing was besmirched with filth. [*Translation:* My coat got dirty as I got out of my car.]
>
> I hate it when he tries ostentatiously to flaunt his accoutrements recently acquired in the haberdashery shop. [*Translation:* I hate it when he tries to show off his new clothes.]

2 Avoiding unnecessary jargon

Jargon is specialized vocabulary of a particular group. Jargon uses words that an outsider might not understand. Specialized language evolves in every field: professions, academic disciplines (see Chapters 37–39), business, and hobbies. As you write, consider your purpose° and audience° to decide whether a word is jargon in the context of your material. For example, a football fan easily understands a sportswriter's use of words such as *punt, sacked,* and *safety,* but they are jargon to people not familiar with football. Avoid using jargon unnecessarily. When you must use jargon for a general audience, be sure to explain the specialized meanings.

This example, showing specialized language used appropriately, is from an undergraduate textbook. The writers assume students know or can decipher the meaning of *eutrophicates, terrestrial,* and *eutrophic.*

As the lake eutrophicates, it gradually fills until the entire lake will be converted into a terrestrial community. Eutrophic change (or eutrophication) is the nutritional enrichment of the water, promoting the growth of aquatic plants.

—DAVIS AND SOLOMON, *The World of Biology*

3 Avoiding euphemisms

Euphemisms attempt to avoid the harsh reality of truth by using more pleasant-sounding, "tactful" words. Euphemisms are necessary for tact in some social situations (using *passed away* instead of *died,* for example). In other situations, euphemisms drain meaning from truthful writing. Unnecessary euphemisms might describe socially unacceptable behaviour (for example, *Johnny has a wonderfully vivid imagination* instead of *Johnny lies*). They also might try to hide unpleasant facts (*She is between assignments* instead of *She lost her job*). Avoid unnecessary euphemisms.

4 Avoiding "doublespeak"

Doublespeak is artificial, evasive language. It aims to distort and deceive. For example, many automobile dealerships today have renamed "used cars" as "pre-owned cars." A major corporation has described its notice that laid off 5000 workers as a "career alternative enhancement package." The military has used "collateral damage" for unintended killing of innocent civilians.

To use doublespeak is to try to hide the truth, a highly unethical practice that seeks to control people's thoughts. Avoid using doublespeak.

5 Avoiding bureaucratic language

Bureaucratic language is stuffy and overblown. The irony in the following example is that the writer seems to be trying to communicate very precisely but nothing is communicated. Bureaucratic language (or *bureaucratese,* the coined word to describe the style) is marked by unnecessary complexity, and is therefore meaningless.

You can include a page that also contains an Include instruction. The page including the Include instruction is included when you paginate the document but the included text referred to in its Include instruction is not included.

EXERCISE 21-4

Consulting section 21e, revise these examples of pretentious language, jargon, euphemism, "doublespeak," and bureaucratic language.

1. In-house employee interaction of a nonbusiness nature is disallowed.
2. An index card posted on the bulletin board advertised a gently worn bridal gown for sale.
3. Your dearest, closest acquaintance, it has been circulated through rumour, is entering into matrimony with her current beloved.
4. The sign in the window called it a pre-loved teddy bear.
5. My male sibling concocted a tale that was entirely fallacious.
6. An individual's cognitive and affective domains are at the centre of his or her personality.
7. He told the police officer that the unanticipated collision occurred as the result of a sudden, involuntary explosive action from his nose and mouth that caused him to momentarily close his eyes, which prevented him from seeing the other motorist's automobile.
8. When the finalization of this negotiation comes through, it will clarify our position in a positive manner.
9. The refuse has accumulated because the sanitation engineers were on strike last month.
10. Employees who are employed by the company for no less than five years in a full-time capacity fulfil the eligibility requirements for participation in the company's savings program.

22 Spelling and Hyphenation

You might be surprised to know this about good spellers: They do not always remember how to spell every word they write, but they are very skilled at sensing when they should check the spelling of a word. Try, therefore, not to ignore your quiet inner voice that doubts a spelling; listen to it and look up the word. At the same time, do not allow spelling doubts to interrupt the flow of your writing during drafting (see 3b). Underline or circle words you want to check, and go back to them when you are editing (see 3d) your writing.

How do you look up a word in the dictionary if you do not know how to spell it? If you know the first few letters, find the general area for the word and browse for it. If you do not know how a word begins, try to find it listed in a thesaurus under an easy-to-spell synonym°. When you are writing on a computer, you can usually use a program that checks spelling.

✚ COMPUTER TIP: Word-processing software usually includes a spell-check program that searches for words that do not match the spellings in the program's dictionary. Each program operates differently, but most allow you to "ask" for a spelling check; some underline a word in colour when it seems to be spelled incorrectly. Such programs alert you to wrong spellings or typing errors (called "typos"), but they have one major drawback. The programs will not identify a misspelled word if that word would be a proper spelling in a different context. For example, if you mean *west* but have typed *rest*, or if you mean *from* and type *form*, no spell-check program will see what you have typed in error as a mistake. Only careful proofreading can spot these errors. ✚

As you spell, be aware that the various origins of words and ways English-speaking people pronounce words make it almost impossible to rely solely on pronunciation to spell a word. What you *can* rely on is using a system of proofreading and using spelling rules.

Note that Canadian spelling, because it is influenced by both British and American spellings, contains elements of both; however, the drift is toward American conventions because of the influence of the media. Both American and British spellings may occur in any given piece of writing. Here are some examples:

labor	*or*	labour	humor	*or*	humour
theater	*or*	theatre	catalog	*or*	catalogue
check	*or*	cheque	realize	*or*	realise
defense	*or*	defence	connection	*or*	connexion

Whatever spelling you choose, be consistent. If you use the spelling *labour* in a document, use *colour* as well; and if you spell *theatre*, use the spelling *centre*.

22a Eliminating careless spelling errors

Many spelling errors are the result of illegible handwriting, slips of the pen, or typographical mistakes. Catching "typos" requires especially careful proofreading, using these techniques:

TECHNIQUES FOR PROOFREADING FOR SPELLING

1. Slow down your reading speed so that you can concentrate on individual letters of words rather than on the meaning of the words.
2. Stay within your "visual span," the number of letters you can identify with a single glance (for most people, about six letters).
3. Put a ruler or large index card under each line as you proofread, to focus your concentration and vision.
4. Read each paragraph *backwards,* from the last sentence to the first. This method helps to prevent your being distracted by the meaning of the material.

22b Spelling homonyms and commonly confused words

Homonyms are words that sound exactly like others *(its, it's; morning, mourning)*. There are also many words that sound so much alike that they are often confused with each other. A comprehensive list appears here (also, the most common sets are included in the Usage Glossary at the back of this handbook).

One source of confusion not covered by this list is "swallowed" pronunciation. For example, if a speaker fails to pronounce the letter *-d* at the end of words ("swallows" it), a writer may put down *use to,* *suppose to,* or *prejudice* when *used to, supposed to,* or *prejudiced* is required.

Another source of confusion is expressions that are always written as two words, not one: for example, *all right,* [not *alright*] and *a lot* [not *alot*].

Homonyms and Commonly Confused Words

accept	to receive
except	with the exclusion of
advice	recommendation
advise	to recommend
affect	to produce an influence on (verb°); an emotional response (noun°)
effect	result (noun); to bring about or cause (verb)
aisle	space between rows
isle	island
allude	to make indirect reference to
elude	to avoid
allusion	indirect reference
illusion	false idea, misleading appearance
already	by this time
all ready	fully prepared
altar	sacred platform or place
alter	to change
altogether	thoroughly
all together	everyone or everything in one place
are	plural form of *to be*
hour	sixty minutes
our	plural form of *my*
ascent	the act of rising or climbing
assent	consent
assistance	help
assistants	helpers
bare	nude, unadorned
bear	to carry; an animal
board	piece of wood
bored	uninterested
breath	air taken in
breathe	to take in air
brake	device for stopping
break	destroy, make into pieces
buy	to purchase
by	next to, through the agency of
capital	major city
capitol	government building (U.S.)

HOMONYMS AND COMMONLY CONFUSED WORDS *(continued)*

choose	to pick
chose	past tense of *to choose*
cite	to point out
sight	vision
site	a place
clothes	garments
cloths	pieces of fabric
coarse	rough
course	path; series of lectures
complement	something that completes
compliment	praise, flattery
conscience	sense of morality
conscious	awake, aware
council	governing body
counsel	advice
dairy	place associated with milk production
diary	personal journal
descent	downward movement
dissent	disagreement
dessert	final, sweet course in a meal
desert	to abandon (verb); dry, sandy area (noun)
device	a plan; an implement
devise	to create
die	to lose life (verb) *(dying);* one of a pair of dice (noun)
dye	to change the colour of something *(dyeing)*
dominant	commanding, controlling
dominate	to control
elicit	to draw out
illicit	illegal
eminent	prominent
immanent	living within; inherent
imminent	about to happen
envelop	to surround
envelope	container for a letter or other papers
fair	light-skinned; just, honest
fare	money for transportation; food
formally	conventionally, with ceremony
formerly	previously
forth	forward
fourth	number four
gorilla	animal in ape family
guerrilla	soldier specializing in unconventional, surprise attacks

➜

HOMONYMS AND COMMONLY CONFUSED WORDS *(continued)*

Word	Meaning
hear	to sense sound by ear
here	in this place
hole	opening
whole	complete; an entire thing
human	relating to the species *Homo sapiens*
humane	compassionate
insure	buy or give insurance
ensure	guarantee, protect
its	possessive form of *it*
it's	contraction for *it is*
know	to comprehend
no	negative
later	after a time
latter	second one of two things
lead	heavy metal substance; to guide
led	past tense of *to lead*
lightning	storm-related electricity
lightening	making lighter
loose	unbound, not tightly fastened
lose	to misplace
maybe	perhaps
may be	might be
meat	animal flesh
meet	to encounter
miner	a person who works in a mine
minor	under age
moral	distinguishing right from wrong; the lesson of a fable, story, or event
morale	attitude or outlook, usually of a group
of	preposition indicating origin
off	away from
passed	past tense of *to pass*
past	at a previous time
patience	forbearance
patients	people under medical care
peace	absence of fighting
piece	part of a whole; musical arrangement
personal	intimate
personnel	employees
plain	simple, unadorned
plane	to shave wood; aircraft
precede	to come before
proceed	to continue

HOMONYMS AND COMMONLY CONFUSED WORDS *(continued)*

presence	being at hand; attendance at a place or in something
presents	gifts
principal	foremost (adjective°); school head (noun°)
principle	moral conviction, basic truth
quiet	silent, calm
quite	very
rain	water drops falling to earth (noun); to fall like rain (verb)
reign	to rule
rein	strap to guide or control an animal (noun); to guide or control (verb)
raise	to lift up
raze	to tear down
respectfully	with respect
respectively	in that order
right	correct; opposite of *left*
rite	ritual
write	to put words on paper
road	path
rode	past tense of *to ride*
scene	place of an action; segment of a play
seen	viewed
sense	perception, understanding
since	measurement of past time; because
stationary	standing still
stationery	writing paper
than	in comparison with; besides
then	at that time; next; therefore
their	possessive form of *they*
there	in that place
they're	contraction for *they are*
through	finished; into and out of
threw	past tense of *to throw*
thorough	complete
to	toward
too	also; indicates degree *(too much)*
two	number following one
waist	midsection of the body
waste	discarded material (noun); to squander, to fail to use up (verb)
weak	not strong
week	seven days

➜

Homonyms and Commonly Confused Words *(continued)*

weather	climatic condition
whether	if
where	in which place
were	past tense of *to be*
which	one of a group
witch	female sorcerer
whose	possessive form of *who*
who's	contraction for *who is*
your	possessive form of *you*
you're	contraction for *you are*
yore	long past

EXERCISE 22-1

Consulting section 22b, select the appropriate homonym from each group in parentheses.

Imagine that you (are, our) standing in the middle of a busy sidewalk with a worried look on (your, you're, yore) face. In your hand (your, you're, yore) holding a map, (which, witch) you are puzzling over. If that happened in real life, (its, it's) almost certain that within (to, too, two) or three minutes a passerby would ask if you (where, were) lost and offer you (assistance, assistants). That helpful passerby, (buy, by) taking a (personal, personnel) interest in your problem, is displaying a quality known as empathy—the ability (to, too, two) put oneself in another person's place. Some researchers claim that empathy is an instinct that (human, humane) beings share with many other animals. (Their, There, They're) theory suggests that we have inherited the ability to empathize from (are, hour, our) distant ancestors. Other scientists wonder (weather, whether) empathy is instead a (conscience, conscious) (moral, morale) choice that people make. Whatever explanation is (right, rite, write) for the origin (of, off) empathy, (its, it's) (affect, effect) can be enjoyed—especially if (your, you're, yore) a person who (maybe, may be) lost and you don't (know, no) (where, were) (to, too, two) turn.

22c Using spelling rules for plurals, suffixes, and *ie, ei* words

Knowing the rules in Chart 104 will help you spell plurals, add suffixes, and spell words that contain *ie* or *ei* combinations.

SPELLING RULES FOR PLURALS, SUFFIXES, AND *IE, EI* WORDS

104

PLURALS

- **Adding *-s* or *-es*:** Most plurals are formed by adding *-s*, including words that end in "hard" *-ch* (sounding like *k*): *leg, legs; shoe, shoes; stomach, stomachs*. For words ending in *-s, -sh, -x, -z*, or "soft" *-ch* (as in *beach*), add *-es* to the singular: *beach, beaches; tax, taxes; lens, lenses.*
- **Words Ending in *-o*:** Add *-s* if the *-o* is preceded by a vowel (*radio, radios; cameo, cameos*). Add *-es* if the *o* is preceded by a consonant (*potato, potatoes*). A few words can be pluralized either way, but current practice favours the *-es* form: *cargo, volcano, tornado, zero.*
- **Words Ending in *-f* or *-fe*:** Some *-f* and *-fe* words are made plural by adding *-s: belief, beliefs*. Others require changing *-f* or *-fe* to *-ves: life, lives; leaf, leaves*. Words ending in *-ff* or *-ffe* simply add *-s: staff, staffs; giraffe, giraffes.*
- **Compound Words:** For most compound words, add *-s* or *-es* at the end of the last word: *chequebooks, player-coaches.* For a few, the word to make plural is not the last one: *sister-in-law, sisters-in-law; kilometre per hour, kilometres per hour.* (For hyphenating compound words, see Chart 106 in 22d.)
- **Internal Changes and Endings Other Than *-s*:** A few words change internally or add endings other than *-s* to become plural: *foot, feet; man, men; mouse, mice; child, children.*
- **Foreign Words:** Plurals other than *-s* or *-es* are listed in good dictionaries. In general, for many Latin words ending in *-um*, form plurals by changing *-um* to *-a: curriculum, curricula; datum, data; medium, media; stratum, strata.* For Latin words that end in *-us*, the plural is often *-i: alumnus, alumni; syllabus, syllabi* (also, *syllabuses).* For Greek *-on* words, the plural is often *-a: criterion, criteria; phenomenon, phenomena.*
- **One-Form Words:** A few spellings are the same for the singular and plural: *deer, elk, quail.* The differences are conveyed by adding words, not endings: *one deer, nine deer; rice, bowls of rice.*

SUFFIXES

- ***-y* Words:** If the letter before the final *y* is a consonant, change the *y* to *i* unless the suffix begins with an *i* (for example, *-ing*): *fry, fried, frying.* If the letter before the *-y* is a vowel, keep the final *y: employ,*

→

104

SPELLING RULES FOR PLURALS, SUFFIXES, AND *IE, EI* WORDS *(continued)*

employed, employing. These rules do not apply to irregular verbs (see Chart 62 in section 8d).

- ***-e* Words:** Drop a final *e* when the suffix begins with a vowel unless doing so would cause confusion (for example, *be* + *ing* does not become *bing*): *require, requiring; like, liking.* Keep the final *e* when the suffix begins with a consonant: *require, requirement; like, likely.* Exceptions include *argument* and *truly.*
- **Words That Double a Final Letter:** If the final letter is a consonant, double it only if it passes these tests: (1) Its last two letters are a vowel followed by a consonant; and (2) the suffix begins with a vowel: *drop, dropped; forget, forgetful, forgettable.* (American spelling adds a third test. The word must have one syllable or be accented on the last syllable: *begin* [accent on last syllable], *beginning* but *travel* [accent on first syllable], *traveling.* British spelling doubles the final consonant in many words even when the accent is not on the last syllable: *travel, travelling; worship, worshipper.)*
- ***-cede, -ceed, -sede* Words:** Only one word ends in *-sede: supersede.* Three words end in *-ceed: exceed, proceed, succeed.* All other words whose endings sound like "seed" end in *-cede: concede, intercede, precede.*
- ***-ally* and *-ly* Words:** The suffixes *-ally* and *-ly* turn words into adverbs°. For words ending in *-ic,* add *-ally: logically, statistically.* Otherwise, add *-ly: quickly, sharply.*
- ***-ance, -ence,* and *-ible, -able:*** No consistent rules govern words with these suffixes. The best advice is "When in doubt, look it up."

THE *IE, EI* RULE: The old rhyme for *ie* and *ei* is usually true:

> "*I* before *e* [*bel**ie**ve, f**ie**ld, gr**ie**f*]
> Except after *c* [*c**ei**ling, conc**ei**t*],
> Or when sounded like *ay* [***ei**ght, v**ei**n*],
> As in *n**ei**ghbour* and *w**ei**gh.*"

You may want to memorize these major exceptions:

ie	conscience	financier	science	species
ei	either	neither	leisure	seize
	counterfeit	foreign	forfeit	sleight
	weird			

EXERCISE 22-2

Consulting section 22c and Chart 104, form the plurals of these words.

1. yourself	6. millennium	11. echo
2. sheep	7. lamp	12. syllabus
3. photo	8. runner-up	13. wife
4. woman	9. criterion	14. get-together
5. appendix	10. lunch	15. crisis

EXERCISE 22-3

Consulting section 22c and Chart 104, follow the directions for each group of words.

1. Add *-able* or *-ible:* (a) profit; (b) reproduce; (c) control; (d) coerce; (e) recognize.
2. Add *-ance* or *-ence:* (a) luxuri _______; (b) prud _______; (c) devi _______; (d) resist _______; (e) independ _______.
3. Drop the final *e* as needed: (a) true + ly (b) joke + ing; (c) fortunate + ly; (d) appease + ing; (e) appease + ment.
4. Change the final *y* to *i* as needed: (a) happy + ness; (b) pry + ed; (c) pry + ing; (d) dry + ly; (e) beautify + ing.
5. Double the final consonant as needed: (a) commit + ed; (b) commit + ment; (c) drop + ed; (d) occur + ed; (e) regret + ful.
6. Insert *ie* or *ei* correctly: (a) rel _______ f; (b) ach _______ ve; (c) w _______ rd; (d) n _______ ce; (e) dec _______ ve.

22d Using hyphens correctly

1 Hyphenating at the end of a line

Generally, try not to divide a word at the end of a line. Following this advice makes reading easier. If you must divide a word, try not to divide the last word on the first line of a paper, the last word in a paragraph, or the last word on a page. Break the word only at a syllable, using the guidelines in Chart 105. If you are unsure of how to divide a word into syllables, consult a dictionary (see 20a).

GUIDELINES FOR END-OF-LINE HYPHENATION 105

- **Do not divide very short words, one-syllable words, or words pronounced as one syllable.**

NO	we-alth	en-vy	scream-ed	
YES	wealth	envy	screamed	

- **Do not leave or carry over only one or two letters.**

NO	a-live	tax-i	he-licopter	helicopt-er
YES	alive	taxi	heli-copter	helicop-ter

- **Divide words only between syllables.**

NO	proc-ede
YES	pro-cede

- **Always follow rules for double consonants.**

NO	ful-lness	omitt-ing	asp-halt
YES	full-ness	omit-ting	as-phalt

- **Divide hyphenated words after the hyphen, if possible, rather than at any other syllable.**

NO	self-con-scious	good-look-ing report
YES	self-conscious	good-looking report

2 Hyphenating prefixes, suffixes, compound words, and numbers

Prefixes and **suffixes** are syllables attached to root words. **Compound words** use two or more words together to express one concept. Some prefixes and suffixes are hyphenated; others are not. Compound words can be written as separate words (*night shift*), hyphenated words (*tractor-trailer*), or one word (*handbook*). Chart 106 gives basic guidelines for word hyphenation.

✤ ALERT: Use figures rather than words for any fraction that needs more than two words to express. If you cannot use figures (for example, if you cannot rearrange a sentence that starts with a multiword

HYPHENATING PREFIXES, SUFFIXES, COMPOUND WORDS, AND NUMBERS

106

- **Use hyphens after the prefixes *all-, ex-, quasi-,* and *self-*.**

  all-inclusive   self-reliant

- **Do not use a hyphen when *self* is a root word, not a prefix.**

NO	self-ishness	self-less
YES	selfishness	selfless

- **Use a hyphen to avoid a distracting string of letters.**

NO	antiintellectual	belllike
YES	anti-intellectual	bell-like

- **Use a hyphen before the suffix *-elect*.**

NO	presidentelect
YES	president-elect

- **Use a hyphen to add a prefix or suffix to a number or a word that starts with a capital letter.**

NO	post1950s	proAmerican	Rembrandtlike
YES	post-1950s	pro-American	Rembrandt-like

- **Use a hyphen to prevent confusion in meaning or pronunciation.**

YES	re-dress ("dress again")	redress ("set right")
	un-ionize ("remove the ions")	unionize ("form a union")

- **Use a hyphen when two or more prefixes apply to one root word.**

YES	pre- and post-war eras	two-, three-, or four-year program

COMPOUND WORDS

- **Use a hyphen between a prefix and a compound word.**

NO	antigun control
YES	anti-gun control

- **Use a hyphen for most compound modifiers that precede the noun. Do not use a hyphen for most compound modifiers after the noun.**

➜

HYPHENATING PREFIXES, SUFFIXES, COMPOUND WORDS, AND NUMBERS *(continued)* 106

YES	well-researched report	two-centimetre clearance
	report is well researched	clearance of two centimetres

- **You do not need to use a hyphen when a compound modifier starts with an *-ly* adverb.**

YES	happily married couple	loosely tied package

- **Do not use a hyphen when a compound modifier is in the comparative or superlative form.**

NO	better-fitting shoe	least-welcome guest most-significant factor
YES	better fitting shoe	least welcome guest most significant factor

- **Do not use a hyphen when a compound modifier is a foreign phrase.**

YES	*post hoc* fallacies

- **Do not use a hyphen with a possessive compound modifier.**

NO	a full-week's work	eight-hours' pay
YES	a full week's work	eight hours' pay

SPELLED-OUT NUMBERS

- **Use a hyphen between two-word numbers from twenty-one through ninety-nine.**

YES	thirty-five (35)	two hundred thirty-five (235)

- **Use a hyphen in a compound-word modifier formed from a number and a word.**

YES	fifty-minute class [also 50-minute class]	three-to-one odds [also 3-to-1 odds]

- **Use a hyphen between the numerator and the denominator of two-word fractions.**

YES	one-half	two-fifths	seven-tenths

fraction), use hyphens between the words of the numerator's number and the words of the denominator's number but not between the numerator and the denominator: two one-hundredths (2/100), thirty-three ten-thousandths (33/10 000). ✤

EXERCISE 22-4

Consulting section 22d, in the blanks write the correct form of the word in parentheses according to the way it is used in the sentence.

EXAMPLE Most people lock the doors of their car when they leave it parked, but many have never thought of protecting their **all-important** [*all-* prefixes hyphenated] computer files.

1. How do (computer users) _______ guard the privacy of their sensitive files?
2. They control access with a (pass word) _______ , often one they invent (them selves) _______ .
3. Clients of automated banking services and Internet surfers also use passwords as an (anti theft) _______ precaution.
4. Unfortunately, computer hackers are always developing new (password cracking) _______ programs.
5. Therefore, if you ever make up a password, think of one that is (hard to crack) _______ .
6. Any program that specializes in cracking passwords can break a code that follows a regular pattern, even if the code has (six hundred) _______ digits and stretches (two metres) _______ when printed out.
7. Other (easily cracked) _______ codes are based on birthdays, Social Insurance numbers, spouses' names, words, and (two word) _______ combinations.
8. You will never (out smart) _______ a determined thief with any of these.
9. Have you ever invented a password so ingenious that after a while it seemed you could not remember it (ninety nine) _______ percent of the time?
10. That kind of password is the (least useful) _______ password of all!

EXERCISE 22-5

The following paragraph contains twelve misspelled words. Circle the words, correct them, and match them to a section in this chapter. If the error does not fall under any particular section, describe the cause of error in your own words.

An invitation arrived last week in a beautyful, crisp white envelop. I knew rite away it was a peace of important mail, unlike all the junk mail I usually recieve. It seemed that the local chapter of the Falcon Club of Canada wanted to hear my thoughts on American car collecting. The prospect of giving a speech through me into a nervous frenzy as I tryed to prepare at the last minute—getting a haircut, memorizing my notes, practiseing in front of my freinds—all designed to insure that I would not humiliate myself publically. As it turned out, my heart-ache was pointless. The club really just wanted the opportunity to inspect my 1965 navy blue Ford Falcon.

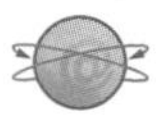

www.rpi.edu/dept/llc/writecenter/web/handouts.html
Types of Writing: Revising Prose

www.wisc.edu/writing/Handbook/ClearConciseSentences.html
Grammar and Style: Clear, Concise Sentences

www.rpi.edu/dept/llc/writecenter/web/genderfair.html
Types of Writing: Gender-Fair Language

www.csuchico.edu/pub/PubGuide/writingstyleguide.html
Writing Style Guide

www2.yourdictionary.com
A Web of Online Dictionaries (and other resources)

Using Punctuation and Mechanics

When you use punctuation and mechanics according to currently accepted practice, you avoid errors that interfere with the delivery of the meaning you want to communicate. Part Four presents and explains the rules and conventions that many readers of academic writing expect you to follow. As you use Chapters 23 through 30, remember that punctuation and mechanics are tools to help you deliver your message clearly to your readers.

23 Periods, Question Marks, and Exclamation Points

Periods, question marks, and exclamation points are called **end punctuation** because they occur at the end of sentences.

I love you. Do you love me? I love you!

PERIODS

23a Using a period at the end of a statement, a mild command, or an indirect question

Unless a sentence asks a direct question°* (23c) or issues a strong command or emphatic declaration (23e), it ends with a period.

STATEMENT A journey of a thousand leagues begins with a single step.

—LAO-TSU

MILD COMMAND Put a gram of boldness into everything you do.

—BALTASAR GRACIAN

INDIRECT QUESTION I asked if they wanted to climb Mt. Everest. [A direct question would end with a question mark: I asked, *"Do you want to climb Mt. Everest?"*]

*Throughout this book, a degree mark (°) indicates that you can find the definition of the word in the Glossary of Terms in this handbook.

23b Using periods with most abbreviations

Most **abbreviations** call for periods, but some do not. Typical abbreviations with periods include *Mt., St., Dr., Mr., Ms., Mrs., Fri, Feb., R.N., a.m.,* and *p.m.* In general, the word *professor* is spelled out, not abbreviated. Abbreviations without periods include the names of some organizations and government agencies (such as *CBC* and *NFB*), and two-letter postal code abbreviations for province names. For more information about abbreviations, see 30h and 30i.

Ms. Yuan, who works at the NFB, lectured to Dr. Benet's film class at 9:30 a.m.

✤ PUNCTUATION ALERT: When the period of an abbreviation falls at the end of a sentence, the period serves also to end the sentence. Put a sentence-ending question mark or exclamation point, however, after the period of an abbreviation.

The phone rang at 4:00 a.m.

Who would call at 4:00 a.m.?

How embarrassing to dial a wrong number at 4:00 a.m.! ✤

QUESTION MARKS

23c Using a question mark after a direct question

A **direct question** asks a question and ends with a question mark. In contrast, an **indirect question** reports a question and ends with a period (see 23a).

How many attempts have been made to climb Mt. Everest?
[An indirect question would be: *The tourists wanted to know how many attempts had been made to climb Mt. Everest.*]

✤ PUNCTUATION ALERT: Do not combine a question mark with a comma, a period, or an exclamation point.

NO She asked, "How are you?."

YES She asked, "How are you?" ✤

Questions in a series are each followed by a question mark, whether or not each question is a complete sentence.

✤ CAPITALIZATION ALERT: When questions in a series are not complete sentences, you can choose whether or not to capitalize the first letter, as long as you are consistent in each piece of writing.

After the fierce storm had passed, the mountain climbers debated what to do next. Turn back? Move on? Rest for a while? ✤

When a request is phrased as a question to achieve a polite tone, it does not always require a question mark: *Would you please send me a copy.*

23d Using a question mark in parentheses

When a date or number is unknown or doubtful even after your very best research, you can use *(?)*.

Mary Astell, an English author who wrote pamphlets on women's rights, was born in 1666 (?) and died in 1731.

The word *about* is often a graceful substitute for *(?)*: *Mary Astell was born about 1666.*

Otherwise, do not use *(?)* to communicate that you are unsure of information. Also, your choice of words, not *(?)*, should communicate irony or sarcasm.

NO Having the flu is a delightful (?) experience.

YES Having the flu is as pleasant as almost drowning.

EXCLAMATION POINTS

23e Using an exclamation point for a strong command or an emphatic declaration

An **exclamation point** can end a strong command or an emphatic declaration. A strong command is a very firm order: *Look out behind you!* An emphatic declaration makes a shocking or surprising statement: *There's been an accident!*

✤ PUNCTUATION ALERT: Do not combine an exclamation point with any other punctuation.

NO "There's been an accident!," she shouted.

YES "There's been an accident!" she shouted. ✤

23f Avoiding the overuse of exclamation points

In academic writing, your words, rather than exclamation points, should communicate the strength of your message. Reserve exclamation points for a short emphatic declaration within a longer passage.

> When we were in Nepal, we tried each day to see Mt. Everest. But each day we failed. Clouds defeated us! The summit never emerged from a heavy overcast.

Frequent use of exclamation points suggests an exaggerated sense of urgency.

NO Mountain climbing can be dangerous. You must learn correct procedures! You must have the proper equipment! Otherwise, you could die!

YES Mountain climbing can be dangerous. You must learn correct procedures. You must have the proper equipment. Otherwise, you could die!

Your choice of words, not *(!)*, should communicate amazement or sarcasm.

NO At 8882 metres (!), Mt. Everest is the world's highest mountain. Yet, Chris (!) wants to climb it.

YES At a majestically staggering 8882 metres, Mt. Everest is the world's highest mountain. Yet, amazingly, Chris wants to climb it.

EXERCISE 23-1

Consulting sections 23a–23f, insert any needed periods, question marks, and exclamation points. Also delete any unneeded ones.

EXAMPLE Have you ever crossed a wide river or a deep canyon on a huge bridge that towered over the landscape.

Have you ever crossed a wide river or a deep canyon on a huge bridge that towered over the landscape?

1. The first (?) modern bridge was built over the Severn River in England in 1781.
2. The fact that it was built out of cast-iron girders might explain why engineers today still call it a "modern" bridge?
3. Earlier bridges had been built from wood or stone!

4. Wooden bridges, however, often burned down when struck by lightning
5. The Severn Bridge used cast-iron girders because iron was a lightweight(!) substitute for stone.
6. "Why would anyone prefer lightweight materials for building a sturdy bridge" is a question you may ask?
7. Strong but light building materials require fewer bridge supports, which looks graceful and keeps costs down!
8. In the 1930s, people wondered if the graceful, narrow bridges that were being built were safe, because they often swayed in the wind?
9. One of them, the Tacoma Narrows Bridge in Washington State, surprised no one (?) when it began to twist in a windstorm. (The date was Nov 7, 1940.)
10. But everyone was shocked when the wind ripped the bridge apart in just a few minutes!

EXERCISE 23-2

Insert needed periods, question marks, and exclamation points.

New York's Ellis Island immigration facility is famous as the place where millions of newcomers arrived in the United States How many people have heard of its Canadian counterpart It may be better to speak of its Canadian counterparts, rather Before the age of airplane travel, there were two important entry points for immigrants taking the Atlantic route to Canada Pier 21 in Halifax, which opened in 1928, was the arrival point for more than one million new Canadians Grosse Île, a small island near Quebec City on the St Lawrence River, was still receiving immigrants when Pier 21 opened, although the island facility closed a few years later What a contrast these two locations make Grosse Île was a quarantine station for severely ill arrivals When it opened in 1832, cholera was raging in the slums of Europe English and Irish immigrants brought this feared disease to Canada Thousands died of cholera in Quebec City and Montreal, despite the quarantine Then, in 1847, more than ninety thousand Irish immigrants arrived, fleeing the potato famine in their homeland Thousands were infected with typhus; the medical staff led by Dr Douglas worked heroically but were unable to save many of the ill This unhappy history may have led Canadians to ignore Grosse Île's heritage until recently In contrast, Pier 21 is celebrated as the place where refugees fleeing Nazism and war reached a safe shore.

24 Commas

Commas are the most frequently used marks of punctuation, occurring twice as often as all other marks of punctuation combined. Rules for the comma are many: The comma *must* be used in certain places, it *must not* be used in other places, and it is *optional* in still other places. This chapter will help you sort through the various rules and uses of the comma.

The comma groups and separates sentence parts, helping to create clarity for readers. Consider the clarity of the following paragraph, which contains all needed punctuation except commas.

NO Among publishers typographical errors known as "typos" are an embarrassing fact of life. In spite of careful editing reviews and multiple readings few books are perfect upon publication. Soon after a book reaches the marketplace reports of errors embarrassments to authors and editors alike start to come in. Everyone laughed therefore although no one thought it was funny when an English textbook was published with this line: "Proofread your writing carefullly."

Here is the same paragraph with commas included.

YES Among publishers, typographical errors, known as "typos," are an embarrassing fact of life. In spite of careful editing, reviews, and multiple readings, few books are perfect upon publication. Soon after a book reaches the marketplace, reports of errors, embarrassments to authors and editors alike, start to come in. Everyone laughed, therefore, although no one thought it was funny, when an English textbook was published with this line: "Proofread your writing carefullly."

In the *Yes* paragraph, the meaning is clear. Each comma in it is used for a specific reason according to a comma rule.

Avoid two practices that can get writers into trouble with commas: (1) As you are writing, do not insert a comma just because you happen to pause to think before moving on. (2) As you reread your writing, do not insert commas according to your personal habits of pausing. Although a comma alerts a reader to a slight pause (except in dates and other conventional material), pausing is not a reliable guide for writers, because people's breathing rhythms, accents, and thinking spans vary greatly.

24a Using a comma before a coordinating conjunction that links independent clauses

When **coordinating conjunctions** (*and, but, or, nor, for, so,* and *yet*) link independent clauses°, they create **compound sentences**°. Use a comma before the coordinating conjunction.

PATTERN FOR COMMAS WHEN COORDINATING CONJUNCTIONS LINK INDEPENDENT CLAUSES 107

Independent clause, { **and** / **but** / **for** / **or** / **nor** / **so** / **yet** } independent clause.

The sky turned dark grey, **and** the wind died suddenly.

The November morning had just begun, **but** it looked like dusk.

Shopkeepers closed their stores early, **for** they wanted to get home.

Soon high winds would start, **or** thick snow would begin silently.

Farmers had no time to continue harvesting, **nor** could they round up their animals in distant fields.

The firehouse whistle blew four times, **so** everyone knew a blizzard was closing in.

People on the road tried to reach safety, **yet** a few unlucky ones were stranded.

When the two independent clauses in a compound sentence are very short, some authorities omit the comma before the coordinating conjunction. However, you will never be wrong, and you avoid the risk of error, if you always use a comma in your academic writing.

✤ COMMA CAUTION: Do not put a comma after a coordinating conjunction that links independent clauses.

NO The sky turned dark grey **and,** the wind died suddenly.

YES The sky turned dark grey, **and** the wind died suddenly. ✤

✤ COMMA CAUTION: Do not use a comma when a coordinating conjunction links two words, phrases°, or dependent clauses° only. Use commas for a series of three or more items (see 24c).

NO Learning a new language demands **time, and patience.** [Two words linked by *and* use no comma.]

YES Learning a new language demands **time and patience.**

NO Each language has **a beauty of its own, and forms of expression** which are duplicated nowhere else. [Two phrases linked by *and* use no comma.]

YES Each language has **a beauty of its own and forms of expression** which are duplicated nowhere else.

—MARGARET MEAD, "Unispeak" ✤

✤ COMMA CAUTION: Do not use a comma to separate independent clauses unless they are linked by a coordinating conjunction. If you use such a comma, you will create the error known as a comma splice (see 14c).

NO **Ten centimetres of snow fell in two hours, driving was hazardous.**

YES Ten centimetres of snow fell in two hours, **and** driving was hazardous. [The coordinating conjunction *and* links the two independent clauses.]

YES Ten centimetres of snow fell in two hours. Driving was hazardous. [Independent clauses can become two separate sentences.] ✤

When independent clauses containing other commas are linked by a coordinating conjunction, you can choose to use a semicolon before the coordinating conjunction (see 25b). Base your decision on what would help your reader understand the material most easily.

Because temperatures remained low all winter, the snow could not melt until well into spring; **and** some people wondered when they would see grass again.

EXERCISE 24-1

Consulting section 24a, combine each pair of sentences using the coordinating conjunction shown in parentheses. When necessary, rearrange words. Insert commas before coordinating conjunctions that separate independent clauses.

EXAMPLE William Lyon Mackenzie King was the grandson of the third prime minister of Canada, Alexander Mackenzie. He himself became the prime minister in 1921. (and)

William Lyon Mackenzie King was the grandson of the third prime minister of Canada, Alexander Mackenzie, and he himself became prime minister in 1921.

1. King studied law at the University of Toronto. He also attended the University of Chicago and Harvard University. (but)
2. King delivered a famous speech to the House of Commons in 1936 in which he said that some countries have too much history. We have too much geography. (but)
3. He was an ardent supporter of Canadian autonomy. He insisted that Canada be treated by its allies in World War II as an equal. (so)
4. In response to French-Canadian protests, King promised that no conscripted soldiers would be sent to fight. Later, he broke his promise and sent conscripts overseas. (but)
5. King is remembered for the wartime slogan "Conscription if necessary, but not necessarily conscription." His tenure as prime minister began long before World War II and continued long after it. (yet)
6. Despite his Canada-first policy, King kept up sentimental connections with England. He would not have had Lester Pearson send him fragments of buildings bombed out by the Blitz to decorate his garden. (or)
7. Although he was often accompanied by women on public occasions, King never married. He had no children. (nor)
8. In public, King was a colourless, pragmatic politician. His secret diaries reveal a man obsessed by strange fears and enthusiasms. (yet)
9. King suffered poor health in his last years. He died at Kingsmere, his estate in Quebec, in 1950. (and)
10. Since his death, King's reputation has suffered. His interest in séances and communing with his dead mother has drawn embarrassing attention to his private life. (for)

24b Using a comma after an introductory clause, phrase, or word

Use a comma to signal the end of an introductory element and the beginning of an independent clause.

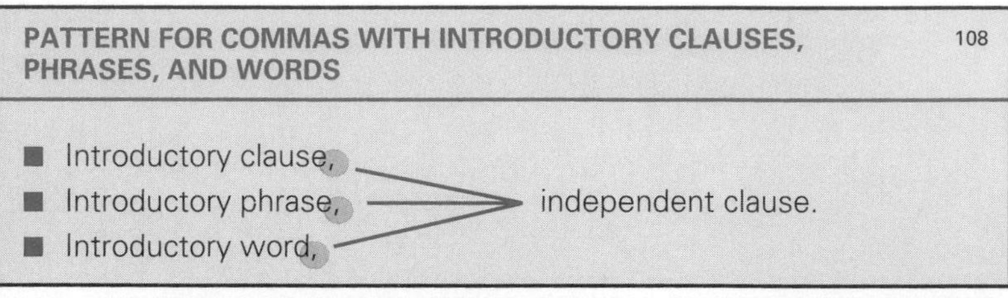

PATTERN FOR COMMAS WITH INTRODUCTORY CLAUSES, PHRASES, AND WORDS
108
Introductory clause,
Introductory phrase,
Introductory word,
independent clause.

Some authorities omit the comma when an introductory element is very short and the sentence is clear without a comma. However, in academic writing, you will never be wrong if you use a comma after an introductory element.

1 Using a comma after an introductory adverb clause

An **adverb clause** is a dependent clause (see 7o-2). It cannot stand alone as an independent unit because it starts with a subordinating conjunction (for example, *although, because, if*; for a complete list, see 7h). When an adverb clause precedes an independent clause, separate the clauses with a comma.

> **When it comes to eating,** you can sometimes help yourself more by helping yourself less.
>
> —RICHARD ARMOUR

2 Using a comma after an introductory phrase

A **phrase** is a group of words that cannot stand alone as a sentence. It lacks a subject°, a predicate°, or both. Use a comma to set off a phrase that introduces an independent clause. (Types of phrases are explained in 7n.)

Between 1544 and 1689, sugar refineries appeared in London and New York. [prepositional phrase°]

Obtained mainly from sugar cane and sugar beets, sugar is also developed from the sap of maple trees. [past participle° phrase]

Beginning in infancy, we develop lifelong tastes for sweet and salty foods. [participial phrase°]

To satisfy a craving for ice cream, timid people sometimes brave midnight streets. [infinitive phrase°]

Eating being enjoyable, we tend to eat more than we need for fuel. [absolute phrase°]

3 Using a comma after introductory words

Introductory words include **transitional expressions** and **conjunctive adverbs.** These words carry messages of relationships between ideas in sentences and paragraphs. Transitional expressions include *for example* and *in addition* (for a complete list, see Chart 25 in section 4d-1). Conjunctive adverbs include *therefore* and *however* (for a complete list, see Chart 51 in section 7f). When these introductory words appear at the beginning of a sentence, most writers follow them with a comma.

For example, fructose is fruit sugar that is metabolized as a blood sugar.

✤ COMMA CAUTION: A comma after a single introductory word may be dropped in some contexts. In most academic writing, however, this comma is still required. Ask your instructor what is required in each class. If the choice is yours, be consistent in each piece of writing. ✤

Interjections are introductory words that convey surprise or other emotions. Use a comma after an interjection at the beginning of a sentence: ***Oh,*** *we did not realize that you are allergic to cats.* ***Yes,*** *your sneezing worries me.*

✤ PUNCTUATION ALERT: Use a comma before and a comma after a transitional expression, conjunctive adverb, or interjection that falls within a sentence. Use a comma before such words that fall at the end of a sentence. ✤

EXERCISE 24-2

Consulting section 24b, and using a comma after each introductory element, combine each set of sentences into one sentence that starts according to the directions in parentheses. You can add, delete, and rearrange words as needed.

EXAMPLE Several magicians have revealed their secrets. They have revealed their secrets recently. (begin with *recently*)

Recently, several magicians have revealed their secrets.

1. One famous trick involves sawing a woman in half. This trick actually uses two women. (begin with *for example*)
2. The magician opens the lid to a large rectangular box. The magician shows the audience that it is empty. (begin with *first*)
3. The brave female assistant lies down in the box. The opened box lid faces away from the audience. (clause beginning *when*)
4. The assistant puts her head outside one end of the box. She seems to put her wiggling feet out the other end. (phrase beginning *locked inside*)
5. Observers watch in astonishment. The magician pushes a saw through the middle of the box. (phrase beginning *in astonishment*)
6. This illusion seems impossible. This illusion is safely performed with two women participating. (clause beginning *although*)
7. The first assistant walks behind the box. This assistant lies down in the box and pulls her knees up to her chest. (phrase beginning *walking*)
8. The first woman now occupies only one side. And the other woman hidden under the box's false bottom gets into position on the second side. (phrase beginning *in the closed box*)
9. The second woman folds her body by bending forward at the waist. She puts her feet out the holes at her end of the box. (phrase beginning *to create the illusion*)
10. Each woman is positioned in a different end of the box. The magician can safely make a grand show of sawing a woman in half. (clause beginning *because*)

24c Using commas to separate items in a series

A **series** is a group of three or more elements—words, phrases°, or clauses°—that match in grammatical form as well as in importance in the same sentence.

PATTERN FOR COMMAS IN A SERIES 109

- word, word, and word
- word, word, word
- phrase, phrase, and phrase
- phrase, phrase, phrase
- clause, clause, and clause
- clause, clause, clause

Marriage requires **sexual, financial, and emotional** discipline.

—ANNE ROIPHE, "Why Marriages Fail"

Culture is a way of **thinking, feeling, believing.**

—CLYDE KLUCKHOHN, *Mirror for Man*

My love of flying goes back to those early days **of roller skates, of swings, of bicycles.**

—TERESA WIGGINS, student

The big world of action is both dangerous and mysterious; you'll never really understand it. **Stay out of it, sit still, don't try.**

—ELIZABETH JANEWAY, "Soaps, Cynicism, and Mind Control"

We have been taught **that children develop by ages and stages, that the steps are pretty much the same for everybody, and that to grow out of the limited behavior of childhood,** we must climb them all.

—GAIL SHEEHY, *Passages*

Some authorities omit the comma before the coordinating conjunction between the last two items of a series. This handbook recommends using this comma, for omitting it can distort meaning and confuse a reader. When the items in a series contain commas or other punctuation, separate them with semicolons instead of commas (see 25d). This practice ensures that your sentence will deliver the meaning you intend.

If it's a bakery, they have to sell cake; if it's a photography shop, they have to develop film; **and** if it's a dry-goods store, they have to sell warm underwear.

—ART BUCHWALD, "Birth Control for Banks"

Numbered or lettered lists within a sentence are items in a series.

Use commas (or semicolons if the items are long) to separate them when there are three or more items.

> To file your insurance claim, please enclose (1) a letter requesting payment, (2) a police report about the robbery, and (3) proof of purchase of the items you say are missing.

✤ COMMA CAUTION: Do not use a comma before the first item or after the last item in a series unless a different rule makes it necessary.

NO Many artists, writers, and composers, have indulged in daydreaming and reverie.

YES Many artists, writers, and composers have indulged in daydreaming and reverie.

NO Such dreamers include, Miró, Debussy, Dostoevsky, and Dickinson.

YES Such dreamers include Miró, Debussy, Dostoevsky, and Dickinson.

YES Such dreamers include, of course, Miró, Debussy, Dostoevsky, and Dickinson. [The comma after *of course* is necessary to set off the transitional expression from the rest of the sentence.] ✤

EXERCISE 24-3

Consulting section 24c, insert commas to separate items in a series. If a sentence needs no commas, circle its number.

EXAMPLE Recent studies show that people who watch television for more than a few straight hours are likely first to feel relaxed then to grow passive and eventually to develop self-contempt.

Recent studies show that people who watch television for more than a few straight hours are likely first to feel relaxed, then to grow passive, and eventually to develop self-contempt.

1. Viewers in the United States Canada West Germany and Italy aged 10 through 82 participated in a carefully designed study.
2. Participants agreed that for one week they would carry beepers listen for a signal about seven times a day and immediately fill in a form about their current mood and mental activity.
3. The participants were told to watch whatever amount of television they normally did and to do nothing special during the week of the study.
4. When viewing stretched on for hours, the viewers' responses showed that they lost their ability to concentrate that they felt increasingly unhappy and lonely and that they experienced guilt and anxiety.

5. A less expected problem was that after seeing so many beautiful competent captivating people on television the viewers felt inadequate and unable to compete.

Using a comma to separate coordinate adjectives

PATTERN FOR COMMAS WITH COORDINATE ADJECTIVES 110
coordinate adjective, coordinate adjective noun

Coordinate adjectives are two or more adjectives° that equally modify a noun°. Separate coordinate adjectives with commas (unless the coordinate adjectives are joined by a coordinating conjunction such as *and* or *but*).

COORDINATE ADJECTIVES

The **huge, restless** crowd waited for the concert to begin. [Both *huge* and *restless* modify *crowd,* so a comma is used.]

The audience cheered happily when the **pulsating, rhythmic** music filled the stadium. [Both *pulsating* and *rhythmic* modify *music,* so a comma is used.]

CUMULATIVE (NONCOORDINATE) ADJECTIVES

The concert featured **several new** bands. [*New* modifies *bands,* but *several* modifies *new bands;* so no comma is used.]

Each had a **distinctive musical** style. [*Musical* modifies *style; distinctive* modifies *musical style*; so no comma is used.]

If you are not sure whether adjectives need a comma between them, use the "Tests for Coordinate Adjectives" in Chart 111.

✤ COMMA CAUTION: (1) Do not put a comma after a final coordinate adjective and the noun it modifies. (2) Do not put a comma between adjectives that are not coordinate. ✤

TESTS FOR COORDINATE ADJECTIVES

111

If either test given here works, the adjectives are coordinate and need a comma between them.

- Can the order of the adjectives be reversed without changing the meaning or creating nonsense? If yes, use a comma.

  NO The concert featured **new several** bands. (Only *several new* makes sense.)

  YES The **huge, restless** (or *restless, huge*) crowd waited for the concert to begin.

  NO Each had a **musical distinctive** style. (Only *distinctive musical* makes sense.)

  YES The audience cheered happily as the **rhythmic, pulsating** (or *pulsating, rhythmic*) music filled the stadium.

- Can the word *and* be inserted between the adjectives? If yes, use a comma.

  NO The concert featured **new and several** bands.

  YES The **large and restless** crowd waited.

EXERCISE 24-4

Consulting section 24d, insert commas to separate coordinate adjectives. If a sentence needs no commas, circle its number.

EXAMPLE Only corn grown for popcorn pops consistently because all other kinds of corn lack tough enamel-like shells.

Only corn grown for popcorn pops consistently because all other kinds of corn lack tough, enamel-like shells.

1. The outside of unpopped popcorn is a hard plastic-like coating.
2. Inside an unpopped kernel is a soft starchy substance combined with water.
3. Applying heat causes the water molecules to expand until the pressure pops the kernel.
4. The popped kernel turns itself inside out and absorbs air into its white pulpy matter.
5. The thinner, softer shells of non-popping corn do not allow water to heat to the high popping temperature.

24e Using commas to set off nonrestrictive (nonessential) elements, but not restrictive (essential) elements

The most difficult comma decisions are those related to **restrictive (essential)** elements and **nonrestrictive (nonessential)** elements. The comma usage rules themselves are easy. The difficult part comes in understanding what *restrictive, essential, nonrestrictive,* and *nonessential* mean. Before trying to master the rules, use Chart 112 to become familiar with the meaning of these terms. Then apply the definitions as you analyze what message you want each of your sentences to deliver.

DEFINITIONS OF "RESTRICTIVE" AND "NONRESTRICTIVE" 112

- A **restrictive element** contains information **essential** for the reader to understand fully the meaning of the word or words that it modifies. It limits ("restricts") what it modifies.

    Some provinces retest drivers **over age sixty-five** to check their driving competency.

    The prepositional phrase° *over age sixty-five* limits the word *drivers* so that a reader understands which drivers are being retested (not all drivers, only those over age sixty-five). Therefore, *over age sixty-five* is restrictive.

- A **nonrestrictive element** is **not essential** for a reader to understand fully the word or words that it modifies. It describes but does not limit (does not "restrict") what it modifies.

    My parents, **who both are over age sixty-five,** took a defensive driving course last year.

    The relative clause° *who both are over age sixty-five* describes *my parents,* but it is not essential to a reader's understanding which parents took a defensive driving course last year. Therefore, *who both are over age sixty-five* is nonrestrictive.

Here are additional examples of restrictive and nonrestrictive elements.

RESTRICTIVE ELEMENTS

Some people **in my neighbourhood** enjoy jogging. [The reader needs the information *in my neighbourhood* to know which people enjoy jogging. The information is essential, so commas are not used.]

Some people **who are in excellent physical condition** enjoy jogging. [The reader needs the information *who are in excellent physical condition* to know which people enjoy jogging. The information is essential, so commas are not used.]

NONRESTRICTIVE ELEMENTS

An energetic person, Anna Hom enjoys jogging. [Without knowing that Anna Hom is energetic, the reader can understand that Anna Hom enjoys jogging. The information is not essential, so commas are used.]

Anna Hom, **who is in excellent physical condition,** enjoys jogging. [Without knowing that Anna Hom is in excellent physical condition, the reader can understand the information that Anna Hom enjoys jogging. The information is not essential, so commas are used.]

Anna Hom enjoys jogging, **which is also my favourite pastime.** [Without knowing about my favourite pastime, the reader can understand the information that Anna Hom enjoys jogging. The information is not essential, so commas are used.]

Once you understand the terms *restrictive, essential, nonrestrictive,* and *nonessential,* use Chart 113 to get to know the patterns for commas with nonrestrictive (nonessential) elements.

PATTERN FOR COMMAS WITH NONRESTRICTIVE ELEMENTS 113

- **Nonrestrictive element,** independent clause.
- Beginning of independent clause, **nonrestrictive element,** end of independent clause.
- Independent clause, **nonrestrictive element.**

✤ COMMA CAUTION: Remember, a restrictive element is essential. Do not set it off with commas (or any other punctuation) from the rest of the sentence. ✤

Using commas to set off nonrestrictive appositives

An **appositive** is a word or group of words that renames a noun°. A **nonrestrictive appositive** is not essential for the identification of the noun it is renaming, so it is set off by commas.

NONRESTRICTIVE APPOSITIVE

The agricultural scientist, **a new breed of farmer,** controls the farming environment. [The appositive *a new breed of farmer* is not essential in identifying who controls the farming environment, so the nonrestrictive appositive is set off with commas.]

Most appositives are nonrestrictive (nonessential). Once the name of something is given, words renaming it are not usually necessary to specify or limit it even more. In some cases, however, appositives are restrictive (essential) and are not set off with commas.

RESTRICTIVE APPOSITIVE

The agricultural scientist **Wendy Singh** has helped develop a new fertilization technique. [The appositive *Wendy Singh* is essential in identifying exactly which agricultural scientist has developed the new fertilization technique, so the restrictive appositive is not set off with commas.]

EXERCISE 24-5

Consulting section 24e and using your knowledge of restrictive and nonrestrictive clauses and phrases, insert commas as needed. If a sentence is correct, circle its number.

EXAMPLE In today's suburban houses many features including front doors imitate parts of the huge aristocratic mansions of past centuries.

In today's suburban houses many features, including front doors, imitate parts of the huge aristocratic mansions of past centuries.

1. The design of ordinary North American homes includes features originally invented for the wealthy who often had different uses for them.
2. Large front doors often approached by a set of stairs allowed noble families to show off as they walked in and out of their houses.
3. Wide indoor staircases which originated in the palaces of fifteenth-century Italy are now found in many large suburban homes.
4. In Italian palaces those staircases led to the ballrooms and dining rooms of the second floor called the "noble floor" because only the upper classes used it.
5. People today who select the latest entertainment equipment are also following the lead of the ultra-wealthy in earlier times.

6. The two silent film stars who built Pickfair a Hollywood mansion of the 1920s created a sensation by including the first-ever private movie theatre in their new home.
7. Families today that own a stereo and a VCR are able to outdo Pickfair in the quality and variety of their home entertainment.
8. Although today's homes often imitate the wealthy mansions of the past, one important exception is the family kitchen unknown in the aristocratic home.
9. In wealthy households of old the kitchen a drab working room was used only by the servants for cooking.
10. Today the kitchen the main gathering place in many homes is used by both rich and poor families for cooking as well as for eating and conversing.

24f Using commas to set off transitional and parenthetical expressions, contrasts, words of direct address, and tag sentences

Words, phrases°, or clauses° that interrupt a sentence but do not change its essential meaning should be set off, usually with commas. (Dashes or parentheses can also set material off; see sections 29a and 29b.)

Conjunctive adverbs such as *however* and *therefore* (for a complete list, see Chart 51 in section 7f) and **transitional expressions** such as *for example* and *in addition* (for a complete list, see Chart 25 in section 4d-1) can express connections within sentences. When they do, set them off with commas.

> The Niagara Peninsula, **therefore,** is well suited to viticulture.
>
> The Hillebrand and Inniskillen wineries are located there, **for example.**

✤ COMMA CAUTION: Use a semicolon or a period—not a comma—before the conjunctive adverb or a transitional expression that falls between independent clauses. If you use a comma, you will create the error known as a comma splice (see Chapter 14). ✤

Parenthetical expressions are "asides," additions to sentences that the writer thinks of as extra. Set them off with commas.

> Sales of Canadian tobacco, **according to recent statistics,** have been steadily decreasing.
>
> Canadian tobacco farmers, **sad to say,** must develop other means of support.

Expressions of contrast describe something by stating what it is not. Set them off with commas.

> Feeding the world's population is a serious problem, **but not an intractable one.**
>
> We must work against world hunger continuously, **not just when emergencies develop.**

Words of **direct address** indicate the person or group spoken to. Set them off by commas.

> Join me, **brothers and sisters,** to end hunger.
>
> Your contribution to the Relief Fund, **Steve,** will help us greatly.

Tag sentences consist of a verb°, a pronoun°, and often the word *not,* generally contracted. Set off tag sentences with commas. If the tag sentence is a question, end it with a question mark.

> Canadians' response to the Manitoba flood was impressive, **wasn't it?**
>
> Response to future crises will be as generous, **I hope.**

EXERCISE 24-6

Consulting section 24f, add necessary commas to set off transitional, parenthetical, and contrasting elements, words of direct address, and tag sentences.

EXAMPLE Writer's block it seems to me is a misunderstood phenomenon.

Writer's block, it seems to me, is a misunderstood phenomenon.

1. Inability to write some say stems from lack of discipline and a tendency to procrastinate.
2. Therefore according to this thinking the only way to overcome writer's block is to exert more willpower.
3. But writer's block can be a complex psychological event that happens to conscientious and hard-working people not just the procrastinators.
4. Strange as it may seem such people are often unconsciously rebelling against their own self-tyranny and rigid standards of perfection.
5. If I told you my fellow writer that all it takes to start writing again is to quit punishing yourself you would think I was crazy wouldn't you.

24g Using commas to set off quoted words from explanatory words

Use a comma to set off quoted words from short explanations in the same sentence. This rule holds whether the explanatory words come before, between, or after the quoted words.

PATTERNS FOR COMMAS WITH QUOTED WORDS 114

- Explanatory words, "Quoted words."
- "Quoted words," explanatory words.
- "Quoted words begin," explanatory words, "quoted words continue."

Speaking of ideal love, the poet William Blake wrote, "Love seeketh not itself to please."

"My love is a fever," said William Shakespeare about love's passion.

"I love no love," proclaimed poet Mary Coleridge, "but thee."

This use of commas is especially important in communicating conversations or other direct discourse. Be aware, however, that words such as *that* or *as* create a different kind of grammatical setting for quoted words. Do not separate them from the quoted words with a comma. (For capitalization in quotations, see 30c.)

Shakespeare also wrote that "Love's not Time's fool."

The duke describes the duchess as being "too soon made glad."

Shaw's quip "Love is a gross exaggeration of the difference between one person and everybody else" delights me.

Sometimes words a person has spoken or written are reported, not given as an exact quotation. Such words are called **indirect discourse.** Often indirect discourse includes the word *that* before the reported words. Do not use a comma after *that* in indirect discourse.

Shakespeare also wrote that people should be true to themselves.

✤ COMMA CAUTION: When quoted words end with a question mark or an exclamation point, keep that punctuation even if explanatory words follow.

QUOTED WORDS *"O Romeo! Romeo!"*

NO "O Romeo! Romeo!," called Juliet as she stood at her window.

NO "O Romeo! Romeo," called Juliet as she stood at her window.

YES "O Romeo! Romeo!" called Juliet as she stood at her window.

QUOTED WORDS *"Wherefore art thou Romeo?"*

NO "Wherefore art thou Romeo?," continued Juliet as she thought of her new-found love.

NO "Wherefore art thou Romeo," continued Juliet as she thought of her new-found love.

YES "Wherefore art thou Romeo?" continued Juliet as she thought of her new-found love. ✤

EXERCISE 24-7

Consulting section 24g, punctuate the following dialogue correctly. If a sentence is correct, circle its number.

EXAMPLE "Can you tell me just one thing?," asked the tourist.

"Can you tell me just one thing?" asked the tourist.

1. "I'm happy to answer any questions you have" said the rancher to the tourist.
2. "Well, then" said the tourist "I'd like to know how you make ends meet on such a tiny ranch."
3. "Do you see that man leaning against the shed over there?" asked the rancher, pointing with a twig.
4. The rancher continued "He works for me, but I don't pay him any money. Instead, I have promised him that after two years of work he will own the ranch."
5. "Then I'll work for him, and in two more years, the ranch will be mine again!," said the rancher with a smile.

24h Using commas in dates, names, addresses, and numbers according to accepted practice

When you write dates, names, and numbers, be sure to use commas according to accepted practice.

RULES FOR COMMAS WITH DATES

115

- Use a comma between the date and the year: **July 20,** 1969.
- Use a comma between the day and the date: **Sunday,** July 20, 1969.
- Within a sentence, use a comma on both sides of the year in a full date.

Everyone wanted to be near a television set on **July 20,** 1969, to watch Armstrong emerge from the lunar landing module.

- Do not use a comma in a date that contains the month with only a day or the month with only a year. Also, do not use a comma in a date that contains only the season and year.

  The major news story during **July 1969** was the moon landing; news coverage was especially heavy on **July 21.**

- An inverted date takes no commas: **20 July 1969.**

  People stayed near their television sets on **20 July 1969** to watch the moon landing.

RULES FOR COMMAS WITH NAMES, PLACES, AND ADDRESSES

116

- When an abbreviated title (Jr., M.D., Ph.D.) comes after a person's name, use a comma between the name and the title—**Rosa Gonzales,** M.D.—and also after the title if it is followed by the rest of the sentence:

  The jury listened closely to the expert testimony of **Rosa Gonzales,** M.D., last week.

- When you invert a person's name, use a comma to separate the last name from the first: **Whiteford,** Robert Karl.
- Use a comma to separate the names of a city and province or territory: **Estevan,** Saskatchewan. If the city and province fall within a sentence, use a comma after the province as well, unless the province name ends the sentence and thus is followed by a period, question mark, or exclamation point.

  Estevan, Saskatchewan, recorded the highest number of hours of sunshine in Canada in 1993.

RULES FOR COMMAS WITH NAMES, PLACES, AND ADDRESSES (*continued*) 116

- When you write a complete address as part of a sentence, use a comma to separate all the items, with the exception of the postal code. The postal code follows the province after a double space but no comma. Also, do not follow the postal code with a comma.

  I wrote to **Mr. U. Lern, 10-01 Rule Road, Toronto, Ontario M1P 2J7** for the instruction manual.

RULES FOR COMMAS WITH LETTERS 117

- For the opening of an informal letter, use a comma:

  Dear Betty,

For the opening of a business or formal letter, use a colon (:).

- For the close of a letter, use a comma:

  Sincerely yours, **Best regards,**
  Love, **Very truly yours,**

RULES FOR COMMAS WITH NUMBERS 118

The SI—the international system of metric measurements used in Canada—does not use commas in large numbers. Instead, it uses spaces to separate sets of three digits. Nevertheless, the use of commas in numbers remains common in Canada. This chart lists rules for both number systems.

1. Rules for numbers in SI

- Counting from the right, put a space after every three digits in numbers with more than four digits: **72 867** **156 567 066**
- A space is optional for most four-digit numbers. Use a consistent style within a given piece of writing.

  $1867 **$1 867**
  1867 km **1 867 km**
  1867 potatoes **1 867 potatoes**

RULES FOR COMMAS WITH NUMBERS (*continued*) 118

Always use a space in four-digit numbers when they are aligned in columns in a table or a chart.

- Do not use a space in four-digit years, in addresses, or in page numbers.

2. Rules for numbers in systems using commas

- Counting from the right, put a comma after every three digits in numbers with more than four digits: **72,867** **156,567,066**
- A comma is optional for four-digit numbers. Use a consistent style within a given piece of writing.

$1867	**$1,867**
1867 km	**1,867 km**
1867 potatoes	**1,867 potatoes**

- Do not use a comma for a four-digit year: **1990** (a year of five digits or more gets a comma if you are using the Imperial system: **25,000 B.C.**); in an address of four digits or more: **12161 Dean Drive;** or in a page number of four digits or more: **see page 1338.**

3. Use a comma to separate related Imperial measurements written as words: **five feet, four inches.**
4. Use a comma to separate a scene from an act in a play: **act 2, scene 4.**
5. Use a comma to separate a reference to a page from a reference to a line: **page 10, line 6.**

EXERCISE 24-8

Consulting section 24h, insert commas (or spaces) where they are needed. Be consistent in the style you choose. If a sentence is correct, circle its number.

EXAMPLE The heaviest hailstone recorded in Canada fell on Cedoux Saskatchewan.

The heaviest hailstone recorded in Canada fell on Cedoux, Saskatchewan.

1. With a rainfall of 6655 mm, Henderson Lake British Columbia has the most annual precipitation in the country.
2. Burgeo Newfoundland has the second highest average annual precipitation with 1699.7 mm.

3. The warmest temperature in Canada—45 degrees Celsius—was recorded on July 5 1937 at Midale Saskatchewan.
4. Windsor Ontario with more than 200000 population holds the record for the highest average number of days per year with thunderstorms: 34 days.
5. Snag Yukon Territory has the record for the coldest temperature ever recorded in Canada; it was minus 63 degrees Celsius on February 3 1947.

24i Using commas to clarify meaning

Sometimes you will need to use a comma to clarify the meaning of a sentence, even though no other rule calls for one.

NO	Of the gymnastic team's twenty five were injured.
YES	Of the gymnastic team's twenty, five were injured.
NO	Those who can practise many hours a day.
YES	Those who can, practise many hours a day.
NO	George dressed and performed for the sellout crowd.
YES	George dressed, and performed for the sellout crowd.

EXERCISE 24-9

Consulting section 24i, insert commas to prevent misreading. If a sentence is correct, circle its number.

EXAMPLE When hunting owls use both vision and hearing.

When hunting, owls use both vision and hearing.

1. During the day flying and hovering over their territories owls create an imaginary "map."
2. Flying at night owls consult this mental map of their surroundings.
3. A team of scientists gave owls distorting eyeglasses to make them re-learn their mental maps.
4. The bespectacled owls scientists found wore their glasses as contentedly as humans do.
5. The owls were soon able to produce new mental maps using their glasses once again spotting and chasing small rodents across the ground.

24j Avoiding misuse of the comma

Using commas correctly helps you deliver your meaning to your reader. As a writer, you frequently have to make decisions about whether a comma is needed. If as you are drafting° you are in doubt about a comma, insert and circle it clearly so that you can go back to it later when you are revising° and think through whether it is correct. Throughout this chapter, most sections that discuss a correct use of the comma include a comma caution to alert you to a related misuse of the comma. This section summarizes the most frequent misuses of the comma.

Because the comma occurs so frequently, advice against overusing it sometimes clashes with a rule requiring it. In such cases, follow the rule that requires the comma.

> The town of Banff, **Alberta,** attracts thousands of tourists each year. [Although the comma after Alberta separates the subject and verb, it is required because the province is set off from the city and from the rest of the sentence; see 24h.]

1 Avoiding misuse of a comma with coordinating conjunctions

Section 24a discusses the correct use of commas with sentences joined by coordinating conjunctions°. Do not put a comma *after* a coordinating conjunction that joins two independent clauses° unless another rule makes it necessary. Also, do not use commas to separate two items joined with a coordinating conjunction.

NO The sky was dark grey **and,** it looked like dusk.

YES The sky was dark grey, and it looked like dusk.

NO **The moon, and the stars** were shining last night.

YES The moon and the stars were shining last night.

2 Avoiding misuse of a comma with subordinating conjunctions and prepositions

Do not put a comma *after* a subordinating conjunction° or a preposition° unless another rule makes it necessary.

NO Although, the storm brought high winds, it did no damage.

YES Although the storm brought high winds, it did no damage.

NO The storm did no damage although, it brought high winds.

YES The storm did no damage although it brought high winds.

NO People expected worse between, the high winds and the heavy downpour.

YES People expected worse between the high winds and the heavy downpour.

3 Avoiding misuse of commas to separate items

Section 24c discusses the correct use of commas with items in a series. Do not use a comma *before* the first or *after* the last item in a series, unless another rule makes it necessary.

NO The gymnasium was decorated with, **pictures of beavers, Mounties, and Canadian prime ministers** for Canada Day.

NO The gymnasium was decorated with **pictures of beavers, Mounties, and Canadian prime ministers,** for Canada Day.

YES The gymnasium was decorated with **pictures of beavers, Mounties, and Canadian prime ministers** for Canada Day.

Section 24d discusses the correct use of commas with coordinate adjectives°. Do not put a comma after the final coordinate adjective and the noun it modifies. Also, do not use a comma between noncoordinate adjectives.

NO The **huge, restless,** crowd waited.

YES The **huge, restless** crowd waited.

NO The concert featured **several, new** bands.

YES The concert featured **several new** bands.

Avoiding misuse of commas with restrictive elements

Section 24e discusses the correct use of commas with restrictive (essential) elements° and nonrestrictive (nonessential) elements°. Do not use a comma to set off a restrictive (essential) element from the rest of a sentence.

NO Vegetables**, stir-fried in a wok,** are uniquely crisp and flavourful. [The information about being stir-fried in a wok is essential, so it is not set off with commas.]

YES Vegetables **stir-fried in a wok** are uniquely crisp and flavourful.

5 Avoiding misuse of commas with quotations

Section 24g discusses the correct use of commas with quoted material. Do not use a comma to set off indirect discourse° (often signalled by *that* or *as*).

NO Jon **said that, he likes stir-fried vegetables.**

YES Jon **said that he likes stir-fried vegetables.**

YES Jon **said, "I like stir-fried vegetables."**

6 Avoiding use of a comma to separate a subject from its verb, a verb from its object, a verb from its complement, and a preposition from its object

NO **Orville and Wilbur Wright, made** their first successful airplane flights on December 17, 1903. [As a rule, do not let a comma separate a subject° from its verb°.]

YES **Orville and Wilbur Wright made** their first successful airplane flights on December 17, 1903.

NO These inventors enthusiastically **tackled, the problems** of powered flight and aerodynamics. [As a rule, do not let a comma separate a verb from its object°.]

YES These inventors enthusiastically **tackled the problems** of powered flight and aerodynamics.

NO Flying has **become, both** an important industry and a popular hobby. [As a rule, do not let a comma separate a verb from its complement°.]

YES Flying has **become both** an important industry and a popular hobby.

NO Air Canada, which was founded in 1937 as Trans-Canada Airlines, today carries passengers **to, destinations worldwide.** [As a rule, do not let a comma separate a preposition° from its object.]

YES Air Canada, which was created in 1937 as Trans-Canada Airlines, today carries passengers **to destinations world-wide.**

EXERCISE 24-10

Some deliberately misused commas have been added in these sentences. Consulting 24j and the other sections in this chapter that are referred to in 24j, delete unneeded commas. If a sentence is correct, circle its number.

EXAMPLE The "Persons Case" is the name of the court case, that finally gave women in Canada the right to serve in the Senate.

The "Persons Case" is the name of the court case that finally gave women in Canada the right to serve in the Senate.

1. In 1919, Judge Emily Murphy asked the prime minister to appoint a woman to the Senate but, she received a disappointing reply.
2. Prime Minister Borden informed her that only "persons" could sit in the Senate, and, the 1867 British North America Act did not recognize women as persons.
3. Murphy, and four other women petitioned the Supreme Court of Canada to decide if the word *persons* in the BNA Act, which served as Canada's constitution, included female persons.
4. After many, long weeks of deliberation, the Court said that, the BNA Act did not count women as persons.
5. The basis of the Court's decision was, the argument that the authors of the 1867 Act, who had not given women the vote, never intended them to become senators.
6. In response, one petitioner tartly expressed the disappointment, shock, and surprise of all those women "who had not known they were not persons" until the Court told them so.
7. The five, anxious petitioners could still appeal the decision of Canada's Supreme Court to, the Privy Council in London.
8. The Privy Council ruled in 1929 that the term *persons*, must be understood in the BNA Act to include women; further, it called, the exclusion of women from politics "a relic of days more barbarous than ours."
9. Ironically, women, had already won the right to be elected to Parliament and to every provincial legislature except Quebec's.
10. To commemorate this court case, someone, who has worked to achieve justice and equality, each year is presented with the cleverly named Persons Award.

Focus on Revising

REVISING YOUR WRITING

If you make comma errors when you write, go back to your writing and locate the errors. Using this chapter as a resource, revise your writing to correct the errors.

CASE STUDY: REVISING FOR CORRECT USE OF COMMAS

In these case studies, you can observe a student writer revising. Then you have the chance to revise other student writing on your own.

Observation

A student wrote the following draft for a course called Introduction to Geography. This material includes excellent specific details, but the draft's effectiveness is diminished by the presence of comma errors.

Read through the draft. The errors are highlighted and explained. Before you look at the student's revision, revise the material yourself. Then compare your version and the student's.

In 1990, Canada produced 68331 tonnes of coal most of it from Alberta British Columbia Saskatchewan and Nova Scotia. Its worth was almost $2 billion, an indication of the continuing importance of this centuries-old industry. Such statistics do not however include the cost in terms of human life. Mining is frequently dangerous but coal mining is particularly hazardous because it exposes miners to deep tunnels soft rock dust explosives and vulnerable ventilation systems. In coal mines accidents and fatalities

space or comma missing in a number of five digits: 24h

commas missing between items in a series: 24c

comma missing to set off nonrestrictive appositive: 24e

commas missing to set off conjunctive adverb: 24f

comma missing before coordinating conjunction linking independent clauses: 24a

commas missing between items in a series: 24c

comma missing after introductory phrase: 24b–2

➜

occur more often than in other mines because the rock strata are usually weaker and methane gas may be present.

Springhill Nova Scotia famous as the birthplace of Anne Murray has been the site of numerous coal-mining disasters. In Springhill a town that once had the deepest mine in Canada 424 mine workers lost their lives from 1881 to 1969. In February 1891 125 miners died in an explosion and in November 1956 an accident killed 39 men, although the tragedy would have been worse if not for the rescue of 88 other trapped men. On October 23 1958 after a tunnel collapse crushed 74 miners 18 were rescued from nearly four kilometres down the deepest rescue operation ever carried out in Canada.

One of the survivors Douglas Jewkes who was rescued nine days after the tunnel caved in is reported to have said "I think this calls for a bottle of 7-Up." He explained that a vision of the soft drink had sustained him while he was trapped underground. Not surprisingly he was later hired by 7-Up. The event moved folk singer Peggy Seeger to compose a ballad "The Springhill Mining Disaster" from which these lines are taken:

In the town of Springhill,
  Nova Scotia,
Down in the dark of the

commas missing with city and province names: 24h

commas missing to set off parenthetical expression: 24f

comma missing to set off nonrestrictive appositive: 24e

comma missing to set off nonrestrictive appositive: 24e

comma missing before coordinating conjunction linking independent clauses: 24a

comma missing after introductory words: 24b-3

commas missing with date: 24h

comma missing after introductory clause: 24b-1

comma missing to set off nonrestrictive appositive: 24e

commas missing to set off nonrestrictive appositive: 24e

comma missing before quoted words: 24g

comma missing to set off nonrestrictive element: 24e

comma missing after introductory words: 24b-3

commas missing to set off nonrestrictive appositive: 24e

Cumberland Mine,
There's blood on the coal
and the miners lie,
In roads that never saw sun nor sky,
Roads that never saw sun nor sky.

Here is how the student revised to correct the comma errors. Compare this version with your revision. Make sure that your revision has eliminated each of the errors highlighted in the draft.

In 1990, Canada produced 68 331 tonnes of coal, most of it from Alberta, British Columbia, Saskatchewan, and Nova Scotia. Its worth was almost $2 billion, an indication of the continuing importance of this centuries-old industry. Such statistics do not, however, include the cost in terms of human life. Mining is frequently dangerous, but coal mining is particularly hazardous because it exposes miners to deep tunnels, soft rock, dust, explosives, and vulnerable ventilation systems. In coal mines, accidents and fatalities occur more often than in other mines because the rock strata are usually weaker and methane gas may be present.

Springhill, Nova Scotia, famous as the birthplace of Anne Murray, has been the site of numerous coal-mining disasters. In Springhill, a town that once had the deepest mine in Canada, 424 mine workers lost their lives from 1881 to 1969. In February 1891, 125 miners died in an explosion, and in November 1956, an accident killed 39 men, although the tragedy would have been worse if not for the rescue of 88 other trapped men. On October 23, 1958, after a tunnel collapse crushed 74 miners, 18 were rescued from nearly four kilometres down, the deepest rescue operation ever carried out in Canada.

One of the survivors, Douglas Jewkes, who was rescued nine days after the tunnel caved in, is reported to have said, "I think this calls for a bottle of 7-Up." He explained that a vision of the soft drink had sustained him while he was trapped underground. Not surprisingly, he was later hired by 7-Up. The event moved folk singer Peggy Seeger to compose a ballad, "The Springhill Mining Disaster," from which these lines are taken:

In the town of Springhill, Nova Scotia,
Down in the dark of the Cumberland Mine,
There's blood on the coal and the miners lie,
In roads that never saw sun nor sky,
Roads that never saw sun nor sky.

→

Participation

A student wrote the following draft for a course called Introduction to Political Science. The assignment was to discuss an example of the power of consumers. The material is clear and logically presented, but the draft's effectiveness is diminished by comma errors.

Read through the draft. Then revise it to eliminate the errors. Also, make any additional revisions you think would improve the content, organization, and style of the material.

Consumers often feel that choosing a new car is a difficult time-consuming matter. Most automobile customers tend to concentrate on the price, the special features the look and the reputation of the car. Truly experienced informed car buyers however carefully investigate the car manufacturer's grievance procedures.

A common mistake that consumers make is to assume that the helpful friendly car salesperson will help resolve problems with the automobile after it is purchased. In fact the salesperson's job is essentially finished once the car is sold so a consumer with a complaint will usually hear "You'll have to talk to the service department."

If a car salesperson offers little or no help a consumer may feel cheated by the indifference. One reaction often felt by many people who end up with a lemon of a car is to write an angry letter to the chief executive officer of the automobile company. Before writing the consumer should realize that complaints to the manufacturers are referred back to the dealership. After all dealerships and manufacturers are not owned and managed by the same people.

In some cases consumers may benefit from legal advice. Different jurisdictions have varying "lemon laws" to help consumers who purchase defective cars. In some U.S. states for example the existence of a problem, that is unresolved, after six repair attempts by the dealership's service department can require a dealer to substitute a new vehicle. Chrysler Motors has the Customer Arbitration Board (CAB), which consists of a consumer advocate, a member of the general public, and an independent, technical expert. Any solution that the CAB proposes is binding on the dealer and Chrysler Motors.

It is comforting to know that a consumer, who buys a lemon of a car, is not always helpless isn't it? Sometimes a lemon can be made into lemonade, right?

25 Semicolons

25a Using a semicolon between closely related independent clauses

When independent clauses° are clearly related in meaning, you can choose to separate them with a semicolon instead of a period. Your choice depends on the meaning you want your material to deliver. A period signals complete separation between independent clauses; a semicolon tells readers that the separation is only partial.

SEMICOLON PATTERN I	119
Independent clause; independent clause.	

This is my husband's second marriage; it's the first for me.

—Ruth Sidel, "Marion Deluca"

A divorce is like an amputation; you survive, but there's less of you.

—Margaret Atwood

✤ COMMA CAUTION: Do not use only a comma between independent clauses, or you will create the error called a comma splice (see Chapter 14). ✤

25b Using a semicolon before a coordinating conjunction joining independent clauses containing commas

When independent clauses° are linked by a coordinating conjunction (*and, but, or, nor, for, yet, so*), a comma should separate them (see 24a), but there is one exception. When one of the independent clauses contains a comma, you can use a semicolon before the coordinating conjunction. Choose according to what would be easier for your reader. As a general rule, you should not start a new sentence with the coordinating conjunction.

SEMICOLON PATTERN II 120

- Independent clause, one that contains a comma; coordinating conjunction independent clause.
- Independent clause; coordinating conjunction independent clause, one that contains a comma.
- Independent clause, one that contains commas; coordinating conjunction independent clause, one that contains a comma.

> When the peacock has presented his back, the spectator will usually begin to walk around him to get a front view; but the peacock will continue to turn so that no front view is possible.
>
> —FLANNERY O'CONNOR, "The King of the Birds"

> For anything worth having, one must pay the price; and the price is always work, patience, love, self-sacrifice.
>
> —JOHN BURROUGHS

25c Using a semicolon when conjunctive adverbs or other transitional expressions connect independent clauses

You can use a semicolon between two independent clauses when the second clause begins with a conjunctive adverb (*therefore, however;* for a complete list, see Chart 51 in 7f) or other transitional expression (*in fact, as a result;* for a complete list, see Chart 25 in 4d-1). Your other option is to use a period, creating two sentences.

SEMICOLON PATTERN III 121

- Independent clause; conjunctive adverb, independent clause.
- Independent clause; transitional expression, independent clause.

The average annual rainfall in the Okanagan Valley is less than 40 cm; **nevertheless,** it lies in the shadow of the rainy Cascade Mountains.

Irrigation came to the semidesert valley in the 1930s; **as a result,** it now produces much of British Columbia's—and even Canada's—fruit and wine.

✤ COMMA ALERTS: (1) Do not use *only* a comma between independent clauses connected by a conjunctive adverb or other words of transition, or you will create the error called a comma splice; see Chapter 14. (2) Usually use a comma *after* a conjunctive adverb or a transitional expression that begins an independent clause, although some writers omit the comma after short words, such as *then, next, soon.* ✤

25d Using a semicolon between items in a series

When a sentence contains a series of items that are long or that already contain commas, use a semicolon, not a comma, to separate the items. Punctuating this way groups the elements, so that your reader can see where one item ends and the next begins. (For information on using commas in a series, see 24c.)

SEMICOLON PATTERN IV 122

Independent clause containing a series of items, any of which contain a comma; another item in the series; another item in the series.

Functioning as assistant chefs, the students chopped onions, green peppers, and parsley; sliced chicken and duck meat into strips; started a broth simmering; and filled a large, low, copper pan with oil before the head chef stepped to the stove.

25e Avoiding misuse of the semicolon

1 Not using a semicolon after an introductory phrase or between a dependent clause and an independent clause

This misuse creates the error known as a fragment; see Chapter 13.

NO Open until midnight; the computer lab is well used.

YES Open until midnight, the computer lab is well used.

NO Although the new dorms have computer facilities; many students still prefer the computer lab.

YES Although the new dorms have computer facilities, many students still prefer the computer lab.

2 Not using a semicolon to introduce a list

To introduce a list, use a colon, never a semicolon.

NO The newscast featured three major stories; the latest pictures of Uranus, a speech by the prime minister, and a series of prairie brush fires.

YES The newscast featured three major stories: the latest pictures of Uranus, a speech by the prime minister, and a series of prairie brush fires.

EXERCISE 25-1

Consulting sections 25a–25e, insert semicolons where they are needed, and change any incorrectly used semicolons to correct punctuation. If a sentence is correct, explain why.

EXAMPLE Writers at a magazine wondered whether people are honest nowadays, they designed an experiment to find out.

Writers at a magazine wondered whether people are honest nowadays; they designed an experiment to find out.

1. If you find a lost wallet you may consider yourself lucky, if you return the wallet along with all the cash in it you are acting honestly.

2. Writers at a magazine tested people's honesty by pretending to lose their wallets, people who returned a wallet with all the money in it passed the test.
3. The writers tried this experiment in many different neighbourhoods, all in all, they left 120 wallets in twelve cities, towns, and suburbs.
4. One writer would stop in a public place and tie a shoelace while intentionally letting the wallet slip out of a pocket, meanwhile, a colleague kept watch from a distance.
5. Every wallet contained the following items; $50 cash, business cards and grocery lists, to make the wallet look authentic, and an identification card with a phone number, so that the person who found the wallet could telephone its owner and offer to return the money.
6. Many people called that telephone number or handed in the wallet to police; although others simply walked off with the money.
7. In a run-down part of one town, a man quickly scooped up the wallet he found on a sidewalk, putting it into his pocket, but the man, who looked as if he could use the money, went straight to the nearest police station with the wallet.
8. A middle-aged woman pushing a baby stroller in a large suburb spotted one wallet, examined its contents, and got into her Cadillac, she unexpectedly kept the wallet.
9. Wallets were returned with all the money in them 67 percent of the time, but small towns usually had more returns than most cities or suburbs.
10. People interviewed by the magazine often expected younger people to be less honest than their elders, however, younger people in the wallet test had the same "honesty score" as older people—exactly 67 percent.

EXERCISE 25-2

Combine each set of sentences into one sentence containing two independent clauses. Use a semicolon between the two clauses. You may add, omit, revise, and rearrange words. Try to use all the patterns in this chapter. More than one revision may be correct, so be ready to explain the reasoning behind your decisions.

EXAMPLE A Canadian-led team of archaeologists has been excavating a site. The site is on the south shore of Crete. Scholars from Greece, the United Kingdom, the United States, and other countries as well have taken part.

A Canadian-led team of archaeologists has been excavating a site on the south shore of Crete; scholars from Greece, the

United Kingdom, the United States, and other countries as well have taken part.

1. Archaeologists have been excavating the site of Kommos in southern Crete for more than twenty-five years. The site has not yet yielded up all its secrets.
2. Ancient Crete was the home of the legendary King Minos. In Crete, according to Greek myth, lived the Minotaur. This was a man with the head of a terrible bull.
3. Kommos was a small seaport. Kommos was far from Knossos. Knossos was the great city at the centre of the Minoan civilization that preceded the Greeks.
4. Only a temple remained at Kommos after Crete passed to Greek rule. Phoenician merchants seem to have been the worshippers at this temple during the early Greek period.
5. The Phoenicians were a seafaring people from the Lebanese coast. They taught the Greeks to use the alphabet. Archaeologists have found few places where Phoenicians and Greeks appear to have lived side by side. Kommos may be one, though.

26 Colons

26a Using a colon after an independent clause to introduce a list, an appositive, or a quotation

You can use a colon to introduce statements that summarize, restate, or explain what is said in an independent clause°. For the use of colons in documenting sources, see 34c–34d.

COLON PATTERN I 123

- Independent clause: list.
- Independent clause: appositive.
- Independent clause: "Quoted words."

A colon can introduce a list only when the words before the colon are an independent clause. After phrases such as *the following* or *as follows,* a colon is usually required. A colon is not called for with the words *such as* or *including* (see 26d).

LISTED ITEMS

> If you really want to lose weight, you need give up only three things: breakfast, lunch, and dinner.
>
> The students' demands included the following: an expanded menu in the cafeteria, improved janitorial services, and more up-to-date textbooks.

A colon can introduce an appositive—a word or words that rename a noun° or pronoun°—but only if the introductory words are an independent clause.

APPOSITIVE

The UBC Museum of Anthropology has one outstanding exhibit: its collection of remarkable Northwest Coast Indian artifacts. [*Collection of ... artifacts* renames *outstanding exhibit*.]

A colon can introduce a quotation, but only if the words before the colon are an independent clause°. Use a comma, not a colon, if the words before the colon are not an independent clause (see 24b).

QUOTATION

The little boy in *E.T.* did say something neat: "How do you explain school to a higher intelligence?"

—GEORGE F. WILL, "Well, *I* Don't Love You, E.T."

26b Using a colon between two independent clauses

When the first independent clause° explains or summarizes the second independent clause, a colon can separate them.

COLON PATTERN II 124
Independent clause: Independent clause.

✤ CAPITALIZATION ALERT: You can use a capital letter or a lower-case letter for the first word of an independent clause that follows a colon. Whichever you choose, be consistent in each piece of writing. This handbook uses a capital letter.

We will never forget the first time we made dinner at home together: He got stomach poisoning and for four days was too sick to go to work.

—LISA BALADENDRUM, student ✤

26c Using a colon in standard formats

TITLE AND SUBTITLE

A Brief History of Time: From the Big Bang to Black Holes

Hours, Minutes, and Seconds

The plane took off at 7:15 p.m.

The track star passed the halfway point at 1:23:02.

In the military services, hours and minutes are written without colons (and with four digits, using the 24-hour clock):

The staff meeting originally scheduled for Tuesday at 0930 will be held Tuesday at 1430 instead.

Chapters and Verses of the Bible

Psalms 23:1–3 Luke 3:13

Memos

To: Dean Kristen Olivero
From: Professor Daniel Black
Re: Student Work-Study Program

Salutation in Formal or Business Letters

Dear Ms. Morgan:

26d Avoiding misuse of the colon

A complete independent clause° must precede a colon, except with standard material (see 26c). When you have not written an independent clause, do not use a colon.

NO The cook bought: eggs, milk, cheese, and bread.

YES The cook bought eggs, milk, cheese, and bread.

The words *such as, including, like,* and *consists of* can be tricky: Do not let them lure you into using a colon incorrectly (see 26a).

NO The health board discussed a number of problems, **such as:** poor water quality, an aging sewage treatment system, and the lack of an alternative water supply.

YES The health board discussed a number of problems, **such as** poor water quality, an aging sewage treatment system, and the lack of an alternative water supply.

YES The health board discussed a number of problems: poor water quality, an aging sewage treatment system, and the lack of an alternative water supply.

Do not use a colon to separate a phrase° or dependent clause° from an independent clause.

NO	Day after day: the drought dragged on.
YES	Day after day, the drought dragged on.
NO	After the drought ended: the farmers celebrated.
YES	After the drought ended, the farmers celebrated.

EXERCISE 26-1

Consulting all sections of this chapter, insert colons where they are needed and delete unnecessary ones. If a sentence is correct, explain why.

EXAMPLE The twentieth century saw a flowering of Irish writing, W. B. Yeats, G. B. Shaw, Samuel Beckett, and Seamus Heaney have all won the Nobel Prize in Literature.

The twentieth century saw a flowering of Irish writing: W. B. Yeats, G. B. Shaw, Samuel Beckett, and Seamus Heaney have all won the Nobel Prize in Literature.

1. They tugged again and saw the reason the rope would not move, a dolphin struggling in the net.
2. The Iroquois of the Great Lakes region lived in fortified villages and cultivated: corn, beans, and squash.
3. Five nations originally formed the Iroquois Confederacy: the Mohawk, the Oneida, the Onondaga, the Cayuga, and the Seneca.
4. Later these five Iroquois nations were joined by: the Tuscarora.
5. Muttering: "What was that?" Doug turned his head just as the form disappeared around a corner.
6. When a jogger breaks through that unavoidable wall of exhaustion, a very different feeling sets in; an intense sense of well-being known as the "jogger's high."
7. However: the "jogger's high" soon disappears.
8. Two new nations were born on the same day in 1947, India and Pakistan achieved their independence from Britain at midnight on August 15.
9. To English 101 Instructors
From Dean of Instruction
Re Classroom Assignments
10. Only a hurricane could have kept Lisa from the appointment she had made with Donald for 800 p.m.; unfortunately, that night there was a hurricane.
11. When he was sixteen, George's interests were the usual ones, cars, music videos, and dating.

12. Like many people who have never learned to read or write, the woman who told her life story in *Aman; The Story of a Somali Girl* was able to remember an astonishing number of events in precise detail.
13. The Greek philosopher Socrates took these words as his motto, "The unexamined life is not worth living."
14. Socrates was executed after being found guilty of: teaching young people new ideas.
15. The voice coming from the radio could belong to only one singer; the great jazz stylist Ella Fitzgerald.

27 Apostrophes

The apostrophe plays four major roles: It creates the possessive case of nouns; it creates the possessive case of indefinite pronouns; it stands for one or more omitted letters in a word; and it can help form the plurals of letters and numerals. It does *not* belong with plurals of nouns or the possessive case of personal pronouns.

27a Using an apostrophe to form the possessive case of nouns and indefinite pronouns

The **possessive case** serves to communicate ownership or close relationship.

OWNERSHIP	The writer's pen
CLOSE RELATIONSHIP	The novel's plot

Possession in nouns° and certain indefinite pronouns° can be communicated by phrases beginning with *of* (*comments of the instructor, comments of Professor Montana*) or by an apostrophe in combination with an *s* (*instructor's comments*).

1 Adding *'s* to show possession when nouns and indefinite pronouns do not end in *s*

The **dean's** duties included working closely with the resident assistants. [*dean* = singular noun not ending in *s*]

In one more year I will receive my **bachelor's** degree. [*bachelor* = singular noun not ending in *s*]

They care about their **children’s** futures. [*children* = plural noun not ending in *s*]

An **indefinite pronoun** refers to nonspecific persons or things (for example, *any, few, someone, no one;* see 7b and 11g).

The accident was really **no one’s** fault. [*no one* = indefinite pronoun not ending in *s*]

2 Adding *’s* to show possession when singular nouns end in *s*

Most academic writers today use *’s* to show possession when singular nouns end in *s,* although some writers prefer to use only the apostrophe. Be consistent in each piece of writing. This handbook uses *’s.*

That **business’s** system for handling complaints is inefficient.

Chris’s ordeal ended.

Lee **Jones’s** insurance is expensive.

When adding *’s* could lead to tongue-twisting pronunciation, practice varies. All writers use the apostrophe. Some writers do not add the *s;* others do, for consistency with other practices.

Charles **Dickens’s** story “A Christmas Carol” is a classic tale.

3 Using only an apostrophe to show possession when a plural noun ends in *s*

The **boys’** statements were recorded.

The newspapers have publicized several **medicines’** severe side effects recently.

Three **months’** maternity leave is in the **workers’** contract.

4 Adding *’s* to the last word in singular compound words and phrases

His **mother-in-law’s** corporation just bought out a competitor.

The **tennis player’s** strategy was brilliant.

They wanted to hear **somebody else’s** interpretation of the rule.

5 Adding *'s* to only the last noun in joint or group possession

Olga and Joanne's books are valuable. [Olga and Joanne own the books together.]

Anne Gagnon and Charles Gagnon's article on solar heating interests me. [Anne Gagnon and Charles Gagnon wrote the article together.]

6 Adding *'s* to each noun in individual possession

Olga's and Joanne's books are valuable. [Olga and Joanne each own some of the valuable books, but they do not own the books together.]

After the fire, **the doctor's and the lawyer's** offices had to be rebuilt. [The doctor and the lawyer had separate offices.]

✤ APOSTROPHE CAUTION: Do not use an apostrophe to indicate the plural form of a noun. For use of the apostrophe with plural nouns, see 27a-3. ✤

27b Not using an apostrophe with the possessive forms of personal pronouns

Some pronouns have specific possessive forms, which do not include an apostrophe. Contrast them with contractions, discussed in 27c.

PERSONAL PRONOUNS	POSSESSIVE FORMS
he	his
she	her, hers
it	its
we	our, ours
you	your, yours
they	their, theirs
who	whose

Be especially alert to *it's* and *its,* as well as *who's* and *whose,* which are frequently confused. (*It's* stands for *it is; its* is a possessive pronoun. *Who's* stands for *who is; whose* is a possessive pronoun.)

NO	The government has to balance **it's** budget.
YES	The government has to balance **its** budget.
NO	The professor **who's** class was cancelled is at a meeting of bird watchers.
YES	The professor **whose** class was cancelled is at a meeting of bird watchers.

✤ APOSTROPHE CAUTION: Do not use an apostrophe within or after a possessive pronoun. Use *its* (not *it's*), *hers* (not *hers'* or *her's*), *theirs* (not *theirs'* or *their's*). ✤

27c Using an apostrophe to stand for omitted letters, numbers, or words in contractions

Contractions are words from which one or more letters have been intentionally omitted and in which apostrophes are inserted to signal the omission. Contractions are common in speaking and in informal writing. In academic writing, some readers dislike them as being too informal, while other readers think contractions are useful if the tone° calls for them. Check with your instructor before using contractions in your academic writing. A major exception is *o'clock* (which stands for *of the clock*).

COMMON CONTRACTIONS

aren't = are not	*she's* = she is, she has
can't = cannot	*there's* = there is
didn't = did not	*they're* = they are
don't = do not	*wasn't* = was not
he's = he is, he has	*we're* = we are
it's = it is	*weren't* = were not
I'd = I would, I had	*we've* = we have
I'm = I am	*who's* = who is
isn't = is not	*won't* = will not
let's = let us	*you're* = you are

Apostrophes also indicate the omission of the first two numerals in years. Avoid this contraction in academic writing.

They moved from Ottawa to Victoria after the blizzard of **'78.**

27d Using ’s to form plurals of letters, numerals, symbols, and words when used as terms

Some writers use *’s* to form plurals of letters, numerals, years, symbols, and words used as terms. Others use *s* alone. Either style is acceptable as long as one style is used throughout a piece of writing. This handbook does not use an apostrophe to indicate such plurals.

WITH *’S*

Billie always has trouble printing ***W’s.***

The address includes six ***6’s.***

These trends lasted through the ***1990’s.***

The ***for’s*** in the paper were all misspelled as ***four’s.***

WITH *S* ALONE

Billie always has trouble printing ***Ws.***

The address includes six ***6s.***

These trends lasted through the ***1990s.***

The ***fors*** in the paper were all misspelled as ***fours.***

✤ UNDERLINING ALERT: Always underline (or use italic type for) letters, numbers, symbols, and words referred to as in the examples above. For plurals, do not underline (or use italics for) the *’s* or *s.*

Many first-graders had trouble writing 8's and pronouncing eight's phonetically.

Many first-graders had trouble writing 8s and pronouncing eights phonetically. ✤

27e Avoiding misuse of the apostrophe

Do not overuse apostrophes by inserting them where they do not belong. Chart 125 lists the major causes of apostrophe errors. Some writers frequently make the same apostrophe error again and again. Learn the causes of your errors, if any, and work consciously on avoiding them.

LEADING CAUSES OF APOSTROPHE ERRORS 125

1. Do not use an apostrophe with the present-tense verb form.
   - **NO** Cholesterol **plays’** an important role in how long we live.
   - **YES** Cholesterol **plays** an important role in how long we live.
2. Do not add an apostrophe at the end of a nonpossessive noun ending in *s*.
   - **NO** Medical **studies’** reveal that cholesterol is the primary cause of coronary heart disease.
   - **YES** Medical **studies** reveal that cholesterol is the primary cause of coronary heart disease.
3. Use an apostrophe after the *s* in the possessive plural of a noun.
   - **NO** The medical community is seeking more information from **doctor’s** investigations into heart disease.
   - **YES** The medical community is seeking more information from **doctors’** investigations into heart disease.
4. Do not use an apostrophe to form a nonpossessive plural.
   - **NO** **Team’s** of doctors are trying to predict who might be most harmed by cholesterol.
   - **YES** **Teams** of doctors are trying to predict who might be most harmed by cholesterol.

EXERCISE 27-1

Consulting sections 27a and 27e, rewrite these sentences to insert *’s* or an apostrophe alone to make the words in parentheses show possession. Delete the parentheses.

EXAMPLE Each box, can, and bottle that shoppers see on a (supermarket) shelves has been designed to appeal to their emotions.

Each box, can, and bottle that shoppers see on a supermarket’s shelves has been designed to appeal to their emotions.

1. A commercial (product) manufacturer designs its packages to appeal to (consumers) emotions through colour and design.
2. Marketing specialists have learned that (people) beliefs about a (product) quality are influenced by their emotional response to the design of its package.
3. Circles and ovals appearing on a (box) design supposedly increase the (product users) feelings of comfort, while bold patterns and colours attract (shoppers) attention.

4. Using both circles and bold designs in (Arm & Hammer) and (Tide) logos produces both these effects in consumers.
5. (Heinz) familiar ketchup bottle and (Coca-Cola) famous label achieve the same effects by combining a bright colour with an old-fashioned, "comfortable" design.
6. Often, a (company) marketing consultants will custom design products to appeal to the supposedly "typical" (adult female) emotions, or to (adult males), (children), or (teenagers) feelings.
7. One of the (marketing business) leading consultants, Stan Gross, tests (consumers) emotional reactions to products and their packages by asking consumers to associate products with well-known personalities.
8. Thus, (test-takers) responses to (Gross) questions might reveal that a particular laundry detergent has (Mark Messier) toughness, (Oprah Winfrey) determination, or (someone else) sparkling personality.
9. Manufacturing (companies) products are not the only ones relying on (Gross) and other corporate (image-makers) advice.
10. (Sports teams) owners also use marketing (specialists) ideas in designing their (teams) images, as anyone who has seen the unforgettable angry bull logo of the Chicago Bulls basketball team will agree.

EXERCISE 27-2

Consulting sections 27a, 27b, and 27e, rewrite these sentences so that each contains a possessive noun.

EXAMPLE Early visitors to Greenland wrote about an unusual custom of the Inuit of that island.

Early visitors to Greenland wrote about an unusual custom of that island's Inuit.

1. The Inuit of Greenland used to settle disputes by insulting each other in public.
2. Each of two people involved in a dispute would sing insulting songs about the faults of the other.
3. The other members of the tribe joined in the singing and decided whose insults were funniest and most embarrassing.
4. After the decision of the tribe members determined the winner in the dispute, the winner and the loser made up.
5. Similar customs, intended to keep the peace among all the members of the community, were also found in medieval Europe, the ancient Arab world, and early China.

28 Quotation Marks

Quotation marks are used most often to enclose **direct quotations**—the exact words of a speaker or writer (see 28a). Quotation marks also set off some titles (see 28b), and they can call attention to words used in special senses (see 28c).

Double quotation marks (" ") are standard. **Single quotation marks** (' ') are used only for quotation marks within quotation marks. (You may have noticed that in materials published in Great Britain, this convention is reversed.) Opening and closing quotation marks look identical in some computer fonts. Always use quotation marks in pairs, and be especially careful not to omit the second (closing) quotation mark.

28a Using quotation marks to enclose short direct quotations

Direct quotations are exact words from a print or nonprint source. When you use a quotation, always check carefully that you have recorded it precisely as it appeared in the original (see also 31c-1).

In MLA style, a quotation is considered "short" if it takes up no more than four typed lines. Short quotations are enclosed in double quotation marks. Longer quotations are usually set off ("displayed") by indentation and line spacing, and they are not enclosed in quotation marks. The requirements for setting off quotations vary with different documentation styles. The examples in this chapter are in MLA parenthetical documentation style, used in most English courses. For advice about setting off quotations in specific documentation styles, see Chapter 34.

✤ DOCUMENTATION ALERT: Whether a quotation is one significant word or occupies many lines, you must always document a quotation so that your reader knows the source you used. ✤

SHORT QUOTATION

Hall explains the practicality of close conversational distances: "If you are interested in something, your pupils dilate; if I say something you don't like, they tend to contract" (47).

Personal space "moves with us, expanding and contracting according to the situation in which we find ourselves" (Fisher, Bell, and Baum 149).

Any quotation marks that appear in the original source should also be used in a long (displayed) quotation.

LONG QUOTATIONS (MORE THAN FOUR LINES)

Robert Sommer, an environmental psychologist, uses literary and personal analogies to describe personal space:

> Like the porcupines in Schopenhauer's fable, people like to be close enough to obtain warmth and comradeship but far enough away to avoid pricking one another. Personal space [...] has been likened to a snail shell, a soap bubble, an aura, and "breathing room." (26)

✤ PUNCTUATION ALERTS: In MLA documentation style, the period goes *after* the parenthetical reference for a short quotation; the period goes *before* the parenthetical reference for a long (displayed) quotation. This rule holds for both prose and poetry quotations.

In MLA style, square brackets are placed around an **ellipsis,** a set of three spaced dots inserted by a writer to indicate that words have been omitted in material that is being quoted (see 29c and 29d). ✤

1 Using quotation marks for quotations within quotations

In a short quotation, when you quote words that themselves contain quotation marks, use double quotation marks at the start and end of the directly quoted words. Then, substitute single quotation marks (‘ ’) wherever there are double quotation marks in the original source.

ORIGINAL SOURCE

Personal space [. . .] has been likened to a snail shell, a soap bubble, an aura, and “breathing room.”

—ROBERT SOMMER, *Personal Space: The Behavioral Bases of Design*, page 26

SINGLE QUOTATION MARKS WITHIN DOUBLE QUOTATION MARKS

Robert Sommer, an environmental psychologist, compares personal space to “a snail shell, a soap bubble, an aura, and ‘breathing room’” (26).

2 Using quotation marks correctly for short quotations of poetry and for dialogue

A quotation of poetry is “short” if it includes three lines or less of the poem. As with short prose quotations, use double quotation marks to enclose the material, and substitute single quotation marks for any internal double quotation marks. If you quote more than one line of poetry, use a slash with one space on each side to show the line divisions (see 29e).

As Auden wittily defined personal space, “some thirty inches from my nose / The frontier of my person goes [. . .]” (*Complete Works*, 205).

A quotation of poetry is considered “long” if it includes more than three lines of the poem. As with long prose quotations, indent all lines as a block, without enclosing the material in quotation marks. Start new lines exactly as they appear in your source. Give documentation information after the text of the long quotation and any punctuation that ends it.

✤ CAPITALIZATION ALERT: When you quote lines of poetry, follow the capitalization of your source. ✤

✤ PUNCTUATION ALERT: All long quotations must be set off (displayed) without being enclosed in quotation marks. Therefore, in a long quotation, use quotation marks exactly as the source does. ✤

Quotation marks are also used to enclose speakers' words in **direct discourse**°. Whether you are reporting the exact words of a real speaker or making up dialogue in, for example, a short story, quotation marks let your readers know which words belong to the speaker and which words do not. Use double quotation marks at the beginning and end of a speaker's words, and start a new paragraph each time the speaker changes.

> Becky Tyde climbed up on Flo's counter, made room for herself beside an open tin of crumbly jam-filled cookies.
>
> "Are these any good?" she said to Flo, and boldly began to eat one. "When are you going to give us a job, Flo?"
>
> "You could go and work in the butcher shop," said Flo innocently. "You could go and work for your brother."
>
> "Roberta?" said Becky with a stagey sort of contempt. "You think I'd work for him?" Her brother who ran the butcher shop was named Robert but often called Roberta, because of his meek and nervous ways.
>
> —ALICE MUNRO, "Royal Beatings"

✤ PUNCTUATION ALERT: If one speaker's words require two or more paragraphs, use double quotation marks at the start of each paragraph *but* double quotation marks at the end of the last quoted paragraph *only*. ✤

Indirect discourse reports what a speaker did. In contrast, direct discourse presents a speaker's exact words. Note that the difference between direct and indirect discourse is not only a matter of punctuation; usually the verb tenses differ. Do not enclose indirect discourse in quotation marks.

DIRECT DISCOURSE

The mayor said, "I intend to vote against that proposal."

INDIRECT DISCOURSE

The mayor said that he intended to vote against that proposal.

For advice on revising incorrect shifts between direct and indirect discourse, see 15a-4.

EXERCISE 28-1

Consulting section 28a, correct the use of double and single quotation marks. If a sentence is correct, explain why.

EXAMPLE As Margaret Laurence writes, "Freedom is more fragile than any of us in Canada would like to believe. I think again of F. R. Scott's words: "Freedom is a habit that must be kept alive by use.""

As Margaret Laurence writes, "Freedom is more fragile than any of us in Canada would like to believe. I think again of F. R. Scott's words: 'Freedom is a habit that must be kept alive by use.'"

1. A Dutch historian has written, "No other modern language known to me has the exact equivalent of the English "fun."
2. In a poem written in 1628, Robert Hayman writes of Newfoundland, Where all are good, Fire, Water, Earth, and Aire, / What man made of these foure would not live there?
3. In his novel *Shoeless Joe*, which became the film *Field of Dreams*, W. P. Kinsella describes the moment of inspiration in the following way: There was silence in the room. Then a voice, stunning as thunder, clear and common as a train whistle—the voice of a ball-park announcer: "If you build it, he will come."
4. Even after 18 years, I have no woman friend I would talk to as I talk to my urban woman friends, writes author Sharon Butala about her move from the city to a ranching community.
5. I've seen them all, recalled Laura, and not a single one impressed me.
6. Romila Thapar opens her history of India with the words, For many Europeans, India evoked a picture of Maharajas, snake-charmers, and the rope-trick.
7. According to an article on James Earl Jones, the actor is "heard all over the world as the voice that dramatically intones "This is CNN" just before all the cable network's station breaks."
8. "I try not to break the rules," said the owner of a major league baseball team, but merely to test their elasticity."
9. "For reasons unknown to me, the meteorologist said, *The Canadian Encyclopedia* contains a statistical analysis of groundhog weather predictions.
10. The philosopher Michel de Montaigne begins his book of personal reflections thus: "This, reader, is an honest book."

EXERCISE 28-2

Consulting section 28a, decide whether each sentence is direct or indirect discourse. Then rewrite each sentence in the other form. Be sure to make any changes needed for grammatical accuracy.

EXAMPLE A medical doctor told some newspaper reporters that he was called into a television studio one day to treat a sick actor. [from indirect to direct discourse]

A medical doctor told some newspaper reporters, "I was called into a television studio one day to treat a sick actor."

1. The doctor was told that he would find his patient on the set of *Side Effects*, a new television series that takes place in a hospital.
2. On his arrival at the television studio, the doctor announced, "I'm Dr. Gatley, and I'm looking for *Side Effects*."
3. The studio security guard asked him if he didn't mean to say that he was auditioning for the part of Dr. Gatley in *Side Effects*.
4. The visitor insisted that he really was Dr. Gatley.
5. The surprised security guard replied, "I like your attitude. With self-confidence like that, you're sure to go far in television."

28b Using quotation marks with titles of short works

When you refer to certain types of works by their titles, enclose the titles in quotation marks. (Other works, usually longer, are put in italics or underlined; see 30f.) Short works include poems, short stories, essays, articles from periodicals, pamphlets, brochures, song titles, and individual episodes of television or radio series.

✤ PUNCTUATION ALERT: Do not put the title of your own paper in quotation marks when you place it on a title page or at the top of a page (see 28d). ✤

Discuss the rhyme scheme of Andrew Marvell's “Delight in Disorder.” [poem]

Have you read “Insecurity” by Neil Bissoondath? [short story]

One of the best sources I have found is “The Myth of Political Consultants.” [magazine article]

“Shooting an Elephant” describes George Orwell's experience in Burma. [essay]

Italics or underlining is used for titles of many other types of works, such as books and plays. A few titles are neither italicized or underlined nor enclosed in quotation marks. (For useful lists showing how to present titles, see Chart 126 in 30e and Chart 127 in 30f.)

✚ COMPUTER TIP: Word-processing programs usually allow you to italicize or underline the words you indicate. Use italics or underlining consistently in a piece of writing. (Underlining in typed or handwritten papers is the equivalent of italics.) ✚

EXERCISE 28-3

Consulting section 28b, correct any quotation mark errors. If a sentence is correct, explain why.

1. Bharati Mukherjee describes a visitor from India who resents being treated as an exotic object in her short story The Lady from Lucknow.
2. Although his poem The Red Wheelbarrow contains only sixteen words, William Carlos Williams creates in it both a strong visual image and a sense of mystery.
3. With her soulful singing and relaxed gestures, Billie Holiday gave a bare television studio the atmosphere of a smoky jazz club in The Sound of Jazz, broadcast in 1957 as part of the television series *The Seven Lively Arts*.
4. Lennie Gallant's song Pieces of You and Natalie MacMaster's Get Me Through December were nominated for the 2001 East Coast Music Awards.
5. In her essay "The Imagination of Disaster, Susan Sontag writes that viewers of disaster movies like to see how these movies succeed in "making a mess"—especially if the mess includes the make-believe destruction of a big city.

28c Using quotation marks for words used in special senses or for special purposes

Writers sometimes enclose in quotation marks words or phrases meant ironically or in some other nonliteral way.

The proposed tax “reform” is actually a tax increase.

Writers sometimes put technical terms in quotation marks and define them the first time they are used. No quotation marks are used once such terms have been introduced and defined.

“Plagiarism”—the unacknowledged use of another person's words or ideas—can result in expulsion. Plagiarism is a serious offence.

Put quotation marks around the English translation of a word or phrase. Italicize (or underline) the word or phrase in the other language.

> My grandfather usually ended arguments with *de gustibus non disputandum est* (“there is no disputing about tastes”).

Words being referred to as words can either be enclosed in quotation marks or be italicized (or underlined). Follow consistent practice throughout a paper.

NO Many people confuse “affect” and *effect.*

YES Many people confuse “affect” and “effect.”

YES Many people confuse *affect* and *effect.*

28d Avoiding the misuse of quotation marks

Writers sometimes enclose in quotation marks words they are uncomfortable about using, such as slang in formal writing or a cliché. Do not use quotation marks around language you sense is inappropriate to your audience or your purpose. Take the time to find accurate, appropriate, and fresh words instead.

NO They “eat like birds” in public, but they “stuff their faces” in private.

YES They eat very little in public, but they consume enormous amounts of food in private.

Do not enclose a word in quotation marks merely to call attention to it.

NO “Plagiarism” can result in expulsion.

YES Plagiarism can result in expulsion.

When you put your paper’s title at the top of a page or on a title page, do not enclose it in quotation marks (or italicize or underline it). However, if the title of *your* paper includes another title or a word that requires setting off in quotation marks, use quotation marks with the included title or word.

NO “The Elderly in Nursing Homes: A Case Study”

YES The Elderly in Nursing Homes: A Case Study

NO Character Development in Anne Hébert’s Story The House on the Esplanade

YES Character Development in Anne Hébert’s Story “The House on the Esplanade”

Do not put a nickname in quotation marks unless you are giving a nickname with a full name. When a person's nickname is widely known and used, write whichever form is appropriate to your audience and purpose: *Joey Smallwood* or *J. R. Smallwood*, for example. You do not have to write *J. R. "Joey" Smallwood.*

EXERCISE 28-4

Consulting sections 28c and 28d, correct any incorrect use of quotation marks. If a sentence is correct, explain why.

EXAMPLE *Bossa nova*, Portuguese for new wave, is the name of both a dance and a musical style originating in Brazil.

Bossa nova, *Portuguese for "new wave," is the name of both a dance and a musical style originating in Brazil.*

1. A "chinook" is a warm wind that blows eastward across the Rockies. "Chinooks" can transform an Alberta winter day into a brief anticipation of spring.
2. Despite the old belief that "where there's a will there's a way," psychologists say that to get results, willingness must be combined with ability and effort.
3. "Observation" and "empathy" are two of the chief qualities that mark the work of the Dutch painter Rembrandt.
4. *Casbah*, an Arabic word meaning fortress, is the name given to the oldest parts of many North African cities.
5. "Flammable" and *inflammable* are a curious pair of words that once had the same meaning but today are often considered opposites.

28e Following accepted practices for quotation marks with other punctuation

Commas and Periods with Quotation Marks

Because the class enjoyed Michel Tremblay's "The Thimble," they were looking forward to his longer works. [comma before closing quotation mark]

Ms. Rogers said, "Don't stand so close to me." [comma before opening quotation mark (see also 24g); period before closing quotation mark]

Edward T. Hall coined the word "proxemics." [period before closing quotation mark]

Semicolons and Colons with Quotation Marks

We have to know “how close is close”: We do not want to offend. [colon after closing quotation mark]

Some experts claim that the job market now offers “opportunities that never existed before”; others disagree. [semicolon after closing quotation mark]

Question Marks, Exclamation Points, and Dashes with Closing Quotation Marks

To use quotation marks with a question mark, exclamation point, or dash, you need to consider the context and the meaning you want to deliver. If the punctuation marks belong to the words enclosed in quotation marks, put that punctuation mark inside the closing quotation mark.

“Did I Hear You Call My Name?” was the winning song.

“I've won the lottery!” he shouted.

“Who's there? Why don't you ans—”

If a question mark, exclamation point, or dash belongs with words that are *not* included in quotation marks, put the punctuation outside the closing quotation mark.

Have you read Al Purdy's poem “The Country North of Belleville”?
If only I could write a story like Audrey Thomas's “Natural History”!

Weak excuses—a classic is “I have to visit my grandparents”—change little from year to year.

EXERCISE 28-5

Consulting section 28e and other sections of this chapter, correct any errors in quotation marks and other punctuation with quotation marks. If a sentence is correct, explain why.

1. What was it that led the Russian novelist Tolstoy to write, "All happy families resemble one another, but each unhappy family is unhappy in its own way?"
2. "No", Michael Ondaatje said, describing how he invented the intricate plot of his novel *The English Patient,*" the plot wasn't there until I finished the book, probably.
3. Prime Minister Trudeau's claim that he used the expression fuddle-duddle, instead of a stronger four-letter word, led a member of Parliament to quip, "Mr. Trudeau wants to be obscene but not heard".
4. After lulling the reader with a description of a beautiful dream palace in his poem Kubla Khan, Coleridge changes the mood abruptly: And 'mid this tumult Kubla heard from far / Ancestral voices prophesying war.
5. Gordie Howe was once asked how hockey players were coping with Canada's "language problem;" he replied, All pro athletes are bilingual. They speak English and profanity.

29 Other Punctuation Marks

This chapter explains the uses of the dash (see 29a), parentheses (see 29b), brackets (see 29c), ellipsis (see 29d), and slash (see 29e). These punctuation marks are not used often, but each serves a purpose and gives you options in your writing.

THE DASH

29a Using the dash

The dash, or a pair of dashes, lets you interrupt a sentence to add information. Such interruptions can fall in the middle or at the end of a sentence.

To make a dash, hit the hyphen key twice (--). Do not put a space before, between, or after the hyphens. Some word-processing programs automatically convert two hyphens into a dash, while others do not; either form is correct. In print, the dash is an unbroken line that is approximately the length of two hyphens joined together (—). In handwritten papers, make a dash no less than twice as long as a hyphen.

1 Using a dash or dashes to emphasize an example, a definition, an appositive, or a contrast

EXAMPLE

Urban centres in Canada—Montreal, Toronto, and Winnipeg—share problems of crime and prostitution in core areas.

—LOVUS DEVINE, student

Definition

Our aboriginal peoples—Inuit, Indian, and Métis—challenge the model of two founding peoples that excludes them.

—William Thorsell, "Let Us Compare Mythologies"

Appositive

And what of our national heroine—Laura Secord—our Paul Revere in drag. The fact is, that craggy face we all know from school books and chocolate boxes is not Laura Secord at all. It's a deception. The portrait was posed for by a grandniece and was painted over a portrait of Premier George Ross.

—Barry Callaghan, "Canadian Wry"

Contrast

What could be funnier—or more offensive—than making a pun on your own friend's name?

—Matthew Pagano, student

Always place the words that you set off in dashes next to or near the words they explain. Otherwise, the interruption will confuse your reader.

NO The current argument **is—one that parents, faculty, students, and coaches all debate fiercely—whether** athletes should have to meet minimum academic standards to play their sports.

YES The current **argument—one that parents, faculty, students, and coaches all debate fiercely—is whether** athletes should have to meet minimum academic standards to play their sports.

2 Using a dash or dashes to emphasize an "aside"

"Asides" are writers' comments within the structure of a sentence or a paragraph. In writing meant to seem objective, asides help writers convey their personal views. Consider your purpose° and audience° when deciding whether to insert an aside.

Another defining phrase is *distinct society*. French-speaking Quebecers—arguably hypersensitive, clearly insecure, but not necessarily separatist—have pleaded for this interpretation of themselves to be stitched into our constitution, but each time it has stuck in the craw of the rest of Canada.

—MORDECAI RICHLER, in *New York Times Magazine*

✤ PUNCTUATION ALERTS: (1) If the words within a pair of dashes require a question mark or an exclamation point, use that punctuation before the second dash: *A first date—do you remember?—stays in the memory forever.* (2) Do not use commas, semicolons, or periods next to dashes. When such a possibility comes up, revise the sentence. (3) Do not enclose dashes in quotation marks except when the meaning or the words quoted require them. Correct form is as follows: *Many of George Orwell's essays—"A Hanging," for example—draw on his experiences as a civil servant. "Shooting an Elephant"—another Orwell essay—appears in many anthologies.* ✤

EXERCISE 29-1

Consulting section 29a, write a sentence about the italicized subject. In your sentence, use dashes to set off the contrast, appositive, aside, example, or definition called for.

EXAMPLE [*health,* definition] Anorexia nervosa—an eating disorder characterized by an aversion to eating and an obsession with losing weight—is extremely common among young female gymnasts and ballet dancers.

1. [*television program,* contrast]
2. [*politician,* appositive]
3. [*food,* aside]
4. [*music,* example]
5. [*recreational sport,* definition]

PARENTHESES

29b Using parentheses

Parentheses let writers interrupt a sentence's structure to add various kinds of information. Parentheses are like dashes in setting off extra or interrupting words. Unlike dashes, which tend to make interruptions stand out, parentheses tend to de-emphasize what they enclose.

Use parentheses sparingly, because their overuse can be very distracting for readers.

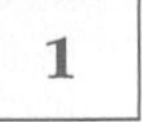

1 Using parentheses to enclose interrupting words

Explanation

After they've finished with the pantry, the medicine cabinet, and the attic, they will throw out the red geranium (too many leaves), sell the dog (too many fleas), and send the children off to boarding school (too many scuffmarks on the hardwood floors).

—Suzanne Britt, "Neat People vs. Sloppy People"

It's hard to explain to Americans what it feels like to be a Canadian. Pessimists among us would say that one has to translate the experience into their own terms and that this is necessary because Americans are incapable of thinking in any other terms—and this in itself is part of the problem. (Witness all those draft dodgers who went into shock when they discovered to their horror that Toronto was not Syracuse.)

—Margaret Atwood, "Canadians: What Do They Want?"

Example

Though other cities (Dresden, for instance) had been utterly destroyed in World War II, never before had a single weapon been responsible for such destruction.

—Laurence Behrens and Leonard J. Rosen, *Writing and Reading Across the Curriculum*

Aside

When it tastes pungent and hot (remember that the pungency will be cut by the beans) stir in a large quantity of molasses. Most people don't put in enough molasses, and yet this is the essence of all good baked bean dishes.

—Pierre Berton, "Baked Beans"

The sheer decibel level of the noise around us is not enough to make us cranky, irritable, or aggressive. (It can, however, affect our mental and physical health, which is another matter.)

—Carol Tavris, *Anger: The Misunderstood Emotion*

Using parentheses with listed items

When you number listed items within a sentence, enclose the numbers (or letters) in parentheses.

✤ PUNCTUATION ALERTS: (1) Use a colon before a list only if the list is preceded by an independent clause; see 26b. (2) Use either commas or semicolons to separate items in a list that falls within a sentence; be consistent within a piece of writing. When any item itself contains punctuation, use a semicolon to separate the items. ✤

> Four items are on the agenda for tonight's meeting: (1) current membership figures, (2) current treasury figures, (3) the budget for renovations, and (4) the campaign for soliciting additional public contributions.

In legal and some business writing, you can use parentheses to enclose a numeral that repeats a spelled-out number.

> The monthly rent is three hundred fifty dollars ($350).
>
> Your order of fifteen (15) gross was shipped today.

3 Using other punctuation with parentheses

Do not put a **comma** before an opening parenthesis even if what comes before the parenthetical material requires a comma.

NO Although clearly different from my favourite film, (*The Wizard of Oz*) *Gone with the Wind* is an important film worth studying.

YES Although clearly different from my favourite film (*The Wizard of Oz*), *Gone with the Wind* is an important film worth studying.

You can use a **question mark** or an **exclamation point** with parenthetical words that occur within the structure of a sentence.

> Looking for clues (what did we expect to find?) wasted four days.

A complete sentence enclosed in parentheses sometimes stands alone and sometimes falls within the structure of another sentence. Those that stand alone start with a capital and end with a period. Those that fall within the structure of another sentence do not start with a capital and do not end with a period.

NO Looking for his car keys (he had left them at my sister's house.) wasted an entire hour.

YES Looking for his car keys wasted an entire hour. (He had left them at my sister's house.)

YES Looking for his car keys (he had left them at my sister's house) wasted an entire hour.

Place quotation marks to enclose words that require them, but do not use quotation marks around parentheses that come before or after those words.

NO Alberta Hunter **"(Down Hearted Blues)"** is better known for her jazz singing than for her poetry.

YES Alberta Hunter **("Down Hearted Blues")** is better known for her jazz singing than for her poetry.

BRACKETS

29c Using brackets

1 Using brackets to enclose words you insert into quotations

When you work quoted words into your own sentences (see 31c), you may have to change the form of a word or two to make the quoted words fit into the structure of your sentence. Enclose any changes you make in square brackets. (The examples with brackets in this section use MLA style° of parenthetical references; see 34c-1.)

ORIGINAL SOURCE

Surprisingly, this trend is almost reversed in Italy, where males interact closer and display significantly more contact than do male/female dyads and female couples.

—ROBERT SHUTER, "A Field Study of Nonverbal Communication in Germany, Italy, and the United States," page 305

QUOTATION WITH BRACKETS

Although German and American men stand farthest apart and touch each other the least, Shuter reported "this trend [to be] almost reversed in Italy" (305).

Enclose your words in brackets if you need to add explanations and clarifications to quoted material.

ORIGINAL SOURCE

This sort of information seems trivial, but it does affect international understanding. Imagine, for example, a business conference between an American and an Arab.

—CHARLES G. MORRIS, *Psychology: An Introduction,* page 516

QUOTATION WITH BRACKETS

"This sort of information [about personal space] seems trivial, but it does affect international understanding" (Morris 516).

Now and then you may find that an author or a typesetter has made a mistake in something you want to quote—a wrong date, a misspelled word, an error of fact. You cannot change another writer's words, but you want your readers to know that you did not make the error. To show that you see the error, insert the Latin word *sic* in brackets, right after the error. Meaning "so" or "thus," *sic* in brackets says to a reader, "It is thus in the original."

The construction supervisor points out one unintended consequence of doubling the amount of floor space: "With that much extra room per person, the tennants [*sic*] would sublet."

✤ PUNCTUATION ALERT: When you use MLA style, place square brackets around an ellipsis that shows that you have omitted words from a quotation (29d). The brackets distinguish between your ellipsis and other spaced periods that may appear in the original work. ✤

2 Using brackets to enclose very brief parenthetical material inside parentheses

From that point on, Thomas Parker simply disappears. (His death [c. 1441] is unrecorded officially, but a gravestone marker is mentioned in a 1640 parish report.)

The abbreviation "c." means "about" when placed next to numerals that refer to time (see Chart 128 in section 30j).

THE ELLIPSIS

29d Using the ellipsis

An **ellipsis** is a set of three spaced dots (use the period key on the keyboard). Its most important function is to show that you have left out some of the original writer's words in material you are quoting. In

MLA style, brackets are used to enclose an ellipsis that is inserted in a quotation. The examples in this section are in MLA style, used in most English courses.

ORIGINAL SOURCE

> Personal space is not necessarily spherical in shape, nor does it extend equally in all directions. (People are able to tolerate closer presence of a stranger at their sides than directly in front.) It has been likened to a snail shell, a soap bubble, an aura, and "breathing room."
>
> —ROBERT SOMMER, *Personal Space: The Behavioral Bases of Design,* page 26

Because ellipses signal readers that you have left out some of the source's words, you do not need an ellipsis to quote a single word. You can also quote a phrase without using an ellipsis as long as you do not omit any words between the first one and the last one that you quote.

> Describing how personal space varies, Sommer says that it "is not necessarily spherical" for it does not "extend equally in all directions" (26).

If you do omit any of the original source's words between the first and the last word you quote, use an ellipsis at each omission.

> Other descriptions of personal space include a "shell [...] and 'breathing room'"(Sommer 26).

Use the same pattern with words omitted from the middle of one sentence to the middle of another.

> "Personal space [...] has been likened to a snail shell, a soap bubble, an aura, and 'breathing room'" (Sommer 26).

✤ PUNCTUATION ALERT: When you omit words from a source you are quoting, omit punctuation that accompanies the omitted words unless it correctly punctuates your sentence.

> Other descriptions of personal space include a "shell [...] and 'breathing room'" (Sommer 26). [comma omitted after *shell*]
>
> Other descriptions of personal space include a "shell, [...] a [...] bubble, [...] and 'breathing room' " (Sommer 26). [commas kept after *shell* and *bubble* to separate three items in a series] ✤

In three situations, use a fourth dot—a sentence-ending period—along with an ellipsis.

1. When an ellipsis falls at the end of your sentence, put a sentence-ending period after the ellipsis.

> Sommer goes on to say that people have described personal space as "a snail shell, a soap bubble, an aura [. . .]."

✤ DOCUMENTATION ALERT: In MLA documentation style, if a parenthetical reference is needed, put it after the ellipsis and closing quotation mark and before the sentence-ending period.

> Sommer goes on to say that people have described personal space as "a snail shell, a soap bubble, an aura [. . .]" (26). ✤

2. When the words you quote complete the source's sentence and you omit one or more complete sentences before continuing the quotation, put a period before the ellipsis.

> "Personal space is not necessarily spherical in shape, nor does it extend equally in all directions.[...] It has been likened to a snail shell, a soap bubble, an aura, and 'breathing room'" (Sommer 26).

3. When you omit words from the middle of one sentence to the beginning of another sentence, put a period after the ellipsis.

> "Personal space is not necessarily spherical [...]. It has been likened to a snail shell, a soap bubble, an aura, and 'breathing room'" (Sommer 26).

These rules apply to omissions of words from both prose and poetry. If you omit a line or more from poetry, however, use a full line of spaced dots.

ORIGINAL SOURCE

Sing a song of sixpence,
A pocket full of rye.
Four and twenty blackbirds
Baked in a pie.
When the pie was opened,
The birds began to sing.
Wasn't that a pleasant dish
To set before the king?

POEM WITH OMITTED LINES

Sing a song of sixpence,
A pocket full of rye.
Four and twenty blackbirds
Baked in a pie
[. . . . .]
Wasn't that a pleasant dish
To set before the king?

THE SLASH

29e Using the slash

The **slash** (/) is a diagonal line also known as a *virgule* or *solidus.*

1 Using the slash to separate quoted lines of poetry

If you quote more than three lines of a poem in writing, set the poetry off with space and indentations as you would a prose quotation of more than four lines (see 28a). For three lines or fewer, run the poetry into your own writing and enclose it in quotation marks, with a slash to divide one line from the next. Leave a space on each side of the slash.

> Consider the beginning of Anne Sexton's poem "Words": "Be careful of words, / even the miraculous ones."

Capitalize and punctuate each line as it is in the original, with this exception: End your sentence with a period if the quoted line of poetry does not have other end punctuation. If your quotation ends before the end of the line, use an ellipsis (see 29d).

2 Using the slash for numerical fractions in typed manuscripts

If you have to type numerical fractions, use the slash to separate numerator and denominator and a hyphen to tie a whole number to its fraction: *1/16, 1-2/3, 2/5, 3-7/8* (For advice on using spelled-out and numerical forms of numbers, see section 30l.)

3 Using the slash for and/or

Try not to use word combinations like *and/or* for writing in the humanities. In academic disciplines where use of such combinations is acceptable, separate the words with a slash. Leave no space before or after the slash. In the humanities, listing both alternatives in normal sentence structure is usually better than separating choices with a slash.

NO The best quality of reproduction comes from 35mm slides/direct-positive films.

YES The best quality of reproduction comes from 35mm slides or direct-positive films.

EXERCISE 29-2

Consulting all sections in this chapter, supply needed dashes, parentheses, brackets, ellipses, and slashes. If a sentence is correct as written, explain why. In some sentences you can choose between dashes and parentheses; when you make your choice, be ready to explain it.

EXAMPLE In Canada, there are almost four times as many managerial and administrative nonclerical workers as there are farmers.

In Canada, there are almost four times as many managerial and administrative (nonclerical) workers as there are farmers.

1. In *The Color Purple* a successful movie as well as a novel, Alice Walker explores the relationships between women and men in traditional African-American culture.
2. The three longest rivers in Canada are 1 the Mackenzie 4241 km, 2 the Yukon 3185 km, and 3 the St. Lawrence 3058 km.
3. Calgary's Saddledome, the broad roof of the arena dips like a saddle, was used in the 1988 Winter Olympic Games, several years after it first opened.
4. All the really interesting desserts ice cream, chocolate fudge cake, pumpkin pie with whipped cream are fattening, unfortunately.
5. Thunder is caused when the flash of lightning heats the air around it to temperatures up to 55 000°F (30 000°C).
6. Christina Rossetti wonders if the end of a life also means the end of love in a poem that opens with these two lines: "When I am dead, my dearest, Sing no sad songs for me."
7. The 2001 Summit of the Americas in Quebec City was accompanied by large-scale protests, and for a few days it seemed to capture the attention of a whole generation.
8. Oscar Peterson has written, "To my way of thinking it the recording his friend Clifford Brown made in 1955 with Max Roach epitomizes the highest achievement in the world of Jazz–spontaneity."
9. Of his decision to resign as prime minister in 1984, Pierre Trudeau said, "I listened to my heart and saw if there were any signs of my destiny in the sky, and there were none there were just snowflakes."

10. Anyone in Canada who performs in public for private profit, of course a play, opera, or musical composition subject to copyright is liable to a fine of two hundred and fifty dollars $250.
11. Kim Campbell does anyone here remember Kim Campbell? seems to have found her niche.
12. Patients who pretend to have ailments are known to doctors as "Munchausens," after Baron Karl Friedrich Hieronymus von Münchhausen, he was a German army officer who had a reputation for wild and unbelievable tales.

EXERCISE 29-3

Follow the directions for each item. Consulting sections 29a, 29b, 29d, and 29e, use dashes, parentheses, ellipses, and slashes as needed.

EXAMPLE Write a sentence using dashes that exclaims about getting something right.

I tried and failed, I tried and failed again—and then I did it!

1. Write a sentence that quotes only three lines of the following sonnet by William Shakespeare:

   Let me not to the marriage of true minds
   Admit impediments. Love is not love
   Which alters when it alteration finds,
   Or bends with the remover to remove.
   O no, it is an ever-fixed mark
   That looks on tempests and is never shaken;
   It is the star to every wand'ring bark
   Whose worth's unknown, although his height be taken.
   Love's not Time's fool, though rosy lips and cheeks
   Within his bending sickle's compass come.
   Love alters not with his brief hours and weeks,
   But bears it out even to the edge of doom.
   If this be error and upon me proved,
   I never writ, nor no man ever loved.
2. Write a sentence in which you use parentheses to enclose a brief example.
3. Write a sentence in which you use dashes to set off a definition.
4. Write a sentence that includes a list of four numbered items.
5. Quote a few sentences from a source. Choose one from which you can omit a few words without losing meaning. Correctly indicate the omission. At the end, give the source of the quotation.

30 Capitals, Italics, Abbreviations, and Numbers

CAPITALS

30a Capitalizing the first word of a sentence

Always capitalize the first letter of the first word in a sentence: *Records show that 1.2 metres of snow fell last year*. Practice varies for using a capital letter to start each question in a series of questions. Whichever practice you choose, be consistent throughout a piece of writing. Of course, if the questions are complete sentences, start each with a capital letter.

YES What facial feature would most people change if they could? Their eyes? Their ears? Their mouth?

YES What facial feature would most people change if they could? their eyes? their ears? their mouth?

Practice varies for using a capital letter for a complete sentence following a colon (see 26b). Whichever practice you choose, be consistent throughout a piece of writing. This handbook uses a capital letter after the colon.

A complete sentence enclosed within parentheses sometimes falls within another sentence. Do not start the sentence within parentheses with a capital letter and do not end it with a period—but do use a question mark or exclamation point if necessary. A sentence within parentheses that does not fall within another sentence starts with a capital letter and ends with a period (or a question mark or exclamation point).

> The men had to get out and haul by ropes attached to bow and stern (two ropes were essential to prevent the canoe from yawing in against the shore), and this meant slithering over wet rocks slimy with vegetable growth, stumbling over the usual litter of fallen trees, and sometimes wading breast high in the stream.
>
> —HUGH MACLENNAN, "The Rivers that Made a Nation"

Reading Hugh MacLennan's account of the early voyageurs reminds me of some canoe trips I've taken. (Portages can be rough!) Luckily, however, I've never had to get out and pull with a rope against the rapids.

–AVRIL WAH, student

30b Capitalizing listed items

A **run-in list** is one in which the items are worked into the structure of a sentence or a paragraph rather than arranged with each item on a new line. When the items in a run-in list are complete sentences, capitalize the first letter of each item. When the items in a run-in list are not complete sentences, begin each with a lower-case letter.

YES We found three reasons for the delay: (1) Bad weather held up delivery of raw materials. (2) Poor scheduling created confusion and slowdowns. (3) Lack of proper machine maintenance caused an equipment failure.

YES The reasons for the delay were (1) bad weather, (2) poor scheduling, and (3) equipment failure.

A **displayed list** is one in which the items are set up vertically, one below the other. If the items are sentences, capitalize the first letter. If the items are not sentences, you may start each with a capital letter or a lower-case letter. Whichever you choose, be consistent in each piece of writing.

✤ ALERTS: If a complete sentence leads into a displayed list, you can end the sentence with a colon. However, if an incomplete sentence leads into a displayed list, use no punctuation.

Make list items parallel in structure (see 18h). For example, if one item is a sentence, use sentences for all the items; if one item starts with a verb, start all items with a verb in the same tense; and so on. ✤

In a **formal outline,** each item must start with a capital letter. Use a period only when the item is a complete sentence (see 2p).

30c Capitalizing the first letter of an introduced quotation

If you use quoted words within the structure of your own sentence, do not capitalize the first quoted word.

Mme Paquette says that when students visit a country whose language they are trying to learn, they "absorb a good accent with the food."

If the words in your sentence serve only to introduce quoted words or if you are directly quoting speech, capitalize the first letter of the quoted words if it is capitalized in the original.

> Mme Paquette says, "Students should always visit a country when they want to learn its language. They'll absorb a good accent with the food."

Do not capitalize the continuation of a one-sentence quotation within your sentence, and do not capitalize a partial quotation.

> "Of course," she added, "the accent lasts longer than the food."

> Smiling, she encouraged me to "travel—and eat—to learn to speak French."

30d Capitalizing short words

In a title or heading, capitalize articles° *(the, a, an)* and short prepositions° (such as *with, of, to*) only when they start the title or heading, or when a source capitalizes them.

Always capitalize the pronoun° *I,* no matter where it falls in a sentence or in a group of words or when it stands alone: *I love you, even though I do not want to marry you.* Always capitalize the interjection° *O: You are, O my fair love, a burning fever.* Do not capitalize the interjection *oh* unless it starts a sentence or is capitalized in material that you are quoting.

30e Capitalizing nouns and adjectives according to standard practice

Capitalize **proper nouns** (nouns° that name specific people, places, and things): *Mexico, World Wide Web.* Also capitalize **proper adjectives** (adjectives° formed from proper nouns): *a Mexican entrepreneur, a Web address.* Do not capitalize articles (*the, a, an*) accompanying proper nouns or proper adjectives.

When a proper noun or adjective loses its very specific "proper" associations, it also loses its capital letter: *french fries, pasteurize.* When a common noun such as *lake* becomes part of a name or title, it is capitalized: *Lake Erie.*

In your reading, expect sometimes to see capitalized words that this book says not to capitalize. How writers capitalize can sometimes depend on audience and purpose. For example, a corporation's written communications usually use *the Board of Directors* and *the Company,* not *the board of directors* and *the company*. Similarly, the administrators of your school might write *the Faculty* and *the College* or *the University,* words you would not capitalize in a paper. In specific contexts, adapt to the situation.

Chart 126 is a Guide to Capitalization. Apply what you find in it to similar items not listed. Also, for information about using capital letters in addresses on envelopes, see the Canada Post guidelines on page 773.

CAPITALIZATION GUIDE 126

	CAPITALS	LOWER-CASE LETTERS
NAMES	Mother Teresa (*also,* used as names: Mother, Dad, Mom, Pa, etc.)	my mother (*relationship*)
	Doctor Who	the doctor (*role*)
TITLES	Prime Minister Campbell	a prime minister
	the Prime Minister (*now in office*)	
	Liberal *(a party member)*	liberal (*a believer in liberal ideals*)
	Member of Parliament Sheila Copps	a member of Parliament
	The Honourable Mr. Justice John Sopinka	the judge
	Queen Elizabeth II	the queen (*also* the Queen, referring to Canada's queen)
GROUPS OF HUMANITY	Caucasian (*race*)	white (*also* White)
	Native Canadian (*ethnic group*)	
	Jew, Catholic, Protestant, Buddhist (*religious affiliation*)	
ORGANIZATIONS	Parliament	parliamentary
	the Supreme Court of Canada	the court (*also* the Court)
	the Progressive Conservative Party	the party
	the Canadian Broadcasting Corporation	the corporation

CAPITALIZATION GUIDE *(continued)* 126

	CAPITALS	LOWER-CASE LETTERS
PLACES	Whitehorse	the city
	the West (*a region*)	turn west (*a direction*)
	King Street	the street
	Atlantic Ocean (*also* the Atlantic)	the ocean
	the Rocky Mountains	the mountains
BUILDINGS	the House of Commons	the legislature (*but* the House; the Commons)
	Pauline Johnson High School	the high school
	China West Café	the restaurant
	St. Peter's Hospital	the hospital
SCIENTIFIC TERMS	Earth (*the planet*)	the earth (*where we live*)
	the Milky Way	the galaxy
		the moon, the sun
	Streptococcus aureus	a streptococcal infection
	Gresham's law	the theory of relativity
LANGUAGES, NATIONALITIES	Spanish	
	Chinese	
SCHOOL COURSES	Chemistry 342	a chemistry course
	Introduction to Photography	my photography class
NAMES OF THINGS	the *Calgary Herald*	the newspaper
	Canadian Living	the magazine
	Lakehead University	the university
	the Dodge Colt	the car
TIMES AND SEASONS	Friday	spring, summer, fall, autumn, winter
	August	
HOLIDAYS	New Year's Day	a new year
	Passover	a festival, a holy day, a holiday
	Ramadan	
HISTORICAL PERIODS	World War II	the war
	the Great Depression (*in the 1930s*)	the depression (*any economic depression*)
	the Reformation	an era, an age
		the eighteenth century
		fifth-century manuscripts

→

CAPITALIZATION GUIDE (*continued*) 126

	CAPITALS	LOWER-CASE LETTERS
RELIGIOUS TERMS	God Buddhism the Torah the Koran the Bible	a god, a goddess a religion
LETTER PARTS	Dear Ms. Tauber: Sincerely, Yours truly,	
TITLES OF PUBLISHED AND RELEASED MATERIAL	"The Painted Door" *The Canadian Encyclopedia* *Under These Rocks and Stones*	[Capitalize the first letter of the first word and all other words except articles°, short prepositions°, and short conjunctions°.]
COMPOUND WORDS	post-Victorian Indo-European	
ACRONYMS AND INITIALISMS	NATO NFB DNA ACTRA NAFTA CD	
SOFTWARE	Microsoft Word DOS WordPerfect	[Capitalize software names as shown in the program documentation. Do not italicize (or underline) these names or enclose them in quotation marks.]

◆ ESL NOTE: When the subject of your paragraph or essay is a proper noun°, capitalize that word or those words. ◆

EXERCISE 30-1

Consulting sections 30a through 30e, add capital letters as needed.

1. When Antonine Maillet was awarded france's prix goncourt in 1979, she said of the acadian people who are the subject of her prizewinning novel, "we don't have much to say. Just that we're alive."

2. Wai-Yee turned to face west and looked out over the pacific, imagining her grandfather's journey across that wide ocean.
3. The fine art course taught by professor Sanzio accepts only students who already have credits in fine art 101 and Renaissance studies 211.
4. For years, a european travel guide written by Arthur Frommer (it advised tourists how to live on five dollars a day) could be found in the backpacks and suitcases of thousands of travellers.
5. The north pole is surrounded by an icy sea; the south pole lies in the middle of a frozen land mass, the continent known as antarctica.
6. At one point in the action, the script calls for the "assembled multitudes" to break into shouts of "hail, o merciful queen Tanya!"
7. How should we think of the start of the french revolution? Was it the best of times? the worst of times? a time of indecision, perhaps?
8. According to the chapter "the making of a new world," among those credited with the discovery of the Americas before Columbus are (1) the vikings, (2) various groups of european fishers and whalers, and (3) the peoples who crossed the Bering strait to Alaska in prehistoric times.
9. People who are accustomed to one of the lovely and powerful English translations of the bible sometimes forget that the bible was not originally written in English.
10. The organization of African unity (OAU) was founded in 1962, when many african nations were winning their independence.

ITALICS (UNDERLINING)

In printed material, **roman type** is the standard; type that slants to the right is called **italic.** If your word-processing program does not give you the option of italics, or when you write by hand, underline. Italics and underlining mean the same thing.

Shampoo Planet [roman]

Shampoo Planet [italic]

Shampoo Planet [underlined]

30f Using standard practice for italicizing titles and other words, letters, or numbers

Chart 127 provides a guide for making decisions about whether to italicize (or underline). Apply what you find in it to similar items not listed.

✚ ONLINE ALERT: In e-mail and other online communications, if underlining is impossible, some writers use an underscore before the first letter and after the last letter of a title.

> See page 15 in the _Simon & Schuster Handbook for Writers_. ✚

✚ ALERT: In documentation° of the sources you use, MLA, APA, and Chicago Manual styles recommend that you underline wherever the rules call for italics. CBE style uses neither underlining nor italics; Columbia online style uses italics in these cases, reserving underlining for hypertext links. Note also that MLA style requires the underline to stop before any punctuation that ends an item, whereas APA style underlines all punctuation (see Chapter 34). ✚

GUIDE TO USE OF ITALICS (OR UNDERLINING) 127

TITLES

ITALICIZE OR UNDERLINE	DO NOT ITALICIZE OR UNDERLINE
The Englishman's Boy [a novel]	your own paper's title
Farther West [a play]	
Who Do You Think You Are? [a collection of short stories]	"Royal Beatings" [one story in the collection]
Simon & Schuster Handbook for Writers [a book]	"Writing Research" [one chapter in the book]
Active Voice: An Anthology of Canadian, American and Commonwealth Prose [a collection of essays]	"The Calgary Stampede" [one essay in the collection]
The Iliad [a long poem]	"Ark Anatomical" [a short poem]
The Lotus Eaters [a film]	
Equinox [a magazine]	"Nanook Passage" [an article in the magazine]
The Barber of Seville [title of an opera]	Concerto in B-flat Minor [identification of a musical work by form, number, and key. Use neither quotation marks nor italics (underlining).]
Symphonie Fantastique [title of a long musical work]	

GUIDE TO USE OF ITALICS (OR UNDERLINING) (continued)

TITLES

ITALICIZE OR UNDERLINE	DO NOT ITALICIZE OR UNDERLINE
The Road to Avonlea [a television series]	"After the Honeymoon" [an episode of a television series]
The Visit [a record album, tape, or CD]	"Greensleeves" [a song or a single selection on an album, a tape, or a CD]
	Lotus 1-2-3 [software program names are neither underlined nor enclosed in quotation marks]

the *Brandon Sun* [a newspaper. Note: Even if *The* is part of the title printed on a newspaper, do not use a capital letter and do not italicize (or underline) it in your writing. In MLA and CM documentation°, omit the word *The*. In APA and CBE documentation, keep *The*.]

OTHER WORDS

ITALICIZE OR UNDERLINE	DO NOT ITALICIZE OR UNDERLINE
the *Haida* [a ship; don't italicize preceding initials like U.S.S. or H.M.S.]	destroyer [a general class of ship]
Voyager 2 [names of specific aircraft, spacecraft, and satellites]	Boeing 747 [general names shared by classes of aircraft, spacecraft, and satellites]
summa cum laude [term in a language other than English]	burrito, chutzpah [widely used and commonly understood words from languages other than English]
What does *our* imply? [a word referred to as such]	
the *abc*'s; confusing *3*'s and *8*'s [letters and numbers referred to as themselves]	

30g Using italics sparingly for special emphasis

Professional writers sometimes use italics to clarify a meaning or stress a point.

> Many people we *think* are powerful turn out on closer examination to be merely frightened and anxious.
>
> —MICHAEL KORDA, *Power!*

In your academic writing, rely on choice of words and sentence structures to convey emphasis.

EXERCISE 30-2

Consulting section 30f, eliminate unneeded underlining and quotation marks, and add needed underlining. Correct capitalization as necessary.

1. The article on "The Canoe" in The Canadian Encyclopedia says that birchbark canoes were "perfectly adapted to summer travel" along the shallow streams and swift rivers of early Canada.
2. According to one source, <u>Canada</u>'s name is derived from the Huron-Iroquois word <u>kanata</u>, meaning a village or settlement.
3. The writer of a humour column in The Globe and Mail described an imaginary paper called The Mop and Pail, where things were just slightly more ridiculous than in real life.
4. For distinguished accomplishments of people over age 70, we can look to Verdi, who composed the operas "Otello" at 74 and "Falstaff" at 80, and Tennyson, who wrote the short poem "Crossing the Bar" at age 80.
5. When a small business chooses a name beginning with the letter a repeated four times, as in AAAAbco Auto Body, we can be sure its marketing plan includes being noticed at the start of the telephone directory.

ABBREVIATIONS

30h Using abbreviations with time and symbols

Some abbreviations are standard in all writing circumstances. In some situations, you may choose whether to abbreviate or spell out a word. When choosing, consider your purpose for writing° and your audience°. Then be consistent in each piece of writing.

Generally, in academic and professional writing, you should spell out words. Sections 30h through 30k provide guidelines to help you decide when it is appropriate to abbreviate.

✤ PUNCTUATION ALERT: Most abbreviations call for periods: *Mr., R.N., a.m.* Some do not, including names of organizations and government agencies (see 23b): *IBM, CBC.* When the period of an abbreviation falls at the end of a sentence, the period serves also to end the sentence.✤

TIME

The abbreviations a.m. (A.M.) and p.m. (P.M.) can be used only with exact times, such as *7:15 A.M., 7:15 a.m.; 3:47 P.M., 3:47 p.m.* You can use capital or lower-case letters, but be consistent in each piece of writing.

✤ USAGE ALERT: Use *a.m.* and *p.m.* only with numbers indicating time. Do not use them instead of the words *morning, evening,* and *night.* ✤

In abbreviations for years, A.D. precedes the year: *A.D. 977.* Conversely, B.C. (or B.C.E.) and C.E. ("common era," an alternative to A.D.) follows the year: *12 B.C.* (or 12 B.C.E.).

SYMBOLS AND SCIENTIFIC TERMS

Symbols are seldom used in the body of papers written for courses in the humanities, but they are used in charts or similar formats. Also, symbols can be appropriate in the sciences.

In the humanities, spell out *percent* and *cent* rather than using the symbols % and ¢. You can use a dollar sign with specific dollar amounts: *$23 billion, $7.85.* Let common sense and your readers' needs guide you.

The conventions of technical and scientific writing require writers in those fields to abbreviate various terms and measurements. As a rule, when you write in the humanities you should avoid such abbreviations. Many writers, however, abbreviate SI (metric) units in almost any context.

✤ USAGE ALERT: If you use the abbreviation for a unit of measurement, use figures for the number that accompanies it: *6 km,* not *six km.* (See section 30l and Chart 131.) ✤

30i Using abbreviations with titles, names and terms, and addresses

TITLES

Use either a title of address before a name (***Dr.*** *Daniel Gooden*) or an academic degree after a name (*Daniel Gooden,* ***Ph.D.***) Do not use both. Because *Jr., Sr., II, III,* and the like are considered part of the name, they can be used with both titles of address and academic degree abbreviations: *Dr. Martin Luther King, Jr.; Arthur Wax, Sr., M.D.* (The title *Professor* is usually not abbreviated.)

✤ COMMA ALERT: When you use an academic degree or *Jr.* or *Sr.*, insert a comma both before it and after it if it falls before the end of a sentence: *Martin Luther King, Jr., was a superb orator.* ✤

Names and Terms

If you use a long name or term frequently in a paper, you may abbreviate it using these guidelines: The first time, give the full term, with the abbreviation in parentheses immediately after the spelled-out form. After that, you can use the abbreviation alone.

> Spain voted to continue as a member of the **North Atlantic Treaty Organization (NATO),** to the surprise of other **NATO** members.

You can abbreviate *U.K.* as a modifier (*the U.K. skating team*), but spell out *United Kingdom* when you use it as a noun. The same rule applies with *U.S.* and *United States.*

NO The **U.K.** has many art galleries and museums.

YES The **United Kingdom** has many art galleries and museums.

Addresses

If you include a full address—street, city, and province—in the body of a paper, you can use the abbreviation for the province name. Both two-letter postal code abbreviations (e.g., AB) and traditional abbreviations (Alta.) are used in writing in Canada. (Only the two-letter abbreviations should be used to address envelopes.) For a list, see Chart 130. Spell out any other combination of a city and a province or a province by itself.

✤ COMMA ALERT: Use a comma before *and* after the province. ✤

NO Wilfrid Laurier University in **Waterloo, Ont.,** used to be called Waterloo Lutheran University.

YES Wilfrid Laurier University in **Waterloo, Ontario,** used to be called Waterloo Lutheran University.

YES Wilfrid Laurier University in **Ontario** used to be called Waterloo Lutheran University.

30j Using abbreviations in documentation according to standard practice

Documentation means giving the source of any material that you quote (see 31c), paraphrase (see 31d), or summarize (see 31e).

Styles of documentation are discussed in Chapter 34. Chart 128 gives scholarly abbreviations that you might find in the sources that you consult, as well as those that you need for documentation in your writing.

COMMON SCHOLARLY ABBREVIATIONS 128

anon.	anonymous	i.e.	that is
b.	born	ms., mss.	manuscript, manuscripts
c. *or* ©	copyright	n.b.	note carefully
c. *or* ca.	about (with dates)	n.d.	no date (of publication, for a book)
cf.	compare	p., pp.	page, pages
col., cols.	column, columns	pref.	preface
d.	died	rept.	report, reported by
ed.; eds.	edited by; editors	sec., secs.	section, sections
e.g.	for example	v. *or* vs.	versus (legal case)
esp.	especially	vol., vols.	volume, volumes
et al.	and others		
f., ff.	and the following page *or* pages		

MONTH ABBREVIATIONS USED IN MLA-STYLE DOCUMENTATION 129

Jan.	January	May	(none)	Sept.	September
Feb.	February	June	(none)	Oct.	October
Mar.	March	Jl.	July	Nov.	November
Apr.	April	Aug., Ag.	August	Dec.	December

POSTAL ABBREVIATIONS 130

CANADA

AB	Alta.	Alberta
BC	B.C.	British Columbia

➜

130

POSTAL ABBREVIATIONS (*continued*)

MB	Man.	Manitoba
NB	N.B.	New Brunswick
NF	Nfld.	Newfoundland
NS	N.S.	Nova Scotia
NT	N.W.T.	Northwest Territories
NU	—	Nunavut
ON	Ont.	Ontario
PE	P.E.I.	Prince Edward Island
QC *or* PQ	Que. *or* P.Q.	Quebec
SK	Sask.	Saskatchewan
YT	Y.T.	Yukon Territory

UNITED STATES

AL	Alabama	MT	Montana
AK	Alaska	NB	Nebraska
AZ	Arizona	NV	Nevada
AR	Arkansas	NH	New Hampshire
CA	California	NJ	New Jersey
CO	Colorado	NM	New Mexico
CT	Connecticut	NY	New York
DE	Delaware	NC	North Carolina
DC	District of Columbia	ND	North Dakota
FL	Florida	OH	Ohio
GA	Georgia	OK	Oklahoma
HI	Hawaii	OR	Oregon
ID	Idaho	PA	Pennsylvania
IL	Illinois	RI	Rhode Island
IN	Indiana	SC	South Carolina
IA	Iowa	SD	South Dakota
KS	Kansas	TN	Tennessee
KY	Kentucky	TX	Texas
LA	Louisiana	UT	Utah
ME	Maine	VT	Vermont
MD	Maryland	VA	Virginia
MA	Massachusetts	WA	Washington (state)
MI	Michigan	WV	West Virginia
MN	Minnesota	WI	Wisconsin
MS	Mississippi	WY	Wyoming
MO	Missouri		

30k Using *etc.*

The abbreviation *etc.* is from Latin *et cetera,* which means "and the rest." Do not use *etc.* in writing in the humanities. Acceptable substitutes are *and the like, and so on,* and *and so forth*.

EXERCISE 30-3

Consulting sections 30h, 30i, and 30j, revise this material so that abbreviations are used correctly.

1. Although she took her coll. degree in a tech. field, Charlene made a point of getting as many lib. arts credits as she could.
2. The U of M in Winnipeg, Man., was the first institution of higher education to be established in W. Can.
3. Graham knew instantly from Lucinda's accent that she came from NS and could not possibly be a native of Alta. as she claimed.
4. Lamont gave generously to all the charities, political orgs., etc. that asked him, until the day he was approached by a rep. of the Natural Law Party.
5. Dozens of hrs. and thousands of $ later, the contractors finally extended the driveway to the main rd., a mere four m away.

NUMBERS

30l Using spelled-out numbers

Depending on how often numbers occur in a paper and what they refer to, you will sometimes express the numbers in words and sometimes in figures. The guidelines here, like those in the *MLA Handbook for Writers of Research Papers,* Third Edition, are suitable for writing in the humanities. For the guidelines other disciplines follow, consult their style manuals (for a list, see 34a).

You may want to reserve numerals for some categories of numbers and spelled-out numbers for other categories. Do not mix spelled-out numbers and numerals in a paper when they both refer to the same thing.

NO In four days, our volunteers increased from **five** to **eight** to **17** to **233**.

YES In four days, our volunteers increased from **5** to **8** to **17** to **233**. [All the numbers referring to volunteers are given in figures, but *four* is still spelled out because it refers to a different quantity—days.]

✤ HYPHENATION ALERT: Use a hyphen between spelled-out two-word numbers from *twenty-one* through *ninety-nine* (see 22d-2). ✤

If you use numbers fairly frequently in a paper, spell out numbers from *one* to *nine,* and use figures for numbers *10* and above. In the humanities, never start a sentence with a figure; spell out the number. You can usually revise a sentence so that the number does not come first. For practices in other disciplines, consult their style manuals (see 34a).

> **Three hundred seventy-five dollars** per credit is the tuition rate for nonresidents.
>
> The tuition rate for nonresidents is **$375** per credit.

If you are using specific numbers often in a paper (temperatures in a paper about climate, for example, or percentages, or any specific measurements of time, distance, or other quantities) use figures. If you are using an occasional approximation, spell out the numbers: *about nine centimetres of snow.*

30m Using numbers according to standard practice

Standard practice requires figures for numbers in the cases covered in Chart 131.

EXERCISE 30-4

Consulting sections 30l and 30m, revise this material so that the numbers are in correct form, either spelled out or in figures.

1. At five fifteen p.m. the nearly empty city streets suddenly filled with 1000's of commuters.
2. Of the forty thousand entries in the *Concise Oxford Dictionary*, only 31 begin with the letter *x*.
3. By the end of act one, scene five, Romeo and Juliet are in love and at the mercy of their unhappy fate.
4. Sound travels through the air at a speed of 331 metres per second, but in water it travels four hundred and fifty percent faster, at 1481 metres per second.
5. 21 years old and unhappily married, Cleopatra met the middle-aged Julius Caesar in forty-eight B.C.E.

GUIDE FOR USING SPECIFIC NUMBERS

131

DATES	August 6, 1941; 1732–1845; 34 B.C. to A.D. 230
ADDRESSES	10 Downing Street 237 North 8th Street London, ON N6A 3K7
TIMES	8:09 A.M.; 6:00 p.m.; six o'clock, *not* 6 o'clock; four in the afternoon (or 4 p.m.), *not* four p.m.
DECIMALS AND FRACTIONS	5.55; 98.6; 3.1416; 7/8; 12-1/4; three quarters, *not* 3 quarters; one-half
CHAPTERS AND PAGES	Chapter 27, page 245; p. 475; pp. 660–62
SCORES AND STATISTICS	a 6–0 score; a 5 to 3 ratio *or* a 5:3 ratio; 29 percent
IDENTIFICATION NUMBERS	94.4 on the FM dial; call 1-416-555-1234
MEASUREMENTS	2 cm *or* two centimetres (*not* two cm); 100 kilometres per hour; 90 km/h; 1.5 L; 2 mL; 3 litres; 8-1/2" x 11" paper *or* 8-1/2 x 11-inch paper
ACT, SCENE, AND LINE NUMBERS	act 4, scene 2, lines 75–79
TEMPERATURES	43°F; 4°C; 7.5°C
MONEY	$1.2 billion; $3.41; 25 cents *or* 25¢

6. An adult blue whale can weigh one hundred tonnes, which is the combined weight of 30 elephants; to get that big a young blue whale gains over three-point-four kilograms an hour.
7. The record for a human's broad jump is eight point five metres (about twenty-eight feet, one-quarter inch), and the record for a frog's broad jump is just over 4 metres (13 feet, 5 inches).
8. 2 out of every 5 people who have ever lived on earth are alive today, according to 1 estimate.

9. The house everyone thought was haunted at six hundred and fifty-three Oak Street stood empty for 8 months, awaiting a purchaser willing to pay its price of $ six hundred forty-nine thousand.
10. The 1912 sinking of the *Titanic*, in which one thousand five hundred and three people drowned, is widely known, but few people seem to remember that more than 3000 people lost their lives aboard the ferry-boat *Doña Paz* when it hit an oil tanker in the Philippines in 1987.

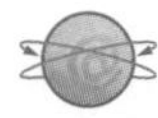

web.uvic.ca/wguide/Pages/EssaysToc.html
Knowing the Basics of Grammar

www.utoronto.ca/writing/advise.html
Grammar and Punctuation

owl.english.purdue.edu/handouts/grammar/index.html
Grammar, Spelling, and Punctuation

Writing Research

Writing research involves first conducting research and then writing a paper based on that research. Chapters 31 through 36 explain how to avoid plagiarism, plan research topics, find and evaluate sources—including online sources, write a paper based on your synthesis of those sources, and document your sources correctly.

31 Using Sources and Avoiding Plagiarism

In the most basic sense, research writing today is the same as it has always been—a process. Research writing as process involves conducting research, understanding and evaluating the results of your research, and writing a properly documented paper. But today, new technology is revolutionizing research writing. The Internet gives researchers immediate access to seemingly limitless information. The advantages are tremendous, but the wise researcher will keep certain cautions in mind.

This handbook teaches you the fundamentals of research—from formulating a research question, compiling a working bibliography, and avoiding plagiarism to drafting, revising, and documenting your paper. You will also learn how to use today's powerful new tools in research while avoiding their pitfalls. Beginning in this chapter, too, you will observe a real student, Lisa Laver, as she moves through the research process.

Sources, often called *outside sources*, are materials from which you learn something you did not know before. Outside sources include books, articles, people, television and radio, and online databases. Research paper assignments require you to use critical thinking to analyze, summarize, and mostly synthesize (see 5f) one or more sources. Using outside sources effectively and efficiently takes practice, so allow yourself time to become familiar with what is involved. The more you follow the guidelines in Chart 132, the better you will succeed.

31a Avoiding plagiarism

To plagiarize°* is to present another person's words or ideas as if they were your own. Plagiarism is like stealing. The word *plagiarize*

*Throughout this book, a degree mark (°) indicates that you can find the definition of the word in the Glossary of Terms in this handbook.

132

GUIDELINES FOR USING OUTSIDE SOURCES IN YOUR WRITING

1. Apply the concepts and skills of thinking critically (see 5a–5b), reading critically (see 5c–5e), and writing critically (see 5g–5k).
2. Avoid plagiarism° by always crediting the source for any ideas and words not your own.
3. Use documentation (see Chapter 34) to credit sources accurately and completely.
4. Know how and when to use these techniques for incorporating material from sources into your own writing:
   - **Quotation:** the exact words of a source set off in quotation marks (see 31c)
   - **Paraphrase:** a detailed restatement of someone else's statement expressed in your own words and your own sentence structure (see 31d)
   - **Summary:** a condensed statement of the main points of someone else's passage expressed in your own words and sentence structure (see 31e)

comes from the Latin word for kidnapper and literary thief. Plagiarism is a serious offence that can be grounds for failing a course or expulsion from a college or university. Plagiarism can be intentional, as when you submit as your own work a paper you did not write. Plagiarism is also intentional when you deliberately incorporate the work of other people in your writing without using documentation to acknowledge those sources. Plagiarism can also be unintentional—but no less serious an offence—if you are unaware of what must be acknowledged and how to do so with documentation.

1 Knowing what not to document

When you write a paper that draws on outside sources, you are not expected to document common knowledge (if there is any on your topic) or your own thinking about the subject.

Common knowledge

You do not have to document common knowledge. Common knowledge is information that most educated people know, although they might need to remind themselves of certain facts by looking up information in a reference book. For example, every educated person knows that the U.S. space program included moon landings. Even though you might have to look in a reference book to recall that Neil Armstrong, the first man to set foot on the moon, landed on July 20, 1969, those facts are common knowledge and do not have to be documented.

You move into *the realm of research and the need to document* as soon as you get into less commonly known details about the moon landing: the duration of the stay on the moon, the size and capabilities of the spaceship, what the astronauts ate during their journey, and similar details. If you feel that you are walking a thin line between knowledge held in common and knowledge learned from research, be safe and document.

Sometimes, of course, a research paper does not happen to contain common knowledge. For example, Lisa Laver, whose research paper appears in Chapter 35, had only very general common knowledge about the broad topic of intelligence. She had even less knowledge of her narrowed topic of "newer theories for defining intelligence." Laver's research paper consists of a little of her common knowledge, much that she summarizes and synthesizes from outside sources, and some of her own thinking based on what she learned from her research.

Your own thinking

You do not have to document your own thinking about your subject. As you conduct your research, you learn new material by building on your *prior knowledge*—what you already know. You are expected to think about that new material, using the sequence for critical thinking in Chapter 5 and summarized in Chart 30. When you synthesize what you have learned from outside sources, you are doing your own thinking. Watch the line carefully: When in doubt, document.

Be particularly careful not to allow plagiarism to slip into a thesis statement° and topic sentences°. It is plagiarism to put a source's main idea into your words and pass that off as your thesis statement or topic sentences. Similarly, it is plagiarism to combine the main ideas of several sources, put them into your own words, and pass that off as your own idea. Your thesis statement and topic sentences must reflect your synthesis of what you have learned from outside sources. Notice how Lisa Laver relied on synthesis and her own thinking in her research paper, presented in Chapter 35.

Examples of Laver's Own Thinking

- The thesis statement: paragraph 1
- Synthesis: most topic sentences (which start all paragraphs except 1 and 10)

- Comments or opinion: opening sentence of paragraph 6 and entire concluding paragraph
- Transitional sentences: opening sentences of paragraphs 2, 3, 4, 8, 9, and 10
- Conclusion: paragraph 11

2 Knowing what to document

What should you document? Everything that is not common knowledge or your own thinking (see 31a-1). Document any material that you quote (see 31c), paraphrase (see 31d), or summarize (see 31e). Remember that writing the exact words of others or the ideas of others in your own words means that you must document.

Careful notetaking is the key to preventing plagiarism. As you conduct research using outside sources, follow these widely used techniques that help researchers avoid plagiarism.

Plagiarism Prevention While Taking Notes

- **Record complete documentation information.** Become entirely familiar with the documentation style° you will need in your paper (see 31b). If you are not sure of exactly which style to use, ask your instructor.

  Next, make a master guide for the specific information your documentation style requires for each type of source. Check for your style's requirements, shown in Chapter 34. Focus especially on the examples in Chart 151 for MLA style; Chart 152 for APA style; Chart 153 for CM style; Chart 154 for CBE style; Chart 155 for Columbia online style.

  Web pages used in your paper require the same level of documentation as a book or a journal. The thoughts and ideas of the author are presented on the Web page and must be acknowledged as another person's work even if the format is less formal than more traditional sources. Because many Web pages are actually self-published and have no editor to ensure quality control or to insist on a standard format, you may have to take extra steps finding and identifying all the components needed for proper documentation (see section 34a). If all the elements of the needed documentation cannot be found, you may have to reconsider whether the particular Web page meets the criteria for a good research source (see Chart 142 in section 32f-3). If it does not, it may have to be discarded or other sources may have to be used to verify the information.

An additional risk with using questionable sources on the Web is that the source itself may be plagiarized. If you unintentionally use such a source, it nonetheless constitutes plagiarism on your part. To become as familiar as you can with your Internet sources, be sure you can answer questions such as those in Chart 142.

Drawing on your master guide, write a bibliography card for each source. Record all the information for the type of source. Also, record any information you need to locate the source again (see 34b).

- **Record documentation information as you go along.** Never forget to write down complete, detailed documentation facts. Use your clearest, most readable handwriting. When you write a research paper, your chances of unintentional plagiarism decrease sharply if you can easily figure out from your notes the exact source you used and the information you found in it. Never expect to relocate a source later—it may be unavailable, or you may not be able to recall where you found it.
- **Use a consistent notetaking system.** Never expect to reconstruct from memory what came from the source and what is the result of your own thinking. Always use different colours of ink or a clear coding system to keep three things separate: (1) material paraphrased or summarized from a source, (2) quotations from a source, and (3) your own thoughts. For quotations, many professional writers use oversized quotation marks so that they are certain to see them later.

31b Understanding the concept of documentation

Documentation means acknowledging your sources. It is a two-part process: You mark the exact place in your paper where you have used an outside source, and you give full and accurate information so that readers can find your sources. This information includes the author, title, publication information or electronic accessing information, and related facts. Whenever you quote (see 31c), paraphrase (see 31d), or summarize (see 31e), you must document your source correctly according to the documentation style° you are using.

Documentation styles vary among the academic disciplines. When you write using outside sources, ask your instructor what documentation style you are expected to use. Chapter 34 explains and illustrates five documentation styles: Modern Language Association (MLA) style; American Psychological Association (APA) style; Chicago Manual (CM) style; Council of Biology Editors (CBE) style; and Columbia online style (COS).

31c Using quotations effectively

Quotations are the exact words of a source set off in quotation marks (see 28a). In contrast to paraphrases (see 31d) and summaries (see 31e), which present your sources' ideas in your words, quotations give your reader the chance to encounter your source's words directly. Chart 133 gives guidelines for using quotations.

Two conflicting demands confront you when you use quotations in your writing. Along with the effect and support of quotations, you also want your writing to be coherent and readable. You might seem to gain authority by quoting experts on your topic, but if you use too many quotations, you lose coherence as well as control of your own paper. If more than a quarter of your paper consists of quotations, you have written what some people call a "Scotch tape special." Having too many quotations gives readers—including instructors—the impression

GUIDELINES FOR USING QUOTATIONS 133

1. Use quotations from authorities in your subject to *support* what you say, not for your thesis statement° or main points.
2. Select quotations that fit your message.
3. Choose a quotation only if
   a. its language is particularly appropriate or distinctive;
   b. its idea is particularly hard to paraphrase accurately;
   c. the authority of the source is especially important to support your material;
   d. the source's words are open to more than one interpretation, so your reader needs to see the original.
4. Do not use quotations for more than a quarter of the text of your paper; rely mostly on paraphrase and summary.
5. Quote accurately.
6. Integrate quotations smoothly into your prose (see 31c-4), paying special attention to the verbs that help you to do so effectively (see 31f).
7. Avoid plagiarism (see 31a). Always document your source. Enclose quotations of four lines or less in quotation marks. Even if you do not use the entire quotation in your paper, the quotation marks signal that all words they enclose are words quoted directly from a source. (See 28a for quotations of five or more lines.)

that you have not synthesized what your sources say and are letting other people do your talking. Use quotations sparingly, therefore. When you draw on support from an authority, rely mostly on paraphrase (see 31d) and summary (see 31e).

1 Quoting accurately

When you use quotations, be very careful to quote a source exactly. Always check your quotations against the originals—and then recheck. Mistakes are extremely easy to make when you are copying from a source into your notes or from your notes into your paper. If you can do so, photocopy a source's words that you think you might want to quote. (Be sure to label the copy with the author's name and complete bibliographic information; see 32j-2.) Mark off on the copy the exact place that caught your attention; otherwise, you might forget your impressions and waste time trying to reconstruct your thought processes.

If you have to add a word or two to a quotation so that it fits in with your prose, put those words in brackets (see 29c). Make sure that your additions do not distort the meaning of the quotation. The quotation below is taken from original material shown in section 31d-2. The bracketed material replaces the word *he* in the original quotation with words that clarify the material.

> "If you hail from western Europe, you will find that [the person you are talking to] is at roughly fingertip distance from you" (Morris 131).*

If you delete a portion of a quotation, indicate the omission with an ellipsis. (MLA style encloses ellipses in brackets; see 29d.) When using ellipses, make sure that the remaining words accurately reflect the source's meaning. Also, make sure that your omission does not create an awkward sentence structure.

ORIGINAL

> Like the porcupines in Schopenhauer's fable, people like to be close enough to obtain warmth and comradeship but far enough away to avoid pricking one another. Personal space is not necessarily spherical in shape, nor does it extend equally in all directions. (People are able to tolerate closer presence of a stranger at their sides than directly in front of them.) It has been likened to a snail shell, a soap bubble, an aura, and "breathing room" (Sommer 26).

*Source information is in MLA style throughout this chapter (see 34c).

WITH ELLIPSES

Like the porcupines in Schopenhauer's fable, people like to be close enough to obtain warmth and comradeship but far enough away to avoid pricking one another. Personal space [...] has been likened to a snail shell [...] (Sommer 26).

2 Selecting quotations from accepted authorities that fit your meaning

Quotations from authorities on your subject can bring credibility to your discussion. You must be able to justify every quotation that you decide to use. If you are unsure whether to quote, follow the criteria in Chart 133, item 3. If you decide not to quote, either paraphrase (see 31d) or summarize (see 31e) the material. For example, Lisa Laver, author of the student research paper in Chapter 35 about definitions of intelligence, quoted Daniel Goleman because he is an accepted authority on her topic. (See Chart 142 in 32f-3.)

Equally important, use a quotation only if its words fit your context. If you force a quotation to fit your material, most readers will quickly discern the manipulation. Also, if you have to hunt for a quotation simply because you want to include a particular authority's words, chances are that the quotation will seem tacked on, not integrated.

3 Keeping long quotations to a minimum

When you use a quotation, your purpose is to supply evidence or support your assertion, not to reconstruct someone else's argument. When a quotation is very long, you may be making this error. Also, if you need to present a complicated argument in detail and thus quote long passages, make absolutely *sure* every word in the quotation counts. Edit out irrelevant parts (using an ellipsis to indicate deleted material; see 31c-1). Otherwise, your readers will likely skip over the long quotation—and your instructor will assume that you did not want to take the time to paraphrase (see 31d) or summarize (see 31e) the material.

✤ FORMAT ALERT: For instructions on how to format the layout of a prose quotation more than four lines long (or more than three quoted lines of poetry) in MLA style, see page 590. For formatting more than forty quoted words in APA style, see pages 620–621. ✤

4 Integrating quotations smoothly into your prose

When you use quotations, you *must* integrate them smoothly into your sentences to avoid choppy, incoherent sentences in which quotations do not mesh with the grammar, style, or logic of your prose. Consider these examples based on the original material in section 31c-1.

NO Sommer says personal space for people "like the porcupines in Schopenhauer's fable, people like to be close enough to obtain warmth and comradeship but far enough away to avoid pricking one another" (26). [grammar problem]

YES Sommer says concerning personal space that "like the porcupines in Schopenhauer's fable, people like to be close enough to obtain warmth and comradeship but far enough away to avoid pricking one another" (26).

Perhaps the biggest complaint instructors have about student research papers is that sometimes quotations are simply stuck in without any reason for their inclusion. Without context-setting information, the reader cannot know how the writer connects the quotation with its surroundings. When words are placed between quotation marks, they take on special significance concerning message as well as language

Also, make sure your readers know *who* said the quoted words; otherwise, you have disembodied quotations (some instructors call them "ghost quotations"). Revise so that more than quotation marks differentiates a quotation from your prose.

A quotation seldom should begin a paragraph; rely on your own topic sentence° to begin. Then use the quotation if it supports or extends what you have said.

Citing the author's name and the title of the work as you introduce a quotation helps to create a context for the quotation. Moreover, if the author is noteworthy, you give additional authority to your message by referring to his or her credentials as part of this introduction. Consider the following treatments of source material:

SOURCE

Gardner, Howard. *The Disciplined Mind: What All Students Should Understand*. New York: Simon & Schuster, 1999: 72.

ORIGINAL MATERIAL

While we all possess all of the intelligences, perhaps no two persons—not even identical twins—exhibit them in the same combination of strengths.

Quotation Using Author's Name

Howard Gardner explains that "while we all possess all of the intelligences, perhaps no two persons—not even identical twins—exhibit them in the same combination of strengths" (72).

Quotation Using Author's Name and Source Title

Howard Gardner explains in *The Disciplined Mind: What All Students Should Understand* that "while we all possess all of the intelligences, perhaps no two persons—not even identical twins—exhibit them in the same combination of strengths" (72).

Quotation Using Author's Name, Credentials, and Source Title

Howard Gardner, a psychologist and author of fifteen books on the human mind, states in *The Disciplined Mind: What All Students Should Understand,* "While we all possess all of the intelligences, perhaps no two persons—not even identical twins—exhibit them in the same combination of strengths" (72).

Occasionally quotations speak for themselves, but at times they do not. Usually the words you are quoting are part of a larger piece, and you know the connection that the quotation has to the original material. Your reader may puzzle over why you included the quotation, so a brief introductory remark provides the needed information.

Quotation Using Author's Name and Introductory Analysis

Psychologist Howard Gardner claims that humans possess eight, or perhaps nine, intelligences, but "while we all possess all of the intelligences, perhaps no two persons—not even identical twins—exhibit them in the same combination of strengths" (72).

Another technique for fitting a quotation into your own writing involves interrupting the quotation with your own words. (Remember that if you insert your own words *within* the quotation, you must put those words between brackets; see 29c.)

"While we all possess all of the intelligences," Howard Gardner explains, "perhaps no two persons—not even identical twins—exhibit them in the same combination of strengths" (72).

✤ ALERT: After using an author's full name in the first reference, in subsequent references you can use the author's last name only, unless another source has that same last name. ✤

EXERCISE 31-1

Read the original material, a passage taken from page 96 of *Misconceiving Canada: The Struggle for National Unity* by Kenneth McRoberts. Then, evaluate the passages that show unacceptable uses of quotations. Describe the problems, and then revise each passage. End the quotations with this MLA parenthetical reference: (McRoberts 96).

ORIGINAL MATERIAL

During the 1980s, the three Prairie provinces were all forced to confront the issue of official bilingualism, in light of Supreme Court decisions upholding their obligations under nineteenth-century statutes. In each case, there was a clear resistance among anglophones to official status for French.

In the case of Manitoba, the resulting conflict was especially acrimonious. In 1979 the Supreme Court ruled that the province was still bound by the Manitoba Act, 1870 and that all laws passed since 1890 were unconstitutional since they had not been enacted in both official languages. The Manitoba government began translating all its statutes into French, but by 1982 it became concerned that the translation was not proceeding fast enough and began to fear that all its laws might soon be declared unconstitutional.

UNACCEPTABLE USES OF QUOTATIONS

1. The Supreme Court ruled that the Prairie provinces were bound by their nineteenth-century legal obligations. "In each case, there was a clear resistance among anglophones to official status for French" (McRoberts 96).
2. With regard to Manitoba, "the Supreme Court ruled that all laws passed since 1890 were unconstitutional since they had not been enacted in both official languages" (McRoberts 96).
3. By 1982, while translating Manitoba's laws into French, the realization "that the translation was not proceeding fast enough and began to fear that all its laws might soon be declared unconstitutional"(McRoberts 96).
4. The 1870 Manitoba Act required the province to enact both French and English versions of its legislation. However, "since they had not been enacted in both official languages" (McRoberts 96), the Supreme Court found that Manitoba had violated the Constitution.
5. As a result of the Supreme Court decision, Manitoba began to translate all its laws, although "in 1982 it became concerned that the French translation was not proceeding fast enough" (McRoberts 96).

EXERCISE 31-2

A. For a paper describing the importance of ritual, write a three- to four-sentence passage that includes your own words and a quotation from this material. After the quoted words, use this parenthetical reference: (Visser 11).

The Aztec cared intensely *how* they ate people and also who they ate, when, and where. Every gesture of the sacrifice was laid down as ritual:

architecture, costumes, sacred weapons, and utensils were carefully prescribed and prepared. People were allowed to eat only the portions of meat assigned to them by their status. In fact the Aztec were terrified by the idea of human sacrifice carried out in chaotic disorder; it could only mean darkness (the failure of the power of the Sun), and destruction: the gods would become violent and brutish themselves, descend to earth, and eat people just as indiscriminately and with as little regard for protocol and etiquette as people had shown earlier. There were a thousand meanings and emotions associated with the sacrifice, besides the wish to eat and enjoy. Eating people was hedged about with ceremony and elaborate care; what they saw as neatness and propriety governed every gesture.

—MARGARET VISSER, *The Rituals of Dinner*

B. For a paper arguing that writers of children's books should not impose their own views on their readers, quote from the Landsberg material in Exercise 31-6. Be sure to include in your quotation some of the strengths that Landsberg sees in the novel she is discussing, in addition to one or more of its weaknesses.

C. Write a three- to four-sentence passage that includes your own words and a quotation from a source you are using for a paper assigned in one of your courses. If you have no such assignment, choose any material suitable for a college-level or university-level paper. Your instructor might request a photocopy of the material from which you are quoting.

31d Paraphrasing accurately

When you paraphrase, you precisely restate in your own words a passage written (or spoken) by another person. A paraphrase is more detailed and longer than a summary (see 31e). A paraphrase is a parallel text, one that goes alongside an original writing. Your paraphrases offer an account of what an authority says, in your own words.

As a bonus, the process of writing a paraphrase helps you untangle difficult passages and come to understand them. Paraphrasing forces you to read closely and to extract precise meaning from complex passages. Guidelines for writing a paraphrase are in Chart 134.

1 Restating material completely using your own words

When you paraphrase, restate the material—and no more. Do not skip points. Do not guess at meaning. Do not insert your own opinions or interpretations. If the source's words trigger your own thinking, preserve your thought right away because you might not

134

GUIDELINES FOR WRITING A PARAPHRASE

1. Say what the source says, but no more.
2. Reproduce the source's emphases.
3. Use your own words, phrasing, and sentence structure to restate the message. If certain synonyms are awkward, quote the material—but resort to quotation only occasionally.
4. Read over your sentences to make sure that they do not distort the source's meaning.
5. Expect your material to be as long as, and possibly longer than, the original.
6. Use verbs that help you integrate paraphrases smoothly into your prose (see 31f).
7. **Avoid plagiarism** (see 31a).
8. As you take notes, record all documentation facts about your source so that you can acknowledge your source accurately and avoid plagiarism.

recall it later. However, *when you write down your thought, make sure it is physically separate from your paraphrase:* in the margin, in a different coloured ink, circled, or differentiated in some other way.

As you paraphrase, use your own words; otherwise you will be quoting. Use your own sentence structures. You can use synonyms, but sometimes synonyms or substitute phrases are not advisable. Consider how each synonym fits into the flow of your sentence. For example, for a basic concept such as *people,* the use of *homo sapiens* might make the material seem strained. In paraphrasing, the farther you get from the original phrasing, the more likely you are to sound like yourself. Do not be surprised to find that when you change language and sentence structure you might also have to change punctuation, verb tense,° and voice°. When you finish, read over your paraphrase to check that it makes sense and does not distort the meaning of the source.

2 Avoiding plagiarism when you paraphrase

You must **avoid plagiarism** (see 31a) when you paraphrase. Even though a paraphrase is not a direct quotation, you *must* use documentation° to credit your source. Also, you *must* reword your source material, not merely change a few words. Compare these passages:

Source

Morris, Desmond. *Manwatching.* New York: Abrams, 1977: 131.

Original

Unfortunately, different countries have different ideas about exactly how close is close. It is easy enough to test your own "space reaction": when you are talking to someone in the street or in any open space, reach out with your arm and see where the nearest point on his body comes. If you hail from western Europe, you will find that he is at roughly fingertip distance from you. In other words, as you reach out, your fingertips will just about make contact with his shoulder. If you come from eastern Europe, you will find you are standing at "wrist distance." If you come from the Mediterranean region, you will find that you are much closer to your companion, at little more than "elbow distance."

Unacceptable Paraphrase (Underscored Words Are Plagiarized)

Regrettably, different nations think differently about <u>exactly how close is close.</u> Test yourself: <u>When you are talking to someone in the street or in any open space,</u> stretch your arm out to measure how close that person is to you. If you are from western Europe, you will find that <u>your fingertips will just about make contact with the person's shoulder.</u> If you are from eastern Europe, your wrist will reach the person's shoulder. If you are from <u>the Mediterranean region, you will find that you are much closer to your companion,</u> when your elbow will reach that person's shoulder (Morris 131).

Acceptable Paraphrase

People from different nations think that "close" means different things. You can easily see what your reaction is to how close to you people stand by reaching out the length of your arm to measure how close someone is as the two of you talk. When people from western Europe stand on the street and talk together, the space between them is the distance it would take one person's fingertips to reach to the other person's shoulder. People from eastern Europe converse at a wrist-to-shoulder distance. People from the Mediterranean, however, prefer an elbow-to-shoulder distance (Morris 131).

The first attempt to paraphrase is not acceptable. All that the writer has done is simply change a few words. What remains is plagiarized because the passage keeps most of the original's language, has the same sentence structure, and uses no quotation marks. The documentation is correct, but its accuracy does not make up for the unacceptable paraphrasing.

The second paraphrase is acceptable. It captures the essence of the original in the student's own words.

EXERCISE 31-3

Read the original material, a paragraph from *The Death and Life of Great American Cities* by Jane Jacobs, published by Random House in 1961, page 141. Then, read the unacceptable paraphrase. Point out each example of plagiarism. Finally, write your own paraphrase, ending it with this parenthetical reference: (Jacobs 141).

Original Material

A good street neighborhood achieves a marvel of balance between its people's determination to have essential privacy and their simultaneous wish for differing degrees of contact, enjoyment, or help from the people around. This balance is largely made up of small, sensibly managed details, practiced and accepted so casually that they normally seem taken for granted.

Unacceptable Paraphrase (Plagiarizes)

A good neighbourhood maintains an impressive balance between the people being determined to have privacy and wishing for varying degrees of contact, pleasure, or assistance from others nearby. People manage this with small details that are normally taken for granted (Jacobs 141).

EXERCISE 31-4

1. For a paper on applied psychology, paraphrase this paragraph. End your paraphrase with this parenthetical reference: (Bender and Tracz 95).

Many border-crossing guards are trained in observing eye movement. A border-crossing guard will ask you questions she can verify on her computer. "What's your name?" "Where do you live?" "How long have you been out of the country?" While you are answering, the guard "maps" your eye movements to see what direction they turn in. She will then ask you something she doesn't know the answer to. If your eyes go the other way, she becomes suspicious you're lying.

–Peter Urs Bender and Robert A. Tracz,
Secrets of Face-to-Face Communication

2. Write a paraphrase of a paragraph of at least 150 words from one of the sources you are using for a paper assigned in one of your courses. If you have no such assignment, choose any material suitable for a college-level or university-level paper. Your instructor may request that you submit a photocopy of the original material to accompany your paraphrase.

31e Summarizing accurately

A summary reviews the main points of a passage and gets at the gist of what an author or speaker says. A summary condenses the essentials of someone else's thought into a few statements. Summaries and paraphrases (see 31d) differ in one primary way: A summary is much shorter than a paraphrase and provides only the main point of the original source. Guidelines for writing a summary are found in Chart 135.

Summarizing forces you to read closely and to comprehend clearly. By writing summaries, you can learn the material because that process helps lock information into your memory. Summarizing is probably the most frequently used technique for taking notes and for incorporating sources into papers.

Here is a summary based on the original material shown in section 31d-2. Compare it with the acceptable paraphrase in that section.

SUMMARY

Expected amounts of space between people when they are talking differs among cultures: in general, people from western Europe prefer fingertip to shoulder distance, from eastern Europe wrist to shoulder, and from the Mediterranean elbow to shoulder (Morris 131).

GUIDELINES FOR WRITING A SUMMARY 135

1. Identify the main points, and condense them without losing the essence of the material.
2. Use your own words to condense the message.
3. Keep your summary short.
4. Use verbs effectively to integrate summaries into your prose (see 31f).
5. **Avoid plagiarism** (see 31a).
6. As you take notes, record all documentation facts about your source so that you can acknowledge your source accurately and avoid plagiarism.

1 Isolating the main points and condensing without losing meaning

A summary captures the entire sense of a passage in very little space, so you must read through all the content before you write. Then isolate the main points by asking these questions: What is the subject? What is the central message on the subject? A summary excludes more than it includes, so you must make substantial deletions. A summary should reduce the original by at least half.

As you summarize, you trace a line of thought. Doing this involves deleting less central ideas and sometimes transposing certain points into an order more suited to summary. In summarizing a longer original—say ten pages or more—you may find it helpful first to divide the original into subsections and summarize each. Then group your subsection summaries and use them as the basis for further condensing the material into a final summary. Until you are experienced at writing summaries, you will likely have to revise them more than once. Always make sure that a summary accurately reflects the source and its emphases.

Condensing information into a table is another option for summarizing, particularly when you are working with numerical data. (For an example, see the student research paper in Chapter 35: Table 1 summarizes many pages of a source.)

As you summarize, you may be tempted to interpret something the author says or make a judgment about the value of the author's point. Your own opinions do not belong in a summary, but do jot them down immediately so that you can recall your reactions later. *Be sure to place your ideas in your notes so that they are physically separate from your summary:* in the margin, in a different coloured ink, circled, or otherwise very different looking.

2 Avoiding plagiarizing when you summarize

Even though a summary is not a direct quotation, you *must* use documentation° to credit your source. Also, you *must* use your own words. Compare these passages:

SOURCE

Gardner, Howard. *The Disciplined Mind: What All Students Should Understand*. New York: Simon & Schuster, 1999: 72.

ORIGINAL

Intelligence tests typically tap linguistic and logical-mathematical intelligence—the intelligences of greatest moment in contemporary schools—perhaps sampling spatial intelligence as well. But as a species we also possess musical intelligence, bodily-kinesthetic intelligence, naturalistic intelligence, intelligence about ourselves (intrapersonal intelligence), and intelligence about other persons (interpersonal intelligence). And it is possible that human beings also exhibit a ninth, existential intelligence—the proclivity to pose (and ponder) questions about life, death, and ultimate realities. Each of these intelligences features its own distinctive form of mental representation; in fact, it is equally accurate to say that each intelligence *is* a form of mental representation.

UNACCEPTABLE SUMMARY (UNDERSCORED WORDS ARE PLAGIARIZED)

<u>Intelligence tests typically tap</u> only two or three of the eight (or possibly nine) human intelligences that Gardner has identified. Furthermore, <u>each of these intelligences features its own distinctive form of mental representation</u> (72).

ACCEPTABLE SUMMARY

Traditional intelligence tests typically evaluate only two or three of the eight (or possibly nine) human intelligences that Gardner has identified. Furthermore, he believes that each intelligence has "its own distinctive form of mental representation" (72).

The unacceptable summary does not isolate the main point, and it plagiarizes by using almost all language used in the source.

The second summary is acceptable because it not only isolates the main idea but also recasts it in the student's words. One phrase (*its own distinctive form of mental representation*) is borrowed, but it is set off in quotation marks. No one would charge this student with plagiarism.

EXERCISE 31-5

Read the original material, a paragraph from *Teaching Your Children Values* by Linda and Richard Eyre, published by Simon & Schuster in 1993, page 42. Then, read the unacceptable summary. Point out each example of plagiarism. Finally, write your own summary, ending it with this parenthetical reference: (Eyre and Eyre 42).

ORIGINAL MATERIAL

Be completely honest with your children. This will show them how always applicable the principle is and will demonstrate your commitment to it. Answer their questions truthfully and candidly unless it is a question that is off-limits, and then tell them simply and honestly why you won't answer it. Never let them hear you tell little "convenient lies" on the phone and never ask them to tell one for you ("My mommy isn't home"). Don't exaggerate. Don't threaten to do things you don't really intend to do.

UNACCEPTABLE SUMMARY

It is best to be completely honest with your children in every situation that is not off-limits; do not exaggerate, threaten children, or ask them to tell little convenient lies for you. This approach will clearly demonstrate to them that the idea of honesty is always applied to every situation and relationship (Eyre and Eyre 42).

EXERCISE 31-6

1. For a paper examining the author's point of view in Canadian children's literature, summarize this material. End your summary with this parenthetical reference: (Landsberg 109).

One-sidedness is a sore (and fatal) temptation for a novelist, to which too many of Canada's accomplished storywriters have succumbed—particularly, alas, those of dissenting views. Perhaps they have been provoked by the national complacency that smothers critics of the status quo like a monstrous clammy blanc mange. Silver Donald Cameron's novel, *The Baitchopper*, about a Nova Scotia fishermen's strike, has a memorable title, an exciting climactic scene at sea in a storm, and some fine salty local language. Unfortunately, it is weakened by a black-and-white finality about heroic proletarian strikers versus the smug establishment. I would share Cameron's conclusions about the rights and wrongs of the strike and about the base self-interest of those who opposed it, but the writer's fixed viewpoint robs his young characters of the opportunity to come to these conclusions for themselves. Ironically, the drama of that inner struggle would have been far more effective in making the point.

—MICHELE LANDSBERG, *Michele Landsberg's Guide to Children's Books*

2. Write a summary of your paraphrase of the Bender and Tracz material in Exercise 31-4. End it with the parenthetical reference given there.
3. Write a one- or two-paragraph-long summary of a source you are using for a paper assigned in one of your courses, or select material suitable for a college-level or university-level paper. Your instructor may request that you submit a photocopy of the original material to accompany your summary.

31f Using verbs effectively to integrate source material into your prose

Many verbs can help you work quotations, paraphrases, and summaries smoothly into your writing. They are listed in Chart 136. Always try to use them without any strain of style. Also, be aware that some of

VERBS USEFUL FOR INTEGRATING QUOTATIONS, PARAPHRASES, AND SUMMARIES 136

agree	complain	emphasize	note	see
analyze	concede	explain	observe	show
argue	conclude	find	offer	speculate
ask	consider	grant	point out	state
assert	contend	illustrate	refute	suggest
believe	declare	imply	report	suppose
claim	deny	insist	reveal	think
comment	describe	maintain	say	write

these verbs imply your position toward the source material (for example, *argue, complain, concede, deny, grant, insist,* and *reveal*); others are general or neutral in meaning (*comment, describe, explain, note, say,* and *write*). Choose them according to the meaning that you want your sentences to deliver. (For examples of verbs being used well in student research papers, see Chapters 35, 36, and 39.)

32 The Processes of Research Writing

32a Understanding research writing

1 Recognizing research writing as a process

Research writing involves you in three processes: conducting research, understanding the results of your research, and writing a paper based on your understanding. These processes are interwoven throughout your research project. All three processes roll ahead and circle back according to what unfolds as you work. To help you, this chapter covers each process. (It is supplemented by Chapter 33, "Successful Online Research.") Also, you can rely on the more general writing explanations in the earlier chapters of this handbook.

For example, the **writing process** for a research paper resembles the process of writing for all academic papers (see Chapters 1–4). Using research simply adds one more dimension. In planning° the paper, you choose a suitable research topic; refine that topic into a research question; use a search strategy to locate, understand, and evaluate sources; and take notes. In drafting° and revising° the paper, you present your synthesis° (see 5f) of the material you found during your search. Then you support your synthesis by quoting, paraphrasing, and summarizing your sources (see Chapter 31). At all stages of research writing, be sure to consult Chapter 5 so that you can apply the principles of critical thinking.

Though few research paper assignments are phrased as questions, research writing is indeed a quest for answers. Regarding it as such makes it clear that you must search to find answers. Your research question gives you focus: You cannot know whether you have found useful material unless you know what you are looking for.

Research questions, whether stated or implied, and the strategies needed to answer them, vary widely. Your purpose might be to present and explain information: "How does penicillin destroy bacteria?" Or your purpose might be to argue one side of an issue: "Is Parliament more important than the Supreme Court in setting social policy?" To find answers, you synthesize material from various sources in an attempt to understand.

Attempt is an important word in relation to research. Some research questions lead to a final, definitive answer, but some do not. In the preceding paragraph, the question about penicillin leads to a definitive answer (you describe how the antibiotic penicillin destroys the cell walls of some bacteria), so your writing has to be informative°. The question about social policy has no definitive answer, but rather, it invites you to present an informed opinion based on information and opinions gathered from your research; so your writing has to be persuasive°.

Research can be an engrossing, creative activity. By gathering information, analyzing its separate elements, and composing a synthesis of them, you come to know your subject deeply. The act of writing can help you make fresh connections and gain unexpected insights. Equally important, you can sample the pleasures of being a self-reliant learner, someone with the self-discipline and intellectual resources to track down, absorb, and synthesize information independently. If you feel overwhelmed by the prospect of research writing, you are not alone. Many researchers, inexperienced and experienced, have such feelings. The best advice is to break research writing into the series of steps described in this chapter so that the project becomes far less intimidating.

2 Understanding the role of the new technologies in research

Not too many years ago, students and other researchers marched through each step in the same way. Today, because of computers, how you carry out the research process becomes a very individual matter. Some students use a computer only for online and CD-ROM research and for writing their papers. (Chapter 33, "Successful Online Research," explains how to go online and conduct research by using the Internet and by connecting to the computerized database of your college or university library.) These students do the rest of the steps by hand on index cards and sheets of paper: keeping their research log (see 32c), compiling their working bibliography (see 32h), taking content notes (32j-2), and so forth.

Other students carry out the entire research process on computer: They set up folders for every phase of their project. To accumulate print sources for their working bibliography, they download them—always carefully recording the origin of the source, and using the documentation style they have selected (32f-4). Another option is to import print sources by scanning them onto disk. Finally, they draft and revise their papers on computer, often using the feature on their word-processing program that lets them keep track of their changes.

Experiment to find whatever method works best for you; there is no right or wrong way to use the new technologies. And always be sure to save and back up your work on the computer.

32b Scheduling for research writing

Research writing takes time. The key to your successfully completing a research project is to plan ahead and budget your time intelligently. As soon as you get a research paper assignment, work out a time schedule. The schedule in Chart 137 lists typical research steps. No two research paper projects are alike, so adapt the schedule to your needs. You might need only one day for some steps but two weeks for others. Be flexible, but always keep your eye on the calendar.

137

SAMPLE SCHEDULE FOR A RESEARCH PAPER PROJECT

Assignment received (date) ______________

Assignment due ______________ Finish by (date)

PLANNING

1. Start a research log (32c). ________
2. Choose a topic suitable for research (32d-1). ________
3. Draft a research question (32a, 32d-2, 32e). ________
4. Decide on purpose and audience (32e). ________
5. Prepare to begin research:
   a. Gather equipment (32f-1). ________
   b. Learn how the library is organized (32f-2). ________
   c. Get to know available online resources (Chapter 33). ________
6. Decide what documentation style to use (32f-4). ________

RESEARCHING

7. Plan a "search strategy," but modify as necessary (32h). ________
8. Consult *Library of Congress Subject Headings* (32m). ________

137

SAMPLE SCHEDULE FOR A RESEARCH PAPER PROJECT *(continued)*

9. Start list of headings and keywords (32i, 33d-2). ________
10. Decide on the kinds of research needed:
    a. Print and/or electronic sources (32f, 32i, 32k through 32p, Chapter 33)? ________
    b. Online sources (32f, 32i, 32k through 32p, Chapter 33)? ________
    c. Field research (32g, 32q)? If yes, schedule tasks. ________
11. Master the concept of evaluating sources (32f-3, 33f) ________
12. Prepare to take notes from sources that prove useful (32c, 32j). ________
13 Do library research:
    a. Consult reference works: general (32k); specialized (32l).
    b. Consult book catalogue and books (32m). ________
    c. Consult periodicals (32n). ________
    d. Consult electronic sources: tapes, CD-ROMs, etc. (32f-3, 32k through 32p). ________
14. Consult online sources (Chapter 33). ________
15. Evaluate all sources before accepting them (32f-3, 33f). ________

WRITING

16. Draft a preliminary thesis statement (32r). ________
17. Outline, as required (32s). ________
18. Draft the paper (32t). ________
19. Use correct in-text (parenthetical) citations (34c through 34g). ________
20. Write the final thesis statement (32r). ________
21. Revise the paper (32t). ________
22. Compile the final bibliography/Works Cited/ References (34c through 34g). ________

Have I planned realistically for my completion date? If not, revise schedule.

32c Using a research log

A **research log** is like a diary. It becomes a record of your research process, especially your evolving thoughts about your work. Start a research log as soon as you get your assignment. Use a separate

Oct 19: Looked for "intelligence" in Library of Congress Subject Headings (LCSH) located in the reference collection. Figured LCSH was one book. Wrong. Four in alpha order, and each is huge and heavy. Found nothing. Ready to give up. Remembered to relax and let myself browse a little. Paid off. Found "intellect." Started going through the listing and writing down key words, especially ones marked with NT for "narrowed topic."

Nov 8: Ready to try online sources. In the computer lab, I used Netscape to start my search, and its home page lists search engines. I chose Yahoo because I have used it to look up sports scores. Searched for 15 minutes but found nothing on "multiple intelligences." Asked the reference librarian for advice. She said Yahoo is only for very general topics. For specific topics, she suggested AltaVista. In minutes I found tonnes of sites and sources. What a relief.

Excerpts from Lisa Laver's Research Log

notebook for the log to bring along wherever you conduct research, or on a laptop, create a new folder. Begin by entering the schedule (see 32b) you intend to follow.

Although much of your research log will never find its way into your research paper itself, what you write in it increases your efficiency. A well-kept log traces your line of reasoning as your project evolves, tells where you ended each work session, and suggests what your next steps should be. Since college and university students take several courses at once, keeping such a record means no wasted time retracing a search path or reconstrucing a thought.

A research log helps you "think on paper," especially when you use the critical thinking sequence of Chart 30 in section 5b. Writing in your log helps you discover insights that only the physical act of writing makes possible.

Excerpts from the research log shown above are by Lisa Laver, whose research paper about multiple intelligences appears in Chapter 35.

32d Transforming a research topic into a research question

1 Choosing and narrowing a topic for research writing

Instructors assign topics for research papers in various ways. Some assign the specific topic. Others assign a general subject area and expect you to narrow it to a topic that can be researched within the constraints of time and length imposed by the assignment. Still other instructors expect you to choose a topic on your own.

When you have free choice of a topic, always choose a topic worthy of research writing. Above all, the topic must give you full opportunity to demonstrate your ability to think critically (see Chapter 5), especially to use synthesis°. What if you develop what some students call a "research topic block"? First, know you can overcome it. Second, force yourself to stay calm. Only then can you think clearly. Next, force yourself to get started by using the suggestions presented in Chart 138. Also try the suggestions in Chart 15, found in Chapter 3. What if you have an assigned topic in a general subject area but you are not sure how to narrow the subject area into a topic appropriate for a research paper? Use the guidelines in Chart 139. Also, note the following story about a student doing research.

WAYS TO FIND IDEAS FOR RESEARCH 138

Before you settle on an idea, "test" it by using Chart 139.

- **Get ready.** Carry a pocket-sized notebook and a pencil or pen at all times. Ideas have a way of popping into your mind when you least expect them. Jot down your thought immediately to prevent its slipping away.
- **Think actively.** Use techniques for gathering ideas (see 2d through 2l).
- **Conquer writing block.** Look back at section 3a for practical suggestions. Avoid thinking about all the steps in a research project at once. Take it one step at a time, according to your research schedule (see 32c).
- **Browse through textbooks.** Pick a field that interests you and look over a textbook or two (look in the bookstore, borrow from a friend, see if any are on reserve at your library's reserve desk). Search for an area that catches your interest and read about it. ➜

138

WAYS TO FIND IDEAS FOR RESEARCH *(continued)*

- **Browse the Internet.** Start with the World Wide Web, a user-friendly resource with millions of sites. Brainstorm a short list of topics that interest you and do subject or keyword searches to see where they lead (see 33c).
- **Look over the *Library of Congress Subject Headings (LCSH)*.** The multivolume *LCSH* lists every single topic (and the call number of the books on each topic) covered by books copyrighted by the U.S. federal government. You can find it in the reference collection of any library (see 32i).
- **Browse general encyclopedias.** Topics range over many subjects, but the articles give only a general sense of each subject. They can be in book form, CD-ROM, or online. Each article is a beginning, but only that (see 32k).
- **Browse specialized encyclopedias.** Each focuses on a specific area (social science, history, philosophy, natural sciences, etc.), and its articles or chapters treat topics in some depth. Most selections mention names of major figures in the field, information that can be helpful in evaluating sources (see 32l).
- **Look through books.** Stroll in the open stacks, if your library has them. If your library has closed stacks, browse through your library's online book catalogue (see 32m).

139

CHOOSING A WORKABLE TOPIC FOR A RESEARCH PAPER

1. **Expect to consider various topics before making your final choice.** Consult Chart 138 for specific ways to find ideas. Avoid rushing; give yourself time to think. Keep your mind open to flashes of insight and to alternative ideas. Conversely, avoid allowing indecision to block you.
2. **Choose a topic about which sufficient appropriate sources are available.** If you cannot find enough useful sources—ones that relate directly to your topic and are credible—drop the topic. Make a preliminary evaluation of the sources you have found so far (32f-3, 33f), so that you do not waste time on an inappropriate topic.
3. **Narrow the topic sufficiently.** Avoid topics that are too broad, such as *communication* or even *nonverbal communication.* Conversely, avoid topics that are too narrow to allow a suitable mix of generalizations and specific details.

CHOOSING A WORKABLE TOPIC FOR A RESEARCH PAPER ***(continued)*** 139

4. **Choose a topic worth researching.** Trivial topics prevent you from doing what student researchers are expected to do—use critical thinking; investigate related ideas; summarize, analyze, and interpret those ideas; and synthesize complex, perhaps conflicting, concepts (see Chapter 5).
5. **Select a topic that interests you.** Know that your topic will be a companion for a while, sometimes most of a semester. Select a topic that arouses your interest and allows you the pleasure of satisfying your intellectual curiosity.
6. **Perhaps confer briefly with a professor in your field of interest.** Ask whether you have narrowed your topic sufficiently and productively. Also, ask for the names of the major books and authorities on your topic.

"Intelligence" was the general subject area assigned to Lisa Laver, the student whose research paper appears in Chapter 35. Her instructor required a paper of 1800 to 2000 words to be written in six weeks based on about a dozen sources. To get started, Laver borrowed from a friend the textbook *Introduction to Psychology*, which contained a chapter on intelligence. She browsed through it. That browsing helped Laver become familiar with the many general aspects of human intelligence. To narrow her search, Laver looked up the term *intelligence* in the *Library of Congress Subject Headings (LCSH).* She discovered several subdivisions under *intellect* (see section 32i for what she saw in the *LCSH*). She then went to specialized reference books for more information. A full narrative of Laver's research process opens Chapter 35. That narrative explains how Laver's research question became "Can there be only one way of describing human intelligence?" The flowchart in section 32e illustrates Laver's process of narrowing her topic.

Although each decision seems to flow smoothly from the one before, the process is rarely neat and tidy. It looks clear-cut only at the end of your thinking, searching, considering alternatives, and choosing. Most likely, you will back out of dead ends and make some sharp turns as you find a suitable path to your research question. To help clarify your thinking, try flowcharting your decision process as you go along.

2 Formulating a research question

Answering a **research question** is the main goal of a research process. To formulate a research question, begin by brainstorming a list of questions that come to mind concerning the topic. Write your brainstormed list in your research log (32c).

Some questions will naturally interest you more than others, so begin with one of those. If a question leads to a dead end, pursue another. When you find yourself accumulating answers—or in the case of unanswerable questions, accumulating viewpoints—you may be looking at a usable research question. Once you have an explicitly stated research question, you can streamline your research by taking notes only on those sources that help you answer your research question.

Stay flexible as you work. The results of your research may lead you to modify your research question slightly. Such revision is part of the moving ahead and circling back that characterizes research writing. When you have finished researching and notetaking based on your final research question, you have a starting place for formulating the preliminary thesis statement° for your research paper.

Suppose, for example, you want to write about homelessness. Here are some typical questions you might ask.

- Why can't a rich country like Canada eliminate homelessness?
- Who is homeless?
- How do people become homeless?
- Is it true that many families—not just adults—are homeless?
- Is the homelessness problem getting better or worse?
- What are we doing to solve the problem?
- What is it like to be homeless?

32e Determining the purpose and audience for your research paper

The question that guides your research process helps you determine whether the **purpose** of your paper is informative° or persuasive°. If your research question asks for facts, information, and explanation, your purpose is to inform. For example, "How have theories of intelligence changed over time?" requires an answer that calls for informative writing. If your research question asks for an informed opinion based on information and other evidence that leads to presenting various contrasting views, your purpose is to persuade. For example, "Why should people be aware of new theories about intelligence?" calls for persuasive writing. Your paper's purpose might shift during your research process, as Lisa Laver's did (see Chapter 35). Remain open-minded as you work, but never forget that you must determine your writing purpose before you get too far along.

The **audience** for your academic writing is primarily, but perhaps not exclusively, your instructor (see section 1c). Sometimes, the audience for a research paper includes other people—students in your class or perhaps specialists on your topic. Your sense of your readers' expertise on your topic helps you make decisions about content, specific details in explanations, and word choice.

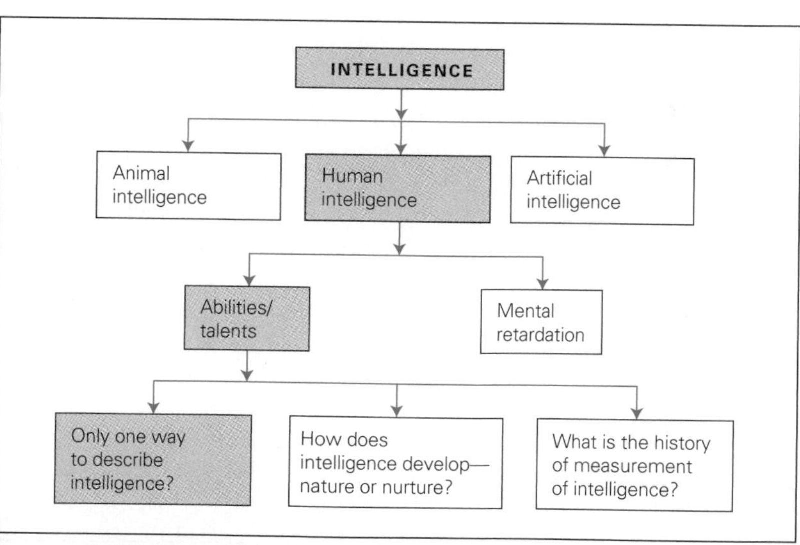

Flowchart of Lisa Laver's Narrowing Process

32f Preparing to undertake research

1 Taking practical steps to prepare

Experienced researchers use equipment that helps them work efficiently. Gather the materials listed in Chart 140 and keep them organized and ready for immediate use. Become familiar with the layout and resources of your college or university library (see section 32f-2 and Chart 141) Finally, develop your skills in online research (Chapter 33) to the point where you are comfortable with the process.

2 Learning how the library is organized

Almost all libraries in Canada and the United States are organized around the same principles for grouping information. But few college or university libraries have similar physical layouts, so be sure to take

BASIC EQUIPMENT FOR CONDUCTING RESEARCH 140

1. A copy of your assignment.
2. This handbook. Its guidelines can help you work efficiently as you evaluate sources, document your sources, and handle other tasks.
3. Your research log (see 32c).
4. Index cards for taking notes (unless you use a laptop). With different colours of index cards, you can colour code different categories of information. Also, with two sizes of cards, you can use one size for bibliographic data and the other for notes. Another coding strategy is to use pens with different-coloured ink or self-sticking dots of different colours.
5. Coins for the library's copy machines and printers.
6. Floppy disks (make sure the library allows downloading to disk).
7. A small stapler, paper clips, and rubber bands if you use index cards and other paper.
8. A separate book bag for you to check out books from the library. Librarians joke about researchers with wheelbarrows. You might need a backpack.

the time—no matter how busy you are—to walk around your library a few times until you know you will feel comfortable and confident there as soon as you walk in.

Some academic libraries provide in-class tours for English courses; some offer out-of-class, individual training sessions; and most offer informative, free flyers designed to help students learn the library layout and what resources the library offers on its shelves and from CD-ROMs and online services. As you learn about your library, be sure to know the answers to the questions in Chart 141.

CHECKLIST FOR TOURING A LIBRARY 141

1. Where is the **general reference** collection? (You cannot check out reference books, so plan time to use them in the library.)
2. Where is the **special reference** collection? (The same pointer applies as for general reference books.)
3. How does the **book catalogue** work?
4. What **periodical indexes** does the library have? (These are lists of articles in journals and magazines, grouped by subject areas.)
5. How and where are the library's collections of **journals and magazines** stored? Most libraries keep periodicals published in the past year on display for easy browsing; periodicals that are older may be kept on CD-ROMs, shelved in binders, or available online. Become adept at using the system in place at your library.
6. Are the **book and journal stacks** open (you can go to the shelves and browse) or closed (you must request each item by filling out a form to hand to library personnel)? If the latter, become familiar with procedures for asking for materials and picking them up when they are ready.
7. What, if anything, is stored on **microfilm** or **microfiche**? If you think you will use that material, take the time to learn how to use the machines.
8. Does the library have any **special collections** such as newspapers, local historical works, or government documents?
9. Does the library make available **access to the Internet**? If not, find out if such access is available in your college or university computer centre. Can you access the library's computerized systems from home or from your dormitory?

3 Preparing to evaluate sources

A **source** can be a book, an article, a World Wide Web page, a CD-ROM, a videotape, or any other form of communication. Sources are rarely of equal value. Your research can be ruined unless you apply the criteria for evaluating research material given in Chart 142. (See Charts 148 and 149 in Chapter 33 for cautions and criteria useful in evaluating online sources.) Do not rush. Evaluate each source with

CRITERIA FOR EVALUATING SOURCES FOR RESEARCH 142

1. **Is it authoritative?** A source can be assumed to be authoritative if it is mentioned repeatedly in respected references such as encyclopedias, textbooks, articles in academic journals, bibliographies, electronic indexes on CD-ROM, online databases, and conversations with experts. To determine whether an author's background qualifies him or her as an authority, consult a fairly current biographical reference book or CD-ROM (see also 32k). You might also look for the author's name in bibliographies at the end of journal articles on your topic.
2. **Is it reliable?** Material is considered reliable when it is published in academic journals (see 32n-2), by university presses, or by publishers that specialize in scholarly books. Material published in newspapers or general-readership magazines and by large commercial publishers may be reliable, but be sure to apply the other criteria in this chart especially carefully and to cross-check names and facts whenever possible. Material obtained online should also be evaluated with care (see Charts 148 and 149).
3. **Is it well known?** Check several sources. If the same information appears, it is probably reliable.
4. **Is it well supported?** Check that each source supports the given assertions or information with sufficient evidence (see 5h). If the material expresses the author's point of view but adds little evidence to back up that position, reject the source.
5. **Is its tone balanced?** Read a source using critical thinking (see 5a–5h). If the tone° (see 1d) is unbiased and the reasoning is logical, the source is probably balanced.
6. **Is it current?** Check that the information is up to date. A source's being current can be important because sometimes long-accepted information is replaced or modified by new research. Check indexes to journals or online databases to see if anything newer has come along.

a cold, critical eye. Apply the principles of critical reading and thinking (see Chapter 5).

As you evaluate sources, remember the difference between a **primary source** and a **secondary source.** Secondary sources report, describe, comment on, or analyze someone else's work. As a result, the information comes to you secondhand. It is influenced by the intermediary between you and that someone else. Consulting secondary sources gives you the opportunity to understand what scholars and other experts believe about your subject. Primary sources include original works, firsthand reports of observations and research, novels, poems, short stories, autobiographies, and diaries. When you use primary sources, no one comes between you and the author's own words. This fact adds to a source's reliability. Note also that you create a primary source yourself when you conduct primary research such as field research (see 32g), including observation, survey, interview, or scientific experiment.

4 Determining your documentation style

Documentation style refers to a specific system for providing information about each source you use in a research paper. Documentation styles vary among the disciplines. The **Modern Language Association (MLA)** has developed a style often used in English and other courses in the humanities (see 34c). The **American Psychological Association (APA)** has developed a style often used in the social sciences (see 34d). **Chicago Manual (CM)** style is used in some of the humanities and other disciplines (see 34e). The **Council of Biology Editors (CBE)** style is used in the life and physical sciences and in mathematics (see 34f). Many disciplines are starting to use **Columbia online style (COS)** to document online sources (34g).

Before you start searching for sources, know what documentation style you need to use. (If your assignment does not specify a documentation style, ask your instructor which to use.) Then, as you take notes on each source, you will know precisely what sorts of information your documentation style demands so you will write down the correct, full facts from the start.

32g Deciding whether to conduct field research

Field research is primary research. It involves going "into the field" to observe, survey, interview, or engage in other activities. Field research yields original data. It becomes a primary source°.

If you intend to do field research, plan time to gather the data or information you need as well as to analyze your gathered information and to synthesize (see sections 5b and 5f) it with any other material. Also, allow extra time if you think you might want to interview an expert on your topic, because many steps are needed. First, gain enough control of your topic to learn who the authorities are and whom you might be able to interview. Have your research question in clear focus so that you can ask worthwhile questions of an expert during the interview. For detailed information about conducting an interview, see 32q.

If you want to survey a group of people on an issue your topic involves, allow time to write, reflect on, and revise a questionnaire. Test the questionnaire on a few people you do not intend to survey so that you can revise any ineffective or ambiguous questions. For detailed information on creating a questionnaire, see Chart 159 in section 39a.

If you need to get tickets to an event such as a concert or play, plan ahead. Be ready to suggest alternative dates if you cannot get your first choice. If you need to visit a museum, do so right away so that you can go back again as needed.

To observe effectively, you must avoid inserting yourself into the situation. Try to remain objective so that you can see things clearly. A report from someone with a bias in one direction or another makes the material useless.

Field research often involves events that cannot be revisited, so expect to record detailed information during an observation or interview. You can decide later whether to use the information. If conditions make it impossible to take notes (for example, darkness in a performance hall), as soon as you have an opportunity, find a quiet place and write down notes as fully as you can.

Remember to document your sources for field research. Interviews and some performances involve the words of other people. For spoken words, use the guidelines in Chapter 31 for documenting quotations, paraphrases, and summaries. If your own work is included, mention that fact in your paper and list it in the Works Cited (MLA style) or References (APA style) at the end of your paper.

32h Using a search strategy for conducting research

A **search strategy** is an organized procedure that leads you step by step from general to specific sources. These sources help you answer your research question (see 32a). You can judge your search to be productive when it leads you to useful sources (see 32f) and allows you to compile a **working bibliography** (see 34b). A working bibliography is a list of possible sources that relate to your research question. Eventually, some of them may not be usable for your research paper, so a working bibliography needs to be about twice as long as the list of sources that you actually use in your finished research paper. If your assignment asks for a minimum of ten to twelve sources, your working bibliography should contain no fewer than twenty to twenty-five items.

Planning a strategy for your search is crucial. When you search for sources according to a plan, you can avoid feeling either at a loss for useful sources or overwhelmed by a seemingly limitless choice of sources. An effective search strategy structures your work so that you do not mistake activity for productivity. Spending days in the library to locate anything even remotely related to a topic is as fruitless as it is exhausting. No two research processes are exactly alike, so expect to be guided by your needs as you adapt the search strategies explained in this chapter. Know also that a search strategy is rarely as tidy as it seems when described. Real life is more messy—and more interesting—than a flowchart or plan.

One useful search strategy is the **expert method.** You start by reading or interviewing an expert in the field. Another is the **chaining method.** It uses reference books and bibliographies from current articles to link to additional sources. A third strategy is the **layering method.** It layers information gathered from general sources to increasingly specific sources. The layering method is especially useful for anyone researching in an unfamiliar field. Lisa Laver, whose research paper is shown in Chapter 35, started with the layering method and soon combined it with the chaining method.

Both the layering strategy and the chaining strategy move from general to specialized reference materials as they uncover the most credible authors and sources. Each time you locate a useful source (see 32f) on your topic, try to use it to find other sources to help you answer your research question.

Try to complete this phase of the research project as soon as possible after you get the assignment. Discovering early in the process which sources are available allows you time to find those that are hard to locate, to use interlibrary loan, and to wait for other people to return books that you want.

32i Using *LCSH* and compiling a list of subject headings and keywords

The *Library of Congress Subject Headings (LCSH)* is a multivolume catalogue available in the reference section of the library. It lists subject headings only; authors and titles are not included. Beginning a search strategy with the *LCSH* helps you see how a subject is broken down. It also guides you to narrow your topic (see 32d). The National Library of

Canada uses the Library of Congress system except for specifically Canadian subjects. If you are researching a Canadian topic, consult the National Library's *Canadian Subject Headings.*

Lisa Laver, whose research paper appears in Chapter 35, looked in the *LCSH* for *intelligence,* which led her to the heading *intellect.* She found the excerpt shown here. In addition to the subject headings, the *LCSH* gives other headings that can lead to additional sources. In the excerpt, *UF* indicates "used for"; *BT* indicates "broader topic"; *RT* indicates "related topic"; *SA* indicates "see also"; and *NT* indicates "narrower topic."

Intellect
[*BF431.BF433 (Psychology)*]
UF Human intelligence
Intelligence
Mind
BT Ability
Psychology
RT Knowledge, Theory of
Mental retardation
Thought and thinking
SA *subdivision* Intelligence levels *under classes of persons and ethnic groups*
NT Age and intelligence
Cognitive styles
Creation (Literary, artistic, etc.)
Heart beat and intelligence
Imagination
Logic
Memory
Mental efficiency
Motor ability and intelligence
Perception
Reason
Self-organizing systems
Social intelligence
Stupidity
Wisdom

Excerpt from *Library of Congress Subject Headings*

Researchers use the *LCSH* to find subject headings and keywords. **Subject headings** are categories describing the content of books and periodical articles. Libraries arrange their collections based on subject headings. **Keywords,** sometimes called *descriptors* or *identifiers,* are the main words that appear in the title, abstract, or full-text source. Keywords can be used to search most book catalogues, periodical indexes, CD-ROMs, and Web sites. When using keywords, chances are you will come up with a large or even overwhelming number of citations. Not all of what turns up will be relevant to your topic. For example, the topic "nuclear energy" is identified with various headings or keywords: *energy, nuclear; atomic energy; energy, atomic; nuclear power; power, nuclear;* and so on. You have to "break the code" to figure out what words identify the category you are seeking in each source. Expect to use a "try and see" approach. Do not get discouraged. If you are totally stumped, ask for help. Keep an ongoing list in your research log of subject headings and keywords that do and do not work for your topic. This practice helps you progress efficiently. (For using keywords for online searches, see 33d-2.)

32j Understanding how to take notes

Your research process includes taking notes as you consult sources. Notetaking has two phases. First, you write preliminary bibliography and summary cards (or create computer files) when you think you have located a useful source for your working bibliography. Second, you create content notes once you have moved from searching to reading your selected sources carefully.

Notetaking is a decision-making process. The criteria in Charts 142, 148, and 149 can help you decide if a particular source is worth notetaking—or photocopying, or printing out from the computer. Even if the source does not appear to be useful, note it in your research log with the title, author, date, and call number; Uniform Resource Locator (URL), or Internet address, for a Web page; or journal source. Add a message to yourself about why you rejected it. What seems useless one day might have potential if you revise the focus of your paper or slightly reshape your topic.

1 Taking preliminary notes

As you find usable sources, write bibliography cards for them (or type them into a computer file) immediately while you have each source in front of you (see 34b). For greatest efficiency, record the information exactly as it will be listed in your finished paper in the documentation style that your instructor has specified (see 32f-4). Doing this can save endless hours of grief later on, because when you compile the list of sources you have referred to in your paper, you have only to put the cards in alphabetical order and type directly from them, or alphabetize the items in the computer file. (See section 34b for pointers that can be useful when you record bibliographic information as you take notes.)

Also, each time you find a useful source, summarize it briefly at the bottom of its bibliography card according to the criteria for evaluating sources in Chart 142. (In a computer file, make sure to group each item with its own summary or to use a coding system that is convenient and foolproof.) An evaluation might read: "This article is by one of the most credible authors writing about my subject" or "Although this book is old, it has good background information and gives good definitions and interesting historical data" or "This article was published only two months ago—it appeared in a scholarly journal and answers my research question perfectly!" or "This Web page has pertinent information, but I must check whether the author is really an authority on the subject." Such evaluative statements can provide direction later for your reading and for further notetaking.

2 Taking content notes

In **content notes,** record information and ideas that relate specifically to your paper. Also, record any understanding you have gained from your reading, using a different colour ink for quotations (see 31c), paraphrases and summaries (see 31d and 31e), and your syntheses (see 5b–5f). If you do your notetaking on a computer, use different fonts, colours, or other means to distinguish these. Always try to sort major information from minor information as it relates to your topic.

Think of taking content notes as a survey process to find out what is available on a particular subject before you commit to extensive reading and notetaking. For this process, set aside more than two to three hours to search on a given subject, write information in your research log, and begin to create a listing of available useful materials on your topic. If you feel confident in the early stages of searching that your topic is going to work, begin to photocopy useful material and make preliminary notes as you go along. Use your bibliography to learn specific author names and sources. Notetaking helps you in three ways: first, to understand and narrow your topic; second, to find answers to your research question; and, third, to help you guard against plagiarism. The third matter is so important that Chapter 31 is devoted to **avoiding plagiarism** (see 31a) and to the skills of quoting (see 31c), paraphrasing (see 31d), and summarizing (see 31e). To plagiarize is to steal someone else's words and pass them off as your own. To avoid the risk of plagiarism, take notes so that you can always tell what is your own thinking and what belongs to a source. Using pens of different colours helps.

If you take notes by hand, use index cards for content notes. In contrast to pages in a notebook, cards provide flexibility for organizing and moving around material to use in writing your paper. Put a heading on each index card that shows a precise link to one of your bibliographic cards (see 34b). Include in your content notes the source's title and the number of the page or pages from which you are taking notes.

Never put notes from more than one source on the same index card. If your notes on a source require more than one index card, number the cards sequentially (if you need two cards, use "1 of 2" for the first card and "2 of 2" for the second card on that same source). If you take notes on more than one idea or topic from a particular source, start a new card for each new area of information. Also, describe the type of note on the card: quotation, paraphrase, or summary. A summary note card written by Lisa Laver, the student whose paper is in Chapter 35, is shown here.

Gray and Viens, "The theory of,"
p. 22

Summary
Evidence that intelligence
is pluralistic

Note Card Summarizing a Source

Urbina, 1330

A review of the 1921 and 1986 surveys shows that the definitions proposed have become considerably more sophisticated and suggests that, as the field of psychology has expanded, the views of experts on intelligence may have grown farther apart. The reader of the 1986 work is left with the clear impression that intelligence is such a multifaceted concept that no single quality can define it and no single task or series of tasks can capture it completely. Moreover, it is clear that in order to unravel the qualities that produce intelligent behavior one must look not only at individuals and their skills but also at the requirements of the systems in which people find themselves.

maybe quote this?

Photocopy of a Source, with Annotations

Photocopying or downloading from a CD-ROM or an online database can save you time. Having a copy of articles, book chapters, or Web pages in your research file can be useful. Such copies allow you to check your paraphrases and your quotations for accuracy. Having a copy of the source also allows you to make certain you have not inadvertently plagiarized (see 31a). Also, some instructors require that students submit copies of any material used for research. Be sure to label each photocopied or downloaded source with the author's name and other bibliographic information so you can prepare a bibliographic card (see 34b). Always underline the section that caught your eye and write why. Many students photocopy or download to create their content notes.

32k Using reference works

The reference book and CD-ROM collection in the library is the starting point for many research studies. This collection is also one of the best places to learn the search words (subject headings and keywords [see 32i]) that are so critical to successful research.

Most widely used reference works are available in electronic versions, usually CD-ROM. Many libraries give students on-site access to electronic-text dictionaries, thesauruses, encyclopedias, bibliographies, and atlases; some libraries allow off-site access to some resources. Online almanacs and statistical works are often kept more up-to-date than their print or CD-ROM counterparts. Check with a librarian to make sure you have used the best source in the best format for your subject.

General reference

The works in this collection are interdisciplinary; they provide basic summaries on vast amounts of information.

General Encyclopedias

General encyclopedia articles can help you get started but usually are not suitable as major sources for postsecondary-level papers. Articles in general encyclopedias such as the *Encyclopedia Britannica* summarize information about a wide variety of subjects. The articles can give you background information and authors' names. General encyclopedias are not the place to look for information on recent events or current research, although sometimes controversies in the field are summarized. Many articles end with a brief bibliography of major works on the subject, which may lead you to the authors' names and their most current works. To locate the information, start with the index volume, which will give you volume and page numbers related to your topic.

The letters *bib* at the end of an index listing mean that article contains a bibliography and so might be worth checking. If you cannot find what you are looking for, try alternative headings or keywords.

One-volume general encyclopedias, such as the *New Columbia Encyclopedia* or the *Random House Encyclopedia,* may cover subjects very briefly. For postsecondary-level work these sources are useful only for you to see whether a general subject area interests you enough for further research.

The Canadian Encyclopedia and *Colombo's Canadian References,* an encyclopedic dictionary, are important sources of information on Canadian topics.

Almanacs, Yearbooks, Fact Books

Almanacs—books such as *The Canadian Global Almanac* and *The World Almanac and Book of Facts*—briefly present a year's events and data in government, politics, sports, economics, demographics, and many other categories. *Facts on File* covers world events in a weekly digest and in an annual one-volume yearbook.

Sources of Canadian information include *Canada Year Book, Canadian Almanac and Directory,* and *Canadian News Facts.* The *Statistical Abstract of the United States* contains a wealth of data about the United States. *Demographic Yearbook* and the *United Nations Statistical Yearbook* carry worldwide data.

Atlases and Gazetteers

Atlases contain maps—and remember that seas and skies and even other planets have been mapped. Gazetteers and comprehensive atlases contain many kinds of geographic information: topography, climates, populations, migrations, natural resources, crops, and so on. Examples include *Canada Gazetteer Atlas, The Historical Atlas of Canada,* and *The National Atlas of Canada.*

Dictionaries

Dictionaries define words and terms (see Chapter 20). In addition to general dictionaries, specialized dictionaries exist in many academic disciplines to define words and phrases specific to a field (see 32l). Examples include *A Dictionary of Canadianisms on Historical Principles* and the various Canadian dictionaries. Many dictionaries are available online and on CD-ROM.

Biographical Reference Works

Biographical reference books give brief factual information about many famous people. They are good places to find dates and brief listings of major events or accomplishments in noted people's lives. (Do not confuse these works with full-length biographies or bestseller accounts about noted people.) Various *Who's Who* series, including *Canadian Who's Who*, cover noteworthy people. *Current Biography: Who's News and Why* is published monthly, with six-month and annual cumulative editions. The *Dictionary of Canadian Biography, Dictionary of American Biography,* and *Webster's Biographical Dictionary* are also widely available. These sources, as well as specialized biographical reference works on famous people in various fields, also list winners of the Nobel Prize and other major awards.

Because of the many different biographical sources, you may want to ask a librarian for assistance in locating biographical references.

Bibliographies

Bibliographies list books. *Books in Print* and *Canadian Books in Print* list all books that are available through their publishers and sometimes other sources in the United States and Canada. These multivolume works classify their entries by author name, title, and general subject headings, but they do not describe a book's content. The database *WorldCat*, available through FirstSearch, lists all the book holdings in most U.S. and some international libraries. It does not describe a book's contents, but it does list the subject headings assigned by librarians to categorize the subjects covered by the book.

The *Book Review Digest* and the *Canadian Book Review Annual* excerpt book reviews that have appeared in major newspapers and magazines. These excerpts of critics' opinions can help you evaluate a source (see 32f-3). These digests are published every year. The reviews appear in the volume that corresponds either to the year a book was published or to the one immediately following. The *Book Review Index* lists where reviews have appeared but does not carry the actual reviews. Other book reviews are available in specialized areas.

Consulting specialized bibliographies—ones that list many books on a particular subject—can be very helpful in your research process (see 32l). Annotated or critical bibliographies describe and evaluate the works that they list and are therefore especially useful.

32l Using specialized reference books

Specialized or subject encyclopedias, which provide more authoritative and specific information than general reference works, are usually appropriate for postsecondary-level research. As you work with the layering strategy (see 32h) in your search for sources, you will soon need to become more focused in your research. The specialized reference collection can assist you at this point. It is an area many students overlook in their preliminary searches. Specialized encyclopedias usually contain short summaries that introduce you to the controversies, the experts, and the keywords for searching that are specific to your topic. Be sure to look for authors' names in the article or in the bibliography so that you can begin to accumulate a list of credible authors. Those names become especially valuable as you search book and periodical catalogues, and if you perform an Internet search. Here are the titles of some of the more commonly used specialized materials categorized by subject area.

BUSINESS AND ECONOMICS

A Dictionary of Economics
Canadian Business Index
Encyclopedia of Advertising
Encyclopedia of Associations
Encyclopedia of Banking and Finance
Handbook of Modern Marketing
Survey of Economic and Social History in Canada

FINE ARTS

Crowell's Handbook of World Opera
Encyclopedia of Music in Canada
International Cyclopedia of Music and Musicians
New Grove Dictionary of Music and Musicians
Oxford Companion to Art

HISTORY

Dictionary of American Biography
Dictionary of Canadian Biography
Encyclopedia of American History
An Encyclopedia of World History
New Cambridge Modern History

LITERATURE

Cassell's Encyclopedia of World Literature
Dictionary of Literary Biography
A Dictionary of Literary Terms
Letters in Canada
Literary History of Canada
MLA International Bibliography of Books and Articles on the Modern Languages and Literature
Oxford Companion to American Literature

Oxford Companion to Canadian Literature
Oxford Companion to English Literature
A Reference Guide to English, American and Canadian Literature

Philosophy and Religion

Dictionary of the Bible
Eastern Definitions: A Short Encyclopedia of Religions of the Orient
Encyclopedia of Philosophy
Encyclopedia of Religion

Political Science

The Canadian Annual Review of Politics and Public Affairs
Foreign Affairs Bibliography
Political Handbook and Atlas of the World
Political Science Bibliographies

Science and Technology

Encyclopedia of Chemistry
Encyclopedia of Computer Science and Technology
Encyclopedia of Physics
Encyclopedia of the Biological Sciences
Larousse Encyclopedia of Animal Life
McGraw-Hill Encyclopedia of Science and Technology

Social Sciences

Canadian Education Index
Dictionary of Anthropology
Dictionary of Education
Encyclopedia of Psychology
International Encyclopedia of the Social Sciences

Film, Television, and Theatre

Canada on Stage: Canadian Theatre Review Yearbook
Film Canadiana
International Encyclopedia of Film
International Television Almanac
Oxford Companion to Canadian Theatre
Oxford Companion to the Theatre

✣ ALERTS: (1) Very specific one-volume works are not listed here. For example, under "social sciences" you would find the *Encyclopedia of Divorce, Encyclopedia of Aging,* and the *Encyclopedic Dictionary of Psychology.* (2) New specialized reference works are published throughout the year. Find the call number for your subject area and browse the collection to see what special references are available in your own library. ✤

32m Using a library's book catalogue

A library's online book catalogue can typically be accessed in four ways: by author, by title, by subject, and by keyword. To use the subject headings, you must use the correct words as search keys (see 32n-3). Usually, these are the ones listed in the *Library of Congress Subject Headings.* If you type in your heading only to have "nothing on this subject" appear on the computer screen, ask a reference librarian to help you, or try another keyword.

Many libraries are connected electronically to other libraries' catalogues, giving you access to the holdings of those libraries. The online TRACEit (formerly REFCATSS) and AMICUS systems, which link the catalogues of many university and other large libraries throughout Canada, are used for interlibrary loans. The Internet gives direct access to the catalogues of many large libraries worldwide. If you need materials not available in your own library, you may be able to find them by accessing these networks or other similar ones.

Each entry in the catalogue contains much useful information. Some libraries allow you to print out this information, and some even let you send the information to your e-mail account or download to a disk. Be sure to record the call number exactly as it appears, with all numbers, letters, and decimal points. The call number tells where the book is located in the stacks. If you are researching in a library with open stacks (you can go where books are shelved), the call number leads you to the area where all books on the same subject can be found. Being there can help you search for sources, even though some books might have been checked out and other books might be at the reserve desk. The call number is also crucial in a library with closed stacks, where you fill in a call slip, hand it in at the call desk, and wait for the book to arrive. If you fill in the wrong number or an incomplete number, your wait will be in vain. Write down all call number information on your preliminary bibliographic cards to make it easier to locate your books and periodicals. You can see an example of an online book catalogue keyword search on page 554.

Additional subject headings are found at the end of the catalogue entry. These are the additional subjects covered in the book you are investigating. They can be valuable hints for further searching. If your library has a card catalogue in drawers for all or part of its collection, you will find the same type of information, but you will not need keywords for access.

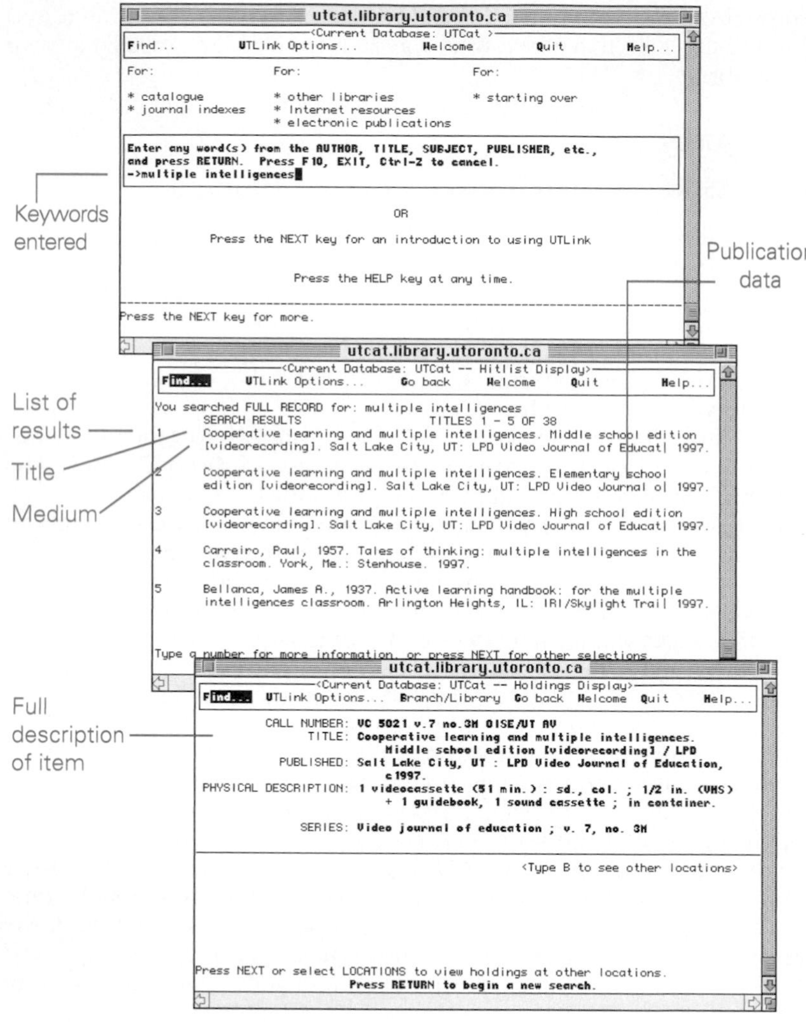

Online Book Catalogue Keyword Search

32n Using periodicals

Periodicals are magazines and journals published at set intervals during the year. The key to using periodicals is to consult **indexes to periodicals** first. The indexes allow articles published in periodicals to be searched by subject and author.

Indexes are updated frequently and packaged in a variety of ways. They are often available in all three of the following formats: print index, CD-ROM index, and online index.

✤ ALERT: Pick the correct index for your subject. If your library has only the print version of the best index for your subject, use it. The fact that an index is on a computer does not necessarily make it the best index. Choosing the wrong index will cause you to miss the best sources for your paper. ✤

1 Using general indexes to periodicals

General indexes list articles in magazines and newspapers. Headings and keywords on the same subject vary among indexes, so think of every possible way to look up the information you seek. Large libraries have many general indexes, among them these two major ones.

- The *New York Times Index* catalogues all articles that have been printed in this important and wide-ranging newspaper since 1851.
- The *Readers' Guide to Periodical Literature* is the most widely used index to over 100 magazines and journals for general (rather than specialized) readers. This index does not include scholarly journals, so its uses are often very limited for post-secondary-level research. It can be useful for getting a broad overview and for thinking of ways to narrow a subject. Lisa Laver used the *Readers' Guide* in the initial stages of working on her research paper, presented in Chapter 35.

For research in Canadian periodicals, see *A Bibliography of Canadian Bibliographies*, *A Guide to Basic Reference Materials for Canadian Libraries*, *Canadian Newspaper Index*, and *Canadian Periodical Index*.

2 Using specialized indexes to periodicals

Specialized indexes are much more helpful for most post-secondary-level research than are general indexes. Specialized indexes help a researcher become a specialist in a particular topic. These indexes list articles published in academic and professional periodicals. Many specialized indexes carry an abstract, or summary, of each listed article. Here is a sampling of specialized indexes:

Business and Economics

Business Periodicals Index
ABI-Inform

Humanities and Fine Arts

Art Index
Essay and General Literature Index
Humanities Index
MLA International Bibliography of Books and Articles in the Modern Languages and Literatures
Music Index

Medicine and Nursing

Cumulative Index of Nursing and Allied Health Literature (CINAHL)
Medline (online only)

Religion and History

Religion Index
Historical Abstracts

Social Science

Education Index
Psychological Abstracts
Social Science Index
PAIS (Public Affairs Information Service)

Science and Technology

General Science Index
Applied Science and Technology Index
Biological Abstracts
Biological and Agricultural Index

A search from *UnCover* (an online periodical index), which Lisa Laver, whose research paper appears in Chapter 35, used in her research on multiple intelligences is shown on page 557.

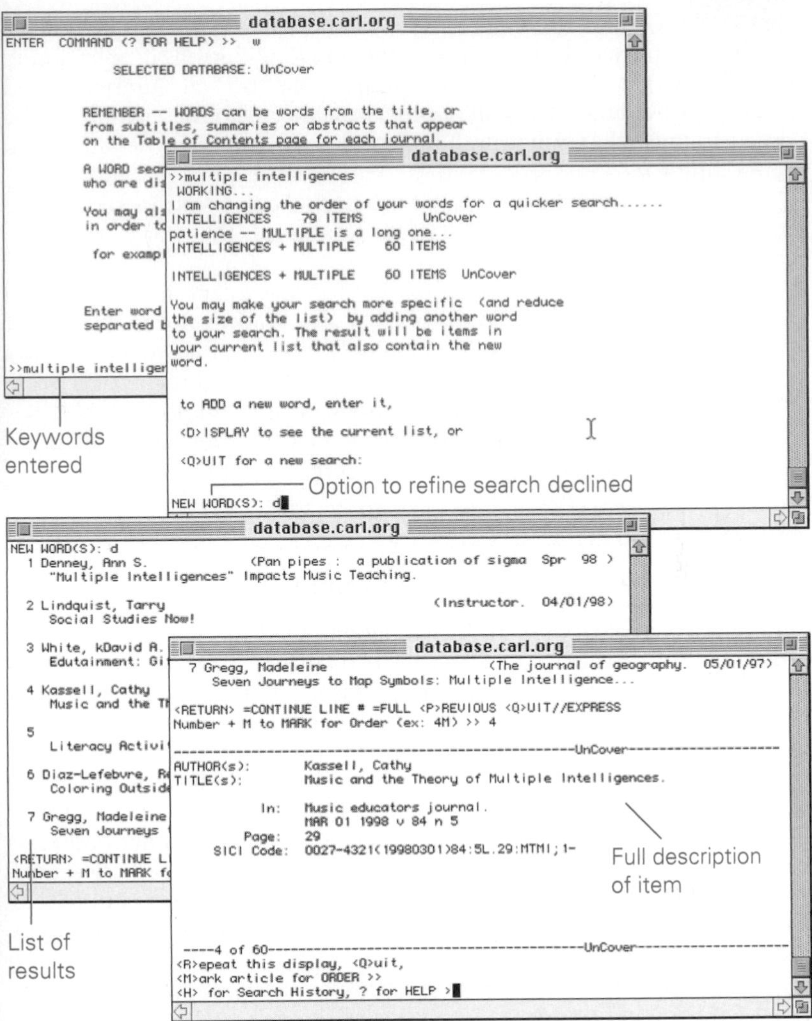

Results of a Search in a Periodical Index

3 Locating periodicals

Indexes help you locate specific articles on your topic. Once you have that listing, though, how do you get your hands on the article itself? Most libraries include periodicals in their online catalogues, although some provide a separate list for periodicals. In either case, what you need to search for is the periodical's name, not the name of the author who wrote the article or the article title itself. If your library subscribes to that periodical, you can then use the call number to find the library's holdings. The call number, together with the citation for the particular article that you found in the index, will get you the article you are looking for.

Few libraries subscribe to all the periodicals listed in specialized indexes. Most libraries have a list of the periodicals they carry; ask at the reference desk.

Although it may not be possible to locate every article you find listed in the indexes, the interlibrary loan system (generally free of charge) or document delivery (generally at a cost to the student) allows you to request articles from other locations. Through the World Wide Web, you can access the online catalogues of several other libraries as well (see Chapter 33). If your library has Internet access to other library collections, use it.

32o Using electronic databases

Electronic databases include bibliographic files of articles, reports, and—less often—books. Each item in these databases provides information about title, author, and publisher. If a database catalogues articles from scholarly journals, the entry might also provide an abstract (a summary) of the material. Once you locate an entry that seems promising for your research, however, you must then track down the source itself. Some databases, including ERIC and Newsbank, provide the full texts of cited articles on microfiche. With such a system, each citation contains an abstract as well as a catalogue number (for example, ERIC ED 139 580), which allows you to look up the microfiche—ask a librarian where this is stored—that contains the entire article. ERIC is also online.

Keywords are essential for searching electronic databases, some of which contain hundreds of millions of references. You must, therefore, choose which databases will be most helpful before you can begin to search. The Dialog system, one of the largest databases, is a compilation of over 200 smaller databases in the humanities, the social sciences, business, science and technology, medicine, economics, and current events. Restrict your search to one database at a time. A reference librarian can usually help you choose the databases best suited to your research, but first you must be able to provide a very specific description of it.

Electronic databases may be online (such as Dialog) or on CD-ROM. CD-ROM is cheaper and easier to use—generally an inexperienced user may follow simple on-screen instructions to search for entries. In contrast, online systems often must be used by trained librarians. Online databases require the library to pay a fee for the time used and the number of entries requested, and your library may pass the fee on to you when you use such a system. Find out whether the service is free for students and, if not, what the charge is. (Some charges are a dollar or more per entry.) Narrowing your search with keywords (see 33d) is important to avoid having to pay for a list of useless sources.

Many databases previously available only online have been transferred to CD-ROM. The most popular databases on the Dialog system (such as the business, psychology, and scientific databases) are available in this format. CD-ROM databases tend to be smaller than those online and are updated less frequently.

32p Using the government documents collection

Canadian government publications are available in astounding variety. Information is available on population figures, weather patterns, agriculture, national parks, education, welfare, and many other topics.

A federal government Web site known as the Canada Site <http://www.canada.gc.ca/> is an excellent starting point for online research into current Canadian government publications. It provides direct access to federal departments, boards, and agencies and their publications, as well as to public records, including parliamentary debates and hearings, and to databases. You can also follow its links to provincial and territorial government sites.

Government document collections are available in reference libraries throughout the country. Ask your reference librarian if your library contains government publications; if it doesn't, ask what library nearest you houses government documents. You can order government publications that are not available to you through your library system by consulting one of the following directories. Ask a reference librarian for the best way to locate the publications you need.

- *Government of Canada Publications: Quarterly Catalogue* ceased publication in 1992; it has been replaced by a cataloguing service available online. The *Weekly Checklist of Canadian Government Publications* <dsp-psd.pwgsc.gc.ca/dsp-psd/Checklist/lists-e.html> is kept up-to-date and is still available in print. You can also access it through the Canada Site.
- The *Canadian Research Index* (formerly the *Microlog Index*) is a monthly index of material selected from the publications

of every level of government in Canada, including parliamentary committees. Also indexed are government-sponsored scientific and technical research reports, statistical reports, and academic theses. Most citations include abstracts. The index is available in print, online <www.micromedia.on.ca/CIRC/CRIndex.htm>, and on CD-ROM. It is put out by a private publisher.

- Federal, provincial, and territorial governments and many of their departments issue catalogues of their publications. Current publications are usually available online
- Statistics Canada collects and analyzes a wide range of data. It publishes an annual *Canada Year Book* and releases daily statistical updates, available online, known as *The Daily* <www.statcan.ca/english/dai-quo/index.htm>. CANSIM II, Statistics Canada's online time-series database retrieval system, is updated continually and is accessible through <cansim2.statcan.ca/>. Statistics Canada maintains an online catalogue of its publications and library collection. You can access its Web site through the Canada Site.

32q Interviewing an expert

An expert can often offer valuable information, points of view concerning your topic, or advice. The faculty at your school or nearby schools have special expertise in many topics. Corporations and professional organizations can often suggest experts in many fields; a customer service department or public relations office is a good place to begin. Public officials are sometimes available for interviews. Many federal and provincial government offices have employees who specialize in providing information to the public. If your topic relates to an event that your family or friends experienced, they qualify as experts.

If you think you might want to interview other people, plan ahead. It takes time to set up appointments and fit your research needs into other people's schedules. You may not always be granted the interviews you seek, but many people remember their own experiences doing academic research and try to help. If you are following the layering strategy, conduct an interview only after you have solid control of your topic. The layering strategy leads you from the most general to the most specific sources on your topic, and you gradually become an expert on your research question. Wait to interview an expert until you have a solid foundation of knowledge about your topic and you know the specific focus your paper is going to take. Do not expect an interview with an expert to save you the work of researching your topic.

Know why you are interviewing the person and what you want to know. Ask questions that elicit information, not merely a "yes" or "no" answer. Be constructive; avoid language that shows bias or a hostile attitude. Keep in mind some basic rules to follow in arranging an interview:

1. Call for an appointment during office hours.
2. Ask permission to use a tape or video recorder at the time you make the appointment. In some cases, the person will refuse permission, for personal or legal reasons. Respect that reaction, and do not assume that the person is unfriendly or unhelpful.
3. Be on time for the interview, and dress appropriately.
4. If you are tape- or video-recording, know your equipment and have it ready when you arrive. Set it up and leave it running until the end of the interview. Avoid periodic checks to see if it is running.
5. Know why you are interviewing the person and what you want to know. Ask questions that elicit information, not merely a "yes" or "no" answer.
6. Be constructive; avoid language that conveys bias or a hostile attitude. At the same time, recognize that no one is ever completely unbiased and that an expert is entitled to his or her point of view. Consider that the person may have a vested interest in what you find out.
7. Go to the appointment prepared with specific questions written out in advance. The more you know about the subject already, the more specific your questions can be.
8. Pace the interview to the time you have been allotted. Be courteous and appreciative and be prepared to leave promptly at the end of your appointment time.
9. Ask permission to use quotations in your paper.
10. If an assistant set up the interview for you, thank that person when you leave.
11. Follow up an interview, no matter how short, with a brief thank-you note (e-mail isn't sufficient—send a handwritten note). A note is not just polite; it helps pave the way for the next student who might ask for an interview.
12. After the interview, allow yourself time to fill in any notes you didn't have time to finish. Write a bibliography entry, and on note cards summarize and evaluate your experience. An expert may have a slanted point of view in line with vested interests.

For details about creating and using questionnaires to gather research data, see section 39a.

32r Drafting a thesis statement for a research paper

Drafting a **thesis statement** for a research paper is the beginning of the transition between the research process and the writing process. A thesis statement in a research paper is like the thesis statement in any essay: It sets out the central theme (see 2n, especially Chart 12). Any paper must fulfil the promise of its thesis statement. Because readers expect unified material, the theme of the thesis must be sustained throughout a research paper.

Most researchers draft a **preliminary thesis statement** before or during their research process. They expect that they will revise the thesis somewhat after their research, because they know that the sources they will consult will enlarge their knowledge of a subject. Other researchers draft a thesis statement after the research process.

No matter when you draft your thesis statement, expect to write many alternatives. Your goal is to draft the thesis carefully so that it delivers the message you intend. In writing a **revised thesis statement,** take charge of your material. Reread your research log (see 32c). Reread your notes (see 32j). Look for categories of information. Rearrange your note cards into logical groupings. Begin to impose a structure on your material.

Remember that one of your major responsibilities in a research paper is to support the thesis. Be sure that the material you gathered during the research process offers effective support. If it does not, revise your thesis statement, conduct further research, or do both.

Lisa Laver, whose research paper appears in Chapter 35, drafted two different preliminary thesis statements before she composed one that worked well with her material.

FIRST PRELIMINARY THESIS STATEMENT There is more than one way of describing human intelligence. [Laver saw this as too close to her research question (Can there be only one way of describing intelligence?) and too broad to prepare readers for the main message of her paper.]

NEXT PRELIMINARY THESIS STATEMENT The intelligence quotient (IQ) tests used today do not measure all aspects of human intelligence. [Laver liked this better but rejected it because it put too much emphasis on IQ tests when her focus was the complexity of human intelligence.]

FINAL THESIS STATEMENT	Human intelligence results from a complex interaction of the riches of many abilities, only a few of which are taken into account by intelligence quotient (IQ) tests widely used today. [Laver felt this got closer to her message; she then checked it to make sure it also satisfied the criteria for a thesis statement listed in Chart 12 in section 2n.]

As you revise your thesis statement, go back to the research question that guided your research process (see 32a). Your **final thesis statement** should be one answer to the question. Here are examples of subjects narrowed to topics, focused into research questions, and then cast as thesis statements.

SUBJECT	*Rain Forests*
TOPIC	The importance of rain forests
RESEARCH QUESTION	What is the importance of rain forests?
THESIS STATEMENT INFORMATIVE	Rain forests provide the human race with many irreplaceable resources.
THESIS STATEMENT PERSUASIVE	Rain forests must be preserved because they offer the human race many irreplaceable resources.

SUBJECT	*Nonverbal Communication*
TOPIC	Personal space
RESEARCH QUESTION	How do standards for personal space differ among cultures?
THESIS STATEMENT INFORMATIVE	Everyone has expectations concerning the use of personal space, but accepted distances for that space are determined by each person's culture.
THESIS STATEMENT PERSUASIVE	To prevent intercultural misunderstandings, people must be aware of cultural differences in standards for personal space.

SUBJECT	*Smoking*
TOPIC	Curing nicotine addiction
RESEARCH QUESTION	Are new approaches being used to cure nicotine addiction?
THESIS STATEMENT INFORMATIVE	Some approaches to curing nicotine addiction are themselves addictive.
THESIS STATEMENT PERSUASIVE	Because some methods of curing addiction are themselves addictive, doctors should prescribe them with caution.

32s Outlining a research paper

Some instructors require an outline of a research paper. To begin organizing your material for an outline, you might write an **informal outline.** Group the subcategories in your material until you are ready to write a formal outline.

A **formal outline** should be in the form discussed in section 2p. Head it with the paper's thesis statement. You can use a **topic outline** (a format that requires words or phrases for each item) or a **sentence outline** (a format that requires full sentences for each item). Do not mix the two types. For a sentence outline of a student's research paper, see Chapter 35.

32t Drafting and revising a research paper

Drafting and revising a research paper have much in common with the writing processes for writing any type of paper (see Chapters 2 and 3). But more is demanded. You must demonstrate that you have followed the research steps in this chapter. You must demonstrate an understanding of the information you have located, and you must organize for effective presentation. Additionally, you must integrate sources into your writing without plagiarizing by properly using the techniques of quotation, paraphrase, and summary (see Chapter 31), and demonstrate that you have moved beyond summary to synthesize your various sources (see 5f). Also, you must use references correctly (see Chapters 31 and 34) to document your sources. So many special demands take extra time for drafting, thinking, redrafting, and rethinking.

Expect to write a number of drafts of your research paper. Successive drafts help you gain authority over the information that you have learned from your research. The **first draft** is your initial attempt to structure your notes into a unified whole. It is also a chance to discover new insights and fresh connections. Only the act of writing makes such discovery possible. A first draft is a rough draft. It is a prelude to later work at revising and polishing. Chart 143 suggests some alternative ways to write the first draft of a research paper.

Second and subsequent drafts result from reading your first draft critically and revising it. If at all possible, get some distance from your material by taking a break of a few days (or a few hours, if you are pressed for time). Then, reread your first draft and think how it can be improved. You might also ask friends or classmates to read it and react.

143

SUGGESTIONS FOR DRAFTING A RESEARCH PAPER

- Some researchers work with their notes in front of them. They use the organized piles made for drafting a thesis statement (see 32r) and for outlining (see 32s). They spread out each pile and work according to the categories of information that have emerged from their material. They proceed from one pile to the next. They expect this process to take time, but they are assured of a first draft that includes much of the results of their research.
- Some researchers gather all their information and then set it aside to write a **partial first draft,** a quickly written first pass at getting the material under control. Writing this way helps researchers get a broad view of the material. The second step is to go back and write a **complete first draft** with research notes at hand. The researchers go over their partial draft slowly to correct information, add material left out, and insert in-text references (see Chapter 34).
- Some researchers write their first draft quickly to get words down on paper when they feel "stuck" about what to say next. When they have a clear idea of how to proceed, they slow down and use their notes. These researchers draw on their experiences with gathering ideas (see 2d through 2j), shaping ideas (see 2k), getting started (see 3a), and drafting (see 3b).
- Some researchers use the computer's cut-and-paste function to move paragraphs and sentences around in the first draft. (If you do this, save a copy of each draft and partial draft, to refer to it in case you need it later.) Others cut up the pages on which they have printed or written their draft. If a new order suggests itself, they tape the paper together in its new form.

As you work, pay attention to any uneasy feelings you have that hint at the need to rethink or rework your material. Experienced writers expect to revise; they know that writing is really rewriting. Research papers are among the most demanding composing assignments, and most writers have to revise their drafts more than a few times. As you revise, consult Charts 16 and 17 in section 3c to remind yourself of general principles of writing. Also, consult the special revision checklist for a research paper, in Chart 144.

The **final draft** shows that you have revised well. It shows also that you have edited (see 3d) and proofread (see 3e) for correct grammar, spelling, and punctuation. No amount of careful research and good writing can make up for a sloppy manuscript. Strive to make the

REVISION CHECKLIST FOR A RESEARCH PAPER 144

If the answer to any question in the list is "no," revise your draft.

1. Does the introductory paragraph lead effectively into the material (see 4g)?
2. Are you fulfilling the promise of the thesis statement (see 32r)?
3. Do the ideas follow from one another?
4. Do you stay on the topic?
5. Have you answered the research question that underlies your paper?
6. Do you avoid writing irrelevant or insignificant information?
7. Do you avoid leaving gaps in information?
8. Have you integrated source material without plagiarizing (see 31a)?
9. Have you used quotations, paraphrases, and summaries well (see Chapter 31)?
10. Have you used parenthetical references correctly, and has each tied in with a source listed in the works cited (or references) list at the end of the paper (see Chapter 34)?
11. Have you used correct documentation forms (see Chapter 34)?
12. Does the concluding paragraph end the material effectively (see 4g)?

paper easy to read. If any page is messy with corrections, retype it. If your instructor accepts handwritten papers, use ruled white paper that has *not* been torn out of a spiral notebook. (If possible, type your work because it will present itself better.) Use black or blue ink and write very legibly.

For a case study of a student writing an MLA-style research paper, including a narrative of the writing process in action, and a sample student research paper, see Chapter 35. For a case study and a sample student research paper using APA style, see Chapter 36.

33 Successful Online Research

33a Knowing about online research

To go online means to connect to the Internet and, indirectly, to the many computers that are linked across that vast network. The Internet offers you immediate access to immense amounts of information: newspapers, periodicals, and books; official government documents; research reports in every field by academic, government, and private organizations and institutions; some music; some videos; and so forth.

Chapter 32 explains how to access electronic sources through your school library, via CD-ROMs or an Internet connection (see especially 32o). This chapter focuses on the sources available on one part of the Internet—the World Wide Web.

The **World Wide Web (WWW)** is the most convenient entry to the Internet. The **Internet** is a network of computers at universities, research centres, government facilities, and businesses around the world. The World Wide Web (often called the **Web**) is organized around pages (called *Web pages*) that are linked together. The main page, called the *home page*, acts as a table of contents to Web pages that are linked in *Web sites*. (*Web page* and *Web site* are often used interchangeably.) For a page to be on the Web, someone has to have created a Web site.

The openness of the Web is good news and bad. The good news is that anyone can have a "place in cyberspace." The bad news is that anyone, no matter what his or her motives or degree of reliability, can create a Web site. Although many Web sites are reliable, many others are untrustworthy, inaccurate and incomplete, advertisements-in-disguise, platforms for hate-mongers, or even material that has been stolen (i.e., plagiarized) from a printed or other Internet source. When an earlier draft of this chapter was being written, the Web had over fifteen million sites; it has far more today and it will have even more when you read this page. Online research demands a careful, critical eye.

The best advice is "online researcher beware." Be sure to evaluate online sources—whether on the Web or the Internet—using the criteria in Chart 148 in section 33f.

In spite of any disadvantages, researching online has several benefits. You can do some of your research from the comfort of your own desk. If your topic is very current, you may be able to augment library research with online research. For example, suppose that you are researching mad cow disease and want to know whether any cases have been discovered in Italy. The World Wide Web and other Internet sites will produce source material more current than you can find in the library. For quick access to many online sources that deal with writing and research, go to these Web sites and use their direct links:

www.pearsoned.ca/troyka

www.prenhall.com/english

As a researcher, you need to depend on your university or college library and other libraries as well as on the Internet. You can find many—but certainly not all—of the same resources online that you can find in a library. Some works are found only in libraries. This is especially true if a source dates from before 1980, when the Internet was becoming prominent. When you use the Web, always know that while sites may provide the most up-to-date information, many sites shut down suddenly. Therefore, always record all the information you need for citing an online source when you access that site in case it has shut down by the time you look for it again (see 31a-2 about creating a master documentation guide).

33b Searching the Web

Before you can search the Web for sites that will help you answer your research question, you must get on the Web. You do this by means of a browser, a program that gives you access to the Web and the search engines located there. Netscape Navigator and Microsoft Internet Explorer are two popular browsers. Once on the Web, you can search for sites by using a search engine or by typing an address into the locator box. Explorer is shown on page 569, and labelled to explain the main features of a browser.

Favorites (or Bookmarks): Lets you save a list of frequently visited sites

History (or Go Button): Shows names of the sites you've visited

Back: Takes you to the previous page visited

Locator box: Contains space for the URL (site address)

Prentice Hall Academic Catalog
Back Forward Stop Refresh Home AutoFill Print Mail
Address: http://vig.prenhall.com/
Prentice Hall
catalog search | customer support | find your PH rep | publish with us | technology solutions | join our mailing list | companion web sites
disciplinefinder | Please Select A Discipline
Favorites History Search Scrapbook Page Holder

Welcome to Prentice Hall

Welcome to prenhall.com, the official Web site of the world's leading publisher of academic and reference textbooks. On this site, you can answer all of your publishing needs from traditional texts to our extensive distance learning offerings.

The perfect course management solution—combining quality Pearson Education content with state-of-the-art Blackboard technology—is CourseCompass! CourseCompass is a dynamic, interactive online course management tool powered by Blackboard. This exciting product allows you to teach with market-leading Pearson Education content in an easy-to-use customizable format.

ph services
- Professor Review Copies
- Customer Support
- Subscribe to Mailing Lists

find out more about:
- Custom Publishing
- Distance Learning
- Longman ELT Connection
- Prentice Hall High School
- Professional Technical Reference
- Our Corporate Portal: Pearson.com

thelearningnetwork
- informIT- The destination for information technology

Internet zone

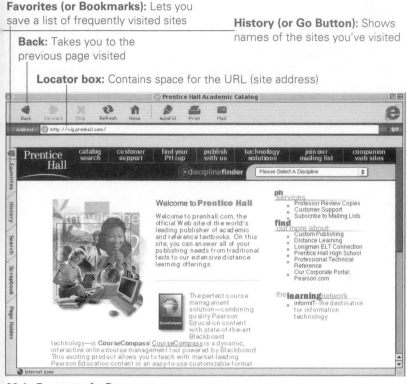

Main Features of a Browser

33c Designing a search strategy for online research

An online search strategy is very much like a library search strategy (see Chapter 32). You start with a broad subject and narrow it to become a suitable topic for an academic research paper. (For a discussion of what makes a suitable topic, consult 2c and 32d.)

1 Using URLs

A **URL** is a Universal Resource Locator. It is a specific "address" on the Internet. Sometimes you have a URL that you know will take you right to a site containing the information you need. To reach that site, type the URL into the locator box near the top of your screen.

2 Using search engines

Search engines are your best entry point for online research. A search engine lists Web sites related to whatever subject or keyword (33d) you have typed into its search box.

Some useful search engines

AltaVista	altavista.com
Excite	www.excite.com
Infoseek	guide.infoseek.com
Lycos	www.lycos.com
Maple Square	maplesquare.ca/
Northern Light	www.nlsearch.com
Yahoo!	www.yahoo.com

Some large U.S.-based search engines also have Canadian versions; Maple Square is a Canadian-based search engine. Some search engines look in Usenet (newsgroups) as well as the Web. Northern Light categorizes Web pages into custom folders—for example, by date.

Most search engines give you the choice of typing in keywords or navigating subject directories. In navigating a subject directory (see 33d-1), you let the search engine guide you in following a process that leads from the general to the specific. When you do a keyword search (see 33d-2), the search engine brings back every page that it can locate containing those keywords. To do efficient keyword searches, you need to choose your keywords carefully and be prepared to weed out rapidly many "hits" (or listings of sites containing your keywords) that are not relevant to your research. Be prepared to revise your search several times. It is always a good idea to explore different approaches: The major search engines are continually adding new capabilities to help their users customize their searches.

Once you finish a search using one search engine, you might want to try another. Amazingly, different search engines find somewhat—or even entirely—different lists of Web sites. This reflects the enormity of choices on the World Wide Web, in addition to the different ways search engines categorize material and carry out their searches. It is up to you to pick and choose from various search engines until you find useful sources.

Metasearch engines search other engines for you. In other words, instead of using one search engine to look for information, you can use a metasearch engine to run simultaneous searches on several search engines and subject directories. This lets you see at a glance which search engines returned the best results without having to search each one individually. Examples of metasearch engines are Ask Jeeves <www.ask.com>, Google <www.google.com>, and MetaCrawler <www.metacrawler.com>.

✤ PUNCTUATION ALERT: When you type or write a URL, surround it with angle brackets. For example, <www.pearsoned.ca/troyka> is the URL for this publisher's Companion Website related to this handbook. However, never use angle brackets when you type a URL in the search box near the top of your computer screen. ✤

33d Narrowing an online search for information

Not every hit will be what you are looking for. To help the search engine find the most relevant sites, therefore, you must narrow your search as much as possible. Subject directories and keyword searches are good ways to begin narrowing.

1 Using a subject directory

A subject directory lists categories of information with links to related Web sites. In this way, directories are similar to print subject catalogues like the *Library of Congress Subject Headings (LCSH)* (see 32i).

One useful directory is the Librarians' Index to the Internet (lii), an easy-to-use guide created by and for librarians. It groups topics both alphabetically and by category. To use this index, type its URL <lii.org/> in the search box. The first screen you see is the home page (shown at the top of page 572). Choose Browse *All* Subjects to get an alphabetical list of topics. Click on a subject that interests you, and you will get a list of Web pages. If you click on an item in the list, you will get a description of that Web page, along with subject headings you can copy down and use in your future research on that topic. In this way, subject directories let you browse subjects and start narrowing a topic.

Suppose, for example, that you are at the alphabetical list in the Librarians' Index, and you click to get to the subject *ballooning*. The new screen lists "Balloon Pages on the World Wide Web" as a link. Clicking on this title takes you to a Web page listing titles of hundreds of Web sites about ballooning (see the second screen shot on page 572). These titles are grouped into five categories: Round the World (1 title),

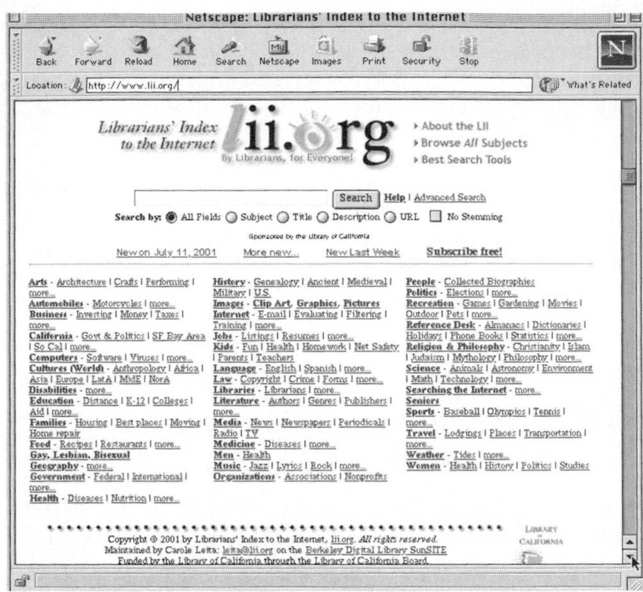

Librarians' Index to the Internet Home Page

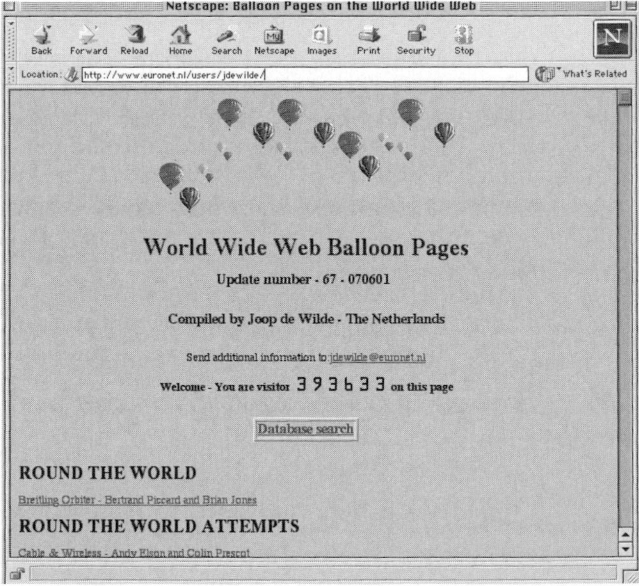

Ballooning Site Index Found Through Librarians' Index

Round the World Attempts (18), Gordon Bennett Race (11), New on This List (23), and Published Before (over 1000). Each title is a link to its Web site. Titles of sites range from "Calgary Balloon Club" to "The European Museum of Balloons and Airships" to "NOAA Profiler-Wind Profiles Data Display" and "Building a Hot Air Balloon." If you visit a few sites, you may get ideas for an aspect of ballooning to write about. Many pages are not in English; often, however, they include an English translation at the end.

Sometimes you can use a search engine as you would an online subject directory. Many search engines list categories such as Government, Health, News, Science, and so forth. Clicking on a general category will take you to lists of increasingly specific categories. Eventually, you will get a list of Web pages on the most specific subtopic you select. These search engines also allow you to click on a category and enter keywords for a search.

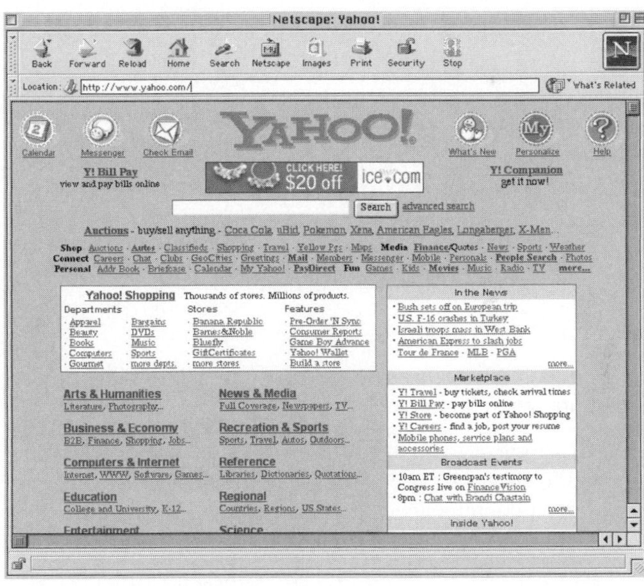

Yahoo! Search Page Allows Subject Directory or Keyword Searches

Some subject directories

AskERIC Virtual Library	ericir.syr.edu
Berkeley Digital Library SunSITE	sunsite.berkeley.edu/
Canadian Information by Subject	www.nlc-bnc.ca/caninfo/ecaninfo.htm
Carnegie Mellon Libraries Online Reference Tools	www.library.cmu.edu/bySubject/CS+ECE/lib/reftools.html
Comprehensive Subject Directories	tug.lib.uwaterloo.ca/internetsearch/subjectdirectories.html
Infomine	infomine.ucr.edu/
Internet Public Library	www.ipl.org
Internet Reference Tools	www2.library.dal.ca/subjects/internetref.htm
Librarians' Index to the Internet	www.lii.org
Library of Congress	lcweb.loc.gov
Search Canada	www.searchcanada.ca/
UBC Library Subject Guides	www.library.ubc.ca/home/subjects/
U of T Internet Resources, by Subject	www.utoronto.ca/subjects.html
Virtual Information Center	www.lib.berkeley.edu
Virtual Desk Reference	www.refdesk.com

EXERCISE 33-1

Consulting sections 33b through 33d-1, carry out the following activities to practise locating online sources.

1. Use a Web browser to find your university's or college's Web site. From here, find the library's Web page. What services does the site offer? Is the page itself searchable? Is online catalogue searching available?
2. Choose a subject that interests you and begin a search. Try using a subject directory to find subtopics for the subject, and type a keyword to limit the search. Did you find relevant Web pages? If not, alone or with a peer-response group, look for ways to improve your search. Try your search again. List at least eight sites that may have useful material for your search and write next to each why it may be helpful. Keep this list to use in Exercise 33-2.
3. Try using a metasearch engine to search for the same topic you used in question 2. What differences do you note in the kinds of hits you receive?

2 Conducting a keyword search

To conduct a keyword search, type your keywords in the search box on the opening page of the search engine. The engine scans Web pages for those words, and then lists sites that contain them. Keywords that consist of very general terms may appear on thousands of Web sites. If a search engine finds thousands of hits for your keywords, do not give up. Instead, use more specific keywords.

For example, a keyword search on *ballooning* yielded 242 hits, or links to Web sites containing that word. A search for the keywords *hot air ballooning* yielded 94 hits. By narrowing more and more, a search for the keywords *hot air ballooning Canada* yielded a manageable 3 hits. The screen shot below shows the beginning of a keyword search on the search engine Yahoo!

As you become more adept at using keywords, your searches will become more directed and less time consuming. Also, the further you are in the process of drafting a thesis statement, the more specific your searches will become. The keywords in your thesis statement are likely to be good keywords for searches. In addition, the opening screens of most search engines provide help in framing your keywords

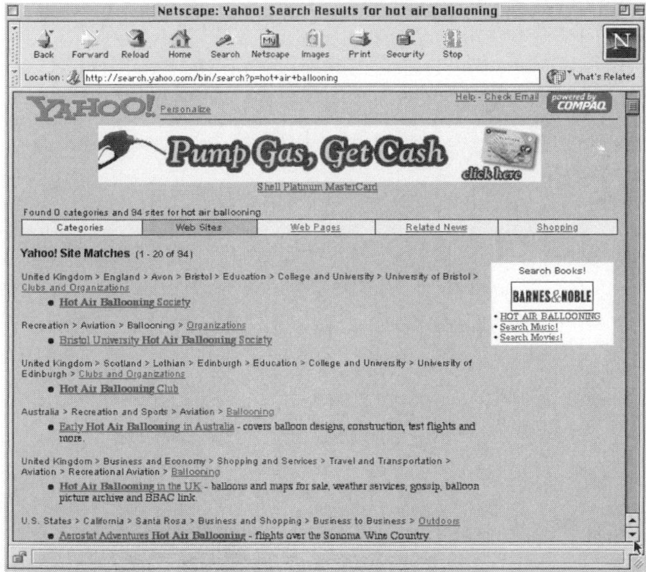

Beginning of a Keyword Search

(click on Help or the search tips feature). And, finally, most keyword search engines permit you to tailor very specific searches by means of Boolean operators, quotation marks, and truncation.

Boolean operators

Some search engines let you create keyword combinations that narrow and refine your search. These searches use **Boolean operators** (or **Boolean expressions**), the words AND, OR, and NOT, or symbols that represent these words. NEAR (which also may be represented by a symbol) is another operator used in structuring searches. Parentheses **( )** can also be used in the Boolean query box to group operators, much as they group mathematical functions. When you use Boolean operators between keywords, you are telling the search engine to list Web sites with your keyword specifications and ignore others.

Chart 145 explains Boolean operators and the operator NEAR in detail, using a keyword search on hot air ballooning as an example. Without Boolean operators, the keywords *hot air ballooning North America* would yield pages that include any of these words, and not necessarily in that order. Note the amount of weeding out that these operators allow.

Chart 145 is not meant to be all-inclusive. It is always a good idea to review the search engine's own search tips, as search engines differ in how they handle operators and formats. For example, some search engines are case sensitive, which means that they look for keywords with upper- and lower-case letters exactly as you type them. To be sure, click on the Help box or search tips feature of any search engine you use.

Quotation marks for online searches

You can also use quotation marks to narrow your search. Enclosing keywords in quotation marks directs the search engine to match the exact word order on a Web page. For example, a search on AltaVista for *"The World of Commercial Ballooning"* nets only about thirty hits, each containing the title or phrase *the world of commercial ballooning*. This is helpful when searching for a name, for example. If you search for *James Joyce* without using quotation marks, most engines would return pages containing *James* and *Joyce* anywhere in the document. A search using *"James Joyce"* would be likely to find Web sites about the Irish writer.

Truncation

Truncation allows you to look for sites by listing only the first few letters of a keyword. You can also tell the search engine to search

USING BOOLEAN OPERATORS AND *NEAR* 145

OPERATOR	FUNCTION
AND	Narrows the focus of your search because both keywords must be found. If you wanted to find information on only North American hot air ballooning you might try **hot air ballooning AND North America**.
NOT	Narrows a search by excluding texts containing the specified word or phrase. If you want to eliminate Canadian ballooning from your search, you might try **North America ballooning NOT Canada**. NOT must sometimes be used with another expression, such as AND. AltaVista, for example, does not accept North America ballooning NOT Canada. Instead, specify North America ballooning AND NOT Canada.
OR	Expands a search's parameters by including more than one keyword. If you want to expand your search to South American ballooning, you might try **hot air ballooning AND North America OR South America**. Pages mentioning North America and ballooning as well as those mentioning South America and ballooning would be returned.
NEAR	Indicates that the keywords may be found in close proximity to each other. If you want to localize your search on ballooning to a specific province you might try **hot air ballooning NEAR Saskatchewan**. The sources returned would contain references to ballooning *in* Saskatchewan, but might also include pages or sites that simply contain the words *hot air ballooning* and *Saskatchewan*. The result will depend on which search engine you are using.
( )	If you use more than two expressions, use parentheses to group them. For example, **(hot air ballooning AND history) AND (Alberta OR Saskatchewan)** would find documents about the history of hot air ballooning in Alberta or Saskatchewan (and both, if possible).

for variants of a keyword by using the wildcard symbol **(*)** in place of the word ending or some of the letters in the word. For example, a truncated search for *wom*n* (or, in some cases, *wom#n*) would return hits for *woman* and *women*. This is helpful when you do not want to exclude the plural form of a noun or when a term comes in varying forms, as in the *balloon/ballooning* example.

Be careful not to use broad truncations, or you will open up your search too much. *Auto**, for example, would return *automobile, automatic, automaton*, and so forth. In this instance, using OR might be more helpful, as in *automatic OR automation.*

Most search engines recognize the symbol (*) for truncation, but a few use specialized symbols such as ?, :, or +. As always, check the Help screen of whichever engine you use for specific details.

If your university or college offers a workshop in using search engines, take it. If it does not, you might try Cornell University's *Lost in Cyberspace? A Workshop on Internet Search Engines* at <www.library.cornell.edu/okuref/websearch.html>. Chart 146 offers additional help in using search engines.

USING SEARCH ENGINES FOR RESEARCH 146

1. Do a keyword search only when you have a very specific, narrow topic with unique keywords. If you enter a general topic, you may be overwhelmed with thousands of returns. If this happens, switch to a subject directory and try a new search, beginning with the general topic.
2. Although most search engines attempt to search as much of the Web as possible, different search engines give different results for the same search. Be prepared to use more than one search engine for your research.
3. Always check the Help screen or search tips feature of the search engine you use. As with the rest of the Web, search engines add or change features frequently.
4. Keep trying to narrow your keywords. This cannot be said often enough.
5. When you do a keyword search, use the capability that some search engines have to rank, or sort, results by relevance. (Check the Help screen or other feature that gives tips on advanced searches.) When results are returned in random order, the most important source may be last.
6. If possible, limit the date range of your search. The date of a Web site tells when it was added to the Web or revised. (Keep in mind, for documenting your sources, that this date may or may not be the same as the copyright date.)
7. When you find a useful site, go to the tool bar at the top of the screen and click on Bookmark (or Favorites) and then click on Add.

USING SEARCH ENGINES FOR RESEARCH (*continued*) 146

The bookmark function allows you to return to a good source easily by opening Bookmarks and double-clicking on the address.

8. Use the search history function to track the sites you visit, in case you want to revisit one you previously thought was not helpful. You can also move a site from History to Bookmark.

33e Avoiding plagiarism of online sources

Easy access to Web sources can be a tremendous help for research. But because Web publishing is unregulated, it creates special responsibilities for the online researcher. To avoid plagiarism in all of its forms, you must become a critical reader and researcher, and carefully follow the instructions in Chapter 31 of this handbook.

The special risks of plagiarism from online sources demand that you take some structured actions. Chart 147 tells how you can take precautions.

GUIDELINES FOR AVOIDING PLAGIARISM OF ONLINE SOURCES 147

- Print out immediately (or download to disk and print out later) whatever sources you find that relate to your topic. Do this once you have narrowed your research focus, so that you have fewer pages to keep track of.
- Make absolutely certain that each printout shows (1) the URL; (2) the name of the source; (3) the date you accessed the source and printed it out (or the date you downloaded the source to print out later).
- Check your required documentation style to see exactly what details you will need for listing the source in your final bibliography or in-text references.
- Note on the printout the exact reason you had for printing out that particular source. Underline or highlight sections you think will be useful to you—and indicate why.
- Never think your instructor will not know when you are plagiarizing. Today, many Web sites are available to reveal plagiarism in a →

GUIDELINES FOR AVOIDING PLAGIARISM OF ONLINE SOURCES (*continued*) 147

click. Most search all full and partial papers for sale on the Web or Internet, all material stored in every search engine, and academic sites that carry scholarly books, articles, and data. An instructor can see what words are plagiarized and from what sources.

- Check all the quotations, paraphrases, and summaries in your final research paper against the material you printed out.

33f Evaluating online sources

Since anyone can post anything on the Web, some sources you find may very well be plagiarized (see 31a). If you unintentionally use such a source, it nonetheless constitutes plagiarism on your part. Also, many sources on the Web have been written by people posing as experts, but giving false information. You are always accountable for the sources you choose. To evaluate a source, use the checklist in Chart 148. This checklist can help you do a general survey to separate the sources worth a closer look from those not likely to be reputable.

JUDGING THE RELIABILITY OF AN ONLINE SITE 148

RELIABLE SITES ARE FROM . . .	QUESTIONABLE SITES ARE FROM . . .
Educational, not-for-profit, or government organizations; Internet addresses ending in *.edu, .ac, .org, .gc, .gov.* These organizations should list their sources. If they do not, don't use them.	Commercial organizations advertising to sell a product (*.com*); Web sites that are advertisements or personal pages; junk mail. These sites may or may not list sources. If they do not, don't use them. If they do, check that they are legitimate, not a front for the commercial enterprise.

JUDGING THE RELIABILITY OF AN ONLINE SITE (*continued*) 148

RELIABLE SITES ARE FROM . . .	QUESTIONABLE SITES ARE FROM . . .
Expert authors. They have degrees or experience in their field that you can check. Do so by seeing if the names appear in other reliable sources, in bibliographies on your topic, or in reference books in your university or college library.	Anonymous authors or authors without identifiable credentials. The reader does not know about them or their motives for posting to the site. Chat rooms, Usenet discussion groups, bulletin boards, and similar networks are questionable for the same reasons.
Reliable print sources online. Online versions of major newspapers, magazines, journals, reports, etc., posted by the publisher or in a full-text index are just as reliable as the print versions.	Excerpts and quotations from newspapers, reports, and other publications that appear on a site that is not the publisher's official site may be edited in a biased or inaccurate manner. Sources may be incomplete and inaccurate.

Most sites also contain material that will help you assess their credibility, such as a bibliography or links to the author or editor. Sites that do not contain such verifying information should be discarded, however useful they may seem. It is far better to err on the side of caution than to use a plagiarized or unreliable source.

Chart 149 gives you details on applying the general guidelines above to individual online sources.

GUIDELINES FOR EVALUATING EACH ONLINE SOURCE

149

EVALUATING AUTHORITY

1. Is an author named? Are credentials listed for the author? (Look for an academic degree, an e-mail address at an academic or other institution, a credentials page, or a list of publications. The last part of an e-mail address can be informative: *.edu* and *.ac* are used in addresses at United States and United Kingdom educational sites, respectively; *.gc* and *.gov* are addresses at Canadian and United States government sites, respectively; and *.com* is an address at a commercial or business site. Be careful: Many universities and colleges now host student Web sites. In the United States, these sites often end with *.edu*, just as regular academic sites do.)
2. Is the author recognized as an authority in reputable print sources? Is the author cited in any bibliographies found in print sources?
3. Do you recognize the author as an authority from other research on your topic? Is the site cross-referenced to other credible and authoritative sites?

EVALUATING RELIABILITY

4. Do you detect evidence of bias or an unbalanced presentation from the language or layout of the information?
5. Ask: Why does the information exist? Who gains from it? Why was it written? Why was it put on the Internet?
6. Are you asked to take action of any kind? If yes, do not use the source unless you are sure the site is not trying to manipulate you toward bias. For example, the World Wildlife Federation can ask for contributions and still contain reliable information. Conversely, a hate group cannot be trusted as objective.
7. Is the material outdated? Is the date recent or was the last update recent?
8. Does the author give an e-mail address for questions or comments?

EVALUATING VALUE

9. Is the information well supported with evidence? Or do the authors express points of view without backing up their position with solid evidence?
10. Remember to read online sources using critical reading and reasoning (see Chapter 5). Is the tone unbiased and the reasoning logical?

For more help with evaluating online sources, try these Web sites:

Evaluating Internet Information (Industry Canada)
www.schoolnet.ca/ln-rb/e/training/eval.html

Evaluating Web Resources
www2.widener.edu/Wolfgram-Memorial-Library/webevaluation/webeval.htm

Thinking Critically about Discipline-Based World Wide Web Resources
www.library.ucla.edu/libraries/college/help/critical/discipline.htm

Thinking Critically about World Wide Web Resources
www.library.ucla.edu/libraries/college/help/critical/index.htm

EXERCISE 33-2

Select three of the Web sites you found for Exercise 33-1. Evaluate these sites by applying the guidelines in Charts 148 and 149. Write out your evaluation. Rank the sites according to their authority, reliability, and value, and explain your ranking.

34 MLA, APA, CM, CBE, and COS Documentation Styles

When you write a research paper, you must **document** your sources. If you do not, you are plagiarizing, which is a serious offence (see 31a). The purpose of documenting sources is to inform your reader of exactly which sources you have taken information from. To prepare to document, you want to create a working bibliography (see 34b), to keep careful track of all the sources on which you take notes. In your research paper itself, you are expected to use the style of documentation required by your instructor. Five major styles are presented in this chapter, including Columbia online style, which many disciplines now use to document electronic sources.

34a Understanding the concept of documentation

Documentation involves marking the exact place in a paper where source material has been used *and* presenting bibliographic information (for example, a book's author, title, year of publication, publisher, and any other required information). Although *bibliography* literally means "description of books," for your research projects you might find yourself compiling a list of sources that includes live interviews, CDs, online information, and films, as well as books and articles.

Bibliographic information is given in a **list of sources** at the end of the paper or in bibliographic notes. When a list of sources includes only the sources actually referred to in a paper, it is called *Works Cited* or *References.* A source list that includes all the works a writer looks at, not just those referred to in the paper, is called *Works Consulted, Bibliography,* or *References.*

Five documentation styles are featured in this chapter. Never mix documentation styles. The most frequently used style in the humanities was developed by the Modern Language Association (**MLA**). It is a **parenthetical citation system** that calls for a source name and page reference to be entered at each place you use a source in your paper. Also, at the end of your paper you include a Works Cited list giving full bibliographic details about each cited source. For full coverage of MLA documentation and editorial style, see the fifth edition of the *MLA Handbook for Writers of Research Papers* by Joseph Gibaldi (1999) and MLA guidelines for online sources at the MLA's Web site <www.mla.org/>. For coverage of MLA documentation in this handbook, see section 34c.

The documentation style used in most social sciences was developed by the American Psychological Association (**APA**). It is a parenthetical citation system that calls for a source name and a publication year, and sometimes a page reference, to be entered at each place you use a source in your paper. Also, at the end of your paper, you include a References list of all cited and "recoverable" sources. (A recoverable source is one that a reader can expect to be able to locate, like a book, and unlike a personal letter.) For full coverage of APA documentation and editorial style, see the fifth edition of the *Publication Manual of the American Psychological Association* (2001) and the Web site that supplements it: <www.apastyle.org>. For coverage of APA documentation in this handbook, see section 34d.

A third style, also used in the humanities and other disciplines, is described in the style manual of the University of Chicago Press and is known as Chicago Manual (**CM**) style. *The Chicago Manual of Style* describes two very different documentation systems: (1) a name-year parenthetical citation system and References list similar to APA's, and (2) a system using bibliographic notes containing full source information. (A separate list of references is usually unnecessary with bibliographic notes.) The University of Chicago Press maintains a Web site where you can find documentation and style FAQs: <www.press.uchicago.edu/Misc/Chicago/cmosfaq.html>. For full coverage of the CM bibliographic note style of documentation as described in the fourteenth edition of *The Chicago Manual of Style* (1993), see section 34e.

The Council of Science Editors—originally known as the Council of Biology Editors (**CBE**) publishes a manual of style and documentation guidelines for mathematics, the physical sciences, and the life sciences. It describes two documentation systems: (1) a **name-year parenthetical citation system** and References list, and (2) a **"numbered reference" system** using numbers in the paper to cite a source and a numbered References list giving full bibliographic details for each source. For coverage of CBE recommendations for citing sources in a paper and for a References list as described in the sixth edition of *Scientific Style and Format: The CBE Manual for Authors, Editors, and Publishers* (1994), see section 34f.

The Columbia Guide to Online Style (**COS**), developed by Janice R. Walker and Todd Taylor (1998) for Columbia University Press, includes new format elements unique to electronic sources. COS for the humanities is similar to MLA style, while COS for the sciences shares elements of APA style. The Columbia University Press Web site contains a brief outline of COS: <www.columbia.edu/cu/cup/cgos/>. For coverage of COS recommendations in this handbook, see section 34g. Be sure to check which documentation style your instructor prefers you to use for citing online sources.

Careful, responsible documentation is an academic obligation. To help you fulfil this obligation, this handbook presents MLA, APA, CM, CBE, and COS documentation guidelines in separate sections. Chart 150 gives a handy list of the places in this handbook where you can find information on each style.

34b Creating a working bibliography

To create a working bibliography, write out a bibliographic card for every source you take notes on. (You may prefer to print out this information, send it to your e-mail account, or download it to a disk, if your library allows. See 32j-1 and 32m.) Include all the information you need to fulfil the requirements of the documentation style you are using. For each library source, record the call number, being careful to copy it exactly. If you conduct research at more than one library, also note the library where you found each source.

Magazines and journals may not have call numbers. Record the exact title of the periodical and article, the date of the issue, the volume and issue numbers, and the pages on which the article appears.

For an online source, record the URL (the Uniform Resource Locator, or the online address), being careful to copy it exactly. Also, record any date related to the source: the most recent update, the date it was originally made available, and so forth. Most importantly, write down the date on which you access and download the material. If you take notes directly from the screen, use the date on which you take notes. This information is required in all documentation styles.

When the time comes to compile bibliographic information for your research paper, arrange your bibliographic cards or sort the items in your computer file in the order required by your documentation style (for example, in alphabetical order for an MLA-style Works Cited list). The bibliographic cards shown on page 588 are for two sources cited in the research paper in Chapter 35.

✤ ALERT: In documentation of the sources you use, MLA, APA, and Chicago Manual styles recommend that you underline wherever the

WHERE TO FIND THE MLA, APA, CM, CBE, AND COS INFORMATION YOU NEED 150

MLA STYLE: *SECTION 34C*

- Parenthetical citations—section 34c-1
- Guidelines for compiling an MLA-style Works Cited list (Chart 151)—section 34c-2
- Directory of MLA Works Cited list models—section 34c-3
- Content or other notes with MLA's parenthetical documentation—section 34c-4

APA STYLE: *SECTION 34D*

- Parenthetical citations—section 34d-1
- Guidelines for compiling an APA-style References list (Chart 152)—section 34d-2
- Directory of APA References list models—section 34d-3
- Abstracts and notes—section 34d-4

CM (CHICAGO MANUAL) STYLE: *SECTION 34E*

- Guidelines for compiling CM-style bibliographic notes (Chart 153)—section 34e-1
- Directory of CM-style bibliographic notes and References models—section 34e-2

CBE (COUNCIL OF BIOLOGY EDITORS) STYLE: *SECTION 34F*

- Guidelines for compiling a CBE-style References list (Chart 154)—section 34f-1
- Directory of CBE-style References list models—section 34f-2

COS (COLUMBIA ONLINE STYLE): *SECTION 34G*

- Parenthetical citations—section 34g-1
- Guidelines for compiling a COS Works Cited list (Chart 155)—section 34g-2
- Directory of COS bibliographic notes models—section 34g-3

rules call for italics. CBE style uses neither underlining nor italics; Columbia online style uses italics in these cases, reserving underlining for hypertext links. ✤

For an overview of this handbook's advice on assembling bibliographic information at various stages in your research, review sections 31a, 32a-2, 32h, 32j, and 33e and Chart 147.

153-G
Gardner, Howard
Frames of Mind: The Theory of Multiple Intelligences
New York: Basic Books, 1993.

http://www.apa.org/monitor/neuralb.html
Azar, Beth
Working out builds the mind's muscles.
APA Monitor, July 1996.
Access date: July 18, 1996.

34c Using MLA-style documentation

In Modern Language Association (MLA) documentation, you are expected to document any source that you quote, paraphrase, or summarize with a two-part system.

1. Within the body of the paper, use in-text citations, as described in 34c-1.
2. At the end of the paper, provide a list of sources titled Works Cited; see 34c-2 and 34c-3.

(For information about using notes for additional content or for extensive citations of sources when you are using MLA-style parenthetical citations, see 34c-4.)

1 Citing sources in the body of a paper in MLA style

For most in-text citations, wherever you use ideas or information you have found in a source, you give a name or a title (whichever is the first information in the source's entry in the Works Cited list) to identify the source and page numbers to show the exact location in the source of the material you are using. In your sentences that set the context for your use of source material, try to include author names and,

when relevant, credentials of authors who are authorities. In such cases, the only part of a citation to put in parentheses is the page number(s). If you cannot incorporate author names into your sentences, give them as part of the parenthetical citation. In a parenthetical citation, use one space between an author name (or title) and page number; do not use a comma or other punctuation between name and page number.

✤ MLA FORMAT ALERT: Position a parenthetical citation at the end of the material it refers to, preferably at the end of a sentence, if that is not too far away from the material. At the end of a sentence, place a parenthetical reference before the sentence's end punctuation. ✤

The examples in this section show how to handle various parenthetical citations in the body of your paper. Remember, however, that you can usually integrate the names and titles of sources into your sentences.

1. Citing a Paraphrased or Summarized Source—MLA

Desmond Morris notes that people from the Mediterranean prefer an elbow-to-shoulder distance from each other (131). [Author name cited in text; page number cited in parentheses.]

In Manwatching: A Field Guide to Human Behavior, zoologist Desmond Morris notes that people from the Mediterranean prefer an elbow-to-shoulder distance from each other (131). [Title of source, author name, and author credentials cited in text; page number cited in parentheses. Note that in MLA style, unlike APA and CM styles, the underline does not extend beneath the end punctuation. See 34d-3 and 34e-2.]

On the other hand, people from the Mediterranean prefer an elbow-to-shoulder distance from each other (Morris 131). [Author name and page number cited in parentheses.]

2. Citing the Source of a Short Quotation—MLA

Hall observes that "if you are interested in something, your pupils dilate; if I say something you don't like, they tend to contract" (47), thus suggesting why in some cultures people stand close to each other when they speak. Personal space "moves with us," according to Fisher, Bell, and Baum, "expanding and contracting according to the situation in which we find ourselves" (149).

✤ MLA FORMAT ALERT: When a quotation is no longer than four handwritten or typed lines, enclose the quoted words in quotation marks to distinguish them from your own words in the sentence. Place the parentheses after the closing quotation mark but before sentence-ending punctuation. If a quotation ends in an exclamation point or a question mark, however, put that punctuation mark before the closing quotation mark, put the parenthetical citation next, and then put a period after the parenthetical citation. ✤

Coles asks, "What binds together a Mormon banker in Utah with his brother, or other coreligionists in Illinois or Massachusetts?" (2).

3. Citing the Source of a Long Quotation—MLA

Robert Sommer, an environmental psychologist, uses literary and personal analogies to describe personal space:

> Like the porcupines in Schopenhauer's fable, people like to be close enough to obtain warmth and comradeship but far enough away to avoid pricking one another. Personal space...has been likened to a snail shell, a soap bubble, an aura, and "breathing room." (26)

✤ MLA FORMAT ALERT: When a quotation is longer than four handwritten or typed lines, do not put quotation marks around the quoted words. Instead, set the quoted words off from your own words by indenting each line of the quotation. In a typed paper, use a 10-space indent for each line of a quotation longer than four lines. If you are handwriting or using a computer, indent each line of the quotation one inch (about 2.5 cm). Put one space after the last punctuation mark of the quotation, and then put in the parenthetical citation. For other examples of long quotations, of prose, and of poetry, see Lisa Laver's research paper in Chapter 35. ✤

4. Citing One Author—MLA

Give an author's name as it appears on the source: for a book, the title page; for an article, directly before the title or at the end of the article. Many nonprint sources also name an author: for a CD, cassette tape, or software, for example, check the printed sleeve or cover. For an online source, identify an author as he or she is identified online.

Males in Germany and the United States stand farther apart and touch less when they talk to other males than when they talk to females (Shuter 305).

5. Citing Two or Three Authors—MLA

Give the names in the order they have in the source. Spell out *and*. For three authors, use commas to separate the authors' names.

```
As children get older, they become more aware of standards for
personal space (Worchel and Cooper 536).
```

```
Personal space gets larger or smaller depending on the circumstances
of the social interaction (Fisher, Bell, and Baum 149).
```

6. Citing More than Three Authors—MLA

With three or more authors, you can name them all or use the first author's name only, followed by *et al.*, either in a parenthetical reference or in your sentence. Do not underline *et al.* No period follows *et*, but do use a period after *al.*

✤ USAGE ALERT: The abbreviation *et al.* stands for "and others"; when an author's name followed by *et al.* is a subject, use a plural verb. ✤

```
Fisher et al. have found that personal space gets larger or smaller
depending on the circumstances of the social interaction (158).
```

```
Personal space gets larger or smaller depending on the
circumstances of the social interaction (Fisher et al. 158).
```

7. Citing More than One Source by an Author—MLA

When you use two or more sources by an author, include the relevant title in each citation. In parenthetical citations, use a shortened version of the title. For example, in a paper using as sources Edward T. Hall's *The Hidden Dimension* and "Learning the Arabs' Silent Language," parenthetical citations use *Hidden* and "Learning." Shorten the titles as much as possible, keeping them unambiguous to readers and starting them with the word by which you alphabetize the works in Works Cited. Separate the author's name and the title with a comma, but do not use punctuation between the title and page number.

```
Although most people are unaware that interpersonal distances exist
and contribute to people's reactions to one another (Hall, Hidden
109), Arabic males seem to understand the practicality of close
conversational distances (Hall, "Learning" 41).
```

When you incorporate the title into your own sentences, you can omit a subtitle, but do not shorten it more than that.

8. Citing Two or More Authors with the Same Last Name—MLA

Use each author's first and last name in each citation, whether in your sentences or in parenthetical citations.

According to British zoologist Desmond Morris, conversational distances vary between people from different countries (131). If a North American backs away from an Arab, the North American is considered cold, the Arab pushy (Charles G. Morris 516).

9. Citing a Work with a Group or Corporate Author—MLA

When a corporation or other group is named as the author of a source you want to cite, use the corporate name just as you would an individual's name.

In a five-year study, the Canadian Institute of Child Health reported that these tests are usually unreliable (11).

A five-year study shows that these tests are usually unreliable (Canadian Institute of Child Health 11).

10. Citing a Work by Title—MLA

If no author is named, use the title in citations. In your own sentences, use the full main title and omit a subtitle, if any. For parenthetical citations, shorten the title as much as possible (making sure the shortened version refers unambiguously to the correct source), and always make the first word the one by which you alphabetize it. The following citation is to an article fully titled "Are You a Day or Night Person?"

The "morning lark" and "night owl" connotations typically are used to categorize the human extremes ("Are You" 11).

11. Citing a Multivolume Work—MLA

When you cite more than one volume of a multivolume work, include the relevant volume number in each citation. (In the Works Cited list, list the multivolume work once and give the total number of volumes; see item 9 in the Works Cited examples in 34c-3). Give the volume number first, followed by a colon and one space, followed by the page number(s).

By 1900, the Amazon forest dwellers had been exposed to these viruses (Rand 3: 202).

Rand believes that forest dwellers in Borneo escaped illness from retroviruses until the 1960s (4: 518-19).

12. Citing Material from a Novel, Play, or Poem—MLA

When you cite material from literary works, part, chapter, act, scene, canto, stanza, or line numbers usually help readers trying to locate what you refer to more than page numbers do. Unless your instructor tells you not to, use arabic numerals for these references, even if the literary work uses roman numerals.

For novels that use them, give part and/or chapter numbers after page numbers. Use a semicolon after the page number but a comma to separate a part from a chapter.

Flannery O'Connor describes one character in The Violent Bear It Away as "divided in two—a violent and a rational self" (139; pt. 2, ch. 6).

For plays that use them, give act, scene, and/or line numbers. Use periods between these numbers.

Among the most quoted of Shakespeare's lines is Hamlet's soliloquy beginning "To be, or not to be: that is the question" (3.1.56).

For poems and plays that use them, give canto, stanza, and/or line numbers. Use periods between these numbers.

In "To Autumn," Keats's most melancholy image occurs in the lines "Then in a wailful choir the small gnats mourn / Among the river swallows" (3.27-28).

✤ MLA ABBREVIATION ALERT: The *MLA Handbook* advises spelling out the word *line* (or *lines*) the first time you cite a line reference because the abbreviation for line (l., plural ll.) can so easily be misread as the numeral 1. After the first citation, you can omit the word. ✤

13. Citing a Work in an Anthology or Other Collection—MLA

You may want to cite a work you have read in a book that contains many works by various authors and that was compiled, written, or edited by someone other than the person you are citing. For example, suppose you want to cite "When in Rome" by Mari Evans, which you have read in a literature text by Pamela Annas and Robert Rosen. Use Evans's name and the title of her work in the in-text citation and as the first block of information for the entry in the Works Cited list (see also item 10 in 34c-3).

In "When in Rome," Mari Evans uses parentheses to enclose lines expressing the houseworker's thoughts as her employer offers lunch, as in the first stanza's "(an egg / or soup / there ain't no meat)" (688-89).

14. Citing an Indirect Source—MLA

When you want to quote words that you found quoted in someone else's work, put the name of the person whose words you are quoting into your own sentence. Indicate the work where you found the quotation either in your sentence or in a parenthetical citation beginning with "qtd. in."

✤ RESEARCH ALERT: When it is possible to do so, find the primary source for words that you want to quote rather than taking a quotation from a secondary source.

```
Martin Scorsese acknowledges the link between himself and his
films: "I realize that all my life, I've been an outsider. I
splatter bits of myself all over the screen" (qtd. in Giannetti and
Eyman 397).
```

```
Giannetti and Eyman quote Martin Scorsese as acknowledging the link
between himself and his films: "I realize that all my life, I've
been an outsider. I splatter bits of myself all over the screen"
(397).
```
✤

15. Citing Two or More Sources in One Reference—MLA

If more than one source has contributed to an idea, opinion, or fact in your paper, acknowledge all of them. In a parenthetical citation, separate each block of information with a semicolon followed by one space.

```
Once researchers agreed that these cultural "distance zones"
existed, their next step was to try to measure or define them (Hall
110-20; Henley 32-33; Fisher, Bell, and Baum 153).
```

Because long parenthetical citations can disturb the flow of your paper, consider using an endnote or footnote for citing multiple sources; see 34c-4.

16. Citing an Entire Work—MLA

References to an entire work usually fit best into your own sentences.

```
In The Clockwork Sparrow, Sue Binkley analyzes studies of circadian
rhythms undertaken between 1967 and 1989.
```

17. Citing an Electronic Source with a Name or Title and Page Numbers—MLA

The principles that govern in-text citations of electronic sources are exactly the same as the ones that apply to books, articles, letters, interviews, or any other source you get information from on paper or in person. You put in your own sentences or in parenthetical references enough information for a reader to be able to locate full information about the source in the Works Cited list.

When an electronically accessed source identifies its author, use the author's name for in-text citations. If an electronic source does not name the author, use its title for in-text citations and for the first block of information in that source's Works Cited entry. (See item 10 in this

section for an example of a work cited by its title and for advice about shortening a title for an in-text citation.)

When an electronic source has fixed page numbers, use them exactly as you would the page numbers of a print source.

18. Citing an Electronic Source that Numbers Paragraphs—MLA

When an electronic source has numbered paragraphs (instead of page numbers), use them for in-text references as you would page numbers, with two differences: (1) Use a comma followed by one space after the name (or title), and (2) use the abbreviation *par.* for a reference to one paragraph or *pars.* for a reference to more than one paragraph, followed by the numbers of the paragraphs you are citing.

```
Artists seem to be haunted by the fear that psychoanalysts might
destroy creativity while it reconstructs personality (Francis,
pars. 22-25).
```

19. Citing an Electronic Source Without Page or Paragraph Numbers—MLA

Many online sources do not number pages or paragraphs. Here is an example from an online source without page numbers or paragraph numbers.

```
From March to April in 1994, violations of this important
disclosure regulation increased 123 percent (Pessan).
```

2 Compiling an MLA-style Works Cited List

In MLA documentation, in-text citations must be accompanied by a list of all the sources referred to in your paper. In a Works Cited list, include only the sources from which you quote or paraphrase or summarize. Do not include sources that you have consulted but do not refer to in the paper unless your instructor asks for a Works Consulted list (which follows the same format as a Works Cited list). Chart 151 gives general information about a Works Cited list. It includes information about MLA editorial style and a documentation model—of a source found on the World Wide Web—from the MLA Web site.

151

GUIDELINES FOR COMPILING AN MLA-STYLE WORKS CITED LIST

- **TITLE**

  `Works Cited`

- **PLACEMENT OF LIST**

  Start a new page numbered sequentially with the rest of the paper, after Notes pages, if any.

- **CONTENT AND FORMAT**

  Include all sources quoted from, paraphrased, or summarized in your paper. Start each entry on a new line and at the regular left margin. If the entry uses more than one line, indent all lines but the first five spaces (or one-half inch—about 1.25 cm) from the left margin. Double-space all lines.

- **SPACING AFTER PUNCTUATION**

  On its Web site*, the MLA explains that computer type fonts have influenced many users of MLA style to leave one space rather than two spaces after punctuation at the ends of sentences. The *MLA Handbook* and the *MLA Style Manual* use one space. Either style is acceptable, so do whichever your instructor prefers.

  Put one space after a comma or a colon.

- **ARRANGEMENT OF ENTRIES**

  Alphabetize by author's last name. If no author is named, alphabetize by the title's first significant word (not *A, An,* or *The*).

- **AUTHORS' NAMES**

  Use first names and middle names or middle initials, if any, as given in the source. Do not use initials for any name that is given in full. For one author or the first-named author in multiauthor works, give the last name first. Use the word *and* with two or more authors. List multiple authors in the order given in the source. Use a comma between the first author's last and first names and after each complete author name except the last. After the last author name, use a period.

  Include *Jr., Sr., II, III,* but do not include other titles and degrees before or after a name.

- **CAPITALIZATION OF TITLES**

  Capitalize all major words in titles.

*The MLA Web site's URL is <www.mla.org/>.

GUIDELINES FOR COMPILING AN MLA-STYLE WORKS CITED LIST *(continued)*

151

■ **SPECIAL TREATMENT OF TITLES**

Use quotation marks around titles of shorter works (poems, short stories, essays, articles). The MLA states that although computers can create italic type, in student papers underlined roman type may be more exact. Underline titles of longer works (books, names of newspapers or journals containing cited articles). For underlining, use an unbroken line like this (unless you use software that underlines only with a broken line, like this).

When a book title includes the title of another work that is usually underlined (such as a novel, play, or long poem), the MLA recommends not to underline the incorporated title: `Decoding Jane Eyre.`

If the incorporated title is usually enclosed in quotation marks (such as a short story or short poem), keep the quotation marks and underline the complete title of the book (do not underline the period): `Theme and Form in "The Waste Land."` (The MLA also allows this as an alternative style for titles that are usually underlined.)

Drop *A, An,* or *The* as the first word of a periodical title.

■ **PLACE OF PUBLICATION**

If several cities are listed for the place of publication, give only the first. If a city name alone would be ambiguous, also give the two-letter postal abbreviation for the province or U.S. state, or an abbreviated country name, if necessary.

■ **PUBLISHER**

Use shortened names as long as they are clear: *Prentice* for *Prentice Hall.* For university presses, use the capital letters *U* and *P* (without periods): for *Oxford University Press* and the *University of Chicago Press*, respectively, `Oxford UP; U of Chicago P.`

■ **PUBLICATION MONTH ABBREVIATIONS**

Abbreviate all publication months except *May, June,* and *July.* Use the first three letters followed by a period: `Dec., Feb.`

■ **PARAGRAPH NUMBERS IN ELECTRONIC SOURCES**

For electronic sources that number paragraphs instead of pages, give the total number of paragraphs followed by the abbreviation *pars.*: `77 pars.`

➜

GUIDELINES FOR COMPILING AN MLA-STYLE WORKS CITED LIST *(continued)* 151

■ **PAGE RANGES**

Give the page range—the starting page number and the ending page number, connected by a hyphen—of any paginated electronic source and any paginated print source that is part of a longer work (for example, a chapter in a book, an article in a journal). A range indicates that the cited work is on those pages and all pages in between. If that is not the case, use the style shown next for discontinuous pages. In either case, use numerals only, without the words *page* or *pages* or the abbreviations *p.* or *pp.*

Use the full second number through 99. Then use only the last two digits for the second number unless it would be unclear: 103–04 is clear, but 567–602 requires full numbers.

■ **DISCONTINUOUS PAGES**

Use the starting page number followed by a plus sign (+): 32+.

■ **WORKS CITED ENTRIES: BOOKS**

Citations for books have three main parts: author, title, and publication information (place of publication, publisher, and date of publication).

AUTHOR — TITLE — PUBLICATION INFORMATION

```
Dudek, Louis. Collected Poetry. Montreal: Delta, 1971.
```

■ **WORKS CITED ENTRIES: PRINT ARTICLES**

Citations for periodical articles contain three major parts: author, title or article, and publication information (usually the periodical title, volume number, year of publication, and page range).

AUTHOR — ARTICLE TITLE

```
Shuter, Robert. "A Field Study of Nonverbal Communication
   in Germany, Italy, and the United States."
```

JOURNAL TITLE — PUBLICATION INFORMATION

```
Communication Monographs. 44 (1977): 298-305.
```

ARTICLE TITLE — JOURNAL TITLE — PUBLICATION INFORMATION

```
"A Start." New Republic 2 May 1994: 7+.
```

GUIDELINES FOR COMPILING AN MLA-STYLE WORKS CITED LIST *(continued)* 151

- **WORKS CITED ENTRIES: SOURCES FROM THE WORLD WIDE WEB**

On its Web site, the MLA sets out a system for documenting sources found on the World Wide Web. This system also applies to FTP and Gopher sites. Citations of these sources contain as much of the following information as you can find: author, title, publication information about a print version if there is one, publication information about the online source, the date you accessed the material, and the URL (electronic address). For these sources, the URL is required in the Works Cited entry. The URL, enclosed in angle brackets <like these>, comes after the access date and before the period at the end of the entry. Here is an entry for an article in a scientific news journal that appears only on the Web.

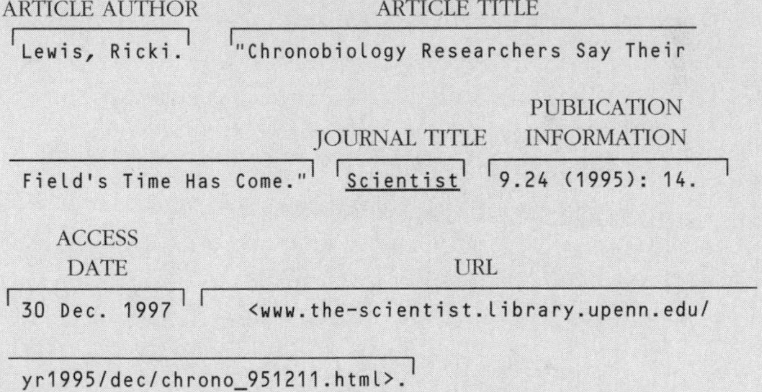

- **WORKS CITED ENTRIES: "PORTABLE" AND OTHER ELECTRONIC SOURCES WITHOUT URLS**

Citations for electronic sources that do not have URLs contain at least the following major parts: publication information, author and title of database, publication medium, name of vendor or computer service, and electronic publication date (add access date if different). Electronic versions of sources that also appear in print start with information about the print version.

Here is an entry for an article from a CD-ROM encyclopedia.

ARTICLE AUTHOR — ARTICLE TITLE — CD-ROM TITLE

Regan, Robert. "Poe, Edgar Allan." <u>Academic American</u> →

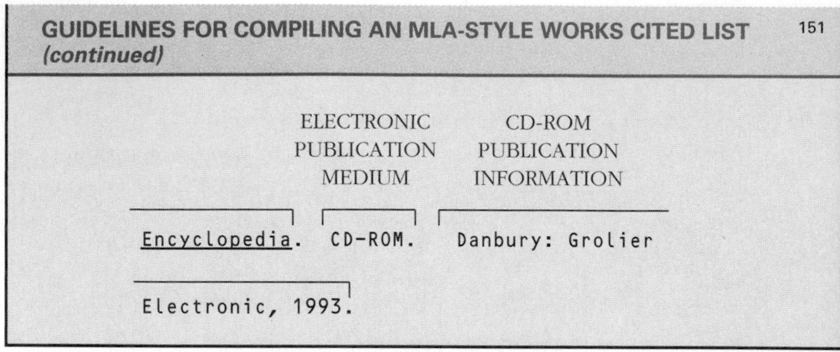
GUIDELINES FOR COMPILING AN MLA-STYLE WORKS CITED LIST (continued) 151

ELECTRONIC PUBLICATION MEDIUM
CD-ROM PUBLICATION INFORMATION

Encyclopedia. CD-ROM. Danbury: Grolier Electronic, 1993.

3 Following models for an MLA-style Works Cited list

Directory

PRINT SOURCES: BOOKS

1. Book by One Author—MLA
2. Book by Two or Three Authors—MLA
3. Book by More than Three Authors—MLA
4. Two or More Books by the Same Author(s)—MLA
5. Book by Group or Corporate Author—MLA
6. Book with No Author Named—MLA
7. Book with an Author and an Editor—MLA
8. Translation—MLA
9. Work in Several Volumes or Parts—MLA
10. Anthology or Collection—MLA
11. One Selection from an Anthology or Collection—MLA
12. More than One Selection from an Anthology or Collection—MLA
13. Signed Article in a Reference Book—MLA
14. Unsigned Article in a Reference Book—MLA
15. Edition—MLA
16. Introduction, Preface, Foreword, or Afterword—MLA
17. Unpublished Dissertation—MLA
18. Reprint of an Older Book—MLA
19. Book in a Series—MLA
20. Book with a Title Within a Title—MLA
21. Government Publication—MLA
22. Published Proceedings of a Conference—MLA

PRINT SOURCES: ARTICLES AND OTHER SHORT DOCUMENTS

23. Signed Article from a Daily Newspaper—MLA
24. Editorial, Letter to the Editor, Review—MLA
25. Unsigned Article from a Daily Newspaper—MLA
26. Signed Article from a Weekly or Biweekly Magazine or Newspaper—MLA
27. Signed Article from a Monthly or Bimonthly Periodical—MLA
28. Unsigned Article from a Weekly or Monthly Periodical—MLA
29. Article from a Collection of Reprinted Articles—MLA
30. Article from a SIRS Collection of Reprinted Articles—MLA
31. Article in a Journal with Continuous Pagination—MLA
32. Article in a Journal that Pages Each Issue Separately—MLA
33. Abstract from a Collection of Abstracts—MLA
34. Published and Unpublished Letters—MLA
35. Map or Chart—MLA

NONPRINT SOURCES

36. Interview—MLA
37. Lecture, Speech, or Address—MLA
38. Film, Videotape, or DVD—MLA
39. Recording—MLA
40. Live Performance—MLA
41. Work of Art, Photograph, or Musical Composition—MLA
42. Radio or Television Program—MLA
43. Microfiche Collection of Articles—MLA

PORTABLE ELECTRONIC SOURCES

44. CD-ROM Database: Abstract with a Print Version—MLA
45. CD-ROM: Article from a Periodical with a Print Version—MLA
46. CD-ROM: Selection from a Book with a Print Version—MLA
47. CD-ROM: Material with No Print Version—MLA
48. Work in More than One Publication Medium—MLA

ONLINE SOURCES: NO URL

49. Online Service Access: Abstract with a Print Version—MLA
50. Online Service Access: Material with No Print Version—MLA
51. Online Service Access with a Keyword: Article from a Periodical with a Print Version—MLA
52. Online Service Access Showing a Path—MLA
53. Online Service Access at a Library—MLA

PRINT SOURCES: BOOKS

1. BOOK BY ONE AUTHOR—MLA

Trudeau, Pierre E. Federalism and the French Canadians. Toronto: Macmillan, 1968.

2. BOOK BY TWO OR THREE AUTHORS—MLA

Scardamalia, Marlene, Carl Bereiter, and Bryant Fillion. Writing for Results: A Sourcebook of Consequential Composing Activities. Toronto: OISE, 1981.

3. BOOK BY MORE THAN THREE AUTHORS—MLA

Cameron, Deborah, et al. Researching Language: Issues of Power and Method. London: Routledge, 1992.

4. TWO OR MORE BOOKS BY THE SAME AUTHOR(S)—MLA

Atwood, Margaret. The Handmaid's Tale. Toronto: McClelland & Stewart, 1985.

---. Survival. Toronto: Anansi, 1972.

---. True Stories. Toronto: Oxford UP, 1981.

5. BOOK BY GROUP OR CORPORATE AUTHOR—MLA

Investors Group. Starting Out: Smart Strategies for Your 20s & 30s. Toronto: Stoddart, 1998.

American Psychological Association. Publication Manual of the American Psychological Association. 4th ed. Washington, DC: APA, 1994.

6. Book with No Author Named—MLA

<u>The Chicago Manual of Style</u>. 14th ed. Chicago: U of Chicago P, 1993.

7. Book with an Author and an Editor—MLA

If your focus is on Eudora Welty as the author of the reviews in *A Writer's Eye* and your paper refers to her or her words, put her name first in the Works Cited entry:

Welty, Eudora. <u>A Writer's Eye: Collected Book Reviews</u>. Ed. Pearl A. McHaney. Jackson: UP of Mississippi, 1994.

If your focus is on Pearl A. McHaney's work as the editor of this collection of reviews and your paper refers to her or her words, put her name first in the Works Cited entry:

McHaney, Pearl A., ed. <u>A Writer's Eye: Collected Book Reviews</u>. By Eudora Welty. Jackson: UP of Mississippi, 1994.

8. Translation—MLA

Maillet, Antonine. <u>La Sagouine</u>. Trans. Luis de Cespedes. Toronto: Simon & Pierre, 1979.

9. Work in Several Volumes or Parts—MLA

When you use more than one volume of a multivolume work, after the title give the total number of volumes. In each parenthetical citation, give both volume and page numbers (see item 11 in 34c-2). MLA style recommends using arabic numerals, even if the source uses roman numerals (*Vol. 6* for *Vol. VI*).

Rand, Enid. <u>Virology</u>. 5 vols. Philadelphia: Lippincott, 1979.

When you use only one volume, give the number of the volume you used. In parenthetical citations, give page numbers only; do not repeat the volume number.

Rand, Enid. <u>Virology</u>. Vol. 2. Philadelphia: Lippincott, 1979.

When you use only one volume of a multivolume work in which each volume is titled separately, you can list it as you would any book, using its individual title and not referring to the rest of the volumes.

Goldman, L. H., Gloria L. Cronin, and Ada Aharoni. <u>Saul Bellow: A Mosaic</u>. New York: Lang, 1992.

If you want to include information about the set of volumes, put it after the basic information about the volume you used.

Goldman, L. H., Gloria L. Cronin, and Ada Aharoni. Saul Bellow: A Mosaic. New York: Lang, 1992. Vol. 2 of Twentieth-Century American Jewish Writers. 14 vols.

10. Anthology or Collection—MLA

When your paper is about a collection of works rather than about the individual selections in an anthology or collection, use this form. Also see item 15.

New, W. H., ed. Canadian Short Fiction: From Myth to Modern. Scarborough, ON: Prentice, 1986.

11. One Selection from an Anthology or Collection—MLA

Morrisseau, Norval. "The Indian That Became a Thunderbird." Canadian Short Fiction: From Myth to Modern. Ed. W. H. New. Scarborough, ON: Prentice, 1986. 26-29.

12. More than One Selection from an Anthology or Collection—MLA

When you use more than one selection from one anthology, in the Works Cited list you can give one entry for the anthology and separate brief entries for each selection cited from the anthology. This plan is more efficient than using the form shown in item 10 for each selection you use. Give full details about the anthology or edited collection, with the editor's name as the first item of information. For each selection cited in your paper, give the name of the selection's author and title. End this information with a period, and then give the name that starts the entry for the anthology and inclusive pages on which the specific selection falls. For citations in your paper, use the name of the author of the selection, not the editor of the anthology. The following entries show first an entry for an anthology followed by entries for two selections in the anthology. Readers who look at the Davies and Engel entries are directed to the Ioannou entry for full information about the anthology and see that the cited material is on pages 40 and 113 respectively.

Ioannou, Greg, and Lynne Missen, eds. Shivers: An Anthology of Canadian Ghost Stories. Toronto: McClelland-Bantam, 1989.

Davies, Robertson. "The Charlottetown Banquet." Ioannou and Missen 40-52.

Engel, Marian. "The Country Doctor." Ioannou and Missen 113-32.

13. Signed Article in a Reference Book—MLA

Shadbolt, Doris. "Emily Carr." The Canadian Encyclopedia. 2nd ed.

Alphabetically arranged collections such as the encyclopedias in this model and the next one do not contain page numbers.

14. Unsigned Article in a Reference Book—MLA

"Russia." Encyclopaedia Britannica. 1994 ed.

15. Edition—MLA

When a book is in some edition other than the first, the edition number appears on the title page. Include this information after the title. Use *2nd ed., 3rd ed., Rev. ed.* (for *Revised edition*), and so on. Put a period after *ed.*, which also acts as the period at the end of the information block.

Buckley, Joanne, and David Gates. Put It in Writing. 2nd ed. Scarborough, ON: Prentice, 1995.

Books are also "editions" when an editor has made an important contribution, such as in selecting works and writing background material about them for an anthology. In this sort of edition, the editor's name (or editors' names) comes first. Also see item 10.

Lantolf, James P., and Gabriela Appel, eds. Vygotskian Approaches to Second Language Research. Norwood, NJ: Ablex, 1994.

Spear, Thomas, and Richard Waller, eds. Being Masai: Ethnicity and Identity in East Africa. Athens: Ohio UP, 1993.

16. Introduction, Preface, Foreword, or Afterword—MLA

Cragg, Catherine, et al. Preface. Editing Canadian English. 2nd ed. By Cragg et al. Toronto: Macfarlane Walter & Ross, 2000. ix–x.

Allmand, Warren. Foreword. The Life and Death of Anna Mae Aquash. By Johanna Brand. Toronto: Lorimer, 1993. v–ix.

When you cite an introduction, preface, foreword, afterword, or appendix, give first the name of the person who wrote it. Then give the name of the cited part, capitalizing it and using a period after it; do not underline it or put it in quotation marks. Then give the title of the book. If the preface, introduction, foreword, afterword, or appendix was written by someone other than the author of the book, write the word *By* and the name of the book's author(s), in normal order. If the book's author(s) wrote the part you are citing, after *By* repeat only the last name or names. After publication information, give inclusive page numbers. If a cited preface or introduction uses roman numerals for page numbers, use roman numerals.

17. Unpublished Dissertation—MLA

Buckley, Joanne. "An Assessment of Kieran Egan's Theory of Educational Development." Diss. U of Western Ontario, 1991.

18. Reprint of an Older Book—MLA

Lampman, Archibald. Lyrics of Earth. 1895. Ottawa: Tecumseh, 1978.

A republished book may be the paperback version of a book originally published as a hardbound, or it may be the reissue of a book. Republishing information can be found on the copyright page. Give the date of the original version before the publication information for the version you used.

19. Book in a Series—MLA

Courchene, Thomas J. In Praise of Renewed Federalism. The Canada Round. Toronto: C. D. Howe Institute, 1991.

Give the book title, underlined, after the author name. Put the series title, neither underlined nor in quotation marks, after the book title.

20. Book with a Title Within a Title—MLA

The MLA recognizes two distinct styles for handling normally independent titles when they appear within an underlined title. In the MLA's preferred style, the embedded title should not be underlined or set within quotation marks.

Lumiansky, Robert M., and Herschel Baker, eds. Critical Approaches to Six Major English Works: Beowulf Through Paradise Lost. Philadelphia: U of Pennsylvania P, 1968.

However, the MLA now accepts a second style for handling such embedded titles. In this alternative style, the normally independent titles should be set within quotation marks, and they should be underlined.

Lumiansky, Robert M., and Herschel Baker, eds. Critical Approaches to Six Major English Works: "Beowulf" Through "Paradise Lost." Philadelphia: U of Pennsylvania P, 1968.

Use whichever style your instructor prefers.

21. Government Publication—MLA

For most government publications, use the name of the government as the first information unit (such as Canada). If no author is named, give the name of the branch of government or the government agency next (such as Department of Finance or Task Force on Program Review).

Canada. Royal Commission on Bilingualism and Biculturalism. Preliminary Report. Ottawa: Queen's Printer, 1965.

Canada. Indian and Northern Affairs Canada. The Inuit. Ottawa: Supply and Services Canada, 1986.

22. Published Proceedings of a Conference—MLA

Smith, Donald B., ed. Forging a New Relationship: Proceedings of the Conference on the Report of the Royal Commission on Aboriginal Peoples. 31 Jan.-2 Feb. 1997. Montreal: McGill Institute for the Study of Canada, 1997.

If the title of the publication of the conference proceedings does not include the name and location of the conference, give that information after the title.

Print Sources: Articles and Other Short Documents

23. Signed Article from a Daily Newspaper—MLA

Tebbutt, Tom. "Showman Agassi Lightly Frolics to Canadian Title." Globe and Mail 1 Aug. 1994: D1.

Omit *A* or *The* as the first word in a newspaper title. If the city of publication is not part of the title, put it in square brackets after the title, not underlined. Give the day, month, and year of the issue. If sections are designated, give the section letter as well as the page number. If an article runs on nonconsecutive pages, give the starting page number followed by a plus sign (for example, *23+* for an article that starts on p. 23 and continues on p. 42).

24. Editorial, Letter to the Editor, Review—MLA

"A Black Mark on Local Government." Editorial. London Free Press 27 July 1994: B8.

Hurka, John. Letter. Calgary Sun 5 July 1994: A18.

Toews, Wendy. "Politics of the Mind." Rev. of They Say You're Crazy by Paula J. Caplan. Winnipeg Free Press 26 Aug. 1995: C3.

25. Unsigned Article from a Daily Newspaper—MLA

"Canadian Adds Flights." Globe and Mail 1 Aug. 1994: B2.

26. Signed Article from a Weekly or Biweekly Magazine or Newspaper—MLA

Wood, Chris. "Storm Clouds over Quebec." Maclean's 6 Nov. 1989: 16-17.

27. Signed Article from a Monthly or Bimonthly Periodical—MLA

O'Malley, Sean. "Make-It-Happen Kinda Dreamer: Theatre Director Diane Dupuy Is Nobody's Puppet." Chatelaine Aug. 1994: 36+.

The + sign shows that the O'Malley article runs on discontinuous pages, starting on page 36.

28. Unsigned Article from a Weekly or Monthly Periodical—MLA

"10 Ways to Sleep Easy." Canadian Living Aug. 1994: 19.

29. Article from a Collection of Reprinted Articles—MLA

Brumberg, Abraham. "Russia after Perestroika." New York Review of Books 27 June 1991: 53-62. Rpt. in Russian and Soviet History. Ed. Alexander Dallin. Vol. 14, The Gorbachev Era. New York: Garland, 1992. 300-20.

30. Article from a SIRS Collection of Reprinted Articles—MLA

Curver, Philip C. "Lighting in the 21st Century." Futurist Jan./Feb. 1989: Energy. Ed. Eleanor Goldstein. Vol. 4. Boca Raton: SIRS, 1990. Art. 84.

Social Issues Resources Series (SIRS) articles are looseleaf collections of reprints from many sources. Give information about the original publication before the information about the article's publication in SIRS. Use the abbreviation *Art.* before the SIRS article number.

31. Article in a Journal with Continuous Pagination—MLA

If the first issue of a volume of a journal with continuous pagination ends on page 228, the second issue starts with page 229. Give only the volume number before the year. Use arabic numerals for all numbers.

La Follette, M. C. "The Politics of Research Misconduct: Congressional Oversight, Universities, and Science." Journal of Higher Education 65 (1994): 261-85.

32. Article in a Journal that Pages Each Issue Separately—MLA

If each issue starts on page 1, give an issue number after the volume number. Use arabic numerals. Separate the two numbers with a period but with no space before or after the period.

Hancock, D. "Prototyping the Hubble Fix." IEEE Spectrum 30.10 (1993): 34-39.

If a journal uses issue numbers but not volume numbers, give the issue number after the journal name.

33. Abstract from a Collection of Abstracts—MLA

To cite an abstract, first give information for the full work: the author's name, the title of the article, and publication information about the full article. If a reader could not know that the cited material is an abstract, write the word *Abstract*, not underlined, followed by a period. Give publication information about the collection of abstracts. For abstracts identified by item numbers rather than page numbers, use the word *item* before the item number.

Marcus, Hazel R., and Shinobu Kitayamo. "Culture and the Self: Implications for Cognition, Emotion, and Motivation." Psychological Review 88 (1991): 224-53. Psychological Abstracts 78: item 23878.

34. Published and Unpublished Letters—MLA

If you cite a letter from a published source, name the author of the letter first. Identify the letter as such, and give its date, if available. Then give publication information.

Lapidus, Jackie. Letter to her mother. 12 Nov. 1975. Between Ourselves: Letters between Mothers and Daughters. Ed. Karen Payne. Boston: Houghton, 1983. 323-26.

If you cite a personal letter that is not in a published source, put *Letter to the author* after the letter writer's name. Then give the date on the letter.

Reilly, Gary Edward. Letter to the author. 26 Dec. 2000.

35. Map or Chart—MLA

Russia and Post-Soviet Republics. Map. Moscow: Mapping Production Association, 1992.

Nonprint Sources

36. Interview—MLA

Friedman, Randi. Telephone interview. 30 June 1998.

For a face-to-face interview, use Personal interview instead of Telephone interview. For a published interview, give the name of the interviewed person first, identify the source as an interview, and then give details as for any published source: author (preceded by the word *By*), title, publication details.

For a radio or television interview, give the name of the interviewed person first, the name of the interviewer next, and then information about the program on which the interview was broadcast.

Gellhorn, Martha. Interview with Daniel Richler. Imprint. TVOntario, Toronto. 7 Dec. 1992.

37. Lecture, Speech, or Address—MLA

Barlow, Maude. Address. League of Canadian Poets. Toronto, 25 May 1991.

38. Film, Videotape, or DVD—MLA

Calendar. Screenplay by Atom Egoyan. Dir. Atom Egoyan. Prod. Ego Filmarts/ZDF. Perf. Atom Egoyan and Arsinee Khanjian. 1993. DVD. Alliance Atlantis, 2001.

Give the title first, and include the director, the distributor, and the year. For older films that were subsequently released on videocassettes, DVDs, or laser disks, provide the original release date of the movie before the name of the distributor. Other information (writer, producer, major actors) is optional. Do not reverse the order of first and last names.

39. Recording—MLA

In a citation of a recording, put first the information important to your use of the source. Here is an entry with the focus on the director of the choral group.

De la Cuesta, Ismael Fernando, dir. Benedictine Monks of Santo Domingo de Silos. Chant. Angel, 1994.

If the use of this source in the paper focused on the performers and the music, the entry would look like this:

Benedictine Monks of Santo Domingo de Silos. Chant. Dir. Ismael Fernando de la Cuesta. Angel, 1994.

If you are citing a recording in some medium other than a CD, name the medium. To cite a specific song, give the song title in quotation marks before the title of the recording.

Cohen, Leonard. "Tower of Song." I'm Your Man. Audiocassette. Columbia, 1988.

40. Live Performance—MLA

The Merchant of Venice. By William Shakespeare. Dir. Richard Monette. Perf. Lucy Peacock and Paul Soles. Festival Theatre, Stratford, ON. 8 May 2001.

41. Work of Art, Photograph, or Musical Composition—MLA

Pratt, Christopher. Shop on an Island. London Regional Art Gallery, London, ON.

Gershwin, George. Porgy and Bess.

Schubert, Franz. Symphony no. 8 in B minor.

Schubert, Franz. Unfinished Symphony.

For musical compositions, give composer and title of work. Underline the title of an opera, ballet, or descriptive word title for music. But if a composition is identified only by musical form, number, and key, do not underline it and do not put it in quotation marks. The entries for Schubert show two ways of identifying the same composition.

42. Radio or Television Program—MLA

For programs that title both the series and each episode, give the episode title first in quotation marks, and then give the series title underlined. If your use of the program focuses on a participant (such as a performer, writer, or director), give that name first, an abbreviated indication of that person's role (*perf., writ., dir.*), and then the programming information. Include the network, the local station and its city, and the date of the broadcast.

"Mountie and Soul." Due South. CTV. CFTO, Toronto. 26 Oct. 1997.

43. Microfiche Collection of Articles—MLA

Wenzell, Ron. "Businesses Prepare for a More Diverse Work Force." St. Louis Post Dispatch 3 Feb. 1990. NewsBank: Employment 27 (1990): fiche 2, grid D12.

Portable Electronic Sources

The following basic blocks of information are used to document a portable electronic source (such as a CD-ROM or a diskette) in MLA style. A period ends each block.

1. Documentation information about the print version, if any. Many sources accessed electronically also exist in published print versions. Follow the models in items 1–35 above for print sources. You may not find all the details about a print version in an electronic version, but provide as much information as you can. Information about a print version usually is given at the beginning or the end of an electronic document.
2. Author (if any) and title (underlined) of the electronic source or database. If there is no print version, start your Works Cited entry with this information.
3. Electronic medium, such as *CD-ROM, Diskette,* or *Magnetic tape.*
4. Name of the producer.
5. Publication date.

44. CD-ROM Database: Abstract with a Print Version—MLA

Marcus, Hazel R., and Shinobu Kitayamo. "Culture and the Self: Implications for Cognition, Emotion, and Motivation." Psychological Abstracts 78 (1991): item 23878. PsycLIT. CD-ROM. SilverPlatter. Sept. 1991.

This model shows a portable database of information that also appears in a print version and that is updated from time to time. All the information through *item 23878* is for the print version. The volume number is 78, and the abstract's number is 23878. All the information from *PsycLIT* to the end of the entry is for the electronic version of the source. PsycLIT is the name of the CD-ROM database, and SilverPlatter is the name of the producer of the CD-ROM. The CD-ROM was issued in September 1991.

45. CD-ROM: Article from a Periodical with a Print Version—MLA

"The Price Is Right." Time 20 Jan. 1992: 38. Time Man of the Year. CD-ROM. Compact, for 1993.

Information for the print version ends with the article's page number, 38. After the publication date for the print version comes a colon followed by the page number for the print version, 38. The title of the CD-ROM is *Time Man of the Year*, its producer is Compact, and its copyright year is 1993. Underline both the title of the print publication and the title of the CD-ROM.

46. CD-ROM: Selection from a Book with a Print Version—MLA

"Prehistoric Humans: Earliest Homo Sapiens." The Guinness Book of Records 1994. Guinness, 1994. The Guinness Multimedia Disk of Records. CD-ROM. Version 2.0. Danbury: Grolier Electronic. 1994.

Version 2.0 signals that this CD-ROM is updated periodically; the producer changes version numbers rather than giving update dates.

47. CD-ROM: Material with No Print Version—MLA

"Spanish Dance." Encarta 2000. CD-ROM. Redmond, WA: Microsoft. 1999.

Encarta 2000 is a CD-ROM encyclopedia with no print version. "Spanish Dance" is the title of an article in this encyclopedia.

48. Work in More than One Publication Medium—MLA

Clarke, David James, IV. Novell's CNE Study Guide. Book. Network Support Encyclopedia. CD-ROM. Alameda: Sybex, 1994.

This book and CD-ROM come together. Each has its own title, but the publication information—Alameda: Sybex, 1994—applies to both.

49. Online Service Access: Abstract with a Print Version—MLA

Marcus, Hazel R., and Shinobu Kitayamo. "Culture and the Self: Implications for Cognition, Emotion, and Motivation." Psychological Abstracts 78 (1991): item 23878. PsycINFO. Dialog. 10 Oct. 1991.

This entry is for the same abstract shown in item 44, but here it is accessed on an online database (PsycINFO) by means of an online service (Dialog). This entry notes PsycINFO, the name of the online database, where item 44 notes PsycLIT, the name of the CD-ROM database; and it notes Dialog, the service through which PsycINFO was accessed, where item 44 notes the CD-ROM producer SilverPlatter. The last information unit—10 Oct. 1991—is the date that the abstract was accessed.

50. Online Service Access: Material with No Print Version—MLA

"Microsoft Licenses OSM Technology from Henter-Joyce." WinNews Electronic Newsletter 2.6 (1 May 1995). Compuserve. 15 May 1995.

The numerals 2.6 mean volume 2, number 6 of this electronic newsletter.

51. Online Service Access with a Keyword: Article from a Periodical with a Print Version—MLA

Kapor, Mitchell, and Jerry Berman. "A Superhighway Through the Wasteland?" New York Times 24 Nov. 1993: Op-ed page. New York Times Online. America Online. 5 May 1995. Keyword: nytimes.

Information applying to the print version of this article in the *New York Times* ends with the words *Op-ed page*, and information about the online version starts with the title of the database, *New York Times Online.* America Online is the service through which the database was accessed, and 5 May 1995 is the access date. The keyword *nytimes* was used to access *New York Times Online,* as noted after the access date.

52. Online Service Access Showing a Path—MLA

When you access a source by choosing a series of keywords, menus, or topics, end the entry with the "path" of words you used. Use semicolons between items in the path, and put a period at the end.

Futrelle, David. "A Smashing Success." Money.com 23 Dec. 1999. America Online. 26 Dec. 1999. Path: Personal Finance; Business News; Business Publications; Money.com.

53. Online Service Access at a Library—MLA

For a source accessed through a library's online service, first give information about the source. Then give the name of the service, the name of the library, and the access date. Give the URL of the online service's home page, if you know it, after the access date. Use angle brackets to enclose this URL, and put a period after the closing bracket.

Dutton, Gail. "Greener Pigs." Popular Science 1999: 38-39. ProQuest Periodical Abstracts Plus Text. ProQuest Direct. Public Lib., Moncton. 7 Dec. 1999 <http://proquest.umi.com>.

URL-Accessed Online Sources

In this section, you will find models for online sources accessed when you enter a URL, or specific Internet address. These guidelines cover Web sites, FTP and Gopher sites, listservs, discussion groups, and other online sources. For such sources, provide as much of the following information as you can.

1. The author's name, if any.
2. In quotation marks, the title of a short work (poem, short story, essay, article, posted message); or underlined, the title of a book.
3. The name of an editor, translator, or compiler, if any, with an abbreviation such as *Ed., Trans.,* or *Comp.* before the name.
4. Publication information for any print version of the source.
5. The underlined title of a scholarly project or reference database. (If the site has no title, describe it: e.g., *Home page.*)
6. The date of electronic publication (including a version number, if any) or posting, or the most recent update.
7. The name of a sponsoring organization, if any.
8. The date you accessed the material.
9. The URL in angle brackets (< >), with a period after the closing bracket.

54. URL Access: Book—MLA

Eaton, Arthur W. Acadian Legends and Lyrics. London and New York: White & Allen, 1889. Early Canadiana Online. 16 Feb. 2000. 25 May 2001 <http://www.canadiana.org/cgi-bin/ECO/mtq?doc=09066>.

55. URL Access: Book in a Scholarly Project—MLA

Herodotus. The History of Herodotus. Trans. George Rawlinson. The Internet Classics Archive. Ed. Daniel C. Stevenson. 11 Jan. 1998. Massachusetts Institute of Technology. 17 Jan. 1998 <http://classics.mit.edu/Herodotus/history.sum.html>.

56. URL Access: Government-Published Book—MLA

Canada. Canadian Heritage. Languages in Canada: 1996 Canadian Census. By Louise Marmen and Jean-Pierre Corbeil. New Canadian Perspectives. 6 Feb. 2001. 11 June 2001 <http://www.pch.gc.ca/offlangoff/perspectives/english/census96/census96.pdf>.

For government publications that name no author, start with the name of the government or government body, and then name the government agency. For a government text, the title is followed by the writer of the publication, if available.

57. URL Access: Article in an Online Periodical—MLA

Ignatieff, Michael. "The Man Who Was Right." Rev. of Reflections on a Ravaged Century, by Robert Conquest. New York Review of Books 23 March 2000. 5 June 2001 <http://nybooks.com/nyrev/WWWarchdisplay.cgi?20000323035R>.

Gold, David. "Ulysses: A Case Study in the Problems of Hypertextualization of Complex Documents." Computers, Writing, Rhetoric and Literature 3.1 (1997): 37 pars. 4 Dec. 1999 <http://www.cwrl.utexas.edu/~cwrl/v3n1/dgold/title.htm>.

Keegan, Paul. "Culture Quake." Mother Jones Nov.-Dec. 1999. 4 Dec. 1999 <http://www.mojones.com/mother_jones/ND99/quake.html>.

Lewis, Ricki. "Chronobiology Researchers Say Their Field's Time Has Come." Scientist 9.24 (1995): 14. 30 Dec. 1997 <http://www.the-scientist.library.upenn.edu/yr1995/dec/chrono-951211.html>.

Pacienza, Angela. "Cities Could Become Treeless Wastelands." Winnipeg Free Press Online Edition 11 June 2001. 9 July 2001 <http://www.winnipegfreepress.com/news/canadaworld/273409436518713.html>.

When you cite online periodicals, give the following information

1. The author's name, if any.
2. In quotation marks, the title of the article or editorial.
3. If applicable, a description of the cited material as a review, an editorial, or a letter, unless the title gives that information.
4. The underlined title of the periodical.
5. Volume and issue numbers, if any.
6. The date of publication.
7. The total number of pages, paragraphs, or other numbered sections, if any.
8. The date you accessed the material.
9. The URL in angle brackets (< >), with a period after the closing bracket.

58. URL Access: Professional Home Page—MLA

"LEARN@PZ." Project Zero. Home page. Harvard Graduate School of Education. 17 Jan. 1998 <http://pzweb.harvard.edu/default.htm>.

LEARN@PZ is the title of the home page for *Project Zero*, sponsored by the Harvard Graduate School of Education.

59. URL Access: Personal Home Page—MLA

Hunter-Kilmer, Melissa. Home page. 15 Feb. 1996. 17 Jan. 1998 <http://www.Idsonline.com/userweb/phantom/index.htm>.

For home pages, include as much of the following information as you can find:

1. If available, the name of the person who created or put up the home page. If first and last names are given, reverse the order of the first author's name.
2. The title, underlined. If there is no title, add the description *Home page*, not underlined, followed by a period.
3. For a professional home page, the name of the sponsoring organization.
4. The date you accessed the material.
5. The URL in angle brackets (< >), with a period after the closing bracket.

Other Online Sources

60. Online Posting—MLA

Woodbury, Chuck. "Free RV Campgrounds." Online posting. 4 Dec. 1999. The RV Home Page Bulletin Board. 21 Dec. 1999 <http://www.rvhome.com/wwwboard/messages/4598.html>.

Be cautious about using online postings as sources. Some postings contain cutting-edge information from experts, but some contain trash. Unfortunately, there is no way to know whether people online are who they claim to be. To cite an online message, include the author name (if any), the title of the message in quotation marks, and then *Online posting*. Give the date of the posting and the name of the bulletin board, if any. Then give the access date and, in angle brackets, the URL.

61. Synchronous Communication—MLA

Bleck, Bradley. Online discussion. "Virtual First Year Composition: Distance Education, the Internet, and World Wide Web." DaMOO. 8 June 1997. 27 Feb. 1998 <http://DaMOO.csun.edu/CW/brad.html>.

Give the name of the speaker, a title for the event ("Virtual First Year Composition: Distance Education, the Internet, and the World Wide Web"), the forum (DaMOO), date, access date, and URL.

62. E-mail Message—MLA

Thompson, Jim. "Bob Martin's Address." E-mail to June Cain. 11 Nov. 1997.

Start with the name of the person who wrote the e-mail message. Give the title or subject line in quotation marks. Then describe the source (e-mail) and identify the recipient. End with the date.

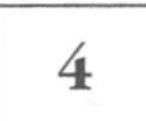

Using content or bibliographic notes in MLA style

In MLA style, footnotes or endnotes serve two specific purposes: (1) You can use them for content (ideas and information) that does not fit into your paper but is still worth relating; and (2) you can use them for bibliographic information that would intrude if you were to include it in your text.

Text of Paper

Eudora Welty's literary biography, <u>One Writer's Beginnings</u>, shows us how both the inner world of self and the outer world of family and place form a writer's imagination.[1]

Content Note—MLA

[1]Welty, who valued her privacy, resisted investigation of her life. However, at the age of 74, she chose to present her own autobiographical reflections in a series of lectures at Harvard University.

Text of Paper

Barbara Randolph believes that enthusiasm is contagious (65).[1] Many psychologists have found that panic, fear, and rage spread more quickly in crowds than positive emotions do, however.

BIBLIOGRAPHIC NOTE—MLA

```
1Others who agree with Randolph include Thurman 21, 84, 155; Kelley
421-25; and Brookes 65-76.
```

✤ MLA FORMAT ALERT: Place a note number at the end of a sentence, if possible. Put it after any punctuation mark except the dash. Do not put any space before a note number, and put one space after it. In typed papers, raise the note number a little above the line of words. In word processing programs, use superscript numbers. ✤

For more examples of MLA-style content notes and to see page format for endnotes, see the student research paper in section 35b.

34d Using APA-style documentation

The American Psychological Association (APA) endorses a name-year parenthetical reference documentation system that is used in its journals and has come to be used by students in the social sciences and some other disciplines. APA in-text citations alert readers to material you have used from outside sources. These citations function with an alphabetical **References list** at the end of your paper containing information that enables readers to retrieve the sources you have quoted from (see 31c), paraphrased (see 31d), or summarized (see 31e).

1 Citing sources in the body of a paper in APA style

In-text citations identify a source by a name (usually an author name) and a year (for copyrighted sources, usually the copyright year). You can often incorporate the relevant name, and sometimes the year, into your sentence. Otherwise, put this information in parentheses, placing the parenthetical reference so that a reader knows exactly what it refers to and is distracted by it as little as possible.

The APA *Publication Manual* recommends that if you refer to a work more than once in a paragraph, you give the author name and date the first time that you mention the work, and then give only the name after that. There is one exception: If you are citing two or more works by the same author, each citation must include the date so that a reader knows which work is being cited.

APA style requires page numbers for direct quotations* and recommends them for summaries. However, some instructors expect page

*When a source is no more than one page long, the page number is included in information about the source in the References list. Therefore, it is unnecessary to repeat the page number in in-text citations.

references for any use made of sources, so find out your instructor's preference. Put page numbers in parentheses, using the abbreviation *p.* before a single page number and *pp.* when the material you are citing falls on more than one page. Item 1 shows citations of a paraphrased source both using and omitting the page number.

For a direct quotation from an electronic source that numbers paragraphs, give the paragraph number (or numbers). Handle paragraph numbers as you do page numbers, but omit *p.* or *pp.*

1. Citing a Paraphrased or Summarized Source—APA

`People from the Mediterranean prefer an elbow-to-shoulder distance from each other (Morris, 1977).` [Name and date cited in parentheses.]

`Desmond Morris (1977, p. 131) notes that people from the Mediterranean prefer an elbow-to-shoulder distance from each other.` [Name cited in text, date and page cited in parentheses.]

2. Citing the Source of a Short Quotation—APA

`A recent report of reductions in SAD-related "depression in 87 percent of patients" (Binkley, 1990, p. 203) reverses the findings of earlier studies.` [Name, date, and page reference in parentheses immediately following the quotation.]

`Binkley reports reductions in SAD-related "depression in 87 percent of patients" (1990, p. 203).` [Name incorporated into the words introducing the quotation and date and page number in parentheses immediately following the quotation.]

3. Formatting a Long Quotation and Citing Its Source—APA

Incorporate a direct quotation of fewer than 40 words into your own sentence and enclose it in quotation marks. Place the parenthetical citation after the closing quotation mark and, if the quotation falls at the end of the sentence, before the sentence-ending punctuation. When you use a quotation longer than 40 words, set it off from your words by starting it on a new line and by indenting each line of the quotation 5 spaces from the left margin. Do not enclose it in quotation marks. Place the parenthetical citation 2 spaces after the end punctuation of the last sentence.

Displayed Quotation (40 or More Words)

`Jet lag, with its characteristic fatigue and irregular sleep patterns, is a common problem among those who travel great distances by jet airplane to different time zones:`

> Jet lag syndrome is the inability of the internal body rhythm to rapidly resynchronize after sudden shifts in the timing. For a variety of reasons, the system attempts to maintain stability and resist temporal change. Consequently, complete adjustment can often be delayed for several days--sometimes for a week--after arrival at one's destination (Bonner, 1991, p. 72).

Interestingly, this research shows that the number of flying hours is not the cause of jet lag.

The following examples show how to handle parenthetical citations for various sources. Remember, though, that you often can introduce source names, including titles when necessary, and sometimes even years in your own sentences.

4. Citing One Author—APA

One of his questions is "What binds together a Mormon banker in Utah with his brother, or other coreligionists in Illinois or Massachusetts?" (Coles, 1993, p. 2).

In a parenthetical reference in APA style, a comma and a space separate a name from a year and a year from a page reference. (Examples 1 through 4 above also show citations of works by one author.)

5. Citing Two Authors—APA

If a work has two authors, give both names in each citation.

One report describes 2123 occurrences (Krait & Cooper, 1994).

The results Krait and Cooper (1994) report would not support the conclusions Davis and Sherman (1992) draw in their review of the literature.

When citing two (or more) authors, use an ampersand (&) between the (final) two names for parenthetical references, but use the word *and* for references in your own sentences.

6. Citing Three, Four, or Five Authors—APA

For three, four, or five authors, use all the authors' last names in the first reference. In all subsequent references, use only the first author's last name followed by *et al.*

First Reference

In one anthology, 35% of the selections had not been anthologized before (Elliott, Kerber, Litz, & Martin, 1992).

SUBSEQUENT REFERENCE

Elliott et al. (1992) include 17 authors whose work has never been anthologized.

7. CITING SIX OR MORE AUTHORS—APA

For six or more authors, use the name of the first author followed by *et al.* for all references, including the first.

8. CITING AUTHOR(S) WITH TWO OR MORE WORKS IN THE SAME YEAR—APA

If you use more than one source written in the same year by the same author(s), alphabetize the works by their titles for the References list, and assign letters in alphabetical order to the years—(1996a), (1996b), (1996c). Use the year-letter combination in parenthetical references. Note that a citation of two or more of such works lists the years in alphabetical order.

Most recently, Jones (1996c) draws new conclusions from the results of 17 sets of experiments (Jones, 1996a, 1996b).

9. CITING TWO OR MORE AUTHORS WITH THE SAME LAST NAME—APA

Include first initials for every in-text citation of authors who share a last name. Use the initials appearing in the References list.

R. A. Smith (1997) and C. Smith (1989) both confirm these results.

These results have been confirmed independently (C. Smith, 1989; R. A. Smith, 1997).

10. CITING A GROUP OR CORPORATE AUTHOR—APA

If you use a source in which the "author" is a corporation, agency, or group, an in-text reference gives that name as author. Use the full name in each citation unless an abbreviated version of the name is likely to be familiar to your audience. In that case, use the full name and give its abbreviation at the first citation; then use the abbreviation for subsequent citations.

After 1949 the federal government took over responsibility for most public housing projects (Canada Mortgage and Housing Corporation [CMHC], 1990).

11. CITING WORKS BY TITLE—APA

If no author is named, use a shortened form of the title in citations. Ignoring *A, An,* or *The,* make the first word the one by which you alphabetize the title in the References. The following citation is to an article fully titled "Are You a Day or a Night Person?"

The "morning lark" and "night owl" connotations are typically used to categorize the human extremes ("Are You," 1989).

12. Citing More than One Source in a Parenthetical Reference—APA

If more than one source has contributed to an idea or opinion in your paper, cite the sources alphabetically in one set of parentheses; separate each block of information with a semicolon.

Conceptions of personal space vary among cultures (Morris, 1977; Worchel & Cooper, 1983).

13. Citing a Personal Communication, Including E-mail and Other Non-retrievable Sources—APA

Telephone calls, personal letters, interviews, and e-mail messages are "personal communications" that your readers do not have access to. Acknowledge personal communications in parenthetical references, but do not include them in your References list. This guideline applies to discussion list postings, as well.

Recalling his first summer at camp, one person said, "The proximity of 12 other kids made me -- an only child with older, quiet parents -- frantic for the entire eight weeks" (A. Weiss, personal communication, January 12, 1996).

14. Reference to an Entire Online Source—APA

For a brief reference to an entire online source, just give the URL (Internet address) in parentheses. Do not include the source in your References list.

Another engaging graphic can be found on the ProjectZero home page (pzweb.harvard.edu/ default.htm).

15. Other References to Retrievable Online Sources—APA

When you quote, paraphrase, or summarize an online source that is available to others, include the work in your References list, and cite the author (if any) or title and the date as you would for a print source.

16. Source Lines for Graphics and Table Data—APA

If you include in your paper a graphic from another source or create a table using data from another source, give a note in the text at the bottom of the table or graphic crediting the original author and the copyright holder. Here are examples of two source lines, one for a graphic from an article, the other for a graphic from a book.

Graphic from an Article

<u>Note.</u> From "Bridge over troubled waters? Connecting research and pedagogy in composition and business/technical communication" by

J. Allen, 1992, Technical Communication Quarterly, 1(4), p. 9. Copyright 1992 by the Association of Teachers of Technical Writing.

Graphic from a Book

Note. From Additive alert: A guide to food additives for the Canadian consumer (p. 28), by Linda R. Pim, 1979, Toronto: Doubleday. Copyright 1979 by Pollution Probe Foundation.

2 Compiling an APA-style References list

In APA documentation, in-text citations must be supported by a list of sources referred to in your paper. Include in this References list the "recoverable" sources that you quote from, paraphrase, or summarize. A recoverable source is one that another person could retrieve with reasonable effort. Do not include in the References list any source not available to others, such as personal letters and other personal communications. (To alert readers to your use of such sources, you use a parenthetical citation marking the source as a personal communication; see, for example, item 34 about personal interviews.) Chart 152 summarizes information about the References list.

GUIDELINES FOR COMPILING AN APA-STYLE REFERENCES LIST 152

- **TITLE**

  References

- **PLACEMENT OF LIST**

  Start a new page numbered sequentially with the rest of the paper, after Notes pages, if any.

- **CONTENT AND FORMAT**

  Include all quoted, paraphrased, or summarized sources in your paper that are not personal communications, unless your instructor tells you to include all the references you have consulted, not just those you have referred to. Start each entry on a new line, and double-space all lines. The APA suggests that whether to use style 1 or 2 (shown below) is a matter of the instructor's (or writer's) preference; check which of the following indent styles your instructor wants you to use.

  1. First line of each entry indented, other lines full width. This style is shown in the fourth edition of the APA *Publication*

→

GUIDELINES FOR COMPILING AN APA-STYLE REFERENCES LIST *(continued)* 152

Manual. Indent the first line of each entry 5 to 7 spaces (or 1 default tab, which is about an inch or 2.5 cm in most word-processing programs). If an entry has more than one line, make all lines after the first full width.

Shuter, R. (1977). A field study of nonverbal communication in Germany, Italy, and the United States. Communication Monographs, 44, 298-305.

2. First line of each entry full width, other lines indented. This "hanging indent" style, shown in the fifth edition (2001) of the APA *Publication Manual*, makes source names and dates prominent. Type the first line of each entry full width, and indent an entry's subsequent lines 5 to 7 spaces (or 1 tab).

Shuter, R. (1977). A field study of nonverbal communication in Germany, Italy, and the United States. Communication Monographs, 44, 298-305.

- **SPACING AFTER PUNCTUATION**

  The 1994 APA *Publication Manual* calls for one space after most punctuation marks: periods at the ends of information units in references (and at the ends of sentences in your paper), commas, semicolons, and colons (except in ratios in your paper [2:1, 100:1]).

- **ARRANGEMENT OF ENTRIES**

  Alphabetize by author's last name. If no author is named, alphabetize by the first significant word (not *A, An,* or *The*) in the title of the work.

- **AUTHORS' NAMES**

  Use last names, first initials, and middle initials if any.

  Reverse the order for all author names, and use an ampersand (&) between the second-to-last and last authors. Mills, J. F., & Holahan, R. H.

  Give names in the order used on the work (title page of book, usually under the article or other printed work). Use a comma between the first author's last name and first initial and after each complete author name except the last. After the last author name, use a period.

- **DATE**

  Put date information after name information, enclosing it in parentheses and using a period followed by one space after the closing parenthesis.

→

GUIDELINES FOR COMPILING AN APA-STYLE REFERENCES LIST *(continued)* 152

For books, articles in journals that have volume numbers, and many other print and nonprint sources, the year of publication or production is the date to use. For articles from most magazines and newspapers, use the year followed by a comma and then the exact date appearing on the issue. Individual entries in 34d-3 show how much information to give for various sources.

- **CAPITALIZATION OF TITLES**

  For books, capitalize the first word, the first word after a colon between a title and subtitle, and any proper nouns. For names of journals and proceedings of meetings, capitalize the first word, all nouns and adjectives, and any other words five or more letters long.

- **SPECIAL TREATMENT OF TITLES**

  Use no special treatment for titles or shorter works (poems, short stories, essays, articles). Underline titles of longer works (books, names of newspapers or journals containing cited articles). For underlining, use an unbroken line if possible. Check with your instructor before using italic type in place of underlining.

  Do not drop *A, An,* or *The* from the titles of periodicals (such as newspapers, magazines, and journals).

- **FORM DESCRIPTION**

  When a source is not a book or an article, a statement about its form is often useful for a reader who wants to retrieve the source. Enclose form information in brackets, and include it after a title and before a period at the end of the block of title information. Do not underline it. Electronically accessed sources should always have a form statement: for example, `[Online]` or `[CD-ROM]`. Also see items 41–45.

- **PUBLISHER**

  Use the full name of a publisher, but drop *Co., Inc., Publishers,* and the like. Retain *Books* or *Press.*

- **PLACE OF PUBLICATION**

  For publishers in the United States, give city and state (use 2-letter postal abbreviations) for all but the largest U.S. cities (such as Boston, Chicago, Los Angeles, and New York). For other countries, give city and country.

  Canadian students and writers publishing in Canada normally use the 2-letter postal abbreviations for Canadian provinces as well as U.S. states. If the country, province, or state is mentioned in the publisher's name, omit it after the city.

GUIDELINES FOR COMPILING AN APA-STYLE REFERENCES LIST *(continued)* 152

- **PUBLICATION MONTH ABBREVIATIONS**
  Do not abbreviate publication months.
- **PAGE NUMBERS**
  Use all digits, omitting none. Use *p.* and *pp.* before page numbers. List all discontinuous pages, with numbers separated by commas: `pp. 32, 44-45, 47-49, 53`.
- **REFERENCES ENTRIES: BOOKS**
  Citations for books have four main parts: author, date, title, and publication information (place of publication and publisher).

AUTHOR	DATE	TITLE	PUBLICATION INFORMATION
Dudek, L.	(1971).	<u>Collected poetry.</u>	Montreal: Delta.

- **REFERENCES ENTRIES: ARTICLES**
  Citations for periodical articles contain four major parts: author, date, title of article, and publication information (usually the periodical title, volume number, and page numbers).

AUTHOR	DATE	ARTICLE TITLE	PERIODICAL TITLE	VOLUME NUMBER	PAGE NUMBERS
Shuter, R.	(1977).	A field of study of nonverbal communication in Germany, Italy, and the United States.	<u>Communication Monographs,</u>	<u>44,</u>	298-305.

- **REFERENCES ENTRIES: ELECTRONIC SOURCES**
  The APA recommends giving information for print forms of sources when print and electronic forms are the same. For Web, FTP, and Gopher sources, give a *Retrieved from* statement with access date and URL. The basic elements of an electronic reference include author(s), date, title and form description (such as `[Online]` or `[CD-ROM]`), periodical title and other information about a print version, producer and database name for a CD-ROM, retrieval statement with an access date, and URL for sources that have them. Here are two typical entries for electronic sources. The first is for an abstract on CD-ROM, and the second is for a journal article found on the World Wide Web.

→

GUIDELINES FOR COMPILING AN APA-STYLE REFERENCES LIST *(continued)* 152

AUTHORS: Marcus, H. F., & Kitayamo, S. — DATE: (1991). — ARTICLE TITLE: Culture and the self: Implications for group dynamics. — FORM DESCRIPTION: [CD-ROM]. — JOURNAL TITLE AND PUBLICATION INFORMATION: Psychological Review, 88(2), 224, 253. — LOCATION INFORMATION: Abstract from: SilverPlatter File: PsycLIT Item: 78-23878.

```
Marcus, H. F., & Kitayamo, S. (1991). Culture and the self:
Implications for group dynamics. [CD-ROM]. Psychological Review,
88(2), 224, 253. Abstract from: SilverPlatter File: PsycLIT
Item: 78-23878.
```

AUTHOR: Lewis, R. — DATE OF PUBLICATION ON THE WEB: (1995, December 11). — TITLE OF ARTICLE: Chronobiology researchers say their field's time has come. — TITLE OF ONLINE JOURNAL: The Scientist, — ISSUE NUMBER: 9, — PAGE NUMBER: 14. — ACCESS DATE: Retrieved December 30, 1997, from the World Wide Web: — URL: www.the-scientist.library.upenn.edu/yr1995/dec/chrono_951211.html

```
Lewis, R. (1995, December 11). Chronobiology researchers say
their field's time has come. The Scientist, 9, 14.
Retrieved December 30, 1997, from the World Wide Web: www.
the-scientist.library.upenn.edu/yr1995/dec/chrono_951211.html
```

Notice that the only punctuation in the URL is part of the address. Do not put a period at the end of a URL unless it belongs to the URL.

3 Following models for an APA-style References list

Directory

PRINT SOURCES

1. Book by One Author—APA
2. Book by Two Authors—APA
3. Book by Three or More Authors—APA
4. Two or More Books by the Same Author(s)—APA

5. Book by Group or Corporate Author—APA
6. Book with No Author Named—APA
7. Book with an Author and an Editor—APA
8. Translation—APA
9. Work in Several Volumes or Parts—APA
10. Anthology or Edited Book—APA
11. One Selection from an Anthology or Edited Book—APA
12. Two Selections from One Anthology or Edited Book—APA
13. Signed Article in a Reference Book—APA
14. Unsigned Article in a Reference Book—APA
15. Edition—APA
16. Introduction, Preface, Foreword, or Afterword—APA
17. Unpublished Dissertation or Essay—APA
18. Reprint of an Older Book—APA
19. Book in a Series—APA
20. Book with a Title Within a Title—APA
21. Government Publication—APA
22. Published Proceedings of a Conference—APA
23. Article from a Daily Newspaper—APA
24. Editorial, Letter to the Editor, or Review—APA
25. Unsigned Article from a Daily Newspaper—APA
26. Article from a Weekly or Biweekly Magazine or Newspaper—APA
27. Article from a Monthly or Bimonthly Periodical—APA
28. Unsigned Article from a Weekly or Monthly Periodical—APA
29. Article from a SIRS Collection of Reprinted Articles—APA
30. Article in a Journal with Continuous Pagination—APA
31. Article in a Journal that Pages Each Issue Separately—APA
32. Letters—APA
33. Map or Chart—APA

NONPRINT SOURCES

34. Interview—APA
35. Lecture, Speech, or Address—APA
36. Film, Videotape, or DVD—APA
37. Recording—APA
38. Live Performance—APA
39. Work of Art, Photograph, or Musical Composition—APA
40. Radio or Television Program—APA
41. Information Services: ERIC and NewsBank—APA

ELECTRONIC AND ONLINE SOURCES

42. Article from an Encyclopedia on CD-ROM—APA
43. Computer Software—APA
44. Book Retrieved from a Database on the Web–APA
45. Article from a Periodical on the Web–APA
46. Personal or Professional Site on the Web–APA

PRINT SOURCES

1. Book by One Author—APA

Trudeau, P. E. (1968). Federalism and the French Canadians. Toronto: Macmillan Canada.

2. Book by Two Authors—APA

Smith, R. J., & Gibbs, M. (1994). Navigating the Internet. Indianapolis, IN: Sams.

3. Book by Three or More Authors—APA

Scardamalia, M., Bereiter, C., & Fillion, B. (1981). Writing for results: A sourcebook of consequential composing activities. Toronto: OISE Press.

Cameron, D., Frazer, E., Harvey, P., Rampton, M. B. H., & Richardson, K. (1992). Researching language: Issues of power and method. London: Routledge.

In an APA References list, include the last names and initials of all authors, even though in your paper you use only the first author's name when a work has six or more authors.

4. Two or More Books by the Same Author(s)—APA

Atwood, M. (1972). Survival. Toronto: Anansi.

Atwood, M. (1981). True stories. Toronto: Oxford University Press.

Atwood, M. (1985). The handmaid's tale. Toronto: McClelland & Stewart.

Repeat the author name(s) for each entry. Arrange the entries by date, from least recent to most recent. To cite two or more works by the same author(s) in the same year, arrange those entries in alphabetical order by title, and then assign a letter to each year (for example, 1993a, 1993b, 1993c). In parenthetical citations, the letter following the year distinguishes one same-year source from another.

5. Book by Group or Corporate Author—APA

Investors Group. (1998). Starting out: Smart strategies for your 20s & 30s. Toronto: Stoddart.

American Psychological Association. (2001). Publication manual of the American Psychological Association (5th ed.). Washington, DC: Author.

When a book is in an edition other than the first, include the edition number in parentheses after the title. Put the period at the end of the block of title information after the closing parenthesis (see also item 6). If the corporate author is also the publisher, use the word *Author* to indicate the publisher.

6. Book with No Author Named—APA

The Chicago manual of style (14th ed.). (1993). Chicago: University of Chicago Press.

In your paper, use a shortened version of the title in parenthetical references (drop *A, An,* or *The* from a shortened title). Underline the words you use for a book title, and capitalize each significant word, even ones that start with lower-case letters in the References list: (Chicago Manual, 1993).

7. Book with an Author and an Editor—APA

Welty, E. (1994). A writer's eye: Collected book reviews (P. A. McHaney, Ed.). Jackson: University Press of Mississippi.

In an APA References list, always capitalize the abbreviation *Ed.* when it stands for the word *Editor* (or *Editors*). (Use a lower-case letter when *ed.* stands for *"edition,"* as in *Rev. ed.* or *2nd ed.*) Note that the state abbreviation is omitted here—the state is mentioned in the publisher's name.

8. Translation—APA

Maillet, A. (1979). La Sagouine. (L. de Cespedes, Trans.). Toronto: Simon & Pierre.

9. Work in Several Volumes or Parts—APA

Rand, E. (1979). Virology (Vols. 1-5). Philadelphia: Lippincott.

Goldman, L. H., Cronin, G. L., and Aharoni, A. (1992). Twentieth-century American Jewish writers: Vol. 2. Saul Bellow: A mosaic. New York: Lang.

10. Anthology or Edited Book—APA

Lantolf, J. P., & Appel, G. (Eds.). (1994). Vygotskian approaches to second language research. Norwood, NJ: Ablex.

New, W. H. (Ed.). (1986). Canadian short fiction: From myth to modern. Scarborough, ON: Prentice Hall.

11. One Selection from an Anthology or Edited Book—APA

Morrisseau, N. (1986). The Indian that became a thunderbird. In W. H. New (Ed.), Canadian short fiction: From myth to modern (pp. 26-29). Scarborough, ON: Prentice Hall.

12. Two Selections from One Anthology or Edited Book—APA

Blank, C. (Ed.). (1992). Language and civilization: A concerted profusion of essays and studies in honor of Otto Heitsch. Frankfurt-am-Main, Germany: Lang.

Middleton, M. (1992). A note on computer jargon. In C. Blank (Ed.), Language and civilization: A concerted profusion of essays and studies in honor of Otto Hietsch (pp. 732-739). Frankfurt-am-Main, Germany: Lang.

Give full publication information in each entry, whether for a selection or for the whole work. In selection entries, after the title of the main work, enclose page numbers for the selection in parentheses, followed by a period. In the main entry, the first information unit is the name of the editor or compiler of the collection. In an entry for each selection entry, the first unit is the name of the author of the selection.

13. Signed Article in a Reference Book—APA

Shadbolt, D. (1988). Emily Carr. In The Canadian encyclopedia (2nd ed.) (Vol. 1, p. 366). Edmonton: Hurtig.

14. Unsigned Article in a Reference Book—APA

Russia. (1994). In Encyclopaedia Britannica.

15. Edition—APA

Buckley, J., & Gates, D. (1995). Put it in writing (2nd ed.). Scarborough, ON: Prentice Hall.

16. Introduction, Preface, Foreword, or Afterword—APA

If the part of the book you are citing was written by the person who wrote the book, do the entry as you would for the entire work with these exceptions. If the part you are citing has a title, give it, without quotation marks or underlining, after the year (for example, a chapter title or the words *Preface, Foreword, Introduction, Afterword,* and *Appendix*). Then, give the title of the book, followed by parentheses enclosing the page numbers of the cited part and ending with a period after the closing parenthesis. Then give publication information.

Troyka, L. Q. (1999). Preface for ESL students. In Simon & Schuster handbook for writers (2nd Canadian ed., pp. 770-772). Scarborough, ON: Prentice Hall.

If the part you are citing does not have a special title, include page numbers in parentheses after the title. If the part you are citing was written by someone other than the person(s) who wrote the book, first give the name of the person who wrote the part, then give the date, then give the title of the part. Then put the word *In* followed by the name(s) of the book's author(s) or editor(s) in normal order, not reversed. Then give the title of the book, page numbers in parentheses of the relevant part, and publication information.

Allmand, W. (1993). Foreword. In J. Brand, The life and death of Anna Mae Aquash (pp. v-ix). Toronto: Lorimer.

17. Unpublished Dissertation or Essay—APA

Buckley, J. (1991). An assessment of Kieran Egan's theory of educational development. Unpublished dissertation, University of Western Ontario, London.

The abbreviation ON (for Ontario) does not follow London in this entry because the name of the university identifies the province.

Stafford, K. M. (1993, January). Trapped in death and enchantment: The liminal space of women in three classical ballets. Paper presented at the annual meeting of the American Comparative Literature Association Graduate Student Conference, Riverside, CA.

18. Reprint of an Older Book—APA

Lampman, A. (1978). Lyrics of earth. Ottawa: Tecumseh Press. (Original work published 1895)

In the text, the citation would read

Lampman (1978/1895).

Republishing information appears on the copyright page.

19. Book in a Series—APA

Courchene, T. J. (1991). In praise of renewed federalism. Toronto: C. D. Howe Institute.

Give the title of the book, but not of the whole series.

20. Book with a Title Within a Title—APA

Lumiansky, R. M., & Baker, H. (Eds.). (1968). Critical approaches to six major English works: Beowulf through Paradise Lost. Philadelphia: University of Pennsylvania Press.

Do not underline an incorporated title even if it would be underlined by itself.

21. Government Publication—APA

Royal Commission on Bilingualism and Biculturalism. (1965). Preliminary report. Ottawa: Queen's Printer.

Indian and Northern Affairs Canada. (1986). The Inuit. Ottawa: Supply and Services Canada.

22. Published Proceedings of a Conference—APA

Smith, D. B. (Ed.). (1997). Forging a new relationship: Proceedings of the conference on the Report of the Royal Commission on Aboriginal Peoples. Montreal: McGill Institute for the Study of Canada.

23. Article from a Daily Newspaper—APA

Christie, J. (1998, March 26). Award bittersweet for hockey women. The Globe and Mail, p. D1.

24. Editorial, Letter to the Editor, or Review—APA

A black mark on local government. (1994, July 27). [Editorial]. The London Free Press, p. B8.

Hurka, J. (1994, July 5). [Letter to the editor]. The Calgary Sun, p. A18.

Toews, W. (1995, August 26). Politics of the mind. [Review of the book They say you're crazy]. Winnipeg Free Press, p. C3.

25. Unsigned Article from a Daily Newspaper—APA

Canadian adds flights. (1994, August 1). The Globe and Mail, p. B2.

26. Article from a Weekly or Biweekly Magazine or Newspaper—APA

Wood, C. (1989, November 6). Storm clouds over Quebec. Maclean's, pp. 16-17.

Use the abbreviations *p.* or *pp.* for newspapers and magazines. Do not use them for journals. Give year, month, and day-date for a periodical published every week or every two weeks.

27. Article from a Monthly or Bimonthly Periodical—APA

When material is not on consecutive pages, give all page numbers.

O'Malley, S. (1994, August). Make-it-happen kinda dreamer: Theatre director Diane Dupuy is nobody's puppet. Chatelaine, pp. 36-39, 90.

Bell, J. (1992, September-October). Kingdom come: Canada's Inuit finally may be getting their own homeland, but at what price? Earthwatch, pp. 10-11.

28. Unsigned Article from a Weekly or Monthly Periodical—APA

10 ways to sleep easy. (1994, August). Canadian Living, p. 19.

29. Article from a SIRS Collection of Reprinted Articles—APA

Curver, P. C. (1989, January-February). Lighting in the 21st century. Futurist, 29-34. Retrieved from SIRS database (SIRS Energy, CD-ROM, 1990 release)

See the models for electronic and online sources, items 41 through 46.

30. Article in a Journal with Continuous Pagination—APA

LaFollette, M. C. (1994). The politics of research misconduct: Congressional oversight, universities, and science. Journal of Higher Education, 65, 261-285.

31. Article in a Journal that Pages Each Issue Separately—APA

Hancock, D. (1993). Prototyping the Hubble fix. IEEE Spectrum, 30 (10), 34-39.

32. Letters—APA

Orlyansky, V. (1991). Letter to the Soviet president. In R. McKay (Ed.), Letters to Gorbachev: Life in Russia through the postbag of "Argumenty i Fakty" (pp. 120-121). London: Michael Joseph.

An *unpublished* letter is not available to your readers. Treat it as a personal communication, acknowledging it in a parenthetical reference in your paper but not including it in the References list.

33. Map or Chart—APA

Russia and post-Soviet republics [Map]. (1992). Moscow: Mapping Production Association.

Nonprint Sources

34. Interview—APA

A personal interview is not available to your readers. Treat it as a personal communication, acknowledging it in a parenthetical reference in your paper but not including it in the References list.

Randi Friedman (personal communication, June 30, 1998) endorses this view.

35. Lecture, Speech, or Address—APA

Barlow, M. (1991, May 25). Address. Speech presented to the League of Canadian Poets, Toronto.

36. Film, Videotape, or DVD—APA

Ego Filmarts/ZDF (Producer), & Egoyan, A. (Director). (1993). Calendar [Film].

Ego Filmarts/ZDF (Producer), & Egoyan, A. (Director). (2001). Calendar [DVD].

37. Recording—APA

The Benedictine Monks of Santo Domingo de Silos. (1994). Chant [CD] (I. F. de la Cuesta, Director; Recording No. CDC 724355513823). Madrid, Spain: Angel Records.

Cohen, L. (Performer). (1988). Tower of song. On I'm your man [CD]. New York: Columbia Records.

38. Live Performance—APA

Shakespeare, W. (Author), Monette, R. (Director), Peacock, L., & Soles, P. (Performers). (2001, May 8). The merchant of Venice [Live performance]. Stratford, ON: Festival Theatre.

39. Work of Art, Photograph, or Musical Composition—APA

Pratt, C. Shop on an island [Artwork]. London, ON: London Regional Art Gallery.

40. Radio or Television Program—APA

Richler, D. (Interviewer). (1992, December 7). [Interview with Martha Gellhorn]. Imprint (Program 72) [Television program]. Toronto: TVOntario.

41. Information Services: ERIC and NewsBank—APA

Chiang, L. H. (1993). Beyond the language: Native Americans' nonverbal communication. Retrieved May 3, 1998, from ERIC online database (ERIC Document Reproduction Service No. ED368540)

Wenzell, R. (1990). Businesses prepare for a more diverse work force. Retrieved March 10, 1999, from NewsBank online database (NewsBank Document Reproduction Service No. EMP 27:DIZ)

Electronic and Online Sources

Information from online sources that your readers probably cannot retrieve for themselves—many e-mail messages and discussion list communications, for example—should be treated as personal communications. Identify the material in your paper, but do not include it in your References list.

The APA system for documenting electronic and online sources in a References list has developed beyond the information in the current, fourth edition of the *Publication Manual* (1994). The models here are based on guidelines APA provides to authors on its Web site <www.apastyle.org>. In general, APA recommends giving author, title, and publication information as for a print source. This information is followed by a "retrieval statement" showing how each source was accessed.

42. Article from an Encyclopedia on CD-ROM—APA

Spanish dance. (2000). Encarta 2000. Retrieved from Encarta database (CD-ROM, 1999 release)

The retrieval statement shows the name of the database and, in parentheses, tells that it is on CD-ROM and gives its release date. Note that the entry does not have end punctuation.

43. Computer Software—APA

Transparent Language Presentation Program (Version 2.0 for Windows) [Computer software]. (1994). Hollis, NH: Transparent Language.

44. Book Retrieved from a Database on the Web—APA

Eaton, A. W. (1889). Acadian legends and lyrics. London & New York: White & Allen. Retrieved May 25, 2001, from Early Canadiana Online database on the World Wide Web: http://www.canadiana.org/cgi-bin/ECO/mtq?doc=09066

The first information block is for the printed version of *Acadian Legends and Lyrics.* The retrieval statement gives the access date, the name of the database, and the URL. The URL is not followed by end punctuation.

45. Article from a Periodical on the Web—APA

Parrott, A. C. (1999). Does cigarette smoking cause stress? American Psychologist, 54, 817-820. Retrieved December 7, 1999, from the World Wide Web: http://www.apa.org/journals/amp/amp5410817.html

46. Personal or Professional Site on the Web—APA

When citing an entire Web site, rather than a particular part of that site, you need only provide the Web address in a parenthetical citation, as in the following example.

The Canada Site is an excellent starting point for online research into current Canadian government publications (http://www.canada.gc.ca/).

4 Writing an abstract and using notes in APA style

You may be asked to include an abstract at the start of a paper you prepare in APA style. An abstract, as described in the 1994 edition of the

APA *Publication Manual*, is "a brief, comprehensive summary" (p. 8). Make this summary accurate, objective, and exact.

✤ APA FORMAT ALERT: If you include an abstract in an APA-style paper, put it on page 2, a separate page after the title page. For an example of an abstract, see the student paper on biological clocks in section 36b. ✤

Content notes can be used in APA-style papers for additional relevant information that cannot be worked effectively into a text discussion. Use consecutive arabic numerals for note numbers, both within your paper and on a separate page following the last text page of your paper. Using the heading *Notes* on this page, number it with your paper, and double-space the notes themselves.

34e Using CM-style documentation

The style manual of the University of Chicago Press endorses two styles of documentation. One is a "name-year" style, similar to the APA's system, using in-text citations that direct readers to an alphabetical References list containing full bibliographic details about each source. Parenthetical references commonly contain an author name and a publication year, separated by a space but no punctuation: (English 1995).

The other style of CM (for *Chicago Manual*) documentation is a note system often used in the disciplines of English, the humanities, and history; that is the style presented here. The CM note system gives complete bibliographic information within a footnote or endnote the first time a source is cited. If that source is cited again, less information is given because the source has already been fully described. A separate Bibliography is usually unnecessary.

TEXT

Welty also makes this point.[1]

NOTE

1. Eudora Welty, <u>One Writer's Beginnings</u> (Cambridge: Harvard University Press, 1984), 17.

Notes may be either at the end of a paper (endnotes) or at the foot of the page on which a citation falls (footnotes). Endnotes are usually easier to format, especially if you are handwriting or typing your paper. Popular word processing programs can format either endnotes or footnotes easily.

Section 34e focuses on the CM bibliographic note system of documentation. In case you are asked to provide a separate

Bibliography, models of various bibliographic entries are shown as well. For complete coverage of bibliographic entries in CM style, see Chapter 15 of *The Chicago Manual of Style*, 14th edition.

1 Creating CM-style bibliographic notes

Chart 153 gives general guidelines for the content and format of CM-style bibliographic notes.

GUIDELINES FOR COMPILING CM-STYLE BIBLIOGRAPHIC NOTES

153

- **TITLE**
  For endnotes, `Notes,` on a new page numbered sequentially with the rest of the paper, after the last text page of the paper. (Footnotes appear at the bottom of the pages where sources are cited.)
- **FORMAT**
  Place endnotes after the text of your paper, on a separate page entitled Notes. Centre the word *Notes* about an inch (2.5 cm) from the top of the page. Double-space after the word *Notes.* Single-space the notes themselves. Indent each note's first line 3 characters (or 1 tab space in your word processing program); do not indent a note's subsequent lines.
  In the body of your paper, use raised (superscript) arabic numerals for the note numbers. Note numbers should be positioned after any punctuation marks except the dash, preferably at the end of a sentence. On the Notes pages, number and note should be the same type size; the number is not raised and a period should follow it. (Not all word processing programs allow you to observe these guidelines.)
- **SPACING AFTER PUNCTUATION**
  Use one space.
- **ARRANGEMENT OF NOTES**
  Arrange notes in numerical order.
- **AUTHORS' NAMES**
  Give the name in standard (not inverted) order, with names and initials as given in the original source. Use the word *and* between (the last) two authors.
- **CAPITALIZATION OF TITLES**
  Capitalize the first word, the last word, and all major words.

➜

GUIDELINES FOR COMPILING CM-STYLE BIBLIOGRAPHIC NOTES *(continued)*

153

- **SPECIAL TREATMENT OF TITLES**
  Underline the titles of long works, and use quotation marks around the titles of shorter works.
  Omit *A, An,* and *The* from the titles of newspapers and periodicals. If the city of publication is not part of a newspaper title, add it before the title and treat it as part of the name: *Prince Albert Herald.* The province or state, where useful for clarity, may be added in parentheses: *Prince Albert* (Sask.) *Herald.*
- **PUBLICATION INFORMATION**
  Enclose publication information in parentheses when using numbered bibliographic notes—but not in a separate Bibliography section. (See also 34e-2.) Use a colon and one space after the city of publication. If it is unclear where the city is located, follow the city with a comma, insert the standard (not postal) abbreviation for the province, state, or country, and end with a colon and one space. Give complete publishers' names or abbreviate them according to standard abbreviations in *Books in Print.* Omit *Co., Inc.,* and *Ltd.* Do not omit *Books* or *Press.*
  Do not abbreviate publication months.
- **PAGE NUMBERS**
  List all page numbers. In ranges of numbers, give the full second number for 2 through 99. For 100 and beyond, give the full second number if a shortened version is ambiguous.
- **SECOND CITATIONS**
  When full bibliographic information has been given in the first note citing a source, subsequent citations can be brief. In short papers, author name(s) and a page reference are usually sufficient information. If you have used more than one work by the author(s), give a shortened title as well.
- **CONTENT NOTES**
  Try to avoid using content notes. If you must use one or two, make them footnotes and use symbols (* and † are standard) rather than numbers. You can repeat these footnote symbols on every page.
- **BIBLIOGRAPHIC NOTES: BOOKS**

  Citations for books include the author, title, publication information, and page numbers if applicable. Note 1 (below) is for the first citation of a book; note 5 is for its second citation in a paper that cites two works by Welty, *One Writer's Beginnings* and *"A Worn Path."*

GUIDELINES FOR COMPILING CM-STYLE BIBLIOGRAPHIC NOTES *(continued)* 153

AUTHOR | TITLE | PUBLICATION INFORMATION | PAGE NUMBERS

1. Eudora Welty, _One Writer's Beginnings_ (Cambridge: Harvard University Press, 1984), 15.

5. Welty, _One_, 21.

■ **BIBLIOGRAPHIC NOTES: ARTICLES**

Citations for articles include the author, article title, journal title, volume number, year, and page numbers. Note 1 (below) shows the first citation of an article, and note 5 shows the second citation for the article in a paper citing only one work by these authors.

AUTHORS | ARTICLE TITLE | JOURNAL TITLE | VOLUME NUMBER | YEAR | PAGE NUMBERS

1. D. D. Cochran, W. Daniel Hale, and Christine P. Hissam, "Personal Space Requirements in Indoor versus Outdoor Locations," _Journal of Psychology_ 117 (1984): 132-33.

5. Cochran, Hale, and Hissam, 133.

2 Following models for CM-style documentation

Directory

PRINT SOURCES: BOOKS

6. Book with No Author Named—CM
7. Book with an Author and an Editor—CM
8. Translation—CM
9. Work in Several Volumes or Parts—CM
10. One Selection from an Anthology or Edited Book—CM
11. Two Selections from One Anthology or Edited Book—CM
12. Signed Article in a Reference Book—CM
13. Unsigned Article in a Reference Book—CM
14. Edition—CM
15. Anthology or Edited Book—CM
16. Introduction, Preface, Foreword, or Afterword—CM
17. Unpublished Dissertation or Essay—CM
18. Reprint of an Older Book—CM
19. Book in a Series—CM
20. Book with a Title Within a Title—CM
21. Secondary Source—CM
22. Government Publication—CM
23. Published Proceedings of a Conference—CM

PRINT SOURCES: ARTICLES

24. Article from a Daily Newspaper—CM
25. Editorial, Letter to the Editor, or Review—CM
26. Unsigned Article from a Daily Newspaper—CM
27. Article from a Weekly or Biweekly Magazine or Newspaper—CM
28. Article from a Monthly or Bimonthly Periodical—CM
29. Unsigned Article from a Weekly or Monthly Periodical—CM
30. Article from a Collection of Reprinted Articles—CM
31. Article in a Journal with Continuous Pagination—CM
32. Article in a Journal that Pages Each Issue Separately—CM

NONPRINT SOURCES

33. Personal Interview—CM
34. Letter—CM
35. Film, Videotape, or DVD—CM
36. Recording—CM

ELECTRONIC SOURCES

37. Computer Software—CM
38. ERIC Information Service—CM
39. Electronic Document—CM

PRINT SOURCES: BOOKS

1. BOOK BY ONE AUTHOR—CM

1. Pierre E. Trudeau, Federalism and the French Canadians (Toronto: Macmillan Canada, 1968), 25.

2. Giuliana Prata, M.D., A Systematic Harpoon into Family Games: Preventive Interventions in Therapy (New York: Brunner/Mazel Publishers, 1990), 63.

Here are Bibliography entries for books by one author. Entries in a Bibliography are arranged alphabetically; in contrast to the style used with numbered notes, publication information is not enclosed in parentheses.

Prata, Giuliana, M.D. A Systematic Harpoon into Family Games: Preventive Interventions in Therapy. New York: Brunner/Mazel, 1990.

Trudeau, Pierre E. Federalism and the French Canadians. Toronto: Macmillan Canada, 1968.

2. BOOK BY TWO OR THREE AUTHORS—CM

1. Marlene Scardamalia, Carl Bereiter, and Bryant Fillion, Writing for Results: A Sourcebook of Consequential Composing Activities (Toronto: OISE Press, 1981), 73.

2. Richard J. Smith and Mark Gibbs, Navigating the Internet. (Indianapolis: Sams, 1994), 15.

Here are Bibliography entries.

Scardamalia, Marlene, Carl Bereiter, and Bryant Fillion. Writing for Results: A Sourcebook of Consequential Composing Activities. Toronto: OISE Press, 1981.

Smith, Richard J., and Mark Gibbs. Navigating the Internet. Indianapolis: Sams, 1994.

3. BOOK BY MORE THAN THREE AUTHORS—CM

1. Deborah Cameron et al., Researching Language: Issues of Power and Method (London: Routledge Publishers, 1992), 102.

Here is a Bibliography entry:

Cameron, Deborah, et al. Researching Language: Issues of Power and Method. London: Routledge, 1992.

4. Multiple Citations of a Single Source—CM

Second and subsequent notes use shortened forms (see Chart 153 in section 34e-1). *Ibid.* can be used when the information in a note is exactly the same as the information in the immediately preceding note. If only the page references differ in two successive notes, you can use *Ibid.* with the respective pages.

2. Schaller, 33.

3. Ibid., 37.

5. Book by Group or Corporate Author—CM

1. Investors Group, Starting Out: Smart Strategies for Your 20s & 30s (Toronto: Stoddart, 1998), 94.

Here is the Bibliography entry:

Investors Group. Starting Out: Smart Strategies for Your 20s & 30s. Toronto: Stoddart, 1998.

6. Book with No Author Named—CM

1. The Chicago Manual of Style, 14th ed. (Chicago: University of Chicago Press, 1993), 241.

7. Book with an Author and an Editor—CM

When the focus in your paper is on Welty and her reviews, use this form:

1. Eudora Welty, A Writer's Eye: Collected Book Reviews, ed. Pearl Amelia McHaney (Jackson: University Press of Mississippi, 1994).

When your focus is on McHaney's work as editor, use this form:

1. Pearl Amelia McHaney, ed., A Writer's Eye: Collected Book Reviews, by Eudora Welty (Jackson: University Press of Mississippi, 1994).

Here are the Bibliography entries. Parenthetical citations use the name that begins the entry.

Welty, Eudora. A Writer's Eye: Collected Book Reviews. Edited by Pearl Amelia McHaney. Jackson: University Press of Mississippi, 1994.

McHaney, Pearl Amelia, ed. A Writer's Eye: Collected Book Reviews, by Eudora Welty. Jackson: University Press of Mississippi, 1994.

8. Translation—CM

1. Antonine Maillet, La Sagouine, trans. Luis de Cespedes (Toronto: Simon & Pierre, 1979).

Here is the Bibliography entry:

Maillet, Antonine. La Sagouine. Translated by Luis de Cespedes. Toronto: Simon & Pierre, 1979.

9. Work in Several Volumes or Parts—CM

The two notes numbered 1 show different ways to give bibliographic information for a specific reference in one volume of a multivolume work. Use whichever you prefer, being consistent throughout a paper. If you are writing about the volume as a whole (as opposed to citing specific pages), end the note with the publication information but no page numbers.

1. L. H. Goldman, Gloria L. Cronin, and Ada Aharoni, Saul Bellow: A Mosaic, vol. 2 of Twentieth-Century American Jewish Writers (New York: Lang, 1992), 97.

1. L. H. Goldman, Gloria L. Cronin, and Ada Aharoni, Twentieth-Century American Jewish Writers, vol. 2, Saul Bellow: A Mosaic (New York: Lang, 1992), 97.

If you are citing an entire work in two or more volumes, use the form shown in note 2.

2. John Herman Randall, Jr., The Career of Philosophy, 2 vols. (New York: Columbia University Press, 1962).

10. One Selection from an Anthology or Edited Book—CM

1. Norval Morrisseau, "The Indian That Became a Thunderbird," in Canadian Short Fiction: From Myth to Modern, ed. W. H. New (Scarborough, Ont.: Prentice Hall, 1986), 26-29.

11. Two Selections from One Anthology or Edited Book—CM

If you cite two or more selections from the same anthology or edited book, give complete bibliographical information in the first note for each selection.

12. Signed Article in a Reference Book—CM

1. Doris Shadbolt, "Emily Carr," in The Canadian Encyclopedia, 2nd ed.

13. Unsigned Article in a Reference Book—CM

1. Encyclopaedia Britannica, 15th ed., s.v. "Russia."

14. Edition—CM

1. Joanne Buckley and David Gates, Put It in Writing, 2nd ed. (Scarborough, Ont.: Prentice Hall, 1995).

15. Anthology or Edited Book—CM

1. W. H. New, ed., Canadian Short Fiction: From Myth to Modern (Scarborough, Ont.: Prentice Hall, 1986).

16. Introduction, Preface, Foreword, or Afterword—CM

1. Warren Allmand, foreword to The Life and Death of Anna Mae Aquash, by Johanna Brand (Toronto: Lorimer, 1993).

17. Unpublished Dissertation or Essay—CM

1. Joanne Buckley, "An Assessment of Kieran Egan's Theory of Educational Development" (diss., University of Western Ontario, 1991), 33-42.

State the author's name first, the title in quotation marks (not underlined), then a description of the work (such as *Ph.D. diss.* or *master's thesis*), then the degree-granting institution, and the date.

18. Reprint of an Older Book—CM

1. Archibald Lampman, Lyrics of Earth (1895; reprint, Ottawa: Tecumseh Press, 1978).

19. Book in a Series—CM

1. Thomas J. Courchene, In Praise of Renewed Federalism, The Canada Round (Toronto: C. D. Howe Institute, 1991).

20. Book with a Title Within a Title—CM

1. Robert M. Lumiansky and Herschel Baker, eds., Critical Approaches to Six Major English Works: "Beowulf" Through "Paradise Lost" (Philadelphia: University of Pennsylvania Press, 1968).

If the name of a work that is usually underlined appears in a title, put quotation marks around it. If the name of a work that is usually in quotation marks appears in a title, keep it in quotation marks and underline it.

21. Secondary Source—CM

When you quote one person's words, having found them in another person's work, give information as fully as you can about both sources. Note 1 shows the form when the focus of your citation is Mary Wollstonecraft's words. If your focus is on what Shrodes, Finestone, and Shugrue have to say about Wollstonecraft's words, handle the information as shown in note 2.

1. Mary Wollstonecraft, A Vindication of the Rights of Woman (1792), 90, quoted in Caroline Shrodes, Harry Finestone, and Michael Shugrue, The Conscious Reader, 4th ed. (New York: Macmillan, 1988), 282.

2. Caroline Shrodes, Harry Finestone, and Michael Shugrue, The Conscious Reader, 4th ed. (New York: Macmillan, 1988), 282, quoting Mary Wollstonecraft, A Vindication of the Rights of Woman (1792), 90.

22. Government Publication—CM

1. Royal Commission on Bilingualism and Biculturalism, Preliminary Report (Ottawa: Queen's Printer, 1965), 127.

2. Indian and Northern Affairs Canada, The Inuit (Ottawa: Supply and Services Canada, 1986), 46.

When a government department, bureau, agency, or committee produces a document, cite that group as the author.

23. Published Proceedings of a Conference—CM

1. Arnold Eskin, "Some Properties of the System Controlling the Circadian Activity Rhythm of Sparrows," in Biochronometry, ed. Michael Menaker (Washington, D.C.: National Academy of Sciences, 1971), 55-80.

Treat published conference proceedings as you would a chapter in a book.

Print Sources: Articles

24. Article from a Daily Newspaper—CM

1. James Christie, "Award Bittersweet for Hockey Women," Globe and Mail 26 March 1998, sec. D, p. 1.

25. Editorial, Letter to the Editor, or Review—CM

1. "A Black Mark on Local Government," editorial, London Free Press, 27 July 1994, sec. B, p. 8.

2. John Hurka, letter, Calgary Sun, 5 July 1994, sec. A, p. 18.

3. Wendy Toews, "Politics of the Mind," review of They Say You're Crazy, by Paula J. Caplan, Winnipeg Free Press, 26 August 1995, p. C3.

26. Unsigned Article from a Daily Newspaper—CM

1. "Canadian Adds Flights," Globe and Mail, 1 August 1994, sec. B, p. 2.

27. Article from a weekly or Biweekly Magazine or Newspaper—CM

1. Chris Woods, "Storm Clouds over Quebec," Maclean's, 6 November 1989, 16–17.

28. Article from a Monthly or Bimonthly Periodical—CM

1. Jim Bell, "Kingdom Come: Canada's Inuit Finally May Be Getting Their Own Homeland, But at What Price?" Earthwatch, September-October 1992, 10–11.

29. Unsigned Article from a Weekly or Monthly Periodical—CM

1. "10 Ways to Sleep Easy," Canadian Living, August 1994, 19.

30. Article from a Collection of Reprinted Articles—CM

1. Phillip C. Curver, "Lighting in the 21st Century," Energy, Social Issues Resources Series, vol. 4 (Boca Raton, Fla.: Social Issues Resources, 1990).

Cite only the publication actually consulted, not the original source. In a Bibliography entry, cite both the reprinted publication you consulted and the publication where the article first appeared.

31. Article in a Journal with Continuous Pagination—CM

1. Marcel C. La Follette, "The Politics of Research Misconduct: Congressional Oversight, Universities, and Science," Journal of Higher Education 65 (1994): 261-85.

Here is the Bibliography entry:

La Follette, Marcel C. "The Politics of Research Misconduct: Congressional Oversight, Universities, and Science." Journal of Higher Education 65 (1994): 261-85.

32. Article in a Journal that Pages Each Issue Separately—CM

1. Dennis Hancock, "Prototyping the Hubble Fix," IEEE Spectrum 30, no. 10 (1993): 34-39.

The issue number of a journal is required only if each issue starts with page 1. In this example, the volume number is 30 and the issue number is 10.

Nonprint Sources

33. Personal Interview—CM

1. Randi Friedman, interview by author, Fredericton, New Brunswick, 30 June 1998.

For an unpublished interview, give the name of the interviewee, identify the interviewer, and then give location and date.

34. Letter—CM

Treat a published letter like any other published document. For an unpublished letter, give the name of the writer, the name of the recipient, and the date of the letter.

1. Gary Edward Reilly, letter to author, 26 December 2000.

35. Film, Videotape, or DVD—CM

1. Atom Egoyan, Calendar (Canada/Armenia/Germany: Ego Filmarts/ZDF, 1993).

1. Atom Egoyan, Calendar (Canada/Armenia/Germany, 1993; Alliance Atlantis, 2001), DVD.

The medium, the use you are making of the material, and the facts necessary to retrieve the source should guide your treatment of it.

36. Recording—CM

1. Benedictine Monks of Santo Domingo de Silos, Chant. Ismael Fernandes de la Cuesta, dir. Angel CDC 724355513823.

Electronic Sources

37. Computer Software—CM

1. Microsoft Word Ver. 8.0, Microsoft, Seattle, Wash.

Place the version or release number, abbreviated as *Ver.* or *Rel.*, directly after the name of the software. Then list the company that owns the rights to the software, followed by the company's location.

38. ERIC Information Service—CM

1. Linda H. Chiang, Beyond the Language: Native Americans' Nonverbal Communication (Anderson, Ind.: Midwest Association of Teachers of Educational Psychology, 1993). ERIC, ED 368540.

Here is the Bibliography entry:

Chiang, Linda H. Beyond the Language: Native Americans' Nonverbal Communication. Anderson, Ind.: Midwest Association of Teachers of Educational Psychology, 1993. ERIC, ED 368540.

39. Electronic Document—CM

At its Web site <www.press.uchicago.edu/Misc/Chicago/cmosfaq. html>, the University of Chicago Press promises more complete coverage of electronic sources in its forthcoming edition. Until then, it endorses documentation guidelines of the International Standards Organization (ISO), the MLA, and the APA for electronic sources.

The ISO recommends listing the following information units: author(s), if any; title; database medium; information about a print version; access or update dates; item or access numbers, if any; paging or other description of length, if any; and location information. It recommends putting information about the database medium, access dates, and length in brackets. For more information, you can consult the ISO guidelines at <www.nlc-bnc.ca/iso/tc46sc9/index.htm>.

1. Dan S. Wallach, "FAQ: Typing Injuries (2/5): General Info.," in typing-injury-faq/general.Z [electronic bulletin board], 1993_[cited 14 November 1993]; available from mail-server@rtfm.mit.edu; INTERNET.

USING AND CITING GRAPHICS—CM

Place the credit line for a table or illustration from another source next to the reproduced material. (If you intend to publish your paper, you must receive permission to reprint copyrighted material from a source.) Spell out the terms *map, plate,* and *table,* but abbreviate *figure* as *fig*.

Reprinted, by permission, from Linda R. Pim, Additive Alert: A Guide to Food Additives for the Canadian Consumer (Toronto: Doubleday, 1979), 28, fig. 2. Copyright 1979 by Pollution Probe Foundation.

34f Using CBE-style documentation

In its 1994 style manual, *Scientific Style and Format,* the (U.S.) Council of Biology Editors (CBE) endorses two documentation systems widely used in mathematics and the physical and life sciences. (The organization is now known as the Council of Science Editors, although its guidelines are still known by the older name.) The first system uses name-year parenthetical citations in the text of a paper together with a References list that gives full bibliographic information for each source. The second system uses numbers to mark citations in the text of a paper that correlate with a numbered References list.

This handbook focuses mainly on CBE's numbered reference system. Here is the way it works:

- The first time you cite each source in your paper, assign it a number in sequence, starting with 1.
- Mark each subsequent reference to the source with the assigned number.
- In your References list, list and number each entry in the order of its appearance in your paper, starting with 1.

The CBE recommends using superscript numbers for marking source citations in your paper, although numbers in parentheses are also acceptable. Here is a brief example showing two sources cited in a paper and a References list arranged in citation sequence.

IN-TEXT CITATIONS

`Sybesma[1] insists that this behaviour occurs periodically, but Crowder[2] claims never to have observed it.`

REFERENCES LIST

1. Sybesma C. An introduction to biophysics. New York: Academic Press; 1977. 648 p.
2. Crowder W. Seashore life between the tides. New York: Dodd, Mead & Co.; 1931. New York: Dover Publications Reprint; 1975. 373 p.

Each citation of Sybesma's *Introduction to Biophysics* is followed by a superscript 1, and each citation of Crowder's *Seashore Life* is followed by a superscript 2 in this paper.

1 Compiling a CBE-style References list

GUIDELINES FOR COMPILING A CBE-STYLE REFERENCES LIST 154

- **TITLE**
  `References` or `Cited References`
- **PLACEMENT OF LIST**
  Start a new page numbered sequentially with the rest of the paper.
- **CONTENT AND FORMAT**
  Include all sources quoted from, paraphrased, or summarized in your paper.
  Centre the title about 1 inch (2.5 cm) from the top of the page.
  Start each entry on a new line. Put the number followed by a space at the regular left margin. If an entry takes more than one line, indent the second and all other lines. The CBE does not specify an indent; unless your instructor specifies an indent, you can indent as for an MLA Works Cited list (see Chart 151 in section 34c-2). Double-space each entry and between entries.
- **SPACING AFTER PUNCTUATION**
  Follow the spacing shown in the models in 34f-2.
- **ARRANGEMENT OF ENTRIES**
  Sequence the entries in the order that you cite the sources in your paper.
- **AUTHORS' NAMES**
  Invert all author names, giving the last name first. You can give first names or use only initials of first and middle names. If you use initials, do not use a period or a space between first and →

GUIDELINES FOR COMPILING A CBE-STYLE REFERENCES LIST *(continued)* 154

middle initials. If you use full first names, separate the names of multiple authors with a semicolon. Do not use *and* or *&*. Place a period after the last author's name.

- **CAPITALIZATION OF TITLES**
  Capitalize a book or an article title's first word and any proper nouns. Do not capitalize the first word of a subtitle unless it is a proper noun.

  Capitalize the titles of academic journals. If the title of a periodical is one word, give it in full; otherwise, abbreviate it according to recommendations established by the *American National Standard for Abbreviations of Titles of Periodicals.*

  Capitalize a newspaper title's major words, giving the full title, but omit *A, An,* or *The.*
- **SPECIAL TREATMENT OF TITLES**
  Do not underline titles or enclose titles in quotation marks.
- **PLACE OF PUBLICATION**
  Use a colon after the city of publication. Add a provincial or state postal abbreviation or a country name to a city that might be ambiguous—for example, `Scarborough (ON); Nijmegen (Netherlands).`
- **PUBLISHER**
  Give publishers' names, omitting *Co., Inc., Press, Ltd.,* and so on. Use a semicolon after the publisher's name.
- **PUBLICATION MONTH ABBREVIATIONS**
  Abbreviate publication months, but omit the period.
- **INCLUSIVE PAGE NUMBERS**
  Shorten the second number as much as possible while keeping it unambiguous—for example, 233–4 for 233 to 234; 233–44 for 233 to 244; 234–304. Use the abbreviation *p* without a period or underlining with designations of pages. Follow the guidelines in the models.
- **DISCONTINUOUS PAGE NUMBERS**
  Give the full numbers of all discontinuous pages, preceding the first number with the *p* abbreviation, and separating successive numbers or ranges with a comma.
- **TOTAL PAGE NUMBERS**
  When citing an entire book, give as the last information unit the total number of pages, followed by the abbreviation *p* and a period.
- **REFERENCES ENTRY: BOOK**
  Citations for books usually list author(s), title, publication information, and pages (either total pages when citing an entire work or ➜

GUIDELINES FOR COMPILING A CBE-STYLE REFERENCES LIST *(continued)* 154

inclusive pages for citing part of a book). Each unit of information ends with a period.

```
1. Stacy RW, Williams DT, Worden RE, McMorris RO. Essentials
   of biological and medical sciences. New York: McGraw-Hill;
   1955. 727 p.
```

■ **REFERENCES ENTRY: ARTICLE**
Citations for articles usually list author(s), article title, journal name and publication information, each section followed by a period. *Sci Am* is the abbreviated form of *Scientific American.* The volume number is 269, and the issue number, in parentheses, is (3).

```
1. Weissman IL, Cooper MD. How the immune system develops. Sci
   Am 1993 Mar;269(3):65-71.
```

2 Following models for a CBE-style References list

Directory

Print Sources: Books

1. Book by One Author—CBE
2. Book by More than One Author—CBE
3. Book by Group or Corporate Author—CBE
4. Anthology or Edited Book—CBE
5. One Selection or Chapter from an Anthology or Edited Book—CBE
6. Translation—CBE
7. Reprint of an Older Book—CBE
8. All Volumes of a Multivolume Work—CBE
9. Unpublished Dissertation or Thesis—CBE

Print Sources: Articles

10. Published Article from Conference Proceedings—CBE
11. Signed Newspaper Article—CBE
12. Unsigned Newspaper Article—CBE
13. Article in a Journal with Continuous Pagination—CBE

14. Article in a Journal that Pages Each Issue Separately—CBE
15. Journal Article on Discontinuous Pages—CBE
16. Article with Author Affiliation—CBE
17. Entire Issue of a Journal—CBE
18. Article with No Identifiable Author—CBE

Other Sources

19. Map—CBE
20. Unpublished Letter—CBE
21. Filmstrip—CBE
22. Videorecording—CBE
23. Slide Set—CBE
24. Electronic Sources—CBE

Print Sources: Books

1. Book by One Author—CBE

1. Hawking SW. Black holes and baby universes and other essays. New York: Bantam; 1993. 320 p.

Use one space but no punctuation between an author's last name and the initial of the first name. Do not put punctuation or a space between a first and a middle initial.

2. Book by More than One Author—CBE

1. Wegzyn S, Gille J-C, Vidal P. Developmental systems: at the crossroads of system theory, computer science, and genetic engineering. New York: Springer; 1990. 595 p.

3. Book by Group or Corporate Author—CBE

1. Canadian Institute of Child Health. Family-centred maternity and newborn care. Ottawa: CICH; 1980. 178 p.

4. Anthology or Edited Book—CBE

1. Heerman B, Hummel S, editors. Ancient DNA: recovery and analysis of genetic material from paleontological, archeological, museum, medical, and forensic specimens. New York: Springer; 1994. 1029 p.

5. One Selection or Chapter from an Anthology or Edited Book—CBE

1. Basov NG, Feoktistov LP, Senatsky YV. Laser driver for inertial confinement fusion. In: Brueckner, KA, editor. Research trends in physics: inertial confinement fusion. New York: American Institute of Physics; 1992: p 24-37.

6. Translation—CBE

1. Magris C. A different sea. Spurr MS, translator. London: Harvill; 1993. 194 p. Translation of: Un mare differente.

7. Reprint of an Older Book—CBE

1. Carson R. The sea around us. New York: Oxford University; 1951. New York: Limited Editions Club Reprint; 1980. 220 p.

8. All Volumes of a Multivolume Work—CBE

1. Crane FL, Moore DJ, Low HE, editors. Oxidoreduction at the plasma membrane: relation to growth and transport. Boca Raton (FL): Chemical Rubber Company; 1991. 2 vol.

Use a two-letter postal abbreviation enclosed in parentheses after the name of a city that might be unfamiliar to your readers.

9. Unpublished Dissertation or Thesis—CBE

1. Baykul MC. Using ballistic electron emission microscopy to investigate the metal-vacuum interface. [dissertation]. Orem (UT): Polytechnic University; 1993. 111 p.

Print Sources: Articles

10. Published Article from Conference Proceedings—CBE

1. Tsang CP, Bellgard MI. Sequence generation using a network of Boltzmann machines. In: Tsang CP, editor. Proceedings of the 4th Australian Joint Conference on Artificial Intelligence; 1990 Nov 8-11; Perth, Australia. Singapore: World Scientific; 1990: p 224-33.

11. Signed Newspaper Article—CBE

1. Hoke F. Gene therapy: clinical gains yield a wealth of research opportunities. Scientist 1993 Oct 4;Sect A:1, 5, 7.

Sect stands for *Section.*

12. Unsigned Newspaper Article—CBE

1. [Anonymous]. Arctic drilling study. Globe and Mail 1995 Sept 2;Sect D:8.

13. Article in a Journal with Continuous Pagination—CBE

1. Lomas J, Woods J, Veenstra G. Devolving authority for health care in Canada's provinces: 1. an introduction to the issues. CMAJ 1997;156(3):371-7.

Give only the volume number before the page numbers.

14. Article in a Journal that Pages Each Issue Separately—CBE

1. Weissman IL, Cooper MD. How the immune system develops. Sci Am 1993 Mar;269(3):65-71.

Give both the volume number and the issue number (here, *269* is the volume number and *3* is the issue number). *Sci Am* is the abbreviation for *Scientific American* based on the standards established by the *American National Standard for Abbreviations of Titles of Periodicals.*

15. Journal Article on Discontinuous Pages—CBE

1. Richards FM. The protein folding problem. Sci Am 1991 Nov;246(1):54-7, 60-6.

16. Article with Author Affiliation—CBE

1. DeMoll E, Auffenberg T (Dept. of Microbiology, Univ. of Kentucky). Purine metabolism in <u>Methanococcus vannielii</u>. J Bacteriol 1993;175:5754-61.

17. Entire Issue of a Journal—CBE

1. Whales in a modern world: a symposium held in London, November 1988. Mamm Rev 1990 Jan;20(9).

November 1988, the date of the symposium, is part of the title of the issue in this case.

18. Article with No Identifiable Author—CBE

1. [Anonymous]. Cruelty to animals linked to murders of humans. AWI Q 1993 Aug;42(3):16.

Other Sources

19. Map—CBE

1. Russia and Post-Soviet Republics [political map]. Moscow: Mapping Production Association; 1992. Conical equidistant projection; 100 x 120 cm; coloured, scale 1:8 000 000.

20. Unpublished Letter—CBE

1. Darwin C. [Letter to Mr. Clerke, 1861]. Located at: University of Iowa Library, Iowa City. IA.

21. Filmstrip—CBE

1. Volcano: the eruption and healing of Mount St. Helens [filmstrip]. Westminster (MD): Random House; 1988. 114 frames: colour; 35 mm. Accompanied by: cassette tape; 22 min.

After the title and description of the filmstrip, give the author, producer, and year. Then give other descriptive information.

22. Videorecording—CBE

1. The discovery of the pulsar: the ultimate ignorance [videocassette]. London: BBC; 1983. 1 cassette: 48 min, sound, colour.

23. Slide Set—CBE

1. Human parasitology [slides]. Chicago (IL): American Society of Clinical Pathologists Press; 1990: colour. Accompanied by: guide.

24. Electronic Sources—CBE

In general, to cite electronic sources, start with a statement of the type of document, and then give the information you would give for a print version. Then, give information that would help a reader to locate the electronic source. End with a date: your access date for online sources or the date of the update you used for CD-ROM databases that are updated periodically.

For a journal accessed online, follow the pattern for a print journal. Insert the note *[serial online]* after the journal's name. End the item with the name or description of the Web site, followed by the URL in parentheses.

```
1. Franch HA, Sooparb S, Du J, Brown NS. A mechanism regulating
   proteolysis of specific proteins during renal tubular cell
   growth J Biol Chem [serial online] 2001;276(22): 19126-31.
   Available from: Journal of Biological Chemistry Web site via
   the Internet (http://www.jbc.org/).
```

34g Using Columbia online-style documentation

The Columbia Guide to Online Style (COS) uses many of the same elements present in predominantly print documentation styles such as MLA and APA to cite works. However, COS includes new format elements unique to electronic publications. COS for the humanities is similar to MLA style, while COS for the sciences shares elements of APA style. Be sure to check with your instructor to find out which documentation style to use. He or she may prefer another style for online sources.

1 Citing sources in the body of a paper in COS

In print publications, parenthetical or in-text references include elements such as the author's last name and the page number of the reference. Many electronic sources lack such elements, so the documentation style needs to allow for these differences. If the author's name is unknown, refer to the source by its title. Since pages in most electronic sources are not numbered, page references may be irrelevant. Commonly, COS parenthetical citations use only the author's name for humanities style and the author's name and date of publication for scientific style.

✤ COS FORMAT ALERT: If page numbers, sections, or other navigational aids are available, include them at the end of the parenthetical citation, preceded by a comma. ✤

HUMANITIES STYLE

```
According to the survey, over 80% of the students on campus waited
until the night before an exam to begin studying (Jani).
```

✤ COS FORMAT ALERT: When the author's name is included in the sentence, the in-text citation is unnecessary. If you cite more than one work by the same author, refer to each by its title. ✤

Scientific Style

```
The research proved conclusively that individuals deprived of
sleep were as dangerous as those driving under the influence of
drugs or alcohol (Rezik, 2000).
```

✤ COS FORMAT ALERT: If the publication date is unavailable, use the date of access (in day-month-year format). ✤

2 Compiling COS bibliographic notes

Chart 155 gives general guidelines for a COS Works Cited list. The labelled screen on page 664 shows how to identify elements needed for reference.

GUIDELINES FOR COMPILING A COS-STYLE WORKS CITED LIST — 155

- **TITLE**

  `Works Cited`

- **PLACEMENT OF LIST**

  If you are producing a print document, number the Works Cited page sequentially with the rest of the paper and begin on a separate page. If your document is a hypertext publication, you may use a separate file and a link to this page in the table of contents.

- **CONTENT AND FORMAT**

  See MLA guidelines, Chart 151.

- **ARRANGEMENT OF ENTRIES**

  See MLA guidelines, Chart 151.

- **AUTHORS' NAMES**

  Finding the author of a source may not be simple. Often, online writers use an alias or go by their login/user name. List a source by these alternative names if they are the only ones you find. If no author name or alias can be identified, cite the source by its title.

  In the humanities style, give the author's full first, middle (if available), and last names; in the scientific style, give the author's full last name and first and middle initials (if applicable). List any second author by first name (humanities) or first initial (scientific), followed by the full last name.

→

GUIDELINES FOR COMPILING A COS-STYLE WORKS CITED LIST (continued) 155

■ **CAPITALIZATION AND SPECIAL TREATMENT OF TITLES**
Use italics rather than underlining for the titles of complete works. Since hypertext links are underlined online, an underlined title may confuse your readers. Also italicize online sites and the names of information services.

In the humanities style, enclose titles of articles/excerpts in quotation marks and capitalize all major words. In the scientific style, do not distinguish titles of articles/excerpts in any way, and capitalize only the first word of the title and proper nouns. (If a title is not available, use the file name.)

■ **PLACE OF PUBLICATION, PUBLISHER, AND ELECTRONIC ADDRESS**
With electronic sources available in fixed formats, such as software and certain electronic publications, a publisher and city are usually listed and should be cited.

In online publishing, the city of publication and publisher often are not relevant to Web sites and other electronic sources that are not in fixed formats. In those cases, provide the Uniform Resource Locator (URL), which is a source's entire electronic address. For addresses that exceed a line in length, follow MLA style: Break only after slashes and do not insert your own hyphens.

■ **VERSION OR FILE NUMBER**
When applicable, provide the specific file number or version of a program.

■ **DOCUMENT DATE OR DATE OF LAST REVISION**
Include a Web page's publication date or date of last revision unless it is identical to the access date.

■ **DATE OF ACCESS**
With the constant updates of online content, readers may have a difficult time finding the content that you cite. To be specific about the version of the Web page you are citing, always provide the date of access.

■ **NAVIGATION POINTS**
On the World Wide Web, a given site is usually one page, regardless of its length. List any helpful navigational aids, such as page references, paragraph numbers, or parts, when they are available. Keep in mind that these aids are often not available. ➜

GUIDELINES FOR COMPILING A COS-STYLE WORKS CITED LIST *(continued)* 155

- **BIBLIOGRAPHIC ENTRIES: HUMANITIES**
  Follow this form as closely as possible in your citations:
  Author's Last Name, First Name. "Title of Document." *Title of Complete Work* [if applicable]. Version or file number [if applicable]. Document date or date of last revision [if different from access date]. Protocol and address, access path or directories (date of access).
- **BIBLIOGRAPHIC ENTRIES: SCIENCES**
  Follow this form as closely as possible in your citations:
  Author's Last Name, Initial(s). (Date of document [if different from date accessed]). Title of document. *Title of complete work* [if applicable]. Version or file number [if applicable]. (Edition or revision [if applicable]). Protocol and address, access path, or directories (date of access).

3 Following models for COS documentation

Directory

The models are first given in humanities style and then repeated in scientific style.

1. Site on the World Wide Web—COS
2. Revised or Modified Site—COS
3. Maintained or Compiled Site—COS
4. Article from a Periodical—COS
5. Article from an Online Journal—COS
6. Work by a Group or Organization—COS
7. Corporate Home Page or Information—COS
8. Government Information or Site—COS
9. Book—COS
10. Graphic, or Video or Audio File on a Page—COS
11. Personal Electronic Mail (E-mail)—COS
12. Posting to a Discussion List—COS

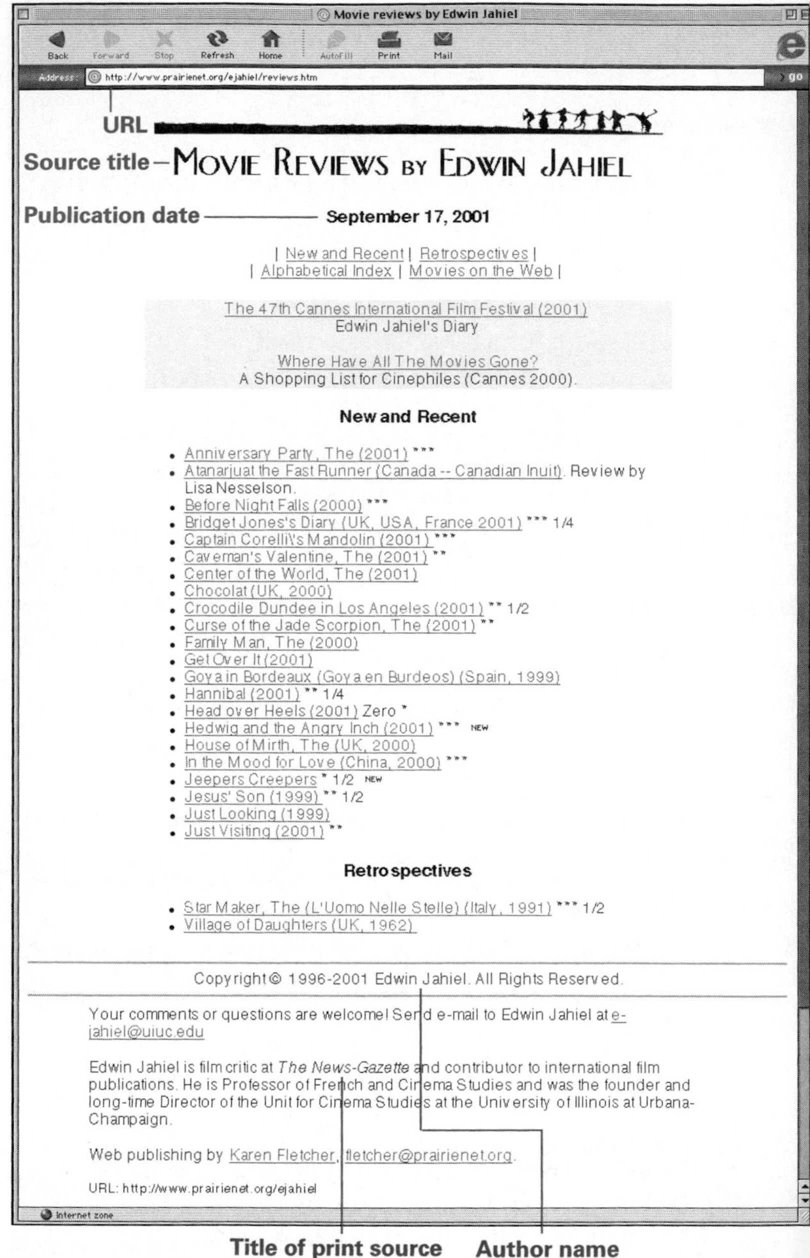

Movie reviews by Edwin Jahiel
Back Forward Stop Refresh Home AutoFill Print Mail
Address: http://www.prairienet.org/ejahiel/reviews.htm
URL
Source title
MOVIE REVIEWS BY EDWIN JAHIEL
Publication date
September 17, 2001
| New and Recent | Retrospectives |
| Alphabetical Index | Movies on the Web |
The 47th Cannes International Film Festival (2001)
Edwin Jahiel's Diary
Where Have All The Movies Gone?
A Shopping List for Cinephiles (Cannes 2000).
New and Recent
Anniversary Party, The (2001) ***
Atanarjuat the Fast Runner (Canada -- Canadian Inuit). Review by Lisa Nesselson.
Before Night Falls (2000) ***
Bridget Jones's Diary (UK, USA, France 2001) *** 1/4
Captain Corelli\'s Mandolin (2001) ***
Caveman's Valentine, The (2001) **
Center of the World, The (2001)
Chocolat (UK, 2000)
Crocodile Dundee in Los Angeles (2001) ** 1/2
Curse of the Jade Scorpion, The (2001) **
Family Man, The (2000)
Get Over It (2001)
Goya in Bordeaux (Goya en Burdeos) (Spain, 1999)
Hannibal (2001) ** 1/4
Head over Heels (2001) Zero *
Hedwig and the Angry Inch (2001) *** NEW
House of Mirth, The (UK, 2000)
In the Mood for Love (China, 2000) ***
Jeepers Creepers * 1/2 NEW
Jesus' Son (1999) ** 1/2
Just Looking (1999)
Just Visiting (2001) **
Retrospectives
Star Maker, The (L'Uomo Nelle Stelle) (Italy, 1991) *** 1/2
Village of Daughters (UK, 1962)
Copyright © 1996-2001 Edwin Jahiel. All Rights Reserved.
Your comments or questions are welcome! Send e-mail to Edwin Jahiel at e-jahiel@uiuc.edu
Edwin Jahiel is film critic at The News-Gazette and contributor to international film publications. He is Professor of French and Cinema Studies and was the founder and long-time Director of the Unit for Cinema Studies at the University of Illinois at Urbana-Champaign.
Web publishing by Karen Fletcher, fletcher@prairienet.org.
URL: http://www.prairienet.org/ejahiel
Internet zone
Title of print source
Author name

Web page with links to author's movie reviews

13. Posting to a Newsgroup or Forum—COS
14. Archived Posting—COS
15. Online Reference Source—COS
16. Computer Information Service or Online Database—COS
17. Gopher Site—COS
18. FTP Site—COS
19. Telnet Site—COS
20. Synchronous Communication—COS
21. Software—COS

HUMANITIES STYLE

1. SITE ON THE WORLD WIDE WEB—COS HUMANITIES

Blackmon, Samantha. *Cows in the Classroom?: MOOs and MUDs and MUSHes ... Oh My!!!* 24 Aug. 2000. http://www.sla.purdue.edu/people/engl/blackmon/moo/index.html (11 Mar. 2001).

2. REVISED OR MODIFIED SITE—COS HUMANITIES

Sheppard, James E., and Arthur Young. *The Canadian 19th Century: A Chronology.* Mod. spring 2000. http://www.ablu.ca/histproj/1800.html (22 Nov. 2000).

For a revised site, use the abbreviation *Rev.* instead of *Mod.*

3. MAINTAINED OR COMPILED SITE—COS HUMANITIES

E-Zine-List. Maint. John Labovitz. 8 Mar. 2000. http://www.meer.net/~johnl/e-zine-list (15 Sept. 2000).

If it is a compiled site, use the abbreviation *Comp.* instead of *Maint.*

4. ARTICLE FROM A PERIODICAL—COS HUMANITIES

Cheadle, Bruce. "Lab Workers Infected with Mysterious Monkey Virus." *Winnipeg Free Press.* 30 June 2001. http://www.winnipegfreepress.com/news/canadaworld/275385538938334.html (9 Oct. 2001).

5. ARTICLE FROM AN ONLINE JOURNAL—COS HUMANITIES

Winickoff, Jonathan P., et al. "Verve and Jolt: Deadly New Internet Drugs." *Pediatrics* 106: 4 (Oct. 2000). http://www.pediatrics. org/cgi/content/abstract/106/4/829 (10 May 2000).

6. Work by a Group or Organization—COS humanities

SIL International. *Ethnomusicology: Studying Music from the Outside In and from the Inside Out.* 7 May 1999. http://www.sil.org/anthro/ethnomusicology.htm (20 Feb. 2000).

7. Corporate Home Page or Information—COS humanities

Pearson PLC. *Pearson Home Page.* 1999. http://www.pearson.com (12 Apr. 2001).

8. Government Information or Site—COS humanities

Citizenship and Immigration Canada. "Staying the Course: 1997 Annual Immigration Plan." 29 Oct. 1996. *Annual Immigration Plans.* http://cicnet.ci.gc.ca/english/pub/index.html (5 Mar. 2001).

9. Book—COS humanities

Use this format for a book previously published in print:

Eaton, Arthur W. *Acadian Legends and Lyrics.* London and New York: White & Allen, 1889. 16 Feb. 2000. *Early Canadiana Online.* http://www.canadiana.org/cgi-bin/ECO/mtq?doc=09066 (25 May 2001).

Use this format for an online book:

Shires, Bob. CPR (Cardiopulmonary Resuscitation) Guide. 17 Jan. 2000. http://www.memoware.com/Category=Medicine_ResultSet=1.htm (17 Apr. 2000).

10. Graphic or Video or Audio File on a Page—COS humanities

owl.gif. 2000. "Original free clipart." *Clipart.com.* http://www. free-clip-art.net/index4.shtml (27 Oct. 2000).

11. Personal Electronic Mail (E-mail)—COS humanities

Torres, Nadia. "Re: Online Translation Programs." Personal e-mail (11 Sept. 2000).

12. Posting to a Discussion List—COS humanities

Sheldon, Amy. "Re: Request for Help on Sexism Inscription." 2 Jan. 2000. *FLING List for Feminists in Linguistics.* http://listserv.linguistlist.org (14 Nov. 2000).

13. Posting to a Newsgroup or Forum—COS humanities

Markowitz, Al. "The Changing Face of Work: A Look at the Way We Work." 28 Sept. 2000. http://yourturn.npr.org/cgi-bin/WebX?50@121.HjNGardZdaj^0@.ee7a9aa (8 Jan. 2001).

14. Archived Posting—COS humanities

Radev, Dragomir R. "Natural Language Processing FAQ." 16 Sept. 1999. *Institute of Information and Computing Sciences.* http://www.cs.ruu.nl/wais/html/na-dir/natural-lang-processing-faq.html (27 Jan. 1999).

15. Online Reference Source—COS humanities

Nordenberg, Tamar. "Make No Mistake! Medical Errors Can Be Deadly Serious." *Britannica.com.* Ebsco Publishing. 2000. http://britannica.com/bcom/original/article/0,5744,12430,00.html (18 Oct. 2000).

Use this model to cite an encyclopedia, dictionary, thesaurus, or style guide.

16. Computer Information Service or Online Database—COS humanities

Raintree Nutrition, Inc. "Pata de Vaca." June 2000. *Raintree Tropical Plant Database.* http://www.rain-tree.com/patadevaca.htm (9 Sept. 2000).

17. Gopher Site—COS humanities

"Elections." May 1996. gopher://israel-info.gov.il/00/facts/state/st4 (27 Dec. 2000).

18. FTP Site—COS humanities

The Treaty of the European Union: The Maastricht Treaty, 7th February, 1992. Oct. 1996. ftp://metalab.unc.edu/pub/docs/books/gutenberg/etext96/maast10.txt (24 Jan. 2001).

19. Telnet Site—COS humanities

Schweller, Kenneth G. "How to Design a Bot." *Collegetown MOO.* 28 May 1999. telnet://galaxy.bvu.edu:7777 (16 Nov. 2000).

20. Synchronous Communication—COS humanities

Dominguez, Jose. "Interchange." *Daedalus Online.* http://daedalus.pearsoned.com (11 Mar. 2001).

21. Software—COS humanities

Wresch, William. *Writer's Helper.* Ver. 4.0. Upper Saddle River: Prentice Hall, 1998.

Scientific Style

1. Site on the World Wide Web—COS scientific

Blackmon, S. (2000, August 24). *Cows in the classroom?: MOOs and MUDs and MUSHes ... Oh my!!!* http://www.sla.purdue.edu/people/engl/blackmon/moo/index html (11 Mar. 2001).

2. Revised or Modified Site—COS scientific

Sheppard, J. E., & Young, A. (2000). *The Canadian 19th century: A chronology.* (Mod. spring 2000). http://www.ablu.ca/histproj/1800.html (22 Nov. 2000).

For a revised site, use the abbreviation *Rev.* instead of *Mod.*

3. Maintained or Compiled Site—COS scientific

E-zine-list. (2000, March 8). (John Labovitz, Maint.). http://www.meer.net/~johnl/e-zine-list (15 Sept. 2000).

If the site has been compiled, use the abbreviation *Comp.* instead of *Maint.*

4. Article from a Periodical—COS scientific

Cheadle, B. (2001, June 30). Lab workers infected with mysterious monkey virus. *Winnipeg Free Press.* http://www.winnipegfreepress.com/news/canadaworld/275385538938334.html (9 Oct. 2001).

5. Article from an Online Journal—COS scientific

Winickoff, J. P., et al. (2000, October). Verve and jolt: Deadly new Internet drugs. *Pediatrics, 106* (4). http://www.pediatrics.org/cgi/content/abstract/106/4/829 (10 May 2000).

6. Work by a Group or Organization—COS scientific

SIL International. (1999, May 7). *Ethnomusicology: Studying music from the outside in and from the inside out.* http://www.sil.org/anthro/ethnomusicology.htm (20 Feb. 2000).

7. Corporate Home Page or Information—COS scientific

Pearson PLC. (1999). *Pearson home page.* http://www.pearson.com (12 Apr. 2001).

8. Government Information or Site—COS scientific

Citizenship and Immigration Canada. (1996, October 29). Staying the course: 1997 annual immigration plan. *Annual immigration plans.* http://cicnet.ci.gc.ca/english/pub/index.html (5 Mar. 2001).

9. Book—COS scientific

Use this format for a book previously published in print:

Eaton, A. W. (1889). *Acadian legends and lyrics.* London & New York: White & Allen. (2000, February 16). Early Canadiana Online. http://www.canadiana.org/cgi-bin/ECO/mtq?doc=09066 (25 May 2001).

Use this format for an online book:

Shires, B. (2000, January 17). *CPR (cardiopulmonary resuscitation) guide.* http://www.memoware.com/Category=Medicine_ResultSet=1.htm (17 Apr. 2000).

10. Graphic or Video or Audio File on a Page—COS scientific

owl.gif [Graphic file] (2000). Original free clipart. *Clipart.com.* http://www.free-clip-art.net/index4.shtml (27 Oct. 2000).

11. Personal Electronic Mail (E-mail)—COS scientific

Torres, N. Re: Online translation programs. [Personal e-mail]. (11 Sept. 2000).

12. Posting to a Discussion List—COS scientific

Sheldon, A. (2000, January 2). Re: request for help on sexism inscription. *FLING List for Feminists in Linguistics.* http://listserv.linguistlist.org (14 Nov. 2000).

13. Posting to a Newsgroup or Forum—COS scientific

Markowitz, A. (2000, September 28). The changing face of work: A look at the way we work. http://yourturn.npr.org/cgi-in/WebX?7@141.MM4qaoT6dgK^3@.ee7a9aa/12 (8 Jan. 2001).

14. Archived Posting—COS scientific

Radev, D. R. (1999, September 16). Natural language processing FAQ. *Institute of Information and Computing Sciences.* http://www.cs.ruu.nl/wais/html/na-dir/natural-lang-processing-faq.html (27 Jan. 1999).

15. Online Reference Source—COS scientific

Nordenberg, T. (2000). Make no mistake! Medical errors can be deadly serious. *Britannica.com.* Ebsco Publishing. http://britannica.com/bcom/original/article/0,5744,12430,00.html (18 Oct. 2000).

Use this model to cite an encyclopedia, dictionary, thesaurus, or style guide.

16. Computer Information Service or Online Database—COS scientific

Raintree Nutrition, Inc. (2000, June). Pata de vaca. *Raintree Tropical Plant Database.* http://www.rain-tree.com/patadevaca.htm (9 Sept. 2000).

17. Gopher Site—COS scientific

Elections. (1996, May). gopher://israel-info.gov.il/00/facts/state/st4 (27 Dec. 2000).

18. FTP Site—COS scientific

The Treaty of the European Union: The Maastricht Treaty, 7th February, 1992. (1996, October). ftp://metalab.unc.edu/pub/docs/books/gutenberg/etext96/maast10.txt (24 Jan. 2001).

19. Telnet Site—COS scientific

Schweller, K. G. (1999, May 28) How to design a bot. *Collegetown MOO.* telnet://galaxy.bvu.edu:7777 (16 Nov. 2000).

20. Synchronous Communication—COS scientific

Dominguez, J. Interchange. *Daedalus Online.* http://daedalus.pearsoned.com (11 Mar. 2001).

21. Software—COS scientific

Wresch, W. (1998). *Writer's Helper.* Ver. 4.0. Upper Saddle River: Prentice Hall.

35 Case Study: A Student Writing an MLA Research Paper

This chapter presents a case study of a student, Lisa Laver, going through the processes of conducting research and writing a paper based on her findings. Section 35a narrates the processes. Section 35b shows the final draft of Laver's paper, along with commentary on the paper's key elements. The commentary includes **process notes** explaining many of Laver's decisions during her writing process.

> *Lisa Laver was given this assignment for a research paper:* Write a research paper on the general subject of intelligence. The paper should be 1800 to 2000 words long and should be based on a variety of sources. The final paper is due in six weeks. Interim deadlines for parts of the work will be announced. To complete this assignment, you need to engage in three interrelated processes: conducting research, understanding the results of that research, and writing a paper based on the first two processes. Consult the *Simon & Schuster Handbook for Writers,* Third Canadian Edition, especially Chapters 32 and 33, which gives you practical, step-by-step guidance on what this assignment entails.

35a Observing the processes of researching and writing an MLA-style research paper

Lisa Laver was eager to dive into her research project and especially wanted to plan her research schedule so that she could budget her time and not end up in a panic at the end. She knew from experience that she would likely have the most trouble in the first stages of her research process as she narrowed her topic and began to find useful sources. She resolved to face up to the challenge calmly and to remain patient with herself as she went along.

The general topic assigned was "intelligence." Laver realized that she had to face many steps to narrow it to a **topic suitable for a research paper** (see 32d). Collecting possible subject headings and key words was her first step. She went to the library reference desk to use the *Library of Congress Subject Headings (LCSH)* books (see 32i). She found nothing under "intelligence" but browsed a bit and found "intellect" as a main category. Its library call number, the code to lead her to all books on the subject, had a range from BF431 to BF433. She wrote down *intellect* and its call numbers in her **research log** (see 32c). She had taken the first step for this project.

Laver then examined the subentries at "intellect" in the *LCSH* and found the listing "human intelligence," which appealed to her as a direction to take. Then, Laver looked at the *LCSH* headings preceded by the code NT (meaning "narrowed topic"). In her research log, she listed all the NT headings as possible keywords. Looking up a few of them, she soon became overwhelmed by the variety of directions she could take. She decided to try another route.

With the call numbers and keywords in hand, Laver looked at **specialized reference books** (see 32l) with call numbers in the range BF431–BF433 (the call numbers she had found in the *LCSH*). In Volume 3 of *Survey of Social Science: Psychology Series*, she found an article called "Intelligence: Definition and Theoretical Models." This proved to be Laver's first big break.

As she read the survey article, Laver was interested by material on a concept of intelligence developed fairly recently by Howard Gardner of Harvard University. She wrote down Gardner's name as a possible **authority** (see 31c-2). Gardner states that human intelligence is not what people think of as IQ, which he believes is a limited concept because it draws on only one or two inborn human abilities. According to Gardner, the totality of human intelligence results from the interaction of eight "intelligences." Laver decided that she would pursue this topic if she could determine that Gardner was a credible authority on the subject of intelligence.

To start checking on Gardner, Laver looked in the *Columbia Encyclopedia*, a **general reference book** she was familiar with from high school. Under "intelligence," Laver found Gardner and his concept of multiple intelligences mentioned. This gave her hope, so next she looked in the library's **book catalogue** (see 32f-2) under the name "Gardner." She was delighted to find several books by him on the subject of multiple intelligences. One of them, *Frames of Reference*, became a **major source** on her topic. She then started writing out **bibliography cards** (see 32j-1).

Because Gardner's work with the concept of multiple intelligences had started somewhat recently, Laver realized that she would have to rely heavily on journals and online sources. The periodicals indexes at Laver's university library were on CD-ROM. Using the keyword "multiple intelligences," she quickly found a number of journal articles whose titles indicated that they had good potential as sources for her research. Laver was able to locate some of the articles in journals that the library had available in print. Others Laver located online using the AltaVista search engine. Each article named Gardner as a major authority.

As Laver read, checked the credibility of her sources, and found additional useful sources, she was at first somewhat skeptical of the concept of multiple intelligences. All her life, she had heard that intelligence was defined by IQ, which was measured by a test. In fact, she had wondered what her IQ and the IQs of her family and friends were. The more Laver thought about the new ideas she was encountering, however, the more open she felt to the possibility of changing her viewpoint. This led Laver to form her **research question** (see 32a and 32d): "Can there be only one way of describing human intelligence?"

As she researched further, Laver saw references to the work of Salovey and Mayer. These names led Laver to research on "emotional intelligence," a concept that encompassed in great detail two of Gardner's eight intelligences: interpersonal and intrapersonal. Laver remembered seeing her parents reading a book by Daniel Goleman titled *Emotional Intelligence.* Browsing through it, she saw that it drew heavily on Salovey and Mayer's work as well as Gardner's. Laver decided to include Salovey and Mayer's work in her paper.

After taking notes, Laver was ready to draft her research paper. Thinking about her purpose, Laver concluded that she should *inform* her readers about the concept of multiple intelligences. (For a discussion of the informative purpose, see section 1b-2.) Soon after she had started her second draft, however, Laver realized that her paper lacked a *focus*—a reason for wanting to explain what she had learned. She decided to include her rationale for why the topic of multiple intelligences was worth writing about: She felt that the concept held benefits especially for students and also for the general population.

As Laver wrote, she used her note cards carefully to make sure she always knew when she was quoting a source and when she was summarizing. She made sure to put in the correct in-text documentation for each source. She also kept a working bibliography (see 32h) so that she would be ready to list each one of her sources in the Works Cited list at the end of her paper. By the time Laver came to the final draft of her research paper, she decided to drop a few of the sources she had found because they repeated what others whom she considered better authorities had said.

Laver struggled with her concluding paragraph. She wanted to assert her conviction that the ideas of Gardner, Salovey and Mayer, and Goleman relating to human intelligence held great promise. At first, she lacked the confidence to state her position outright; after a while, the strength of her convictions overrode her hesitancy. Here is an early draft of Laver's concluding paragraph, which you can compare with the one in her final draft that appears in section 35b.

> Today, there is no longer a single definition of intelligence. Scientists have found new ways of describing human intelligence and seeing it in operation. Educators, in turn, can use those findings to give students more avenues to school success and, as a result, to acquiring greater self-esteem.

35b Analyzing an MLA-style research paper

Lisa Laver followed MLA style for format decisions on this paper.

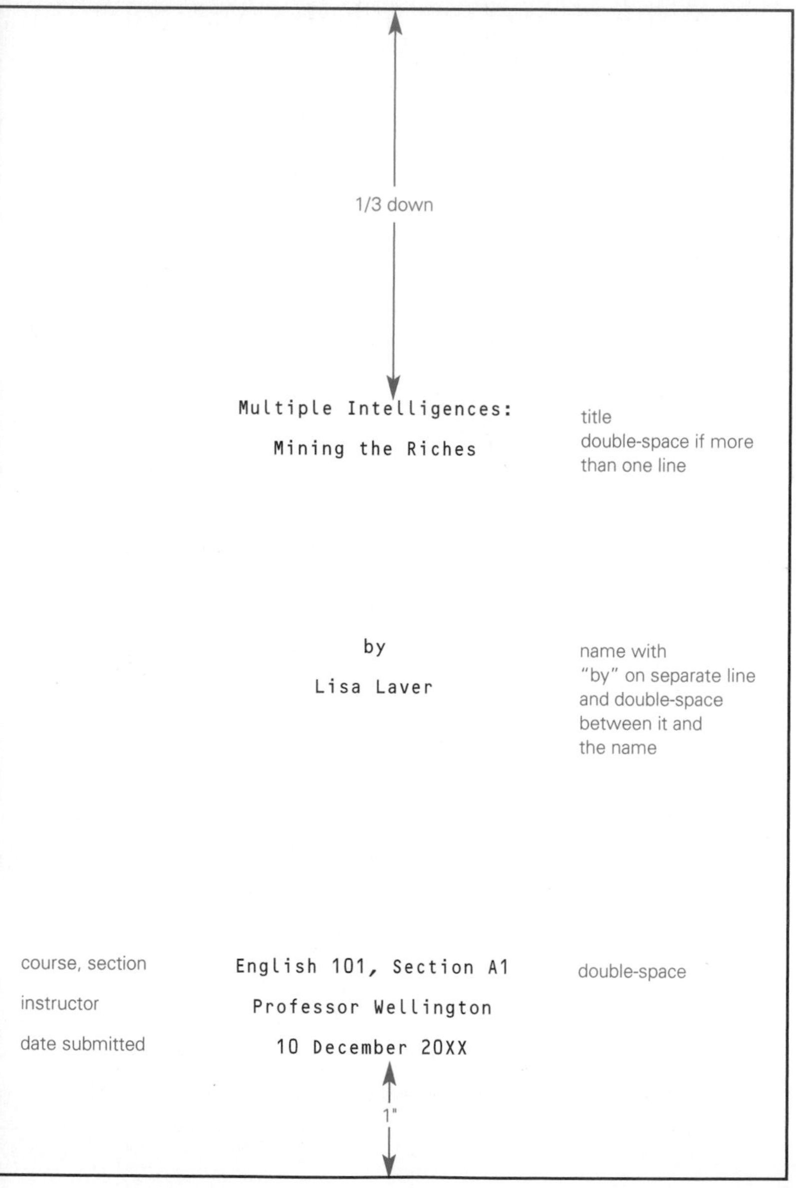

Title page and first page of essay with a title page. If your instructor requires a title page, you can use the format and types of information shown on page 675 for Lisa Laver's title page. Then, on page 1 of your paper, put your last name followed by a space followed by the numeral 1 in the upper right corner 1/2 inch (about 1.25 cm) below the top edge of the page. Double-space below this heading, and then type the paper's title, centring it. Double-space after the title, and then start your paper, indenting the first line of each paragraph 5 characters. If you are using a computer, format for double line spacing and set tabs for indents.

First page without a title page. If your instructor does not require a title page, follow MLA format style, shown below, for the first page of your paper.

FIRST PAGE FOR A PAPER WITHOUT A TITLE PAGE

1/2"

Laver 1

Lisa Laver — name

Professor Wellington — instructor

English 101, Section A1 — course, section

10 December 20XX — date submitted

double-space

Multiple Intelligences:

Mining the Riches

A first-year student, Claire Barbry, takes two final exams on the same day. During her first exam, for Chemistry 101, she doodles tiny test tubes in her exam booklet's margins as she thinks. During her second exam, for Canadian History, she jump-starts her energies by sketching tiny outlines of the Peace Tower in Ottawa on the cover of her text booklet. Barbry gets a good grade on each test, but she is surprised that one professor wrote, "Loved the pictures. Great way to stimulate your thinking," while the other wrote, "Lose those pictures. They waste your time." Barbry knew her second professor was wrong. By drawing, Barbry had

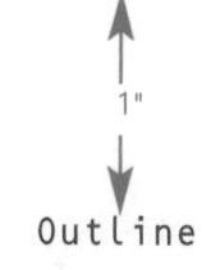

Laver i

Outline

<u>Thesis statement</u>: Human intelligence results from a complex interaction of the riches of many abilities, only a few of which are taken into account by intelligence quotient (IQ) tests used widely today.

I. The history of IQ testing dates to the late nineteenth century.
   A. Galton made a first attempt at IQ measurement.
   B. Binet wrote the first practical intelligence test.
   C. Binet's test was revised at Stanford University to create the Stanford-Binet IQ test, widely used today.

II. Opinions of IQ tests vary.
   A. Many parents and others tend to accept them.
   B. Many psychologists and other academics tend to reject them.

III. Brain research has inspired more complex theories of intelligence.
   A. Concepts of learning and of teaching are multifaceted.
   B. Aspects of brain function operate simultaneously.
      1. Intelligence includes thought.
      2. Intelligence includes emotions.
      3. Intelligence includes imagination.
      4. Intelligence includes predispositions.

→

Laver ii

IV. The theory of multiple intelligences (MI) is the work of Howard Gardner.

   A. Gardner has identified eight separate intelligences.

      1. Musical intelligence is one.
      2. Bodily-kinesthetic intelligence is another.
      3. Logical-mathematical intelligence, one of two abilities today's IQ tests measure, is another.
      4. Linguistic intelligence, the other of the abilities today's IQ tests measure, is another.
      5. Spatial intelligence is another.
      6. Interpersonal intelligence is another.
      7. Intrapersonal intelligence is another.
      8. Naturalistic intelligence is another.

   B. Gardner developed criteria for considering an ability to be an intelligence.

      1. It must have an identifiable core set of information-processing operations.
      2. It must have a distinctive developmental history, with a set of "end state" performances.
      3. It must have evolutionary plausibility.
      4. It must be supported by experimental and psychological tasks.

   C. MI theory has affected educational practices.

      1. One school reports an example of using one intelligence to encourage development of another.
      2. A U.S. school reports using a variety of intelligences to study American history.

Laver iii

V. Other researchers have developed the concept of emotional intelligence.

A. Emotional intelligence builds on two of Gardner's eight intelligences.

1. Interpersonal intelligence is one.

2. Intrapersonal intelligence is the other.

B. Salovey and Mayer did pioneering work in the area.

C. Daniel Goleman wrote a bestselling book on the subject.

Name and page-number heading. Except for a title page, give each page of a paper you prepare according to MLA format guidelines a heading in the upper right corner 1/2 inch (about 1.25 cm) below the top edge of the paper. Use your last name, followed by a space, followed by the page number. Number pages that come before your essay begins, such as outline pages, with lowercase roman numerals (see Lisa Laver's outline). Use arabic numeral 1 on the page on which your essay begins, and then number each page consecutively through to the last page of Works Cited. Double-space below the name and page number to whatever comes next on the page.

Outline. Laver's instructor required a formal outline in the final draft of each student's research paper. To format her outline, Laver referred to sections 2p and 32s in this handbook. In the upper right corner heading consisting of her last name and the page number, she used lowercase roman numerals for the page numbers, a conventional way of showing that the outline comes before the first page of the essay itself. She double-spaced below the name-number heading and then centred the word *Outline*, using a capital letter to start it. She double-spaced and then typed the words *Thesis statement* at the left margin, underlining them. The thesis statement matches the last sentence of the first paragraph of her paper.

Laver used a **sentence outline,** not a topic outline (see 2p). To reflect the organization of her paper, she divided the material in the outline into five major parts, numbered I, II, III, IV, and V. The main items in each part are marked A, B, C, etc. In places where she went into more detail, she used 1, 2, 3, etc., for the new level of information.

Laver 1

Multiple Intelligences:
Mining the Riches A

1 A first-year student, Claire Barbry
takes two final exams on the same day. During B
her first exam, for Chemistry 101, she
doodles tiny test tubes in her exam booklet's
margins as she thinks. During her second
exam, for Canadian History, she jump-starts
her energies by sketching tiny outlines of
the Peace Tower in Ottawa on the cover of her
test booklet. Barbry gets a good grade on
each test, but she is surprised that one
professor wrote, "Loved the pictures. Great
way to stimulate your thinking," while the
other wrote, "Lose those pictures. They waste
your time." Barbry knew her second professor
was wrong. By drawing, Barbry had been
consciously applying discoveries from
research into the psychology of brain
functioning. She knew that school success can
increase greatly when students tap into their
talents not usually associated with academic
work. Human intelligence results from a C
complex interaction of the riches of many
abilities, only a few of which are taken into
account by intelligence quotient (IQ) tests
widely used today.

2 A context for such an assertion can be
found by briefly reviewing the history of D

COMMENTARY

A. **Title.** Laver uses her title to prepare her readers for the paper's major theme (multiple intelligences) and central focus (that the concept offers rich benefits). ◆ PROCESS NOTE: Laver drafted a few titles as she was revising. She started with "Everyone Is Smart in Some Way," but that oversimplified the point. She later tried and rejected "Evolving Theories of Human Intelligence" because she was not writing a historical survey of human intelligence theories but rather a discussion of such theories of more recent interest. ◆

B. **Introductory device.** Laver tells this anecdote, based on the experience of a friend, because it illustrates her point dramatically.

C. **Thesis statement.** The last sentence of Laver's introductory paragraph is her thesis statement. In writing it, she wanted to prepare her readers, in more detail than her title does, for the message of her paper. ◆ PROCESS NOTE: Laver tried out a few thesis statements as she moved from early to later drafts, each time trying to get closer to her central message. For evolving versions of this thesis statement, see 32r. ◆

D. ◆ PROCESS NOTE: In an earlier draft of this paper, Laver wrote four paragraphs about the history of definitions and measurements of human intelligence. Then, as she read over her draft, she realized that her coverage of history should not consume nearly a third of her paper when her central goal was to discuss in some detail a new theory of great potential. For this final draft, Laver condensed the history into one paragraph. ◆

Laver 2

human intelligence being defined and tested. Interest in such matters dates back to the nineteenth century. Sir Francis Galton attempted in the late 1800s to create a test that supported his view that mental ability is determined solely by heredity. His assumption and the test he wrote were never widely accepted. However, building on his notion that testing for intelligence levels was possible, Alfred Binet in 1905, at the request of the French government, which wanted schools to place students into correct ability levels, wrote the first reasonably
practical intelligence test. In 1916, a E
significant revision of Binet's test was undertaken at Stanford University in California, and the test was renamed the
Stanford-Binet Intelligence Test ("History"). F
This test, which has been updated every few decades since 1916, is designed to measure only two abilities: computing numbers and thinking in structured patterns. The Stanford-Binet Intelligence Test introduced such innovations as "scaling" and "standardizing" of scores so that by applying a formula, the test can compare one person's score with the scores of other people of the same age who answered the same questions ("Intelligence").

3 The Stanford-Binet Intelligence Test, G
and others like it, caught on quickly with

→

COMMENTARY

E. **Summary.** In her final draft, Laver condensed her historical information from four paragraphs to one. To do so, she summarized the information to cover only the major events that relate to the central message of her paper.

F. **Using an online encyclopedia.** Laver needed to make sure that this reference source, *Grolier Multimedia Encyclopedia,* is a reliable, respected collection of information. She decided to ask her university librarian how to determine whether a specific encyclopedia is considered a reliable source. The librarian suggested that Laver read a review of encyclopedias on CD-ROMs and online. Laver learned that such reviews appear fairly often in computer magazines as well as library journals. She searched those sources and quickly located an encyclopedia review article that compared different CD-ROM and online encyclopedias. After reading the review and finding that *Grolier* is a reliable source, Laver felt confident about the material it contained.

G. **Topic sentences.** Laver placed her topic sentences at the start of most of her paragraphs. She felt that they provided a useful guide to her line of reasoning and presentation of information.

Laver 3

3 the public. People liked the idea that a
single number could define someone's
intelligence. IQ tests have become hugely
respected. The notion that a single number
can describe a person's intelligence seems H
firmly fixed in people's thinking about
intelligence today. Many people want to know
the exact number of their IQ. When IQ tests
are given in school, students and parents are
rarely told the outcome, yet many people
manage to find out or to retake the test
privately. Then, they carry their IQ number
for the rest of their lives, either as a
secret burden when the score is not as high
as they had hoped or as a badge of honour
allowed sometimes "accidentally to slip out"
during conversations. So deeply ingrained is
public respect for IQ testing that some U.S.
parents expect their preschoolers, usually at I
age three, to take the Stanford-Binet
Intelligence Test. Scores, and scores alone,
determine whether their children will qualify
for one of the limited openings at
prestigious prekindergarten schools that
exist in parts of the United States. Parents
who do this--and there are many--are highly
competitive and often insist that much of
their children's time be spent on activities
and games that they believe will prepare them
for the test (Hartocollis B1).

➜

COMMENTARY

H. **Using her own thinking.** Laver learned this information through personal experience. As she was growing up, she had heard people talking about IQ tests and scores. She had even worried at times about whether her IQ was high or low. But as she progressed through high school and met all kinds of people with all sorts of different abilities, she began to suspect that intelligence involved more than what one IQ test could measure. Laver does not use sources to support this section because it is drawn from her own knowledge.

I. **Incorporating a very current source.** ◆ PROCESS NOTE: The morning that Laver was planning to edit her final draft of this paper, she saw, to her surprise, an article in that day's *New York Times* about the Stanford-Binet test being given to three-year-old children. The issues of the accuracy of IQ testing and the prestige of high scores were a major part of the article. Because the information in the article provided strong, timely support for this section of her paper, Laver decided, even though it would take her a little extra writing time, to integrate the article into her paper. ◆

Laver 4

4 Opponents of such a worshipful emphasis
on IQ scores say their overuse is a disaster.
One such opponent, Brent Staples, argues in
"The IQ Cult": "Most scientists concede that J
they don't really know what 'intelligence'
is. Whatever it might be, paper and pencil
tests aren't the tenth of it" (293).
Experiences like Claire Barbry's on the day K
of her two final exams show that today's IQ
tests are indeed severely limited and their
underlying assumptions actually can hamper a
student's success in school. A review of a
1986 survey of definitions of intelligence in
scholarly publications reveals that the
reviewer "is left with the clear impression
that intelligence is such a multifaceted
concept that no single quality can define it
and no single task or series of tasks can
capture it completely" (Urbina 1330). L

5 To everyone's benefit, the last ten
years of brain research have inspired
theories of human intelligence that
increasingly are getting respectful
attention. Caine and Caine, summarizing a
number of recent studies into the nature of
intelligence, urge that educators should
enlarge their concepts of learning and of
teaching to move beyond simplistic IQ scores.
Caine and Caine, however, do not claim that
all new theories of diversity in

→

COMMENTARY

J. **Quotation from a source.** This is Laver's first quotation from a source. (Before this, she has paraphrased or summarized her sources.) She decided to use the quotation because she felt that its down-to-earth language would reinforce her message. In addition, she believed that the prestige of the well-respected journalist Brent Staples, who wrote often on issues of race and class, would bring greater authority to the point she was trying to make.

K. ◆ PROCESS NOTE: Laver mentions Barbry again to show the explicit relationship between the anecdote in her introductory paragraph and the message of paragraph 4; she again mentions Barbry in paragraph 10. ◆

L. **Major source.** Laver considered the Urbina material a major source. She found the essay in the specialized reference book that she located through the *Library of Congress Subject Headings (LCSH)* under "intellect." The essay, listed in the Works Cited at the end of Laver's essay, introduced Laver to the concept of "multiple intelligences," the topic of her paper, and to the name Howard Gardner, the main authority on that topic.

Laver 5

intelligences are equally valid. For example,
one new theory, considered "the answer" for a M
short time, held that each person's brain
consists of two hemispheres, one of which is
dominant: The right side controls creative,
artistic talents and the left side controls
logical, language-based talents (67). By now,
more widely accepted and respected theories,
based on careful research, show that the
human brain continuously performs many
functions simultaneously: "Thought, emotions,
imagination, and predisposition occur
concurrently. They interact with other brain
processes such as health maintenance and the
expansion of general social and cultural
knowledge" (66).

6 The researcher who has had the strongest
impact on theories of human intelligence is
Howard Gardner. In 1979, he was a junior N
member of a research team at the Harvard
Graduate School of Education that
investigated human potential and cognition.
That experience, along with his years of
additional research as a developmental
psychologist, led Gardner to theorize that
humans possess many different intelligences.
In his book *Frames of Mind*, Gardner strives
to disprove the idea that human intelligence
consists of only one or two abilities. He
offers his alternative: the theory of

➜

COMMENTARY

M. ◆ PROCESS NOTE: Laver debated about including the information that the "answer" had once rested almost entirely on the theory of right brain/left brain dominance. On the one hand, she worried that it might be off the topic; on the other hand, she felt that her paper needed to reflect a little of the scholarly debates that go on concerning descriptions of human intelligence. Therefore, she decided to include it. ◆

N. **Major source.** Howard Gardner is the psychologist who originated the theory of multiple intelligences. Laver decided that the central section of her paper should focus on Gardner and his work. She found discussions of his theories in his book *Frames of Mind* and in the work of other people who refer to Gardner as the top authority.

Laver 6

multiple intelligences. He argues that his
"theory challenges the classical view of
intelligence that most of us have absorbed
explicitly (from psychology or educational
texts) or implicitly (by living in a culture
with a strong but possibly circumscribed view
of intelligence)" (5). Based on this view,
Gardner developed his theory of multiple
intelligences (MI). At first, in 1983, he
delineated seven intelligences: musical, O
bodily-kinesthetic, logical-mathematical,
linguistic, spatial, interpersonal, and
intrapersonal (*Frames* 73-276). Later, in
1995, he added an eighth intelligence to his
list: naturalistic (Campbell). Table 1 P
defines the characteristics of each and then
describes behaviours typical of a person with
such an intelligence. The only two
intelligences that IQ tests consider are,
most of all, logical-mathematical and,
somewhat less, linguistic.

7 Gardner has established criteria by
which to judge whether an ability deserves to
be categorized as an "intelligence." Those
criteria entail "a set of skills of problem
solving--enabling the individual to resolve
genuine problems or difficulties [author's Q
emphasis] that he or she encounters and
laying the groundwork for the acquisition of
new knowledge" (*Frames* 60-61). These criteria

COMMENTARY

O. ◆ PROCESS NOTE: Laver almost made a serious error as a researcher while she was searching for information about Howard Gardner's theory of multiple intelligences. Early in her online research process, she found a Web site featuring a photograph of Gardner along with information about a videotape on his theories. At first, Laver was thrilled to have found something online about Gardner. But when she applied the information in Charts 142, 148, and 149 for evaluating sources, she discovered that (1) the information was two years old and included only seven of the eight intelligences Gardner had identified, (2) the material was presented by a commercial enterprise that wanted to sell the videotape, and (3) the many misspellings showed that the material had not been issued by a professionally responsible group. She put the material aside and looked for more credible sources. ◆

P. **Online source.** Campbell is a source that Laver found on the World Wide Web. Because Campbell's article does not have page numbers, Laver cannot give a page reference for her information here or in the Works Cited entry. In the Works Cited entry at the end of her paper, Laver includes complete information according to new MLA guidelines for documenting World Wide Web sources, including the URL enclosed in angle brackets.

Q. **Author's emphasis.** Laver knows that when underlining (or italic type) appears in a quotation, it may not be clear who is doing the emphasizing, so it is prudent to insert [*author's emphasis*] or [*emphasis added*], between brackets, the standard way to insert information into quotations.

Laver 7

Table 1

Gardner's Eight Intelligences

Type of Intelligence	Definition	Behaviour
Musical	Refers to musical ability, perhaps a biological advantage. Requires the use of symbols that are read, heard internally, and interpreted to create harmonic melody.	Person enjoys listening to music; expresses eagerness to learn from music and musicians; responds to music by conducting, performing, and/or dancing.
Bodily-kinesthetic	Refers to physical skill, including the ability to play sports, express emotions in dance, or otherwise display masterful use of the body.	Person enjoys touching and exploring objects; learns best by direct involvement and participation; displays skill in acting, athletics, and dance.
Logical-mathematical	Necessitates problem solving and synthesizing a solution in one's mind before actually articulating it.	Person enjoys logical problem solving and complex operations such as calculus, physics, and computer programming; likes to study the concepts of quantity and time.

R

➜

COMMENTARY

R. **Table.** Table 1 is a condensation of information that Laver at first wrote in paragraphs. She decided to present the material in a table because it is more concise and useful in this form.

Laver 8

Table 1 Continued

Type of Intelligence	Definition	Behaviour
Linguistic	Encompasses the ability to master language by comprehending words and the desire to use them effectively and in a variety of ways to form grammatically correct and well-styled sentences.	Person enjoys and responds to the rhythm and variety of language; listens and reads well with the ability to comprehend, summarize, and interpret ideas.
Spatial	Refers to the capacity to visualize objects without experiencing their actual existence and to recognize people, places, and fine detail.	Person enjoys navigating self and objects through space; produces mental imagery; thinks in pictures and visualizes detail; perceives space from multiple perspectives.
Inter-personal	Involves the ability to interact well with others, seek out or follow leadership, encourage human interaction, and enhance each individual's place in society.	Person enjoys relating and interacting with others to form social relationships; communicates well verbally and nonverbally; recognizes and appreciates diverse perceptions on social and other issues.

Laver 9

Table 1 Continued

Type of Intelligence	Definition	Behaviour
Intra-personal	Involves knowledge of the inner self, including the ability to use feelings and emotions as a rationale for one's behaviour.	Person enjoys opportunities to explore the inner self; tends not to conform to popular opinion or peer pressure; works independently to discover meaning in experiences and thoughts.
Naturalistic	Refers to the ability to observe, understand, and organize patterns in nature; involves interest in collecting and sorting natural objects.	Person enjoys doing experiments in nature, learning names of natural objects, classifying and labelling articles from nature, and recognizing small changes in nature.

Source: Based on Howard Gardner, <u>Frames of Mind: The Theory of Multiple Intelligences</u> (New York: Basic, 1993).

→

Laver 10

call for, in part, an identifiable core set of operations--basic kinds of information-processing operations or mechanisms that deal with specific kinds of input; a distinctive developmental history, along with a set of "end state" performances; an evolutionary plausibility; and support from experimental and psychological tasks (Hoerr, "Naturalist Intelligence").

8 Although MI theory emerged from research in psychology, educators--and their students--have eagerly begun to adopt the concept. Teachers using Gardner's ideas and methods are demonstrating that when students who do not usually do well in school are encouraged and taught how to tap the rich mine of their other intelligences to learn traditional classroom tasks, the students succeed. Specific illustrations are easy to find in reports of teachers. For example, a S
teacher drew on the highly developed spatial-mechanical intelligence of Jacob, a first-grader who refused to take part in writing activities.

> The teacher asked that during "journal time" Jacob create a tool dictionary to be used as a resource in the mechanical learning center. After several entries T
> in which he drew and described tools and other materials, Jacob confidently moved

→

COMMENTARY

S. **Specific examples.** Laver knows that well-chosen specific examples can be clarifying and confirming illustrations of a point. Of the many examples she found during her research, she chose the ones here and in paragraph 9 because they are memorable and convincing.

T. **Displayed quotation.** Because the quotation by Gray and Viens is more than four lines long, MLA style calls for it to be "displayed." This means that the quotation must have all lines in a "block" indented from the left margin. (See 34c-1.)

Laver 11

> on to writing about other things of import to him, such as his brothers and a recent birthday party. Rather than shy away from all things linguistic--he had previously refused any task requiring a pencil--Jacob became invested in journal writing. (Gray and Viens 23-24)

Traditional theory asks, "Is this student intelligent?" MI theory allows Jacob's teacher to ask, "In what way is this student intelligent?" and "How can I use his strongest intelligence to help him develop other abilities?" (Hoerr, "Focusing").

9 Another illustration comes from a class of high school students in the United States studying American history. The students got an assignment to choose a topic from a list prepared by the teacher, to research the topic, and to respond to the topic by using what they had learned about MI theory. Students chose a format that allowed them to use their strongest intelligence so that they could successfully learn the history they were studying. The projects in this class included writing and performing a skit about early explorers in the West (linguistic and interpersonal intelligences); painting watercolours of birds and other wildlife for a project on naturalist John J. Audubon (visual-spatial intelligence); creating a

➜

working telegraph (logical-mathematical and bodily-kinesthetic intelligences); giving a eulogy of Davy Crockett (interpersonal intelligence); and taking on the role of a historical figure and speaking to the class "in character" (intrapersonal, linguistic, and interpersonal intelligences). Their teacher found that her students had "successfully learned not only historical information, but also a great deal about themselves. The theory of multiple intelligences offers hope to all students that they will be valued for their unique qualities, that they can succeed in their own way, and that they can have a successful future" (Lambert).

10 Clearly, whether students adopt the concepts of multiple intelligences on their own, as Barbry did, or work on them together with teachers, a new chance exists for students to excel in school and eventually in their jobs and lives. Interestingly, many people in the general public are beginning to become interested in the concept of multiple intelligences. For example, strong popular interest recently emerged concerning two of Gardner's intelligences: interpersonal and intrapersonal. Starting with the 1990 publication of their journal article "Emotional Intelligence," Peter Salovey and

U. ◆ PROCESS NOTE: Laver discovered the work of Salovey and Mayer and of Goleman by chance. A while before she wrote her paper, she had seen the title *Emotional Intelligence* on a book that her parents were reading. It had been recommended by friends who liked to read bestsellers. As Laver was learning about Gardner's concepts of different types of intelligence, the Goleman book popped into her mind, and so she checked it out of the library. It turned out to be an excellent source, and its bibliography led her to the very useful scholarly article by Salovey and Mayer. ◆

Laver 13

John Mayer led the way among scientists to a substantial expansion of Gardner's concepts of intrapersonal and interpersonal intelligences. Salovey and Mayer avoid overusing technical language and so make their ideas more generally accessible. For example, here is their straightforward definition of emotional intelligence: "the ability to monitor one's own feelings and emotions, to discriminate among them, and to use this information to guide one's thinking and actions" [authors' emphasis] (189). In 1995, a general-audience "pop psychology" book, Emotional Intelligence, became an immediate bestseller upon publication and remained one for many months. Its author, Daniel Goleman, a journalist and writer, fleshes out Gardner's concepts of interpersonal and intrapersonal intelligences. But he also emphasizes the close interaction between them and the other intelligences that Gardner has identified:

> These two minds, the emotional and the rational, operate in tight harmony for the most part, intertwining their very different ways of knowing to guide us through the world. Ordinarily there is a balance between emotional and rational minds, with emotion feeding into and informing the operations of the rational mind, and the rational mind refining and sometimes vetoing the inputs of the emotions. (9)

Goleman, drawing mainly from the work of Salovey and Mayer and a few others, asked

→

Laver 14

Gardner for his reaction to the new public interest in emotional abilities. Gardner said he applauded the interest as a balance to trends in his work. He said that "when I first wrote about personal intelligences, I *was* talking about emotion." However, Gardner's theory of multiple intelligences eventually came to focus more on cognition (which Goleman defines as "awareness of one's mental processes"), and not, as Gardner put it, "on the full range of emotional abilities" (41).

11 Additional new discoveries about the brain and human intelligence will likely emerge as scientists continue their investigations. In turn, changes in public attitudes toward IQ scores are likely to follow. Most educators and members of the general public will begin to accept the idea that human intelligence is far-ranging, involving much more than the logical-mathematical intelligence and, to a lesser extent, linguistic intelligence IQ tests claim to measure. The greatest benefit will be that more students can start to excel in all subjects through avenues built on talents not traditionally valued in schools. In turn, those students can enjoy the greater self-esteem that leads to better personal and family lives and to more satisfying jobs.

→

COMMENTARY

V. **Concluding paragraph.** Laver decided to end her paper with her opinion coupled with a prediction for the future.

Laver 15

Works Cited W

Caine, Renate Nummela, and Geoffrey Caine. "Understanding a Brain-Based Approach to Learning and Teaching." Educational Leadership 48 (1990): 66-70. X

Campbell, Bruce. "The Naturalist Intelligence." The Building Tool Room. Home page. 10 Oct. 1996 <http://www.newhorizons.org/article_eightintel.html>. Y

Gardner, Howard. Frames of Mind: The Theory of Multiple Intelligences. New York: Basic, 1993. Z

---. "Reflections on Multiple Intelligences: Myths and Messages." Phi Delta Kappan 77 (1995): 200-09. AA

Goleman, Daniel. Emotional Intelligence. New York: Bantam, 1995.

Gray, James, and Julie Viens. "The Theory of Multiple Intelligences: Understanding Cognitive Diversity in School." National Forum: Phi Kappa Phi Journal 74 (1994): 22-25.

Hartocollis, Anemona. "The Big Test Comes Early." New York Times 12 Dec. 1997: B1. BB

"History of Intelligence." Grolier Multimedia Encyclopedia. America Online. 12 Dec. 1997. CC

➜

COMMENTARY

W. **General format.** Laver provides an alphabetically arranged list of all the sources referred to in the paper. It is headed "Works Cited" and follows MLA documentation style (see 34c). Entries are alphabetized by each author's last name; if no author's name is given, the work's title is the first information unit and is alphabetized by its first word (excluding *A, An,* or *The*). Any entry more than one line long is indented five spaces (or one-half inch—about 1.25 cm) for each line after the first. Double-spacing is used within and between entries, including after the name-page line to the Works Cited heading.

X. **Journal article by two authors.** The name of the first author is inverted (last name, first name, middle name, if any) but the name of the second author is not. Article title is in quotation marks, and journal title is underlined. Volume, year (in parentheses), and page numbers are given. (The same format is used for the entries Gray and Viens and for Salovey and Mayer.)

Y. **Article published on a professional site on the World Wide Web.** Author's name is inverted. Article title is in quotation marks. Title of the professional site is underlined, and the site is identified as a *home page*. The access date is followed by the URL enclosed in angle brackets. (The same format is used for the second entry for Hoerr.)

Z. **Book by one author.** Author's name is inverted. Title is underlined. Publisher is identified in as brief a form as possible.

AA. **Second work by an author.** Three hyphens followed by a period indicate that the author is the same as in the preceding entry. Multiple works by the same author are listed in alphabetical order by title. (This device is also used for the second entry for Hoerr.)

BB. **Article in a daily newspaper.** Article title is in quotation marks. Name of newspaper is underlined. Date of newspaper is given as day, abbreviated month, and year, followed by a colon and inclusive page numbers.

CC. **Unsigned article in an online encyclopedia.** Entry is alphabetized by article title, which is given first, in quotation marks. Encyclopedia name is underlined. America Online is the computer service through which the encyclopedia was accessed, on the date given last.

Laver 16

Hoerr, Thomas. "Focusing on the Personal Intelligences as a Basis for Success." NASSP Bulletin 80.583 (1996). Periodical Abstracts. FirstSearch. 4 Oct. 1997. DD

---. "The Naturalist Intelligence." The Building Tool Room. Home page. 10 Oct. 1997 <http://www.newhorizons/.org/trm_hoerrmi.html>.

"Intelligence." Columbia Encyclopedia. 1963 ed. EE

Lambert, Endy Ecklund. "From Crockett to Tubman: Investigating Historical Perspectives." Educational Leadership 55 (1997). Periodical Abstracts. FirstSearch. 5 Oct. 1997.

Salovey, Peter, and John D. Mayer. "Emotional Intelligence." Imagination, Cognition and Personality 9 (1989-90): 185-211.

Staples, Brent. "The IQ Cult." The Bell Curve Debate: History, Documents, Opinions. Ed. Russell Jacoby and Naomi Glauberman. New York: Times, 1995. 293-95. FF

Urbina, Susana P. "Intelligence: Definition and Theoretical Models." Survey of Social Science: Psychology Series. Ed. Frank Magill. Vol. 3. Pasadena: Salem, 1994. 1328-33. GG

COMMENTARY

DD. **Abstract accessed online.** After the author's name, the title of the work is in quotation marks, followed by the name of the original publication *(NASSP Bulletin)*, underlined; its volume, issue number, and year. The database *Periodical Abstracts* is underlined. FirstSearch is the service by which *Periodical Abstracts* was accessed on the date given last. (This format is also used for the entry for Lambert.)

EE. **Unsigned article in a print encyclopedia.** Entry is alphabetized by article title, given first, in quotation marks. Encyclopedia title is underlined. No publication information is required for familiar reference books, other than the edition number or the year of publication. When articles are arranged in alphabetical order, as they are in this encyclopedia, no page numbers need be given.

FF. **Essay in an edited book.** Name of essay author is given first, followed by essay title in quotation marks. Title of the book is underlined. Abbreviation *Ed.* (for "Edited by") is followed by the names of the editors in regular order. Publication information is given in briefest form, and page range uses last two digits of the second number.

GG. **Signed article in a multivolume reference work.** Author of article is followed by title of article in quotation marks. Title of book is underlined. Abbreviation *Ed.* (for "Edited by") is followed by the editor's name in regular order. Volume number uses arabic numerals, even if the volumes are numbered with roman numerals. Publication information is followed by inclusive page numbers for the article.

36 Case Study: A Student Writing an APA Research Paper

This chapter presents a student research paper written in the documentation style° of the American Psychological Association (APA). Section 36a discusses the researching (see Chapters 32 and 33), planning (see Chapter 2), drafting (see 3b and 32t), and revising (see 3c and 32t) processes of the student, Samuel Fung. Section 36b shows the final draft of the paper, including its abstract.

> *Samuel Fung was given this assignment for a research paper in a course called Introduction to Psychology:* Write a research paper of 1800 to 2000 words about an unconscious process in humans. For guidance, refer to the *Simon & Schuster Handbook for Writers,* Third Canadian Edition, Chapters 31 through 34. Use the documentation style of the American Psychological Association (APA) explained in Chapter 34. Your topic and working bibliography are due in two weeks. An early draft of your paper is due two weeks later (try to get it close to what you hope will be your last draft, so that comments from me and your peers can concretely help you write an excellent final draft). Your final draft is due one week after the early draft is returned to you with comments.

36a Observing the processes of researching and writing an APA-style research paper

After Samuel Fung had read his assignment, he started **planning** by listing various unconscious processes in humans so that he could pick the one most interesting to him. Referring to his class notes and the textbook from his psychology course, he found these topics: sleep, dreams, insomnia, biological clocks, daydreams, hypnosis, and meditation. He favoured biological clocks because of his experiences with jet lag whenever he travelled between his home in Vancouver and his grandparents' home in Hong Kong.

Fung then checked to see whether the library at his university had enough sources useful for research on biological clocks. He was pleased to find books, journal articles, magazine and newspaper articles, and even a videotape of a U.S. Public Broadcasting System program on the subject. So that he could compile a working bibliography (see 32h) and, at the same time, try to find an approach to the topic suitable for a paper of 1800 to 2000 words, Fung began to read and take notes (see 32j). He saw entire books about biological clocks, so he realized that he would need to narrow the topic (see 32d) sufficiently to shape a thesis statement° (see 2n and 32r). The narrowing process worried him because he had been told in other courses that his topics for research papers were too broad. He was determined this time to avoid that same problem.

The working bibliography that Fung submitted consisted of twenty-six sources, though he had read and rejected about six others (he knew that this represented real progress for him). He did not intend to use them all in his paper, but he wanted them available as he wrote his early drafts. Not surprisingly, his instructor urged him to reduce the list once drafting began; otherwise Fung would risk writing too little about too much. He redoubled his efforts to read even more critically to evaluate his sources (see 32f and 33f) and weed out material. He omitted some of the sources on his list, took detailed notes (see 32j) on each remaining source, and began to group his material into emerging subtopics.

To start **drafting** his paper, Fung spread his notecards around him for easy reference, but he felt somewhat overwhelmed by the amount of information at hand, and he wrote only a few sentences. To break through, he decided to write a "discovery draft" (see 3b) to see what he had absorbed from his reading and notetaking. That very rough draft became his vehicle for many things, including creating an effective thesis statement°, inserting source information according to APA documentation style, and checking the logical arrangement of his material.

Revising for Fung started with his thesis statement°, a process that helped him further narrow his focus. He started with "Biological clocks are fascinating," which expressed his feelings but said nothing of substance. His next version served well as he revised his discovery draft into a true first draft: "Biological clocks, our unconscious timekeepers, affect our lives in many ways including compatibility in marriage, family life, jet travel, work schedules, illnesses, medical treatments, and the space program." That version proved to Fung that he was covering too much for an 1800- to 2000-word research paper, and he wanted to drop material. He decided first to inform his readers about the phenomenon of biological clocks and then to discuss the effects of those clocks on people's alertness in the morning and later in the day, on travellers on jet airplanes, and on workers' performance. For his final draft, Fung used this more focused thesis statement: "Biological clocks, which are a significant feature of human design, greatly affect personal and professional lifestyles."

Using APA documentation style made Fung attend very closely to the details of correct parenthetical references (see 34d-1) within his paper and a correct References list (see 34d-2 and 34d-3) at the end. Because he had used MLA documentation style° in other courses, he made sure not to confuse the two styles. For example, he saw that APA-style parenthetical citations require a page reference for a quotation but not for a paraphrase or summary (whereas MLA style requires a page reference for all three). For format and style details of the References list at the end of his paper, he found Chart 152 in section 34d-2 especially helpful.

As Fung checked the logical arrangement of his material, he realized that because he had dropped some aspects of biological clocks when he finally narrowed his topic sufficiently, he needed a little more depth about those aspects that he was retaining. A few hours at the computer led him to what he needed, including examples about baseball players and emergency room physicians. Fung learned from his research experiences the difference between researching a topic too broadly (and therefore gathering too many sources for the assignment) and researching a few aspects of a topic in depth by focusing on selected sources. His final draft, which appears in 36b, draws on sixteen sources, a number that is down drastically from the twenty-six with which he started.

Part of Fung's title page and his abstract page follow. For guidelines on writing an abstract, see section 34d-4.

36b Looking at the final draft of an APA-style research paper

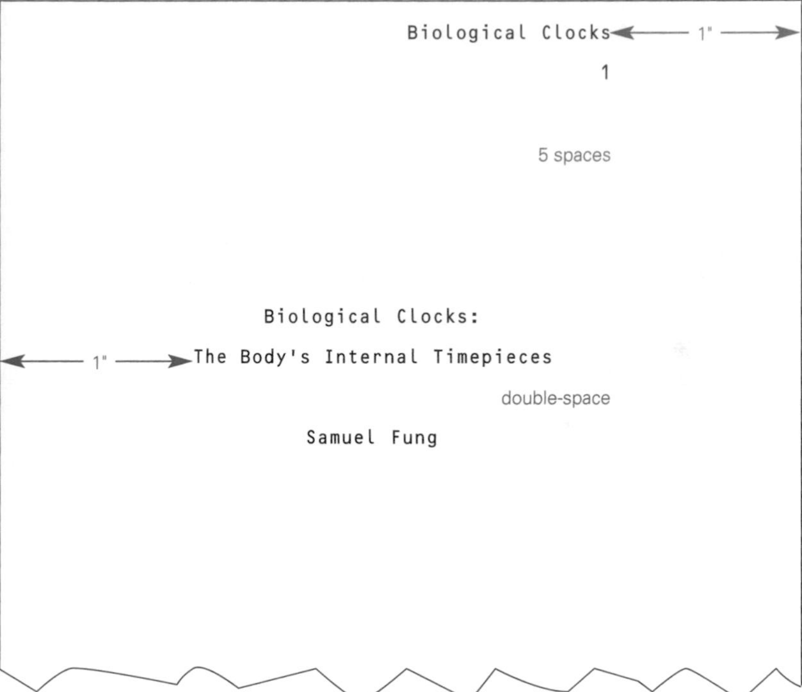

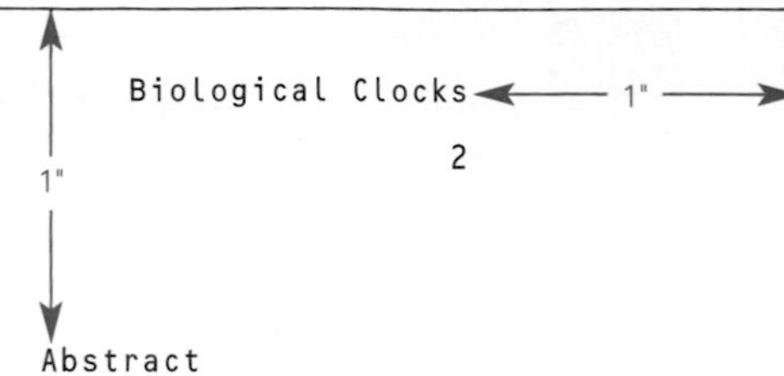

Abstract

double-space

Circadian rhythms, which greatly affect human lives, often suffer disruption in technological societies, resulting in such disorders as jet lag syndrome and seasonal affective disorder (SAD). With growing scientific awareness of both natural circadian cycles and the effects of disturbances of these cycles, individuals are learning how to control some negative effects.

Biological Clocks

3

Biological Clocks:

The Body's Internal Timepieces

Life in modern, technological societies is built around timepieces. People set clocks on radios, microwave ovens, VCRs, and electric coffee makers. Students respond to bells that start and end the school day as well as dividing it into blocks of time. Almost everyone relies on clocks to manage time well. While carefully managing the minutes and hours each day, individuals are often encouraged or forced by current styles of family and work life to violate another kind of time: their body's time. Biological clocks, which are also known as circadian cycles, are a significant feature of human design that greatly affect personal and professional lifestyles.

The term "circadian," which is Latin for "about a day," describes the rhythms of people's internal biological clocks. Circadian cycles are in tune with external time cycles such as the 24-hour period of the earth's daily rotation as signalled by the rising and setting of the sun. In fact, says William Schwartz, professor of neurobiology and a researcher in the field of chronobiology (the study of circadian rhythms), "All such biological clocks are adaptations to life on a rotating world" (Lewis, 1995). Usually, humans set their biological clocks by seeing these cycles of daylight and darkness. Carefully designed studies conducted in caves or similar environments that let researchers control light and darkness have shown that most people create

➜

Biological Clocks
4

cycles slightly over 24 hours when they are not exposed to natural cycles of day and night (Allis & Haederle, 1989; Enright, 1980). Human perception of the external day-night cycle affects the production and release of a brain hormone, melatonin, which is important in initiating and regulating the sleep-wake cycle, as Alfred Lewy and other scientists at the National Institute of Health in Bethesda, Maryland, have found (Winfree, 1987).

An individual's lifestyle reflects that person's own circadian cycle. Scientists group people as "larks" or "owls" based on whether individuals are more efficient in the morning or at night. The idea behind the labels is that "in nature certain animals are diurnal, active during the light period; others are nocturnal, active at night. The 'morning lark' and 'night owl' connotations typically are used to categorize the human extremes" ("Are You," 1989, p. 11).

"Larks" who must stay up late at night and "owls" who must awaken early in the morning experience mild versions of the disturbances, called "jet lag," that time-zone travellers often encounter. Jet lag, which is characterized by fatigue and irregular sleep patterns, results from disruption of circadian rhythms, a common problem among those who travel great distances by jet airplane to different time zones:

> Jet lag syndrome is the inability of the internal body rhythm to rapidly resynchronize after sudden shifts in the timing. For a variety of reasons, the system attempts to maintain stability and resist

> temporal change. Consequently, complete adjustment can often be delayed for several days--sometimes for a week--after arrival at one's destination. (Bonner, 1991, p. 72)

Interestingly, research shows that the number of flying hours is not the cause of jet lag. Rather, "the number, rate, and direction of time-zone changes are the critical factors in determining the extent and degree of jet lag symptoms," according to Richard Coleman (1986, p. 67) in <u>Wide Awake at 3 a.m.: By Choice or by Chance?</u> Eastbound travellers find it harder than westbound travellers to adjust. Proof of this theory can be found in professional baseball. Three researchers analyzed win-lose records to discover whether jet lag affected baseball players' performance (Recht, Lew, & Schwartz, 1995). They focused on the records of eastern and western teams over a period of 3 years. If a visiting team did not have to travel through any time zones, it lost 54% of the time. If the visiting team had travelled from east to west, it lost 56.2% of the time. But if the visitors had travelled from west to east, the home team beat the visitors 62.9% of the time.

Another group that suffers greatly from biological-clock disruptions consists of people whose livelihoods depend on erratic schedules. This situation affects 20 to 30 million U.S. workers whose work schedules differ from the usual morning starting time and afternoon or early evening ending time (Weiss, 1989). Charles Czeisler, director of the Center for Circadian and Sleep

→

Disorders at Brigham and Woman's Hospital in Boston, reports that 27% of the U.S. workforce does shift work (Binkley, 1990). Shift work can mean, for example, working from 7:00 a.m. to 3:00 p.m. for 6 weeks, from 3:00 p.m. to 11:00 p.m. for 6 weeks, and from 11:00 p.m. to 7:00 a.m. for 6 weeks. Many shift workers endure stomach and intestinal-tract disorders, and, on average, they have a 3 times higher risk of heart disease than non-shift workers (Bingham, 1989). In a 1989 report to the American Association for the Advancement of Science, Czeisler states that "police officers, [medical] interns, and many others who work nights perform poorly and are involved in more on-the-job accidents than their daytime counterparts" (Binkley, 1990, p. 26).

Other researchers confirm that safety is at risk during late-shift hours (Chollar, 1989). In a study of 28 medical interns observed during late-night shifts over a 1-year period, 25% admitted to falling asleep while talking on the phone, and 34% had at least one accident or near-accident during that period (Weiss, 1989). Investigations into the <u>Challenger</u> Shuttle explosion and the nuclear-reactor disasters at Three-Mile Island and Chernobyl reveal critical errors made by people undergoing the combined stresses of lack of sleep and unusual work schedules (Toufexis, 1989).

Emergency room physicians experience these two stresses all the time. A U.S. professional group, the American College of Emergency Physicians (ACEP), after investigating circadian rhythms and shift work, drafted a formal policy statement, approved by ACEP's Board of Directors in 1994. The policy calls for "shifts... consistent with circadian principles" to prevent "burnout" and keep emergency physicians from leaving the field, as well as to enable them to take the best care of patients (Thomas, 1996).

If jet lag and circadian disruptions caused by shift work are obvious ways to upset a biological clock, a less obvious disruption is increasingly recognized as a medical problem: the disorder known as seasonal affective disorder (SAD). Table 1 lists some of the major symptoms of SAD.

Table 1

Common Symptoms of Seasonal Affective Disorder

Sadness	Later waking
Anxiety	Increased sleep time
Decreased physical activity	Interrupted, unrefreshing sleep
Irritability	Daytime drowsiness
Increased appetite	Decreased sexual drive
Craving for carbohydrates	Menstrual problems
Weight gain	Work problems
Earlier onset of sleep	Interpersonal problems

Note. From The Clockwork Sparrow (p. 204), by S. Binkley, 1990, Englewood Cliffs, NJ: Prentice Hall. Copyright 1990 by Prentice Hall.

SAD appears to be related to the short daylight (photoperiod) of winter in the temperate zones of the

→

northern and southern hemispheres. The phenomenon of SAD not only illustrates the important role of circadian rhythms, but also dramatically proves that an understanding of circadian principles can help scientists improve the lives of people who experience disruptions of their biological clocks. Binkley claims that exposure to bright light for periods of up to two hours a day during the short photoperiod days of winter reduces SAD-related "depression in 87 percent of patients ... within a few days; relapses followed" (pp. 203-204) when light treatment ended.

Lengthening a person's exposure to bright light can also help combat the effects of jet lag and shift work. Specific suggestions for using light to help reset a jet traveller's biological clock include "a late-afternoon golf game or early-morning walk"; for night-shift workers, staying in the dark during the day and being in artificial light that mimics daylight at night are helpful (Mayo Clinic, 1997).

Establishing work schedules more sensitive to biological clocks can increase workers' sense of well-being and reduce certain safety hazards. A group of police officers in Philadelphia were studied while on modified shift schedules (Locitzer, 1989; Toufexis, 1989). These officers changed between day shifts and night shifts less frequently than they had on former shift schedules; they rotated forward rather than backward in time; and they worked 4 rather than 6 consecutive days. Officers reported 40% fewer patrol-car

Biological Clocks

9

accidents and decreased use of drugs or alcohol to get to sleep. Overall, the police officers preferred the modified shift schedules. Charles Czeisler, who conducted the study, summarizes the importance of these results: "When schedules are introduced that take into account the properties of the human circadian system, subjective estimates of work schedule satisfaction and health improve, personnel turnover decreases, and worker productivity increases" (Locitzer, 1989).

Scientists like Charles Czeisler are helping individuals to live harmoniously with their biological clocks. Growing awareness of the effects of such situations as shift work and travel across time zones is one significant step toward control. The use of light to manipulate the body's sense of time is another. As more people become aware of how circadian rhythms affect lifestyles, the day might soon come when we can fully control our biological clocks instead of their controlling us.

References

Allis, T., & Haederle, M. (1989, June 12). Ace in the hole: Stefania Follini never caved in. People, p. 52.

Are you a day or night person? (1989, March). USA Today Magazine, p. 11.

Bingham, R. (Writer & Director). (1989). The time of our lives [Television production]. KBTC Public Television of Seattle, PBS.

Binkley, S. (1990). The clockwork sparrow. Englewood Cliffs, NJ: Prentice Hall.

Bonner, P. (1991, July). Travel rhythms. Sky Magazine, pp. 72-73, 76-77.

Chollar, S., (1989, November). Safe solutions for night work. Psychology Today, p. 26.

Coleman, R. (1986). Wide awake at 3:00 a.m.: By choice or by chance? New York: Freeman.

Enright, J. T. (1980). The timing of sleep and wakefulness. Berlin: Springer.

Lewis, R. (1995, December 11). Chronobiology researchers say their field's time has come. The Scientist, 9, 14. Retrieved December 30, 1997, from the World Wide Web: http://www.the-scientist.library.upenn.edu/yr1995/dec/chrono_951211.html

Locitzer, K. (1989, July/August). Are you out of sync with each other? Psychology Today, p. 66.

Mayo Clinic. (1997, December 30). Tricks to try when you're out of sync. Mayo Health Oasis. Mayo Clinic Health Letter, March 1995.

Biological Clocks

11

Retrieved December 30, 1997, from the World Wide Web: http://mayohealth.org/mayo/9503/htm/sync_sb.htm

Recht, L., Lew, R., & Schwartz, W. (1995, October 19). Baseball teams beaten by jet lag [Letter]. Nature, 377, 583.

Thomas, H. (1996). Circadian rhythms and shift work [American College of Emergency Physicians policy resource and education paper]. Retrieved December 30, 1997, from the World Wide Web: http://www.acep.org/POLICY/PR004166.HTM

Toufexis, A. (1989, June 5). The times of your life. Time, pp. 66-67.

Weiss, R. (1989, January 21). Safety gets short shrift on long night shift. Science News, p. 37.

Winfree, A. (1987). The timing of biological clocks. New York: Freeman.

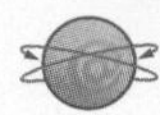

owl.english.purdue.edu/handouts/research/index.html
Research Papers

www.bedfordstmartins.com/online/
Online! A Reference Guide to Using Internet Sources

owl.english.purdue.edu/handouts/research/r_quotprsum.html
Quoting, Paraphrasing, and Summarizing

www.windweaver.com/searchguide.htm
Using the Best Directories and Search Engines

www.english.uiuc.edu/cws/wworkshop/bibliostyles.htm
Bibliography Style Handbook (APA and MLA)

www.lib.ohio-state.edu/guides/chicagogd.html
Chicago Manual of Style Form Guide

www.lib.ohio-state.edu/guides/cbegd.html
CBE Style Form Guide

www2.gasou.edu/facstaff/jwalker
Columbia Online Style (follow links)

PART

VI Writing Across the Curriculum and in the Public World

When you write for the different disciplines, you become familiar with the perspectives and assumptions that underlie each discipline. Part Six compares and contrasts the various disciplines so that you can respond effectively to the major types of writing assignments each discipline involves. The information in Part Six serves as a resource for your entire academic career and beyond.

37 Comparing the Different Disciplines

37a Recognizing similarities and differences among the disciplines

The humanities, the social sciences, and the natural sciences each have their own perspectives on the world and their own philosophies about academic thought and research. To understand some of the differences among the disciplines, consider these three quite different paragraphs about a mountain.

HUMANITIES

The mountain stands above all that surrounds it. Giant timbers—part of a collage of evergreen and deciduous trees—conceal the expansive mountain's slope, where cattle once grazed. At the base of the mountain, a cool stream flows over rocks of all sizes, colours, and shapes. Next to the outer bank of the stream stands a shingled farmhouse, desolate, yet suggesting its active past. Unfortunately, the peaceful scene is interrupted by billboards and chairlifts, landmarks of a modern, fast-paced life.

SOCIAL SCIENCES

Among the favourite pastimes of Canadian city dwellers is the "return to nature." Many outdoor enthusiasts hope to enjoy a scenic trip to the mountains, only to be disappointed. They know they have arrived at the mountain that they have travelled hundreds of kilometres to see because huge billboards are directing them to its base. As they look up the mountain, dozens of people are riding over the treetops in a chairlift, littering the slope with paper cups and food wrappers. At the base of the mountain stands the inevitable refreshment stand, found at virtually all Canadian tourist attractions.

Land developers consider such commercialization a way to preserve and utilize natural resources, but environmentalists are appalled.

NATURAL SCIENCES

The mountain is approximately 2100 metres in height. The underlying rock is igneous, of volcanic origin, composed primarily of granites and feldspars. Three distinct biological communities are present on the mountain. The community at the top of the mountain is alpine in nature, dominated by very short grasses and forbs. At middle altitudes, a typical northern boreal coniferous forest community is present, and at the base and lower altitudes, deciduous forest is the dominant community. This community has, however, been highly affected by agricultural development along the river at its base and by recreational development.

These examples illustrate that each discipline has its writing traditions and preferences. The paragraph written for the humanities describes the mountain from the individual perspective of the writer—a perspective both personal and yet representative of a general human response. The paragraph written for the social sciences focuses on the behaviour of people as a group. The paragraph written for the natural sciences reports observations of natural phenomena.

As you study and write in each of the academic disciplines, you become familiar with alternative ways of thinking. As you come to know the habits of mind that characterize each discipline, you develop specialized vocabularies that allow you to participate in the conversations of each discipline. As your perspectives are broadened, you gain lifelong access to the pleasures of informed insight—among the major benefits of a postsecondary education.

No matter what differences exist among the academic disciplines, all subject areas interconnect and overlap. Chart 156 lists similarities and differences.

For example, in a humanities class you might read *Lives of a Cell,* by Lewis Thomas, a collection of essays about science and nature written by the late noted physician and prize-winning author. As you consider the art of the writer, you will also be thinking deeply about biology and other sciences.

The four differences listed in Chart 156 are discussed in detail here.

SIMILARITIES AND DIFFERENCES IN WRITING ACROSS THE DISCIPLINES 156

SIMILARITIES

1. Consider your purpose, audience, and tone.	Chapters 1–2
2. Use the writing process to plan, shape, draft, revise, edit, and proofread.	Chapters 2–3
3. Develop a thesis.	Chapters 2–3
4. Arrange and organize your ideas.	Chapter 2
5. Use supporting evidence.	Chapters 2–4
6. Develop paragraphs thoroughly.	Chapter 4
7. Critically think, read, and write, and use correct reasoning and logic.	Chapter 5
8. Argue well.	Chapter 6
9. Write effective sentences.	Chapters16–19
10. Choose words well.	Chapters 20–21
11. Use correct grammar.	Chapters 7–15
12. Spell correctly.	Chapter 22
13. Use correct punctuation and mechanics.	Chapters 23–30

DIFFERENCES

1. Conduct research and select sources according to each discipline (see 37a-1).
2. Select a style of documentation appropriate to each discipline (see 37a-2 and Chapter 34).
3. Follow manuscript format requirements, if any, in each discipline (see 37a-3).
4. Use specialized language, when needed, in each discipline (see 37a-4).

1 Conducting research and selecting sources according to each discipline

Primary sources offer you first-hand exposure to information. No one comes between you and the exciting experience of discovering and confronting material on your own. Research methods differ among the disciplines when primary sources are used. In the humanities, existing documents are primary sources; the task of the researcher is to analyze and interpret these primary sources. Typical primary-source material for research could be a poem by Dylan Thomas, the floor plans of Egyptian pyramids, or early drafts of music manuscripts. In the social and natural sciences, primary research entails the design and undertaking of experiments involving direct observation. The task of the researcher in the social and natural sciences is to conduct the experiments or to read the first-hand reports of experiments and studies written by people who conducted them.

Secondary sources—articles and books about a primary source—are also important in all disciplines. In the humanities, you can learn much from the examples of others who have analyzed and interpreted primary sources. In the social and natural sciences, secondary sources can usefully synthesize findings in many areas and draw parallels that offer new insights.

2 Selecting a style of documentation appropriate to each discipline

Writers use **documentation** to give credit to the sources they have used. A writer who does not credit a source is guilty of **plagiarizing**—a serious academic offence (see 31a). Styles of documentation differ among the disciplines.

In the humanities, many fields use the documentation style of the Modern Language Association (MLA), as explained and illustrated in section 34c. The student research paper in Chapter 35 and the student literary analysis in Chapter 38 use MLA documentation style. CM (Chicago Manual) style, also used in the humanities, is described in 34e. In the social sciences, most fields use the documentation style of the American Psychological Association (APA). APA documentation style is explained and illustrated in 34d. The student research paper in Chapter 36 uses APA documentation style. In the natural sciences, documentation styles vary, as is explained in 34f and 39g.

3 Following manuscript format requirements in each discipline

As a reflection of the differences among academic disciplines, different formats are sometimes expected for presentation of material. These special formats have evolved to communicate a writer's purpose, to emphasize content by eliminating distracting variations in format, and to make the reader's work easier. Writing in the humanities is less often subject to set formats, although the writing is expected to be well organized and logically presented. Writing in the social and natural sciences often calls for set formats for specific types of writing.

4 Using specialized language, when needed, in each discipline

Specialized language is often referred to as **jargon**. Jargon is useful when it helps people who are specialists communicate easily with each other in a kind of "verbal shorthand." When specialized material is communicated to the general reading public, however, any jargon has to be defined so that everyone can understand the message. Jargon is not useful when it is unnecessarily obscure and overblown (see 21e-2).

All disciplines use specialized language to some extent. The specialized terms in the social and natural sciences are generally more technical and less accessible to nonspecialists than are those in the humanities. The more important that exactness is to a discipline, the more likely that many words will have specialized meanings. For example, consider the word *niche*. It has two generally known meanings: "a place particularly suitable to the person or thing in it," and "a hollowed space in a wall for a statue or vase." *Niche* in the natural sciences, however, has a very specialized meaning: "the set of environmental conditions—climate, food sources, water supply, enemies—that permit an organism or species to survive."

✤ USAGE ALERT: Many writers in scientific disciplines make a habit of writing in the passive voice. Yet style manuals for scientific writing agree with the advice you will find in 8o: Use the active voice except for purposes best fulfilled by the passive.* ✤

*You may want to look at section 2.06 in the *Publication Manual of the American Psychological Association,* Fourth Edition (36).

38 Writing About Literature

Literature, which includes **fiction** (novels and stories), **drama** (plays and scripts), and **poetry** (poems and lyrics), has developed from age-old human impulses to discover and communicate meaning by telling stories, re-enacting events, and singing or chanting. Reading and then writing about literature can deliver a related satisfaction: You have the chance to think about meaning and to tell others what you have found.

38a Understanding methods of inquiry into literature

All questions about literature require you to read a work closely. Some questions then ask you to deal with the material on a literal level (see 5d-1). You might be asked to explain the meaning of a passage in a novel, or to find out what historical events were going on when the work was written or what other scholars have said about some element of the work.

Other questions call for inferential reasoning (see 5d-2) and evaluative thinking (see 5d-3). You might be asked to discuss the effect of sound or rhythm or rhyme in a poem, or to compare characters in two plays by a particular playwright. Unlike inquiry in many other disciplines, literary inquiry may also involve you in being asked to describe your response or reaction to a work of literature after a close, careful reading.

In each case, your answers must be thorough, well reasoned, well supported with evidence, and informed by knowledge of the work.

38b Understanding purposes and practices in writing about literature

1 Using first and third person appropriately

Instructors usually have students use the first person°* (*I, we, our*) to write about their points of view or personal evaluations, and the third person° (*he, she, it, they*) for other assignments. Be sure to inquire about and adapt to your instructor's requirements. In research papers, the first person is usually acceptable only when you present your personal experience, your own conclusions, or your personal views contrasted with those of the sources that you have consulted and documented°.

2 Using verbs in the present tense and the past tense correctly when writing about literature

When you describe or discuss a literary work or any of its elements, use the present tense°: *Constance's adventures in Cyprus and Verona—the settings of the Shakespearean tragedies—**are** framed by two brief scenes set in her campus office.* The present tense is also correct for discussing what the author has done in a specific work: *By transforming Desdemona into a warrior, MacDonald **is playing** upon an imaginary implication of Desdemona's taste for Othello's gory tales and of her wish to accompany Othello to the battlefield in Cyprus.*

If you are discussing events that take place before the action of a literary work has begun, a past-tense° verb is correct: *But her own career **has come*** [before the action starts] *to a dead end.* Also use past tenses, as appropriate, to discuss historical events or biographical information: *MacDonald's play opens with an epigraph taken from the psychologist Carl Gustav Jung, who **theorized** that our unconscious combines archetypal characters found in myth and literature: the Fool, the Hero, and so on.*

* Throughout this book, a degree mark (°) indicates that you can find the definition of the word in the Glossary of Terms in this handbook.

3 Using your own ideas and using secondary sources

Some assignments call only for your own ideas about the subject of your essay. Other assignments ask you to support your analysis with **secondary sources.** Secondary sources include books and articles in which an expert discusses material related to your topic. You can locate secondary sources by using the research process discussed in Chapters 32 and 33.

Whenever you use secondary sources, **avoid plagiarism** (see 31a and 33e). So that no reader thinks that the ideas of another person are yours, always document your sources (see 31b and Chapter 34). Also, to work material from secondary sources skilfully and gracefully into your writing, use the techniques of quotation (see 31c), paraphrase (see 31d), and summary (see 31e).

38c Using documentation style for writing about literature

If you use secondary sources° when you write about literature, you are required to credit your sources by using documentation. Many instructors require their students to use the documentation style of the Modern Language Association (MLA), an organization of scholars and teachers of language and literature. MLA documentation style is described in section 34c. Two other documentation styles sometimes required in the humanities are APA (American Psychological Association), presented in section 34d, and CM (Chicago Manual), presented in section 34e.

38d Writing different types of papers about literature

Before you write a paper in which you refer or react to a literary work, be sure to read the work closely. To read well, use your understanding of the reading process (see 5d) and engage in critical reading (see 5e).

1 Writing reaction papers

In a paper in which you react to a work of literature, you might ask and try to answer a central question that the work made you think about, criticize a point of view in the work, or present a problem that you see in the work. For example, if you are asked to respond to a play, you might write about why you did or did not enjoy reading the play, how the play does or does not relate to your personal experience or to your view of life, what the play made you think about and try to puzzle through. You can focus on the entire play or on a particular scene, character, or set of lines.

2 Writing book reports

A book report informs readers about the content of a book—by summarizing its plot and its theme and by discussing (1) the significance and purpose of the book, (2) how the book presents its content, and (3) who might be most interested in the book. When you discuss the significance of the book, try to relate it to your field of study. For example, if the book is a classic in children's literature, your focus for a literature class would differ somewhat from your focus for a course in psychology or education.

3 Writing interpretations

An interpretation discusses either what the author means by the work or what the work means personally to the reader. When you are writing an interpretation paper, always consider the questions in Chart 157.

QUESTIONS FOR AN INTERPRETATION PAPER 157

1. What is the theme of the work?
2. How are particular parts of the work related to the theme?
3. If patterns exist in various elements of the work, what do they mean?
4. What message does the author convey through the use of major aspects of the work, listed in Chart 158?
5. Why does the work end as it does?

4 Writing analyses

Analysis is the examination of the relationship of a whole to its parts. In a **literary analysis,** you are expected to discuss your well-reasoned ideas about a work of fiction, poetry, or drama. To get to know the work well and to gather ideas for your analysis, read the work thoroughly, again and again. Watch for patterns in the aspects of literary analysis listed in Chart 158. Write notes as you go along so that you have a record of two important resources for your writing: the patterns you find in the material, and your reactions to the patterns and to the whole work.

MAJOR ASPECTS OF LITERARY WORKS TO ANALYZE 158

PLOT	The events and their sequence
THEME	Central idea or message
STRUCTURE	Organization and relationship of parts to each other and to the whole
CHARACTERIZATION	Traits, thoughts, and actions of the people in the plot
SETTING	Time and place of the action
POINT OF VIEW	Perspective or position from which the material is presented—sometimes by a narrator or a main character
STYLE	How words and sentence structures present the material
IMAGERY	The pictures created by the words (similes, metaphors, figurative language) [for a list and definitions, see Chart 103 in section 21c]
TONE	The attitude of the author toward the subject of the work—and sometimes toward the reader—expressed through the choice of words and through the imagery
FIGURES OF SPEECH	Includes metaphor and simile
SYMBOLISM	The meaning beneath the surface of the words and images
RHYTHM AND RHYME	Beat, metre, repetition of sounds, etc.

38e Three case studies of students writing about literature

This section includes three student essays of literary analysis. The last two essays use secondary sources°, and all three use MLA documentation style (see sections 34c and 38c).

1 Student essay interpreting a plot element in a short story

The following essay interprets a plot element in Edgar Allan Poe's story "The Tell-Tale Heart."

Born in 1809, Edgar Allan Poe was an important American journalist, poet, and fiction writer. In his short, dramatic life, Poe gambled, drank, lived in terrible poverty, saw his young wife die of tuberculosis, and died himself under mysterious circumstances at age 40. He also created the detective novel and wrote brilliant, often bizarre short stories that still stimulate the reader's imagination.

When the student who wrote this essay read Poe's "The Tell-Tale Heart," first published in 1843, she was fascinated by one of the plot elements: the sound of a beating heart that compels the narrator of the story to commit a murder and then to confess it to the police. In the following paper, the student discusses her interpretation of the source of the heartbeat.

The Sound of a Murderous Heart

In Edgar Allan Poe's short story "The Tell-Tale Heart," several interpretations are possible as to the source of the beating heart that causes the narrator-murderer to reveal himself to the police. The noise could simply be a product of the narrator's obviously deranged mind. Or perhaps the murder victim's spirit lingers, heart beating, to exact revenge upon the narrator. Although each of these interpretations is possible, most of the evidence in the story suggests that the inescapable beating heart that haunts the narrator is his own.

The interpretation that the heartbeat stems from some kind of auditory hallucination is flawed. The narrator clearly is insane--his killing a kind old man because of an "Evil Eye" demonstrates this--and his psychotic behaviour is more than sufficient cause for readers to question his truthfulness. Even so, nowhere else in the story does the narrator imagine things that do not exist. Nor is it likely that he would intentionally attempt to mislead us since the narrative is a confessional monologue through which he tries to explain and justify his actions. He himself describes his "disease" as a heightening of his senses, not of his imagination. Moreover, his highly detailed account of the events surrounding the murder seems to support this claim. Near the end of the story, he refutes the notion that he is inventing the sound in his mind when he says, "I found that the noise was not within my ears" (792). Although the narrator's reliability is questionable, there seems to be no reason to doubt this particular observation.

Interpreting the heartbeat as the victim's ghostly retaliation against the narrator also presents difficulties. Perhaps most important, when the narrator first hears the heart, the old man is still alive. The structure of the story also argues against the retaliation interpretation. Poe uses the first-person point of view to give readers immediate access to the narrator's strange thought processes, a choice that suggests the story is a form of psychological study. If

→

"The Tell-Tale Heart" were truly a ghost story, it would probably be told in the third person, and it would more fully develop the character of the old man and explore his relationship with the narrator. If the heartbeat that torments the narrator is his own, however, these inconsistencies are avoided.

The strongest evidence that the tell-tale heart is really the narrator's is the timing of the heartbeat. Although it is the driving force behind the entire story, the narrator hears the beating heart only twice. In both of these instances, he is under immense physical and psychological stress--times when his own heart would be pounding. The narrator first hears the heartbeat with the shock of realizing that he has accidentally awakened his intended victim:

> Meantime the hellish tattoo of the heart increased. It grew quicker and quicker, and louder every instant. The old man's terror must have been extreme! It grew louder, I say, louder every moment!--do you mark me well? I have told you that I am nervous: so I am. And now at the dead hour of the night, amid the dreadful silence of that old house, so strange a noise as this excited me to uncontrollable terror. (791)

As the narrator's anxiety increases, so does the volume and frequency of the sound, an event easily explained if the heartbeat is his own. Also, the sound of the heart persists even after the old man is dead, fading slowly into the background, as would the murderer's own heartbeat after his short, violent struggle with the old man. This reasoning can also explain why the narrator did not hear the heart on any of the seven previous nights when he looked into the old man's bedchamber. Because the old man slept and the "Evil Eye" was closed, no action was necessary (according to the narrator-murderer's twisted logic), and therefore he did not experience the rush of adrenaline that set his heart pounding on the fatal eighth visit.

The heart also follows a predictable pattern at the end of the story when the police officers come to investigate a neighbour's report of the dying old man's scream. In this encounter the narrator's initial calm slowly gives way to irritation and fear. As he becomes increasingly agitated, he begins to hear the heart again. The narrator clearly identifies it as the same sound he heard previously, as shown by the almost word-for-word repetition of the language he uses to describe it, calling it "_a low, dull, quick sound--much such a sound as a watch makes when enveloped in cotton_" [Poe's italics] (792). As the narrator-murderer focuses his attention on the sound, which ultimately overrides all else, his panic escalates until, ironically, he is betrayed by the very senses that he boasted about at the start of the story.

Work Cited

Poe, Edgar Allan. "The Tell-Tale Heart." _American Literature: A Prentice Hall Anthology_. Vol. 1. Ed. Emory Elliott, Linda K. Kerber, A. Walton Litz, and Terence Martin. Englewood Cliffs: Prentice, 1991. 789-92.

2 Student essay analyzing character in a play

The following essay examines *Goodnight Desdemona (Good Morning Juliet)* by Ann-Marie MacDonald, a playwright, novelist, and actor. MacDonald won the Governor General's Award for Drama for this comic play in 1990. Although the play's protagonist is apparently on a quest for the key to a strange manuscript that could unlock a literary mystery, her search takes her into the unexplored territory of her own personality. MacDonald shifts playfully among scenes, characters, and scripts, tantalizing us with clues to the play's deeper mystery. The student's paper examines how MacDonald uses the framework of the quest to "take apart" elements in two Shakespearean tragedies and in the process allow the main character to construct her own fully developed personality.

The Construction of the Protagonist in Goodnight Desdemona (Good Morning Juliet)

On the surface, Ann-Marie MacDonald's comedy Goodnight Desdemona (Good Morning Juliet) is the story of an imaginary literary puzzle. Constance, a talented but ineffectual academic, believes that the two Shakespearean tragedies Othello and Romeo and Juliet were originally written as comedies by an unknown author. By deciphering a mysterious manuscript, Constance hopes to find the original texts of the two plays and the identity of their author. MacDonald does not show us Constance's literary labours, however. Instead, most of the play is a dream sequence in which Constance becomes a character in the two Shakespearean tragedies. Only at the play's end do we learn that Constance's true search is not a literary quest at all: The dream sequence is a descent into Constance's unconscious, and her literary puzzle is a metaphor for her quest for herself.

Constance's adventures in Cyprus and Verona--the settings of the Shakespearean tragedies--are framed by two brief scenes set in her campus office. There we see her as a comical figure, timid and socially awkward; her nickname, we discover later on, is "Mouse." Constance's talents are exploited by the suave Professor Claude Night, with whom she is hopelessly in love, and who has built a successful career by plagiarizing Constance's work. But her own career has come to a dead end.

Her colleagues ridicule her bizarre theory about the two Shakespearean tragedies. From her observation that the tragic outcomes of the two plays turn on "flimsy mistakes--a lost hanky, a delayed wedding announcement" (21), Constance reasons that Shakespeare (as plagiarist) eliminated the role of a fool from each play. This "Wise Fool" would have been the unknown author's agent in concocting and then correcting the "mistakes" in the original comic versions of _Othello_ and _Romeo and Juliet_. By confronting the characters and situations in the plays, Constance believes, the Wise Fool would have engineered happy endings for them.

No sooner does Constance set this part of her thesis down on paper than Professor Night arrives to collect the latest scholarly pieces she has ghostwritten for him. He casually announces that he is eloping with one of his students and is taking the post at Oxford University that Constance has coveted. She takes it all quietly, as usual.

Betrayed in love and blocked in her career, Constance has reached the lowest point in her life. She imagines herself falling into a decline and dying pathetically. In her vision she is awarded a posthumous doctorate; a chastened Claude Night lays roses daily on →

her grave. Rousing herself from this hallucination, Constance immediately begins to discard the paraphernalia of her trivial and unsatisfying identity, tossing keepsakes into the wastebasket. When a few pages of the mysterious manuscript fall into the trash as well, the inscription on its cover catches her eye:

> You who possess the eyes to see
> this strange and wondrous alchemy,
> where words transform to vision'ry,
> where one plus two makes one, not three;
> open this book if you agree
> to be illusion's refugee,
> and of return no guarantee--
> unless you find your true identity.
> And discover who the Author be. (28-29)

Sent on her search with these words, Constance falls into her own wastebasket and directly into the action of <u>Othello</u>.

Constance enters Shakespeare's plots at two crucial moments: just as the jealous Othello is about to murder his innocent wife, Desdemona, in Cyprus, and at the moment when family hatreds in Verona lead Romeo to fight Juliet's cousin in the duel that sets in motion the lovers' downfall. Constance struggles to set things right between the characters while she hunts unsuccessfully for the key to the original manuscript of the two plays. A comedy of errors and incongruities is the result.

As Constance stumbles through <u>Othello</u> and then <u>Romeo and Juliet</u>, we witness odds and ends of famous Shakespearean speeches and scenes. MacDonald's playing on stage reality and our reality is reminiscent of Tom

Stoppard's absurdist version of _Hamlet_ in _Rosencrantz and Guildenstern Are Dead_. When Constance hears gunfire at the siege of Cyprus, she wonders, "They can't use real blood, can they?" (37) She is an incongruous visitor, knowing more about the characters and their circumstances than they believe possible, intruding on their lives, demolishing Shakespeare's plots, answering Shakespearean speeches in colourless Canadian English. (At one point she remembers how she ought to be speaking as a character in an Elizabethan play and starts counting iambic pentameter on her fingers.) By interfering in their plots, Constance inadvertently transforms the two plays into the comedies she believes they were intended to be. She saves Desdemona by revealing the trap that Iago had set to make Othello murderously jealous.

> CONSTANCE [...] I've preempted the Wise Fool!
> He must be here somewhere--I'll
> track him down and reinstate him
> in the text, [...] (38)

She cannot find her fool, however. Constance barely escapes with her life from _Othello_, falling suddenly into _Romeo and Juliet_ where she stops Romeo's fateful duel.

Revisiting these two plays with Constance forces us to reimagine their two heroines. As Constance suspected, in the "pre-Shakespearean" comic versions of their plays (that is, the plays as MacDonald shows them), Desdemona and Juliet are not innocent, helpless, doomed victims. Rather, Constance finds Desdemona to be a warlike woman who advises her:

> If thou wouldst know thyself an Amazon,
> acquire a taste for blood. [...] (36-37)

➜

In Shakespeare's <u>Othello</u>, the Venetian general has wooed Desdemona with stories of military victories in exotic lands. By transforming Desdemona into a warrior, MacDonald is playing upon an imaginary implication of Desdemona's taste for Othello's gory tales and of her wish to accompany Othello to the battlefields in Cyprus.

The teenaged characters Constance meets in Verona really are teenagers--randy, brawling, and rather shallow. In MacDonald's version of her story, Juliet is independent and sexually adventurous. A piece of quasi-Shakespearean stage nonsense has Constance impersonating a man, and Romeo a woman; both Romeo and Juliet become infatuated with Constance/Constantine. A flustered Constance exclaims at the insistent Juliet:

> Heavenly days, what's come over you?!
> You're supposed to be all innocence. (69)

Desdemona and Juliet, as transformed by MacDonald, represent possible models for Constance as an autonomous twentieth-century woman.

Meanwhile, MacDonald has been dropping hints at the progress of Constance's quest.

> CONSTANCE [...] I have to find the Author first; or else the Fool to lead me to the bard.
> JULIET Author? Fool?
> CONSTANCE And Self. It is my quest, and means more to me than love or death. (71)

These hints are for the audience, but not for Constance. Bound up in the pursuit of her thesis, she follows false trails and misconstrues the message contained in the introduction to the manuscript: "where one plus two makes one, not three [...]." She does not yet recognize that these words bid her to reconstruct her one-dimensional personality by reassembling the neglected parts of her "self," and that this is her true quest.

Earlier on, in her office, Constance had tossed the signs of her mouse-like identity into her wastebasket. Now she is inspired by the two not-quite-Shakespearean heroines. Desdemona, who knows the scholarly Constance as "the pedant," adds another dimension to Constance's personality by dubbing her an Amazon and inciting her to admit her hatred for her betrayer, Professor Night. Thinking of her own betrayer, Constance nearly kills the traitorous Iago in a swordfight.

I saw a flash of red before my eyes.
I felt a rush of power through my veins.
I tasted iron blood inside my mouth.
I loved it! (50)

Then, in Verona, Constance begins to reclaim her sexual and passionate side. Constance had earlier admitted to only a delayed adolescent crush on Claude Night--now Juliet coaxes her to proclaim that she once truly loved him. Juliet and Romeo nearly succeeded in drawing Constance into their romantic escapades. Finally, Desdemona and Juliet confront each other and stage a tug-of-war over Constance, who refuses to surrender completely to the obsessions of either one. In an instant, Constance realizes who the Wise Fool is. She is the Fool. And the Author.

In following her supposed scholarly quest, Constance has deconstructed Shakespeare's two plays, helped us to reimagine Desdemona and Juliet, and constructed her own identity. The Amazon in Desdemona ➔

and the sexual being in Juliet combine, in proper measure, with the pedant. The end of Constance's search is the integration of her personality followed by a symbolic rebirth--all three women have their birthday on the day the play ends. MacDonald's play opens with an epigraph taken from the psychologist Carl Gustav Jung, who theorized that our unconscious combines archetypal characters found in myth and literature: the Fool, the Hero, and so on. Hints scattered throughout the play seem to point to this idea of the self and its construction. Other hints, as we have seen, lead to the interpretation of Constance's quest as a quest for herself. Her dreamed adventures in Cyprus and Verona, therefore, may be seen as a healing journey into her unconscious. As Constance learns to act as an autonomous and complete personality, it becomes clear that she is the Author of the tale by the same token that she has become the author of her own life.

Works Cited

MacDonald, Ann-Marie. _Goodnight Desdemona (Good Morning Juliet)_. Toronto: Playwrights Canada, 1997.

Stoppard, Tom. _Rosencrantz and Guildenstern Are Dead_. New York: Grove, 1968.

3 Student research paper analyzing a poem

The following essay is a literary analysis of a poem. It uses secondary sources°. E. J. Pratt, a major figure in Canadian poetry, was born in 1882 in Western Bay, Newfoundland. Pratt's narrative poetry attempts to mythologize Canadian history, a subject he takes up in *Towards the Last Spike,* for which he won his third Governor General's Award. In this paper, the student discusses Pratt's reconciliation of epic tradition and modern Canadian historical events. (Note that the title of a long poem is given in italics, not in quotation marks.)

Towards the Last Spike: A Canadian Epic?

In a review of Towards the Last Spike that appeared in the University of Toronto Quarterly, Northrop Frye made this comment: "The poem is in the epic tradition, without any of the advantages of epic to sustain it" (270). Pratt took a subject that was "epic" in scope and size, and created instead the "verse panorama," as he called it in its lengthy subtitle. It can be argued that Canadian poets lack the poetic tradition that would turn their history into epic poetry. Pratt comes close to the epic in Towards the Last Spike, but through his choice of dramatic technique, he has, in effect, originated a style of narrative poetry that works against the ultimately unifying vision of the epic. The poem anthologizes the past in a series of vignettes linked by historical "progress reports." This structure enables Pratt to achieve variety and contrast without distorting the remainder of the poem; the work ultimately has the cumulative effect of richness and a textured quality. At the same time, the fragmentation of the narrative mirrors the political divisiveness and lack of national unity that the poem portrays, finally subverting Pratt's epic aim. →

In keeping with his panoramic vision, Pratt sets up a complex web of themes through the course of the poem. The poem has two protagonists, mankind and nature. Not only do these two contend with each other, but man also quarrels with man, and natural elements are in conflict with each other as well. The two protagonists are equated as "two fortresses: the mind, the rock" (65). The conflicts take place in two different worlds, each carefully characterized by Pratt: the political realm of Macdonald and the natural one of the nameless Canadian workers and the landscape--the "Laurentian monster."

The poem is as much a reflection of how politicians operate as it is an account of the building of the railroad. In his political sections, Pratt illustrates

> [. . .] the battle of ideas and metaphors
> And kindred images called by the same name
> Like brothers who with temperamental blood
> Went to it with their fists. (51)

This political struggle is waged between the imaginative, emotional man represented by Macdonald and Van Horne, and the cerebral, practical man typified by Blake and Mackenzie. The characterization is not as simple as this opposition would imply, however, for Macdonald in his own way is as calculating as Blake. One of Pratt's major accomplishments in this poem is the credible portrait of the political consciousness in action. Pratt describes Macdonald's political awareness at length in the section entitled "The Gathering" and shows the politician at work concocting his platform:

> He could make use of that--just what he needed
> A Western version of the Arctic daring,
> Romance and realism, a double dose. (43)

Pratt continually emphasizes the power of metaphors and words in the political context. Macdonald recognizes the potency of Blake's phrase "To build a Road over that sea of mountains" (53), with its implication that the task is impossible. This idea frightens Macdonald more than the rest of Blake's massive rhetoric, for

> This carried more than argument. It was
> A flash of fire which might with proper kindling
> Consume its way into the public mind. (53)

The theme of control runs as a corollary to Pratt's concept of words and metaphors. Macdonald is able to gain control in the House of Commons through his vision and his use of words, while Blake, "the homicidal master of the opiates," loses his audience and therefore his support through boredom (53). Van Horne is shown to be a master of control to rival Macdonald, since he is able to manage both the resources of nature and the inventions of man:

> [. . .] Electricity
> And rock, one novel to the coiling hand,
> The other frozen in the lap of Age,
> Were playthings for the boy, work for the man. (57)

Macdonald and Van Horne also share the passion of the visionary man; symbolically each spends a sleepless night gazing at the stars and at the landscape. Blake, in ironic comparison, needs help to see the country around him:

> Though with his natural eyes
> Up to this time he had not sighted mountains
> He was an expert with the telescope. (52)

At the same time Pratt undercuts the vision of Macdonald because it originates in liquor, "his medicine": ➜

A blessed sleep fell like a dew upon him,
And soon, in trance, drenched in conciliation,
He hiccupped gently--"Now let S-S-Stephen come!" (76)

Pratt's ability and craftsmanship as a poet are reflected clearly in the poem. He uses various patterns of images to draw the poem together: The metaphor of music is one example of this technique and further elaboration of the drive to control. The image is first applied to the vision of the railroad:

The airs had long been mastered like old songs
The feet could tap to in the galleries.
But would they tap to a new rhapsody,
Whose ear could be assured of absolute pitch
To catch this kind of music in the West? (49)

Political language is equated with music as well, so that the battle between Blake and Macdonald is not just of rival visions, but also of rival musical expressions:

Blake had returned to the attack and given
Sir John the ague with another phrase
As round and as melodious as the first:
"The Country's wealth, its millions after millions
Squandered--LOST IN THE GORGES OF THE FRASER":
A beautiful but ruinous piece of music
That could only be droned with drums and fifes. (65)

Pratt also uses the image of the orchestra as a description of the Conservatives in defeat, with Macdonald shown as the "old conductor off the podium" (50). The metaphor returns to conclude the poem effectively, as the completion of the railroad becomes the new beginning for the young nation: "Merely the tuning-up!" (80). The image is appropriate in this context, for it implies that the railroad has finally organized Canada into a new harmony. The tone rises in the last section to a pitch of excitement and optimism in its celebration of the achievement. Occasionally, like Macdonald, Pratt uses a phrase that provides a striking visual image for the reader. An example of this occurs in his treatment of Blake, in the expression "Rumours he heard had gangrened into facts" (46).

The elemental conflict between humans and the landscape is contrasted with the sophisticated battle of political visions. The landscape is splendidly characterized by Pratt as a primeval reptile whose primary weapon is its immense size:

> Whose tail had covered Labrador and swished
> Atlantic tides, whose body coiled itself
> Around the Hudson bay, then curled up north
> Through Manitoba and Saskatchewan
> To Great Slave Lake. In continental reach
> The neck went past the Great Bear Lake until
> Its head was hidden in the Arctic Seas. (61)

Traditionally, the epic hero battles the monster to defend or reach his home; here, however, the homeland is the monster. The characterization of home as alien or "other" makes identification with the land in the interests of a national vision impossible and undercuts the poet's epic ambition. In addition, Pratt points to the apparently indissoluble link between terror and beauty in the Canadian scene:

> They needed miles to render up their beauty
> As if the gods in high aesthetic moments
> Resenting the profanity of touch
> Chiselled this sculpture for the eye alone. (64) ➜

Here Pratt would seem to be anticipating the ambivalent relationship to the natural world, at once home and enemy, illustrated in the work of later writers like Margaret Atwood in The Journals of Susanna Moodie or Charles Lillard and Barry McKinnon in their "Bushed" poems.

The landscape is a living thing that wrestles not only with man, but with itself as well. The conflict exists on many levels at one time:

> The men were fighting foes which had themselves
> Waged elemental civil wars and still
> Were hammering one another at this moment. (65)

Although the men are ultimately successful in the combat, and the poem is, in part, a celebration of the triumph of human will over nature, Pratt, in concluding his poem, chooses to focus on the landscape rather than on his "hero." The "Laurentian monster" endures and has the ability to adapt to the new conditions that humans have imposed on it:

> [. . .] To drown
> The traffic chorus, she must blend the sound
> With those inaugural, narcotic notes
> Of storm and thunder which would send her back
> Deeper than ever in Laurentian sleep. (80)

Pratt makes certain, though, that the reader is aware of the cost of the railroad in terms of human life and strength. His interlude "Ring, Ring the Bells" underlines this by illustrating the process of metamorphosis that changes men into landscape.

The title Towards the Last Spike emphasizes not the final event, but rather the movement toward the climax. This is reflected in the anticlimactic treatment of the driving of the last spike, which undercuts the epic and heroic quality of the previous events. Pratt creates a realistically human scene. Donald Smith does not drive the spike home with one superhuman or legendary blow: He fumbles it.

The poem is uneven in quality, and Pratt can be amazingly trite in some of his images. The following part of his description of Van Horne can be cited as an example of Pratt's verse at its most overworked:

Here he could clap the future on the shoulder
And order Fate about as his lieutenant
For he would take no nonsense from a thing
Called Destiny--the stars had to be with him. (57)

These are understandable flaws in a work of this range, and Pratt is for the most part successful in bringing his immense work and all its characters vividly to life. He can write convincingly as an observer of Canadian nature or as a political cartoonist in his depiction of British Columbia as "the Lady" wavering between the respective lures of Macdonald and the Americans. Pratt's modern awareness of discords and divisions admits irony into the poem and diminishes its epic world view. His diversity becomes in itself an impediment to the realization of epic coherence. The question that the poem, with its contradictory impulses, asks is whether epic form and feeling can be sustained in the twentieth century.

Towards the Last Spike is epic in proportions and in its universal theme, but it lacks the conventions and formulaic devices that characterize the earlier epic style. It moves toward the epic vision just as the country moves toward national unity with the creation of the railroad, but the conflicts that are still ➔

unresolved prohibit anything beyond a momentary glimpse of a binding national identity, one of the prerequisites of epic vision. _Towards the Last Spike_ is unique in Canadian poetry, for it is a compendium of our historical experience, and as such, it becomes almost by default our Canadian "epic."

Works Cited

Frye, Northrop. "Poetry." _University of Toronto Quarterly_ 22 (1953): 270-73.

Pratt, E. J. _Towards the Last Spike_. 1952. _Poets Between the Wars_. Ed. M. T. Wilson. Toronto: McClelland & Stewart, 1967.

39 Writing in the Social Sciences and Natural Sciences

39a Understanding methods of inquiry in the social sciences

Disciplines in the **social sciences** include subject areas such as economics, education, geography, political science, psychology, and sociology. At some colleges and universities, history is included in the social sciences; at others it is included in the humanities. The social sciences focus on the behaviour of people as individuals and in groups.

Observation is a common method for inquiry in the social sciences. To make observations, take along whatever tools or equipment you might need: writing or sketching materials, and perhaps recording or photographic equipment. As you make observations, take very accurate and complete notes. If you use abbreviations to speed your notetaking, make sure you will later understand them when you need to write up your observations. In a report of your observations, tell what tools or equipment you used, because your method might have influenced what you saw (for example, your taking photographs may make people act differently than usual).

Interviewing is another common technique that social scientists use. Interviews are useful for gathering people's opinions and impressions of events. If you interview, remember that interviews are not always a completely reliable way to gather factual information, because people's memories are not precise. If your only source for facts is interviews, try to interview as many people as possible so that you can cross-check the information. Before you interview anyone, practise with whatever notetaking tools you might need, so that they do not intrude on the interview process (see also 32q).

Questionnaires can be useful for gathering information in the social sciences. When you administer a questionnaire, be sure that you ask a sufficient number of people to respond, so that you do not reach conclusions based on too small a sample of responses. To write questions for a questionnaire, use the guidelines in Chart 159.

159

GUIDELINES FOR WRITING QUESTIONS FOR A QUESTIONNAIRE

1. First, define what you want to find out, and then write questions that will elicit the information you seek.
2. Phrase questions so that they are easy to understand.
3. Use appropriate language (see 21a), and avoid artificial language (see 21e).
4. Be aware that how you phrase your questions will determine whether the answers that you get truly reflect what people are thinking. Make sure that your choice of words does not imply what *you* want to hear.
5. Avoid questions that invite one-word answers about complex matters that call for a range of responses.
6. Test a draft of the questionnaire on a small group of people before you use it. If any question is misinterpreted or hard to understand, revise and retest it.

39b Understanding writing purposes and practices in the social sciences

Social scientists write to inform readers by presenting and explaining information (see 1b-2) or to persuade readers by arguing a point of view (see 1b-3).

Analysis (see 4f-6 and 5a) helps social scientists write about problems and their solutions. For example, an economist writing about a major automobile company in financial trouble might first break the situation into parts, analyzing employee salaries and benefits, the selling price of cars, and the costs of doing business. Next, the economist might show how these parts relate to the financial status of the whole company. Then the economist might speculate about how specific changes would help solve the company's financial problems.

Social scientists are particularly careful to **define their terms** when they write, especially when they discuss complex social issues. For example, if you are writing a paper on substance abuse in the medical profession, you first have to define what you mean by the terms *substance abuse* and *medical profession*. By *substance* do you mean alcohol and drugs or only drugs? How are you quantifying *abuse*? When you refer to the medical profession, are you including nurses and lab technicians or only doctors? Without defining these terms, you can confuse your readers or lead them to wrong conclusions.

Social scientists often use **analogy** (see 4f-8) to make unfamiliar ideas clear. When an unfamiliar idea is compared with one that is more familiar, the unfamiliar idea becomes easier to understand. For example, sociologists may talk of the "culture shock" that some people feel when they enter a new society. The sociologists might compare this "shock" to the reaction that someone living today might have if suddenly moved hundreds of years into the future or the past.

In college and university courses in the social sciences, some instructors ask students to write their personal reactions to information or experiences, in which case the first person (*I, we, our*) is acceptable. In most writing for the social sciences, however, writers use the third person (*he, she, it, one, they*). Also, because the emphasis is on people or groups being observed rather than on the person doing the observing, some social scientists use the passive voice° (see 8n and 8o) rather than the active voice°. The *Publication Manual of the American Psychological Association,* the most commonly used style manual in the social sciences (see 39c), however, recommends the active voice whenever possible.

39c Using documentation style in the social sciences

If you use sources° when you write about the social sciences, you are required to credit these sources by using documentation°. The most commonly used documentation style° in the social sciences is that of the American Psychological Association (APA). The APA documentation style uses parenthetical references in the body of a paper and a References list at the end of a paper. APA documentation style is described in section 34d. For an example of a student research paper that uses APA documentation style, see Chapter 36.

The *Chicago Manual* (CM) style of documentation is sometimes used in the social sciences. CM bibliographic note style is described in section 34e.

39d Writing different types of papers in the social sciences

Two major types of papers in the social sciences are case studies and research papers.

1 Writing case studies in the social sciences

A **case study** is an intensive study of one group or individual. It is usually presented in a relatively fixed format, but the specific parts and order of case-study formats vary. Most case studies contain the following components: (1) basic identifying information about the individual or group; (2) a history of the individual or group; (3) observations of the individual's or group's behaviour; and (4) conclusions and perhaps recommendations as a result of the observations.

In writing a case study, describe situations; do not interpret them unless your assignment allows you to interpret *after* you report. Be sure to differentiate between fact and opinion (see 5d-3). For example, you may observe nursing-home patients lying in bed on their sides facing the door. Describe exactly what you see; do not interpret this observation as, say, patients watching for visitors. Perhaps medicines are injected in the right hip, and patients are more comfortable lying on their left side, thus facing the door.

2 Writing research papers in the social sciences

You may be assigned a **research paper** in the social sciences for which you must consult secondary sources°. (See 32l on using specialized reference books and 32n-2 on using specialized indexes.) These sources are usually articles and books that report, summarize, and otherwise discuss the findings of other people's research. For an example of a student research paper written for an introductory psychology course, see Chapter 36.

39e Understanding ways of gathering information in the sciences

Disciplines in the **natural sciences** include astronomy, biology, chemistry, geology, and physics. The sciences focus on natural phenomena. The purpose of scientific inquiry is discovery. Scientists formulate and test hypotheses in order to explain cause and effect (see 5f) systematically and objectively.

The **scientific method,** commonly used in the sciences to make discoveries, is a procedure for gathering information related to a specific hypothesis. The scientific method is the cornerstone of all inquiry in the sciences. Guidelines for using the scientific method are shown in Chart 160.

GUIDELINES FOR USING THE SCIENTIFIC METHOD 160

1. Formulate a tentative explanation—known as a **hypothesis**—for a scientific phenomenon. Be as specific as possible.
2. Read and summarize previously published information related to your hypothesis.
3. Plan and outline a method of investigation to uncover the information needed to test your hypothesis.
4. Experiment, exactly following the investigative procedures you have outlined.
5. Observe closely the results of the experiment, and write notes carefully.
6. Analyze the results. If they prove the hypothesis to be false, rework the investigation and begin again. If the results prove the hypothesis to be true, say so.
7. Write a report of your research. At the end, you might suggest additional hypotheses that might be investigated.

39f Understanding writing purposes and practices in the natural sciences

Scientists usually write to inform their audiences about factual information.

Exactness is extremely important in scientific writing. Readers expect precise descriptions of procedures and findings, free of personal biases. Scientists expect to be able to *replicate*—repeat step-by-step—the experiment or other process and get the same outcome as the writer.

Completeness is also essential in scientific writing. Without complete information, the reader might come to wrong conclusions. For example, a researcher may investigate how different types of soil affect plant growth. The researcher should report not only the analysis of each soil type, but also the amount of daylight each plant receives, the moisture content of the soil, the amount and type of fertilizer used, and all other related facts. Having all this information may lead the researcher to unexpected insights. For instance, plant growth may be less dependent on soil type than on a combination of soil type, fertilizer, and watering. This observation could be made only if the researcher had carefully noted all the facts.

The sciences generally focus on the experiment rather than the experimenter and on objective observation rather than subjective interpretation. Unless you are writing a personal-reaction paper, generally avoid using the first person (*I, we, our*) in writing science papers.

When writing for the sciences, you are often expected to follow fixed formats, which are designed to summarize a project and present its results efficiently. In your report, organize the information to achieve clarity and precision. Writers in the sciences sometimes use charts, graphs, tables, diagrams, and other illustrations to present material. In fact, illustrations can sometimes explain complex material more clearly than words can.

39g Using documentation style in the natural sciences

If you use sources° when you write about the sciences, you are required to credit your sources by using documentation°. Documentation styles° in the various sciences differ somewhat. Ask your instructor which style you should use. If your instructor has no preference, research the various style manuals in the sciences. If you cannot locate the manual you need, or if the science you are writing in does not have a style manual, find a journal that publishes research in that science and imitate its documentation style.

The Council of Science Editors—originally known as the Council of Biology Editors (CBE)—publishes style and documentation guidelines for the life sciences, the physical sciences, and mathematics in *Scientific Style and Format: The CBE Manual for Authors, Editors, and Publishers,* 6th edition (1994). CBE documentation guidelines are described in section 34f.

39h Writing different types of papers in the natural sciences

Two major types of papers in the sciences are reports and reviews.

1 Writing science reports

Science reports tell about observations and experiments. Such reports may also be called "laboratory reports" when they describe laboratory experiments. Formal reports include the eight sections (including the title) described in Chart 161. Less formal reports, which are sometimes assigned in introductory courses, might not include an abstract or a review of the literature. Ask your instructor which sections to include in your report.

PARTS OF THE SCIENCE REPORT 161

1. **Title.** This is a precise description of what your report is about.
2. **Abstract.** This is a short overview of the report.
3. **Introduction.** This section states the purpose behind your research and presents the hypothesis. Any needed background information and a review of the literature appear here.
4. **Methods and material.** This section describes the equipment, material, and procedures used.
5. **Results.** This section provides the information obtained from your efforts. Charts, graphs, and photographs help present the data.
6. **Discussion.** This section represents your interpretation and evaluation of the results. Did your efforts support your hypothesis? If not, can you suggest why not? Use concrete evidence in discussing your results.
7. **Conclusion.** This section lists conclusions about the hypothesis and the outcomes of your efforts, with particular attention to any theoretical implications that can be drawn from your work. Be specific in suggesting further research.
8. **References cited.** This list presents references cited in the review of the literature, if any. Its format conforms to the requirements of the documentation style in the particular science.

SAMPLE SCIENCE REPORT (EXCERPTS)

An Experiment to Predict Vestigial Wings in an F_2 *Drosophila* Population

INTRODUCTION

The purpose of this experiment was to observe second filial generation (F_2) wing structures in *Drosophila*. The hypothesis was that abnormalities in vestigial wing structures would follow predicted genetic patterns.

METHODS AND MATERIALS

On February 7, four *Drosophila* (P_1) were observed. Observation was made possible by etherizing the parents (after separating them from their larvae), placing them on a white card, and observing them under a dissecting microscope. The observations were recorded on a chart.

On February 14, the larvae taken from the parents on February 7 had developed to adults (F_1), and they were observed using the same methods as on February 7. The observations were recorded on the chart.

On February 19, the second filial generation (F_2) was supposed to be observed. This was impossible because they did not hatch. The record chart had to be discontinued.

RESULTS

No observations of F_2 were possible. For the F_1 population, according to the prediction, no members should have had vestigial wings. According to the observations, however, some members of F_1 did have vestigial wings.

[DISCUSSION SECTION OMITTED]

CONCLUSIONS

Two explanations are possible to explain vestigial wings in the F_1 population. Perhaps members from F_2 were present among the F_1 generation. This is doubtful since the incubation period is 10 days, and the time between observations was only 8 days. A second possible explanation is that the genotype of the male P_1 was not WW (indicating that both genes were for normal wings) but rather heterozygous (Ww). If this were true the following would be the first filial products in a 1:1 ratio:

P_1 Ww x ww

F_1 Ww ww

Thus, the possibility for vestigial wings would exist. The problem remains, however, that the ratio was not 1:1, but rather 2:1 (i.e., 24 normal to 12 abnormal). One explanation could be that the total number was not large enough to extract an average.

The hypothesis concerning predicted genetic patterns in F_2 could not be confirmed because the F_2 generation did not hatch. This experiment should be repeated to get F_2 data. A larger F_1 sample should be used to see if the F_1 findings reported here are repeated.

2 Writing science reviews

A **science review** is a paper discussing published information on a scientific topic or issue. The purpose of the review is to gather together for readers the current knowledge about the topic or issue.

Sometimes the purpose of a science review is to suggest a new interpretation of the old material. Any reinterpretation is based on a synthesis of old information with new, more complete information. In such reviews, the writer must marshal evidence to persuade readers that the new interpretation is valid.

If you are required to write a science review, (1) choose a very limited scientific issue currently being researched; (2) use information that is current—the more recently published or updated the articles, books, journals, and Web sites you consult, the better; (3) accurately summarize and paraphrase material—as explained in 31e and 31d; (4) document your sources (see Chapter 34). If your review is more than two or three pages, you might want to use headings to help your reader understand the organization and idea progression of your paper. See Chapters 32 and 33 for advice on finding sources.

40 Business Writing

Business and public writing require of you what other kinds of writing call for: understanding your audience and your purpose. This chapter explains how to write business letters (see 40a), job application letters (see 40b), résumés (see 40c), e-mail (see 40d), and memos (see 40e). As you write for business, or for any other public purpose, use the guidelines listed in Chart 162.

GUIDELINES FOR BUSINESS AND PUBLIC WRITING 162

- Consider your audience's needs and expectations.
- Show that you understand the purpose for a business communication and the context in which it takes place.
- Put essential information first.
- Make your points clearly and directly.
- Use conventional formats.

40a Writing and formatting a business letter

Business letters are written to give information, to build good-will, or to establish a foundation for discussions or transactions. Experts in business and government agree that the letters likely to get results are short, simple, direct, and human. Here is good, basic advice: (1) Call the person by name; (2) tell what your letter is about in the first paragraph; (3) be honest; (4) be clear and specific; (5) use correct English; (6) be positive and natural; (7) edit ruthlessly.

For business letters, use the guidelines in Chart 163 and the format on page 769. To avoid sexist language in the salutation of your letter, use the guidelines in Chart 164. For a business envelope, see page 773.

GUIDELINES FOR BUSINESS LETTERS 163

LETTERHEAD	If printed stationery is not available, type the company name and address centred at the top of white paper, 8 1/2 x 11".
DATE	Put the date at the left margin under the letterhead, when typing in block form as shown in the example. When using paragraph indentations, type the date so that it ends at the right margin.
INSIDE ADDRESS	Direct your letter to a specific person. Be accurate in spelling the name and the address. If unsure of your information, telephone and ask questions of a secretary or other assistant.
SUBJECT LINE	Place at the left margin. In a few, concise words state the letter's subject.
SALUTATION	Use a first name only if you personally know the person. Otherwise, use *Mr.* or *Ms.* or whatever title is applicable with the person's last name. Avoid sexist language.
CLOSING	*Sincerely* or *Sincerely yours* is generally appropriate, unless you know the person very well and wish to use *Cordially*. Leave about four lines for your signature.
NAME LINES	Type your full name and title below your signature. The title can be on the same line as your name or on the next line.
SECOND PAGE	Head a second page with three items of information: the name of the person or company to which your letter is addressed, the number *2* or *page 2*, and the date. Place the information on three lines at the top left margin or on one line spaced across the top of the page.

BUSINESS LETTER FORMAT

letterhead	**ALPHAOMEGA INDUSTRIES, INC.** **1234 Emily Carr Blvd.** **Vancouver BC V6M 2C3**
date	December 28, 20XX
inside address	Ron R. London, Sales Director Seasonal Products Corp. 270 18th St. Brandon MB R7A 6A9
subject line	Subject: Spring Promotional Effort
salutation	Dear Ron:
message	Since we talked last week, I have completed plans for the spring promotion of the products that we market jointly. AlphaOmega and Seasonal Products should begin a direct mailing of the enclosed brochure on January 28. I have secured several mailing lists that contain the names of people who have a positive economic profile for our products. The profile and the outline of the lists are attached. Do you have additional approaches for the promotion? I would like to meet with you on January 6 to discuss them and to work out the details of the project. Please call me and let me know if a meeting next week at your office accommodates your schedule.
closing	Sincerely, Alan Stone
name, title	Alan Stone, Director of Special Promotions
writer's/typist's initials	AS/kw
copies	cc: Yolanda Lane, Vice President, Marketing
enclosures	enclosures Enc: Brochure; Mailing Lists; Customer Profile

GUIDELINES FOR WRITING A NONSEXIST SALUTATION 164

You may want to send a business letter when you do not have a specific person to whom it should be addressed. Use the following steps to prepare a salutation.

1. Telephone the company to which you are sending the letter. State your reason for sending the letter, and ask for the name of the person who should receive it.
2. Use a first name only if you know the person. Otherwise, use *Mr.* or *Ms.* or an applicable title. Avoid a sexist title such as *Dear Sir.*
3. If you cannot find out the name of the person who should read your letter, use a generic title.

NO Dear Sir: [obviously sexist]
Dear Madam/Sir or Dear Sir/Madam: [few women want to be addressed as "Madam"]

YES Dear Personnel Officer:
Dear IBM Sales Manager:

In addressing an envelope, remember that the best written letter means nothing if it does not reach its destination. In the illustration on page 773, you will see the Canada Post guidelines for addressing envelopes so that they can be processed by machine. (Envelopes that must be sorted by hand add several days to mail-delivery time.)

40b Writing and formatting a job application letter

Chart 165 gives guidelines for a job application letter. A sample job application letter appears on page 772.

165

GUIDELINES FOR JOB APPLICATION LETTERS

YOUR ADDRESS	Type your address in block style as you would on an envelope. Use as your address (with a postal code) a place where you can be reached **by letter**.
DATE	Put the date below your address. Make sure that you mail the letter on either the same day or the next day; a delayed mailing can imply lack of planning.
INSIDE ADDRESS	Direct your letter to a specific person. Telephone the company to find out the name of the person to whom you are writing. Be accurate. A misspelled name can offend the receiver. A wrong address usually results in a lost letter.
SALUTATION	Be accurate. No one likes to see his or her name misspelled. In replying to an ad that gives only a post-office box number, omit the salutation and start your opening paragraph directly below the inside address. To avoid sexist language, use Chart 164.
INTRODUCTORY PARAGRAPH	State your purpose for writing and your source of information about the job.
BODY PARAGRAPH(S)	Interest the reader in the skills and talents you offer by mentioning whatever experience you have *that relates to the specific job.* Mention your enclosed résumé, but do *not* summarize it.
CLOSING PARAGRAPH	Suggest an interview, stating that you will call to make arrangements.
CLOSING	*Sincerely* or *Sincerely yours* is generally appropriate.
NAME LINES	Type your full name below your signature. Leave about four lines for your signature.
NOTATION	If you are enclosing any material with your letter, type *Enc:* and briefly list the items.

JOB APPLICATION LETTER

248 Woodbridge Hall
Wilfrid Laurier University
75 University Ave. W
Waterloo ON N2L 3C5
May 15, 20XX

Rae Clemens, Director of Human Resources
Taleno, Ward Marketing, Inc.
1471 Summit Blvd.
London ON N6G 1E9

Dear Ms. Clemens:

I am answering the advertisement for a marketing trainee that Taleno, Ward placed in today's London Free Press.

Marketing has been one of the emphases of my course work here at Wilfrid Laurier University, as you will see on my enclosed résumé. This past year, I gained some practical experience as well, when I developed marketing techniques that helped to turn my typing service into a busy and profitable small business.

Successfully marketing the typing service (with flyers, advertisements in university publications, and even a two-for-one promotion) makes me a very enthusiastic novice. I can think of no better way to become a professional than working for Taleno, Ward.

I will be here at Laurier through August 1. You can reach me by phone at (519) 555-1976. Unless I hear from you before, I'll call on May 25 about setting up an interview.

Sincerely yours,

Lee Chen

Lee Chen

Enc: Résumé

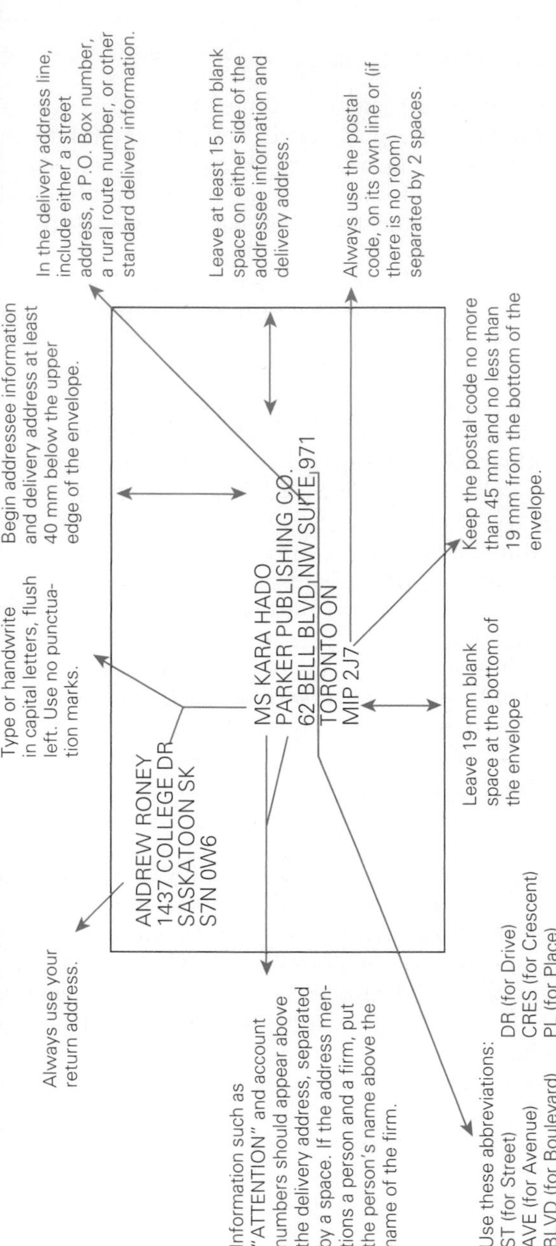
Always use your return address.
ANDREW RONEY
1437 COLLEGE DR
SASKATOON SK
S7N 0W6
Type or handwrite in capital letters, flush left. Use no punctuation marks.
Begin addressee information and delivery address at least 40 mm below the upper edge of the envelope.
In the delivery address line, include either a street address, a P.O. Box number, a rural route number, or other standard delivery information.
Leave at least 15 mm blank space on either side of the addressee information and delivery address.
Always use the postal code, on its own line or (if there is no room) separated by 2 spaces.
MS KARA HADO
PARKER PUBLISHING CO.
62 BELL BLVD NW SUITE 971
TORONTO ON
MIP 2J7
Keep the postal code no more than 45 mm and no less than 19 mm from the bottom of the envelope.
Leave 19 mm blank space at the bottom of the envelope
Information such as "ATTENTION" and account numbers should appear above the delivery address, separated by a space. If the address mentions a person and a firm, put the person's name above the name of the firm.
Use these abbreviations:
ST (for Street)
AVE (for Avenue)
BLVD (for Boulevard)
DR (for Drive)
CRES (for Crescent)
PL (for Place)
CIR (for Circle)
N (for North)
S (for South)
E (for East)
W (for West)
RM (for Room)
APT (for Apartment)
2-letter postal abbreviations
names of provinces:

Canada Post Guidelines for Business Envelope Format

40c Writing and formatting a résumé

A **résumé** is an easy-to-read, factual document that presents your qualifications for employment. All résumés cover certain standard items: name, address, phone number; education; past experience; skills and talents; publications, awards, honours, membership in professional organizations; a list of references or a statement that they are "available upon request."

A résumé gives you an opportunity to present a positive picture of yourself to a prospective employer. Employers understand that college and university students may have limited experience in the business world. Think of headings that allow you to emphasize your strengths. For example, if you have never done paid work, do not use *Business Experience.* You can use *Work Experience* if you have done volunteer or other unpaid work. If the experience you offer an employer is that you have run school or social events, you might use *Organizational Experience.* If your greatest strength is your academic record, put your educational achievements first.

You may choose to arrange your résumé in emphatic order with the most important information first and the least important last. Or you may choose to arrange information in chronological (time) order, a sequence that is good for showing a steady work history or solid progress in a particular field. Lee Chen's résumé, which was sent with the job application letter on page 772, is on page 775. It uses emphatic order. Stephen Schmit's résumé, on page 776, uses chronological order.

When you are applying for a specific job, modify your basic résumé to emphasize your qualifications for that job. Lee Chen added the *Marketing Trainee* heading and the statement about relevant experience for becoming a marketing trainee to her basic résumé and positioned the *Marketing Experience* section first. These modifications help to send a message that Chen's qualifications for the marketing trainee position are better than other applicants'. If you keep your résumé on computer, you can easily tailor it to specific job opportunities.

Your résumé usually has to fulfil only one purpose: It has to convince the person who first looks at it to put it into the "Call for an interview" pile rather than into the wastebasket. To do that best, a résumé should be eye-catching and informative, and it should make its readers think, "We should talk to this person; seems like someone who would be an asset to our business."

EMPHATIC RÉSUMÉ

MARKETING TRAINEE

Lee Chen
248 Woodbridge Hall
Wilfrid Laurier University
75 University Ave. W
Waterloo ON N2L 3C5
519-555-1976

The experience I acquired marketing my typing service provided me with a good practical background for a position as a marketing trainee.

MARKETING EXPERIENCE (program for campus typing service)
Evaluated typing-service capabilities; analyzed market for service; drew up and implemented marketing plan; produced 2-colour flyer, designed print ads and wrote copy, developed and ran special promotion. August 19XX to February 20XX.

BUSINESS EXPERIENCE
Type-Right Typing Service: Ran campus typing service for two years. Duties included word processing (Word, PageMaker, WordPerfect), proofreading, billing and other financial record-keeping, and customer contact. August 19XX to present.

Archer & Archer Advertising: Worked as general assistant in the copy department under direct supervision of John Allen, Director. Duties included proofreading, filing, direct client contact. June 19XX to August 19XX.

ADDITIONAL EXPERIENCE
Coordinated student-employment service at Pauline Johnson High School, Brantford, Ontario. Duties included contacting students to fill jobs with local employers, arranging interviews, and writing follow-up reports on placements.

EDUCATION
Wilfrid Laurier University
B.A. May 20XX, Psychology, Marketing

EXTRACURRICULAR
Marketing Club, Computer Graphics Society

References available upon request.

CHRONOLOGICAL RÉSUMÉ

Stephen L. Schmit
5163 Duke St.
Halifax NS B3J 3J6

(902)555-8165

CAREER QUALIFICATIONS Technical writer trained in preparation of manuals, catalogues, and instructional materials. Experienced in writing computer documentation containing syntax formats.

WORK EXPERIENCE Dalhousie University, Halifax, NS, Reading and Writing Specialist, English Language Centre, March-July 20XX, January-March 20XX.

Created individual lesson plans for each student assigned to the Reading and Writing Laboratory and developed materials for use in Laboratory programs. Ran the Laboratory for approximately 100 students 20 hours a week. Kept all records of students' work and prepared written and oral reports on student progress and laboratory operations.

Tutor of International Students, September 19XX-present. Integrated students into an urban school and community and was a positive role model educationally and socially.

W. M. Mercer, Inc., Halifax, NS, September-December 20XX.
Data processing and general office duties. Created and implemented a CRT search system for office personnel.

SPECIAL SKILLS C++ programming language; Word, WordPerfect, Lotus 1-2-3, Excel.

EDUCATION Dalhousie University, Halifax, NS, Bachelor of Arts, June 20XX.

Concentration: English with minors in Economics and Technical Communications.

Activities: Selected to serve on the Residence Judicial Board, a faculty-staff-student group that adjudicates residence-hall disputes; campus newspaper reporter; yearbook staff.

40d Writing e-mail

E-mail stands for "electronic mail." A great deal of business and local communication is conducted by e-mail. An e-mail message is less formal than a letter, but certain conventions still apply. Chart 166 gives guidelines for e-mail messages.

GUIDELINES FOR E-MAIL MESSAGES 166

- Include a subject line to tell your reader the topic.
- Single-space within paragraphs; double-space between paragraphs.
- Do not use ALL CAPITALS. They are hard to read and generally considered the written equivalent of shouting.
- Use bulleted or numbered lists when itemizing.
- Keep your message brief and your paragraphs short. (Reading a screen is harder on the eyes than reading from a printed document, so people have a tendency to skim e-mail.)
- Be cautious of what you say in e-mail. You may send it to the wrong person by mistake. Also, e-mail can be forwarded to others without your permission, although this practice is severely frowned upon. Never give personal information to strangers. Never give credit information on a non-secure site.
- Forward an e-mail message only if you have the permission of the original sender.
- Check your document to make sure that your message is clear and your tone is appropriate, and that spelling, grammar, and punctuation are correct.
- Use "emoticons" only if you are sure the reader appreciates them. :-) Some people do not. :-(
- Never "flame" (make personal attacks on others).
- Never "spam" (send unsolicited or junk mail).

For longer documents, such as academic papers, you can compose in a word-processing program and then *attach* the document to an e-mail message to be sent to your instructor or others. Attached documents maintain their original formatting (margins, spacing, fonts). One word of caution: Be sure your intended recipient will be able to download your attached file.

40e Writing a memo

Memos can be sent on paper or via e-mail. Readers need to quickly determine the importance of a memo by reading the headings at the top. A memo from a supervisor asking for sales figures will receive prompt attention, whereas a memo from the office manager about new forms for ordering supplies probably will not receive a careful reading until it is time to order more supplies.

The audience° for a memo is usually "local." For example, in the workplace, local audiences can be senior management, other levels of supervisors or managers, people at your level, all employees, or customers. Other audiences can be people who share interests (religious, political, or leisure-time groups) or causes (environment, education, or health care). Be as specific as possible in naming your memo's audience.

Memos are written to present new information; summarize, clarify, or synthesize° known information; put information officially on the record; make a request or suggestion; and record recent activities and outcomes. Most word-processing software provides formats for memos. For example, in Microsoft Word™, you can click on File, and then New, and then Memo. Select the style you want—"professional" is a good choice for workplace use.

A memo has these parts:

HEADINGS

TO: [Your audience, named as specifically as possible]

FROM: [Your name]

DATE: [Month, day, and year you are writing]

SUBJECT: [Memo's topic, concisely stated]

CONTENTS

Introductory paragraph. State the memo's purpose and give needed background information.

Body paragraph(s). State the point you are making in the memo and why it is worth your readers' time. Alternatively, present the required data.

CONCLUSION

End with a one- to two-sentence summary or a specific recommendation. If the memo is short, end with instructions or a "thank you" line.

One or at most two pages is the expected length of a memo. If you need more pages, you are writing a report.

41 Writing Under Pressure

The demands of writing under pressure can sometimes seem overwhelming, but if you break the challenge into small, sequential steps and then focus on each step in turn, you can succeed. When you write under the pressure of time constraints, you are expected to write as completely and clearly as possible. If you tend to freeze under pressure, force yourself to take some slow, deep breaths and use a relaxation technique such as counting backwards from ten. When you turn to the task, remember to break the whole into parts so that the process is easier to work through.

Writing answers for essay tests is one of the most important writing tasks that you face in your postsecondary education. Essay tests are common in all disciplines, including the natural sciences. They demand that you recall information and also put assorted pieces of that information into contexts that lead to generalizations you can support. Essay tests give you the chance to synthesize° and apply your knowledge, helping your instructor determine what you have learned.

41a Understanding cue words and key terms

Most essay questions contain what is sometimes called a **cue word,** a word of direction that tells what the content of your answer is expected to emphasize. Knowing the major cue words and their meanings can increase your ability to plan efficiently and to write effectively. Be guided by the list of cue words and sample essay-test questions in Chart 167.

Each essay question also has one or more **key terms** that tell you the information, topics, and ideas you are to write about. For example, in the question "Criticize the architectural function of the modern football stadium," the cue word is "criticize," and the key terms are "architectural function" and "football stadium." To answer the question successfully, you must define "architectural function," then describe the typical modern football stadium (mentioning major variations when important), and then discuss how well the typical modern football stadium fits your definition of "architectural function."

167

CUE WORDS FOUND IN QUESTIONS FOR ESSAY TESTS

- **Analyze** means to separate something into parts and then discuss the parts and their meanings.

  Analyze Socrates's discussion of "good life" and "good death."

- **Clarify** means to make clear, often by giving a definition of a key term and by using examples to illustrate it.

  Clarify T. S. Eliot's idea of tradition.

- **Classify** means to arrange into groups on the basis of shared characteristics.

  Classify the different types of antipredator adaptations.

- **Compare and contrast** means to show similarities and differences.

  Compare and contrast the reproductive cycles of a moss and a flowering plant.

- **Criticize** means to give your opinion concerning the good points and bad points of something.

  Criticize the architectural function of the modern football stadium.

- **Define** means to give the definition of something and thereby to separate it from similar things.

  Define the term "yellow press."

- **Describe** means to explain features to make clear an object, procedure, or event.

  Describe the chain of events that constitutes the movement of a sensory impulse along a nerve fibre.

- **Discuss** means to consider as many elements as possible concerning an issue or event.

  Discuss the effects of television viewing on modern attitudes toward violence.

167

CUE WORDS FOUND IN QUESTIONS FOR ESSAY TESTS *(continued)*

- **Evaluate** means to give your opinion about the value of something.

  Evaluate Nellie McClung's contribution to feminism in Canada.

- **Explain** means to make clear or intelligible something that needs to be understood or interpreted.

  Explain how the amount of carbon dioxide in the blood regulates rates of heartbeat and breathing.

- **Illustrate** means to give examples of something.

  Illustrate the use of symbolism in Thomas King's novel *Green Grass, Running Water.*

- **Interpret** means to explain the meaning of something.

  Give your interpretation of Margaret Avison's poem "The Swimmer's Moment."

- **Justify** means to show or prove that something is valid or correct.

  Justify the existence of labour unions in today's economy.

- **Prove** means to present evidence that cannot be refuted logically or with other evidence.

  Prove that smoking is a major cause of lung cancer.

- **Relate** means to show the connections between two or more things.

  Relate increases in specific crimes in 1932–33 to the prevailing economic conditions.

- **Review** means to re-examine, summarize, or reprise something.

  Review the structural arrangements in proteins to explain the meaning of the term *polypeptide.*

- **Show** means to point out or demonstrate something.

  Show what effects pesticides have on the production of wheat.

- **Summarize** means to repeat briefly the major points of something.

  Summarize the major benefits of compulsory education.

- **Support** means to argue in favour of something.

  Support the position that destruction of rain forests is endangering the planet.

41b Writing effective responses to essay-test questions

An effective response to an essay-test question is complete and logically organized. Here are two answers to the question "Classify the different types of antipredator adaptations." The first one is successful; the second is not. The sentences are numbered for your reference, and they are explained on page 783.

Answer 1

(1) Although many antipredator adaptations have evolved in the animal kingdom, they all can be classified into four major categories according to the prey's response to the predator. (2) The first category is hiding techniques. (3) These techniques include cryptic coloration and behaviour in which the prey assumes characteristics of an inanimate object or part of a plant. (4) The second category is early enemy detection. (5) The prey responds to alarm signals from like prey or other kinds of prey before the enemy can get too close. (6) Evasion of the pursuing predator is the third category. (7) Prey that move erratically or in a compact group are displaying this technique. (8) The fourth category is active repulsion of the predator. (9) The prey kills, injures, or sickens the predator, establishing that it represents danger to the predator.

Answer 2

(1) Antipredator adaptations are the development of the capabilities to reduce the risk of attack from a predator without too much change in the life-supporting activities of the prey. (2) There are many different types of antipredator adaptations. (3) One type is camouflage, hiding from the predator by cryptic coloration or imitation of plant parts. (4) An example of this type of antipredator adaptation is the praying mantis. (5) A second type is the defence used by monarch butterflies, a chemical protection that makes some birds ill after eating the butterfly. (6) This protection may injure the bird by causing it to vomit, and it can educate the bird against eating other butterflies. (7) Detection and evasion are also antipredator adaptations.

An explanation of what happens, sentence by sentence, in the two answers to the question about antipredator adaptations is shown on page 783.

Answer 1 sets about immediately answering the question by introducing a classification system as called for by the cue word, *classify*. Answer 2, on the other hand, defines the key word, a waste of time on a test that will be read by an audience of specialists. Answer 1 is tightly organized, easy to follow, and to the point. Answer 2 rambles, never manages to name the four categories, and says more around the subject than on it.

	ANSWER 1	ANSWER 2
Sentence 1	Sets up classification system and gives number of categories based on key term	Defines key term
Sentence 2	Names first category	Throwaway sentence—accomplishes nothing
Sentence 3	Defines first category	Names and defines first category
Sentence 4	Names second category	Gives an example for first category
Sentence 5	Defines second category	Gives an example for second (unnamed) category
Sentence 6	Names third category	Continues to explain example
Sentence 7	Defines third category	Names two categories
Sentence 8	Names fourth category	
Sentence 9	Defines fourth category	

41c Using strategies when writing under pressure

If you use specific strategies when writing under pressure, you can be more comfortable and your writing will likely be more effective. As you use the strategies listed in Chart 168, remember that your purpose in answering questions is to show what you know in a clear, direct, and well-organized way. When you are studying for an essay exam, write out one-sentence summaries of major areas of information. This technique helps to fix the ideas in your mind, and a summary sentence may become a thesis sentence for an essay answer.

The more you use the strategies in the chart and adapt them to your personal needs, the better you will use them to your advantage. Try to practise them, making up questions that might be on your test and timing yourself as you write the answers. Doing this offers you another benefit: If you study by anticipating possible questions and writing out the answers, you will be very well prepared if one or two of them show up on the test.

EXERCISE 40-1

Look back at an essay that you have written under time pressure. Read it over and decide whether you would change the content of your answer or the strategies you used as you were writing under pressure. List these specific strategies, and, if you think they were useful, add them to Chart 168.

STRATEGIES FOR WRITING ESSAY TESTS

168

1. Do not start writing immediately.
2. If the test has two or more questions, read them all at the start. Determine whether you are supposed to answer all the questions. Doing this gives you a sense of how to budget your time either by dividing it equally or by allotting more for some questions. If you have a choice, select questions about which you know the most and can write about most completely in the time limit.
3. Analyze each question that you answer by underlining the cue words and key terms (see 41a) to determine exactly what the question asks.
4. Use the writing process as much as possible within the constraints of the time limit. Try to allot time to plan and revise. For a one-hour test of one question, take about 10 minutes to jot down preliminary ideas about content and organization, and save 10 minutes to reread, revise, and edit your answer. If you suddenly are pressed for time—but try to avoid this—consider skipping a question that you cannot answer well or a question that counts less toward your total score. If you feel blocked, try freewriting (see 2f) to get your hand and your thoughts moving.
5. Support any generalizations with specifics (see 4c about using the formula RENNS for being specific).
6. Be aware of "going off the topic." Respond to the cue words and key terms (see 41a) in the question, and do not try to reshape the question to conform to what you might prefer to write about. Remember, your reader expects a clear line of presentation and reasoning that answers the given question.

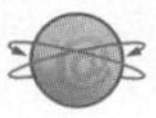

www.utoronto.ca/writing/advise.html
Advice on Academic Writing

planet-hawaii.com/hch/hday/essays.html
Writing Essays that Make Historical Arguments

writingcenter.gmu.edu/resources/onlinehandouts.html
Writing About Literature; Writing About Film

filebox.vt.edu/eng/mech/writing/
Writing Guidelines for Engineering and Science Students

owl.english.purdue.edu/handouts/index2.htm#bw
Writing in the Job Search/Professional Writing

english.byu.edu/writingcenter/Handouts/Handouts.htm
Writing Timed Essays (five basic principles)

PART VII Writing When English Is a Second Language

When English is your second language, you face the special challenge of needing to learn characteristics of English that native-born writers take for granted. Part Seven begins with a special ESL Preface to set the context for the rest of Part Seven, which explains the features of English that tend to give non-native writers the most trouble. As you use Chapters 42 through 47, remember that learning to write English involves much more than studying separate features. As is the case with any writer in any language, the more time you spend writing, the faster you can become a fluent writer.

Preface for ESL Students

Do you sometimes worry when you write in English? If you ever do worry about your English writing, let me assure you that you have much in common with me and with many college and university students. But as an ESL writer, you face a special challenge because you must attend to every word, every phrase, every sentence, and every paragraph in a way that native speakers of English do not.

You may be reassured to know that any errors you make as an ESL writer indicate that you are progressing through necessary stages of second-language development. Eventually, when you have passed through all the stages that all language learners must, you should be a proficient writer of English.

Unfortunately, there are no shortcuts. As with progress in speaking, listening, and reading comprehension in a new language, passing through the various stages of language development takes time. Some students have more available time than others, and some students have a home or study environment that enables faster learning of a new language. However, no matter how fast a language skill is learned, all the stages of language development must be experienced. Just as most adults make mistakes when they learn to play a new sport, few people write fluently and without error when they compose a first draft of a piece of writing. In fact, only rarely have even the most noted and experienced writers ever written something perfectly the first time.

What can you do to progress as quickly as possible from one writing stage to another? You might start by trying to remember what the typical school writing is like in your first language. Try to recall how ideas are presented in writing in your native language, especially when information has to be explained and when a matter of opinion has to be argued.

In recalling the typical style of school writing in your native language, compare it with what you are learning about writing style in Canadian English. For example, most college and university writing has a very direct, straightforward basic structure. In a typical essay or research paper, the reader expects to find a **thesis statement**°*, which clearly states the overall message of the piece of writing, by the end of the first or second paragraph. Usually, each paragraph that follows relates directly to the thesis statement and starts with a sentence, called a **topic sentence**°, that tells the point of the paragraph. The rest of each paragraph usually supports the point by using reasons, examples, and other specific details. The final paragraph brings the essay or research paper to a reasonable, logical conclusion.

This handbook contains many examples of writing by college and university students. For essays, see sections 3f, 6i, and 38e. For research papers, see Chapters 35 and 36 and section 38e. Also, this handbook explains paragraph structures typically expected in college and university writing; see Chapter 4. By the way, these typical academic structures do not apply to novels, plays, poems, or articles in most newspapers and magazines.

Writing structures typical of your native language probably differ from those in this country. Always honour your culture's writing traditions and structures, for they reflect the richness of your heritage. At the same time, try to adapt to and practise the academic writing style characteristic of English-speaking Canada. Later, when you are writing fluently, your instructors likely will encourage you to practise other writing styles that are less common and that allow greater liberty in organization and expression.

Over the past twenty years, many interesting observations have been made about the distinctive variations in school writing styles among people of different cultures and language groups. Research about these contrasts is ongoing, so scholars hesitate to generalize about them. Even so, interesting differences seem to exist. Traditional French school essays usually begin with a series of points that are discussed in the body of the essay and then repeated in reverse order in the conclusion. Japanese school writing customarily begins with references to nature. In some African nations, a ceremonial, formal opening is expected to start school writing as an expression of respect for the reader.

The ESL chapters following this special ESL Preface are designed to help you focus on errors that many ESL writers make. I hope that Chapters 42 through 47 can be of great use to you.

I hope also that the rest of this handbook will become your trusted companion. Throughout its pages, ESL Notes (signalled by the symbol ◆ preceding and following them) and various kinds of Alerts (signalled by the symbols ✤ and ✚ preceding and following them)

*Throughout this book, a degree mark (°) indicates that you can find the definition of the word in the Terms Glossary in this handbook.

present information in related contexts that can help you as you acquire Canadian English-language writing skills. A directory of selected ESL Notes and Alerts follows this Preface to help you locate ones that may be especially useful to you.

LYNN QUITMAN TROYKA

DIRECTORY OF ESL NOTES AND SELECTED ALERTS

42 ESL Singulars and Plurals

How to Use Chapter 42ESL Effectively

1. Use this chapter together with these handbook sections:
   - 7a nouns°
   - 8c *-s* forms of verbs°
   - 11a–11l subject–verb agreement°
   - 12f nouns as modifiers°
2. Remember that throughout this handbook, **a degree mark** (°) after a word indicates that you can find the definition of the word in the Glossary of Terms toward the back of the book.
3. Use any **cross-references** (often given in parentheses) to find full explanations of key concepts.

This chapter can help you choose between using singulars° (one) and plurals° (more than one). Section 42a discusses the concept of count and noncount nouns°. Section 42b discusses determiners° and nouns. Section 42c discusses particularly confusing instances of the choice between singular and plural. Section 42d discusses some nouns with irregular plural forms.

42a Understanding the concept of count and noncount nouns

Count nouns name items that can be counted: *radio, street, idea, fingernail.* Count nouns can be singular° or plural° (*radios, streets*).

Noncount nouns name things that are thought of as a whole and not separated into separate, countable parts: *rice, knowledge, traffic.* Two important rules to remember about noncount nouns are that (1) they are never preceded by *a* or *an*, and (2) they are never plural.

Chart 169 lists eleven categories of uncountable items, giving examples in each category.

UNCOUNTABLE ITEMS 169

- **Groups of similar items making up "wholes":** *clothing, equipment, furniture, jewellery, junk, luggage, mail, money, stuff, traffic, vocabulary,* etc.
- **Abstractions:** *advice, equality, fun, health, ignorance, information, knowledge, news, peace, pollution, respect,* etc.
- **Liquids:** *blood, coffee, gasoline, water,* etc.
- **Gases:** *air, helium, oxygen, smog, smoke, steam,* etc.
- **Materials:** *aluminum, cloth, cotton, ice, wood,* etc.
- **Food:** *beef, bread, butter, macaroni, meat, park,* etc.
- **Particles or grains:** *dirt, dust, hair, rice, salt, wheat,* etc.
- **Sports, games, activities:** *chess, homework, housework, reading, sailing, soccer,* etc.
- **Languages:** *Arabic, Chinese, Japanese, Spanish,* etc.
- **Fields of study:** *biology, computer science, history, literature, math,* etc.
- **Events in nature:** *electricity, heat, humidity, moonlight, rain, snow, sunshine, thunder, weather,* etc.

Some nouns can be countable or uncountable depending on their meaning in a sentence. Most of these nouns name things that can be meant either individually or as "wholes" made up of individual parts.

COUNT — You have a **hair** on your sleeve. [In this sentence, *hair* is meant as an individual, countable item.]

NONCOUNT — Kioko has black **hair**. [In this sentence, *hair* is meant as a whole.]

COUNT — The **rains** were late last year. [In this sentence, *rains* is meant as individual, countable occurrences of rain.]

NONCOUNT — The **rain** is soaking the garden. [In this sentence, particles of *rain* are meant as a whole.]

When you are editing your writing (see Chapter 3), be sure that you have not added a plural *-s* to any noncount nouns, for they are always singular in form.

✤ VERB ALERT: Be sure to use a singular verb with any noncount noun that functions as a subject° in a clause. ✤

To check whether a noun is count or noncount, look it up in a dictionary that notes the distinction. For example, in the *Longman Dictionary of American English,* count nouns are indicated by [C] and noncount nouns are indicated by [U] (for uncountable). Nouns that have both count and noncount meanings are marked [C;U].

42b Using determiners with singular and plural nouns

Determiners, also called *expressions of quantity,* are used to tell "how much" or "how many" about nouns. Other names for determiners include *limiting adjectives°, noun markers,* and *articles°*. (For information about articles—the words *a, an,* and *the*—see Chapter 43ESL.)

Choosing the right determiner with a noun can depend on whether the noun is noncount° or count° (see 42a). For count nouns, you must also decide whether the noun is singular or plural. Chart 170 lists many determiners and the kinds of nouns that they can accompany.

170

DETERMINERS TO USE WITH COUNT AND NONCOUNT NOUNS

GROUP 1: DETERMINERS FOR SINGULAR COUNT NOUNS

With every **singular count noun,** always use one of the determiners listed in Group 1.

a, an, the

a house	**an egg**	**the car**

one, any, some, every, each, either, neither, another, the other

any house	**each egg**	**another car**

my, our, your, his, her, its, their, nouns with *'s* or *s'*

your house	**its egg**	**Connie's car**

this, that

this house	**that egg**	**this car**

one, no, the first, the second, etc.

one house	**no egg**	**the fifth car**

➜

DETERMINERS TO USE WITH COUNT AND NONCOUNT NOUNS *(continued)* 170

GROUP 2: DETERMINERS FOR PLURAL COUNT NOUNS

All the determiners listed in Group 2 can be used with **plural count nouns**. Plural count nouns can also be used without determiners, as discussed in section 43b.

the

the bicycles — **the rooms** — **the ideas**

some, any, both, many, more, most, few, fewer, the fewest, a number of, other, several, all, all the, a lot of

some bicycles — **many rooms** — **all ideas**

my, our, your, his, her, its, their, nouns with *'s* or *s'*

our bicycles — **her rooms** — **students' ideas**

these, those

these bicycles — **those rooms** — **these ideas**

no, two, three, four, the first, the second, the third, etc.

no bicycles — **four rooms** — **the first ideas**

GROUP 3: DETERMINERS FOR NONCOUNT NOUNS

All the determiners listed in Group 3 can be used with noncount nouns (always singular). Noncount nouns can also be used without determiners, as discussed in section 43b.

the

the porridge — **the rain** — **the pride**

some, any, much, more, most, other, the other, little, less, the least, enough, all, all the, a lot of

enough porridge — **a lot of rain** — **more pride**

my, our, your, his, her, its, their, nouns with *'s* or *s'*

their porridge — **India's rain** — **your pride**

this, that

this porridge — **that rain** — **this pride**

no, the first, the second, the third, etc.

no porridge — **the first rain** — **no pride**

✣ USAGE ALERT: The phrases *a few* and *a little* convey the meaning "some": *I have* ***a few*** *rare books* means "I have *some* rare books." *They are worth* ***a little*** *money* means "They are worth *some* money."

Without the word *a*, the words *few* and *little* convey the meaning "almost none": *I have **few*** [or *very few*] *books* means "I have *almost no* books." *They are worth **little** money* means "They are worth *almost no* money." ✤

42c Using correct forms in *one of* constructions, for nouns used as adjectives, and with *States* in names or titles

One of *constructions*

One of constructions include *one of the* and a noun° or *one of* followed by an adjective°-noun combination (*one of my hats, one of those ideas*). Always use a plural noun as the object° when you use *one of the* with a noun or an adjective-noun combination.

NO	One of the **reason** to live here is the beach.
YES	One of the **reasons** to live here is the beach.
NO	One of her best **friend** has moved away.
YES	One of her best **friends** has moved away.

The verb° in these constructions is always singular because it agrees with the singular *one*, not with the plural noun: *One of the most important inventions of the twentieth century **is*** [not *are*] *television.*

For advice about verb forms that go with *one of the . . . who* constructions, see section 11j.

Nouns used as adjectives

Adjectives° in English do not have plural forms. When you use an adjective with a plural noun, make the noun plural but not the adjective: *the **green*** [not *greens*] *leaves*. Be especially careful when you use as an adjective a word that can also function as a noun.

The bird's wingspan is 25 **centimetres**. [*Centimetres* is functioning as a noun.]

The bird has a 25-**centimetre** wingspan. [*Centimetre* is functioning as an adjective.]

Do not add *-s* (or *-es*) to the adjective even when it is modifying a plural noun or pronoun.

NO	Many **Canadians** students are avid fans of off-road racing.
YES	Many **Canadian** students are avid fans of off-road racing.

***Names or titles that include the word* States**

States is a plural word. However, names such as the *United States* or the *Organization of American States* refer to singular things—one a country and one an organization, even though made up of many states. When *States* is part of a name or title referring to one thing, the name is a singular noun and therefore requires a singular verb.

NO	The United **States** have a large entertainment industry. The United **State** has a large entertainment industry.
YES	The United **States has** a large entertainment industry.

Using nouns with irregular plurals

Some English nouns have irregular spellings. In addition to those discussed in Chart 104 in section 22c, here are others that often cause difficulties.

Plurals of foreign nouns and other irregular nouns

Whenever you are unsure whether a noun is plural, look it up in a dictionary. If no plural is given for a singular noun, add an *-s*.

Many nouns from other languages that are used unchanged in English have only one plural. If two plurals are listed in the dictionary, look carefully for differences in meaning. Some words, for example, keep the plural form from the original language for scientific usage and have another English-form plural for nonscientific contexts: *formula, formulae, formulas; appendix, appendices, appendixes; index, indices, indexes; medium, media, mediums; cactus, cacti, cactuses;* and *fungus, fungi, funguses.*

Words from Latin that end in *-is* in their singular form become plural by substituting *-es: parenthesis, parentheses; thesis, theses; oasis, oases,* for example.

Other words

Medical terms for diseases involving an inflammation end in *-itis: tonsillitis, appendicitis*. They are always singular.

The word *news,* although it ends in *s,* is always singular: *The* ***news is*** *encouraging*. The words *people, police,* and *clergy* are always plural even though they do not end in *s: The* ***police are*** *prepared.*

EXERCISE 42-1

Consulting Chapter 42ESL, select the correct choice from the words in parentheses and write it in the blank.

EXAMPLE The debate over global (warmings, warming) **warming** is heating up.

1. One of the hottest (year, years) ________ in history was recorded in the 1980s, and (many, much) ________ other warm years have followed.
2. Scientists believe that these (temperature, temperatures) ________ patterns prove that the earth's climate is getting hotter.
3. If the news of a global warming trend (is, are) ________ true, Canadians who are tired of shovelling (snow, snows) ________ should not start to dream of banana plantations in Saskatchewan.
4. Even a (three-degrees, three-degree) ________ rise in the average temperature may bring damaging dry spells to the (Canadian, Canadians) ________ Prairies.
5. In addition, coastal regions would be hit by (floodings, flooding) ________ if warmer (weather, weathers) ________ began to melt the polar icecaps.

EXERCISE 42-2

Consulting Chapter 42ESL, select the correct choice from the words in parentheses and write it in the blank.

EXAMPLE A work that the British mathematician George Boole published in 1847 has had remarkable (influence, influences) **influence**.

(1) George Boole had the (inspiration, inspirations) ________ to link mathematical notation to the rules of human (thought, thoughts) ________ (2) He noticed that nearly every (statement, statements)________ can be expressed in a kind of algebra with the three logical operators AND, OR, and NOT. (3) After Boole's death, (much, many) ________ philosophers adopted similar systems to analyze (argument, arguments) ________ as either true or false. (4) In 1938, an engineering student named Claude Shannon wrote one of the most important master's (thesis, theses) ________ ever. (5) Shannon realized that when the categories *true* and *false* are stated as *on* and *off*, Boolean algebra can be used to run the (switching, switchings) ________ processes of electronic circuits. (6) This discovery has had several important (application, applications) ________, especially in computers. (7) Today, one of the (way, ways) ________ in which we are reminded of Boole is when we perform a "Boolean search" on the Web: This means that we refine the search topic using Boole's logical operators AND, OR, and NOT.

43 ESL Articles

HOW TO USE CHAPTER 43ESL EFFECTIVELY

1. Use this chapter together with these handbook sections:
   - 7a articles° and nouns°
   - 42a singulars° and plurals° with count nouns° and noncount nouns°
   - 42b determiners° with count and noncount nouns
2. Remember that throughout this handbook, **a degree mark** (°) after a word indicates that you can find the definition of the word in the Glossary of Terms toward the back of the book.
3. Also, use any **cross-references** (usually given in parentheses) to find full explanations of key concepts.

This chapter gives you guidelines for using articles. Section 43a discusses using articles with singular count nouns. Section 43b discusses using articles with plural count nouns and with noncount nouns (which are always singular). Section 43c discusses using articles with proper nouns° and with gerunds°.

43a Using *a, an,* or *the* with singular count nouns

The words *a* and *an* are called **indefinite articles.** The word *the* is called a **definite article.** Articles are one type of determiner. (For other determiners, see Chart 170 in 42b.) Articles signal that a noun will follow and that any modifiers between the article and the noun refer to that noun.

a chair	**the** computer
a cold metal chair	**the** lightning-fast computer

Every time you use a singular count noun, a common noun that names one countable item, the noun requires some kind of determiner; see Group 1 in Chart 170 (in Chapter 42) for a list. To choose between *a* or *an* and *the*, you need to determine whether the noun is **specific** or **nonspecific**. A noun is considered specific when anyone who reads your writing can understand from the context of your message exactly and specifically to what the noun is referring.

For nonspecific singular count nouns, use *a* (or *an*). When the singular noun is specific, use *the* or some other determiner. Chart 171 can help you decide when a singular count noun is specific and therefore requires *the*.

✤ USAGE ALERT: Use *an* before words that begin with a vowel sound. Use *a* before words that begin with a consonant sound. Words that begin with *h* or *u* can have either a vowel or a consonant sound. Make the choice based on the sound of the first word after the article, even if that word is not the noun.

an idea	**an h**onour	**a u**seless umbrella
an umbrella	**a g**ood idea	**a h**istory book ✤

WHEN A SINGULAR COUNT NOUN IS SPECIFIC AND REQUIRES *THE* 171

- **Rule 1: A noun is specific and requires *the* when it names something unique or generally known.**

  The sun has risen above **the horizon**. [Because *sun* and *horizon* are generally known nouns, they are specific nouns in the context of this sentence.]

- **Rule 2: A noun is specific and requires *the* when it names something used in a representative or abstract sense.**

  I would like to know who chose **the unicorn** to be **the symbolic animal** on Canada's coat of arms. [Because *unicorn* and *symbolic animal* are representative references rather than references to a particular unicorn or animal, they are specific nouns in the context of this sentence.]

- **Rule 3: A noun is specific and requires *the* when it names something defined elsewhere in the same sentence or in an earlier sentence.**

  The ship ***St. Roch*** was the first vessel to navigate the Northwest Passage in both directions. [The name *St. Roch* denotes a specific ship.]

  The carpet in my bedroom is new. [*In my bedroom* defines exactly which carpet is meant, so *carpet* is a specific noun in this context.] ➜

WHEN A SINGULAR COUNT NOUN IS SPECIFIC AND REQUIRES *THE* *(continued)*	171

I have **a computer** in my office. **The computer** is often broken. [*Computer* is not specific in the first sentence, so it uses *a*. In the second sentence, *computer* has been made specific by the first sentence, so it uses *the*.]

- **Rule 4: A noun is specific and requires *the* when it names something that can be inferred from the context.**
  Monday, I had to call **the technician** to fix it. [If this sentence follows the two sentences about a computer in Rule 3 above, *technician* is specific in this context.]

One common exception affects Rule 3 in Chart 171. A noun may still require *a* (or *an*) after the first use if one or more descriptive adjectives come between the article and the noun: *I bought* ***a sweater*** *today. It was* ***a*** [not *the*] ***red sweater***. Other information may make the noun specific so that *the* is correct. For example, *It was* ***the red sweater that I saw in the store yesterday*** uses *the* because the *that* clause makes specific which red sweater is meant.

43b Using articles with plural nouns and with noncount nouns

With plural nouns and noncount nouns, you must decide whether to use *the* or to use no article at all. (For guidelines about using determiners° other than articles with nouns, see Chart 170 in 42b.)

What you learned in section 43a about nonspecific and specific nouns can help you make the choice between using *the* or using no article. Chart 171 in section 43a explains when a singular count noun's meaning is specific and calls for *the*. Plural nouns and noncount nouns with specific meanings usually use *the* in the same circumstances. However, a plural noun or a noncount noun with a general or nonspecific meaning usually does not use *the*.

Geraldo grows **flowers** but not **vegetables** in his garden. He is thinking about planting **corn** sometime.

Plural nouns

A plural noun's meaning may be specific because it is widely known.

The oceans are being damaged by pollution. [Because the meaning of *oceans* is widely understood, *the* is correct to use. This example is related to Rule 1 in Chart 171.]

A plural noun's meaning may also be made specific by a word, phrase°, or clause° in the same sentence°.

Geraldo sold **the daisies from last year's garden** to the florist. [Because the phrase *from last year's garden* makes *daisies* specific, *the* is correct to use. This example is related to Rule 3 in Chart 171.]

A plural noun's meaning usually becomes specific by being used in an earlier sentence.

Geraldo planted **tulips** this year. **The tulips** will bloom in April. [*Tulips* is used in a general sense in the first sentence, without *the.* Because the first sentence makes *tulips* specific, *the tulips* is correct in the second sentence. This example is related to Rule 3 in Chart 171.]

A plural noun's meaning may be made specific by the context.

Geraldo fertilized **the bulbs** when he planted them last October. [In the context of the sentences about tulips, *bulbs* is specific and calls for *the.* This example is related to Rule 4 in Chart 171.]

Noncount nouns

Noncount nouns are always singular in form (see 42a). Like plural nouns, noncount nouns use either *the* or no article. When a noncount noun's meaning is specific, use *the* before it. If its meaning is general or nonspecific, do not use *the.*

Kalinda served **rice** to us. She flavoured **the rice** with curry. [*Rice* is a noncount noun. This example is related to Rule 3 in Chart 171: By the second sentence, *rice* has become specific, so *the* is used.]

Kalinda served us **the rice that she had flavoured with curry.** [*Rice* is a noncount noun. This example is related to Rule 3 in Chart 171: *Rice* is made specific by the clause *that she had flavoured with curry,* so *the* is used.]

Generalizations with plural or noncount nouns

Rule 2 in Chart 171 tells you to use *the* with singular count nouns used in a general sense. With generalizations using plural or noncount nouns, omit *the.*

NO **The tulips** are **the flowers** that grow from **the bulbs.**
YES **Tulips** are **flowers** that grow from **bulbs.**

NO **The dogs** require more care than **the cats** do.
YES **Dogs** require more care than **cats** do.

43c Using *the* with proper nouns and with gerunds

Proper nouns

Proper nouns name specific people, places, or things (see 7a). Most proper nouns do not require articles°: *We visited* ***Lake Rossignol*** *with* ***Asha*** *and* ***Larry.*** As shown in Chart 172, however, certain types of proper nouns do require *the*.

Gerunds

Gerunds are present participles (the *-ing* form of verbs°) used as nouns: ***Skating*** *is invigorating*. Gerunds usually are not preceded by *the*.

PROPER NOUNS THAT USE *THE* 172

- **Nouns with the pattern *the* ... *of* ...**
  - **the** Dominion **of** Canada
  - **the** President **of** Mexico
  - **the** eleventh **of** November
  - **the** University **of** Paris
- **Plural proper nouns**
  - **the** United Arab Emirates
  - **the** Johnsons
  - **the** Rocky Mountains [but Mount Fuji]
  - **the** Vancouver Canucks
  - **the** Falkland Islands [but Long Island]
  - **the** Great Lakes [but Lake Louise]
- **Collective proper nouns (nouns that name a group)**
  - **the** Modern Language Association
  - **the** Society of Friends
- **Some (but not all) geographical features and regions**
  - **the** Amazon
  - **the** Beauce [Quebec]
  - **the** Gobi Desert
  - **the** Outback
  - **the** Indian Ocean
  - **the** Lake District
- **A few countries and cities**
  - **the** Congo
  - **the** Hague [capital of the Netherlands]
  - **the** Czech Republic
  - **The** Pas

NO The **constructing** new bridges is necessary to improve traffic flow.

YES **Constructing** new bridges is necessary to improve traffic flow.

Use *the* before a gerund when two conditions are met: (1) the gerund is used in a specific sense (see 43a) and (2) the gerund does not have a direct object°.

NO **The designing** fabric is a fine art. [*Fabric* is a direct object of *designing*, so *the* should not be used.]

YES **Designing** fabric is a fine art. [*Designing* is a gerund, so *the* is not used.]

YES **The designing of fabric** is a fine art. [*The* is used because *fabric* is the object of the preposition° *of* and *designing* is meant in a specific sense.]

EXERCISE 43-1

Consulting Chapter 43ESL, select the correct choice from the words in parentheses and write it in the blank.

EXAMPLE Be forewarned: (A, An, The) **The** camera as we know it may soon be obsolete.

1. At (a, an, the) ________ dawn of (a, an, the) ________ twenty-first century comes (a, an, the) ________ invention so advanced that it may completely rid (a, an, the) ________ industrialized world of every camera ever used.
2. (A, An, The) ________ digital camera, which allows photos to appear on (a, an, the) ________ computer monitor, takes up virtual space, not physical space.
3. As (a, an, the) ________ result, if you see (a, an, the) ________ bad photo on (a, an, the) ________ screen, you can simply erase (a, an, the) ________ photo to make room for (a, an, the) ________ new one.
4. With this new technology (a, an, the) ________ aunt can e-mail photos to her niece or nephew, or she can put them on (a, an, the) ________ Web page.
5. Digital cameras also allow people to alter (a, an, the) ________ appearance of people or things, which, according to many critics, is (a, an, the) ________ chief disadvantage of this kind of camera.

EXERCISE 43-2

Consulting Chapter 43ESL, select the correct choice from the words in parentheses and write it in the blank. You may have the option of leaving one or more blanks empty

EXAMPLE If you are (a, an, the) **a** student from (a, an, the) **a** foreign country, what can you do to learn about (a, an, the) **the** Canadian way of life?

1. Some people say that (a, an, the) ________ best thing (a, an, the) ________ newcomer can do to discover (a, an, the) ________ new culture is to watch (a, an, the) ________ local television programs.
2. (A, An, The) ________ entertainment that Canadians like to watch on television reveals much about (a, an, the) ________ culture in this country.
3. News and public affairs are also important, which is why it is (a, an, the) ________ good idea to subscribe to (a, an, the) ________ newspaper or (a, an, the) ________ magazine.
4. (A, An, The) ________ student who wants to learn more about Canada may also consider finding (a, an, the) ________ activities to do outside (a, an, the) ________ walls of (a, an, the) ________ campus–tutoring or volunteering, perhaps.
5. Finally, (a, an, the) ________ excellent way to soak up (a, an, the) ________ culture is to live with (a, an, the) ________ local family, as long as (a, an, the) ________ family involves (a, an, the) ________ student in its activities.

Word Order

HOW TO USE CHAPTER 44ESL EFFECTIVELY

1. Use this chapter together with these handbook sections:
   - 7k–7o sentence° patterns
   - 7e adjectives°
   - 7p sentence types
   - 7f adverbs°
   - 7m modifiers°
   - 11f verbs° in inverted word order
   - 7o clauses°
2. Remember that throughout this handbook, **a degree mark** (°) after a word indicates that you can find the definition of the word in the Glossary of Terms toward the back of the book.
3. Also, use any **cross-references** (usually given in parentheses) to find full explanations of key concepts.

This chapter can help you with several issues of word order in sentences. Section 44a discusses standard word order for English sentences and important variations. Section 44b discusses the placement of adjectives. Section 44c discusses the placement of adverbs.

44a Understanding standard and inverted word order in sentences

In **standard word order,** the most common pattern for declarative sentences in English, the subject° comes before the verb°. (To better understand these concepts, review sections 7k–7o.)

With **inverted word order,** the main verb° or an auxiliary verb° comes before the subject. The most common use of inverted word order in English is forming **direct questions**. Questions that can be answered with "yes" or "no" begin with a form of *be* used as a main verb, or with an auxiliary verb (*be, do, have*), or with a modal auxiliary (*can, should, will*, and others—see Chapter 47ESL).

QUESTIONS THAT CAN BE ANSWERED WITH "YES" OR "NO"

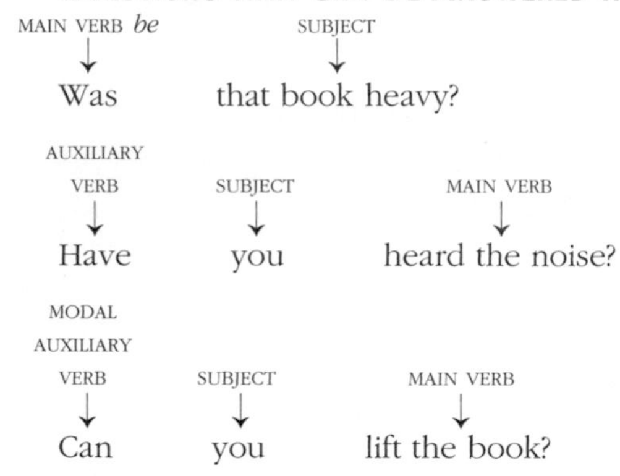

To form a yes/no question with a verb other than *be* as the main verb and when there is no auxiliary or modal as part of a verb phrase, use the appropriate form of the auxiliary verb *do*.

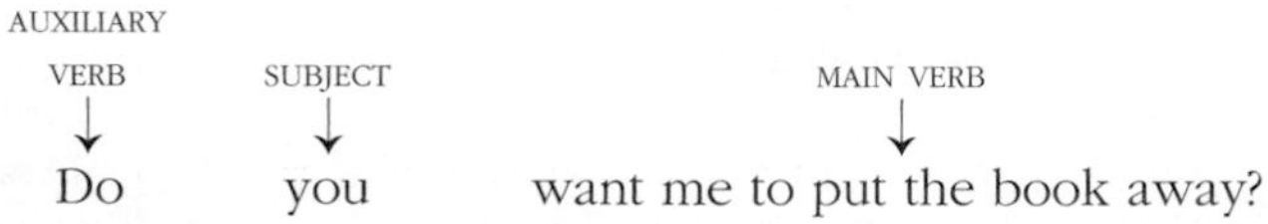

A question that begins with a **question-forming word** like *why, when, where*, or *how* cannot be answered with "yes" or "no": ***Why** did the book fall?* Some kind of information must be provided to answer such a question; the answer cannot be "yes" or "no." Information is needed: for example, *It was too heavy for me.*

Most information questions follow the same rules of inverted word order as yes/no questions.

INFORMATION QUESTIONS: INVERTED ORDER

QUESTION WORD ↓ Why | MAIN VERB *be* ↓ is | SUBJECT ↓ that book open?

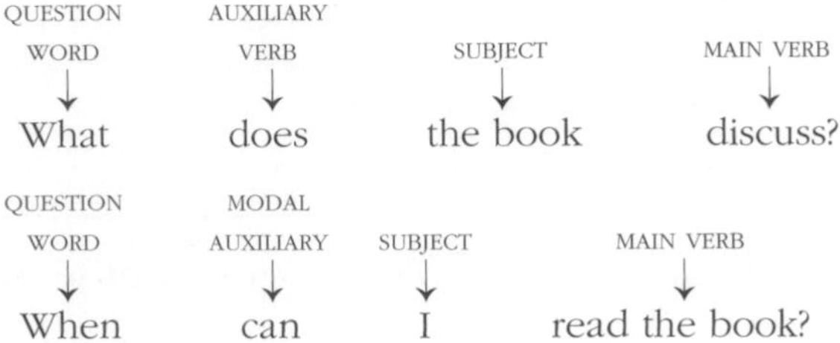

When *Who* or *What* functions as the subject in a question, however, use standard word order.

Information Questions: Standard Order

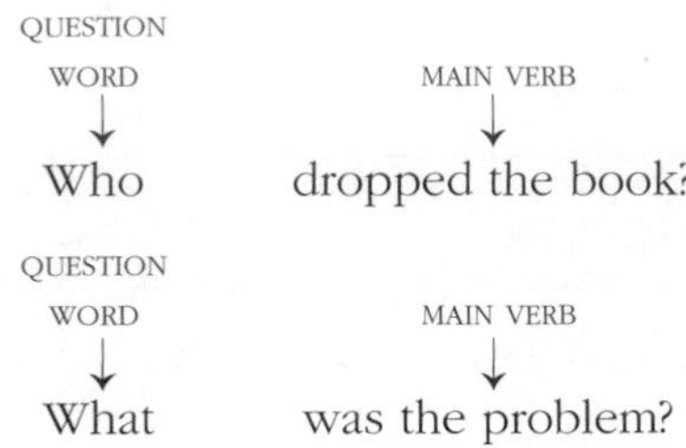

✤ ALERT: When a question has more than one auxiliary verb, put the subject after the first auxiliary verb.

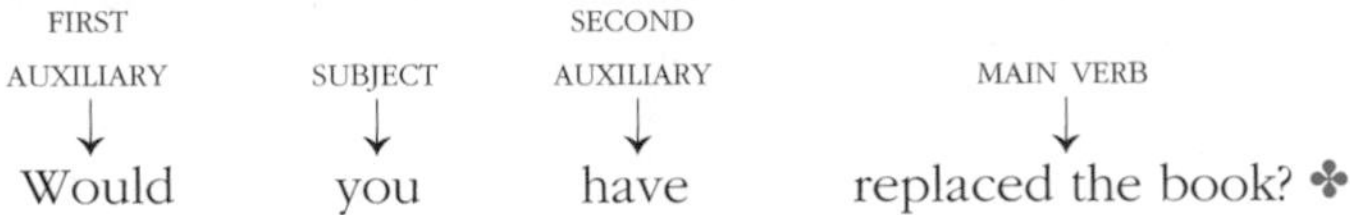

The same rules apply to emphatic exclamations: ***Was*** *that book heavy!* ***Did*** *she enjoy that book!*

Also, when you use negatives such as *never, hardly, ever, seldom, rarely, not only,* or *nor* to start a clause, use inverted order. These sentence pairs show the differences.

I have never seen a more exciting movie. [standard order]

Never have I seen a more exciting movie. [inverted order]

She is not only a talented artist **but also** an excellent musician.

Not only is she a talented artist, but **she is also** an excellent musician.

I didn't like the book, and **my husband didn't either**.

I didn't like the book, and **neither did my husband**.

✤ USAGE ALERT: With indirect questions, use standard word order: *She asked* ***how I dropped the book*** (not *She asked* ***how did I drop the book***). ✤

✤ STYLE ALERT: Word order deliberately inverted can be effective, when used sparingly, to create emphasis in a sentence that is neither a question nor an exclamation (also see 19f). ✤

44b Understanding the placement of adjectives

Adjectives modify—that is, they describe or limit—nouns°, pronouns°, and word groups that function as nouns (see section 7e). In English, an adjective comes directly before the noun it describes. However, when more than one adjective describes the same noun, several sequences may be possible. Chart 173 shows the most common order for positioning several adjectives.

173

WORD ORDER FOR MORE THAN ONE ADJECTIVE

1. **Determiners, if any:** *a, an, the, my, your, Jan's, this, that, these, those,* and so on
2. **Expressions of order, including ordinal numbers, if any:** *first, second, third, next, last, final,* and so on
3. **Expressions of quantity, including cardinal (counting) numbers, if any:** *one, two, three, few, each, every, some,* and so on
4. **Adjectives of judgment or opinion, if any:** *pretty, happy, ugly, sad, interesting, boring,* and so on
5. **Adjectives of size and/or shape, if any:** *big, small, short, round, square,* and so on
6. **Adjectives of age and/or condition, if any:** *new, young, broken, dirty, shiny,* and so on
7. **Adjectives of colour, if any:** *red, green, blue,* and so on
8. **Adjectives that can also be used as nouns, if any:** *French, Protestant, metal, cotton,* and so on
9. **The noun**

1	2	3	4	5	6	7	8	9
A		few		tiny		red		ants
The	last	six					Thai	carvings
My			fine		old		oak	table

44c Understanding the placement of adverbs

Adverbs modify—that is, describe or limit—verbs°, adjectives°, other adverbs, or entire sentences (see section 7f). Adverbs are usually positioned first, in the middle, or last in clauses. Chart 174 summarizes adverb types, what they tell about the words they modify, and where each type can be placed.

TYPES OF ADVERBS AND WHERE TO POSITION THEM 174

- **Adverbs of manner**
  - **describe *how* something is done**
  - **usually are in middle or last position**

    Nick **carefully** groomed the dog.
    Nick groomed the dog **carefully.**

- **Adverbs of time**
  - **describe *when* or *how long* about an event**
  - **usually are in the first or last position**

    First, he shampooed the dog.
    He shampooed the dog **first**.

  - **include *just, still,* and *already,* and similar adverbs, which usually are in the middle position**

    He had **already** brushed the dog's coat.

- **Adverbs of place**
  - **describe *where* an event takes place**
  - **usually are in the last position**

    He lifted the dog **into the tub.**

- **Adverbs of frequency**
  - **describe *how often* an event takes place**
  - **usually are in the middle position**

    Nick has **never** been bitten by a dog.

  - **are in the first position when they modify an entire sentence** (see "Sentence adverbs" below)

    Occasionally, he is scratched while shampooing a cat.

- **Adverbs of degree or emphasis**
  - **describe *how much* or *to what extent* about other modifiers**
  - **are directly before the word they modify**

➜

174

TYPES OF ADVERBS AND WHERE TO POSITION THEM *(continued)*

Nick is **extremely** calm around animals. [*Extremely* modifies *calm*]

- **include *only,* which is easy to misplace** (see 15b-1)

■ **Sentence adverbs**

- **modify the entire sentence rather than just one word or a few words**
- **include transitional words and expressions** (see 4d-1) **as well as *maybe, probably, possibly, fortunately, unfortunately, incredibly,* and others**
- **are in first position**

Incredibly, he was once asked to groom a rat.

✤ PUNCTUATION ALERT: Unless they are very short (fewer than five letters), adverbs in the first position are usually followed by a comma. ✤

✤ USAGE ALERT: Do not let an adverb in a middle position separate a verb from its direct object° or indirect object° (see section 15b-2). ✤

EXERCISE 44-1

Consulting Chapter 44ESL, find and correct any errors in word order.

1. The antique glass beautiful vase shattered on the floor.
2. Lu Mi had not meant to break her favourite mother's jar.
3. She was so upset that almost she cried.
4. When Lu Mi's mother heard the sound of shattering glass, she ran into the room asking, "You are all right?"
5. Knowing that Lu Mi had broken accidentally the vase, her mother was not angry extremely.

EXERCISE 44-2

Consulting Chapter 44ESL, find and correct any errors in word order.

1. A beautiful few flowers began to bloom in my garden this week.
2. A neighbour asked me, "You did grow all these yourself?"
3. "Yes," I replied, "the roses are my favourite husband's, but my favourite are the tulips."
4. My neighbour, who extremely was impressed with my gardening efforts, decided to grow some flowers of her own.
5. Weeks later, as I strolled by her house, I saw her planting happily seeds from her favourite type of plant—petunias.

Prepositions

How to Use Chapter 45ESL Effectively

1. Use this chapter together with these handbook sections:
   - 7g prepositions°
   - 21a using appropriate language
2. Remember that throughout this handbook, **a degree mark** (°) after a word indicates that you can find the definition of the word in the Glossary of Terms toward the back of the book.
3. Also, use any **cross-references** (usually given in parentheses) to find full explanations of key concepts.

Prepositions function with other words in prepositional phrases°. Prepositional phrases usually indicate **where** (direction or location), **how** (by what means or in what way), or **when** (at what time or how long) about the words they modify.

This chapter can help you with several uses of prepositions, which function in combination with other words in ways that are often idiomatic. An idiom's meaning differs from the literal meaning of each individual word (see 20a-1). For example, *Yao-Ming* ***broke into*** a smile means that a smile appeared on Yao-Ming's face. However, the dictionary definitions of *break* and *into* imply that *broke into a smile* means "shattered the form of" a smile. Knowing which preposition to use in a specific context takes much experience reading, listening to, and speaking the language. A dictionary like the *Longman Dictionary of Contemporary English* or the *Oxford Advanced Learner's Dictionary* can be especially helpful when you need to find the correct preposition to use in cases not covered by this chapter. Section 45a lists many common prepositions. Section 45b dicusses prepositions with some expressions of time and place. Section 45c discusses combinations of verbs and prepositions called phrasal verbs°. Section 45d discusses common expressions using prepositions.

45a Recognizing prepositions

Chart 175 shows many common prepositions.

COMMON PREPOSITIONS 175

about	before	except for	near	through
above	behind	excepting	next	throughout
according to	below	for	of	till
across	beneath	from	off	to
after	beside	in	on	toward
against	between	in addition to	onto	under
along	beyond	in back of	on top of	underneath
along with	but	in case of	out	unlike
among	by	in front of	out of	until
apart from	by means of	in place of	outside	up
around	concerning	inside	over	upon
as	despite	in spite of	past	up to
as for	down	instead of	regarding	with
at	during	into	round	within
because of	except	like	since	without

45b Using prepositions with expressions of time and place

Chart 176 shows how to use the prepositions *in, at,* and *on* to deliver some common kinds of information about time and place. The chart, however, does not cover every preposition that indicates time or place, nor does it cover all uses of *in, at,* and *on*. For example, it does not explain the subtle difference in meaning delivered by the prepositions *at* and *in* in these two correct sentences: *I have a chequing account* ***at*** *that bank* and *I have a safe-deposit box* ***in*** *that bank.* Also, the chart does not include expressions that operate outside the general rules. (Both these sentences are correct: *You ride* ***in*** *the car* and *You ride* ***on*** *the bus.*)

176

USING *IN, AT,* AND *ON* TO SHOW TIME AND PLACE

TIME

- ***in* a year or a month** (*during* is also correct but less common)

  in 1995 **in** May

- ***in* a period of time**

  in a few months (seconds, days, years)

- ***in* a period of the day**

  in the morning (afternoon, evening)
  in the daytime (morning, evening) *but* **at** night

- ***on* a specific day**

  on Friday **on** my birthday

- ***at*** a specific time or period of time

  at noon **at** 2:00 **at** dawn **at** nightfall
  at takeoff (the time a plane leaves)
  at breakfast (the time a specific meal takes place)

PLACE

- ***in* a location surrounded by something else**

  in Alberta
  in Utah
  in downtown Bombay
  in the kitchen
  in the apartment **in** the bathtub

- ***at* a specific location**

  at your house **at** the bank
  at the corner of Third Avenue and Main Street

- ***on* the top or the surface of something**

  on page 20
  on the second floor, but **in** the attic or **in** the basement
  on Wellington Street
  on the mezzanine
  on street level

45c Using prepositions in phrasal verbs

Phrasal verbs, also called *two-word verbs* and *three-word verbs,* are verbs° that combine with prepositions to deliver their meaning.

In some phrasal verbs, the verb and the preposition should not be separated by other words: ***Look at*** *the moon* [not ***Look*** *the moon* ***at***]. In **separable phrasal verbs,** other words in the sentence can separate the verb and the preposition without interfering with meaning: *I* ***threw away*** *my homework* is as correct as *I* ***threw*** *my homework* ***away.***

Here is a list of some common phrasal verbs. The ones that cannot be separated are marked with an asterisk (*).

LIST OF SELECTED PHRASAL VERBS

ask out	get along with*	look into
break down	get back	look out for*
bring about	get off	look over
call back	go over*	make up
drop off	hand in	run across*
figure out	keep up with*	speak to*
fill out	leave out	speak with*
fill up	look after*	throw away
find out	look around	throw out

Position a pronoun° object° between the words of a separable phrasal verb: *I threw **it** away.* Also, you can position an object phrase of several words between the parts of a separable phrasal verb: *I threw* ***my research paper*** *away.* However, when the object is a clause, do not let it separate the parts of the phrasal verb: *I threw away* ***all the papers that I wrote last year***.

Many phrasal verbs are informal and are used more in speaking than in writing. For academic writing, a more formal verb may be more appropriate than a phrasal verb. In a research paper, for example, *propose* or *suggest* might be better choices than *come up with*. For academic writing, acceptable phrasal verbs include *believe in, benefit from, concentrate on, consist of, depend on, dream of* (or *dream about*), *insist on, participate in, prepare for,* and *stare at.* None of these phrasal verbs can be separated.

EXERCISE 45-1

Consulting Chapter 45ESL and using the list of phrasal verbs in section 45c, write a one- or two-paragraph description of a typical day at work or school in which you use at least five phrasal verbs. After checking a dictionary, revise your writing, substituting for the phrasal verbs any more formal verbs that you think may be more appropriate for academic writing.

45d Using prepositions in common expressions

In many common expressions, different prepositions convey great differences in meaning. For example, four prepositions can be used with the verb *agree* to create five different meanings.

agree to = to give consent [I cannot ***agree to*** buy you a new car.]

agree about = to arrive at a satisfactory understanding [We ***agree about*** your needing a car.]

agree on = to arrive at a satisfactory understanding [You and the seller must ***agree on*** a price for the car.]

agree with = to have the same opinion. [I ***agree with*** you that you need a car.]

agree with = be suitable or healthful [The idea of such a major expense does not ***agree with*** me.]

You can find entire books filled with English expressions that include prepositions. The list below shows a few that you are likely to use often.

List of Selected Expressions with Prepositions

ability in
access to
accustomed to
afraid of
angry with *or* at
authority on
aware of
based on
capable of
certain of
confidence in
dependent on
different from
faith in
familiar with
famous for
frightened by
happy with
in charge of
independent of
in favour of
influence on *or* over
interested in
involved in [*something*]
involved with [*someone*]
knowledge of
made of
married to
opposed to
patience with
proud of
reason for
related to
suspicious of
time for
tired of

46 ESL Gerunds, Infinitives, and Participles

HOW TO USE CHAPTER 46ESL EFFECTIVELY

1. Use this chapter together with these handbook sections:
   - 7d verbals°
   - 11a subject–verb agreement°
   - 7k and 7l subjects° and objects°
   - 18a–18c parallelism
   - 8b principal parts° of verbs
2. Remember that throughout this handbook, **a degree mark** (°) after a word indicates that you can find the definition of the word in the Glossary of Terms toward the back of the book.
3. Also, use any **cross-references** (usually given in parentheses) to find full explanations of key concepts.

Participles are verb forms (see 8b). A verb's *-ing* form is its present participle. The *-ed* form of a regular verb is its **past participle**; irregular verbs form their past participles in various ways (for example, *bend, bent; eat, eaten; think, thought*—for a complete list, see Chart 62 in section 8d). Participles can function as adjectives° (*a **smiling** face, a **closed** book).*

A verb's *-ing* form can also function as a noun (***Sneezing** spreads colds*), which is called a **gerund**. Another verb form, the infinitive, can also function as a noun. An **infinitive** is a verb's simple or base form usually preceded by the word *to* (*We want everyone **to smile***). Verb forms—participles, gerunds, and infinitives—functioning as nouns or modifiers are called **verbals,** as explained in section 7d.

This chapter can help you make the right choices among verbals. Section 46a discusses gerunds and infinitives used as subjects. Section 46b discusses verbs that are followed by gerunds, not infinitives. Section 46c discusses verbs that are followed by infinitives, not gerunds. Section 46d discusses meaning changes depending on whether certain verbs are followed by a gerund or an infinitive. Section 46e explains that meaning does not change for certain sense verbs° no matter whether they are followed by a gerund or an infinitive. Section 46f discusses differences in meaning between the present-participle form and the past-participle form of some modifiers.

46a Using gerunds and infinitives as subjects

Gerunds are used more commonly than infinitives as subjects. Sometimes, however, either is acceptable.

Choosing the right health club is important.

To choose the right health club is important.

✤ VERB ALERT: When a gerund or an infinitive is used alone as a subject, it is singular° and requires a singular verb. When two or more gerunds or infinitives create a compound subject°, they require a plural verb. (See sections 7k and 11d.) ✤

46b Using a gerund, not an infinitive, as an object after certain verbs

Some verbs° must be followed by gerunds° used as direct objects°. Other verbs must be followed by infinitives°. Still other verbs can be followed by either a gerund or an infinitive. (A few verbs can change meaning depending on whether they are followed by a gerund or an infinitive; see 46d.) Chart 177 lists common verbs that must be followed by gerunds, not infinitives.

Yuri **considered** ***calling*** [not *to call*] the mayor.

He **was having trouble** ***getting*** [not *to get*] a parking permit.

Yuri's boss **recommended** ***taking*** [not *to take*] someone who speaks English and Russian to the office that issues the permits.

Gerund after go

Go is usually followed by an infinitive: *We can* ***go to see*** [not *go seeing*] *a movie tonight*. Sometimes, however, *go* is followed by a gerund in phrases such as *go swimming, go fishing, go shopping,* and *go driving: I will* ***go shopping*** [not *go to shop*] *after work.*

177

VERBS AND EXPRESSIONS THAT USE GERUNDS AFTER THEM		
acknowledge	detest	mind
admit	discuss	object to
advise	dislike	postpone
anticipate	dream about	practise
appreciate	enjoy	put off
avoid	escape	quit
cannot bear	evade	recall (remember)
cannot help	favour	recommend
cannot resist	finish	regret
complain about	give up	resent
consider	have trouble	resist
consist of	imagine	risk
contemplate	include	suggest
delay	insist on	talk about
deny	keep (on)	tolerate
deter from	mention	understand

Gerund after be + *complement* + *preposition*

Many common expressions use a form of the verb *be* plus a complement° plus a preposition. In such expressions, use a gerund, not an infinitive, after the preposition. Here is a list of some of the most frequently used expressions in this pattern.

LIST OF SELECTED *BE* + COMPLEMENT + PREPOSITION EXPRESSIONS

be (get) accustomed to	be interested in
be angry about	be prepared for
be bored with	be responsible for
be capable of	be tired of
be committed to	be (get) used to
be excited about	be worried about

We **are excited about** ***voting*** [not *to vote*] in the next election.

Who will **be responsible for** ***locating*** [not t*o locate*] our polling place?

✤ USAGE ALERT: Always use a gerund, not an infinitive, as the object of a preposition. Be especially careful when the word *to* is functioning as a preposition in a phrasal verb (see 45c): *We are* ***committed to changing*** [not *to change*] *the rules.* ✤

46c Using an infinitive, not a gerund, as an object after certain verbs

Chart 178 lists selected common verbs° and expressions that must be followed by infinitives°, not gerunds°, as objects°.

She **wanted *to go*** [not *wanted going*] to the lecture.

Only three people **decided *to question*** [not *decided questioning*] the speaker.

178 VERBS AND EXPRESSIONS THAT USE INFINITIVES AFTER THEM

afford	claim	hope	promise
agree	consent	intend	refuse
aim	decide	know how	seem
appear	decline	learn	struggle
arrange	demand	like	tend
ask	deserve	manage	threaten
attempt	do not care	mean	volunteer
be left	expect	offer	vote
beg	fail	plan	wait
cannot afford	give permission	prepare	want
care	hesitate	pretend	would like

Infinitives after be + *complement*

Gerunds are common in constructions that use forms of the verb *be,* a complement°, and a preposition° (see 46b). However, use an infinitive, not a gerund, when *be* plus a complement is not followed by a preposition.

We **are eager *to go*** [not *going*] camping.

I **am ready *to sleep*** [not *sleeping*] in a tent.

Infinitives to indicate purpose

Use an infinitive in expressions that indicate purpose: *I read a book* ***to learn*** *more about Mayan culture*. This sentence means "I read a book for the purpose of learning more about Mayan culture." *To learn*

delivers the idea of purpose more concisely (see Chapter 16) than expressions such as "so that I can" or "in order to."

Infinitives with the first, the last, the one

Use an infinitive after the expressions *the first, the last,* and *the one: Soon-yi is **the first to arrive*** [not *arriving*] *and the last to leave* [not *leaving*] *every day.*

Unmarked infinitives

Infinitives used without the word *to* are called **unmarked infinitives** or **bare infinitives**. An unmarked infinitive may be hard to recognize because it is not preceded by *to*. Some common verbs followed by unmarked infinitives are *feel, have, hear, let, listen to, look at, make* (meaning "compel"), *notice, see,* and *watch*.

Please let me **take** [not *to take*] you to lunch. [unmarked infinitive]

I want **to take** you to lunch. [marked infinitive]

I can have Kara **drive** [not to *drive*] us. [unmarked infinitive]

I will ask Kara **to drive** us. [marked infinitive]

The verb *help* can be followed by either a marked or an unmarked infinitive. Either is correct: *Help me **put*** [or ***to put***] *this box in the car.*

✤ USAGE ALERT: Be careful to use parallel structure (see Chapter 18) correctly when you use two or more gerunds or infinitives after verbs. If two or more verbal objects° follow one verb, put the verbals into the same form.

NO	We went **sailing** and **to scuba dive**.
YES	We went **sailing** and **scuba diving**.
NO	We heard the wind **blow** and the waves **crashing**.
YES	We heard the wind **blow** and the waves **crash**.
YES	We heard the wind **blowing** and the waves **crashing**.

Conversely, if you are using verbal objects with compound predicates°, be sure to use the kind of verbal that each verb requires.

NO	We enjoyed **scuba diving** but do not plan **sailing** again. [*Enjoyed* requires a gerund object and *plan* requires an infinitive object; see Charts 177 and 178.]
YES	We enjoyed **scuba diving** but do not plan **to sail** again. ✤

46d Knowing how meaning changes when certain verbs are followed by a gerund or an infinitive as an object

With stop

The verb *stop* followed by a gerund° means "finish, quit." *Stop* followed by an infinitive means "stop or interrupt one activity to begin another."

We **stopped eating**. [We finished our meal.]

We **stopped to eat**. [We stopped another activity, such as driving, in order to eat.]

With remember *and* forget

The verb *remember* followed by an infinitive means "not to forget to do something": *I must* ***remember to talk*** *with Isa. Remember* followed by a gerund means "recall a memory": *I* ***remember talking*** *in my sleep last night.*

The verb *forget* followed by an infinitive means "to not do something": *If you* ***forget to put*** *a stamp on that letter, it will be returned. Forget* followed by a gerund means "to do something and not recall it": *I* ***forget having put*** *the stamps in the refrigerator.*

With try

The verb *try* followed by an infinitive means "make an effort": *I* ***tried to find*** *your jacket.* Followed by a gerund, *try* means "experiment with": *I* ***tried jogging*** *but found it too difficult.*

46e Understanding that meaning does not change whether a gerund or an infinitive follows certain sense verbs

Sense verbs° include words such as *see, notice, hear, observe, watch, feel, listen to,* and *look at.* The meaning of these verbs is usually not affected whether they are followed by a gerund° or an infinitive° as an object°. *I* ***saw*** *the water* ***rise*** and *I* ***saw*** *the water* ***rising*** both have the same meaning in English.

EXERCISE 46-1

Consulting sections 46a through 46e, write the correct form of verbal object (either a gerund or an infinitive) for each verb in parentheses.

EXAMPLE On some campuses, it seems as if nearly every student wants **to find** a better apartment or dormitory room.

1. Often, students become as anxious over (find) ______ a suitable apartment as they do over (write) ______ a final exam.
2. In many places, senior undergraduates and graduate students tend (avoid) ______ dormitories.
3. Some students consider (live) ______ off campus a sign of maturity and independence.
4. Others just seem (need) ______ the extra physical and mental space.
5. In later life, people who were able (share) ______ a big, roomy house with school friends often remember the experience fondly.
6. We rarely see students (come) ______ up with an ideal solution, though, if they have left their search to the last minute.
7. The idea is to plan ahead and actively try (find) ______ a place that suits you; otherwise, you may be forced to try (sleep) ______ on your friend's couch for a few weeks.
8. Most colleges and universities recognize that they must help their students (locate) ______ living space they can afford.
9. The housing problem at one large Ontario university became known after a student acknowledged (live) ______ hidden in a campus stairwell.
10. (Explain) ______ this situation was a huge embarrassment for university officials, even after social workers attempted (blame) ______ this student's predicament on personal problems.

46f Choosing between *-ing* forms and *-ed* forms for adjectives

Deciding whether to use the *-ing* form (present participle°) or the *-ed* form (past participle° of a regular verb°) as an adjective° in a specific sentence can be difficult. For example, *I am* ***amused*** and *I am* ***amusing*** are both correct in English, but their meanings are very different. To make the right choice, decide whether the modified noun° or pronoun° is causing or experiencing what the participle describes.

Use a present participle (*-ing*) to modify a noun or pronoun that is the agent or the cause of the action.

Mica described your **interesting** plan. [The noun *plan* causes what its modifier describes—interest; so *interesting* is correct.]

I find your plan **exciting**. [The noun *plan* causes what its modifier describes—excitement; so *exciting* is correct.]

Use a past participle (*-ed* in regular verbs) to modify a noun or pronoun that experiences or receives whatever the modifier describes.

An **interested** committee wants to hear your plan. [The noun *committee* experiences what its modifier describes—interest; so *interested* is correct.]

Excited by your plan, I called a board meeting. [The pronoun *I* experiences what its modifier describes—excitement; so *excited* is correct.]

Here are frequently used participles that convey very different meanings, depending on whether the *-ed* or the *-ing* form is used.

amused, amusing
annoyed, annoying
appalled, appalling
bored, boring
confused, confusing
depressed, depressing
disgusted, disgusting
fascinated, fascinating
frightened, frightening
insulted, insulting
offended, offending
overwhelmed, overwhelming
pleased, pleasing
reassured, reassuring
satisfied, satisfying
shocked, shocking

EXERCISE 46-2

Consulting section 46f, choose the correct participle.

EXAMPLE It can be a (satisfied, satisfying) **satisfying** experience to learn about the lives of artists.

1. Artist Frida Kahlo led an (interested, interesting) ______ life.
2. When she was eighteen, (horrified, horrifying) ______ observers say Kahlo was (injured, injuring) ______ in a streetcar accident.
3. A (disappointed, disappointing) ______ Kahlo had to abandon her plan to study medicine.
4. Instead, she began to create paintings filled with (disturbed, disturbing) ______ images.
5. Some art critics consider Kahlo's paintings to be (fascinated, fascinating) ______ works of art even though many people find them (overwhelmed, overwhelming) ______ .

EXERCISE 46-3

Consulting section 46f, choose the correct participle.

EXAMPLE Learning about the career of a favourite actor is always an (interested, interesting) **interesting** exercise.

1. Jim Carrey is an actor/comedian with a very (fascinated, fascinating) ________ history.
2. (Raised, Raising) ________ by his parents in Southern Ontario, Carrey grew up in one of the most media-rich areas in North America.
3. Bios of Carrey reveal the (surprised, surprising) ________ news that this bright and talented student dropped out of school in grade ten.
4. After relocating to Los Angeles in the 1980s, a (disappointed, disappointing) ________ Carrey discovered the difficulties of acting after his first (cancelled, cancelling) ________ TV series left him briefly out of work.
5. Carrey's career skyrocketed with his (amused, amusing) ________ appearances on *In Living Color*, a TV show that led to numerous box office hits like *Ace Ventura: Pet Detective* and *The Mask*.

EXERCISE 46-4

Consulting section 46f, choose the correct participle.

EXAMPLE Studying popular myths that turn out to be false can be a (fascinated, fascinating) **fascinating** experience.

1. While doing research for a paper about birds, I discovered some (interested, interesting) ________ information about ostriches.
2. I encountered an (unsettled, unsettling) ________ passage in a book that said ostriches do not, in fact, stick their heads into the sand for protection when they feel fear.
3. This myth about (frightened, frightening) ________ ostriches began among the ancient Arabs and has since been passed on by many reputable writers.
4. In reality, an ostrich does not have to do something as useless as burying its head in the sand when a predator approaches, because a (hunted, hunting) ________ ostrich can reach speeds of nearly 55 kilometres an hour and can thus outrun most other animals.
5. A (threatened, threatening) ________ ostrich can also kick its way out of most dangerous situations with its powerful legs, and, at a height of well over two metres, it presents itself as a (frightened, frightening) ________ opponent.

47 ESL Modal Auxiliary Verbs

HOW TO USE CHAPTER 47ESL EFFECTIVELY

1. Use this chapter together with these handbook sections:
   - 7c recognizing verbs°
   - 8j progressive forms°
   - 8e auxiliary verbs°
   - 8g verb tense°
   - 8l and 8m subjunctive mood°
2. Remember that throughout this handbook, **a degree mark** (°) after a word indicates that you can find the definition of the word in the Glossary of Terms toward the back of the book.
3. Also, use any **cross-references** (usually given in parentheses) to find full explanations of key concepts.

Auxiliary verbs are known as *helping verbs* because adding an auxiliary verb to a main verb° helps the main verb convey additional information (see 8e). For example, the auxiliary verb *do* is important in turning sentences into questions. *You have to sleep* becomes a question when *do* is added: *Do you have to sleep?* The most common auxiliary verbs are forms of *be, have,* and *do.* (Charts 63 and 64 in section 8e list the forms of these three verbs.)

Modal auxiliary verbs are one type of auxiliary verb. They include *can, could, may, might, should, had better, must, will, would,* and others discussed in this chapter. They have only two forms: the present-future and the past. Modals differ from *be, have,* and *do* used as auxiliary verbs in the ways discussed in Chart 179.

This chapter can help you use modals to convey shades of meaning. Section 47a discusses using modals to convey ability, necessity, advisability, possibility, and probability. Section 47b discusses using modals to convey preferences, plans or obligations, and past habits. Section 47c introduces modals in the passive voice°.

SUMMARY OF MODALS AND THEIR DIFFERENCES FROM OTHER AUXILIARY VERBS 179

- Modals in the present or future are always followed by the simple form of a main verb: *I might* ***go*** *tomorrow.*
- One-word modals have no *-s* ending in the third-person singular: *She* ***could*** *go with me, you* ***could*** *go with me, they* ***could*** *go with me.* (The two-word modal *have to* changes form to agree with its subject: *I* ***have to*** *leave, she* ***has to*** *leave.*) Auxiliary verbs other than modals usually change form for third-person singular: *I* ***have*** *talked with her, he* ***has*** *talked with her.*
- Some modals change form in the past. Others (*should, would, must,* which convey probability, and *ought to*) use *have* + a past participle. *I* ***can*** *do it* becomes *I* ***could*** *do it* in past-tense clauses about ability. *I* ***could*** *do it* becomes *I* ***could have*** *done it* in clauses about possibility.
- Modals convey meaning about ability, necessity, advice, possibility, and other conditions: For example, *I can go* means "I am able to go." Modals do not indicate actual occurrences.

47a Conveying ability, necessity, advisability, possibility, and probability with modals

Conveying ability

The modal *can* conveys ability now (in the present), and *could* conveys ability before (in the past). These words deliver the meaning of "able to." For the future, use *will be able to.*

We **can** work late tonight. [*Can* conveys present ability.]

I **could** work late last night, too. [*Could* conveys past ability.]

I **will be able to** work late next Monday. [*Will be able* is future; *will* here is *not* a modal.]

Adding *not* between a modal and the main verb makes the clause° negative: *We* ***can not*** (or ***cannot***) *work late tonight; I* ***could not*** *work late last night; I* ***will not be able*** *to work late next Monday.*

✤ USAGE ALERT: You will often see negative forms of modals turned into contractions°: *can't, couldn't, won't, wouldn't,* and others. Because contractions are considered informal usage by some instructors, you will never be wrong if you avoid them in academic writing except for reproducing spoken words. ✤

Conveying necessity

The modals *must* and *have to* convey the message of a need to do something. Both *must* and *have to* are followed by the simple form of the main verb. In the present tense, *have to* changes form to agree with its subject.

You **must** leave before midnight.

She **has to** leave when I leave.

In the past tense, *must* is never used to express necessity. Instead, use *had to.*

PRESENT TENSE

We **must** study today.

We **have to** study today.

PAST TENSE

We **had to** [not *We must*] take a test yesterday.

The negative forms of *must* and *have to* also have different meanings. *Must not* conveys that something is forbidden; *do not have to* conveys that something is not necessary.

You **must not** sit there. [Sitting there is forbidden.]

You **do not have to** sit there. [Sitting there is not necessary.]

Conveying advisability or the notion of a good idea

The modals *should* and *ought to* express the idea that doing the action of the main verb is advisable or is a good idea.

You **should** go to class tomorrow morning.

In the past tense, *should* and *ought to* convey regret or knowing something through hindsight. They mean that good advice was not taken.

You **should have** gone to class yesterday.

I **ought to have** called my sister yesterday.

The modal *had better* delivers the meaning of good advice or warning or threat. It does not change form for tense.

You **had better** see the doctor before your cough gets worse.

Need to is often used to express strong advice, too. Its past-tense form is *needed to.*

You **need to** take better care of yourself.

Conveying possibility

The modals *may, might,* and *could* can be used to convey an idea of possibility or likelihood.

We **may** become hungry before long.

We **could** eat lunch at the diner next door.

The past-tense forms for *may, might,* and *could* use these words followed by *have* and the past participle of the main verb.

I **could have studied** German in high school, but I studied Spanish instead.

Conveying probability

In addition to conveying the idea of necessity (see Conveying Necessity, page 826), the modal *must* also can convey probability or likelihood. It means that a well-informed guess is being made.

Marisa **must** be a talented actress. She has been chosen to play the lead role in the school play.

When *must* conveys probability, the past tense is *must have* plus the past participle of the main verb.

I did not see Boris at the party; he **must have left** early.

EXERCISE 47-1

Consulting section 47a, fill in the blanks with the past-tense modal that expresses the meaning given in parentheses.

EXAMPLE I (advisability) **should have** gone to bed at the regular time last night.

1. I (advisability) ______ learned my lesson after what happened in class today.
2. Because I (necessity, no choice) ______ finish writing a paper, I stayed up until 3:00 a.m.
3. In class today, I (ability) ______ not stay awake.
4. The instructor (making a guess) ______ seen my eyes close.
5. I woke up instantly when I heard him say, "You (advice, good idea) ______ stayed in bed if you (necessity, no choice) ______ sleep, Mr. Lee."

EXERCISE 47-2

Consulting Section 47a, select the correct choice from the words in parentheses and write it in the blank.

EXAMPLE When I was younger, I (ability) **could** ride my bicycle for hours.

1. You (advisability) ________ asked about the library's policy on overdue materials.
2. Considering the size of your bill, you (probability) ________ want a receipt.
3. Ingrid (making a guess) ________ not ________ been as eager to come as she thought she was.
4. After all the studying you have done, you (advisability) ________ less frightened by tomorrow's exam.
5. Ernesto is astounded at all the paperwork he (necessity, no choice) ________ fill out.

47b Conveying preferences, plans, and past habits with modals

Conveying preferences

The modals *would rather* and *would rather have* express a preference. *Would rather* (present tense°) is used with the simple form° of the main verb° and *would rather have* (past tense°) is used with the past participle° of the main verb.

We **would rather see** a comedy than a mystery.

Carlos **would rather have stayed** home last night.

Conveying plan or obligation

A form of *be* followed by *supposed to* and the simple form of a main verb delivers a meaning of something planned or of an obligation.

I **was supposed to meet** them at the bus stop.

Conveying past habit

The modals *used to* and *would* express the idea that something happened repeatedly in the past.

I used to hate going to the dentist.

I would dread visiting the dentist each time.

✤ USAGE ALERT: Both *used to* and *would* can be used to express repeated actions in the past, but *would* cannot be used for a situation that lasted for a duration of time in the past.

NO	I **would** live in Corner Brook.
YES	I **used to** live in Corner Brook. ✤

47c Recognizing modals in the passive voice

Modals use the active voice°, as shown in sections 47a and 47b. In the active voice, the subject does the action expressed in the main verb° (see 8n–8o).

Modals can also use the passive voice°. In the passive voice, the doer of the main verb's action is either unexpressed or is expressed as an object° in a prepositional phrase° starting with the word *by*.

PASSIVE	The waterfront **can be seen** from my window.
ACTIVE	I **can see** the waterfront from my window.
PASSIVE	The tax form **must be signed by** the person who fills it out.
ACTIVE	The person who fills out the tax form **must sign** it.

EXERCISE 47-3

Consulting Chapter 47ESL, select the correct choice from the words in parentheses and write it in the blank.

EXAMPLE I (should, should have) **should have** taken kayaking lessons my first summer in British Columbia.

1. I (would, used to) ________ live far from the ocean and the mountains.
2. In those days I (can, could) ________ only dream of kayaking down the coast where the Rocky Mountains meet the Pacific.
3. Sometimes I think I (must be come, must have come) ________ to the world's most beautiful landscape.
4. My move to the West Coast (should not have been, should not have) ________ put off for so long.
5. If you have a dream, you (cannot, should not) ________ leave it unfulfilled.

EXERCISE 47-4

Consulting Chapter 47ESL, select the correct choice from the words in parentheses and write it in the blank.

EXAMPLE We (must have, must) **must** study this afternoon.

1. I have heard that Natasha (should not, cannot) ________ go skiing with us because she has a research paper due.
2. Juan (would have, would have been) ________ granted a fellowship if he had completed his course work.
3. You (ought not have, ought not to have) ________ arrived while the meeting was still in progress.
4. Louise (must be, must have been) ________ sick to miss the party last week.
5. Had I not found a roommate, I (might not have, might not have been) ________ able to afford the rent on my apartment.

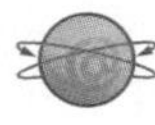

owl.english.purdue.edu/handouts/esl/index.html
English as a Second Language (ESL) Handouts and Resources

www.utoronto.ca/writing/advise.html#5
Some Answers for Writers of English as a Second Language

www.go-ed.com/english/practice/rside/Home.html
Hypertext English Language Practice

www.pacificnet.net/~sperling/quiz/#grammar
ESL Grammar Quiz

www.aitech.ac.jp/~iteslj/quizzes/
Self-Study Quizzes for ESL Students

Usage Glossary

This usage glossary presents the customary manner of using particular words and phrases. *Customary manner*, however, is not as firm in practice as the term implies. Usage standards change. If you think a word's usage might differ from what you read here, consult a dictionary published more recently than this book.

As used here, *informal* indicates that the word or phrase occurs commonly in speech but should be avoided in academic writing. *Nonstandard* indicates that the word or phrase should not be used in standard spoken English and in writing.

Some commonly confused words appear in this Usage Glossary. For an extensive list of homonyms and other commonly confused words, see 22b. Parts of speech, sentence structures, and other grammatical terms mentioned in this Usage Glossary are defined in the Terms Glossary, which follows this Glossary.

a, an Use *a* before words beginning with consonants (***a*** *dog,* ***a*** *grade,* ***a*** *hole*) or consonant sounds (***a o****ne-day sale,* ***a E****uropean*). Most North American English uses *a*, not *an*, with words starting with a pronounced *h*: ***a*** [not *an*] *historical event.*

accept, except *Accept* means "agree to; receive." As a verb, *except* means "exclude, leave out"; as a preposition, *except* means "leaving out": ***Except*** [preposition] *for one detail, the striking workers were ready to* ***accept*** [verb] *management's offer*: *They wanted the no-smoking rule* ***excepted*** [verb] *from the contract.*

advice, advise *Advice,* a noun, means "recommendation"; *advise*, a verb, means recommend; give advice": *My* ***advice*** *is to do what your physician* ***advises***.

affect, effect As a verb, *affect* means "cause a change in; influence" (*affect* also functions as a noun in the discipline of psychology). As a noun, *effect* means "result or conclusion"; as a verb, it means "bring about": *Many groups* ***effected*** [verb] *amplification changes at their concerts after discovering that high decibel levels* ***affected*** [verb] *their hearing. Many fans still choose to ignore sound's harmful* ***effects***.

aggravate, irritate *Aggravate* is used colloquially to mean "irritate." Use *aggravate* to mean "intensify; make worse." Use *irritate* to mean "annoy; make impatient."

all ready, already *Already* means "before; by this time"; *all ready* means "completely prepared": *The ballplayers were* ***all ready*** *and the manager had* ***already*** *given the lineup card to the umpire.*

all right Two words, never one (not *alright*).

all together, altogether *All together* means "in a group, in unison"; *altogether* means "entirely, thoroughly": *The sopranos, altos, and tenors were supposed to sing* ***all together,*** *but their first attempt was not* ***altogether*** *successful.*

allude, elude *Allude* means "refer to indirectly or casually"; *elude* means "escape notice": *They were* ***alluding*** *to budget cuts when they said that "constraints beyond our control enabled the suspect to* ***elude*** *us."*

allusion, illusion An *allusion* is an indirect reference to something; an *illusion* is a false impression or idea.

a lot Informal for *a great deal* or *a great many*; avoid it in academic writing.

a.m., p.m. (or **A.M., P.M.**) Use only with numbers, not as substitutes for the words *morning, afternoon,* or *evening*: *We will arrive in the* ***afternoon*** [not *in the p.m.*].

among, between Use *among* for three or more items and *between* for two items: *My roomates and I discussed* ***among*** *ourselves the choice* ***between*** staying in school and getting full-time jobs.

amount, number Use *amount* for uncountable things (*wealth, work, corn, happiness*); use *number* for countable items: *The* ***amount*** *of rice to cook depends on the* ***number*** *of dinner guests.*

and/or Appropriate in business and legal writing when either or both items it connects can apply: *This process is quicker if you have a modem* ***and/or*** *a fax machine.* Writing in the humanities usually expresses alternatives in words: *This process is quicker if you have a modem, a fax machine, or* ***both***.

anymore Use *anymore* with the meaning "now, any longer" in negations or questions only: *No one knits* ***anymore***. *For positive statements, use an adverb such as now: Summers are so hot* ***now*** [not *anymore*] *that holding yarn is unbearable.*

anyplace Informal for *any place* or *anywhere.*

anyways, anywheres Nonstandard for *anyway, anywhere.*

apt, likely, liable *Apt* and *likely* are used interchangeably. Strictly, *apt* indicates a tendency or inclination: *Allen is* ***apt*** *to leave early on Friday. Likely* indicates a reasonable expectation or greater certainty than *apt*: *I will likely go with him to the party.* (Some authorities in Canada do not allow this use of *likely* and prefer to use *probably* here.) *Liable* denotes legal responsibility or implies unpleasant consequences: *Maggie and Gabriel are* ***liable*** *to be angry if neither of us shows up.*

as, like, as if, as though Use *as*, not *like*, as a subordinating conjunction introducing a clause: *This hamburger tastes good,* **as** [not *like*] *a hamburger should.* Use *as if* (or *as though*), not *like*, to introduce a subjunctive or other conditional clause. *That hamburger tastes* **as if** [not *like*] *it had been grilled all day. As* and *like* can both function as prepositions in comparisons. Use *like* to suggest a point of similarity or an area of resemblance, but not complete likeness, between nouns or pronouns: *Alaska, **like*** [not *as*] *Hawaii, belongs to the United States.* Use *as* to show equivalence: *Beryl acted **as*** [not *like*] *the moderator of our panel.* Also if the items are in prepositional phrases, use *as* even if you are suggesting only one point of similarity: *In Mexico, **as*** [not *like*] *in Argentina, Spanish is the main language.*

assure, ensure, insure *Assure* means "promise, convince"; *ensure* means "make certain or secure," *insure* means "indemnify or guarantee against loss" and is reserved for financial or legal certainty, as in insurance: *The agent **assured** me that he could **insure** my rollerblades but that only I could **ensure** that my elbows and knees would outlast the skates.*

as to Avoid as a substitute for *about: They answered questions **about*** [not *as to*] *their safety record.*

awful, awfully The adjective *awful* means "causing fear." Avoid it as a substitute for intensifiers such as *very* or *extremely*. In academic writing, also avoid the informal usage of the adverb *awfully* for *very* or *extremely.*

a while, awhile As two words, *a while* is an article and a noun that can function as a subject or object. As one word, *awhile* is an adverb; it modifies verbs. In a prepositional phrase, the correct form is *a while: for a while, in a while, after a while.*

bad, badly *Bad* is an adjective; use it after linking verbs. (Remember that verbs like *feel* and *smell* can function as either linking verbs or action verbs.) *Badly* is an adverb and is nonstandard after linking verbs; see 12d: *Farmers feel **bad** because a **bad** drought has **badly** damaged the crops.*

been, being *Been* is the past participle of the verb *be*; *being* is the present participle of *be*, used in the progressive form: *You **are being*** [not *been*] *silly if you think I believe you **have been*** [not *being*] *to Sumatra.*

being as, being that Nonstandard for *because* or *since: We forfeited the game **because*** [not *being as* or *being that*] *our goalie has appendicitis.*

beside, besides *Beside* is a preposition meaning "next to, by the side of": *She stood **beside** the new car, insisting that she would drive.* As a preposition, *besides* means, "other than, in addition to": *No one **besides** her had a driver's licence.* As an adverb, *besides* means "also, moreover": ***Besides,** she owned the car.*

better, had better Used in place of *had better, better* is informal: We **had better** [not *We better*] be careful.

breath, breathe *Breath* is a noun; *breathe* is a verb.

bring, take Use *bring* for movement from a distant place to a near place or to the speaker; use *take* for movement from a near place or from the speaker to a distant place: *If you **bring** a leash when you come to my house, you can **take** Vicious to the vet.*

but, however, yet Use *but, however,* and *yet* alone, not in combination with each other: *The economy is strong, **but*** [not *but yet* or *but however*] *unemployment is high.*

calculate, figure, reckon Informal or regional for *estimate, imagine, expect, think,* and similar words.

can, may *Can* indicates ability or capacity; *may* requests or grants permission. In negations, however, *can* is acceptable in place of *may: You **cannot*** [or *may not*] *leave yet.*

can't hardly, can't scarcely Nonstandard; double negatives.

censor, censure The verb *censor* means "delete objectionable material; judge"; *censure* means "condemn; reprimand officially."

chairman, chairperson, chair Many writers and speakers prefer the gender-neutral terms *chairperson* and *chair* to *chairman*; *chair* is more common than *chairperson.*

choose, chose *Choose* is the simple form of the verb; *chose* is the past-tense form: *I **chose** the movie last week, so you **choose** it tonight.*

cloth, clothe *Cloth* is a noun meaning "fabric"; *clothe* is a verb meaning "cover with garments or fabric; dress."

complement, compliment *Complement* means "bring to perfection, go well with; complete"; *compliment* means "praise; flatter": *They **complimented** us on the design of our experiment, saying that it **complemented** work done twenty years ago.*

conscience, conscious The noun *conscience* means "a sense of right and wrong"; the adjective *conscious* means "being aware or awake."

consensus of opinion Redundant; use *consensus* only.

continual(ly), continuous(ly) *Continual* means "occurring repeatedly"; *continuous* means "going on without interruption": *Intravenous fluids were given **continuously** for three days after surgery; nurses were **continually** hooking up new bottles of saline.*

data Plural of *datum,* a rarely used word. Informal usage commonly treats *data* as singular, but it should be treated as plural in academic writing.

different from, different than *Different from* is preferred for formal writing; *different than* is common in speech.

disinterested, uninterested *Disinterested* means "impartial"; *uninterested* means "indifferent; not concerned with."

emigrate from, immigrate to *Immigrate to* means "enter a country to live there"; *emigrate from* means "leave one country to live in another."

enthused Nonstandard substitution for the adjective *enthusiastic: Are you **enthusiastic*** [not *enthused*] *about seeing a movie?*

etc. Abbreviation for the Latin *et cetera,* meaning "and the rest." For writing in the humanities, avoid in-text use of *etc.*; acceptable substitutes are *and the like, and so on, and so forth.*

everyday, every day The adjective *everyday* means "daily" and modifies nouns; *every day* is an adjective-noun combination that functions as a subject or object: *I missed the bus **every day** last week. Being late for work has become an **everyday** occurrence.*

explicit, implicit *Explicit* means "directly stated or expressed"; *implicit* means "implied, suggested": *The warning on cigarette packs is **explicit:** "Smoking can kill you." The **implicit** message is "Don't smoke."*

fewer, less Use *fewer* for anything that can be counted (with count nouns): ***fewer** dollars, **fewer** fleas, **fewer** haircuts.* Use *less* with collective or other noncount nouns: ***less** money, **less** scratching, **less** hair.*

former, latter When two items are referred to, *former* signifies the first one and *latter* signifies the second. Do not use *former* and *latter* for references to more than two items.

go, say *Go* is nonstandard for *say, says,* or *said: After he stepped on my hand, he* ***said*** [not *he goes*], *"Your hand was in my way."*

good and Nonstandard intensifier: *They were exhausted* [not *good and tired*].

good, well *Good* is an adjective (***good*** *idea*). Using it as an adverb is nonstandard. *Well* is the equivalent adverb: *run* ***well*** [not *run good*].

got, have *Got* is nonstandard in place of *have: What do we* ***have*** [not *got*] *for supper?*

have, of Use *have*, not *of*, after such verbs as *could, should, would, might, must: You should* ***have*** [not *should of*] *called first.*

have got, have got to Avoid using *have got* when *have* alone delivers your meaning: **I have** [not *have got*] *two more sources to read.* Avoid *have got to* for *must: I* ***must*** [not *have got to*] *turn in a preliminary thesis statement by Monday.*

hopefully An adverb meaning "with hope, in a hopeful manner" or "it is hoped that," *hopefully* can modify a verb, an adjective, or another adverb: *They waited* ***hopefully*** *for the plane to land. Hopefully* is commonly used as a sentence modifier with the meaning "I hope," but you should avoid this usage in academic writing: ***I hope*** [not *Hopefully*] *the plane will land safely.*

if, whether Use either *if* or *whether* at the start of a noun clause: *I don't know* ***if*** [or *whether*] *I want to dance with you.* In conditional clauses, use *whether* (or *whether or not*) when alternatives are expressed or implied: *I will dance with you* ***whether or not*** *I like the music.* Similarly: *I will dance with you* ***whether*** *the next song is fast or slow.* Use *if* in a conditional clause that does not express or imply alternatives: ***If*** *you promise not to step on my feet, I will dance with you.*

imply, infer *Imply* means "hint or suggest without stating outright"; *infer* means "draw a conclusion from what is being expressed." A writer or speaker implies; a reader or listener infers: *When the Member of Parliament implied that she might begin taking intensive French lessons, reporters* ***inferred*** *that she had decided to run for leader of her party.*

incredible, incredulous *Incredible* means "extraordinary; not believable"; *incredulous* means "unable or unwilling to believe." A person would be *incredulous* in response to finding something *incredible: Listeners were* ***incredulous*** *as the freed hostages described* ***incredible*** *hardships they had experienced.*

inside of, outside of Nonstandard for *inside* or *outside: She waited* ***outside*** [not *outside of*] *the dormitory.*

irregardless Nonstandard for *regardless.*

is when, is where Avoid these constructions in giving definitions: *Defensive driving* ***involves drivers' staying alert*** [not *is when drivers stay alert*] *to avoid accidents that other drivers might cause.*

its, it's *Its* is a personal pronoun in the possessive case: *The dog buried* ***its*** *bone. It's* is a contraction of *it is* or *it has* (***It's*** *a hot day;* ***it's*** *hotter than usual because the humidity is high.*

kind, sort Use *this* or *that* with these singular nouns; use *these* or *those* with the plural nouns *kinds* and *sorts*. Also, do not use *a* or *an* after *kind of* or *sort of*: *Drink* ***these kinds*** *of fluids* [not *this kind of fluids*] *on* ***this sort*** *of* [not *sort of a*] *day*.

kind of, sort of Informal as adverbs meaning "in a way; somewhat": *The bikers were* ***somewhat*** [not *kind of*] *dehydrated by the time they got back to camp.*

later, latter *Later* means "after some time; subsequently"; *latter* refers to the second of two: *The college library stays open* ***later*** *than the town library; also, the* ***latter*** *is closed on weekends.*

lay, lie *Lay (laying, laid)* means "place or put something, usually on something else" and needs a direct object; *lie (lying, lay, lain)*, meaning "recline," does not take a direct object; see 8f. Substituting *lay* or *lie* is nonstandard: ***Lay*** [not *lie*] *the blanket down, and then* ***lay*** *the babies on it so they can* ***lie*** [not *lay*] *in the shade.*

leave *Leave* means "depart"; *let* means "allow, permit." *Leave* is nonstandard for *let*: ***Let*** [not *leave*] *me use your car tonight.*

lots, lots of, a lot of Informal for *many, much, a great deal:* ***Many*** [not *A lot of*] *bees were in the hive.*

may be, maybe *May be* is a verb phrase; *maybe* is an adverb: Our team ***may be*** tired, but ***maybe*** we can win anyway.

media Plural of *medium*. In most cases, a more specific word is preferable: ***Television reporters*** *offend* [not *The media offend*] *viewers by shouting questions at grief-stricken people.*

morale, moral *Morale* is a noun meaning "a mental state relating to courage, confidence, or enthusiasm." As a noun, *moral* means "ethical lesson implied or taught by a story or event"; as an adjective, *moral* means "ethical": *One* ***moral*** *to draw from corporate downsizings is that overstressed employees suffer from low* ***morale***. *Under such stress, sometimes even employees with high* ***moral*** *standards steal time, supplies, or products from their employers.*

Ms. A woman's title free of reference to marital status, equivalent to *Mr.* for men.

off of Nonstandard for *off:* Don't fall ***off*** [not *off of*] the piano.

OK, O.K., okay All three forms are acceptable in informal writing. In academic writing, try to express meaning more specifically: *The weather was* ***satisfactory*** [not *okay*] *for the race.*

on account of Wordy; use *because* or *because of*: ***Because of*** [not *On account of*] *the high humidity, paper jams occur in the photocopier.*

percent, percentage Use *percent* with specific numbers: *2 percent, 95 percent.* Use *percentage* when descriptive words accompany amounts that have been expressed as percentages: *Less than* ***6 percent*** *of Canada's land is legally protected as wilderness, a smaller* ***percentage*** [not **percent**] *than is commonly believed.*

plus Nonstandard as a substitute for *and: The band will do three concerts in Hungary,* ***and*** [not *plus*] *it will tour Poland for a month*. Nonstandard as well as a substitute for *also, in addition, moreover:* ***Also*** [not *Plus*], *it may be booked to do one concert in Vienna.*

precede, proceed *Precede* means "go before"; *proceed* means "advance, go on, undertake, carry on": ***Preceded*** *by elephants and tigers, the clowns* ***proceeded*** *into the tent.*

pretty Informal qualifying word; use *rather, quite, somewhat,* or *very* in academic writing: *The flu epidemic was* ***quite*** [not *pretty*] *severe.*

principal, principle *Principle* means "a basic truth or rule." As a noun, *principal* means "chief person; main or original amount"; as an adjective, *principal* means "most important": "*During assembly, the* ***principal*** *said "****A principal*** *value in this society is the* ***principle*** *of free speech.*

raise, rise *Raise* (*raised, raising*) needs a direct object; *rise* (*rose, risen, rising*) does not take a direct object. Using these verbs interchangeably is nonstandard: *What if the mob* ***rises*** [not *raises*] up and runs amok?

rarely ever Informal; in academic writing, use *rarely* or *hardly ever: The groups* ***rarely*** [not *rarely ever*] *meet, so they* ***hardly ever*** [not *rarely ever*] *interact.*

real, really Nonstandard intensifiers.

reason is because Redundant; use *reason is that: One* ***reason*** *we moved away* ***is that*** [not *is because*] *we changed jobs.*

reason why Redundant; use either *reason* or *why*: *I still do not know the* ***reason*** *that* [or *I still do not know* ***why***, not *the reason why*] they left home.

regarding, in regard to, with regard to Too stiff or wordy for most writing purposes; use *about, concerning,* or *for: What should I do* ***about*** [not *with regard to*] dropping this course?

respective, respectively The adjective *respective* relates the noun it modifies to two or more individual persons or things; the adverb *respectively* refers to a second set of items in a sequence established by a preceding set of items: *After the fire drill, Dr. Pan and Dr. Moll returned to their* ***respective*** *offices, on the second and third floors,* ***respectively***. (Dr. Pan has an office on the second floor; Dr. Moll has an office on the third floor.) Do not confuse *respective* and *respectively* with *respectful* and *respectfully*, which refer to showing regard for or honour to something or someone.

shall, will *Shall* was once used with *I* or *we* for future-tense verbs, and *will* was used with all other persons (*We* ***shall*** *leave Monday, and he* ***will*** *leave Thursday*); but *will* is commonly used for all persons now. Similarly, distinctions were once made between *shall* and *should. Should* is much more common with all persons now, although *shall* is used about as often as *should* in questions asking what to do: ***Shall*** [or *Should*] *I get your jacket?*

should, would Use *should* to express condition or obligation: *If you* ***should*** *see them, tell them that they* ***should*** *practise what they preach.* Use *would* to express wishes, conditions, or habitual actions: *If you* ***would*** *buy a VCR for me, I* ***would*** *tape all the football games for you.*

sometime, sometimes, some time The adverb *sometime* means "at an unspecified time"; the adverb *sometimes* means "now and then"; *some time* is an adjective-noun combination meaning "an amount or span of time": ***Sometime*** *next year we have to take qualifying exams. I* ***sometimes*** *worry about finding* ***some time*** *to study for them.*

stationary, stationery *Stationary* means "not moving"; *stationery* refers to paper and related writing products.

such Informal intensifier; avoid it in academic writing unless it precedes a noun introducing a *that* clause: *That play got terrible* [not *such bad*] *reviews. It was* ***such*** *a dull drama that it closed after one performance.*

supposed to, used to The final *d* is essential: *We were* ***supposed to*** [not *suppose to*] *leave early. I* ***used to*** [not *use to*] *wake up as soon as the alarm rang.*

sure Nonstandard for *surely* or *certainly: I was* ***certainly*** [not *sure*] *surprised at the results.*

than, then *Than* indicates comparison: *One is smaller* ***than*** *two. Then* relates to time: *He tripped and* ***then*** *fell.*

that, which Use *that* with restrictive (essential) clauses only; *which* can be used with both restrictive and nonrestrictive clauses, but many writers reserve *which* for nonrestrictive clauses only. *The house* ***that*** *Jack built is on Beanstalk Street,* ***which*** [not *that*] *runs past the reservoir.*

their, there, they're *Their* is possessive; *there* means "in that place" or is part of an expletive; *they're* is a contraction of *they are:* ***They're*** *going to* ***their*** *accounting class in the building* ***there*** *behind the library.* ***There*** *are twelve sections of Accounting 101.*

theirself, theirselves, themself Nonstandard for *themselves.*

thusly Nonstandard for *thus.*

till, until Both are acceptable; except in expressive writing, avoid the contracted form *'til* in academic writing.

to, too, two *To* is a preposition; *too* is an adverb meaning "also; more than enough"; *two* is the number: *When you go* ***to*** *Prince Edward Island, visit Green Gables. Go* ***to*** *one of the seaside restaurants for dinner,* ***too****. It won't be* ***too*** *expensive, because* ***two*** *people can share a lobster.*

toward, towards Both are acceptable; *toward* is somewhat more common in North America.

try and, sure and Nonstandard for *try to* and *sure to: If you* ***try to*** [not *try and*] *find a summer job, be* ***sure to*** [not *sure and*] *list on your résumé all the software programs you can use.*

unique An absolute adjective; use it without *more, most,* or other qualifiers, or use a different adjective: *Solar heating is* ***uncommon*** [not *rather unique*] *in northern latitudes. In only one home in Vermont, a* ***unique*** [not *very unique*] *heating system uses hydrogen for fuel.*

wait on Informal for *wait for*; appropriate in the context of persons giving service to others: *I had to* ***wait*** *a half hour for that clerk to* ***wait on*** *me.*

where Nonstandard for *that: I read in the newspaper* ***that*** [not *where*] *Michael Jordan might return to basketball again.*

-wise The suffix *-wise* means "in a manner, direction, or position." Be careful not to attach *-wise* indiscriminately to create new words rather than using good words that already exist. When in doubt, check your dictionary to see that a *-wise* word you want to use is acceptable.

your, you're *Your* is possessive; *you're* is the contraction of *you are:* ***You're*** *generous to share* ***your*** *Internet time with us.*

Terms Glossary

This glossary defines important terms used in this handbook, including the ones marked with a degree symbol (°). Many of these glossary entries end with parenthetical references to the handbook section(s) or chapters where the specific term is most fully discussed.

absolute adjective An adjective that cannot express degrees of intensity and so has no comparative and superlative forms: *unique, perfect.* See also *positive, comparative, superlative.* (12e)

absolute phrase A phrase containing a subject and a participle and modifying an entire sentence: ***The semester*** [subject] ***being*** [present participle of *be*] ***over,*** *the campus looks deserted.* (7n)

abstract noun A noun that names things not knowable through the five senses: *idea, respect.* (7a)

active voice An attribute of verbs showing that the action or condition expressed in the verb is done by the subject, in contrast with the passive voice, which conveys that the action or condition of the verb is done to the subject (8n and 8o)

adjective A word that describes or limits (modifies) a noun, a pronoun or a word group functioning as a noun: *silly, three.* (12).

adjective clause A dependent clause also known as a *relative clause.* An adjective clause modifies a preceding noun or pronoun and begins with a relative word (such as *who, which, that,* or *where)* that relates the clause to the noun or pronoun it modifies. Also see *clause.* (7o-2)

adverb A word that describes or limits (modifies) verbs, adjectives, other adverbs, phrases, or clauses: *loudly, very, nevertheless, there.*

adverb clause A dependent clause beginning with a subordinating conjunction that establishes the relationship in meaning between the adverb clause and its independent clause. An adverb clause modifies the independent clause's verb or the entire independent clause. Also see *clause, conjunction.* (7o-2)

agreement The required match of number and person between a subject and verb or a pronoun and antecedent. A pronoun that expresses gender must match its antecedent in gender also. (11)

analogy An explanation of the unfamiliar in terms of the familiar. Like a simile, an analogy compares things not normally associated with each other; but unlike a simile, an analogy does not use *like* or *as* in making the comparison. Analogy is also a rhetorical strategy for developing paragraphs. (21c, 4f-8)

analysis A process of critical thinking that divides a whole into its component parts in order to understand how the parts interrelate. Sometimes called *division,* analysis is also a rhetorical strategy for developing paragraphs. (5, 4f-6)

antecedent The noun or pronoun to which a pronoun refers. (10, 11m–11r)

antonym A word opposite in meaning to another word. (20a)

APA style See *documentation style.*

appositive A word or group of words that renames a preceding noun or noun phrase: *my favorite month,* ***October.*** (7m-3)

argument A rhetorical attempt to persuade others to agree with a position about a topic open to debate. (1b, 6)

articles Also called *determiners* or *noun markers,* articles are the words *a, an,* and *the. A* and *an* are indefinite articles, and *the* is a definite article; also see *determiner.* (7a, 42)

assertion A statement. In developing a thesis statement, an assertion is a sentence that makes a statement and expresses a point of view about a topic. (2n)

audience The readers to whom a piece of writing is directed. (1c)

auxiliary verb Also known as a *helping verb,* an auxiliary verb is a form of *be, do, have, can, may, will,* and others, that combines with a main verb to help it express tense, mood, and voice. Also see *modal auxiliary verb.* (8e)

base form See *simple form.*

bibliography A list of information about sources. (34)

brainstorming Listing all ideas that come to mind on a topic, and then grouping the ideas by patterns that emerge. (2g)

case The form of a noun or pronoun in a specific context that shows whether it is functioning as a subject, an object, or a possessive. In modern English, nouns change form in the possessive case only (*city* = form for subjective and objective cases; *city's* = possessive-case form). Also see *pronoun case.* (9)

cause and effect The relationship between outcomes (effects) and the reasons for them (causes). Cause-and-effect analysis is a rhetorical strategy for developing paragraphs. (5i, 5k, 4f-9)

chronological order Also called *time order,* an arrangement of information according to time sequence; an organizing strategy for sentences, paragraphs, and longer pieces of writing. (4e)

citation Information to identify a source referred to in a piece of writing. See also *documentation.* (31, 34)

clause A group of words containing a subject and a predicate. A clause that delivers full meaning is called an *independent* (or *main*) *clause.* A clause that lacks full meaning by itself is called a *dependent* (or *subordinate*) clause. See also *adjective clause, adverb clause, nonrestrictive element, noun clause, restrictive element.* (7o)

cliché An overused, worn-out phrase that has lost its capacity to communicate effectively: *smooth as silk, ripe old age.* (21d)

climactic order Sometimes called *emphatic order,* climactic order is an arrangement of ideas or information from least important to most important. (4e)

clustering See *mapping.*

coherence The clear progression from one idea to another using transitional expressions, pronouns, selective repetition, and/or parallelism to make connections between ideas. (4d)

collective noun A noun that names a group of people or things: *family, team.* (11h, 11r)

comma fault See *comma splice.*

comma splice The error that occurs when only a comma connects two independent clauses. (14)

common noun A noun that names a general group, place, person, or thing: *dog, house.* (7a)

comparative The form of a descriptive adjective or adverb that reflects a different degree of intensity between two: *blue, less blue; more easily, less easily.* See also *positive, superlative.* (12e)

comparison and contrast A rhetorical strategy for organizing and developing paragraphs by discussing a subject's similarities (comparison) and differences (contrast). (4f-7)

complement An element after a verb that completes the predicate, such as a direct object after an action verb or a noun or adjective after a linking verb. Also *see object complement, predicate adjective, predicate nominative, subject complement.*

complete predicate See *predicate.*

complete subject See *subject.*

complex sentence See *sentence types.*

compound predicate See *predicate.*

compound sentence See *sentence types.*

compound subject See *subject.*

concrete noun A noun naming things that can be seen, touched, heard, smelled, or tasted: *smoke, sidewalk.* (7a)

conjunction A word that connects or otherwise establishes a relationship between two or more words, phrases, or clauses. Also see *coordinating conjunction, correlative conjunction,* and *subordinating conjunction.*

coordinating conjunction A conjunction that joins two or more grammatically equivalent structures: *and, or, for, nor, but, so, yet.*

coordination The use of grammatically equivalent forms to show a balance or sequence of ideas. (17a–17d)

correlative conjunction A pair of words that joins equivalent grammatical structures, including *both ... and, either ... or, neither ... nor, not only ... but.*

COS See *documentation style.*

count noun A noun that names items that can be counted: *radio, street, idea, fingernail.* (42a–42b, 43a–43b)

critical response Formally, an essay summarizing a source's central point or main idea and then presenting the writer's synthesized reactions in response. (5g)

cumulative sentence The most common structure for a sentence, with the subject and verb first, followed by modifiers adding details; also called a *loose sentence.* (19e)

dangling modifier A modifier that attaches its meaning illogically, either because it is closer to another noun or pronoun than to its true subject or because its true subject is not expressed in the sentence. (15c)

declarative sentence A sentence that makes a statement: *Sky diving is exciting.* Also see *exclamatory sentence, imperative sentence, interrogative sentence.*

deduction The process of reasoning from general claims to a specific instance. (5j-2)

definite article See *articles.*

demonstrative pronoun A pronoun that points out the antecedent: *this, these, that, those.*

denotation The dictionary definition of a word. (20a, 20b-1)

dependent clause A clause that cannot stand alone as an independent grammatical unit. See also *adjective clause, adverb clause, noun clause.*

descriptive adjective An adjective that describes the condition or properties of the noun it modifies and (except for a very few such as *dead* and *unique*) has comparative and superlative forms: *flat, flatter, flattest.* See also *absolute adjective*

descriptive adverb An adverb that describes the condition of properties of whatever it modifies and has comparative and superlative forms: *happily, more happily, most happily.*

determiner A word or word group, traditionally identified as an adjective, that limits a noun by telling "how much" or "how many" about it. Also called *expression of quantity, limiting adjective,* or *noun markers.* (42b, 42)

diction Word choice. (20, 21)

direct address Words naming a person or group being spoken to; written words of direct address are set off by commas: *The answer,* ***my friends*****,** *lies with you. Go with them,* ***Gene.*** (24f)

direct discourse In writing, words that repeat speech or conversation exactly, and so are enclosed in quotation marks.

direct object A noun or pronoun or group of words functioning as a noun that receives the action (completes the meaning) of a transitive verb. (7l)

direct question A sentence that asks a question and ends with a question mark: *Are you going?*

direct quotation See *quotation.*

documentation The acknowledgment of someone else's words and ideas used in any piece of writing by giving full and accurate information about the person whose words were used and where those words were found; for

example, for a print source, documentation usually includes author name(s), title, place and date of publication, and related information. (31, 34)

documentation style Any of various systems for providing information about the source of words, information, and ideas quoted, paraphrased, or summarized from some source other than the writer. Documentation styles discussed in this handbook are MLA, APA, CM, CBE, and COS. (34)

double negative A nonstandard negation using two negative modifiers, rather than one. (12c)

drafting A part of the writing process in which writers compose ideas in sentences and paragraphs. (3b)

edited English English language use that conforms to established rules of grammar, sentence structure, punctuation, and spelling; also called *standard English*. (21a-2)

editing A part of the writing process in which writers check the technical correctness of their grammar, spelling, punctuation, and mechanics. (3d)

elliptical construction A sentence structure that deliberately omits words expressed elsewhere or that can be inferred from the context.

euphemism Language that attempts to blunt certain realities by speaking of them in "nice" or "tactful" words. (21e-3)

evidence Facts, data, examples, and opinions of others used to support assertions and conclusions.

exclamatory sentence A sentence beginning with *What* or *How* that expresses strong feeling: *What a ridiculous statement!*

expletive The phrase *there is (are), there was (were), it is,* or *it was* at the beginning of a clause, changing structure and postponing the subject: ***It is*** *Mars that we hope to reach* (compare *We hope to reach Mars).*

expository writing See *informative writing.*

expression of quantity See *determiner.*

faulty predication A grammatically illogical combination of subject and predicate. (15d-2)

finite verb A verb form that shows tense, mood, voice, person, and number while expressing an action, occurrence, or state of being.

first person See *person.*

freewriting Writing nonstop for a specified time in order to generate ideas by free association of thoughts. Focused freewriting may start with a set topic or may build on one sentence taken from earlier freewriting. (2f)

fused sentence See *run-together (run-on) sentence.*

future perfect progressive tense The form of the future perfect tense that describes an action or condition ongoing until some specific future time: *they will have been talking.*

future perfect tense The tense indicating that an action will have been completed or a condition will have ended by a specified point in the future: *they will have talked.*

future progressive tense The form of the future tense showing that a future action will continue for some time: *they will be talking.*

future tense The form of a verb, made with the simple form and either *shall* or *will,* expressing an action yet to be taken or a condition not yet experienced: *they will talk.*

gender Concerning languages, the classification of words as masculine, feminine, or neutral. In English, a few pronouns show changes in gender in third-person singular: *he, him, his; she, her, hers; it, its its.* A few nouns naming roles change form to show gender difference: *prince, princess,* for example. (11q, 21b)

gender-neutral language See *sexist language.*

gerund A present participle functioning as a noun: ***Walking*** *is a good exercise.* Also see *verbal.*

gerund phrase A gerund, its modifiers, and/or object(s), which functions as a subject or an object. (7n)

helping verb See *auxiliary verb.*

homonyms Words spelled differently that sound alike: *to, too, two.* (22b)

idiom A word, phrase, or other construction that has a different meaning from its usual meaning: *He lost his head. She hit the ceiling.*

illogical predication See *faulty predication.*

imperative mood The mood that expresses commands and direct requests, using the simple form of the verb and often implying but not expressing the subject, *you: Go.* (8l)

imperative sentence A sentence that gives a command: *Go to the corner and buy me a newspaper.*

indefinite article See *articles, determiner.*

indefinite pronoun A pronoun such as *all, anyone, each,* and *others,* that refers to a nonspecific person or thing. (11p)

independent clause A clause that can stand alone as an independent grammatical unit. (7o-1)

indicative mood The mood of verbs used for statements about real things, or highly likely ones: *I think Grace is arriving today.* (8l)

indirect discourse Reported speech or conversation that does not use the exact structure of the original and so is not enclosed in quotation marks. (15a-4)

indirect object A noun or pronoun or group of words functioning as a noun that tells to whom or for whom the action expressed by a transitive verb was done. (7l)

indirect question A sentence that reports a question and ends with a period: *I asked if you are going.*

indirect quotation See *quotation.*

induction The reasoning process of arriving at general principles from particular facts or instances. (5j-1)

infinitive A verbal made of the simple form of a verb and usually, but not always, *to,* that functions as a noun, adjective, or adverb.

infinitive phrase An infinitive, its modifiers, and/or object. It functions as a noun, adjective, or adverb.

informal language Word choice that creates a tone appropriate for casual writing or speaking. (21a-1)

informative writing Writing that gives information and, when necessary, explains it; also known as *expository writing.* (1b)

intensive pronoun A pronoun that ends in *-self* and that intensifies its antecedent: *Vida* ***himself*** *argued against it.*

interjection An emotion-conveying word that is treated as a sentence, starting with a capital letter and ending with an exclamation point or a period: *Oh! Ouch!*

interrogative pronoun A pronoun such as *whose* or *what,* that implies a question: ***Who*** *called?*

interrogative sentence A sentence that asks a direct question: *Did you see that?*

intransitive verb A verb that does not take a direct object. (8f)

invention techniques Ways of gathering ideas for writing.

inverted word order In contrast to standard order, the main verb or an auxiliary verb comes before the subject in inverted word order. Most questions and some exclamations use inverted word order.

irony Words used to imply the opposite of their usual meaning. (21c)

irregular verb A verb that forms the past tense and past participle in some way other than by adding *-ed* or *-d.* (8d)

jargon A particular field's or group's specialized vocabulary that a general reader is unlikely to understand. (21e-2)

levels of formality The degree of formality reflected by word choice and sentence structure. A highly formal level is used for certain ceremonial and other occasions when stylistic flourishes are appropriate. A medium level, which is neither too formal nor too casual, is acceptable for most academic writing. (21a-1)

levels of generality In grouping information or ideas, moving from the most general to the most specific. (2l)

limiting adjective See *determiner.*

linking verb A main verb that connects a subject with a subject complement that renames or describes the subject. Linking verbs convey a state of being, relate to the senses, or indicate a condition. (8a)

logical fallacies Flaws in reasoning that lead to illogical statements (5k).

loose sentence See *cumulative sentence.*

main clause See *independent clause.*

main verb A verb that expresses action, occurrence, or state of being and that shows mood, tense, voice, number, and person. (8)

mapping An invention technique based on thinking about a topic and its increasingly specific subdivisions; also known as *clustering* and *webbing.* (2i)

mechanics Conventions regarding the use of capital letters, italics, abbreviations, and numbers. (30)

metaphor A comparison implying similarity between two things. A metaphor does not use words such as *like* or *as*, which are used in a simile and which make a comparison explicit: *a mop of hair* (compare the simile *hair like a mop*). (21c)

misplaced modifier Describing or limiting words that are wrongly positioned in a sentence so that their message is either illogical or relates to the wrong word(s). (15b)

mixed construction A sentence that unintentionally changes from one grammatical structure to another, incompatible one, thus garbling meaning. (15d)

mixed metaphors Incongruously combined images. (21c)

MLA style See *documentation style.*

modal auxiliary verbs A group of auxiliary verbs that add information such as a sense of needing, wanting, or having to do something or a sense of possibility, likelihood, obligation, permission, or ability. (47)

modifier A word or group of words functioning as an adjective or adverb to describe or limit another word or word group. (12, 19e)

mood The attribute of verbs showing a speaker's or writer's attitude toward the action by the way verbs are used. English has three moods: imperative, indicative, and subjunctive. Also see *imperative mood, indicative mood, subjunctive mood.* (8l and 8m)

noncount noun A noun that names "uncountable" things: *water, time.* (42, 43)

nonessential element See *nonrestrictive element.*

nonrestrictive element A descriptive word, phrase, or dependent clause that provides information not essential to understanding the basic message of the element it modifies and so is set off by commas. (24e)

nonsexist language See *sexist language.*

nonstandard Language usage other than edited English. Also see *edited English* (21a-2)

noun A word that names a person, place, thing, or idea. Nouns function as subjects, objects, or complements.

noun clause A dependent clause that functions as a subject, object, or complement. (7o-2)

noun complement See *complement.*

noun determiner See *determiner.*

noun phrase A noun and its modifiers functioning as a subject, object, or complement. (7n)

number The attribute of some words indicating whether they refer to one (singular) or more than one (plural).

object A noun, pronoun, or group of words functioning as a noun or pronoun that receives the action of a verb (direct object); tells to whom or for whom something is done (indirect object); or completes the meaning of a preposition (object of a preposition). (7l)

object complement A noun or adjective renaming or describing a direct object after a few verbs including *call, consider, name, elect,* and *think: I call joggers* ***fanatics***.

objective case The case of a noun or pronoun functioning as a direct or indirect object or object of a preposition or of a verbal. A few pronouns change form to show case *(him, her, whom).* Also see *case.* (9)

paragraph A group of sentences that work together to develop a unit of thought. (4)

paragraph development Using specific, concrete details (RENNS) to support a generalization in a paragraph; rhetorical strategies for arranging and organizing paragraphs. (4f)

parallelism The use of equivalent grammatical forms or matching sentence structures to express equivalent ideas. (18)

paraphrase A restatement of someone else's ideas in language and sentence structure different from those of the original. (31d)

parenthetical documentation See *parenthetical reference.*

parenthetical reference Information enclosed in parentheses following quoted, paraphrased, or summarized material from a source to alert readers to the use of material from a specific source. Parenthetical references function together with a list of bibliographic information about each source used in a paper to document the writer's use of sources. (34c-1, 34d-1)

participial phrase A phrase that contains a present participle or a past participle and any modifiers and that functions as an adjective. See also *verbal.*

passive construction See *passive voice.*

passive voice The form of a verb in which the subject is acted upon; if the subject is mentioned in the sentence, it usually appears as the object of the preposition *by: I was frightened by the thunder* (compare the active-voice version *The thunder frightened me*). The passive voice emphasizes the action, in contrast to the active voice, which emphasizes the doer of the action. (8n, 8o)

past participle The third principal part of a verb, formed in regular verbs, like the past tense, by adding *-d* or *-ed* to the simple form. In irregular verbs, it often differs from the simple form and the past tense: *break, broke,* ***broken***. (8b)

past perfect progressive tense The past perfect tense form that describes an ongoing condition in the past that has been ended by something stated in the sentence: *I had been talking.* (8j)

past perfect tense The tense that describes a condition or action that started in the past, continued for a while, and then ended in the past: *I had talked.*

past progressive tense The past tense form that shows the continuing nature of a past action: *I was talking.* (8j)

past tense form The second principal part of a verb, in regular verbs formed by adding *-ed* or *-d* to the simple form. In irregular verbs, the past tense may change in several ways from the simple form.

perfect tenses The three tenses—the present perfect (*I have talked*), the past perfect, (*I had talked*) and the future perfect (*I will have talked*) that help to show complex time relationships between two clauses. (8i)

periodic sentence A sentence that begins with modifiers and ends with the independent clause, thus postponing the main idea—and the emphasis—for the end; also called a *climactic sentence.* (19e)

person The attribute of nouns and pronouns showing who or what acts or experiences an action. First person is the one speaking (*I, we*); second person is the one being spoken to (*you, you*); and third person is the person or thing spoken about (*he, she, it; they*). All nouns are third person.

personal pronoun A pronoun that refers to people or things, such as *I, you, them, it.*)

persuasive writing Writing that seeks to convince the reader about a matter of opinion. (1b)

phrasal verbs A verb that combines with one or more prepositions to deliver its meaning: *ask out, look into.* (45c)

phrase A group of related words that does not contain a subject and predicate and thus cannot stand alone as an independent grammatical unit. A phrase functions as a noun, verb, or modifier. (7n)

plagiarism A writer's presenting another person's words or ideas without giving credit to that person. Documentation systems allow writers to give proper credit to sources in ways recognized by scholarly communities. Plagiarism is a serious offence, a form of intellectual dishonesty that can lead to course failure or expulsion. (31)

planning An early part of the writing process in which writers gather ideas. Along with shaping, planning is sometimes called *prewriting.* (2)

plural See *number.*

positive The form of an adjective or adverb when no comparison is being expressed: *blue, easily.* Also see *comparative, superlative.* (12e)

possessive case The case of a noun or pronoun that shows ownership or possession. Also see *case.* (9, 27a–27d)

predicate The part of a sentence that contains the verb and tells what the subject is doing or experiencing or what is being done to the subject. A *simple predicate* contains only the main verb and any auxiliary verb(s). A *complete predicate* contains the verb and all its modifiers, objects, and other related words. A *compound predicate* contains two or more verbs and their objects and modifiers, if any. (7k)

predicate adjective An adjective used as a subject complement: *That tree is **leafy***.

predicate nominative A noun or pronoun used as a subject complement: *That tree is a **maple***.

premises In a deductive argument expressed as a syllogism, statements presenting the conditions of the argument from which the conclusion must follow. (5j)

preposition A word that conveys a relationship, often of space or time, between the noun or pronoun following it and other words in the sentence. The noun or pronoun following a preposition is called its *object.* (7g, 45)

prepositional phrase See *phrase, preposition.*

present participle A verb's *-ing* form. Used with auxiliary verbs, present participles function as main verbs. Used without auxiliary verbs, present participles function as nouns or adjectives. (8b, 7d)

present perfect progressive tense The present perfect tense form that describes something ongoing in the past that is likely to continue into the future. *I have been talking.*

present perfect tense The tense indicating that an action or its effects, begun or perhaps completed in the past, continue into the present: *I had talked.*

present progressive tense The present tense form of the verb that indicates something taking place at the time it is written or spoken about: *I am talking.*

present tense The tense that describes what is happening, what is true at the moment, and what is consistently true. It uses the simple form (*I **talk***) and the *-s* form in the third person singular, (*he, she it **talks***). (8h)

prewriting A term for all activities in the writing process before drafting. See *planning* and *shaping.* (2)

primary sources "Firsthand" work: write-ups of experiments and observations by the researchers who conducted them; taped accounts, interviews, and newspaper accounts by direct observers; autobiographies, diaries, and journals; expressive works (poems, plays, fiction, essays); also known as *primary evidence.* Also see *secondary source.* (5h, 32g)

progressive forms Verb forms made in all tenses with the present participle and forms of the verb ***be*** as an auxiliary. Progressive forms show that an action, occurrence, or state of being is ongoing. (8j)

pronoun A word that takes the place of a noun and functions in the same ways that nouns do. Types of pronouns are *demonstrative, indefinite, intensive, interrogative, personal, reciprocal, reflexive,* and *relative.* The word (or words) a pronoun replaces is called its *antecedent.* (9, 10, 11m–11r)

pronoun–antecedent agreement The match in expressing number and person, and for personal pronouns, gender as well, required between a pronoun and its antecedent. (11m–11r)

pronoun case The way a pronoun changes form to reflect its use as the agent of action (subjective case), the thing being acted upon (objective case), or the thing showing ownership (possessive case). (9)

pronoun reference The relationship between a pronoun and its antecedent. (10)

proofreading Reading a final draft to find and correct any spelling or mechanics mistakes, typing errors, or handwriting illegibility; the final step of the writing process. (3e)

proper adjective An adjective formed from a proper noun: *Victorian, Canadian.*

proper noun A noun that names specific people, places, or things and is always capitalized: *Moose Jaw, Eli Mandel, Corvette.*

purpose The goal or aim of a piece of writing: to express oneself, to provide information, to persuade, or to create a literary work. (1b)

quotation Repeating or reporting another person's words. *Direct quotation* repeats another's words exactly and encloses them in quotation marks. *Indirect quotation* reports another's words without quotation marks except around any words repeated exactly from the source. Both direct and indirect quotation require documentation of the source to avoid plagiarism. See also *indirect discourse*. (28a, 31c)

reciprocal pronoun The pronouns *each other* and *one another* referring to individual parts of a plural antecedent: *We respect* ***each other***.

References In many documentation styles, including APA, the title of a list of sources cited in a research paper or other written work. (34d, 34e, 34f)

reflexive pronoun A pronoun that ends in *-self* and that reflects back to its antecedent: *They claim to support* ***themselves***.

regular verb A verb that forms its past tense and past participle by adding *-ed* or *-d* to the simple form. Most English verbs are regular. (8d)

relative adverb An adverb that introduces an adjective clause: *The lot* ***where*** *I usually park my car was full.*

relative clause See *adjective clause.*

relative pronoun A pronoun such as *who, which, that, what,* and *whoever,* that introduces an adjective clause or sometimes a noun clause.

restrictive clause A dependent clause that gives information necessary to distinguish it from others in the same category. In contrast to a nonrestrictive clause, a restrictive clause is not set off with commas. (24e)

restrictive element A word, phrase, or dependent clause that provides information essential to the understanding of the element it modifies. In contrast to a nonrestrictive element, a restrictive element is not set off with commas. (24e)

revision A part of the writing process in which writers evaluate their rough drafts and, based on their decisions, rewrite by adding, cutting, replacing, moving, and often totally recasting material. (3c)

rhetoric The area of discourse that focuses on arrangement of ideas and choice of words as a reflection of the writer's purpose and sense of audience. (4)

Rogerian argument An argument technique adapted from the principles of communication developed by psychologist Carl Rogers. (6c)

run-together (run-on) sentence The error of running independent clauses together without the required punctuation that marks them as complete units. (14)

secondary source A source that reports, analyzes, discusses, reviews, or otherwise deals with the work of someone else, as opposed to a primary source, which is someone's original work or first-hand report. A reliable secondary source should be the work of a person with appropriate credentials, should appear in a respected publication or other medium, should be current, and should be well reasoned. (5h, 32g)

second person See *person.*

sentence See *sentence types.*

sentence fragment A portion of a sentence that is punctuated as though it were a complete sentence. (13)

sentence types A grammatical classification of sentences by the kinds of clauses they contain. A *simple sentence* consists of one independent clause. A *complex sentence* contains one independent clause and one or more dependent clauses. A *compound sentence* contains two or more independent clauses joined by a coordinating conjunction. A *compound-complex sentence* contains at least two independent clauses and one or more dependent clauses. Sentences are also classified by their grammatical function; see *declarative sentence, exclamatory sentence, imperative sentence,* and *interrogative sentence.* (7j, 7p)

sexist language Language that unfairly assigns roles or characteristics to people on the basis of gender. Language that avoids gender stereotyping is called *nonsexist language* or *gender-neutral language.* (11q, 21b)

shaping An early part of the writing process in which writers consider ways to organize their material. Along with planning, shaping is sometimes called *prewriting.* (2)

simile A comparison, using *like, or, as,* between otherwise dissimilar things. (21c)

simple form The form of the verb that shows action, occurrence, or state of being taking place in the present. It is used in the singular for first and second person and in the plural for first, second, and third person. It is also the first principal part of a verb. The simple form is also known as the *dictionary form* or *base form.* (8b)

simple predicate See *predicate.*

simple sentence See *sentence types.*

simple subject See *subject.*

simple tenses The present, past, and future tenses, which divide time into present, past, and future. (8g)

singular See *number.*

slang Coined words and new meanings for existing words, which quickly pass in and out of use; not appropriate for most academic writing. (21a-3)

source A book, article, document, other work, or person providing information. (1e, 31, 32, 33, 34)

split infinitive One or more words coming between the two words of an infinitive. (15b-2)

standard English See *edited English.*

standard word order The most common order for words in English sentences: the subject comes before the predicate.

subject The word or group of words in a sentence that acts, is acted upon, or is described by the verb. A *simple subject* includes only the noun or pronoun. A *complete subject* includes the noun or pronoun and all its modifiers. A *compound subject* includes two or more nouns or pronouns and their modifiers. (7k)

subject complement A noun or adjective that follows a linking verb, renaming or describing the subject of the sentence; also called a *predicate nominative.* (7m-1)

subjective case The case of the pronoun functioning as subject. Also see *case.* (9)

subject–verb agreement The required match between a subject and verb in expressing number and person. (11a–11l)

subjunctive mood The verb mood that expresses wishes, recommendations, indirect requests, speculations, and conditional statements: *I wish you were here.* (8m)

subordinate clause See *dependent clause.*

subordinating conjunction A conjunction that introduces an adverbial clause and expresses a relationship between the idea in it and the idea in the independent clause. (7h)

subordination The use of grammatical structures to reflect the relative importance of ideas. A sentence with logically subordinated information expresses the most important information in the independent clause and less important information in dependent clauses or phrases. (17e–17i)

summary An extraction of the main message or central point of a passage or other discourse; a critical thinking activity preceding synthesis. (5f, 31e)

superlative The form of the adjective or adverb that expresses comparison among three or more things: *bluest, least blue; most easily, least easily.* (12e)

syllogism The structure of a deductive argument expressed in two premises and a conclusion. The *first premise* is a generalized assumption or statement of fact. The *second premise* is a different assumption or statement of fact based on evidence. The *conclusion* is also a specific instance that follows logically from the premises. (5j)

synonym A word that is close in meaning to another word. (20a-1)

synthesis A component of critical thinking in which material that has been summarized, analyzed, and interpreted is connected to what is already known (one's prior knowledge). (5b, 5f)

tag question An inverted verb-pronoun combination added to the end of a sentence, creating a question, that "asks" the audience to agree with the assertion in the first part of the sentence: *You know what a tag question is,* ***don't you?*** A tag question is set off from the rest of the sentence with a comma. (24f)

tag sentence See *tag question.*

tense The time at which the action of the verb occurs: in the past, present, or future. (8g–8k)

tense sequence In sentences that have more than one clause, the accurate matching of verbs to reflect the logical time relationships. (8k)

thesis statement A statement of an essay's central theme that makes clear the main idea, the writer's purpose, the focus of the topic, and perhaps the organizational pattern. (2n)

third person See *person.*

tone The writer's attitude toward his or her material and reader, especially as reflected by word choice. (1d)

topic The subject of discourse.

topic sentence The sentence that expresses the main idea of a paragraph. (4b)

Toulmin model for argument A model that defines the essential parts of an argument as the *claim* (or *main point*), the *support* (or *evidence*), and the *warrants* (or *assumptions behind the main point*). (6e)

transition The connection of one idea to another in discourse. Useful strategies for creating transitions include transitional expressions, parallelism, and planned repetition of key words and phrases. (4d)

transitional expressions Words and phrases that signal connections among ideas and create coherence. (4d-1)

transitive verb A verb that must be followed by a direct object. (8f)

unity The clear and logical relationship between the main idea of a paragraph and the evidence supporting the main idea. (4b)

usage A customary way of using language. (21, Usage Glossary)

valid A term applied to a deductive argument when the conclusion follows logically from the premises. Validity describes the structure of an argument, not its truth. (5j-2)

verb A class of words that shows action or occurrence or describes a state of being. Verbs change form to show time (tense), attitude (mood), and role of the subject (voice). Verbs occur in the predicate of a clause and can be in verb phrases, which consist of a main verb, any auxiliary verbs, and any modifers. Verbs can be described as transitive or intransitive depending on whether they take a direct object. (8)

verbal A verb part functioning as a noun, adjective, or adverb. Verbals include *infinitives, present participles* (functioning as adjectives), *gerunds* (present participles functioning as nouns), and *past participles.* (7d)

verbal phrase A group of words that contains a verbal (an infinitive, participle, or gerund) and its modifiers.

verb phrase A main verb, any auxiliary verb(s), and any modifiers.

voice An attribute of verbs showing whether the subject acts (active voice) or is acted upon (passive voice). (8n and 8o)

webbing See *mapping.*

Works Cited In MLA documentation style the title of a list of all sources cited in a research paper or other written work. (34c-2 and 34c-3)

writing process Stages of writing in which a writer gathers and shapes ideas, organizes material, expresses those ideas in a rough draft, evaluates the draft and revises it, edits the writing for technical errors, and proofreads it for typographical accuracy and legibility. The stages often overlap. See *planning, shaping, drafting, revision, editing, and proofreading.* (1, 2, 3)

Index

All entries in boldface italics (***advice, advise***, for example) are discussed in the Usage Glossary and any other place listed. Section numbers are in boldface tpe and page numbers in regular type. The listing **30h:** 509 thus refers you to page 509, which is in section **30h**.

Index

G

H

I

Chart List

LIST OF CHARTS BY CONTENT

LIST OF CHARTS BY CONTENT *(continued)*

→

LIST OF CHARTS BY CONTENT (*continued*)

Response Symbols

Here are two lists of symbols your instructor might write on your papers. The first list shows traditional correction symbols; the second list shows complimentary symbols. You can find material related to each item by consulting the handbook sections or chapters given.

CORRECTION SYMBOLS

ab	abbreviation error, **23b, 30h–30k**
ad	adjective or adverb error, **12**
agr	agreement error, **11**
ca	case error, **9**
cap	needs capital letter, **30a–30e**
cl	avoid cliché, **21d**
coh	needs coherence, **4d**
coord	faulty coordination, **17a–17d**
cs	comma splice, **14**
dev	needs development, **4a, 4c, 4f**
dm	dangling modifier, **15c**
e	needs exact language, **20b**
emph	needs emphasis, **19**
frag	sentence fragment, **13**
fs	fused sentence, **14**
hyph	hyphenation error, **22d**
inc	incomplete sentence, **15e**
ital	italics (underlining) error, **30f–30g**
k	awkward construction, **15, 16, 21e**
lc	needs lower-case letter, **30a–30e**
mixed	mixed construction, **15d**
mm	misplaced modifier, **15b**
num	number use error, **30l–30m**
¶	start new paragraph, **4**
no ¶	do not start new paragraph, **4**
//	parallelism, **18**
pl	plural error, **22c**
pro agr	pronoun agreement error, **11m–11r**
pe	punctuation error, **23–29**
ref	pronoun reference error, **10**
rep	repetitious (redundant), **16c**
rt	run-together sentence, **14**
shift	shift, **15a**
sl	avoid slang, **21a-3**
sp	spelling error, **22**
sub	faulty subordination, **17e–17h**
sxt	sexist language use, **11q, 21b**
t	verb tense error, **8g–8k**
trans	needs transition, **4d-1, 4d-5**
u	needs unity, **4b, 4c**
us	usage error, **Usage Glossary**
v	verb form error, **8b–8f**
v agr	verb agreement error, **11a–11l**
var	needs sentence variety, **19**
w	wordy, **16**
wc	word choice error, **20, 21**
ww	wrong word, **20, 21**
^	insert
~	delete
∾	transpose
#	space needed
◠◡	close up
?	meaning unclear

COMPLIMENTARY SYMBOLS

gd coh	good coherence, **4d**
gd coord	good coordination, **17a–17d**
gd dev	good development, **4f**
gd log	good logic, **5j–5k**
gd //	good parallelism, **18**
gd rea	good reasoning, **5i–5k**
gd rev	good revising, **3c**
gd sub	good subordination, **17e–17h**
gd th	good thesis statement, **2n, 3c-2, 6b, 32r**
gd trans	good transitions, **4d-1, 4d-5**
gd ts	good topic sentence, **4a, 4b**
gd u	good unity, **4b, 4c**
gd var	good sentence variety, **19**
gd wc	good word choice, **20, 21**
gd wp	good writing process, **1, 2, 3**

How to Use Your Handbook

You can use your *Simon and Schuster Handbook for Writers* as a reference book, just as you use a dictionary or an encyclopedia. At each step, use one or more suggestions to find the information you want.

STEP 1: USE lists to decide where to go.

- Scan the Overview of Contents (on inside front cover).
- Scan the longer Contents that starts on page v.
- Scan the Index at the back of the book for a detailed alphabetical list of all major and minor topics.
- Scan the list of Charts in Tinted Boxes that highlight and summarize all major subjects.

STEP 2: LOCATE the number that leads to the information you seek.

- Find a chapter number.
- Find a number-letter combination for a subsection of a chapter, explaining a rule or guiding principle.
- Find a chart number.
- Find a page number.

STEP 3: CHECK elements on each page to confirm where you are in the book. (See opposite.)

- Look for the shortened title at the top of each page (left page for chapter title and right page for section title).
- Look for a chapter number and section number in the coloured tab at the top corner of each page.
- Look for a page number at the bottom of the page.

STEP 4: LOCATE and read the information you need. Use special features, illustrated opposite, to help you.

- Use cross-references (usually given in parentheses) to related key concepts.
- Find the definition for any word followed by a degree mark (°) in the Terms Glossary at the back of the book.
- Use ✤ ALERT ✤ notes for pointers about related matters of usage, grammar, punctuation, and writing. Watch for ✚ COMPUTER TIPS ✚ and ◆ ESL NOTES ◆ as well.